C000133514

Street by Street

TYNE & WEAR

PLUS ASHINGTON, BLYTH, CHESTER-LE-STREET, CONSETT, CRAMLINGTON, DURHAM, MORPETH, PETERLEE, PRUDHOE, SEAHAM, STANLEY

Enlarged Areas Gateshead, Newcastle upon Tyne, South Shields, Sunderland

1st edition May 2001

© Automobile Association Developments Limited 2001

This product includes map data licensed from Ordnance Survey® with the permission of the Controller of Her Majesty's Stationery Office. © Crown copyright 2000. All rights reserved. Licence No: 399221.

All rights reserved. No part of this publication may be reproduced, stored in a retrieval system, or transmitted in any form or by any means-- electronic, mechanical, photocopying, recording or otherwise – unless the permission of the publisher has been given beforehand.

Published by AA Publishing (a trading name of Automobile Association Developments Limited, whose registered office is Norfolk House, Priestley Road, Basingstoke, Hampshire, RG24 9NY. Registered number 1878835).

Mapping produced by the Cartographic Department of The Automobile Association.

A CIP Catalogue record for this book is available from the British Library.

Printed by G. Canale & C. S.P.A., Torino, Italy

The contents of this atlas are believed to be correct at the time of the latest revision. However, the publishers cannot be held responsible for loss occasioned to any person acting or refraining from action as a result of any material in this atlas, nor for any errors, omissions or changes in such material. The publishers would welcome information to correct any errors or omissions and to keep this atlas up to date. Please write to Publishing, The Automobile Association, Fanum House, Basing View, Basingstoke, Hampshire, RG21 4EA.

Ref: MX053

Key to map pages — ii-iii

Key to map symbols — iv-1

Enlarged scale pages — 2-17

Street by Street — 18-185

Index – towns & villages — 186

Index – streets — 187-218

Index – featured places — 218-222

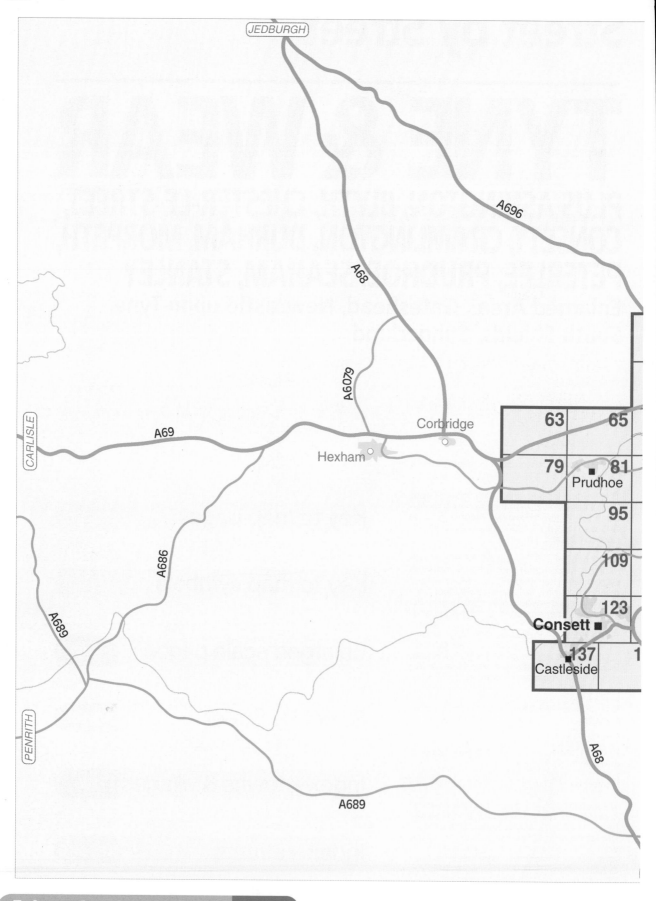

JEDBURGH

A696

A68

A6079

CARLISLE

A69

Corbridge

Hexham

63   65

79   81
Prudhoe

95

A686

109

A689

123

Consett ■

PENRITH

137
Castleside

A68

A689

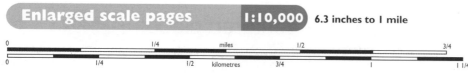

Enlarged scale pages   **1:10,000**   6.3 inches to 1 mile

0   1/4   miles   1/2   3/4
0   1/4   1/2   kilometres   3/4   1   1 1/4

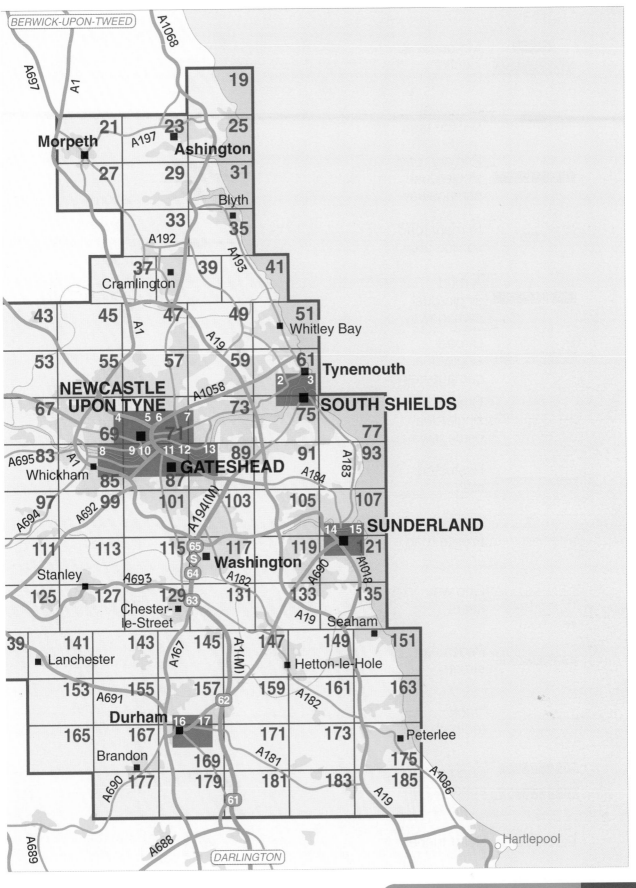

BERWICK-UPON-TWEED

A1068

A697

A1

19

21 23 25
Morpeth A197 Ashington

27 29 31
Blyth

33 35
A192

A193

37 39 41
Cramlington

43 45 47 49 51
A1 A19 Whitley Bay

53 55 57 59 61
NEWCASTLE Tynemouth
UPON TYNE A1058 2 3
67 73 75
SOUTH SHIELDS
4 5 6 7
69 71 77
A695 83 8 9 10 11 12 13 89 91 93
A1 A183
Whickham GATESHEAD
85 87 A184
97 99 101 103 105 107
A694 A692 A194(M)
111 113 115 65 117 119 14 15 121
S SUNDERLAND
Stanley A693 64 Washington A690 A1018
125 127 129 63 131 A182 133 135
Chester- A19 Seaham
le-Street
39 141 143 145 147 149 151
Lanchester A167 A1(M) Hetton-le-Hole
153 155 157 159 161 163
A691 62 A182
Durham 16 17
165 167 171 173 Peterlee
Brandon 169 A181 175
A690 177 179 181 183 185
61 A19 A1086

A689 A688 DARLINGTON Hartlepool

0 1/4 miles 1/2 3/4 1

0 1/4 1/2 kilometres 3/4 1 1 1/4 1 1/2 1 3/4

Junction 9	Motorway & junction
Services	Motorway service area
	Primary road single/dual carriageway
Services	Primary road service area
	A road single/dual carriageway
	B road single/dual carriageway
	Other road single/dual carriageway
	Restricted road
	Private road
← ←	One way street
	Pedestrian street
	Track/ footpath
	Road under construction
	Road tunnel
P	Parking
P+	Park & Ride
	Bus/coach station
	Railway & main railway station
	Railway & minor railway station
	Underground station
	Light railway & station
+++++++++++	Preserved private railway
LC	Level crossing
•–•–•–•–•	Tramway
----------	Ferry route
....	Airport runway
–·–·–·–·	Boundaries- borough/ district
ᴠᴠᴠᴠᴠᴠᴠᴠ	Mounds
93	Page continuation 1:15,000
7	Page continuation to enlarged scale 1:10,000

Symbol	Description	Symbol	Description
	River/canal lake, pier		Toilet with disabled facilities
	Aqueduct lock, weir		Petrol station
465 ▲ Winter Hill	Peak (with height in metres)	PH	Public house
	Beach	PO	Post Office
	Coniferous woodland		Public library
	Broadleaved woodland	i	Tourist Information Centre
	Mixed woodland		Castle
	Park		Historic house/ building
	Cemetery	Wakehurst Place NT	National Trust property
	Built-up area	M	Museum/ art gallery
	Featured building	†	Church/chapel
	City wall		Country park
A&E	Accident & Emergency hospital		Theatre/ performing arts
	Toilet		Cinema

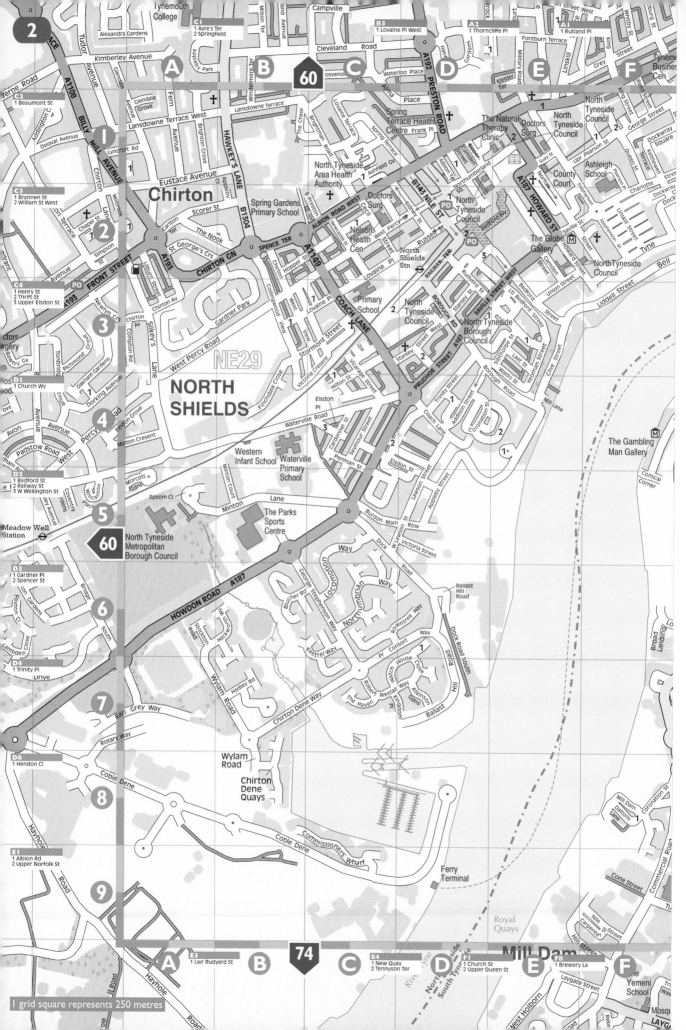

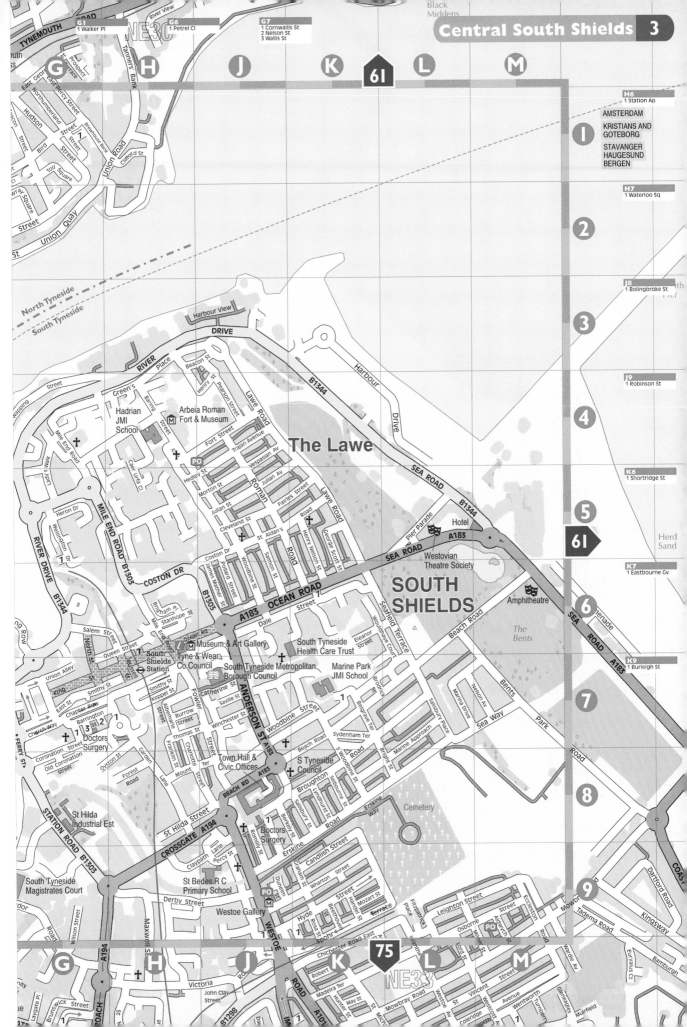

G
1 Walker Pl

G6
1 Petrel Cl

G7
1 Cornwallis St
2 Nelson St
3 Wallis St

H6
1 Station Ap

AMSTERDAM

KRISTIANS AND
GOTEBORG

STAVANGER
HAUGESUND
BERGEN

H7
1 Waterloo Sq

J8
1 Bolingbroke St

J9
1 Robinson St

K6
1 Shortridge St

K7
1 Eastbourne Gv

K9
1 Burleigh St

TYNEMOUTH

NE30

North Tyneside

South Tyneside

Black Middens

Harbour View

RIVER DRIVE

Green's

Hadrian JMI School

Arbeia Roman Fort & Museum

The Lawe

B1344

SEA ROAD

B1344

Herd Sand

Pier Parade

Hotel

A183

Westovian Theatre Society

SOUTH SHIELDS

Amphitheatre

The Bents

OCEAN ROAD A183

Museum & Art Gallery

Tyne & Wear Co Council

South Shields Station

South Tyneside Metropolitan Borough Council

South Tyneside Health Care Trust

Marine Park JMI School

Beach Road

Sea Way

Bents Park

SEA ROAD A183

Doctors Surgery

Town Hall & Civic Offices

S Tyneside Council

Cemetery

St Hilda Industrial Est

STATION ROAD B1303

South Tyneside Magistrates Court

CROSSGATE A194

BEACH RD A183

St Hilda Street

St Bedes R C Primary School

Westoe Gallery

Doctors Surgery

WESTOE ROAD A183

NE33

Leighton Street

Chichester Road East

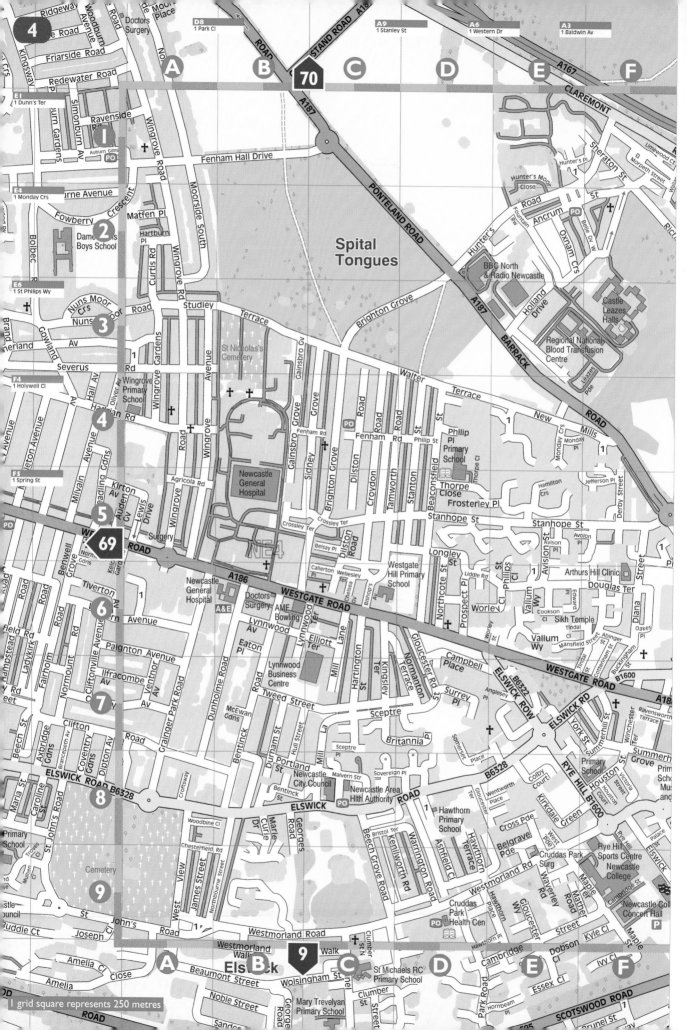

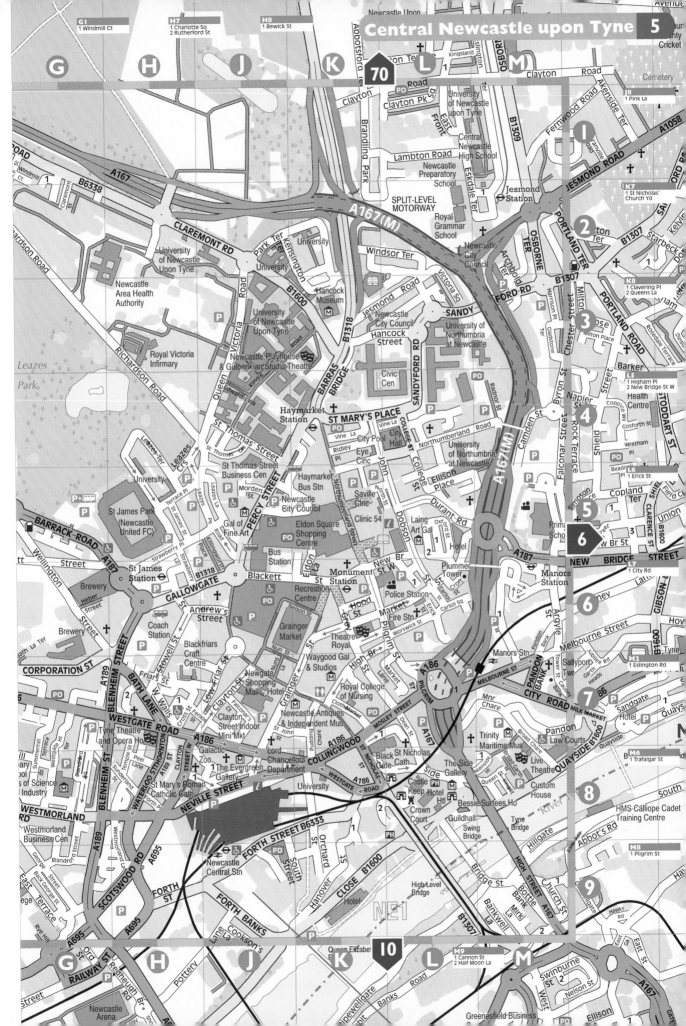

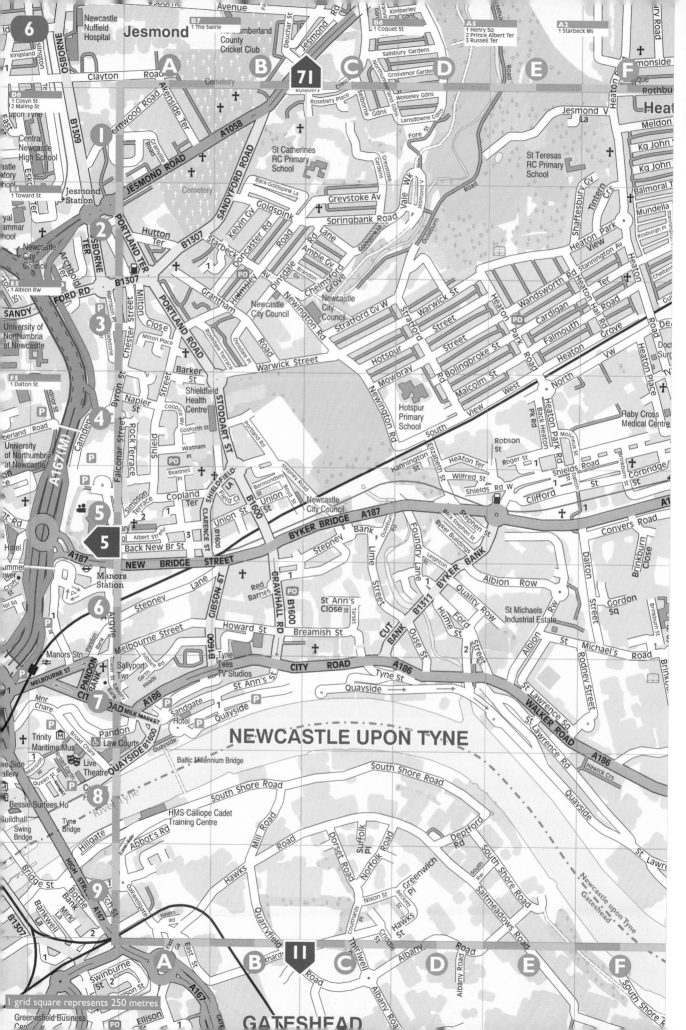

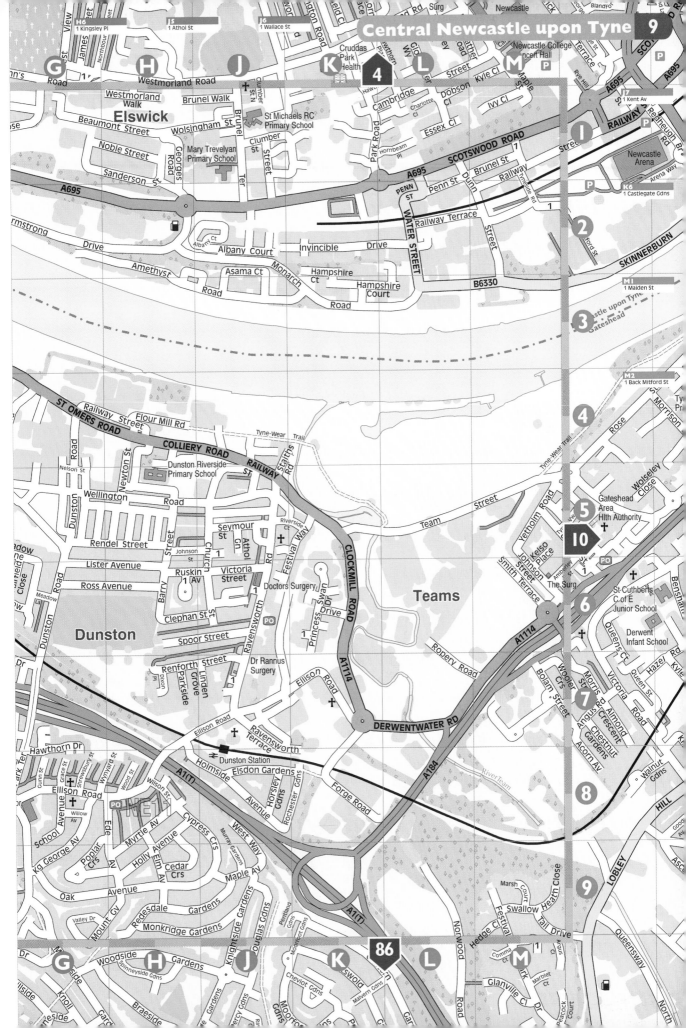

G   H   J   K   **4**   L   M

Elswick

Newcastle College
Concert Hall

Newcastle Arena

RAILWAY

SKINNERBURN

Cruddas Park Health

Westmorland Road

1 Kingsley Pl
1 Athol St
1 Wallace St

Westmorland Walk

Brunel Walk

St Michaels RC Primary School

Cambridge

Beaumont Street

Wolsingham St

Mary Trevelyan Primary School

Noble street

Georges Road

Sanderson

A695

Albany Court

Invincible   Drive

WATER STREET

Scotswood Road   A695

Penn St   Brunel St

Railway Terrace

PENN ST

Dunn St

Railway

Railway Street

1 Kent Av

1 Castlegate Gdns

Armstrong   Drive

Asama Ct   Monarch

Hampshire Ct

Hampshire Court

B6330

1 Maiden St

Amethyst   Road

Road

stle upon Tyne Gateshead

St OMERS ROAD

Railway Street

Flour Mill Rd

COLLIERY ROAD

RAILWAY ST

Tyne-Wear Trail

Tyne-Wear Trail

1 Back Mitford St

Rose

Morrison

Nelson St

Dunston Riverside Primary School

Gaiths Rd

Team   Street

Wolseley Close

Wellington   Road

Dunston

Seymour St

Athol Gn

Riverside Ct

Festival Way

Gateshead Area Hlth Authority

Rendel Street

Johnson St

Church Rd

Victoria Street

Doctors Surgery

10

Vetholm Road

Kelso Place

Smith Terrace

Lister Avenue

Barry St

Ruskin 1 AV

Swan Drive

Princess

The Surg

St-Cuthberts C of E Junior School

Ross Avenue

Clephan St

CLOCKMILL ROAD

Teams

Benshan

Meadow La

Dunston

Spoor Street

Ravensworth

A1114

Ropery Road

Derwent Infant School

Queens Ct

Renforth Street

Linden Grove

Dixon Pl

Dr Rannus Surgery

Ellison   Road

A1114

A1114

Wooler Crs

Bolam Street

Hazel Rd

Queen St

Hawthorn Dr

Ellison Road

Holmside

A1(T)

Ravensworth Terrace

Dunston Station

Elsdon Gardens

DERWENTWATER RD

A184

Morris St

Angus Rd

Almond Crescent

Chestnut Gardens

Acorn Av

Victoria Road

Shrewsbury St

Gunn St

Grace St

Wynyard St

Wood St

Wilson St

Cypress Crs

Horsley Gdns

Rochester Gdns

Forge Road

A1(T)

RiverTeam

walnut Gdns

Ellison Road

Willow Av

Murray Gardens

West Way

Kg George Av

Poplar Crs

Myrtle Av

Holly Avenue

Elm Av

Cedar Crs

Maple Av

Marsh Court

Swallow

LOBLEY HILL

School Avenue

Ede

Oak   Avenue

Redesdale   Gardens

Knightside Gardens

Douglas Gdns

Festival

Heath Close

Trail Drive

Queensway

Valley Dr

Mount Gv

Monkridge Gardens

Spinneyside Gdns

Pentland Gdns

Norwood

Hedge Gdns

Glanville Cl

G   H   J   K   **86**   L   M

Woodside Gardens

Cheviot Gdns

Moorhead

Malvern Gdns

Cotswold

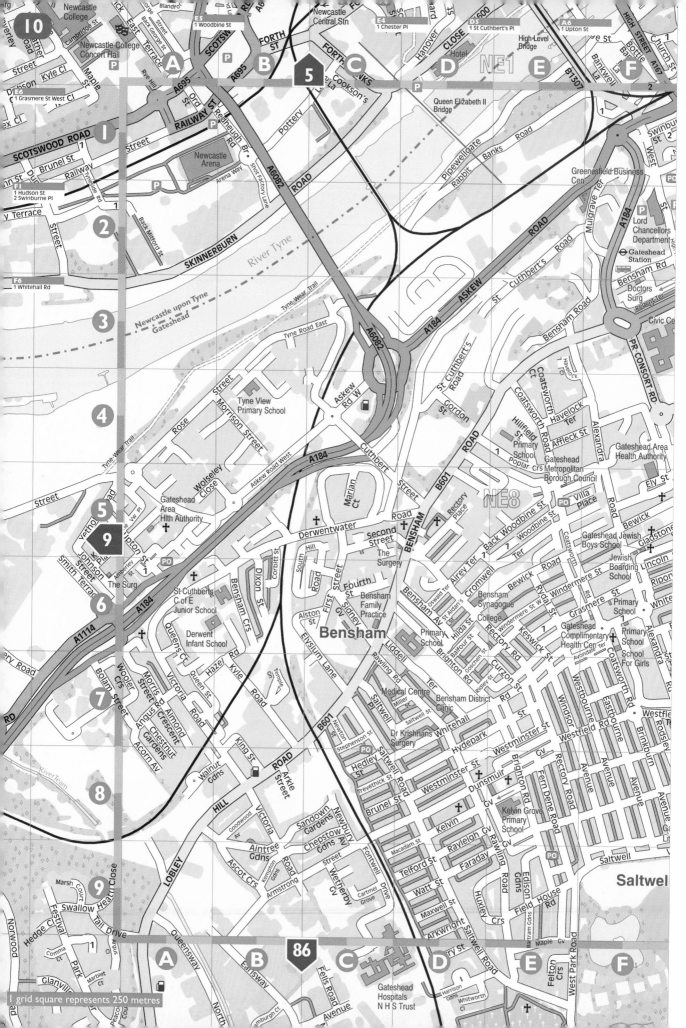

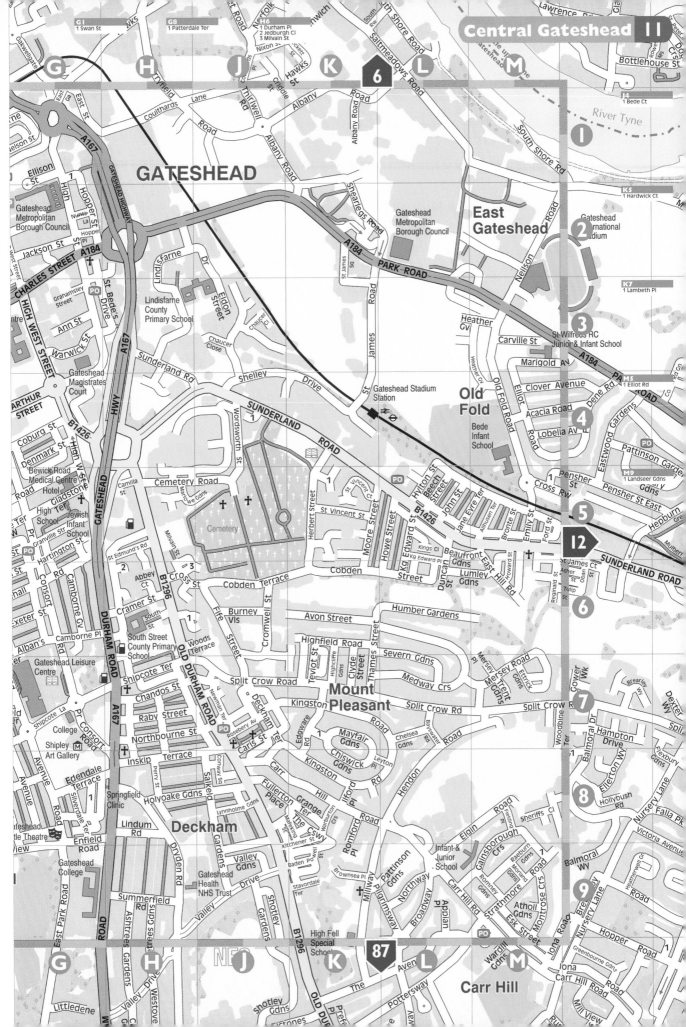

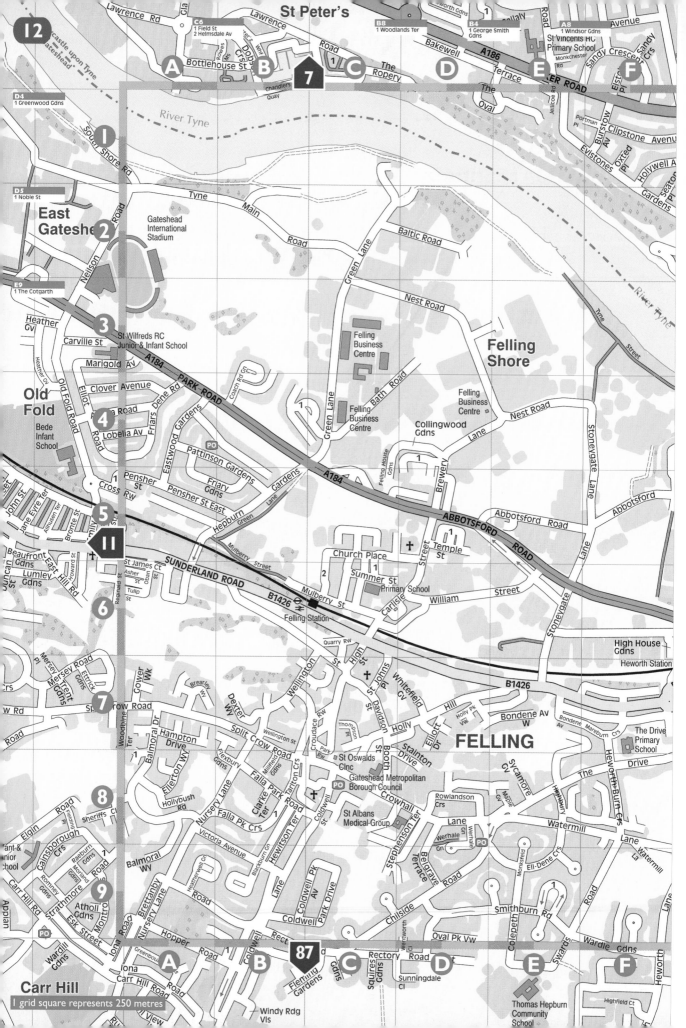

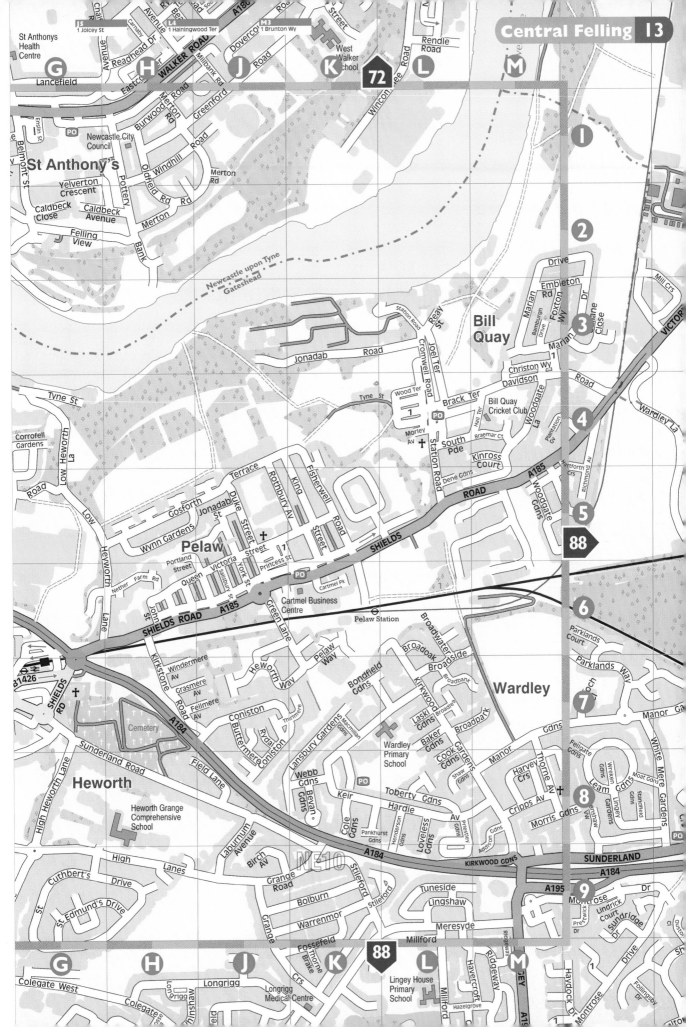

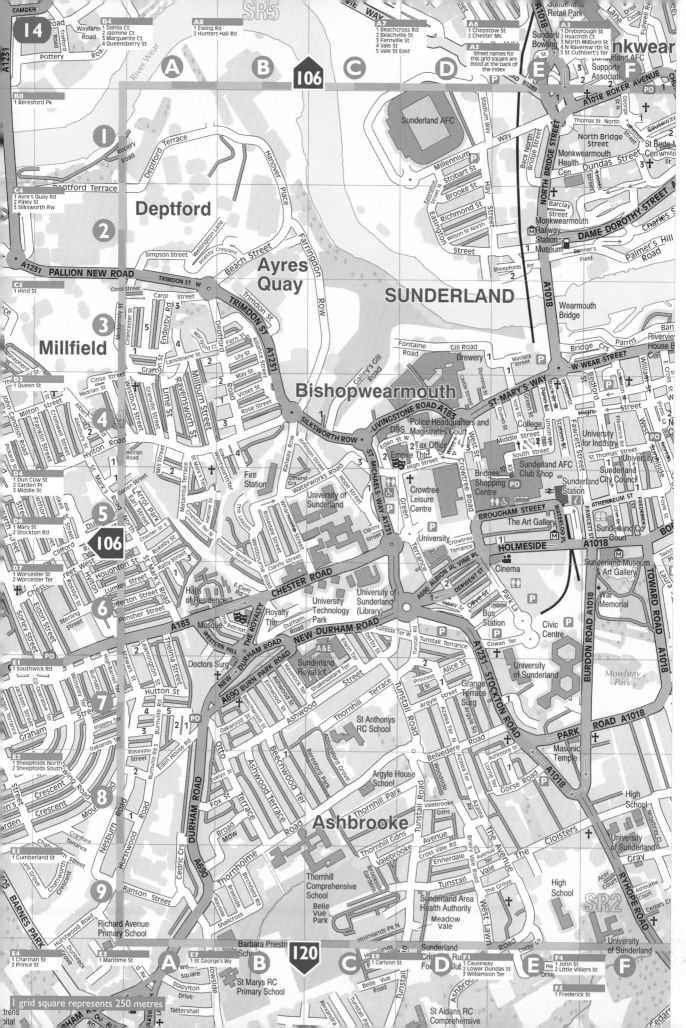

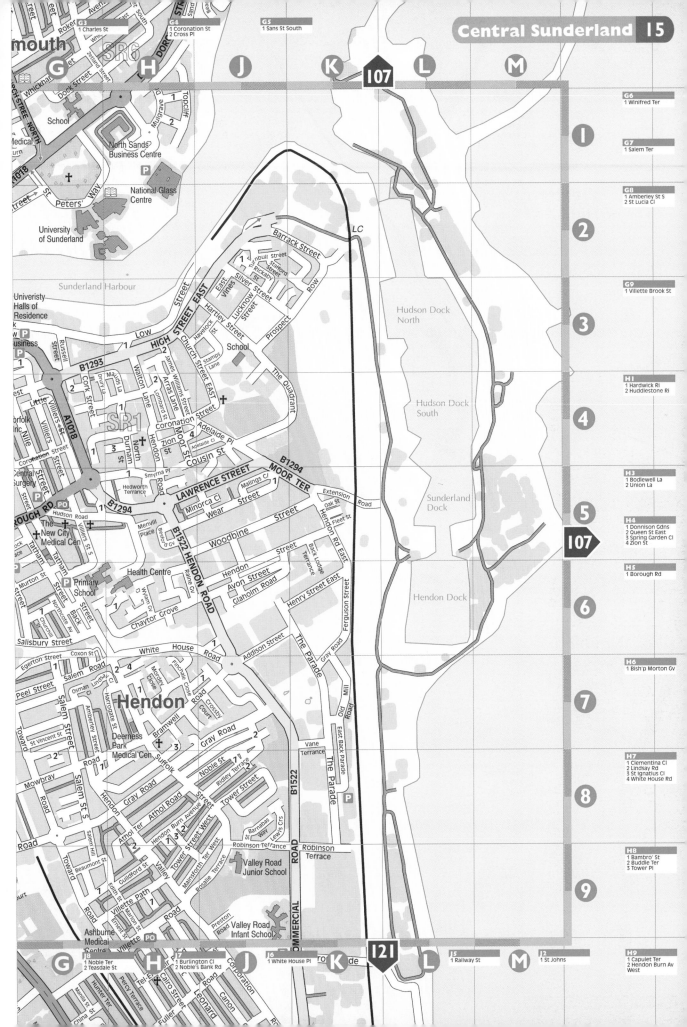

mouth

G H J K **107** L M

SR6

G3
1 Charles St

G4
1 Coronation St
2 Cross Pl

G5
1 Sans St South

G6
1 Winifred Ter

G7
1 Salem Ter

G8
1 Amberley St S
2 St Lucia Cl

G9
1 Villette Brook St

School

North Sands
Business Centre

National Glass
Centre

Peters'

University
of Sunderland

Univeristy
Halls of
Residence

Sunderland Harbour

H1
1 Hardwick Ri
2 Huddlestone Ri

H3
1 Bodlewell La
2 Union La

H4
1 Donnison Gdns
2 Queen St East
3 Spring Garden Cl
4 Zion St

107

H5
1 Borough Rd

H6
1 Bish'p Morton Gv

H7
1 Clementina Cl
2 Lindsay Rd
3 St Ignatius Cl
4 White House Rd

H8
1 Bambro' St
2 Buddle Ter
3 Tower Pl

H9
1 Capulet Ter
2 Hendon Burn Av West

Barrack Street

Turnbull Street
Stafford
Rickaby

East
Vines
Silver Street
Lucknow Street
Hartley Street
Havelock
Stamps
Lane
School

LC

HIGH STREET EAST
Low
Russell Street
Church Street EAST
James Williams Street
Arras Lane
Lombard St
Coronation Street
Adelaide Pl
Zion
St
Moor St
Adelaide Cl
Cousin St

Prospect Row

The Quadrant

Hudson Dock
North

Hudson Dock
South

Sunderland
Dock

B1293
Cork Street
Maude La
Drury La
Durham
St
North
Hendon Road
Smyrna Pl

SR1

A1018
Villiers Street
Norfolk
Villiers
Street
Nile
Street
Coronation
Street
Central
Surgery

LAWRENCE STREET
Hedworth
Terrace
Minorca Cl
Wear Street
Mallings Cl
MOOR TER
B1294
Extension Road
Oak St
Fleet St

Hendon Rd East

B1294
Hudson Road
The
New City
Medical Cen
Menvill
Place
Beston
B1522 HENDON ROAD
Woodbine Street

Health Centre
Hendon
Street
Avon Street
Glaholm Road
Raine Gv
Back Lodge
Terrace

Back
Lodge
Terrace

Henry Street East
Ferguson Street

Gray Road
Mill Dio Road

Sunderland
Dock

Hendon Dock

Primary
School
Chaytor Grove
Northcote Av
Churchill
Salisbury street

White House Road
Coxon St
Finchale Road
Crossby
Court
Addison Street

The Parade

Egerton Street
Peel Street
Salem Road
Osman Cl
Lindsay
Morley
Close
Toward
St Vincent St
Amberley Street
Harrogate st
Bramwell
Hendon
Deerness
Park
Medical Cen
Gray Road
Suffolk
Noble St
Ridley Terrace

Vane
Terrace

East Back Parade

Mowbray
Salem St S
Hendon
Ter
Athol Road
Gray Road
Tower Street West
Street
Hendon Burn Avenue
Barnabas
St Way
Lew's Crs
Tower Street

B1522
The Parade

Robinson Terrace
Robinson
Terrace

Toward
Beaumont St
Salem Hill
Guildford St
Edith St
Villette Path
Marion Rd
Ernest St
Mainsforth Ter West
Rosalie Terrace
Preston
Road

Valley Road
Junior School

Valley Road
Infant School

COMMERCIAL ROAD

Ashburne
Medical
Centre
Villette
Hunter Ter
Percy Terrace
Tel-El-
Cairo Street
Manila St
China St
Leonard
Canon
Fuller
Corporation

121

G H J K **121** L **J5** M **J2**

G
1 Noble Ter
2 Teasdale St

H
1 Burlington Cl
2 Noble's Bank Rd

J
1 White House Pl

J5
1 Railway St

J2
1 St Johns

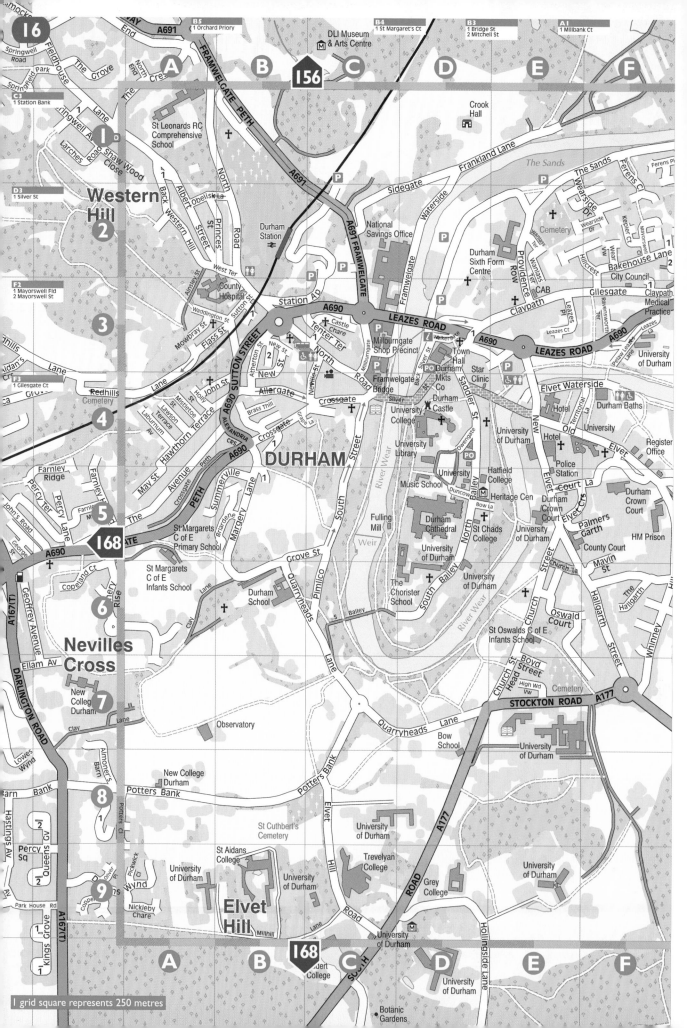

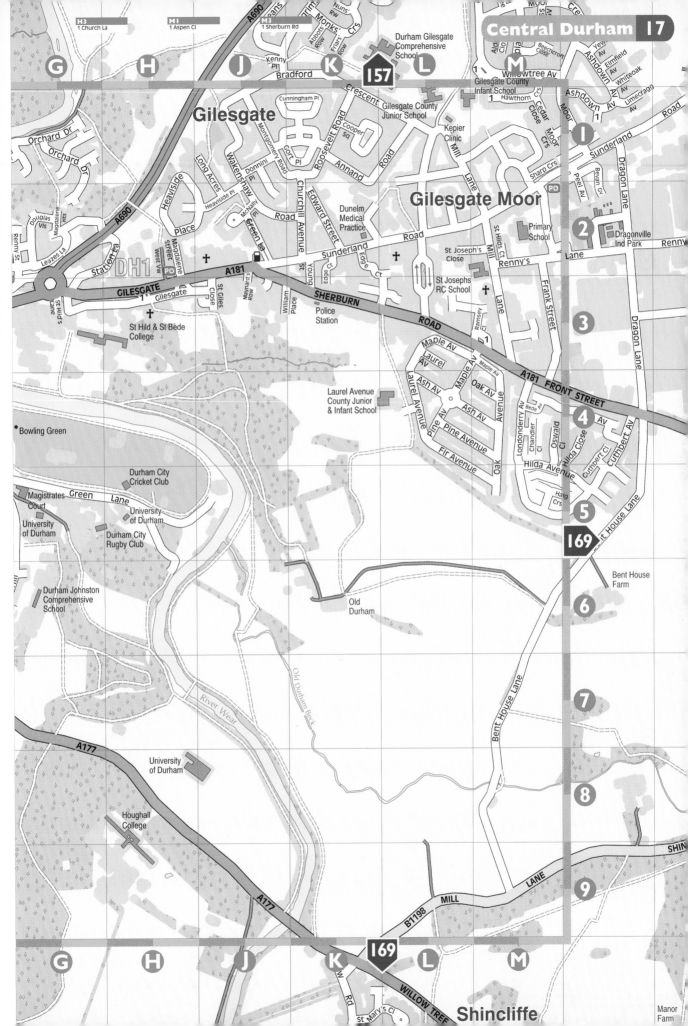

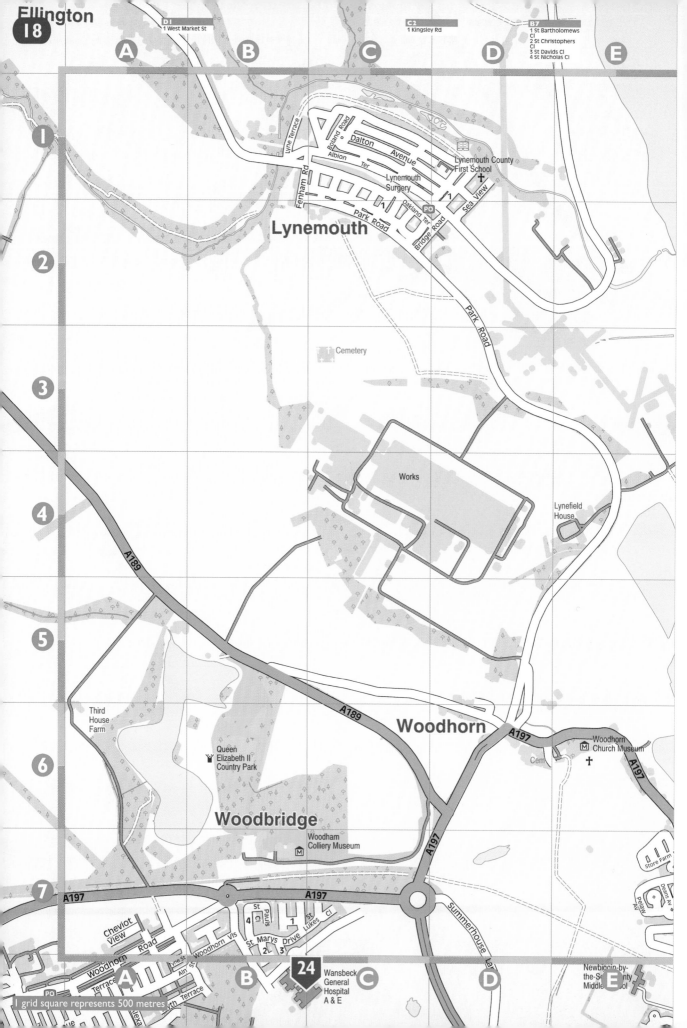

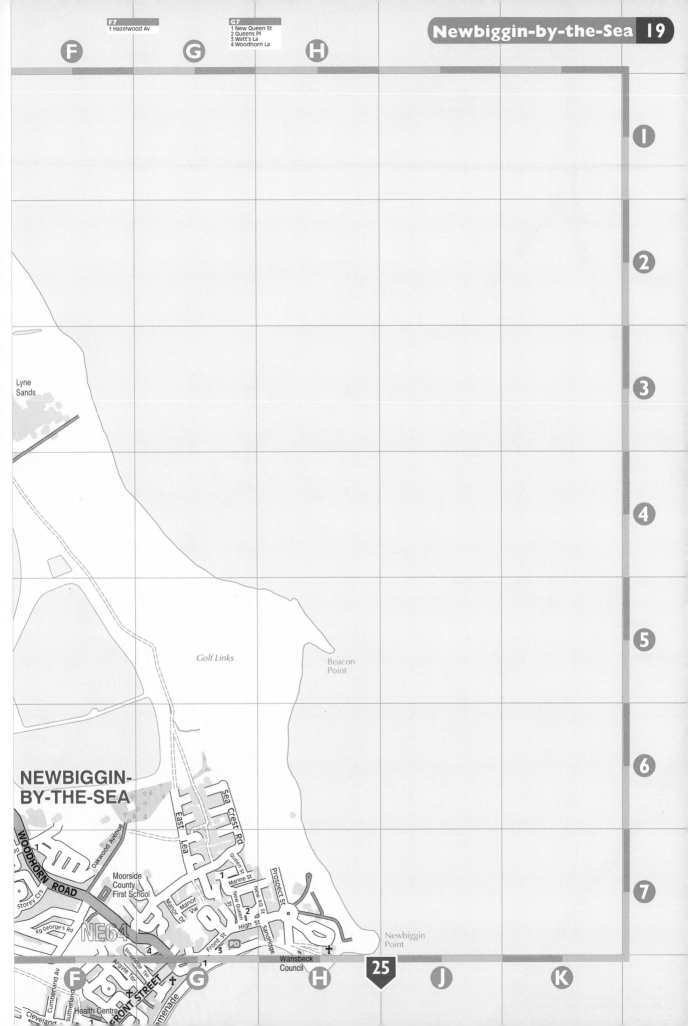

F7
1 Hazelwood Av

G7
1 New Queen St
2 Queens Pl
3 Watt's La
4 Woodhorn La

F   G   H

1
2
3
4
5
6
7

Lyne
Sands

Golf Links

Beacon
Point

**NEWBIGGIN-
BY-THE-SEA**

Sea Crest Rd

East Lea

Oakwood Avenue

WOODHORN ROAD

Storey Crs

Moorside
County
First School

Manor Dr

Manor
Vw

Marine St

Queen St

High St

New Queen

New Kg St

Prospect St

Sandridge

Newbiggin
Point

NE64

Kg George's Rd

Front St

Simonside Ter

Wansbeck
Council

25

Cumberland Av

Argyle Ter

Sutherland

Cleveland

Health Centre

FRONT STREET

Promenade

F   G   H   J   K

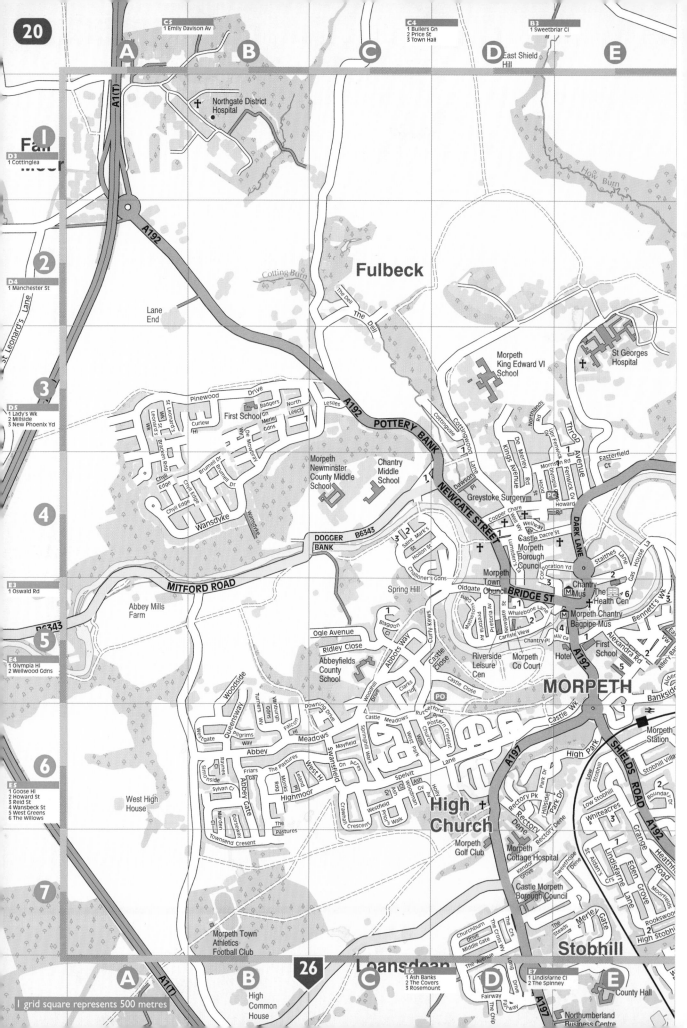

A   B   C   D   East Shield   E
Hill

Fa
Moor

1

D3
1 Cottinglea

Northgate District
Hospital

2

D4
1 Manchester St

A192

Lane
End

Cotting Burn

Fulbeck

The Dell

The Dell

How Burn

St Leonard's Lane

3

D5
1 Lady's Wk
2 Millside
3 New Phoenix Yd

Pinewood   Drive

Badgers   North
Gn   Leech
St Leonard's   Curlew   First School   Meriel
Wk   Hl   De Mowbray   Gdns
Brumell Dr

Leslies

A192

POTTERY BANK

Cottingwood

Morpeth
King Edward VI
School

Northlands
Rd

St Georges
Hospital

Easterfield
Ct

Cottingrate

E3
1 Oswald Rd

Chvil
Edge

Chvil Edge

Chvil Edge

Brumell Dr

Wansdyke

Wansdyke

Morpeth
Newminster
County Middle
School

Chantry
Middle
School

Dawson
Pl

NEWGATE STREET

Greystoke Surgery

De Merley
Rd
Morrison
Rd
Hood

Olympia St

Kings Avenue

Fenwick Cl

Throp

Avenue

Howard
Rd

Copper Chare

Well Wy
Wellway
Castle
Dacre St

PO

4

**DOGGER
BANK**

B6343

Saint Mark's
St
Hollon St

Challoner's Gdns

Castle
Morpeth
Borough
Council

Staithes
Lane

Gas House La

MITFORD ROAD

Abbey Mills
Farm

Spring Hill

Oldgate
supc

Morpeth
Town
Council

Corporation Yd

Chantry
Mus

The
Health Cen

Bennett's Wk

Dark Lane

E4
1 Olympia Hl
2 Wellwood Gdns

B6343

5

Ogle Avenue

Ridley Close

Abbeyfields
County
School

Blaggon
Cl

Curly Kews

Matheson St
pretoria Av

Whalebone Lane

Carlisle View

Chantry Pl

Hill Ga

BRIDGE ST

Morpeth Chantry
Bagpipe-Mus

First
School

Alexandra Rd

Allery Bank

Riverside
Leisure
Cen

Morpeth
Co Court

Hotel

A192

MORPETH

Banksid

Woodside

Turners Wy

Castle
Close

PO

Castle Close

Castle WK

Morpeth
Station

6

E3
1 Goose Hl
2 Howard St
3 Reid St
4 Wansbeck St
5 West Greens
6 The Willows

West High
House

Queensway

Westgate

Pilgrims
Way

Vanburgh
Gdns
Falcon
Hl

Meadows

Raynes
Way

Friars
Ga

Simonside

Sylvan Cl

The Pastures

Abbey

West Hl

Highmoor

Marden

Corseway

The Pastures

Townsend Cresent

Abbey Gate

Mayfield
Gn   Aces

Leland

Crawhall

Westfield
Crescent

Swansfield

Springhill Wark

Spelvit

Moor
Gv

Woodman

Ash
Gv

Castle Meadows

West Park

Holly
Lane

Rutherford

Postern Crescent

Pylon
Walk

Castle
Meadows

Woodhill Drive

Downing drive

Clarks
Fld

Morpeth
Golf Club

High Church

Rectory Pk

Rectory
Dene

Park Dr

Rectory
Dene

Low Stobhill

Whiteacres

Low
Stobhill

St Aidan's

Lindisfarne
Lane

Grange Rd

Stobhill Villa

Boundary Dr

Eden Grove

Moorfields

Rookswood

High Stobhill

A197

High Park

SHIELDS ROAD

Heathfield

Merley Gate

A192

A197

7

West High
House

Morpeth
Cottage Hospital

Castle Morpeth
Borough Council

Churchburn
Drive

Middle Gate

Kendor
Grove

Sweethope

The Crts
Dene

The Steads

Rectory
Dene

Stobhill

Morpeth Town
Athletics
Football Club

The Avenue

Long Drive

The Chip

Northumberland
Business Centre

County Hall

A   A1(T)   B   **26**   Loansdean   C   D   E

High
Common
House

E6
1 Ash Banks
2 The Covers
3 Rosemount

Fairway

The

Fark'way

E7
1 Lindisfarne Cl
2 The Spinney

Pegswood

A   B   C   D   E

E5
1 Sheepwash Bank

1

E6
1 Byron Cl
2 Cleaswell Hl
3 Fern Ct
4 Laburnum Ct
5 Morpeth Rd
6 Rutherford Cl
7 South Vw
8 The Square
9 Welbeck Rd

Terrace
Lindisfarne
Terrace

Dilston

Bothal
Park

Coney
Garth

A197

Castleway

Kworth
Dr

Belsay

2

E7
1 Gladewell Ct
2 Greenfield Dr

gswood
tion

A1068

SHEEPWASH ROAD

Bothal Bank

Bothal
Barns

Sheepwash Rd

3

Whitefield

Bothal

4

21

Bothalhaugh

Sheepwash

Glebe Farm

5

SHEEPWASH

Sheepwash Bk
9

7

A1068

Olly

6

A196

Paddock Hall
Farm

North
Choppington

A196

Avenue

Riverside

West Av

Pine Av

Welbeck

North Av

Central

Sycamore Av

Road

Dene

Saraben

Sheepwash Avenue

Bothal
Av

Front St

3
4

5

FRONT ST.

P.O

Police
Station

Morpeth
Road

Morpeth Cl

High Stre

eywood

Meadow Bank Dr

1

2

Underhill Dr

Overdale

Overdale
Ct

Acreford
Court

7

Chop
Coun
First

A   B   C   D   E

28

1 grid square represents 500 metres

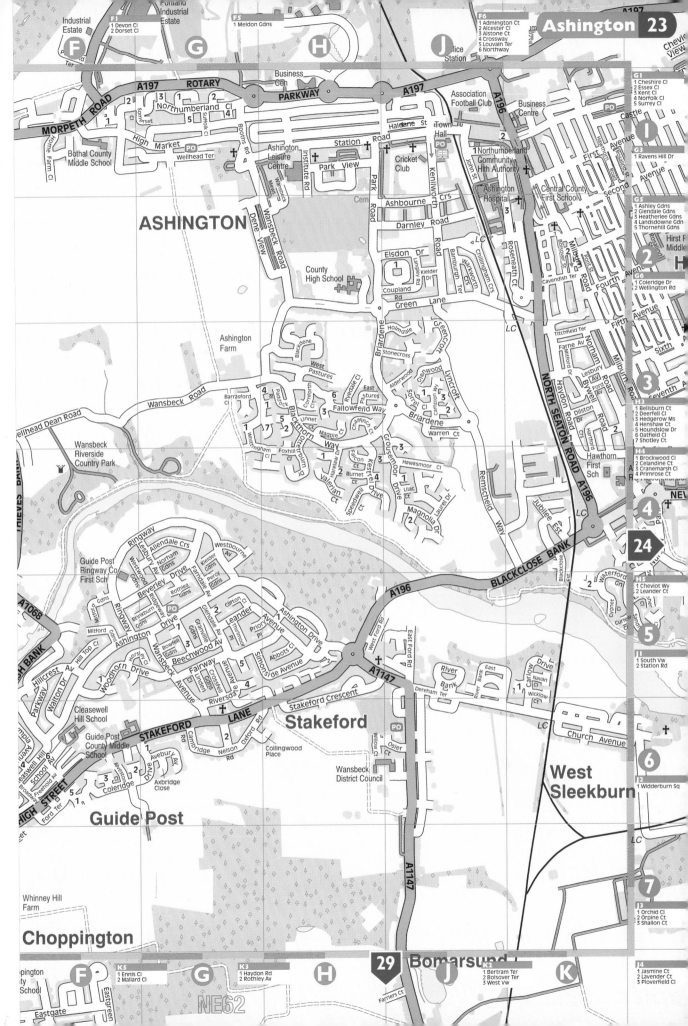

ROAD

County
First School

F1
1 Buteland Ter
2 Windsor Rd

Kg George's

Storey Crs

Argyle Ter

Simonside Ter

Front St

Manor Dr

Manor Vw

New St

High St

Sandridge

G1
1 Bridge St

PO

Wansbeck
Council

Health Centre

Cleveland Av

Cumberland Av

Sutherland Av

Aqua Ter

GISBON ST FRONT STREET

Promenade

Newbiggin
Bay

Westmorland Av

Northumberland Av

Seaton Av

Westfield Ch

North View

PO

Windsor County
First School

NORTH SEATON ROAD

Melrose Ter

Beach Ter

Beach

Spital Carrs

Spital
Point

Beach Terrace

Newbiggin
nt

1

2

3

4

5

6

7

A B 20 C D E

Morpeth
Athletics
Football Club

Loansdean

Castle Morpeth
Borough Council

1 Chathill Cl

Stobhill

High
Common
House

Churchburn
Drive
Middle Ga
The Avenue
The Turn
Fairway
The Chip
Long Drive
Fairway
The Steads
Merle Gat
High Stobhi
Grove
Moorfields
Lane
Rookswoo

County Hall

Northumberland
Business Centre

A1(T)

B6524

Tranwell

A197

Catchburn
Farm

Catch Burn

Clif

Gubeon Wood

A1(T)

Ber's Lane

Well Hill

Glororum

A197

The Drive

North
Whitehouse
Farm

Stannington
Children's Hospital

Green Lane

Dovecote
Farm

Green Lane

St Marys
Hospital

A B C D E

I grid square represents 500 metres

F1
1 Norham Cl
2 Rennington Cl

F

G

H

21

J

LC

The Orchard

Fieldhouse Lane

Fieldhouse Cl

Crofts park

I

Hepscott

Edgehill

Norham

Ellingham Drive

Wfthnham Way

Wrefton Cl

Crookham Gv

Glanton Cl

Catch Burn

High Stobhill Farm

Barmoor Farm

Coalburn Farm

2

Thornlea

Briarlea

Stoneleigh

Coal Burn

Hazeldene

A192

A192

Field House Farm

3

Hepscott Manor Farm

4

LC

Clifton Lane

Hepscott Manor

A192

28

ton

5

High Clifton Farm

A1(T)

Hepscott Park

The Grange

6

Stannington Station Road

Stannington Station Road

A192

Stannington Station

LC

Netherton Wood

7

Stannington Station Road

Pegwhistle Burn

Moor Lane

F

G

H

J

K

Netherton Park

30

A   B   **24**   C   D   E

B6
1 Avondale Cl

West Sleekburn County
Middle School

B3
1 Havelock Crs

A3
1 Burt Rd
2 Moorland Ct
3 Moorland Crs

LC

Cambois

1

B7
1 Chase Ms

Cambois
County
First School

2

C6
1 Cowpen Rd
2 Ferndale Cl
3 Greendale Cl
4 Ribblesdale Av
5 Thorndale Pl
6 Tweedy St

A189

Brock Lane

Havelock
Mews

Barrington Park

**East
Sleekburn**

Northfield

Brock Lane

Sandfield
Rd
Waterfield
Rd
Wilson Av

Sleek Burn

Grange Park Av

Parkside

Welwyn Av

Park Avenue

Revlyn Avenue

Legg

3

C7
1 Callerdale Rd
2 Coverdale Av
3 Milldale Av

Grange Avenue

Moorland Av

Moorland
Vis

Moorland
Dr

St John's Crs
St John's Rd

ables
al Group

King's
Crs

King's
Rd

Albert

Queen's   Road

Bedlington
Community
High School

ce Road

4

29

A189

Mount Pleasant
Farm

Cowley Road

Blyth Valley
Borough Council

D5
Buttermere Wy

B1331

River Blyth

Spencer Road

Spencer
Court

Cowley Rd

A193

Cowpen Road

5

D6
Burnside Cl

Kitty Brewster
Farm

Coniston Road

Ennerdale Rd

Loweswater
Cl

Coniston Road

Thirlmere
Way

John St

Beecher
Street

Lindsay Av

Alwinton
Close

Walton Avenue

Bebside

6

7
1 Cragton Gdns
2 Hartleigh Pl
3 Malton Cl
4 Redesdale Pl

Ullswater
Close

Northumberland
County Council

Avondale
Clendale Av
Longsdale Avenue

Kitty
Brewster

Maple Crescent
Bells

A193

Lyndon
Wk

Middle
School

First School

Weardale
AV

Teesdale
Pl

Escdale Av

Whorledale Av

Borrowdale

Windmill Cr

Park

Nidderdale
Cl

Craig Mill

Cowpen Hall

Cowley
Pl

Norcale

PO

Brandon

Eston

Dunston

Brierley Road

Langley Av

Edendale Avenue

Cowpen Road

The Orchards

Dean View Drive

Cowpen
Road

Cemetery

King's Gdns

Queen's Gdns

Prince's Gdns

Malvins
Rd

The Paddock

Albion

Priory Gra

Malvins
Close County
First School

COWPEN   ROAD

Cowpen

Malvins

Beal Cl

Bamburgh

Cambo

7

side Social
b House

FRONT ST

A193

LC

Chase Farm Dr

A189

Inglewood Cl

Thorntree Way

Huntford
Grn

Beaumont Manor

Blyth Tynedale
Co High
School

Tynedale

Patterdale Road

Bradale

Dovedale Av

Ravensdale Grove

Middle
School

Lynndale Av

Prestdale Av

Wettondale Av

Pettondale Av

Swaledale Avenue

Kingsdale Avenue

Bishopdale Av

Stardale

Devonworth Place

Bankdale
Gdns

Hall Green

Hortondale Grove

Northumberland
Area Hlth Authority

Garestone
Cl

Brookside Av

Rookery Cl

Wallside Road

Ingram
Dr

Matfen
Cl

Elsdon

Ryal Cl

Axwell
Drive

Ingram Drive

Albion Way

Budle Cl

Craster Cl

Ford Drive

Ingoe Cl

Norham
Drive

Ogle

Isabella Rd

Bebside

34

Monkdale

E6
1 Earl's Gdns

E7
1 Belsay Ct
2 Thorneyburn Wy
3 Whithorn Ct

LYE

Leaholme Crs

hester Cl

Trevelyan Av

A   B   **34**   C   D   E

F5
1 Grieve St
2 Millfield Gdns

F6
1 Goschen St
2 Hambledon St
3 Sweethope Av
4 Thompson St

F7
1 High St
2 Rosebery Av

G5
1 Goschen St
2 Thompson St
3 Worsdell St

G6
1 Arthur St
2 Boyne Ct
3 Cummings St
4 Davison St
5 French St
6 Gatacre St
7 Kerry Cl
8 Merton Sq
9 Seaforth St
10 Simpson St
11 Thompson St

G7
1 Aldborough St
2 Back Croft Rd
3 Barnard St
4 Crofton St

H6
1 Ballast Hi
2 Beaconsfield St
3 Plessey Rd
4 Post Office St
5 Quay Rd
6 Quayside
7 Ridley St
8 Sussex St
9 Tate St

H7
1 Carlton St
2 Coburg St
3 Crown St
4 Hawthorne Rd
5 Oxford St
6 Percy St South
7 Rosamond Pl
8 St Cuthberts Ct
9 Wellington St

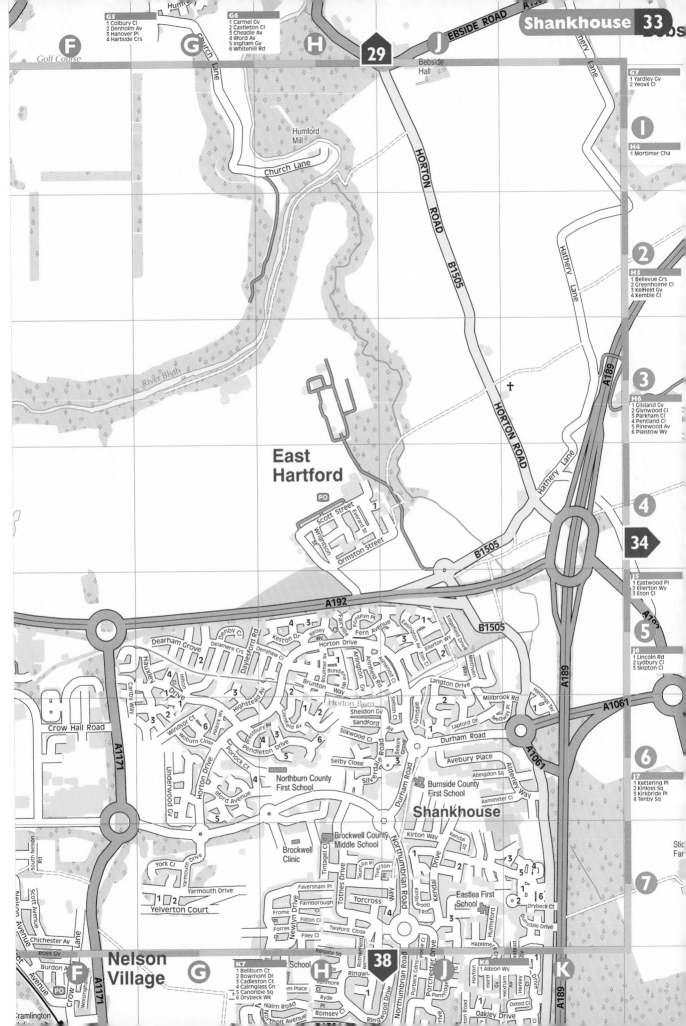

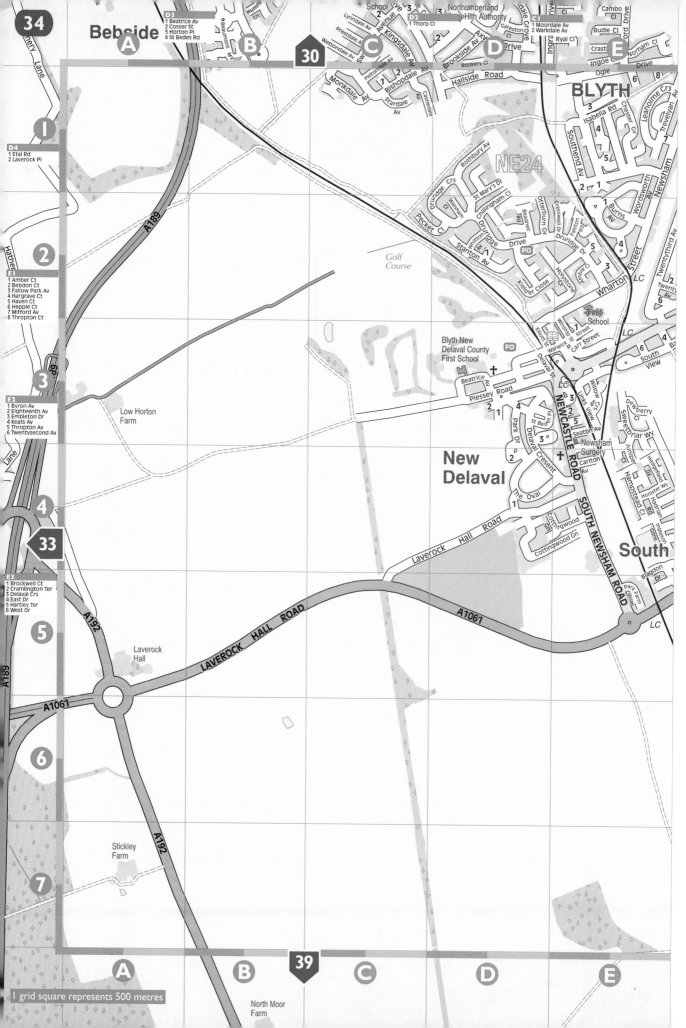

Sports Centre
Marr Road · Middle St
St Wilfrids
Middle School
Blyth Valley
Borough
Council
F
Princess Louise
First School
Prs
PO

1 Cherry Trees
2 Elm Trees
3 Kendal Av
4 Kendal Av
5 Rowan Ct
6 Second Av

Collingwood
Winch
G
First
School

Bowley St
Haughton St

F2
1 Eighth Av
2 Fenwick Av
3 Newlands Av
4 Newlands Pl
5 Twentieth Av
6 Twentyfifth Av

Cumberla
Co Council

Park Vw
East
View

H

Stannington St

J

F3
1 Clifton Gdns
2 Glendford Pl

31

Third Av

Kingsway

Blyth Spartans
AFC
PO

PLESSEY RD

Plessey Ter

Dalmatia Ter
Hunter Av

Rosemary Ter
Woodbine Ter
Briarwood Rd

B1329

WENSLEYDALE TERRACE

I

F4
1 Elstree Gdns

First Av
Seventh
Sixth Av
Ninth Av
Tenth Avenue

Twelfth Avenue
Fifteenth Av

A193 BROADWAY

A193 ROTARY WAY

Arcadia Ter
Grimsby Ter
Bohemia Ter

Solingen
Estate

Grantham St

Dent St

Allendale Ter
Brinkburn

Rosemary Ter

2

G1
1 Broadway Crs
2 Columbia Ter
3 Eleventh Av
4 George St
5 Kingsway
6 Rutherford St

Isabella
Pit

B1523

Newlands Rd
Middle
School

Barras Av

Warkworth

Wansbeck Av
Alconbury
Addington

Appledore Rd
Amersham Rd

Crebe

Matthew
Rd

Wolmer Rd

Solingen
Est

Sixth
PLESSEY ROAD

Melville
Av

Carrick Dr
Burnham
Banbury
Banbury Wy
Bromley
Gdns

Curfew Way
Plover
Dunkel Cl
Dunbane Dr

Guillemot
Osprey Dr

Kingfisher
Wy

Link House

LINKS ROAD

Beachway

South Beach

3

G2
1 Amberley Wy
2 Ashford Cl
3 Aylesford Sq
4 Bexhill Sq
5 Coquet Av
6 Guillemot Cl
7 Seafield Rd

Barras Av West
Farnham
Fairfield Av
Grange
Pastures
The
Gosport Wy
Gateley Av
Garasdale Av

Deal
Cl
Dorking
Close

Lapwing Cl
Dunlin
Sandpiper Cl
Petrel Wy

Teal Avenue
Cormorant

Osprey Dr

ROTARY WAY A193

B1329

Newsham

Earlswood
Gv
Esher Gdns
Epsom Wy
Eastwood
Av

Kittiwake Close
Herring Gull
Albatross
Way

Heron
Close
Avocet
Fulmar

Shearwater
Way
Elder Close
Drive

Shearwater
Way

Tern Cl
Mallard Wy

Links Road

4

Sandringham Drive

Newsham

NEWSHAM SOUTH

NEWSHAM ROAD

LINKS ROAD

G3
1 Dalston Pl
2 Downe Cl
3 Redshank Dr

A1061

Malay
Wy

Cemetery

A193

Gloucester Lodge
Farm

5

H1
1 Chamberlain St
2 Nixon Ter
3 Twizell St
4 Woodside

6

Lysdon
Farm

LINKS ROAD

A193

7

Hartley
Links

F

G

H

40

J

Seaton S
Middle Sc
Conway Grove
Benfield

Alston
Grove
Astley Gdns
Astley

K

Seaton Red
House Farm

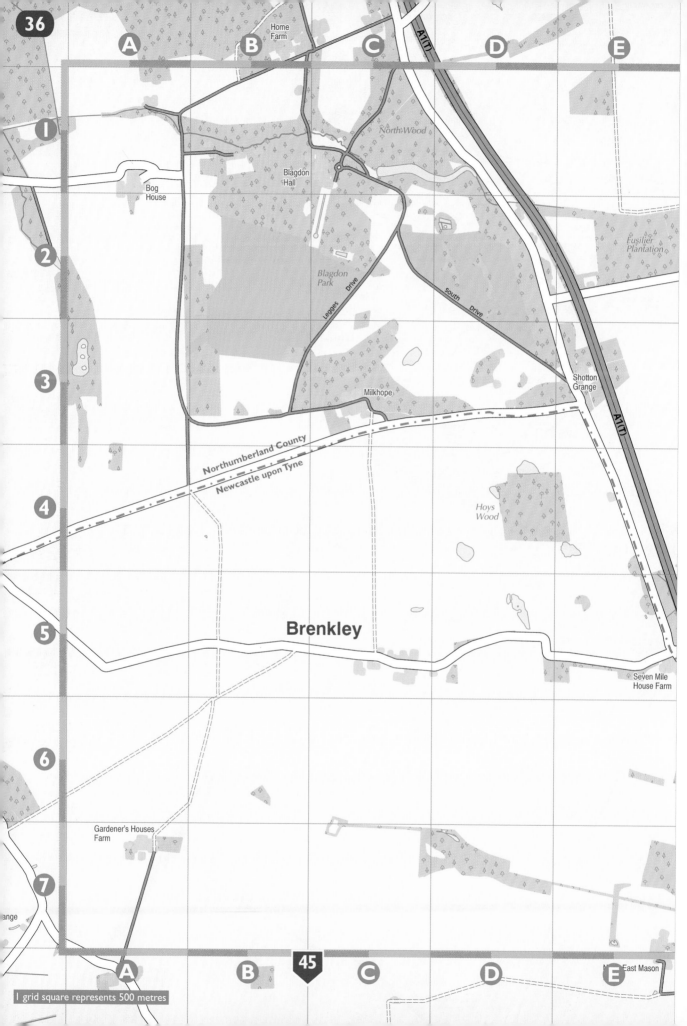

A B C D E

I

Home Farm

North Wood

Bog House

Blagdon Hall

Fusilier Plantation

2

Blagdon Park

Ledges Drive

South Drive

3

Milkhope

Shotton Grange

Northumberland County
Newcastle upon Tyne

Hoys Wood

A1(T)

4

Brenkley

5

Seven Mile House Farm

6

Gardener's Houses Farm

7

Grange

East Mason

I grid square represents 500 metres

F
G
H
J
I

K

G7
1 Garden Cl

K2
1 Ladykirk Wy
2 Lytham Cl
3 Selbourne Cl
4 Shanklin Pl
5 Southwold Pl

A1068

32

A1172

A1172

Nelson Drive

Bassington Drive

Business Park

Northumberland Co Council

Chichester Av
Ross Gv
Burdon Av
PO

Cram Station
I

Bassington Avenue

Plessey North Moor Farm

Moor Plantation

A1068

Beacon Lane

Kielder Av

Sudbury Way
Statford Cl
3
Shiel Gdns
Salisbury
Sheringham Dr
5
4

Lockerbie Rd
2
1
2
Loughrigg Avenue
3
2
1
Longridge Way

Langdale Drive

Lindsey Drive
1

2

White Hall Farm

Beaconhill

Beaconhill County First School

CRAMLINGTO

3

Beacon Lane

Waterloo Plantation

A1068

Plessey South Moor Farm

4

38

5

LO

Club House

Arcot Hall Golf Course

A1(T)

Hotel

Damdykes

A19(T)

A19(T)

6

FISHER LANE

Sandy's Letch

B1318 FRONT STREET

Brenkley Way

Thorntree Avenue

High Barnes

7

Seaton Burn

1

F
G
46
H
J
K

A1(T)

Brenkley Ct

BRIC

DUDLEY

Cemetery

West Park V

Western T

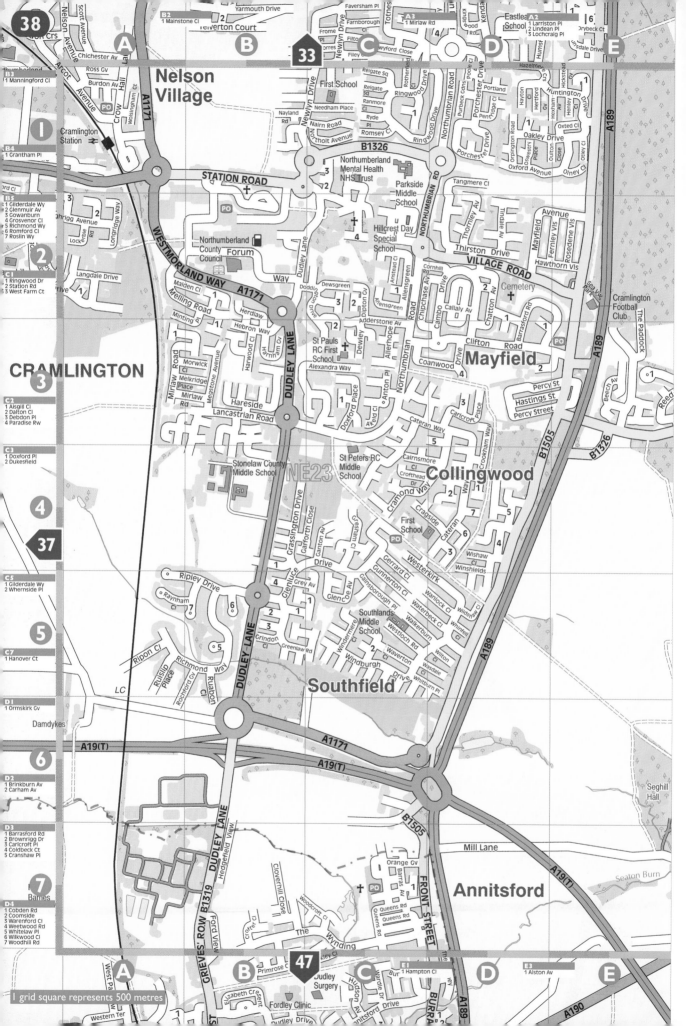

40

A   B   **35**   C   D   E

Hartley Links

I
C6
1 Bardon Crs
2 Horsley Gdns

Farm
1 Vanborough Ct

A6
1 Ambleside Cl
2 Kearsley Cl
3 Wallington Ct

A2
1 Maple Ct
2 Wansbeck Gv

Seaton Sluice
Middle School

Conway Grove
Benfield
Grove
Denway
Grove
Franklyn
Avenue
Naylor
Pl

Alston
Grove

Waring
Av
St Ronan's Dr
Meadow

Astley Gdns
Astley Gardens

Seaton Red
House Farm

New Hartley

Montrose
Close
Mountford Rd
Hastings Terrace
Hastings Gdns
Melton
Drive
Lysdon Av
Alston Rd
Gloria
Av
Seaburn View
Bradbury Ct
PO
Clinic
Hester Av
Meadow View
Avon Court
Street
St Michael's   Avenue
LC

2
E1
1 Hastings Av
2 Marden Ct

Dorchester Ct
Bristol

Lysdon Burn
St Michael's Avenue

Lookout
Farm

FOUNTAIN HEAD

A190
Seaton

3
E2
1 Aidan Av

THE AVENUE
A190

SEATON DELAVAL
4
39

ROAD
A190

Greenlands Ct
Avenue Head
Farm
Seaton
Terrace
Sinclair Gdns
Hartley St
Park View
Park Road
Ridsdale Cl
Park View
Whitton Pl
Hallington
A192

tors Surg
PO

5

Astley
Community
High School
Whitstead Rd
Elsdon
Rd
Fontburn Road
Mindrum Wy
Bavington
Road
Swinburn
Road
Acomb
Avenue
Avenue
Swarland Road
Kyloe
Av
Staward Av
Paston Rd
Chiswick
Rd
Tranwell
Tillmouth
Drive
Dunsdale Rd
Medburn Rd
Ryal Cl

Holywell County
First School

Holywell

Henshaw
Grove
Valley Rd
Seaton Crs
Holywell Avenue
East Gra
Holywell Dene Rd

6
Newb
Av
Melrose
Av
Ashkirk Wy
Thornhill
Ct
Denham
Drive
Woodside Av
Cragham Av
Stamford Av
Brentwood
Hedley
Hollinghill
Rd
Northside
Pl
Avenue
Southward Wy
Sandown Cl
Wylam Av
Branchland
Dr
Cholerford
Ms
Holywell
PO

Crow Hall
Farm

North Tyneside
Northumberland County

7
Wallridge Drive
Ridge Way
Seaton Burn
Dale Top
Bank Top

NE25

West Field
A   B   **49**   C   A192   D   E

I grid square represents 500 metres

F G H J

1 Collywell Ct
2 Waterford Cl
G2

1 Southward Cl
G3

I
2
3
4
5
6
7

Drewent Rd

BANK

Park Field Ter

Easedale

Westlands

The Seaburn Cl

Cresswell

The Links

Links

West Ter

Collywell

Queens Road

PH

Ochiltree Ct

A193

2

Taylor Cotts

Albert Rd

1

PO

Southward

Clarence St

7

Millway

Elwyn Close

Millfield

Elwin Cl

Budworth Av

Malvern Road

Dereham Av

Granville Av

Dereham Rd

BERESFORD ROAD

Bay Rd

Melton Crs

Dereham Rd

Rosewood Crs

Simonside

The Crest

The Rise

St Mary's Wynd

Seaton Sluice

Hartley

East End

Crag Point

NE26

Seaton Burn

Hartley West Farm

HARTLEY LANE

A193

BLYTH ROAD

St Mary's or Bait Island

St Mary's Lighthouse

B1325

Cemetery

The Links

Gerrard Road

Garsdale Road

Gerrard Cl

Linton Rd

Brierdene Rd

Westley Cl

Westley Avenue

Craneswater Av

THE LINKS

Gorsedene Road

Hinns Avenue

PO

Brier Dene Farm

Brierdene

Br   Crescent

Astley Drive

50

A193

F G H J K

Whitley Lodge First School

2 4 5
Grenada Drive 1

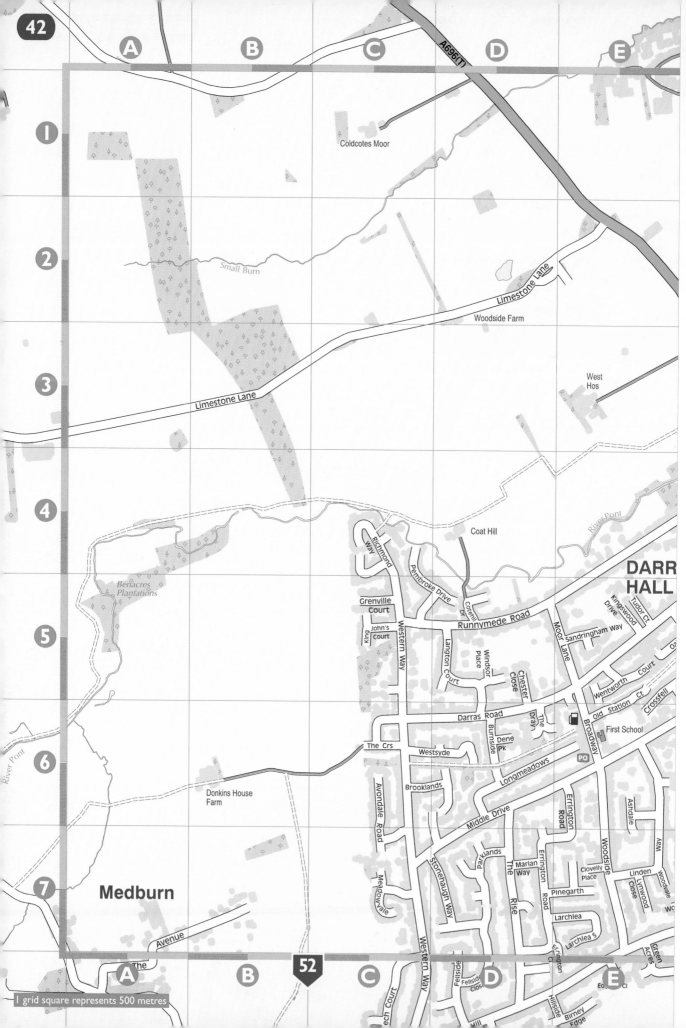

A **B** **C** A696(T) **D** **E**

1

Coldcotes Moor

2

Small Burn

Limestone Lane

Woodside Farm

3

Limestone Lane

West
Hos

4

Coat Hill

River Pont

Richmond Way

DARR
HALL

Benacres
Plantations

Pembroke Drive

Grenville
Court

Runnymede Road

Tudor Ct
Kingswood
Drive

King's Court

Windsor Place

Moor Lane

Sandringham Way

5

Western Way

Langton Court

Chester
Close

Wentworth Court

Crossfell

Old Station Ct

Darras Road

The Dray

River Pont

The Crs

Westsyde

Burnside

Dene
Pk

Broadway

First School

6

Brooklands

Longmeadows

PO

Errington Road

Ashdale

Donkins House
Farm

Avondale Road

Middle Drive

Woodside

Parklands

The
Way

Marian
Place

Errington Road

Clovelly
Place

Linden Close

Lynwood
Close

Woodvale Way

Stonehaugh Way

Meadowvale

The
Rise

Pinegarth

Larchlea

7

Medburn

Larchlea S

Avenue

Green
Acres

A The **B** **52** **C** Western Way **D** **E**
Egg... Cl

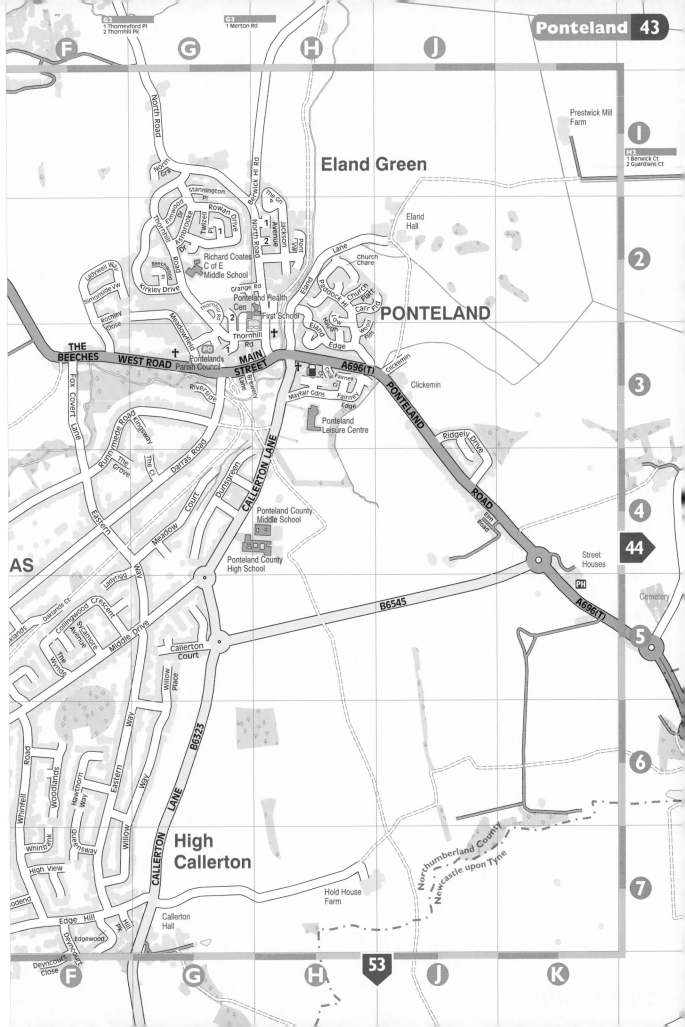

G2
1 Thorneyford Pl
2 Thornhill Pk

G3
1 Merton Rd

F G H J

Prestwick Mill
Farm

I

H2
1 Berwick Ct
2 Guardians Ct

North
Gra

North Road

Stannington
Pl

Elmwood
Dr

Rowan Drive

Thornhill
Road

Ashbrooke
Dr

Twizell
Pl

1

Berwick Hl Rd

North Road

Jackson
Avenue

1
2

Pont
Vw

The Gn

Eland Green

Eland
Hall

Eland
Lane

Church
Chare

2

Ladywell Way

Simonside Vw

Beechwood
Pl

Kirkley Drive

Rothley
Close

Richard Coates
C of E
Middle School

Meadowfield

Thornhill Rd

Grange Rd

2

Ponteland Health
Cen

First School

Thornhill
Rd

Paddock Hl

Church
Flatt

Carr
Fld

Eland

Low
Haugh

Wood
Flds

PONTELAND

Eland
Edge

THE
BEECHES

WEST ROAD

Ponteland
Parish Council

PO

MAIN
STREET

Brewery
Lane

Riverside

A696(T)

Cecil
Ct

Fairney
Cl

Mayfair Gdns

Fairney
Edge

Clickemin

Clickemin

PONTELAND

Fox Covert
Lane

Runnymede Road

Kingsway

The
Grove

The Cl

Darras Road

Eastern

Dunsgreen

CALLERTON LANE

Meadow
Court

Ponteland
Leisure Centre

Ridgely Drive

ROAD

3

Ponteland County
Middle School

Ponteland County
High School

Elm
Road

4

AS

Oaklands Ct

Collingwood
Crescent

Sycamore
Avenue

Ladyrigg

Middle Drive

Way

Callerton
Court

Willow
Place

B6545

Street
Houses

44

PH

Cemetery

A696(T)

5

cklands

The
Wynde

Willow Place

B6323

CALLERTON LANE

Whinfell
Road

Woodlands

Hawthorn
Way

Eastern

Way

Willow

Way

Queensway

Whinbank

High View

odend

Edge Hill

Edgewood

Deyncourt
Close

Deyncourt

Hill
Pk

**High
Callerton**

Callerton
Hall

Hold House
Farm

Northumberland County

Newcastle upon Tyne

6

7

F G H 53 J K

F1
1 West Acres

F2
1 Brenkley Cl
2 Farndale Cl
3 Horton Crs
4 The Winding

F G H **36** J

North East Mason
Farm

I
F3
1 Havannah Crs
2 Merlay Dr

Mason

North Mason Lodge

Oakfield Grange
PO

East Acres

Beech Avenue

North Vw

Front Street

Elm Av Ash Av Oak Av Av Poplar Pine Av

Sycamore Av

NE13

Hartley Burn

Big Waters
Nature Reserve

2
K4
1 Lola St

Dunsley Gdns

Church Cl

Dinnington
Village
First School

The Crest

Mitford Way

Castleway

Bracken Cl

Main Road

Mill Hill

Sandy Lane

Hack Hall

Waterford Pk

3

Westfield Av

Wallington Avenue

Hawthorn Av

Sandison
Court

Morley Hill
Farm

Brunswick
Village

Sandford Ms

4

1

5

Main Road

Coach Lane

46

1

3 2 3 10

4

1

Newsham Av

5 Hazle

6

West Brunton
Farm

Sunnyside

Brunton Lane

Middle
Brunton West
Farm

7

F G H **55** J K

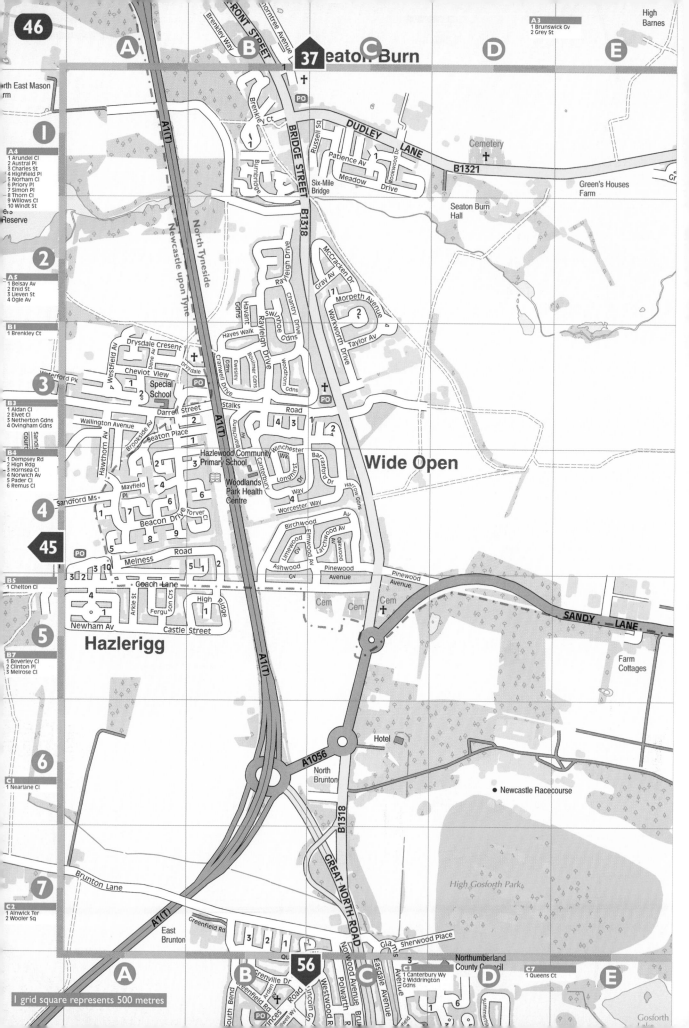

Annitsford

Fordley

DUDLEY

Burradon

Camperdown

Killingworth

George Stephenson High School

Killingworth Middle School

Forest Hall

High Weetslade

Gosforth Wood

Seaton Burn

MAIN STREET

KILLINGWORTH WAY

BURRADON ROAD

WEETSLADE ROAD

GREAT LIME ROAD

STATION ROAD

KILLINGWORTH DRIVE

LIME ROAD

A189
A190
A1056
B1321
B1319
B1505
B1505

38
48
57
47
2
3
4
5
6
7

F1
1 Bamborough Ct
2 Green Crs

G1
1 Southfields

G7
1 Dene Av

H1
1 Briarwood
2 Burn Vw
3 Burt Crs
4 Owen Brannigan Dr

H2
1 March Rd

H4
1 Attlee Cl
2 Front St
3 Shillaw Pl

H5
1 Bell Gv
2 Chestnut Cl
3 Garth Thirteen

J1
1 Bridge Cottages
2 Seaton Cft

J5
1 Eastwood Cl
2 Hall Dr
3 Netherton
4 Redford Pl
5 Stagshaw

J6
1 Alder Wy
2 Beech Wy
3 Cowans Av
4 Ettrick Cl
5 Garth Sixteen
6 Garth Twelve
7 Hawthorn Pl
8 Kielder Cl
9 Laburnum Cl
10 Redwood Cl
11 Rothbury Cl
12 Thompson Av
13 West Clifton
14 Willow Gdns

J7
1 Coniston Cl
2 Grasmere Ct

K6
1 Bolam Rd
2 East Bailey
3 West Bailey

K5
Street names for this grid square are listed at the back of the index

K4
1 Algernon
2 Callerton
3 Hauxley
4 Havanna

North Tyneside Council

North Tyneside Area Health Authority

Moor Edge First School

Bailey Green First Sch

First Kirklands School

Dudley Surgery

Fordley Clinic

Newcastle upon Tyne

North Tyneside

Burradon House

Cheviot Grange

F G H 40 J

NE25

1 Collingwood Rd
2 Wellington Av

K5
1 Harewood Crs

Bank Top

I

West Field

Northumberland County
North Tyneside

Holywell Grange
Farm

2

3

East Holywell

West Holywell

Fenwick's Close
Farm

Brierdene Burn

Cemetery

Church
WY
Front Street

Woodlands
CI

Gdn Ter

John St

Earsdon

A192

HARTLEY LANE

Monkseaton Rd

Holly Av

Hesleyside Rd

EARSDON ROAD

Westgate Rd

The Ridings

North

MONK

4

Nelson

Waterloo Rd

Whitley

Redheugh Rd

Greystead Rd

Tarset Rd

Burnbank

Walwick Rd

Haddon

Kielder Ho

First
School

Hatfield Gdns

Ludlow Dr

Wilton

Haddon Ct

Arundel Drive

Wentworth

Carnoustie

50

Kielder
Road

PO

Otterburn Avenue

Thorntree

Sandringham Drive

Marina Dr

Marina
Drive

5

LC

Shamrock
CI

West
Wy

Road

NE27

kworth

Moor Edge
Farm

Moor Edge Rd

EARSDON ROAD

Shiremoor
Middle School

Hector St

South St

Wark Av

Grange Av

Earsdon Vw

Seaton Rd

Otterburn

Harewood
Crs

West
Monks

6

Hartside

Harle Rd

Havelock

Hartside
Crs

Harlow Av

STATION ROAD

A186

Shiremoor
Station

PO

Etal Crs

Ford

Avenue

Beadnell

Belford Gdns

Milfield Avenue

Park Avenue

Park Grove

Craster Avenue

Felton

Witton Rd

Fame

Park

Park Crs

Park Rd

Park Lane

Shiremoor

Allendale Crs

Glendale Rd

PO

Langley Av

Alwinton Rd

Mitten Av

Murton

Well Lane

7

A186

B1322

Brandon Av

Emmerson Pl

Lesbury

Kirkland Wk

Brenkley Av

Stanton Road

Carthington Av

Lilburn

Colwell Rd

Kirkey Rd

Brunton Av

Brenkley Av

Shiremoor First
School

Horsley Av

Ditton

Harbottle Av

Angerton
Av

Horton Av

Beal Rd

Sherwood Close

The Bridle

Murton Lane

NEW YORK ROAD

Holyfields

BENTON ROAD

A191

A191(T)

A191(T)

Frayfields

West St

Turner St

PO

Berlink North

NEW YORK ROAD

St Albans View

Brunswick Rd

Park La

New Yo

A191

New Yo

F4
1 Ocean Vw

F6
1 Cranbourne Gv

F **G** **H** **J**

1
F7
1 Ellersmere Gdns
2 Grange Cl

2
G5
1 Simpson St

3

4

5

6

7

WHITLEY
BAY

Brook St
Promenade
ebrew
ynagogue
oxfo
North Pde
South Pde Hotel
Esplanade
York Rd
Victoria Ter
Clifton Ter
Percy Rd
ond Ter
North Tyneside
Council Offices
Doctors
Surgery
Station Rd
Algernon Pl
Whitley
Edwards Rd
Rockcliffe St
Gordon
Sq
Hotel
Windsor Ter
Whitley
Bay Station
Felton
Plessey
Dilston
Av
Etal Av
Egremont
Alma Pl
Delaval Rd
Margaret Rd
Grafton Rd
Windsor Crs
Crescent
Holystone Av
Chollerford
Avenue
Belsay Av
Amble Av
Marden Crs
Eskdale Ter
Naters St
Norma
Cliff
RW
Burnside Road
North
View
Eleanor
Street
John St
PO
Shorestone Av
St George's Road
Foxton Av
Station Rd
Cullercoats
Station
Marden
Front St
Hatterton Av
Newton Av
Longston
AV
Marden
AV
Beverley Terrace
Broadway
Sandfield
Cl
The Broadway
Mast Lane
Seacombe
Wansbeck
Cullercoats
Primary School
Links
Beverley Gdns
Marden
Kendal Avenue
Fairfield
Dr
Keswick Dr
Seacrest
Av
Sunlea
Avenue
Sandhurst Av
Links
Road
Links Avenue
Medburn
Av
A193
THE BROADWAY
Derwent
Rd
Deepdale Road
Road
Silloth Pl
Thursby
Av
Fairbrk
Av
Lambley
PI
Wintinan
Rd
Beach Croft Avenue
Challen
Gdns
Rennington Av
Beach Rd
Ealing
Dr
ne Av
 Road
allington
Marden High
School
Monkhouse
School
Green

Cullercoats

Marden

Long
Sands

61

F **G** **H** **J** **K**

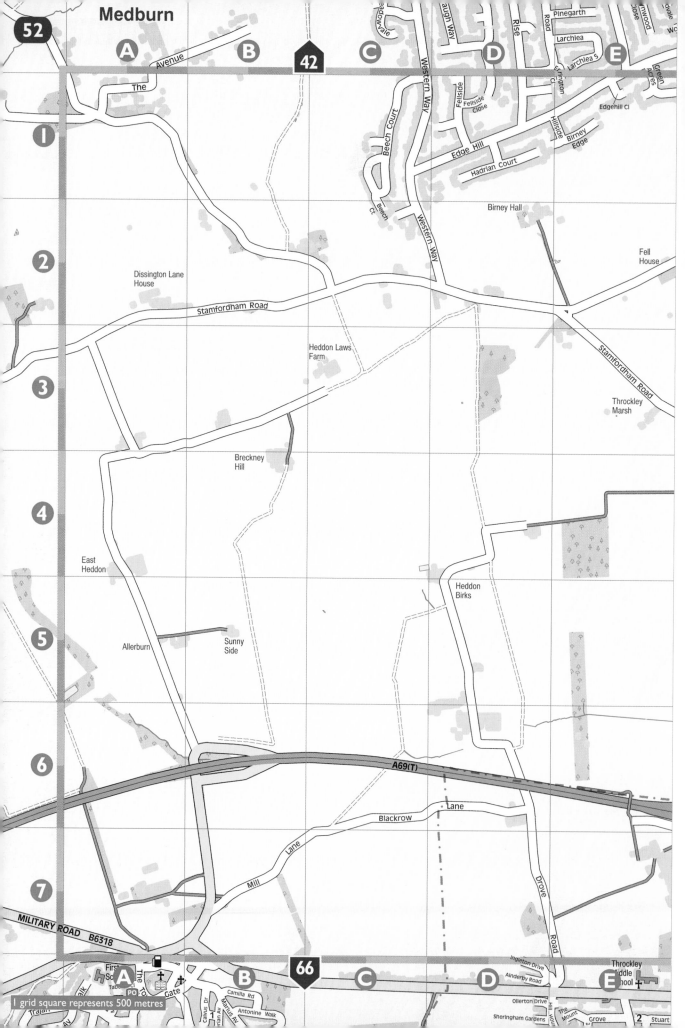

Medburn

52

42

66

A B C D E

1 2 3 4 5 6 7

The Avenue

Dissington Lane House

Stamfordham Road

Heddon Laws Farm

Breckney Hill

East Heddon

Allerburn

Sunny Side

Beech Court

Beech Ct

Western Way

Edge Hill

Hadrian Court

Fellside

Fellside Close

Pinegarth

Larchlea

Larchlea S

Rise

Errington Cl

Hillside

Birney Edge

Green Acres

Edgehill Cl

Birney Hall

Fell House

Stamfordham Road

Throckley Marsh

Heddon Birks

A69(T)

Lane

Blackrow

Mill Lane

Drove Road

MILITARY ROAD B6318

Ingleton Drive

Ainderby Road

Throckley Middle School

First School

PO

The Towne Gate

Camilla Rd

Antonine Walk

Calvus Dr

Martius Av

Hadrian Av

Trajan Walk

Ollerton Drive

Sheringham Gardens

Hill House

The Grove

Stuart

I grid square represents 500 metres

K6
1 Abbey Dr
2 Ashford Gv
3 Callerton Vw
4 Claverdon St
5 Lilac Cl
6 Nedderton Cl
7 Newsham Cl

K7
1 Aberford Cl
2 Aicroft Cl
3 Amesbury Cl
4 Dorchester Cl
5 Dunstable Pl

Hold House
Farm

F

Edge Hill
Deyncourt Close
Ridgewood
Limecourt

Callerton Hall

G

43

H

J

I

2

3

4

54

5

Black Callerton

Callerton Grange

Callerton Lane End

B6323
Northumberland County
Newcastle upon Tyne

Broomhall Farm

Callerton

STAMFORDHAM ROAD
B6324

Crescent Farm

Lough House

B6323
PONTELAND ROAD

Dewley Burn

Dewley Farm

Fell House Farm

Mandarin Close
Magenta
Malaga Cl
Madeira Cl
Marquis Close
Mangrove

6

Throckley Industrial Estate

North Walbottle

North Walbottle Road
Aylsham Cl
Nuneaton Way
Ladybank
Kinver Dr
Kenmoor
Coronation Road
Northumberland Gdns
Lotus Close
Dover Cl
Casterton
Chadderton
Caversham Rd
Cottersdale
Coldside Gdns
Dalto
Dawlish
Hillhead
Par
Me
Cen

7

PONTELAND ROAD
A6085

Westway
Laurel St
Sycamore St
Wesley Wy
Finchale Gdns
Alston Gdns
Northway
Lancercost Gdns
Brampton Gdns
Ambleside Gdns
Ambleside

Throckley

F

HEXHAM ROAD
B6528

G

Talbot House Special School

H

67

J

Cardinal Cl
Minster Gv
Monkridge
The Old
Queensbury Dr
Chetham Gdns
Chudleigh Gdns

K

Knoplaw Fi
School
Par

Gardens
Throckley
Vallum

Cotter Riggs Pl

PO

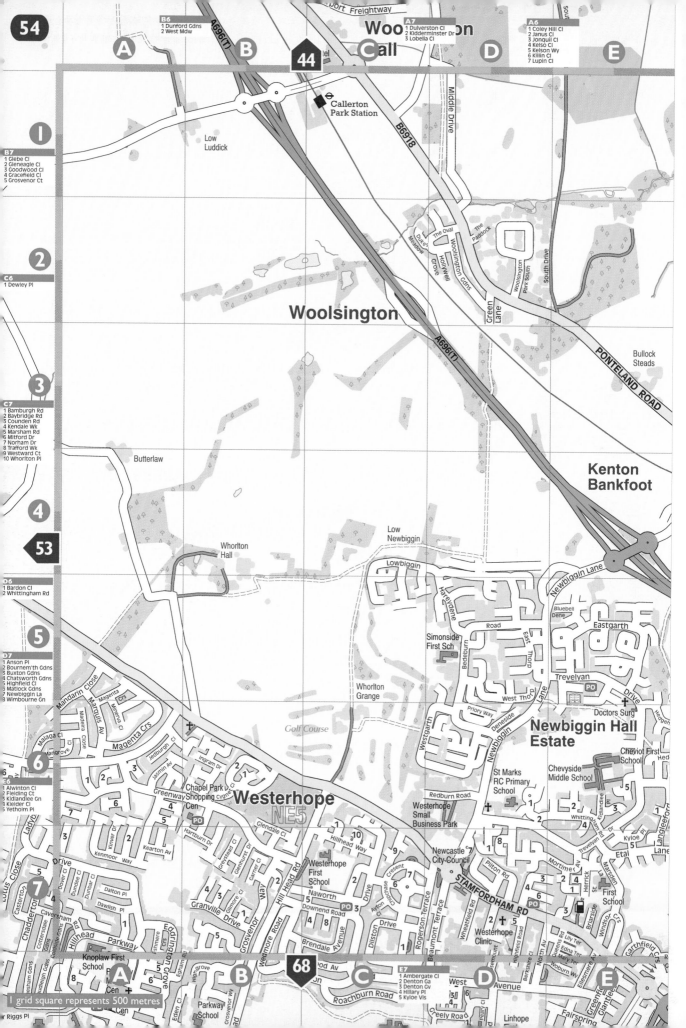

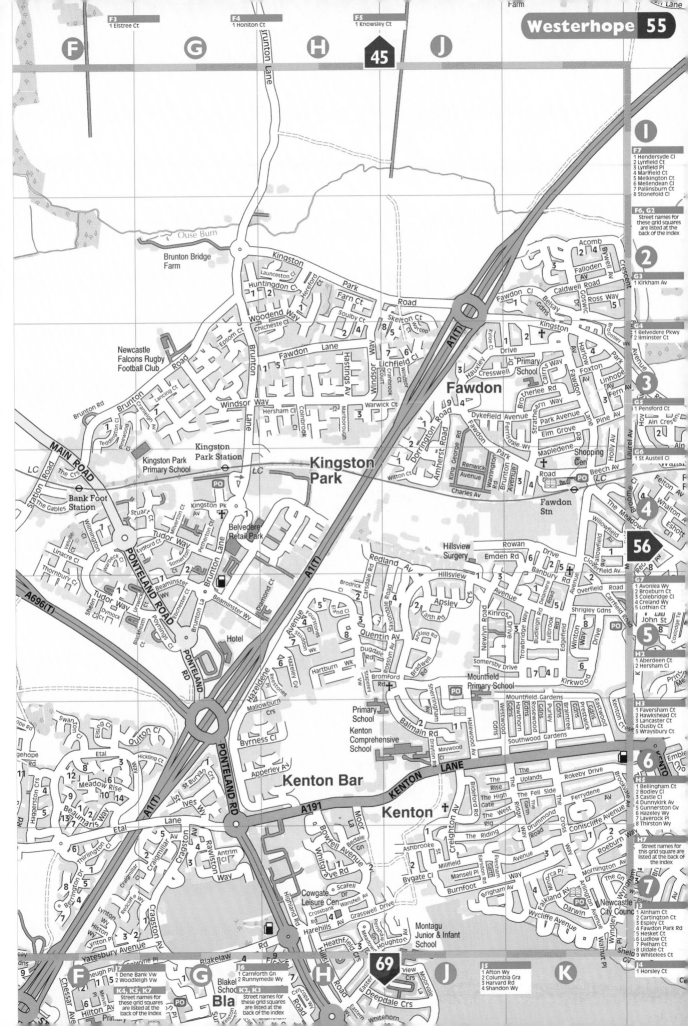

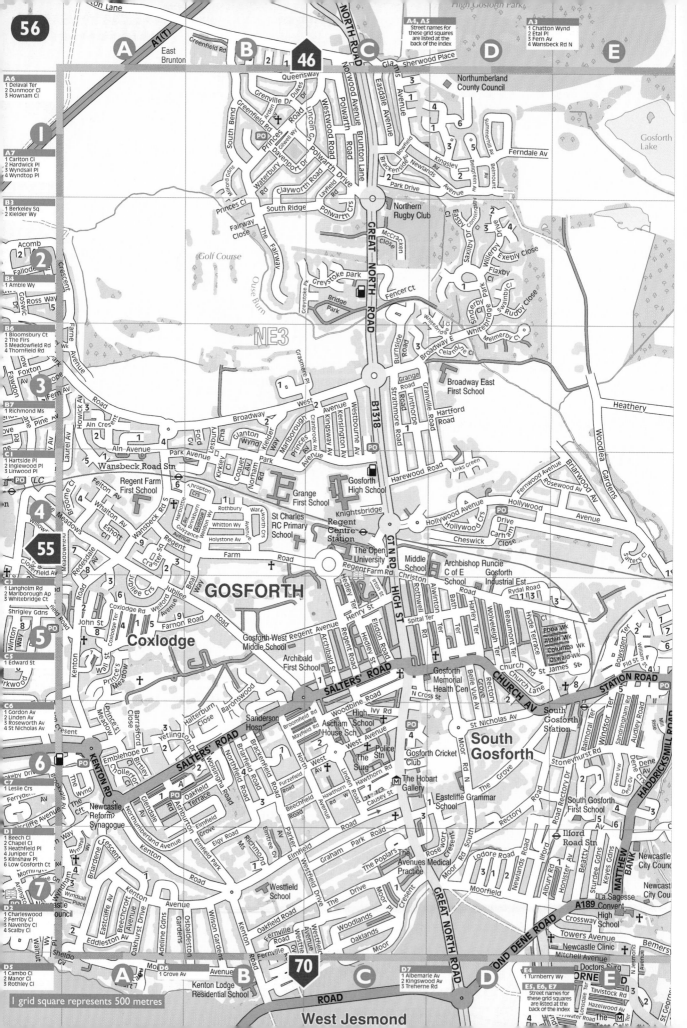

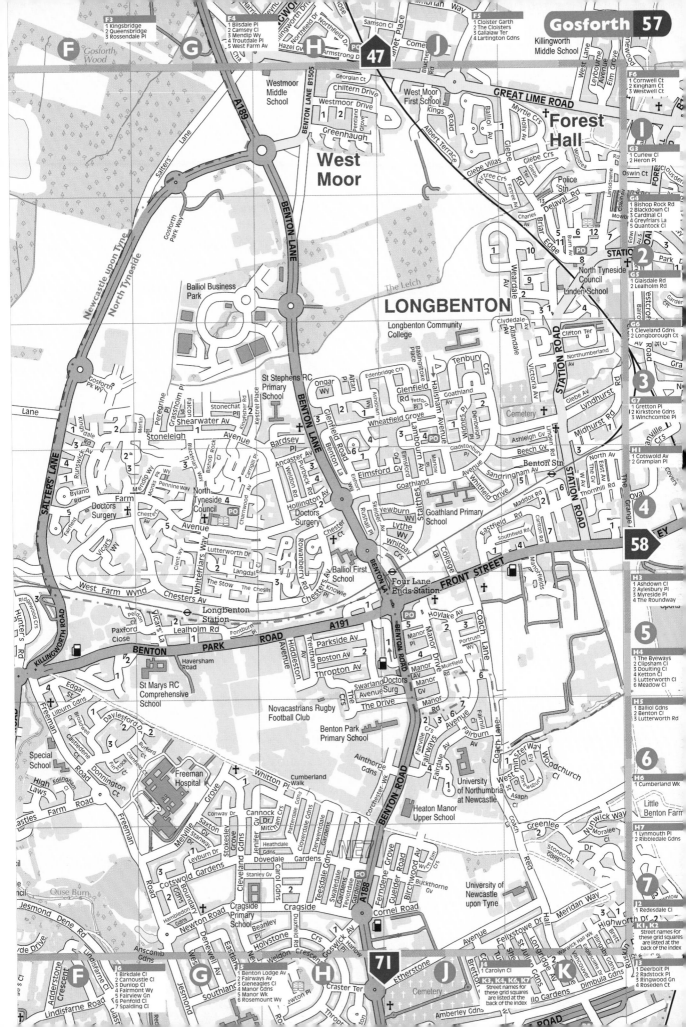

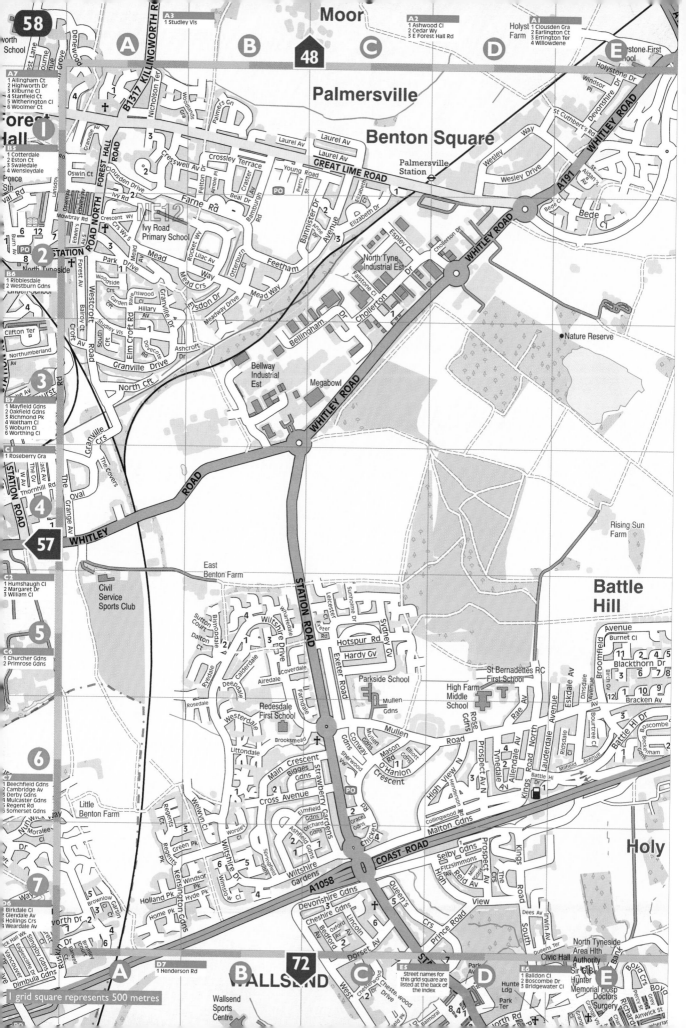

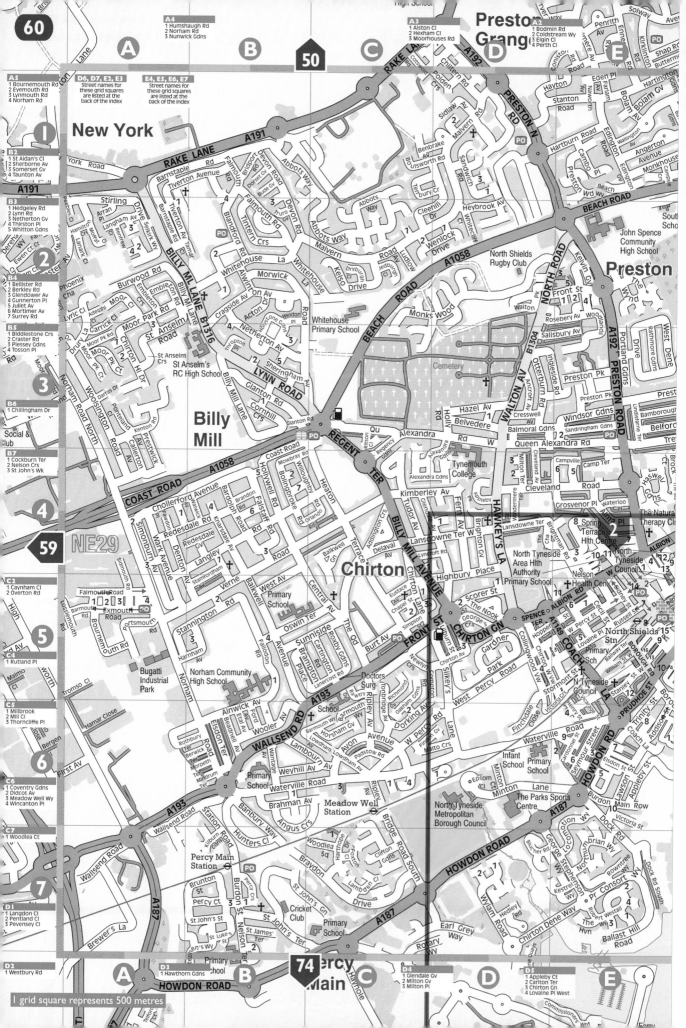

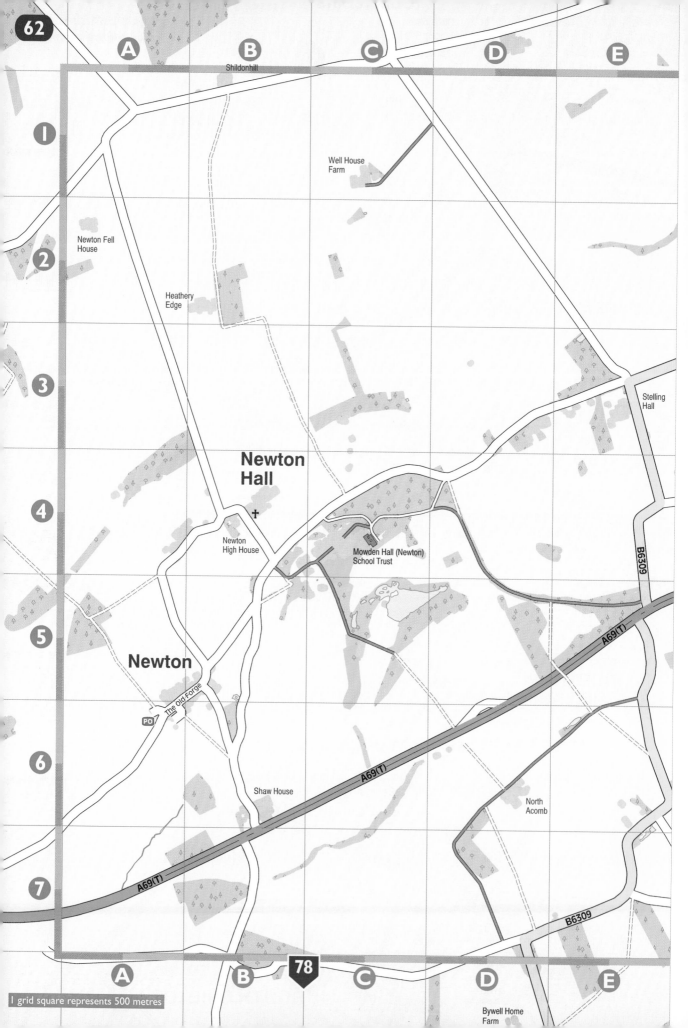

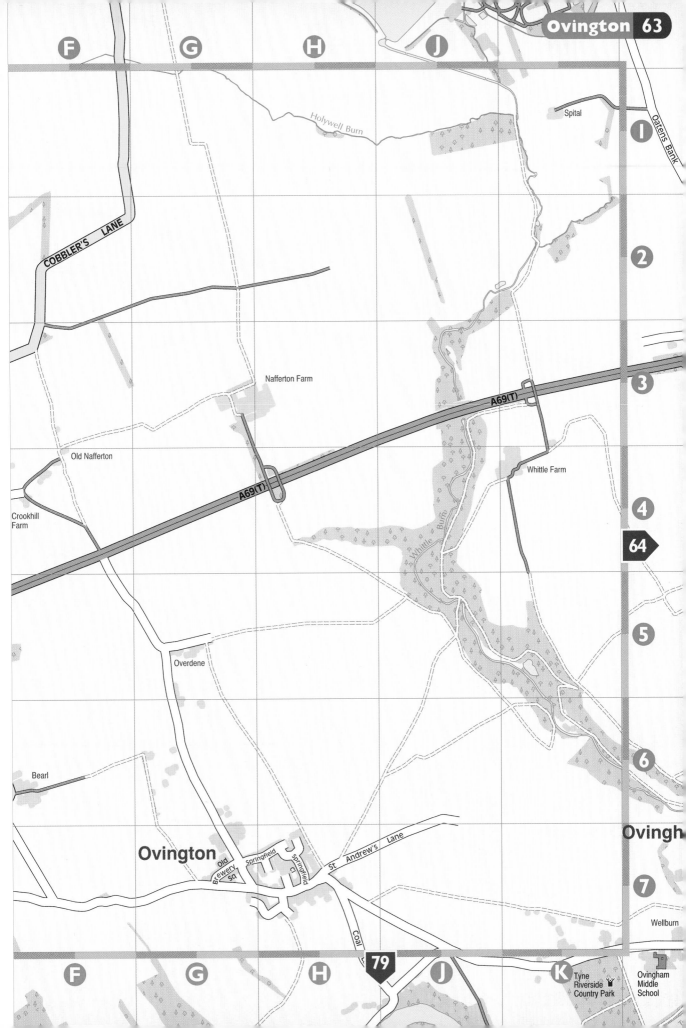

F G H J

Oakens Bank

1

Spital

2

COBBLER'S LANE

3

Nafferton Farm

A69(T)

Old Nafferton

A69(T)

Whittle Farm

Crookhill Farm

4

64

Whittle Burn

5

Overdene

6

Bearl

Ovingh

Ovington

Old Brewery Sq

Springfield

Springfield Ct

St Andrew's Lane

7

Wellburn

Coal

79

F G H J K Tyne Riverside Country Park

Ovingham Middle School

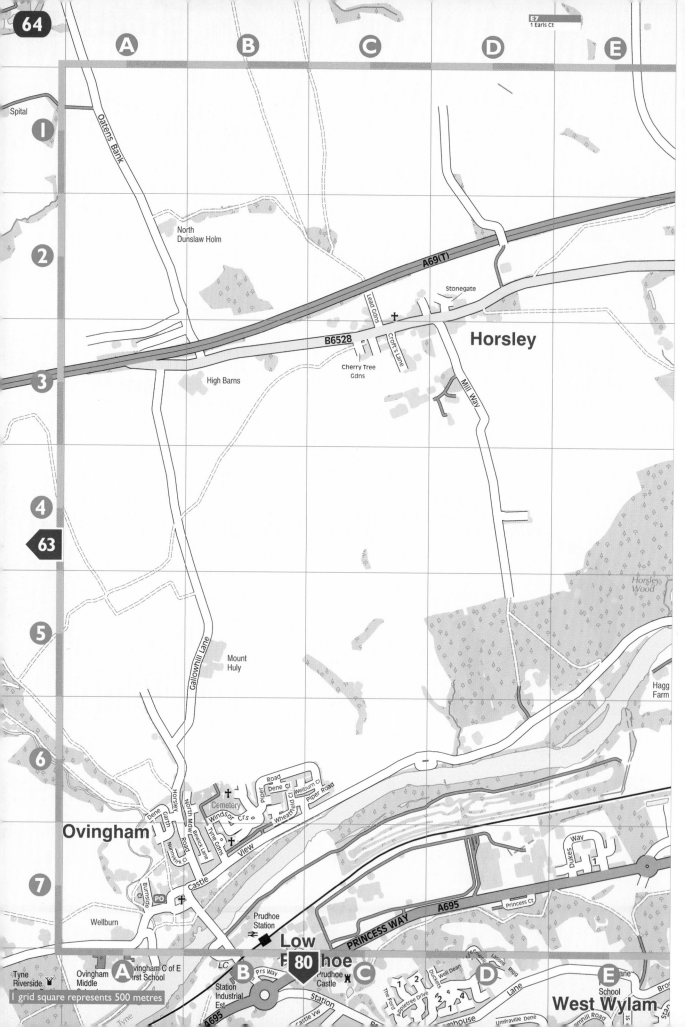

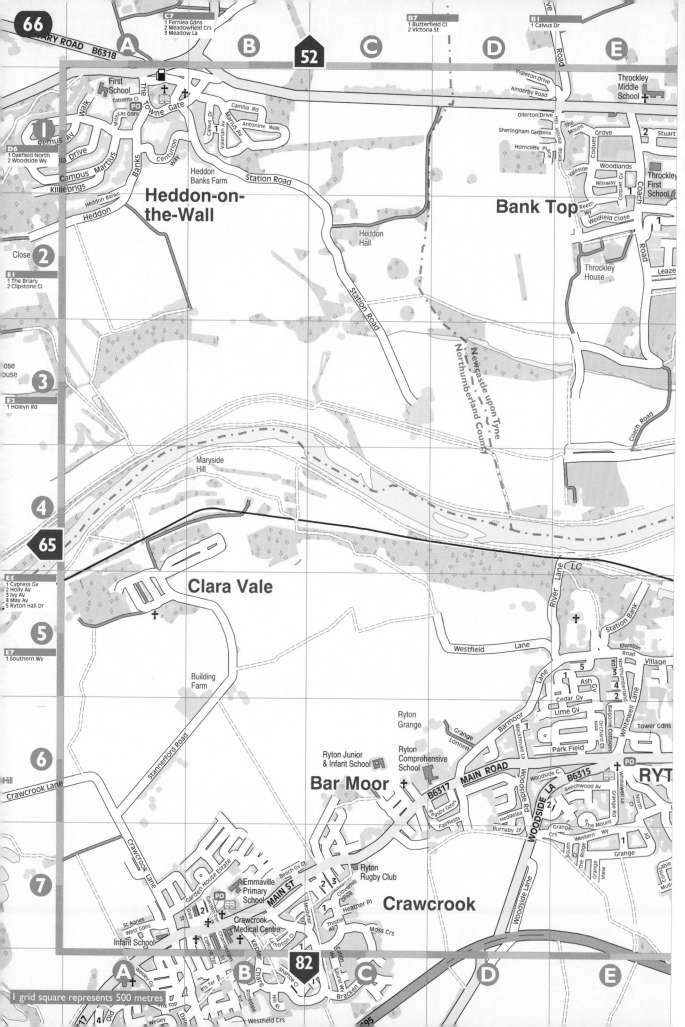

C7
1 Fernlea Gdns
2 Meadowfield Crs
3 Meadow La

B7
1 Butterfield Cl
2 Victoria St

B1
1 Calvus Dr

A　**B**　**C**　**D**　**E**

ARY ROAD B6318

First School

PO The Towne Gate

Taberna Cl

Mithras Gdns

1
Remus Av

Campus

D6
1 Oakfield North
2 Woodside Wy

Walk

Calla Drive

Martius Av

Killiebrigs

Centurion Way

Calvus Dr

Valerian Av

Martius Av

Camilla Rd

Antonine Walk

Heddon Banks Farm

Station Road

Heddon-on-the-Wall

Heddon Banks

Heddon

Heddon Hall

Ingleton Drive

Alnderby Road

Ollerton Drive

Sheringham Gardens

Horncliffe Place

House Road

Coquet

The Mount

Grove

Wilsway

Woodlands

2
Stuart

Hill

Vaiside

Reeth

Coquet Gv

Wy

Coach

Throckley Middle School

Throckley First School

1

Close

2

E1
1 The Briary
2 Clipstone Cl

Wellfield Close

Throckley House

Leaze

Station Road

ose
house

3

E2
1 Holeyn Rd

Maryside Hill

Newcastle upon Tyne

Northumberland County

Bank Top

4

Coach Road

65

E5
1 Cypress Gv
2 Holly Av
3 Ivy Av
4 May Av
5 Ryton Hall Dr

Clara Vale

River Lane

LO

Station Bank

5

E7
1 Southern Wy

Westfield   Lane

Elvaston Road

Village

Building Farm

Lane

5

Ash Gv

Northumberland

4

Whitewell Lane

Tower Gdns

Cedar Gv

Lime Gv

Barmoor

2

Balgonie Cottages

Orchard Ct

Ryton Grange

Grange Lonnen

Blackhouse La

Park Field

Stannerford Road

6

Hill

Crawcrook Lane

Ryton Junior & Infant School

Ryton Comprehensive School

Bar Moor

MAIN ROAD

B6317

Rugby Gdns

Fairfields

Woodside Rd

Woodside C

B6315

Beechwood Av

PO

Whitewell La

RYT

Hedgelea

Burnaby Dr

2

Granger Crs

The Mount

Grange Rd

North

Crawcrook Lane

Garden House Estate

Emmaville Primary School

PO

Garden Ter

MAIN ST

Beech Gv Ct

3

Cloverhill Drive

Molyfair

7

Heather Pl

Thistle Av

Ryton Rugby Club

Crawcrook

Western Wy

South

The Ridge

Grange View

1

Grange

St Agnes'
West Gdns

Infant School

Dale

Clifford Ter

Crawcrook Medical Centre

Kepier Ter

Chamberlain

Lambton La

1

Moss Crs

Shafto St

Chare

82

Capitol

Laurel Wy

Bracken

A　**B**　**C**　**D**　**E**

Wesley Gv

Iris Ter

Rosedale

Hill Ri

Dale

nk Top

Wesley

Westfield Crs

F
G
Throckley
H
53
J

F1
1 The Crescent
2 Mt Pleasant Ct

F2
1 The Causeway
2 Collier Cl
3 Hawkwell Ri
4 Isabella Wk
5 The Wynd

F6
1 Holburn Cl
2 Holburn Ct

G1
1 Ferndown Ct
2 Sandpiper Cl
3 Whernside Wk

I
1 Appian Pl
2 Elmfield Rd
3 Eversleigh Pl
4 St Mary's Pl

G2
1 Briar La
2 Mayfield Gdns
3 Rye Cl

2

G3
1 Westmacott St

3

Shamrock Cl

Southfork
G7
1 Clifton Cl
2 Curlew Cl
3 Dunlin Cl
4 Sanderling Cl

H2
1 Bankhead Rd

4

68

H3
1 Berkley St
2 Millfield Cl

5

H4
1 Church Bank
2 Church Rd
3 Clarks Hill Wk

6

J2
1 Village Farm

7

J4
1 Berwick St

HEXHAM ROAD
Throckley Surgery
PO
Newcastle City Council
A6085
B6528
Talbot House Special School
Primary School
George Street
Whitehall Rd
HAWTHORN
Walbottle
N Walbottle Road
North Walbottle Road
TERRACE
Chapel House Middle School
Cotter Riggs Pl
Beckside Gdns

Richard Browell Road
Fosse Law
Parkside
New Burn
PO
The Paddock
The Green
Walbottle
Percy Way
Queens Road
Queen's Ct

Tyne Riverside Country Park
Grange Farm
Doctors Surgery
Townfield Gdns
Alnwick
Park Rd
Newburn Hall Motor Mus
First School
Newburn
Hospital
Lane
Burnham Avenue
Combe Drive
Blanchland Av
Medburn Rd

Newburn Leisure Centre
Grange Rd
Boyd St
Davison St
Newcastle City Council
Manor Gv
Millfield Lane
Ellington Cl
Doddington Cl
Crofton Way
Burnham Av
Malven
Park Ri

Station Rd
Water Rw
PO
HIGH STREET
Golf Course
LEMINGTON ROAD
A6085
Aln Grove

River Tyne
Newcastle upon Tyne
Gateshead
Shelley Road
Newburn Industrial Estate
Keats Road

Haugh Lane
LC
Newburn
Bridge
Road
Ryton Industrial Est
LC

East Peth
Willow Ct
Holburn
Dene Crs
Dene Cl
Meadow Cl
The Meadows
Thorpe Dr
Holburn Wy
Holburn Crs
Holburn Gdns
B6317
Crookhill
Crookhill Junior School
Stella Bank
Stella Lane
Parkland
The Fairway
STELLA ROAD
B6317
BRIDGE STREET

ON
Watermill
Hexham Old Road
Runhead Estate
Runhead Est
Church
Hexham Old Road
Stella Lane
Stella
Cromwell Ct
Cowan Close
Stella Hall
Hall Pk
Staith La
The Rise
Path Head
Summerhill
Fountain Lane

Cemy
North Gv
High Gv
South Grove
The Crescent
Stargate
Kg Edward Rd
PO
Ashton Cl
Cow Lane

K4
1 Allerdean Cl
2 Grasmoor Pl
3 Hamsterley Crs
4 Helston Ct

K1
1 Deacon Cl
2 Marcross Cl
3 Meltham Cl
4 Milsted Cl

J7
1 Storey La
2 Tempest St

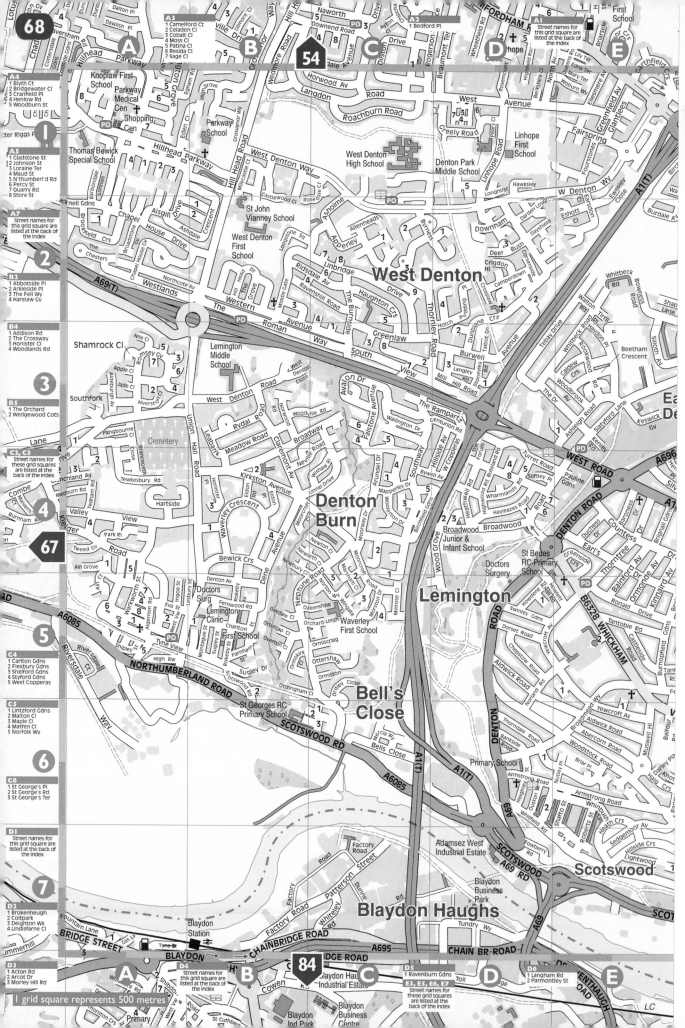

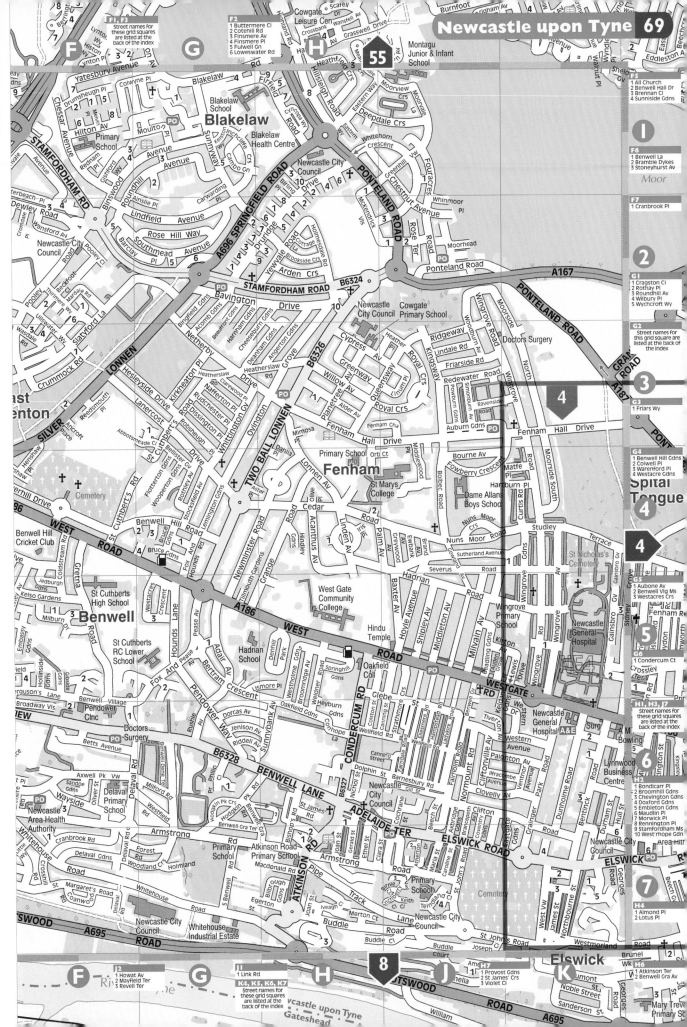

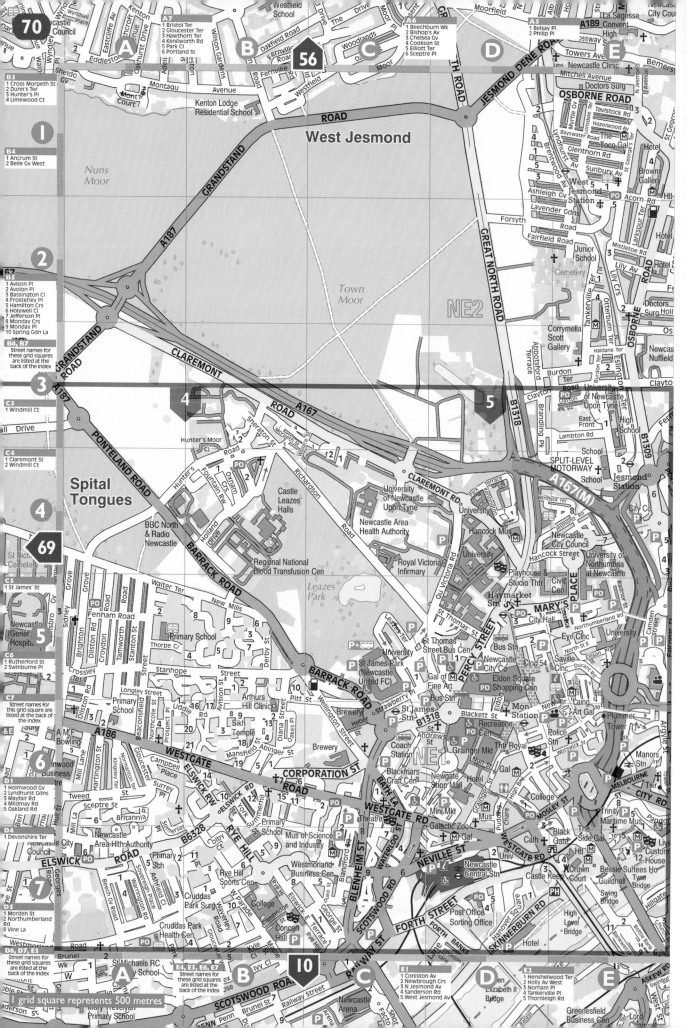

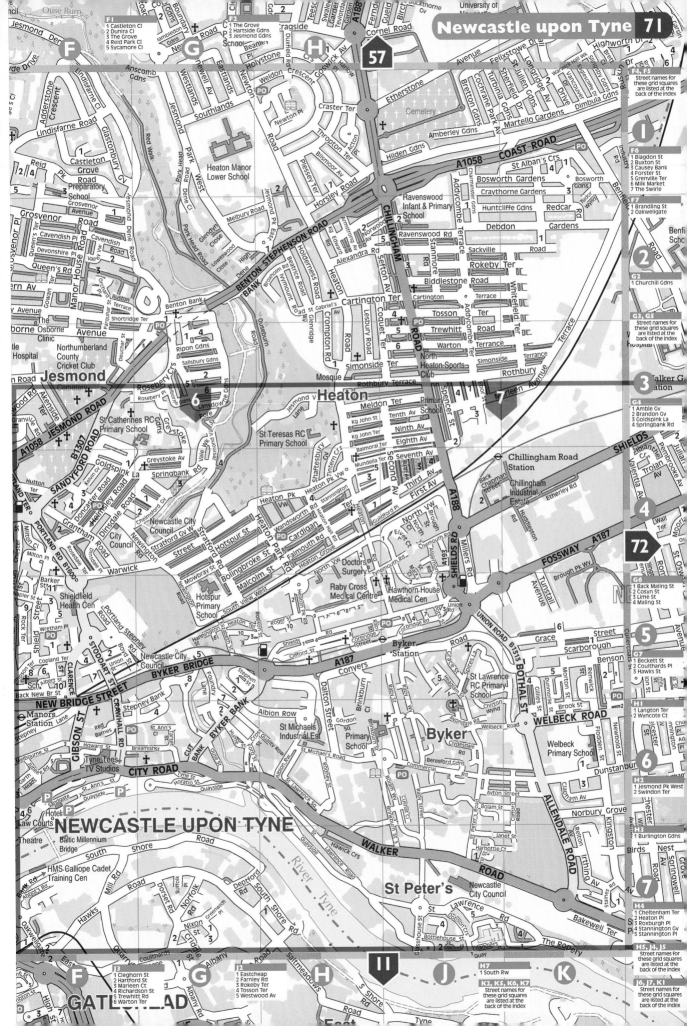

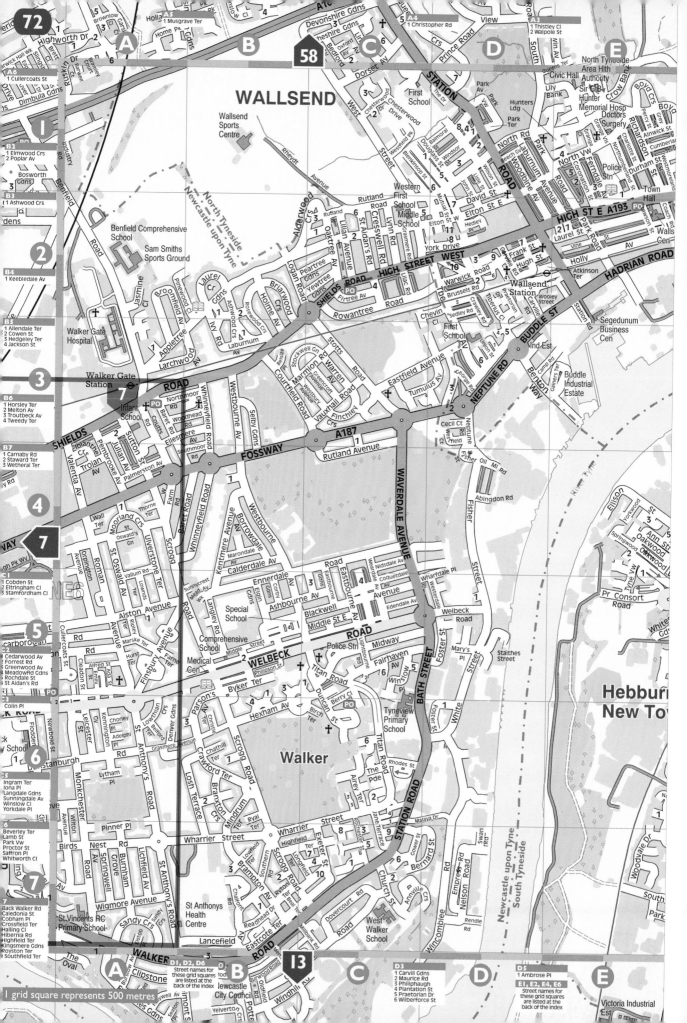

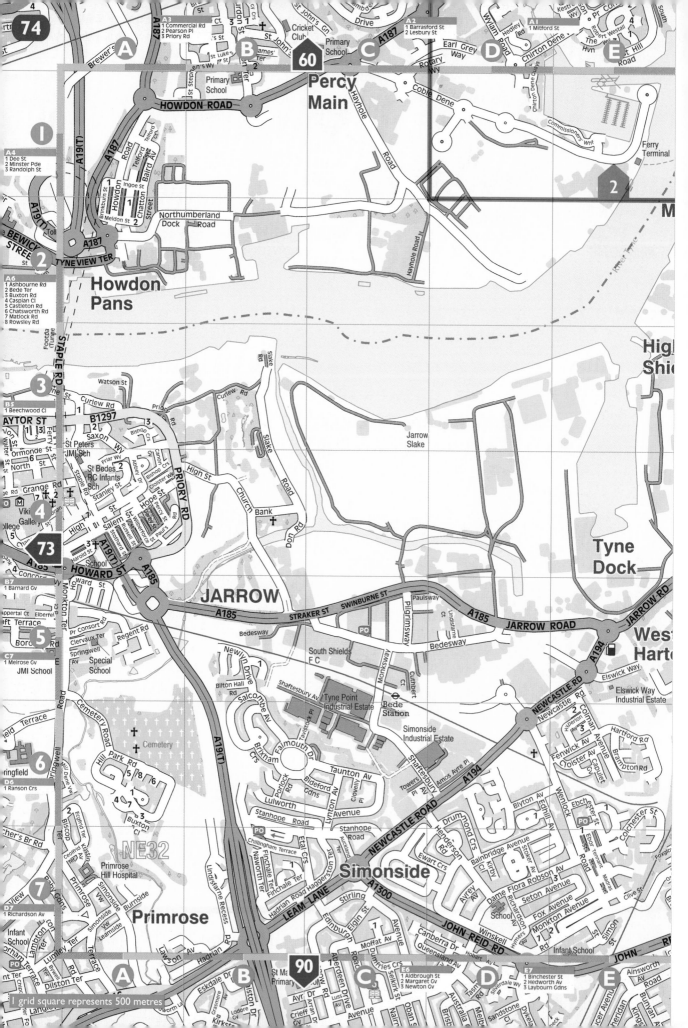

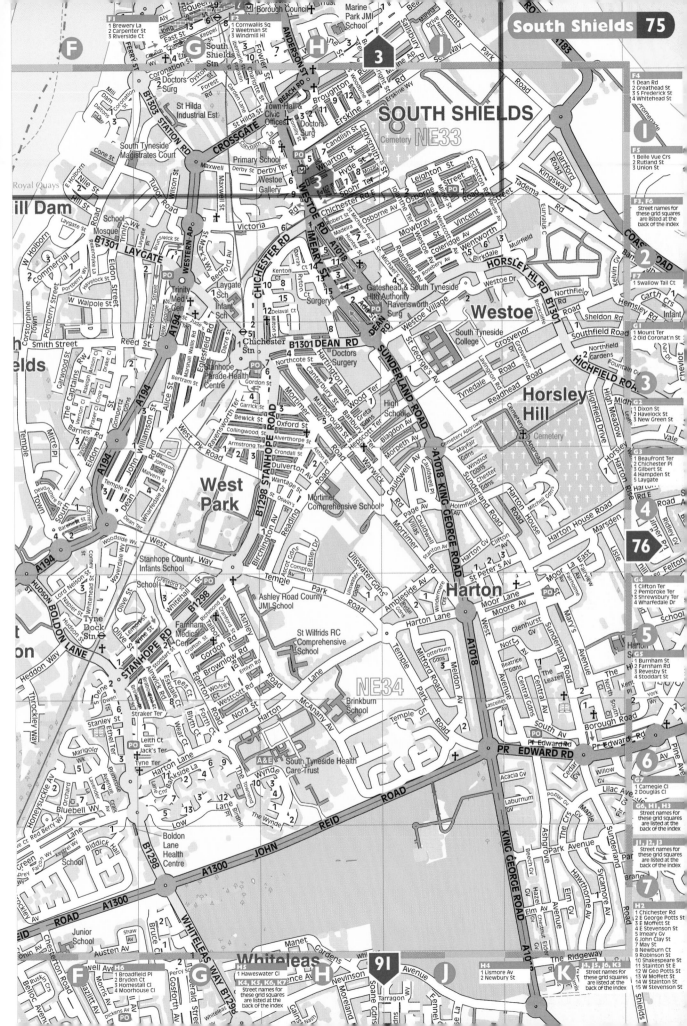

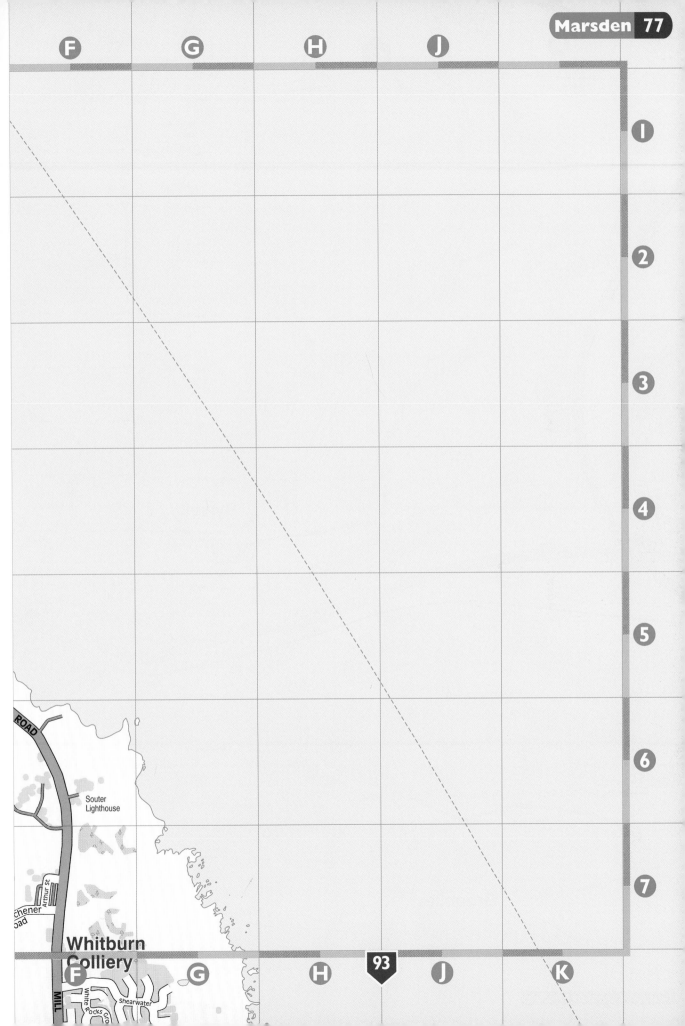

F G H J

I
2
3
4
5
6
7

ROAD

Souter
Lighthouse

Arthur St

chener
oad

**Whitburn
Colliery**

F G H 93 J K

MILL

White Rocks Gro

Shearwater

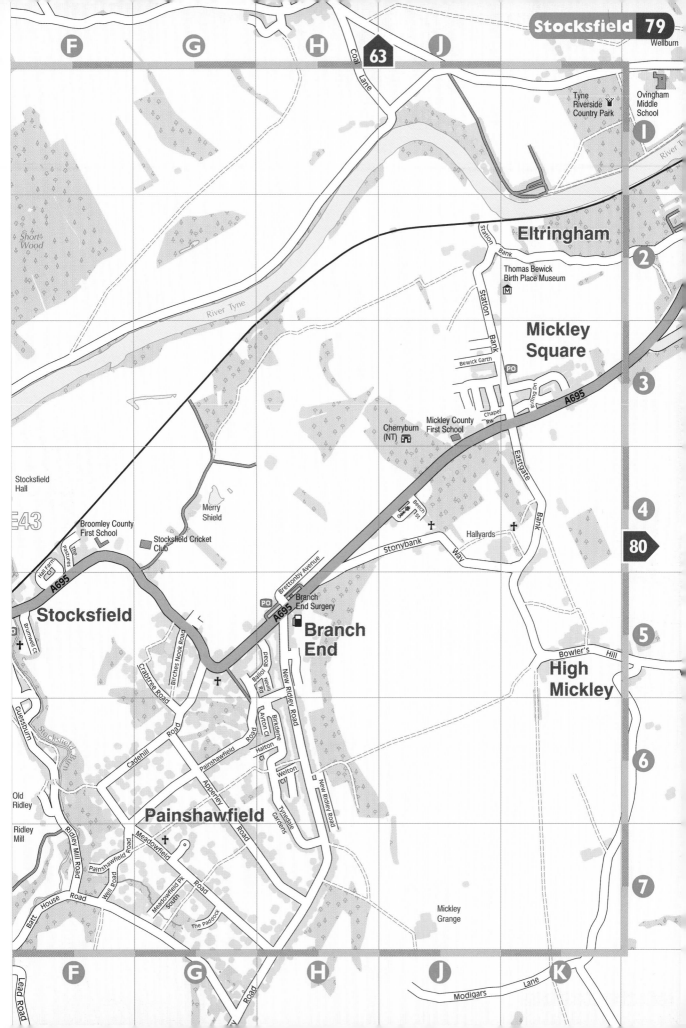

Wellburn

F G H **63** J

Tyne Riverside Country Park

Ovingham Middle School

1

River T

Station Bank

Eltringham

2

Thomas Bewick Birth Place Museum

Mickley Square

Bewick Garth

PO

Station Bank

Ridling Dn

A695

3

Cherryburn (NT)

Mickley County First School

Chapel Rw

Eastgate

River Tyne

Short Wood

Stocksfield Hall

E43

Broomley County First School

Stocksfield Cricket Club

Merry Shield

The pastures

Hall Farm Cl

Oaklea

Beech St

Stonybank

Hallyards

Way

Bank

4

80

5

Bowler's Hill

High Mickley

A695

Stocksfield

Brunwell Cl

Crabtree Road

Birches Nook Road

Road

Cadehill

Apperley

Brettonby Avenue

PO

A695

Branch End

Branch End Surgery

Nevill Rd

Balliol Road

New Ridley Road

Birkdene

Ayton Cl

Halton Cl

Welton Cl

Painshawfield

Road

Tynedale Gardens

New Ridley Road

6

Guessburn

Old Ridley

Ridley Mill

Stocksburn

Ridley Mill Road

Painshawfield Road

Well Road

Meadowfield

Painshawfield

Road

Meadowfield Pk South

Road

The Paddock

Mickley Grange

7

Batt House Road

Lead Road

F G H J K

Modigars Lane

A B C D E

Prudhoe

C1
1 Cockshott Dean
2 Orchard HI

B3
1 Greener Ct
2 Linnheads

B2
1 Sandysykes

Prudhoe Station

PRINCESS WAY

64

Wellbu

Ovingham Middle School

Ovingham C of E First School

Prudhoe Castle

Prudhoe

Adderlane First School

West Wylam

Tyne Riverside Country Park

C2
1 Edgewell Gra
2 St Cuthberts Cl

Station Road

Station Industrial Est

A695

Station Road

River Tyne

Cherry Gv

Holly Grove

Lime Gv

Maple Gv

Castle

Castle Vw

Dene Gv

Cheyne Rd

Western Av

Castle Road

Master's Cres

Cheyne Rd

Avenue

Kepwell Rd

Kepwell Road

Castle Surgery

Umfraville Dene

Greenwell Dr

Lassell Rigg

Well Dean

Broomhouse Lane

The Ford

Appletree Drive

Duckets

Northumberland Area Health Authority

Broomhill Road

Adderlane Road

Dene st

Bilverfield

PO

B6395

PRUDHOE

NE42

Northumberland County Council

STONYFLAT BANK

B639

Stancley Rd

D1
1 Grey Lady Wk
2 The Haughs
3 Holyoake St
4 Spetchells

Prudhoe Castle First School

Western Road

WEST ROAD

Leaway

Edgewell Grange

Milton Gv

Edgewell Rd

Prudhoe West County First School

St Matthews RC First School

Cemetery

Swalwell Cl

Wesley Ter

Oakfield Pk

Hillcrest

St Thomas St

Cameron Rd

The Hvn

Priestclose Rd

Target

Redwell Ct

Redwell Road

FRONT ST

Tyne View Ter

Cheviot View

Paddock Cl

Paddock Wood

cranbrook Dr

Sycamore Gv

Rowan

Simonside

Cranbrook Dr

Broom

High Shaw

Highfield County Middle School

Highfield Lane

South Road

Highfield

Prudhoe County High School

Homedale

Valley View

Park La

Park Lane

Orchard Ct

Park Av

Moorlands

695
D2
1 Drawback Cl
2 Grange Ct
3 John Wesley Ct
4 Oakfield Ter
5 St Mathews La

Beaumont Way

Tennyson Ct

Ruskin

Ovington Vw

Cemetery

Cem

Otter Burn Way

Broom

Cemetery

Moor Road

H
Northg
NHS T

Edgewell House Farm

79

E1
1 Bilverfield Rd
2 The Close
3 Low Cl
4 West Wylam Dr

Edgewell House Road

Mickley Moor

Durham Riding

E3
1 Homedale Pl

gh
ickley

Lumley's Lane

A B 94 C D E

1 grid square represents 500 metres

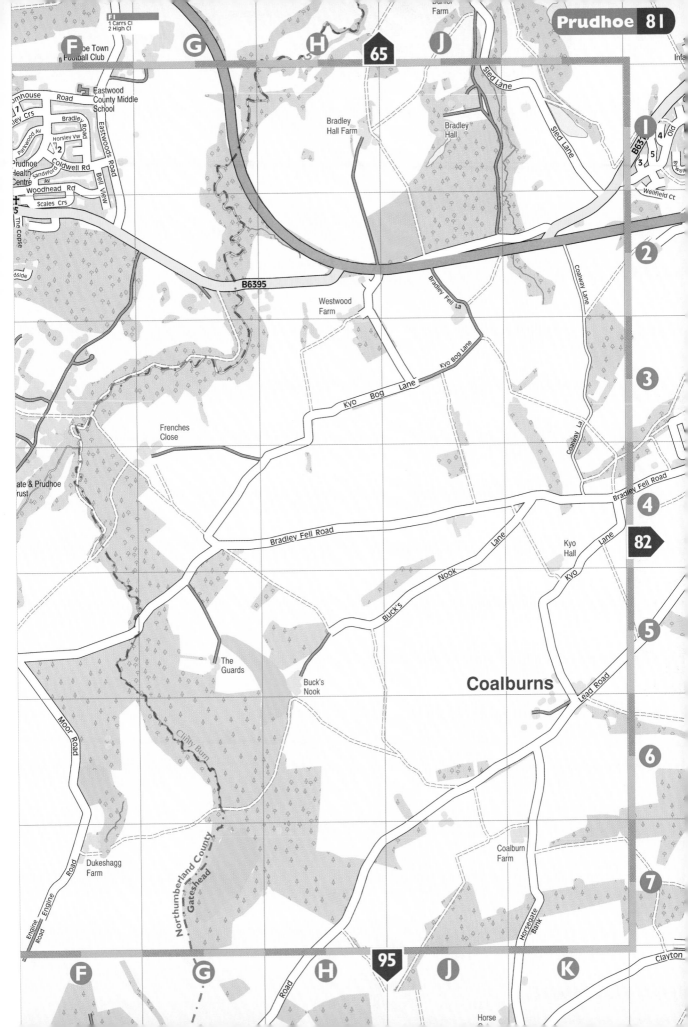

F1
1 Carrs Cl
2 High Cl

F

Prudhoe Town
Football Club

G

H

65

J

Infa

Sled Lane

Bradley
Hall Farm

Bradley
Hall

I

B63

4
5
3

Crnhouse
Road

Eastwood
County Middle
School

Bradley Road

Horsley Vw

Eastwoods Road

Prudhoe
Health
Centre

Sandyford

Coldwell Rd

Woodhead Rd

Av

Bell View

Scales Crs

2

Parkwood Av

ey Crs

7

The Copse

5

dside

Wellfield Ct

2

Sled Lane

Coalway Lane

B6395

Westwood
Farm

Bradley Fell La

Kyo Bog Lane

3

Coalway La

Kyo Bog Lane

Frenches
Close

Coalway La

ate & Prudhoe
rust

Bradley Fell Road

4

Bradley Fell Road

Kyo
Hall

Kyo Lane

82

Nook Lane

Buck's

Kyo

5

The
Guards

Buck's
Nook

Coalburns

Lead Road

6

Moor Road

Clinty Burn

Dukeshagg
Farm

Northumberland County
Gateshead

Coalburn
Farm

7

Engine Road

Engine Road

Horsegate Bank

Clayton

F

G

H

95

J

K

Horse

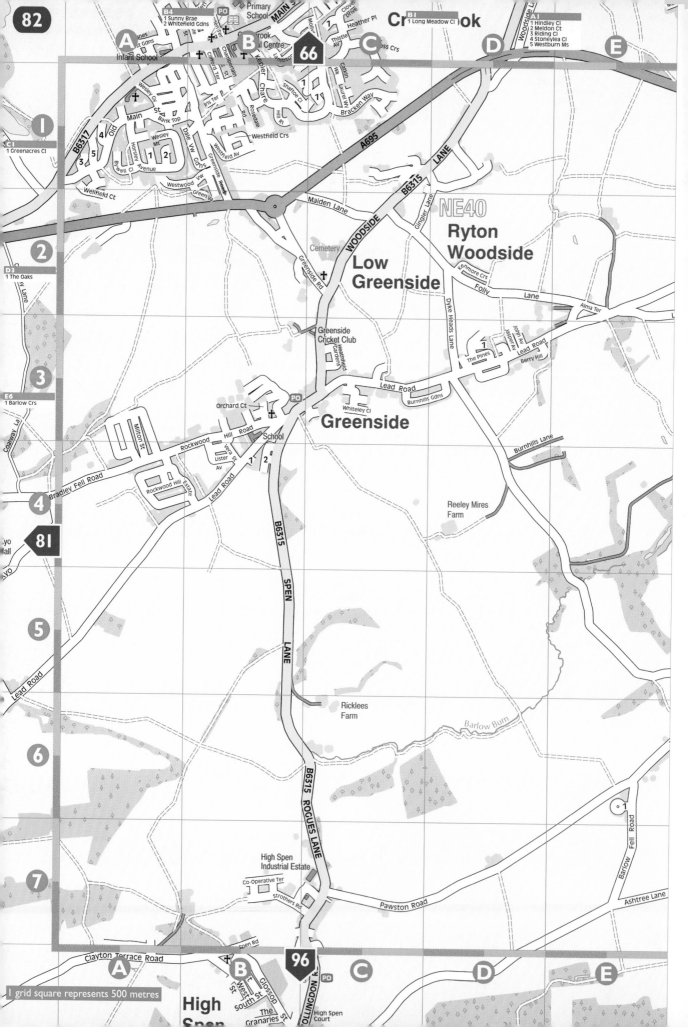

A B C D E

66

Cr 1 Long Meadow Cl ok

A1
1 Hindley Cl
2 Meldon Ct
3 Riding Cl
4 Stoneylea Cl
5 Westburn Ms

B4
1 Sunny Brae
2 Whitefield Gdns

Primary School
MAIN ST

Infant School

CI
1 Greenacres Cl

B6317

Main St
Wesley Cl
Horsley Avenue
Bywell Cl
Wellfield Ct
Wesley Mt
Bank Top
Old Dale Vw Gdns
Iris Ter
Roseale
Westfield Av
Westfield Crs
Westwood
Green Va
Greenside Road

Clover Drive
Heather Pl
Thistle Av
Catkin Wk
Laurel Av
Bracken Way
Cross Crs
Shaftoe Cl
Hill Rl

A695

Malden Lane

WOODSIDE

B6315

Gingler Lane

LANE

NE40

Ryton Woodside

Kenmore Crs

Folly   Lane

Alma Ter

Cemetery

Greenside Rd

Low Greenside

Dyke Heads Lane

D3
1 The Oaks

E6
1 Barlow Crs

Coalway La

Greenside Cricket Club

Heathfield Gardens

The Pines

John Av
Jasper Av
Lead Road
Berry Hill

Lead Road

Whiteley Cl

Burnhills Gdns

PO

Orchard Ct

School

Greenside

Milton St
Rockwood Hill Road
Vera St
Lister Av
Rockwood Hill Estate

Bradley Fell Road

Lead Road

81

Reeley Mires Farm

Burnhills Lane

B6315

SPEN

LANE

Lead Road

Ricklees Farm

Barlow Burn

B6315 ROGUES LANE

1

Barlow Fell Road

High Spen Industrial Estate

Co-Operative Ter

strothers Rd

Pawston Road

Ashtree Lane

Clayton Terrace Road

Spen Rd

96

PO

High Spen Court

GLOSSON RD

Glosson St
West St
South St
The Granaries

High Spen

1
2
3
4
5
6
7

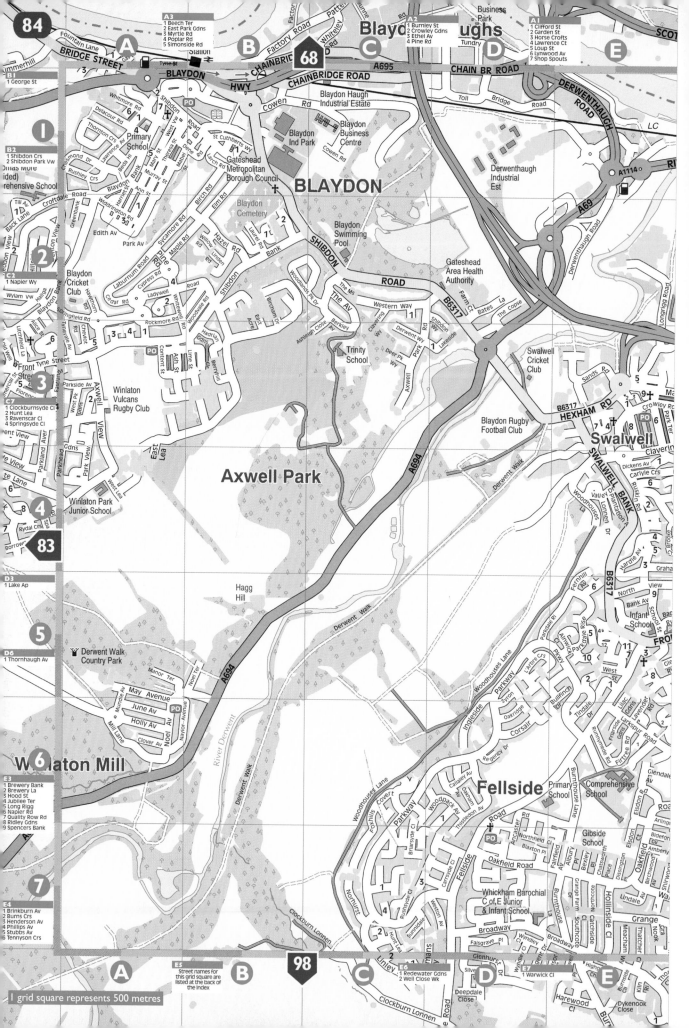

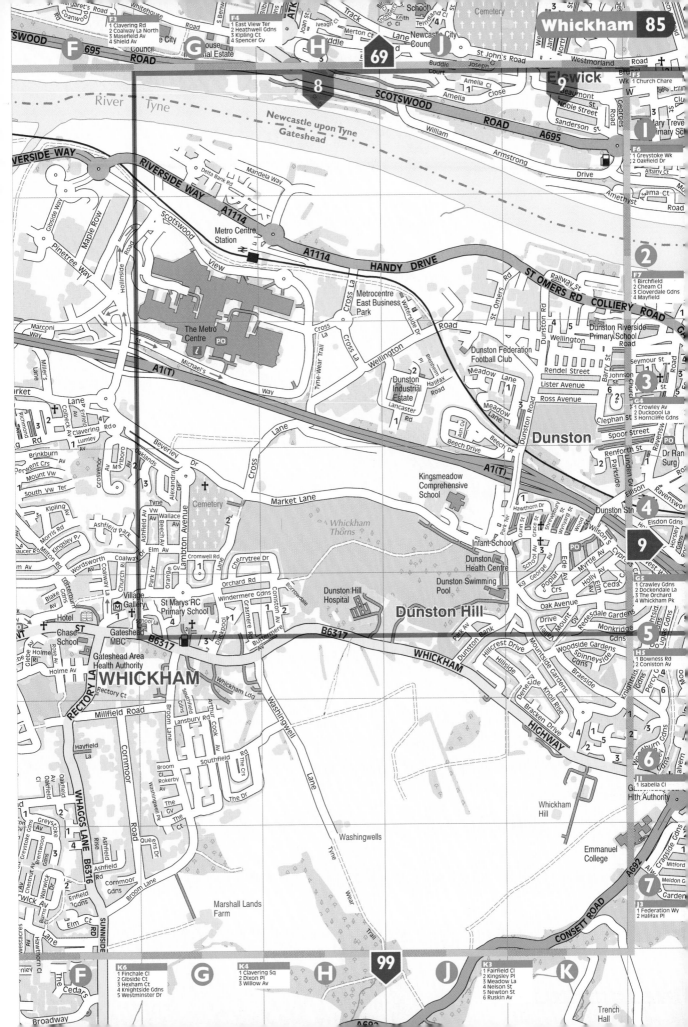

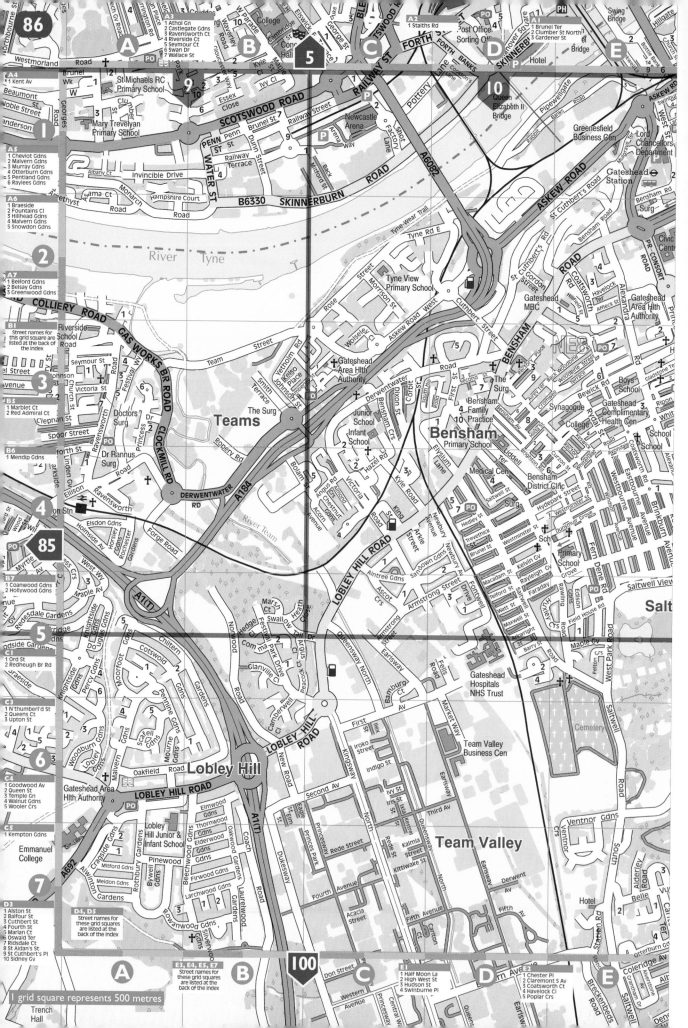

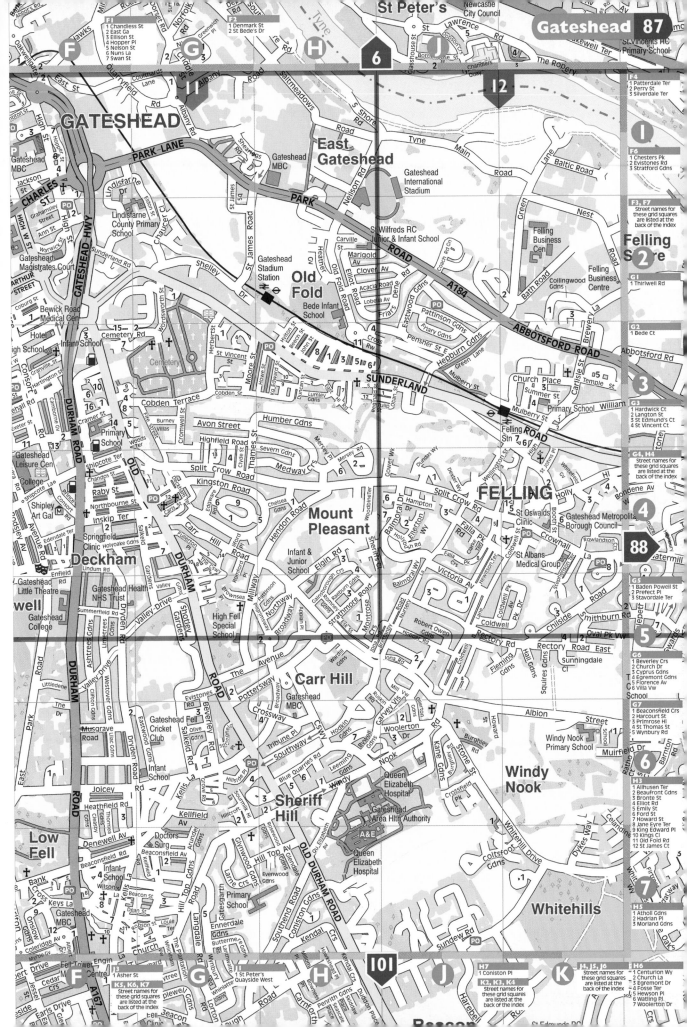

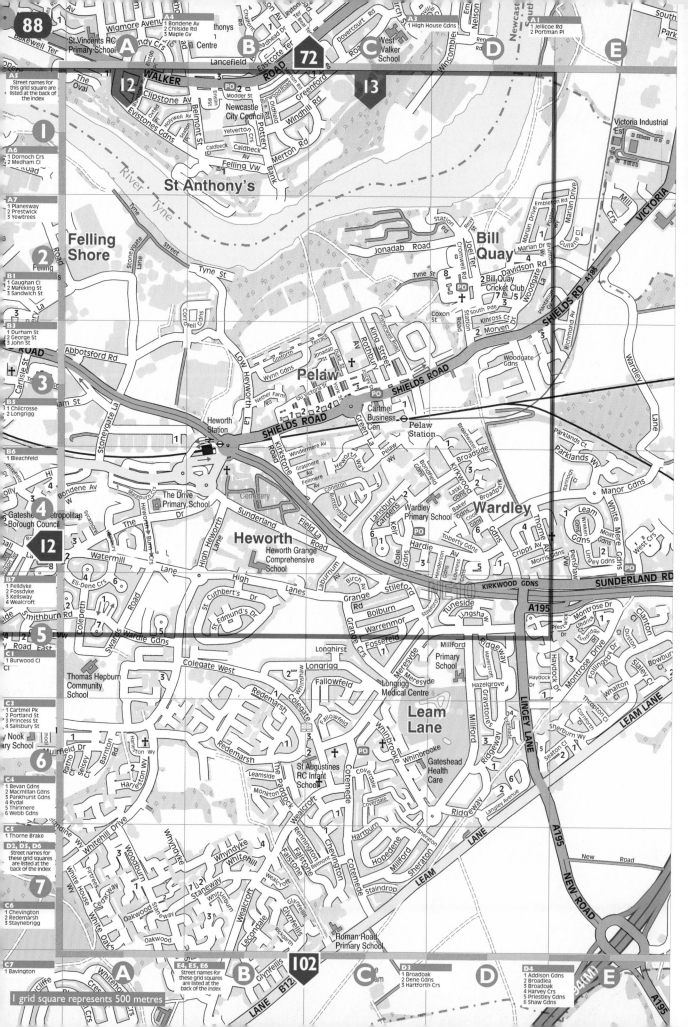

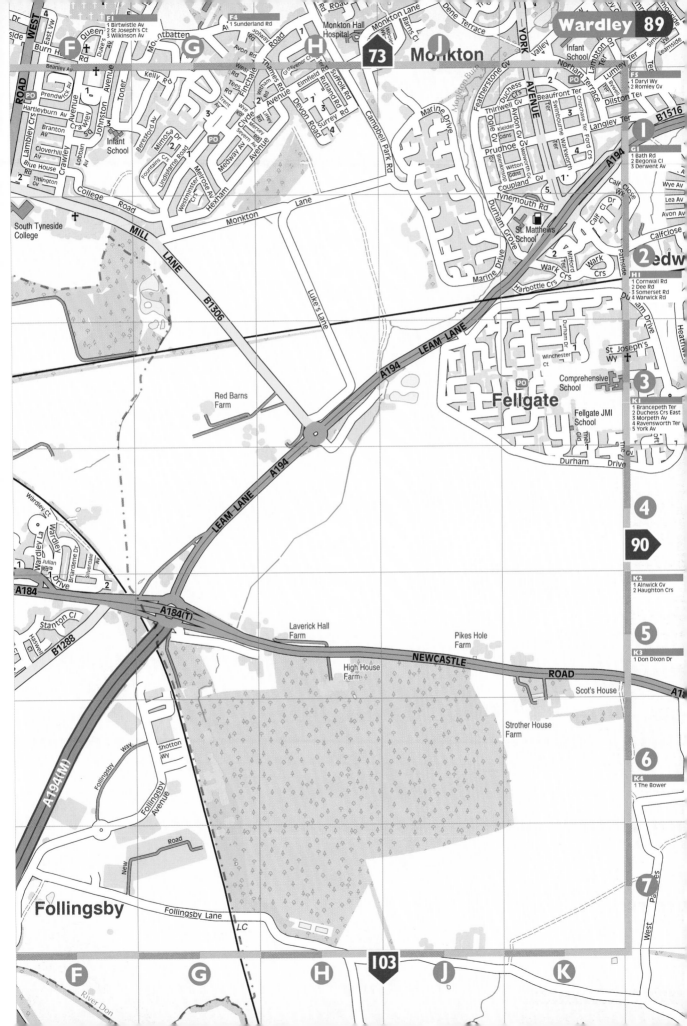

Monkton

Fellgate

Follingsby

Red Barns Farm

Laverick Hall Farm

High House Farm

Pikes Hole Farm

Strother House Farm

Scot's House

South Tyneside College

Monkton Hall Hospital

St. Matthews School

St Joseph's Comprehensive School

Fellgate JMI School

Infant School

MILL LANE

B1306

LEAM LANE

A194

A194

A184

A184(T)

A194(M)

NEWCASTLE ROAD

Durham Drive

Monkton Lane

Luke's Lane

Campbell Park Rd

Marine Drive

Follingsby Lane

Follingsby Avenue

New Road

73

103

90

F1
1 Birtwistle Av
2 St Joseph's Ct
3 Wilkinson Av

F4
1 Sunderland Rd

F5
1 Daryl Wy
2 Romley Gv

G1
1 Bath Rd
2 Begonia Cl
3 Derwent Rd

H1
1 Cornwall Rd
2 Dee Rd
3 Somerset Rd
4 Warwick Rd

K1
1 Brancepeth Ter
2 Duchess Crs East
3 Morpeth Av
4 Ravensworth Ter
5 York Av

K2
1 Alnwick Gv
2 Haughton Crs

K3
1 Don Dixon Dr

K4
1 The Bower

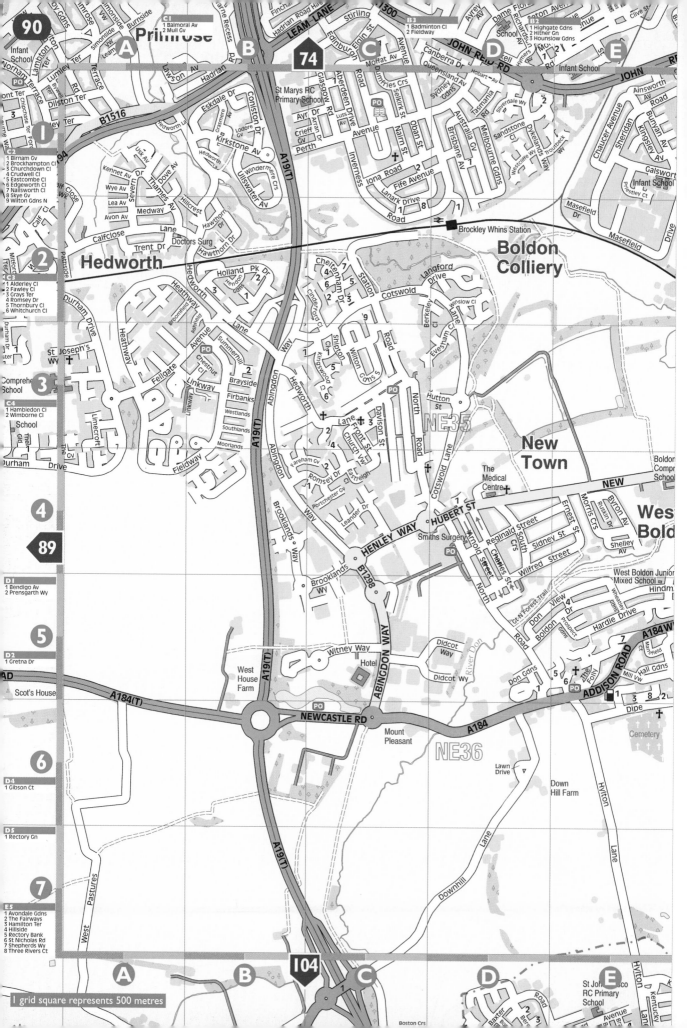

Whiteleas

Biddick Hall

East Boldon

Witherwack

F4
1 Wilson Dr

F5
1 Alpine Gv
2 Claremount Ct
3 Everest Gv
4 Grampian Gv
5 Rosemount Ct
6 Snowdon Gv
7 Stewart Dr

King George Comprehensive School

Cleadon Grange

G5
1 Bowness Cl
2 The Fairways
3 Patterdale Cl

Cleadon Village County JM School

G4
1 Borrowdale Cl

1 Brodie Cl
2 Cameron Cl

H1
1 Romney Av
2 Sandalwood

Albert Elliott County Junior Mixed School

Boldon North Bridge

ROAD B1298

Boker Lane Health Centre

Junior School

WESTERN TERRACE

FRONT STREET A184

Low House Farm

Belle Vue Villa

Field House

Blue House Farm

H2
1 Sutherland Ct

H5
1 Beatrice Gdns
2 Charlcote Crs
3 Coulton Dr
4 Grange Ter
5 St Chad's Vls

J3
1 Celtic Crs
2 Kelvin Gv
3 Paddock Cl
4 Saxon Cl

East Boldon Station

SUNDERLAND ROAD A184

K3
1 East Boldon Rd
2 South Dr

K1
1 Carnoustie Dr
2 Ganton Ct
3 Heartsbourne Dr

J5
1 Bede Ter
2 Crossways

F3
1 Buckingham Cl
2 Marina Ter
3 Robinson Gdns

F4
1 Cornthwaite Dr
2 Staffords La

F5
1 Whitburn Bents
Rd

F

G

H

77

J

Whitburn
Colliery

MILL LANE

Shearwater

White Rocks Grove

Lilac Av

Lily Crs

May Gdl

Marsden Av

Rose Crs

Rose Crs

Fern Avenue

Wheatall Drive

field Dr

Fulmar Wk

Cedar Gv

Poplar Drive

A183

Birch Av

Sycamore Rd

Geoffrey St

Rupert St

WHITBURN

Maple Gv

High Crft

High St

Bryers St

Bowman St

Whitburn Cem

Myrtle Av

Myrtle Av

Larch Av

Oak Crs

Elm Dr

Beech Av

1

2

3

Croftside Av

Rackly Wy

Adolphus Street

Holly Av

← Guards

2

Front St

STREET

EAST STREET

East Flds

Whitburn
Comprehensive School

Church Lane

urn ery

Whitburn
Cricket Club

Newark Dr

Hill Wk

Markham Av

Nicholas Av

WHITBURN BENTS ROAD

Blisdale

Swaledale Av

Ryedale Av

ansdale Av

Farndale Av

Eskdale Rd

ents Av

1

A183

Whitby Av

otel
1

A183 W

F

G

H

107

J

K

I

F6
1 Hart Ter

2

G4
1 Ash Gv

3

4

5

6

7

94

A B 80 C D E

I

Hedley Park
Farm

High V...

2

PH

Airey Hill
Farm

3

Currock
Hill

Engine Road

Bowser's
Hole

Labourn's
Fell

4

Northumberland County

Gateshead

Ravenside

Woodhead

Hollings

5

Hollings
Hill

Milkwell Burn

Lead Lane

6

Mill Burn

Wood
House

Whittonstall Hall
Farm

B6309

7

Park
Wood

A B 108 C D E

1 grid square represents 500 metres

F   G   H   81   J

1

2

3

4

96

5

6

7

Northumberland
Gateshead

Engine
Road

Engine

Leadgate

Lead
Road

Greenhead
Road

Ashtree

Horse
Gate

Broomfield Farm

Clayton Terrace Road

Ramsay Road

Hall Rd

Meadow Brook
Drive

Whittonstall Rd

PO

Derwent   Street

Wear St

Doctors
Surgery
South

Road

Tay St

Mersey St

1

Clyde St

William St

Chopwell
County
Primary School

Chopwell

Broomfield
Crs

Milkwellburn
Wood

Moorland Vw

Mill Road

Valley Dene

NE17

Carr
House

Gateshead
Northumberland County

Runnymede Gdns

Blackhall
Mill

Connolly Ter

PO   1

Chopwell Rd

Armondside Rd

Moraine Crs

Mill Race

Riversdale
Ct

Derwent St

Nursery
Ct

River
View

Broad Oak
Farm

A694

PO   Dene
Ct

Derwent
Crs

109

Hamsterley

Derwentcote
Steel Furnace

Forge Lane

F   G   H   J   K

Doctors
Surgery

Cemetery

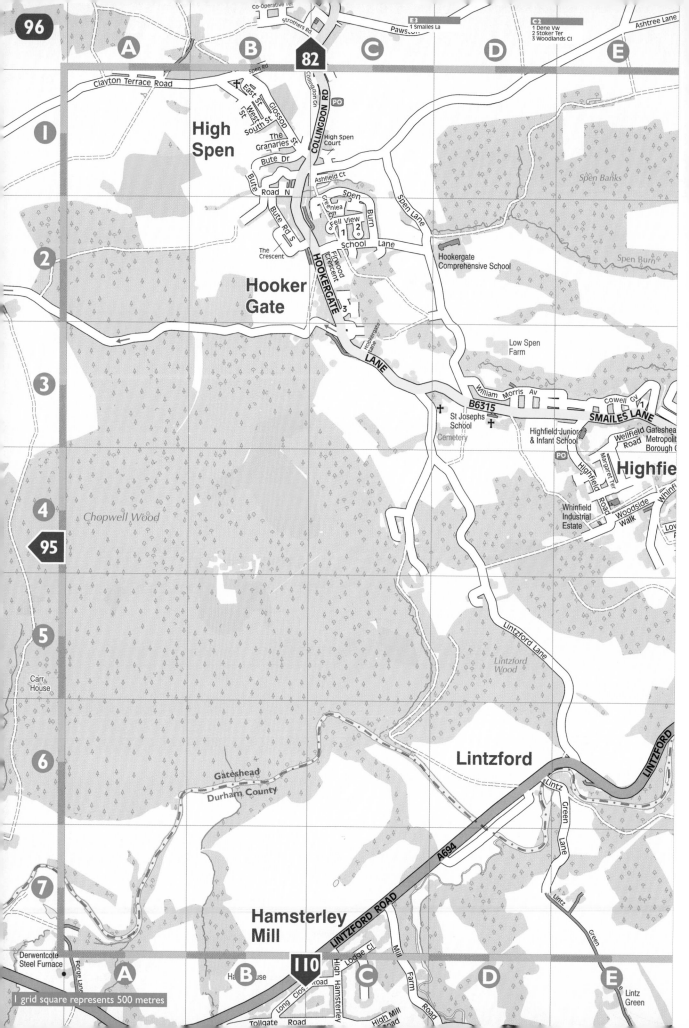

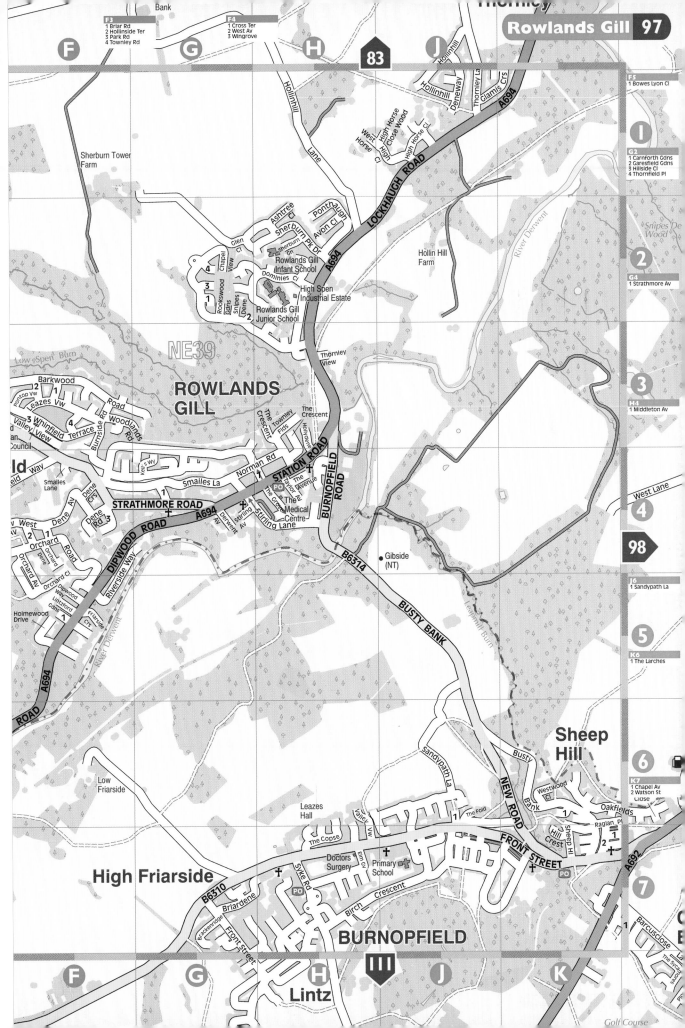

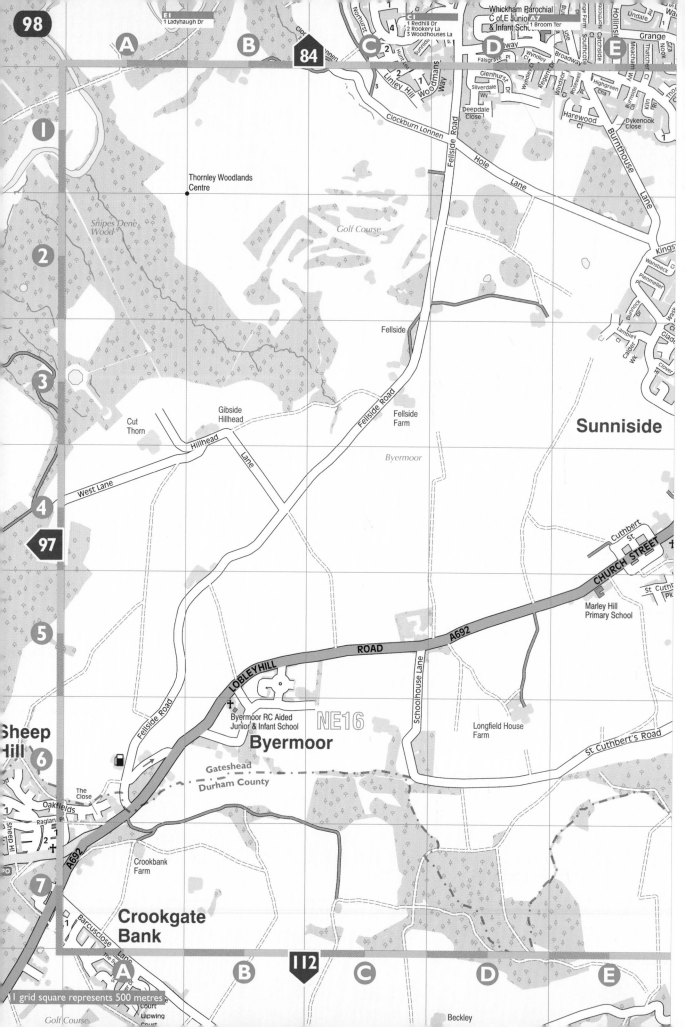

A B 84 C D E

1 Ladyhaugh Dr

Whickham Parochial
C of E Junior
& Infant School

C1
1 Redhill Dr
2 Rookery La
3 Woodhouses La

A7
1 Broom Ter

Norhurst
Linley Hill Road
Woodmans Way
Hunt Lea
Sunnie
Falsgrave Pl
Glenhurst Dr
Silverdale
Wyndley Cl
Broadway
Southcote
Regent Ct
Windsor
Iliswood
Highgreen
Burnside
Meacham Wk
Lindale
Grange
Cra Nook

1

Thornley Woodlands
Centre

Snipes Dene
Wood

Golf Course

Clockburn Lonnen
Fellside Road
Hole Lane
Burnthouse Lane

Deepdale
Close

Harewood
Cl

Dykenook
Close

Sunniside

Kings

Wansbeck
Plenmeller
Pl

2

3

Cut
Thorn

Gibside
Hillhead

Hillhead

Lane

Fellside

Fellside Road

Fellside
Farm

Byermoor

Dunnock
Lambley
Calder
Wk
Clover

Gladel
Way

4

97

West Lane

Cuthbert
St

CHURCH STREET

St Cuthbert
PK

Marley Hill
Primary School

5

LOBLEYHILL ROAD A692

Schoolhouse Lane

Longfield House
Farm

St Cuthbert's Road

Sheep
Hill

6

Fellside Road

Byermoor RC Aided
Junior & Infant School

Byermoor

NE16

The
Close

Oakfields

Raglan Pl

Sheep
Hi

Gateshead
Durham County

A692

Crookbank
Farm

7

Crookgate
Bank

Barcusclose Lane

The S

A B 112 C D E

Golf Course

Court
Lapwing
Court

Beckley

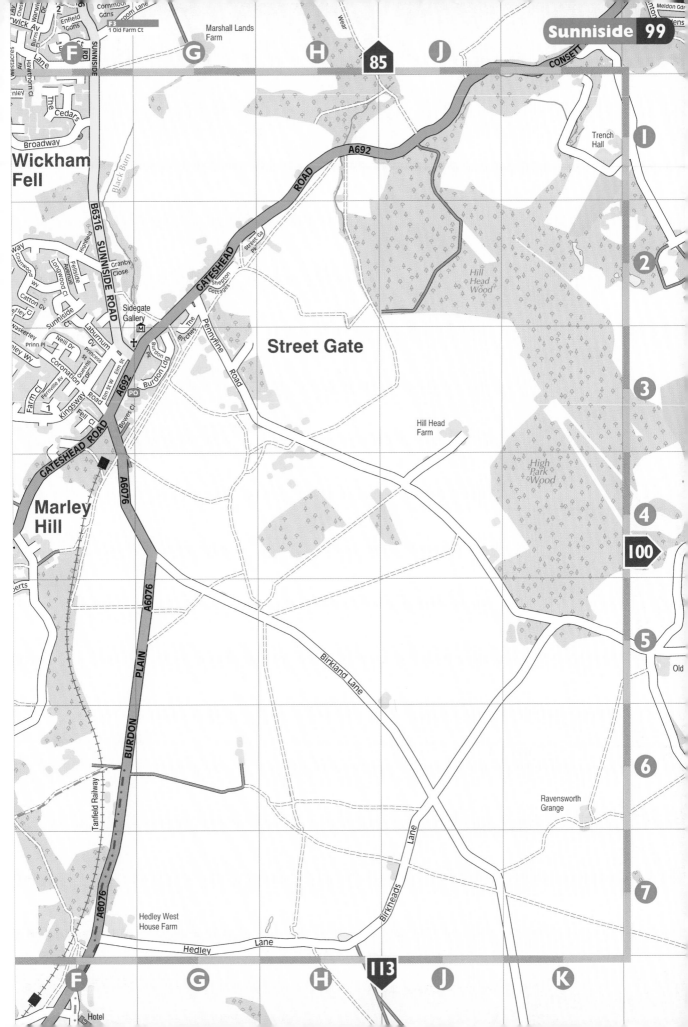

Wickham
Fell

Street Gate

Marley
Hill

Wear

CONSETT

Trench
Hall

Hill
Head
Wood

High
Park
Wood

Hill Head
Farm

Ravensworth
Grange

Old

Marshall Lands
Farm

1 Old Farm Ct
F3

Enfield
Gdns

Cornmoor Lane

Meldon Gdr

The
Cedars

Broadway

B6316

SUNNISIDE ROAD

Black Burn

Highfield

Granby
Close

Sidegate
Gallery

GATESHEAD ROAD

Street Ca
Pk

Shepton
Cottages

The
Arches

Pennyfine Road

Cornwood
W

Longwood Cl

Catton Gv

Sunniside
Ct

Fellside

Avenue

Laburnum
Gv

Neill Dr

Princes

Prinn Pl

Coronation

Naskerley

Farm Cl

Kingsway

A692

PO

Fernville Av

Fell Cl

Bowes Cl

Burdon Ldg

Burdon
Rd

Elm St W Elm St

Queens
Dr

Roberts

GATESHEAD ROAD

A6076

A6076

BURDON PLAIN A6076

Tanfield Railway

Hedley West
House Farm

Hedley   Lane

Birkland Lane

Birkheads   Lane

Hotel

85

100

113

F   G   H   J

I

2

3

4

5

6

7

F   G   H   J   K

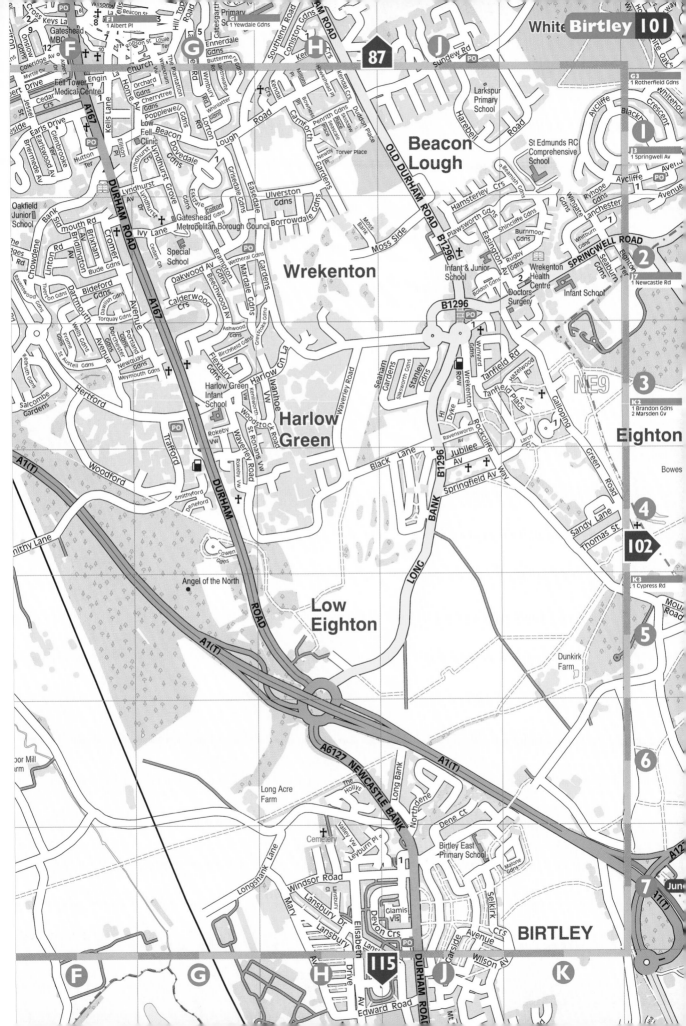

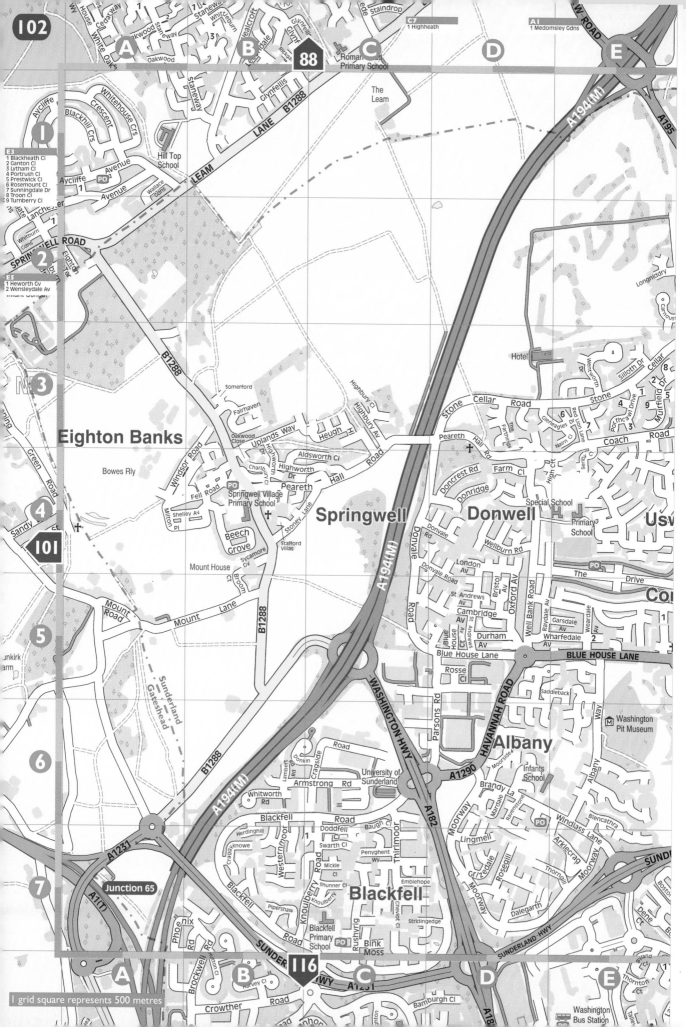

Follingsby

F

G

H

89

J

F2
1 Downfield

F3
1 Cumberland Wy
2 Rutland Pl

F4
1 Essex Dr
2 Hampshire Pl
3 Sussex Pl

I

F5
1 Laurens Ct

2

F7
1 Trenton Av

3

G3
1 Marwell Dr
2 Whitbourne Cl
3 Wimpole Cl

4

104

G4
1 Wylam Cl

5

G5
1 Front St
2 Hall Rd
3 Usworth Station Rd

6

H3
1 Watcombe Cl

7

Follingsby Lane

LC

River Don

East House

Waterloo Road

South Tyneside
Sunderland

North Moor
Farm

NORTHUMBERLAND WAY

The Fairway
Dalmahoy
Gullane
Hall
Foxton
Gv
Road

Northumbria
Sports
Centre

Merevale Cl

Barton
Cl

Maxwell Dr

Stephenson

Steatham

Usworth
Hall
Road

Waterloo Road

A1290

Cherry Blossom Way

Usworth
Secondary
School

Heworth Road

Norfolk

Wiltshire Pl

Warwick

Westmorland Av

Essex

Monterey

Drive

St Bedes
RC Primary
School

Rutherford

Baird Cl

Rainhill Road

Rainhill

Sulgrave

Usworth Grange
Primary School

NE37

Barmston

Lane

worth

Inkerman Road

Tyne Gardens

Park Gv

Manor

Violia
St

Vernon st

Road

Helmdon

Foxley

Marlborough Road

Silverstone Road

Usworth Colliery
Junior School

Capron Rd

Brackley

Waterloo

Sulgrave

ncord

House Ter

Victoria Road
Health Centre

Victoria Rd

PO

1 2 3

Manor Vw

Mnt Vw

Banbury

Mandeville

PO

Usworth Station Rd

Edgecote

Cherwell

LC

Nissan

Spout La

1

VERMONT

GLOVER ROAD

Spire

Industrial

Road

Tower Rd

Bridgewater Rd

NORTHUMBERLAND WAY

Glover
Industrial
Estate

Barmston

Washington
Football
Club

Spout
Lane

Washington
Secondary
School

Brindley Road

WASHINGTON

ERLAND HIGHWAY

A1231

SUNDERLAND HIGHWAY

A1231

7

Pattinson Road

Barmsto

Richmond Av

Valley Forge

Spout Lane

Hill Rise

Washington
Village Primary School

Barmston Way

Stockley Rd

Horsley Rd

Alston Road

Faraday Cl

Burnhope Road

NORTHUMB

Glebe

Barmston
Medical Centre

PO

Kerley Road

Westerhope

117

mston

Primary
School

Lee Rd

Walton Road

F

G

H

J

K

St Josephs
School

Cemetery

H7
1 Thornhope Cl

H4
1 Shaistone
2 Trafalgar Rd

Primary
School

Washington
Village

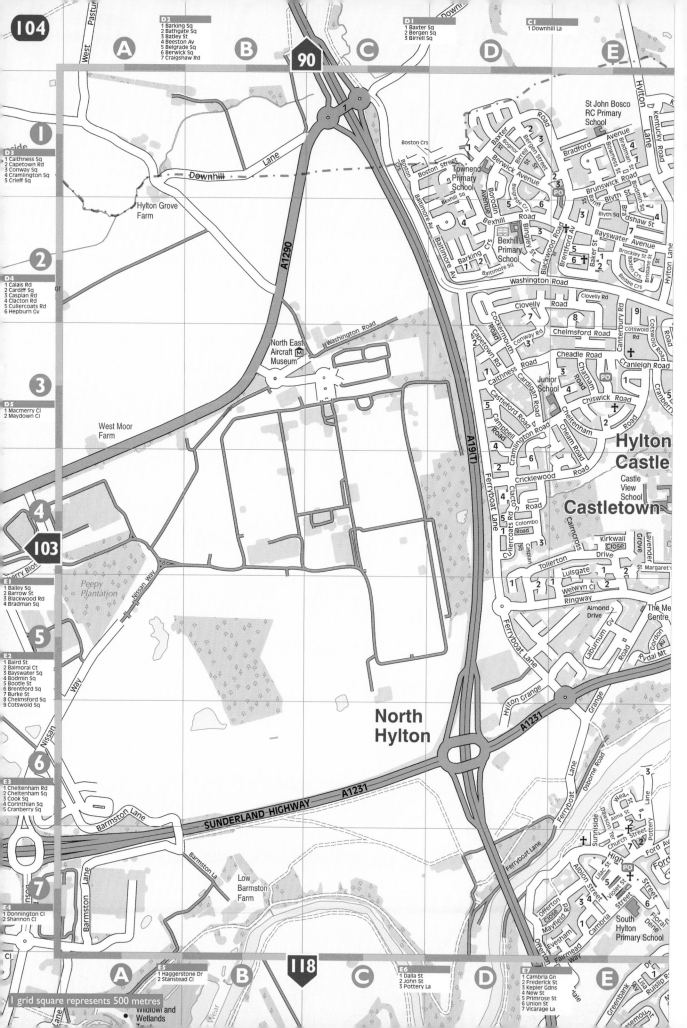

A **B** **C** **D** **E**

1

2

3

4

103

5

6

7

A **B** 118 **C** **D** **E**

1 grid square represents 500 metres

St John Bosco RC Primary School

North East Aircraft Museum

Hylton Grove Farm

West Moor Farm

Peepy Plantation

North Hylton

Hylton Castle

Castletown

Castle View School

Low Barmston Farm

South Hylton Primary School

SUNDERLAND HIGHWAY

A1231

A1290

A19(T)

A1231

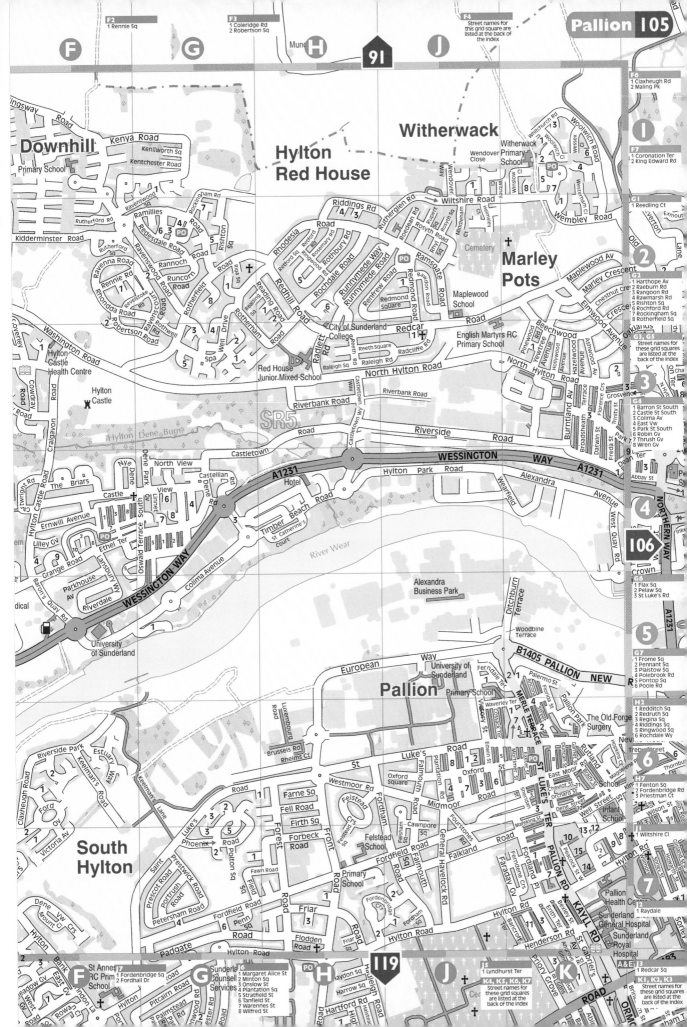

Downhill

Hylton
Red House

Witherwack

Marley
Pots

Pallion

South
Hylton

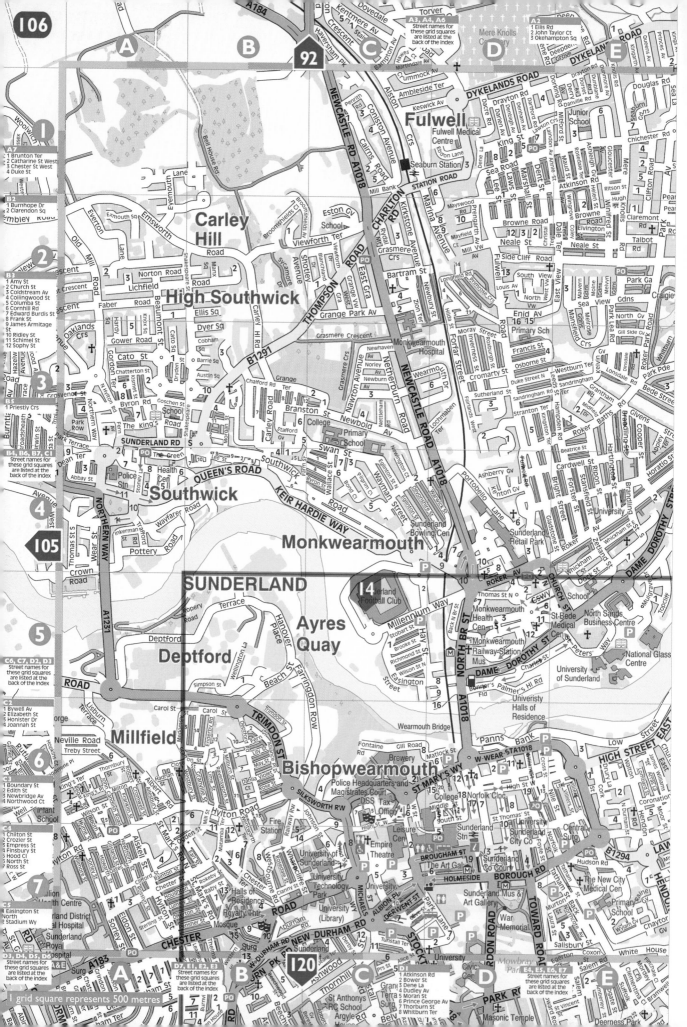

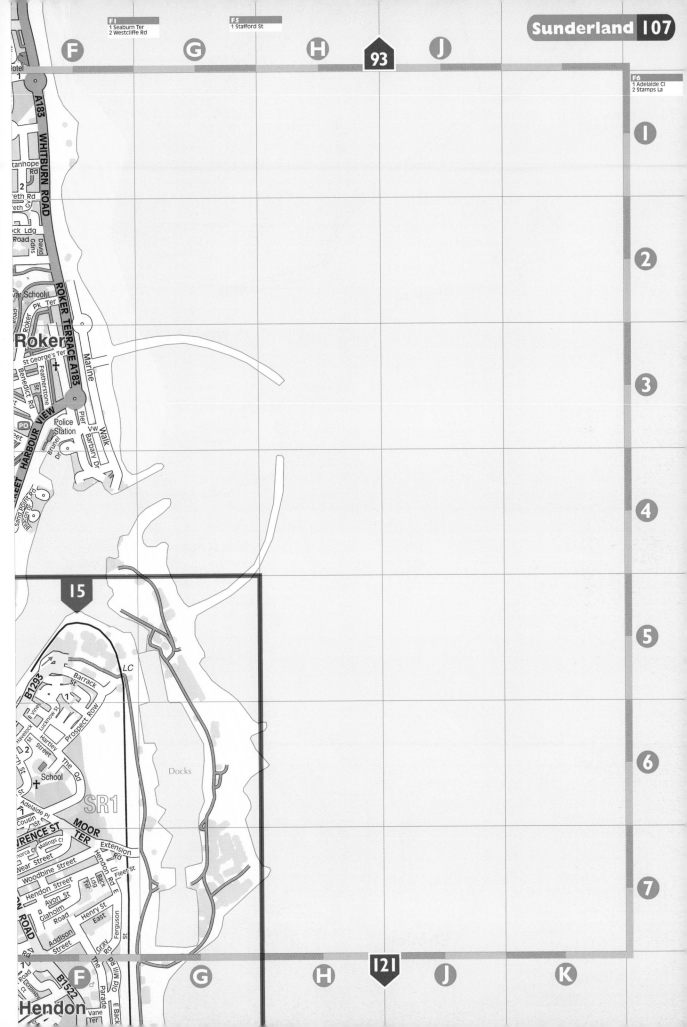

F1
1 Seaburn Ter
2 Westcliffe Rd

F5
1 Stafford St

F
G
H
93
J

F6
1 Adelaide Cl
2 Stamps La

I

2

3

4

15

5

6

7

F
G
H
121
J
K

Roker

WHITBURN ROAD
A183
Stanhope Rd
reth Rd
reth Gr
ck Ldg
Road
David Gdns
var School
Roker Pk Ter
ROKER TERRACE A183
Marine
St George's Ter
Featherstone
Benedict Rd
St
Pier
Vw Walk
Barbary Dr
Brunel Dr
Police Station
PO
Sand POINT RD
Beacon Dr
HARBOUR VIEW

B1293
Barrack St
E Vine
Lucknow St
Hartley Street
Prospect Row
LC
Docks
Havelock St
The Old
School
SR1
Adelaide Pl
Cousin St
LAWRENCE ST
MOOR TER
Minorca cl
Mallings Cl
Near Street
Woodbine Street
Hendon Street
Avon St
Glanolm Road
Henry St East
Addison Street
Extension Rd
Hendon Rd E
Fleet St
Ldg
Gray Rd
Ferguson
E Mill Dl
The Parade
Vane Ter
E Back
ROAD
B1522
Hendon

A   B   **94**   C   D   E

E7
1 Epsom Cl
2 Newbury Dr
3 Salisbury Cl

D7
1 Chepstow Cl
2 Kempton Cl
3 Wetherby Cl

1

2

Morrowfield Farm

Small Burn

B6309

Newlands

Northumberland County
Durham County

B6309

PO

C of E Junior
Mixed & Infant
School

dary Lane

Fine Lane

3

Northumberland County
Durham County

A694

Chesters Dene
Ebba's
St
Cohort
Cl
Hadrian's Way
The Chesters
Foss
Way

Church
Cl

Springhouse Cl

4

Mere Burn

East
Law

Lane

Springhouse

askerleyedge
antation

5

Whinny

West Law Road

6

Panshield

River Derwent

A694

High
Waskerley

Spa Drive

Shotley
Park

7

Low
Waskerley

Pike Hill

Oley Mdw

FRONT STREET

Shotley Bridge
Junior School

SNOW'S GREEN RD

B6310

Ascot Rd

Goodwood
Dr

2
Aintree Dr
7
3
1

Cl
Shel
Woodlan

School

Shotley
Bridge

PO

Wood St

Green St

The
er
Lane
Oak

Piele Pk
Briary
ns

Summerdale

Churchill
Cl
The
Briary

Road

Woodlar

The Mount
Mountside
Glenside
Drive

Shotley Bridge
General Hospital

B6278

1 grid square represents 500 metres

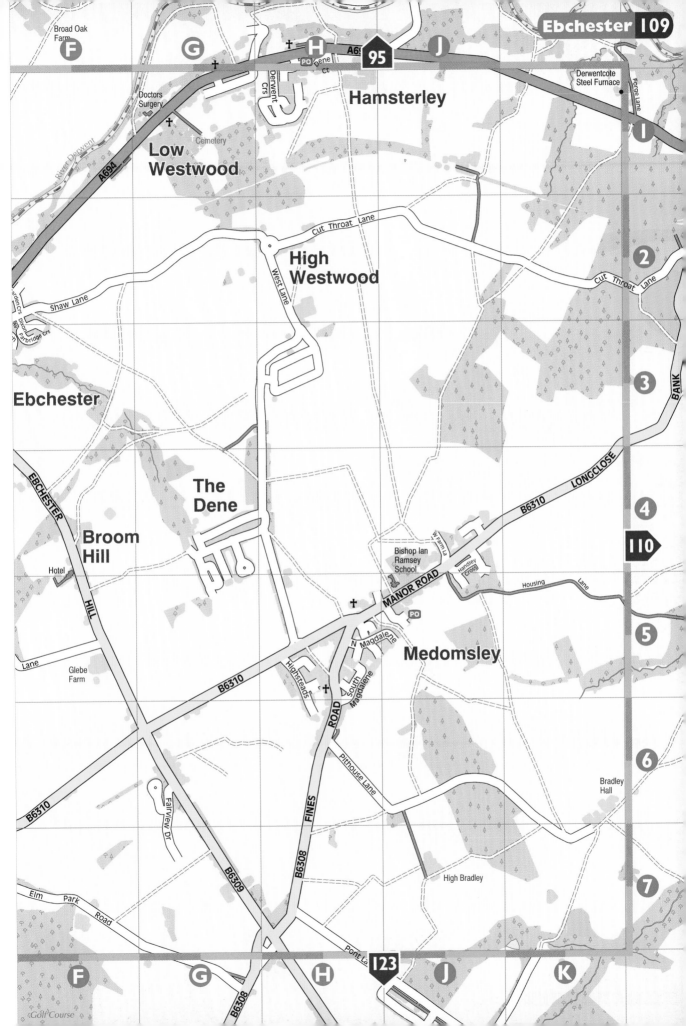

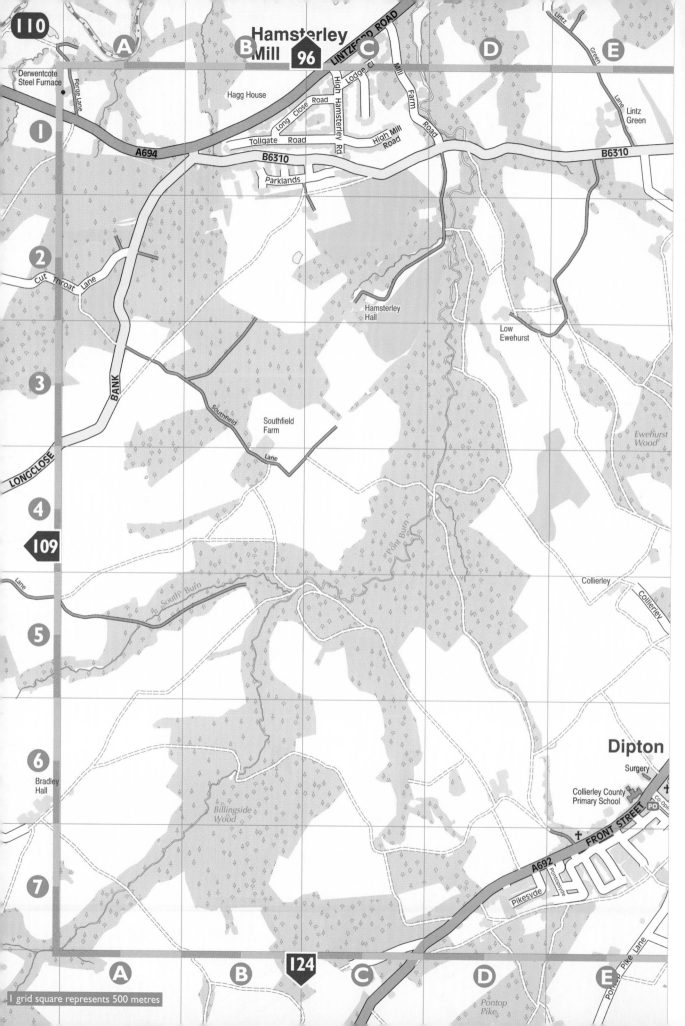

A

B **Hamsterley Mill** 96

LINTZFORD ROAD

C

D

E

Derwentcote
Steel Furnace

Forge Lane

Hagg House

Lodge Cl

High Hamsterley Rd

High Mill
Road

Mill Farm Road

Lintz
Green

Lintz
Green

1

A694

Long Close Road

Tollgate Road

B6310

B6310

Lane

Parklands

2

Cut Throat Lane

BANK

Hamsterley
Hall

Low
Ewehurst

3

LONGCLOSE

Southfield

Southfield
Farm

Lane

Ewehurst
Wood

4

109

Pont Burn

South Burn

Collierley

Collierley

5

6

Bradley
Hall

Billingside
Wood

Dipton

Surgery

Collierley County
Primary School

PO

Co-op

FRONT STREET

7

A692

Pikesyde

Pontopsyde

Pontop Pike Lane

A

B

C

D

E

Pontop
Pike

1 grid square represents 500 metres

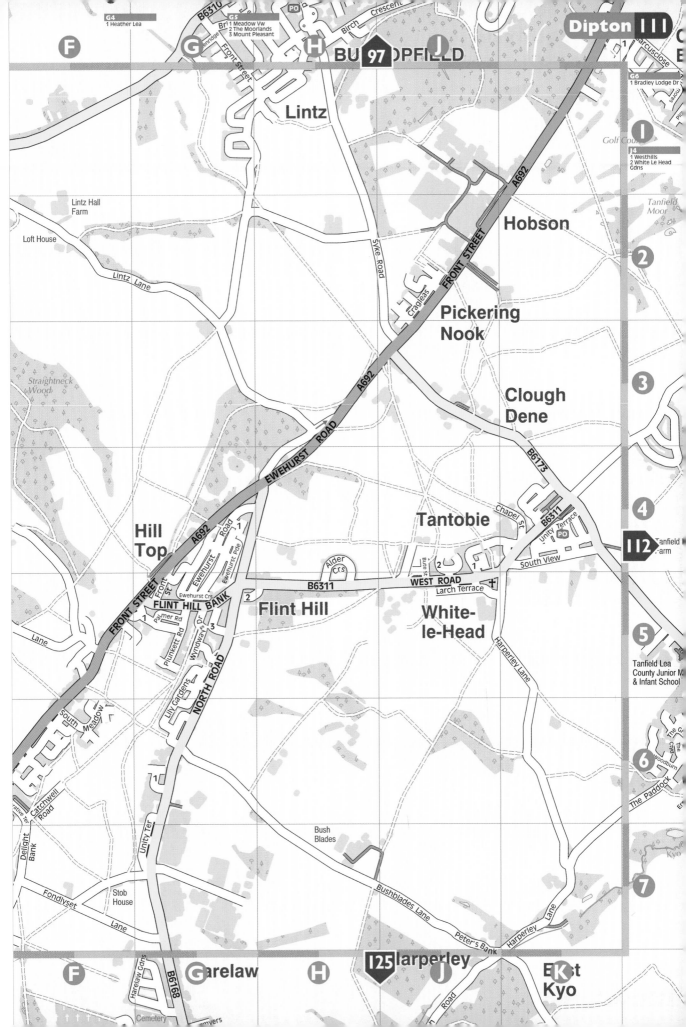

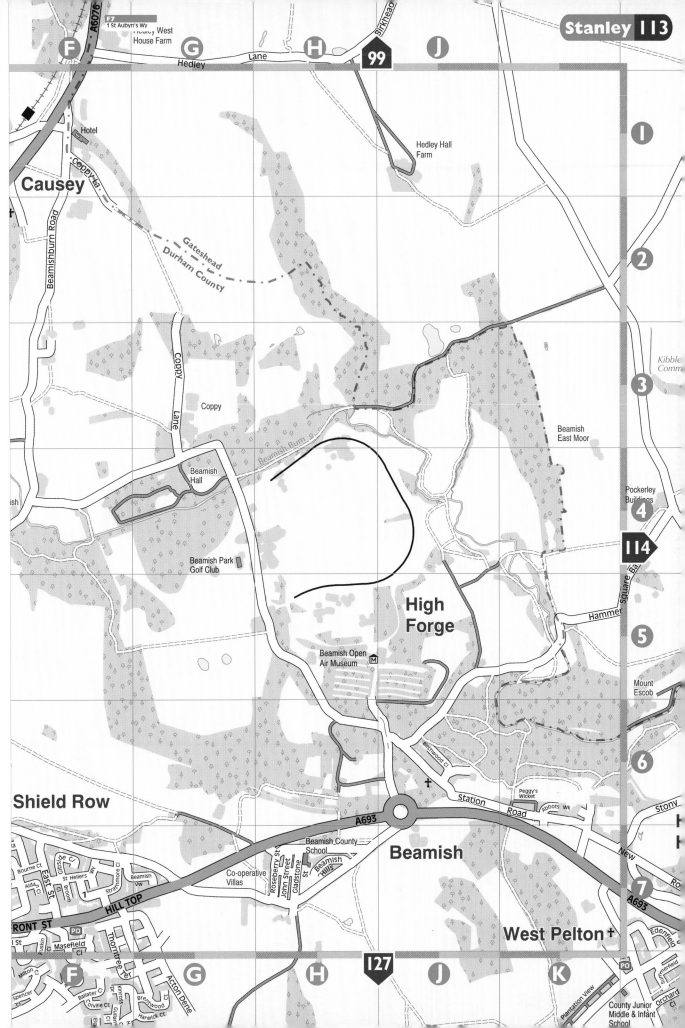

Causey

Shield Row

West Pelton †

Beamish

High Forge

Beamish Hall

Beamish Park Golf Club

Beamish Open Air Museum

Beamish East Moor

Hedley Hall Farm

Hedley West House Farm

Coppy

Pockerley Buildings

Mount Escob

Kibble Comm

Gateshead Durham County

Beamish Burn

Beamish County School

Co-operative Villas

Peggy's Wicket

Abbots Wk

Station Road

Birchwood Cl

County Junior Middle & Infant School

Beamishburn Road

Coppy Lane

Hedley Lane

Birkhead

Beamish Hills

Hill Top

Front St

East St

Acton Dene

Thorntree Ter

Square Ba

Hammer

New Ro

Stony

Edenfield

Roseberry St

John Street

Gladstone

Bourne Ct

St Hellers Wy

Beamish Vw

Strathmore Ter

Aida Cl

Milton

Ruskin

Masefield Cl

Spencer

Ballater Cl

Colville Ct

Kinross

Brentwood

Harwick Ct

Plantation View

Orchard

A6076

A693

99

114

127

F7
1 St Aubyn's Wy

Hotel

PO

Coppy La

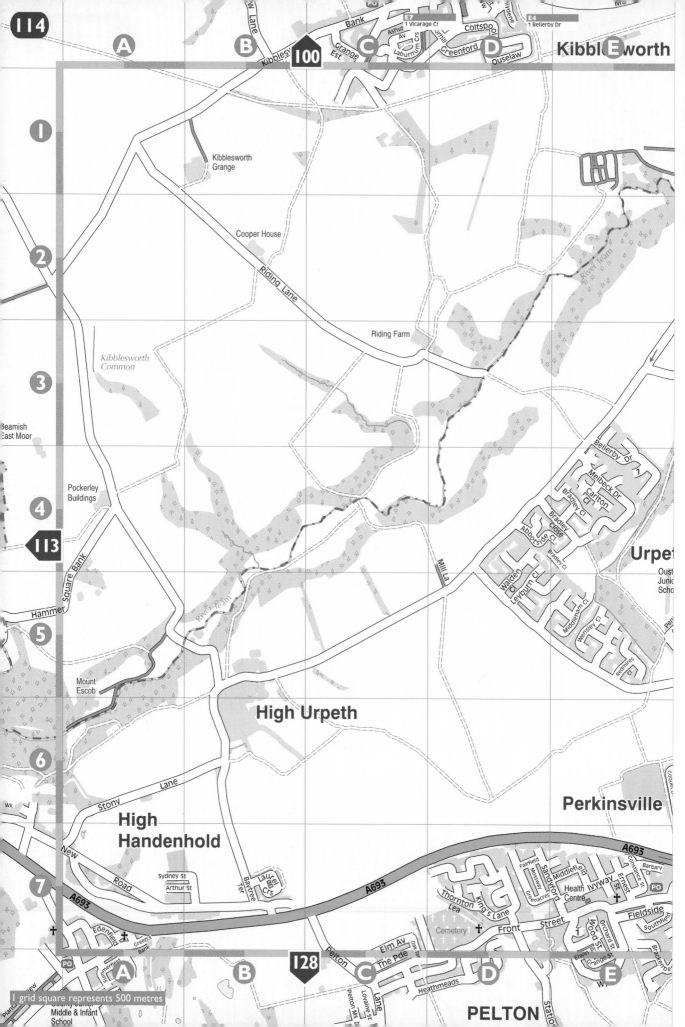

(A) (B) **100** (C) (D) **Kibbl E worth**

1

Kibblesworth
Grange

2

Cooper House

Riding Lane

River Team

Riding Farm

Kibblesworth
Common

3

Beamish
East Moor

4

Pockerley
Buildings

113

Square Bank

Hammer

River Team

Mill La

Bellerby Dr

Melbeck Dr
Carlton
Bradley Cl
Bradley
Close
Abbotside Cl
Bradley Cl

Urpet

Oust
Junic
Scho

Walden Cl
Leyburn Cl

5

Middleham Cl
Wensley Cl

Redmires

Mount
Escob

6

High Urpeth

Stony   Lane

Perkinsville

**High
Handenhold**

New   Road

Sydney St
Arthur St

Baytree Ter

Laurel Crs

A693

A693

A693

Fairfield
Mossway
Sandyford
Middlef ld
Constance St
Ernest St
Barbary
Cl
PO

Thornton
Lea
King's Lane
Greenacres
Ivy Way
Health
Centre

Fieldside
Southfield

7

A693

Cemetery
Front   Street

Orchard St
Wood St

Edenfield
Green's
Bank

PO

(A) (B) **128** (C) The Pde (D) (E)

Elm AV
Heathmeads
Pelton

County Junior
Middle & Infant
School

PELTON

I grid square represents 500 metres

F   G   H   101   J   **BIRTLEY**

J2
1 Birtley La
2 Holyoake Gdns
3 Ruskin Rd

St Josephs Infant School

Gateshead Metropolitan Borough Council

Birtley Lane Surg

Primary School

Portobello

Lord Lawson of Beamish Secondary School

Rowletch Burn Industrial Estate

Birtley St Josephs RC School

Harras Bank

Birtley Medical Group Practice

Birtley Swimming Baths

Radcliffe St

Leafield House School

Wilfrid St

Low Urpeth

Rowletch Burn

King St

George St

Morris St

Station

The Av

Durham Road

A6127

FELL BANK

The Uplands

Penshaw-Way

Shadon Way

Birtley La

Hartland Dr

Tamerton Dr

Portobello County Junior Infant School

Dunvegan

Thirlmere

116

Coniston Road

Ouston

Barley Mow

Barley Mow Primary School

Dorset Avenue

Pembroke Av

Norfolk Avenue

Cambridge Pl

Cheshire Av

Oxford Pl

Cumberland

Durham Pl

Athlone Pl

Suffolk Pl

The Dr

Bedford Avenue

Vigo La

Errol

Kirkstone

Colebrook

Scafell

Nairn Ct

Moray Cl

Sandray Close

Hartside

Kharesdale

Lodge

Picktree

The Oval
The Oval
Viola Crs
Angus
Alford
Athull
Abernethy
Turnberry
Coldstream
Callander
Ross
Cromarty
Cannock
Coldstream

Iris Crs
Aberfoyle

Arisaig
Ardrossan
Aberdeen
Rothsay

St Benets Primary RC School

Ouston County Infant School

Carnoustie

Byron

Milbanke Close

Milbanke Close

Drum Road

First Av

Second Av

Drum

Third Av

Road

Drum Rd

Pelton Health Clinic

Pelton County Junior & Infant School

Lyne Cl
Alice
Tweed
W
Institute Ter
Conway Rd
Brecon Pl
Ascot Pl
Ouston Lane
Caithness Dr
Wansbeck Cl

Park View Comprehensive School

Lombard Drive

Sinclair Drive

Leander Av

Hampton

Merlin Dr

Ash Mdw

North Drive

Lintfort

Picktree Lane

A1(M)

A6127

DURHAM ROAD

York Rd

NORTH ROAD

Wear Lodge

Pelaw Gro

Kingsbury

Queen's Gdns

F   G   **129**   H   J   K

A693

Pelton La

Low Flatts

Lyndhurst

Longean Pk

Vigo Lane

B1288

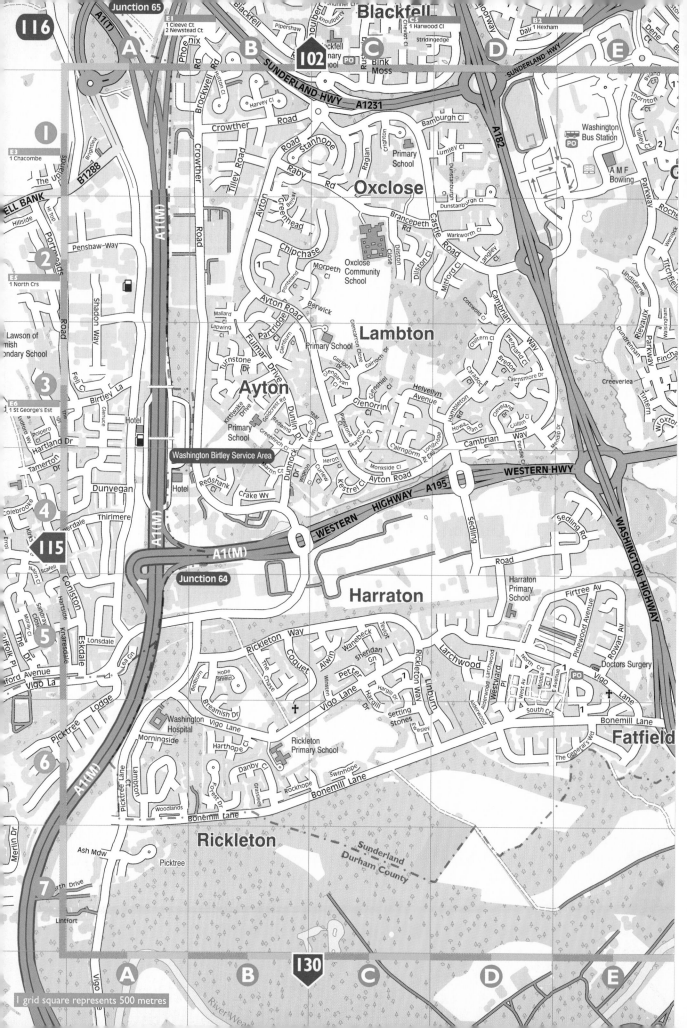

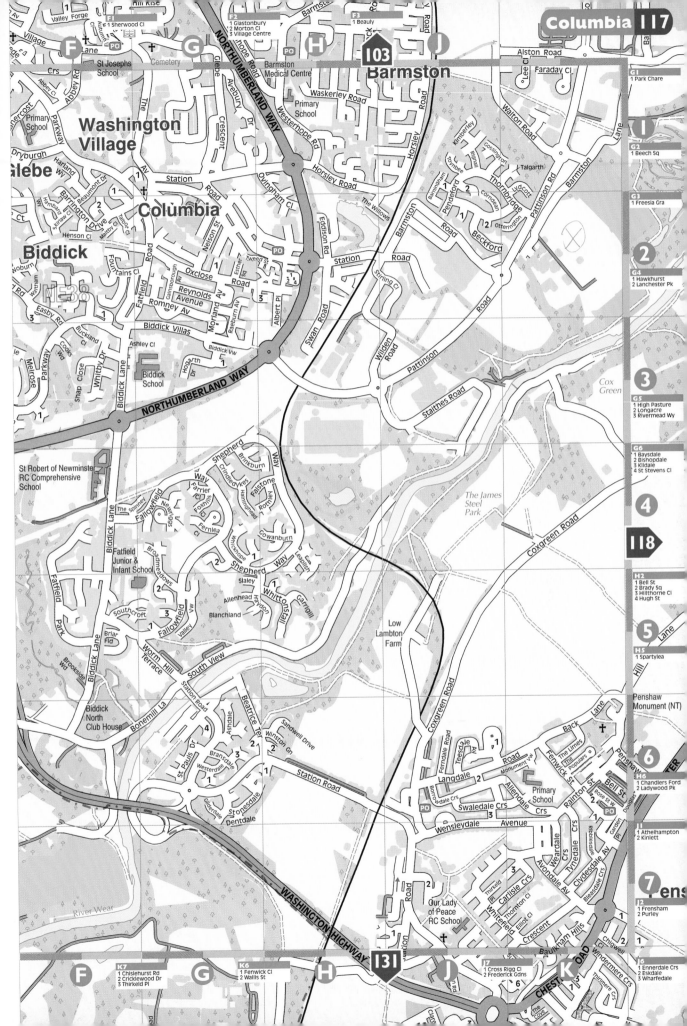

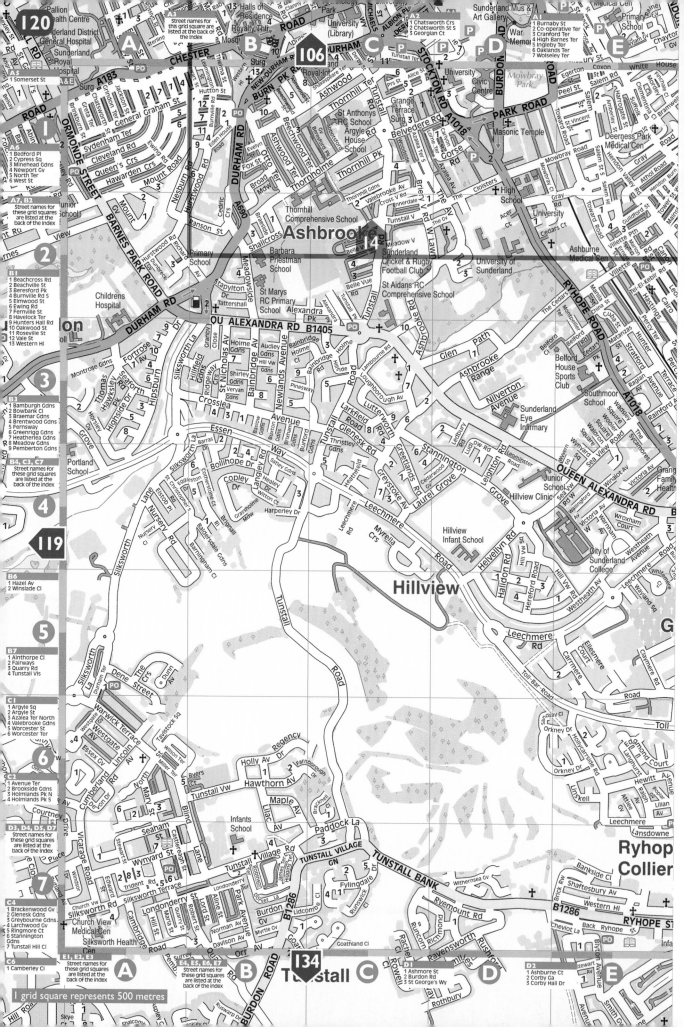

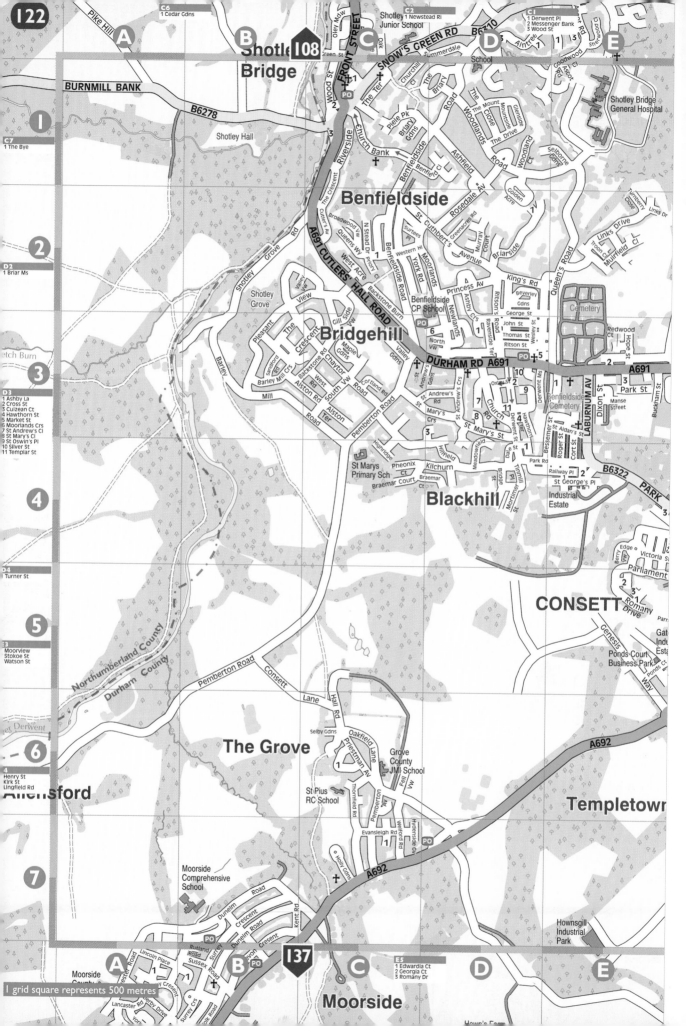

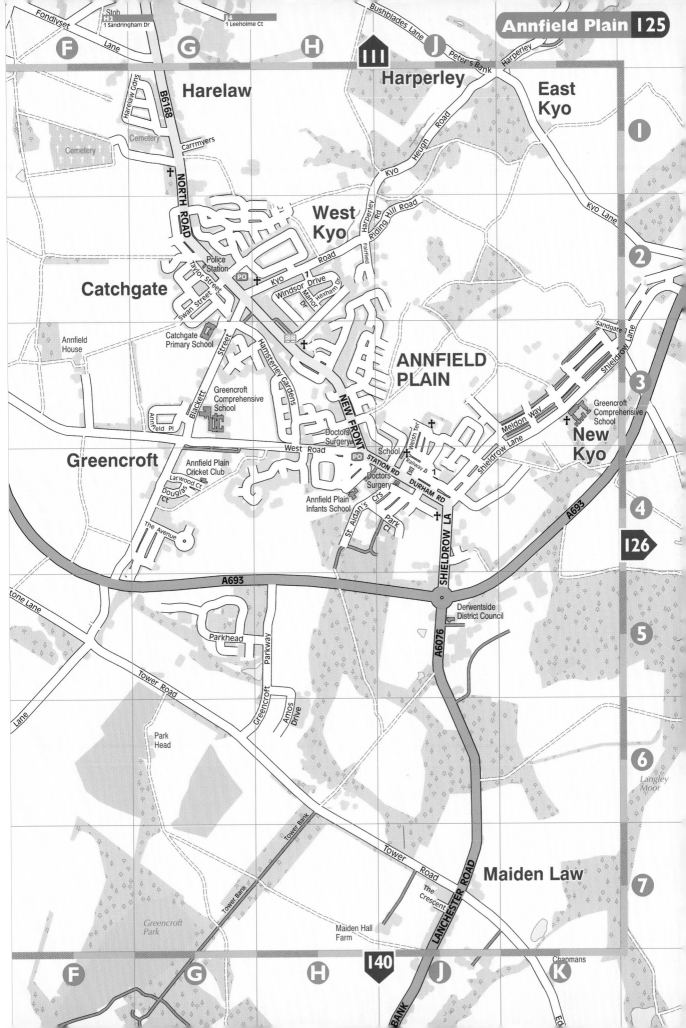

Fondlyset Lane
Stob
H2
1 Sandringham Dr
J4
1 Leeholme Ct
Bushblades Lane
Peter's Bank
Harperley

F **G** **H** **III** **J** **I**

Harelaw
Harperley
East Kyo

B6168
Harelaw Gdns
Cemetery
Cemetery
Carrmyers
NORTH ROAD

Kyo
Heugh Road
Harperley Rd
Riding Hill Road
Kyo Lane

2

West Kyo
Fairfield

Police Station
Taylor Street
Swan Street
PO
Kyo
Windsor Drive
Manor Dr
Hexham Dr
Kyo Road
7

Sandgate
Shieldrow Lane

3

Catchgate
Catchgate Primary School
Street

ANNFIELD PLAIN

Greencroft Comprehensive School
New Kyo
Meldon Way
Shieldrow Lane

Annfield House
Hamsterley Gardens
Blackett
Greencroft Comprehensive School
Annfield Pl

Greencroft
West Road
Larwood Ct
Douglas Ct
Annfield Plain Cricket Club
NEW FRONT STREET
Doctors Surgery
School
Welsh Ter
Railway St
1
STATION RD
DURHAM RD
St Aidan's Crs

4

126

The Avenue
Annfield Plain Infants School
PO
Doctors Surgery
Park Ct
SHIELDROW LA

A693

Derwentside District Council

5

Parkhead
Parkway
Greencroft
Amos Drive
A693
A6076

stone Lane
Lane

Tower Road

Park Head

6

Langley Moor

Greencroft Park
Tower Bank
Tower Road
Tower Road
LANCHESTER ROAD
Maiden Law
The Crescent

7

Maiden Hall Farm
Chapmans
BANK

F **G** **H** **140** **J** **K**

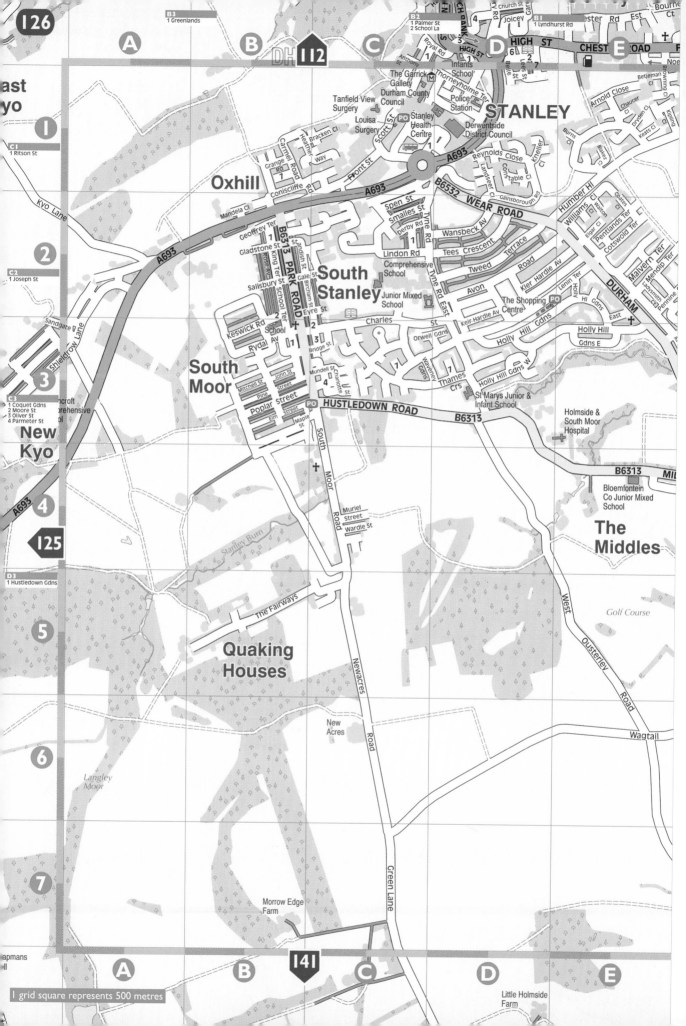

126

A3
1 Greenlands

DH 112

A B C D E

1

C1
1 Ritson St

2

C2
1 Joseph St

Kyo Lane

A693

3

C3
1 Coquet Gdns
2 Moore St
3 Oliver St
4 Parmeter St

New
Kyo

Sandgate

Shieldrow Lane

Oxhill

Carmel Road
Grange Rd
Coniscliffe Rd
Mandela Cl
Geoffrey Ter
Gladstone St
Salisbury St
Keswick Rd
Rydal Av
School Av

B6313 PARK ROAD

King Ter
Roseay
Gale St
Bircham St
Eyre St
Mitchell St
John St
Pine street
Poplar street
Elm street
Maple St
South Moor Road

Front St

Spen St
Smailes St
Derby Rd
Lindon Rd
Tyne Rd
Tyne Rd East
Charles St
Bridge St
Mundell St
Charlotte St

A693

A693

B6532 WEAR ROAD

Tanfield View
Surgery
Louisa
Surgery

The Garrick
Gallery
Durham County
Council
Stanley
Health
Centre

Infants
School
Police
Station
Derwentside
District Council

STANLEY

Reynolds Close
Landseer Cl
Constable Cl
Gainsborough Rd
Kneller Cl
Burns Cl

Humber Hl
Williams Cl
Eigar Cl
Pentlands Ter
Cotswold Ter
Malvern Ter
Mendip Tce
Pennine

DURHAM

Arnold Close
Chaucer Cl
Dryden Cl
Kipling Cl
Keats Cl
Blakes Cl

B2
1 Palmer St
2 School La

HIGH ST
CHEST ROAD

B1
1 Lyndhurst Rd

Royal Rd
Anthony St
Thorneyholme Ter
Belle St

Wansbeck Av
Tees Crescent
Tweed
Terrace
Road
Avon
Kier Hardie Av
Keir-Hardie Av

Orwell Gdns
Waveney Gdns
Thames Crs

Holly Hill
Holly Hill Gdns
Lenin Ter
Holly Hl Gdns East
Holly Hill Gdns W
Holly Hill Gdns E

The Shopping
Centre

St Marys Junior &
Infant School

Holmside &
South Moor
Hospital

South
Stanley

Comprehensive
School

Junior Mixed
School

South
Moor

HUSTLEDOWN ROAD
B6313

PO

B6313
MIL

The
Middles

Bloemfontein
Co Junior Mixed
School

4

A693

125

D3
1 Hustledown Gdns

Stanley Burn

Muriel
Street
Wardle St

West Ousterley Road

Golf Course

5

The Fairways

Quaking
Houses

Newacres Road

Green Lane

Wagtail

6

Langley
Moor

New
Acres

7

Morrow Edge
Farm

Little Holmside
Farm

Chapmans

141

A B C D E

1 grid square represents 500 metres

West Pelton †

Craghead

Holmside

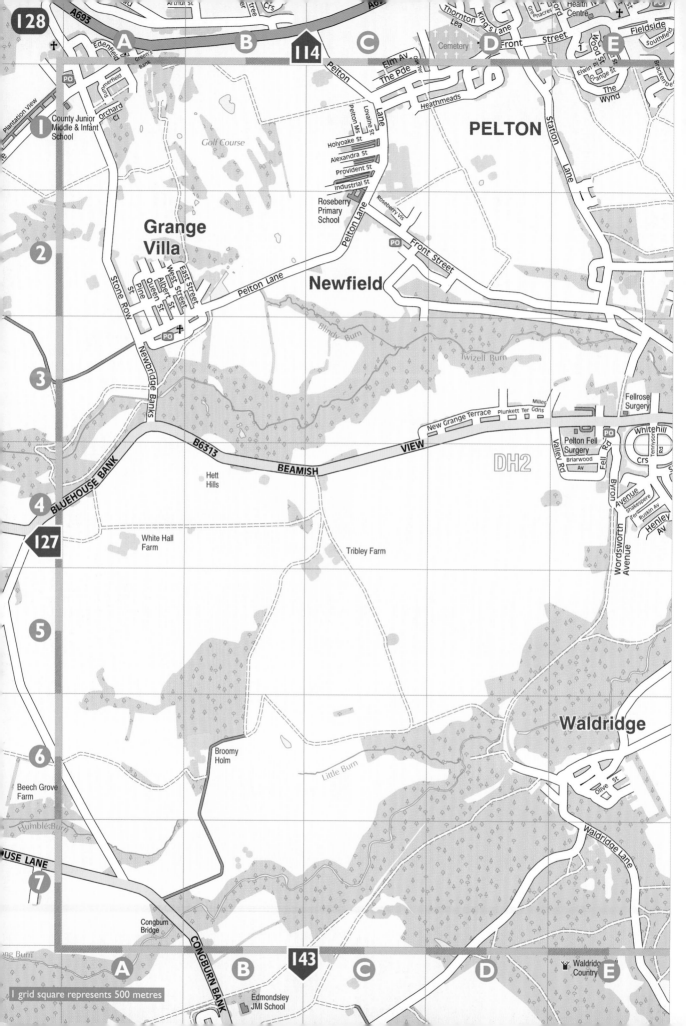

A693

A
B
114
C
D
E

Thornton
Lea
King's Lane
greenacres
Health
Centre
Fieldside
Southfield
Front
Street
Woo...
Southfield
Arthur St
tree
Crs
Edenfield
Green's
Bank
Cemetery
Elm Av
The Pde
Elwin Pl
Grange St
The
Wynd

Plantation View
PO
Summerfield
Orchard Cl
County Junior
Middle & Infant
School
Pelton
Pelton
Lane
Lovaine St
Heathmeads
PELTON
Station
Lane
Brackenfi...

1

Golf Course
Pelton Ms
Holyoake St
Alexandra St
Provident St
Industrial St
Roseberry Vis

**Grange
Villa**
Stone Row
West Street
East Street
Albert St
Queen St
Pine St
Roseberry
Primary
School
Pelton Lane
PO
Front Street
PO

2

Pelton Lane
Newfield

Newbridge Banks
Blindy Burn
Twizell Burn

3

BLUEHOUSE BANK
B6313
Hett
Hills
BEAMISH
VIEW
New Grange Terrace
Plunkett Ter
Miller
Gdns
Fellrose
Surgery
Whitehill
Crs
Tennyson...
Rd
Pelton Fell
Surgery
Briarwood
Av
PO
Valley Rd
Fell Rd

4

127
White Hall
Farm
Tribley Farm
DH2
Byron
Avenue
Shakespere
Terrace
Ruskin Av
Henley
Av
Wordsworth Avenue

5

Waldridge

6
Broomy
Holm
Little Burn

Beech Grove
Farm
Olive St

...USE LANE
Humble Burn

7

Congburn
Bridge
Waldridge
Lane

A
B
143
C
D
Waldridge
Country
E

...ng Burn
CONGBURN BANK
Edmondsley
JMI School

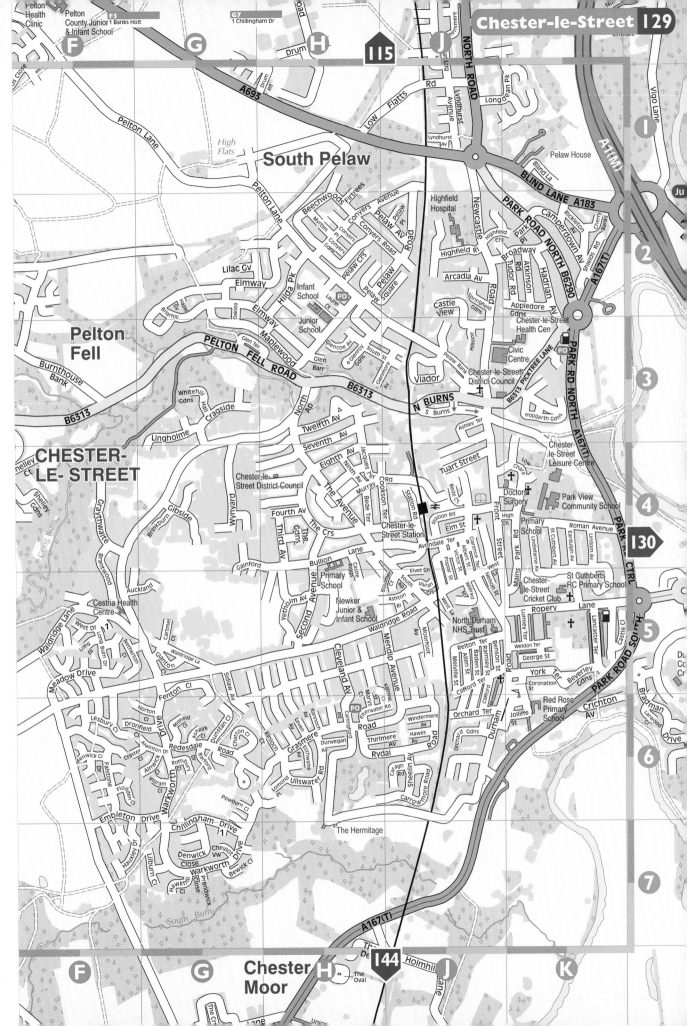

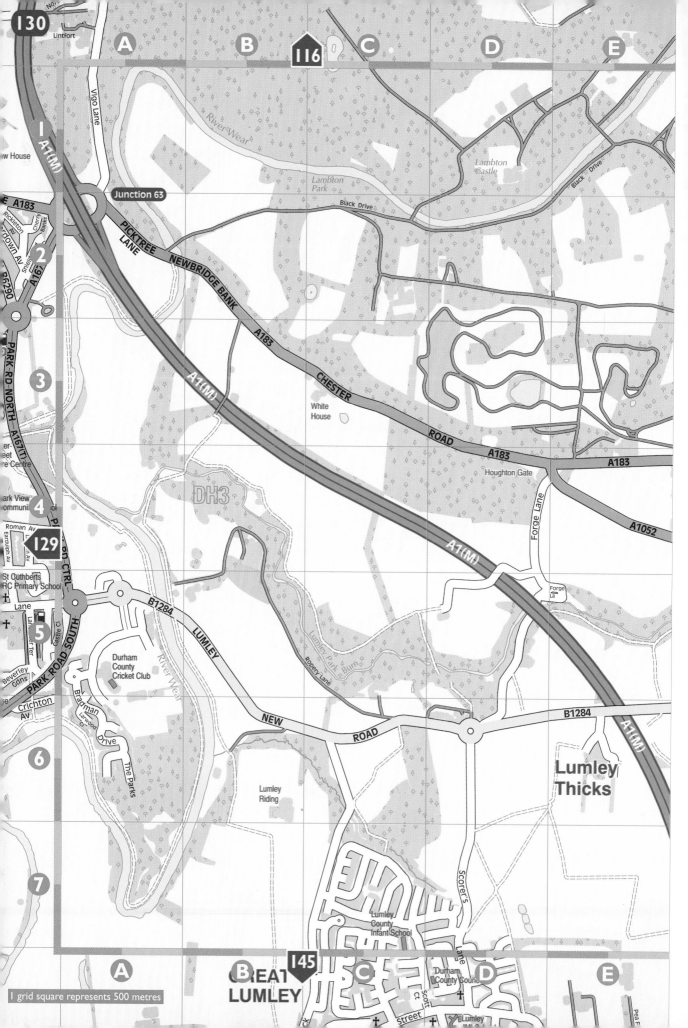

130

116

A   B   C   D   E

Lintfort

Vigo Lane

A1(M)

1

Junction 63

PICKTREE LANE

NEWBRIDGE BANK

River Wear

Lambton Park

Lambton Castle

Black Drive

Black Drive

A183

A183

CHESTER

ROAD

A183

White House

Houghton Gate

A183

Forge Lane

A1052

A1(M)

A183

Rickleton Av

Cherry Banks

Shield Av

A167

B6290

2

3

PARK RD NORTH

A167(T)

4

ark View ommunit chool

Roman Av

Eardulph Av

129

St Cuthberts RC Primary School

Lane

5

Castle Cl

Lower Ter

Beverley Gdns

Crichton Av

PARK ROAD SOUTH

B1284

LUMLEY

Durham County Cricket Club

River Wear

Bradman Drive

Larwood Cl

The Parks

6

NEW

ROAD

Ropery Lane

Lumley Park Burn

B1284

A1(M)

Lumley Thicks

Forge La

7

Lumley Riding

Lumley County Infant School

Scorers

Lane

A   B   C   D   E

GREAT LUMLEY

145

Durham County Counci

Lumley

Street

DH3

1 grid square represents 500 metres

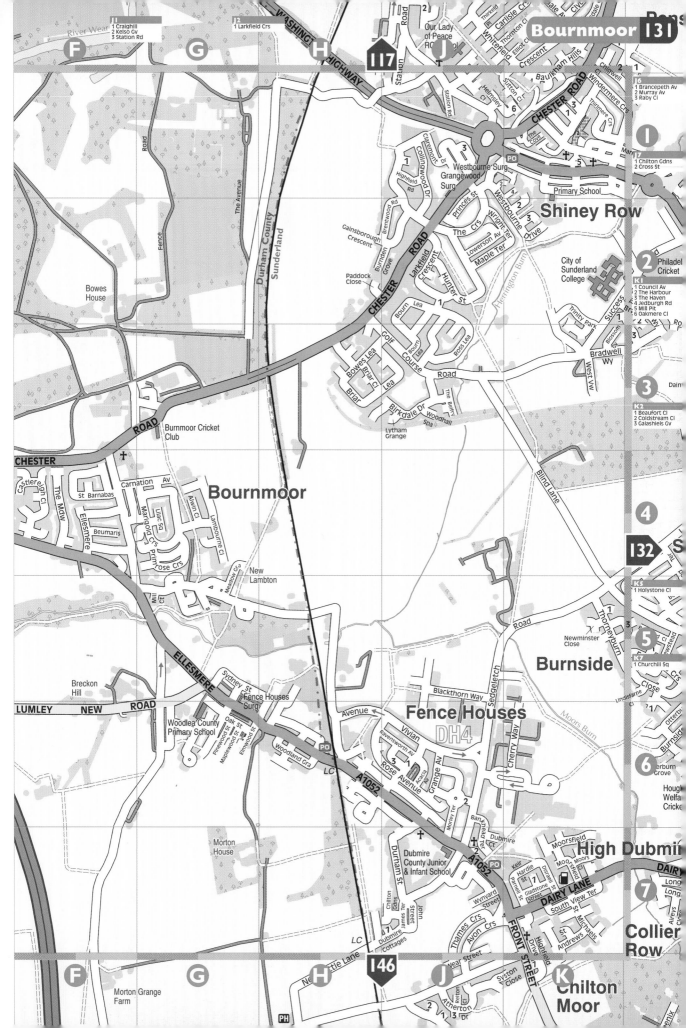

East Herrington

Foxcove
Crow Lane
Herrington Road
B1286
DURHAM ROAD
Park Lea
West Park
Pk Lea
Meadow Dr
Meadow View
Broadmeado
Drumoyne Close
Elmfield Cl
Silksworth Road
Oakfield Cl
Woodside Terrace
Longmeadows
Ashton Close
Briardene
Glendale
Cranborne
CITY WAY
CITY WAY
Admiral Way
Monarch Way
Victory Way
Camberwell Way
Moorside
Glanville Rd
Career Crs
1 Braemar Gdns
Amelia Gdns
Arundel Gdns
Silksworth
Balmoral Carter
Caernar
Dudley Gdns
Aldwych Sq
Primary School
Launceston Drive
Warwick
Raby D
Augusta Sq
Grayling Ct
Farringdon School
Silksworth Road
Morpeth Dr
Manston
Morval Cl
Marcross Dr
Machurst
Melgarve Dr
Benedict Biscop C of E School
Madgley Dr
Marlow Dr
Glodlynn
Bowlynn Dr
Maclynn Cl
Brenlynn Cl
Maree
Melvdig
Manningford
Maree
College Road
Burn Road
Chantry Cl
Moorside Road
Englemann Way
Lacepark
Corbiere Cl
Birch Ct
Vicarsholme
Friarsfield Cl
Bishops Wy
Priestfield
Hightree Close
Fairgreen
Knollside Cl
Brookbank Cl
Canonsfield Cl
Plough Road
Woodland Rise
Normont
Silksworth Wy
DOXFORD PK WY
Baffin Cl
Frobisher Ct
Laxford
Trool Ct
DOXFORD PARK WAY
Hall Farm Road
Warden Law La
Silksworth Dr
Silksworth Hall Drive
Mill Hill Road
Church View Medical Cen
Silksworth Hea
PO
Foxfair Cl
Cortesto
Silver

A19(T)

Low Haining

Haining

Warden Law North Farm

Hangmans Lane

Salter's Lane

Lane

Thristley House Farm

Clubhouse
B1404
Warden Law

F · + G PO
F Golf Course G
H
119
J
H
J
K
High Sharpley

I

2

3

4
134

5

6

7

H1
1 Maidstone Cl
2 Marbury Cl
3 Matfen Dr
4 Melsonby Cl
5 Merrington Cl
6 Merrion Cl

H2
1 Maplebeck Cl
2 Maxton Cl
3 Midsomer Cl
4 Milsted Cl
5 Minskip Cl
6 Montford Cl

J1
1 Aspen Ct
2 Bordeaux Cl
3 Bowlynn Cl
4 Dunnlynn Cl
5 Plane Tree Ct

J2
1 Bristlecone
2 Cottonwood
3 Elsdonburn Rd
4 Markby Cl
5 Mayo Dr
6 Medina Cl
7 Meltham Dr
8 Membury Cl
9 Milrig Cl
10 Monterey

J3
1 Whitebark

K1
1 Crawford Ct
2 Hawkins Cl

K2
1 Abbotsfield Cl
2 Cardinals Cl
3 Deaconsfield Cl
4 Deansfield Cl
5 Harvest Cl
6 Hightree Cl
7 Honeycomb Cl
8 Monksfield Cl

A   B   120   C   D   E

RYHOPE ST

Tunstall

I

1

2

3

133

4

5

6

7

Doxford Park

Tunstall Lodge Farm

Lodgeside Meadow

East Farm

Burdon

Burn Hall Farm

A19(T)

Old Burdon

Pacific Hall Farm

Sunderland
Durham County

Sharpley Hall Farm

B1404

Seaton Grove

Seaton

B1404   SEATON LANE

Westlea Junior School

A   B   149   C   D   E

Seaton Moor House

Oak

Northumberland County
Durham County

Wharnley
Burn

A **B** **C** **D** **E**

1

Combfield
House

Derwent
Grange

ALLENSFORD BANK

A68

FRONT ST

Castleside

2

Dean Howl
Farm

Wharnley Way

CONSE

Moorland
School

Hillcrest

PO

ROWLEY B

Watergate
Road

Street

Church

3

Healeyfield

Horsleyhope Burn

Healeyfield Lane

4

Goldhill Lane

Goldhill

5

Horsleyhope

Healeyfield Lane

Greenside

Honey
Hill

6

Middles
Farm

Whitehall
Moss

7

Lindisfarne

A **B** **C** **D** **E**

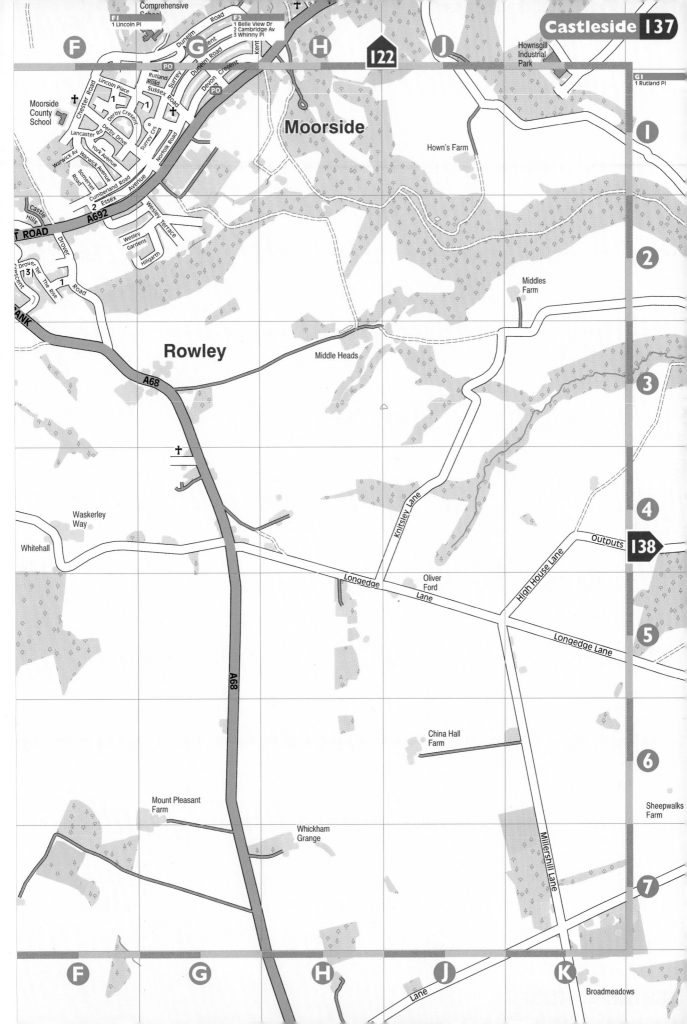

F

1 Lincoln Pl

Comprehensive School

Duneim Road

Kent Road

G

F2
1 Belle View Dr
2 Cambridge Av
3 Whinny Pl

Duneim Road

Devon Cresent

PO

Rutland Road

PO

H

122

J

Hownsgill Industrial Park

G1
1 Rutland Pl

Moorside County School

Chester Road

Lincoln Place

1

Derby Cresent

1

Rutland Road

Surrey

Sussex Road

Norfolk Road

Hown's Farm

I

Warwick AV

Warwick Avenue

Lancaster Rd

Derby Drive

York Avenue

Surrey Crs

Moorside

2

Somerset Road

Cumberland Road

2

Essex

Avenue

Middles Farm

Castle Hills

A692

Drover Road

Wesley Terrace

Middles Farm

ROAD

Drover Ter

3

Wesley Gardens

Hillgarth

2

The Rise

1

Rowley

A68

Middle Heads

3

BANK

Waskerley Way

Knitsley Lane

4

Whitehall

Outputs

138

Longedge Lane

Oliver Ford

High House Lane

A68

China Hall Farm

Longedge Lane

5

Mount Pleasant Farm

Whickham Grange

Millershill Lane

6

Sheepwalks Farm

7

F

G

H

J

Lane

K

Broadmeadows

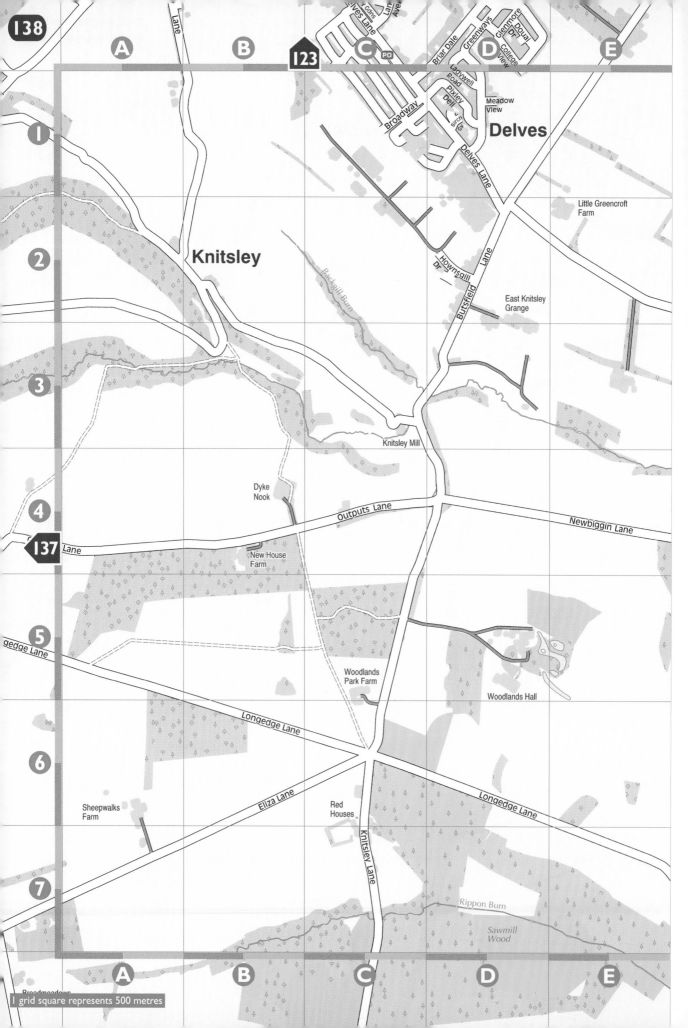

138

A   B   **123**   C   PO   D   E

Lane

Delves

1

Knitsley

2

Little Greencroft Farm

Backsill Burn

Butsfield Lane

Hownsgill Dr

East Knitsley Grange

3

Knitsley Mill

Dyke Nook

4

Outputs Lane

Newbiggin Lane

137 Lane

New House Farm

Woodlands Park Farm

5

gedge Lane

Woodlands Hall

Longedge Lane

6

Sheepwalks Farm

Eliza Lane

Red Houses

Longedge Lane

Knitsley Lane

7

Rippon Burn

Sawmill Wood

A   B   C   D   E

Broadmeadows

1 grid square represents 500 metres

F
G
H
124
J
I
2 A691
3
Lizards
4
140
5
L
6
7
F
G
H
J
K

Woodside
Esp Green
A691

Stockerley
Bridge
Stockerley Lane
Stockerley Burn

Hurbuck
Cottages

Humberhill Lane

Low
Meadows
Smallthorpe Burn

Newbiggin
Newbiggin Lane

Yeckhouse Lane

Upper
Houses

Humber House
Farm

Hollinside

Middlewood
Farm

Colepike
Hall

Longedge L

berhill La

B6296

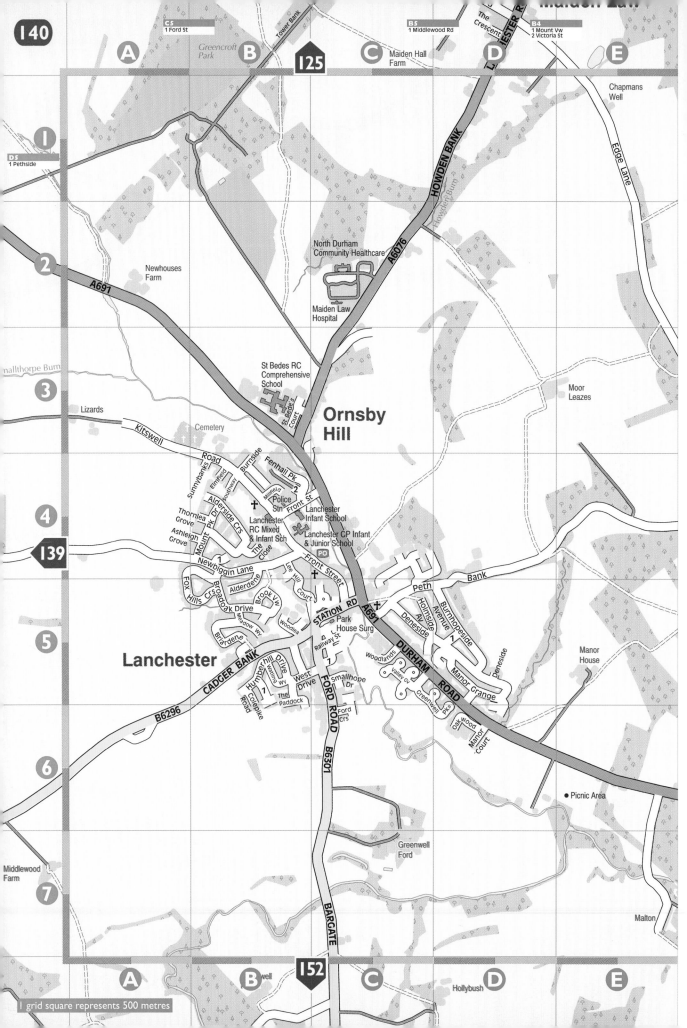

A

B

C

D

E

125

C5
1 Ford St

B5
1 Middlewood Rd

B4
1 Mount Vw
2 Victoria St

The Crescent

LESTER R

Maiden Law

Tower Bank

Greencroft Park

Maiden Hall Farm

Chapmans Well

I

D5
1 Pethside

Edge Lane

HOWDEN BANK

Howden Burn

2

A691

Newhouses Farm

North Durham Community Healthcare

A6076

Maiden Law Hospital

mallthorpe Burn

3

Lizards

St Bedes RC Comprehensive School

St Bede's Court

Ornsby Hill

Moor Leazes

Kitswell

Cemetery

Road

Sunnybanks

Burnside

Fenhall Pk

2

Millfield

Front St

Police Stn

Elmfield

Southway

Alderside Crs

4

Thornlea Grove

Mount Pk Dr

Lanchester Infant School

Lanchester CP Infant & Junior School

Lanchester RC Mixed & Infant Sch

Ashleigh Grove

139

1

The Close

PO

Front Street

Peth

Bank

Newbiggin Lane

Fox Hills

Broadoak Drive

Alderdene

Brook Vw

Lee Hill Court

Woodlea

STATION RD

Park House Surg

Railway St

A691

Holmside

Deneside

Av

Burnhopeside Avenue

1

Deneside

Manor House

5

Lanchester

Meadow Wy

Briardene

Humberhill Drive

Watling Wy

West Drive

7

The Paddock

Woodlands

valley cv

DURHAM ROAD

Manor Grange

CADGER BANK

Colepike Road

Smallhope Dr

Greenwell

Greenwell Pk

Oak Wood

Manor Court

6

B6296

FORD ROAD

Ford Crs

B6301

Picnic Area

Middlewood Farm

7

Greenwell Ford

BARGATE

Malton

A

B

152

well

C

D

Hollybush

E

1 grid square represents 500 metres

Holmside Hall

G4
1 The Gables

Morro
Farm

H3
1 Co-operative Ter

126

I

Little Holmside
Farm

Green La

Holmside Lane

Whiteside
Farm

2

Whiteside Burn

Holmside Fall Road

Parkside

Vale View

The Avenue

PO

The Villas

Langley Avenue

Holmside Lane

Whitehouse Avenue

The
Haven

Pleasant
View

Holmlea

Braeside

Burnhope
Primary
School

Burnhope

3

White
House

Edge Lane

Peth Lane

Beech Gv

Langley
Lane

Greenwood
Av

4

142

Long E

Long Edge

5

High
Burnhopeside

Langley West
House

6

Langley Lane

A691

Langley

7

Burnhopeside
Hall

F
G
H
153
J
A691
K

River Brown

F G1
1 Stobart St

Congburn
Bridge

G H5
1 Graham Ct

H

128

J

H6
1 Fynway

I

Waldridge Fell
Country Park

CONGBURN BANK

B6532

Edmondsley
JMI School

Tyzack

Street

Jubilee Cl

2

Edmondsley

*Sacriston
Wood*

Bruce St

Hamilton
Terrace

EDMONDSLEY LANE

Westhills

Close   Daleside

Nettlesworth
West House

3

Black Burn

Ashford   Cross

Dene

Deneside

Lane

Nettlesworth

Ugly Lane

4 PARK

Hill heads

Charlaw   Close

Acorn Close

Derwent   Coniston Dr

B6532

RC JMI
School

† **SACRISTON**

Church   Street

Morningside

Brookside

Parkside

Springside

B6312

144

Tan

Hills

Rydal
Close

Coningham
Ct

St Cuthberts   FRONT STREET
Dr

† Cemetery

Ripon
Cl

Gregson St

Witton Av

Findon

Avenue

Sacriston
Swimming
Baths

Plawsworth Road
County Infant School

Barras Hill

5

Kimblesw

Sacriston
Cricket
Club

Water

St John St

PLAWSWORTH ROAD

Rose
Crs

Fern
Rd

Lavender
Gardens

Industrial
Est

PO

Iveson St

Highfield

Lilac Av

Viola Crs

6

**Kimblesw
Grange**

VALLEY VIEW

WITTON ROAD

Sacriston
Junior
School

DURHAM ROAD

Priory Ct

Crossfield

Holly Crescent

Penshaw
Vw

Hill Crest

Eastwood

Redhouse
Close

Browbank

Cathedral
View

7

Fulforth

B6532

FINDON HILL

B6532

Fyndoune
Community
College

*Wellsprings
Farm*

Kimblesw
Grange

Tre   Crescent

Norburn Park

Rose   Lea

Hillside   Findon Av

Briar Lea

May Lea

Oak   Lea   Fyndoune Wy

Durham Gdns

Dene Ct

Waterson Wy

SACRISTON LANE

View

Fair

South   Lea

**Witton
Gilbert**

Brookside

F
Witton Gilbert
County School

Chapel Ct

G

Friarside

Glebeside

Brookside

Burns

H
155

Fyndoun
Cottage

J

K

Potter
House

FRONT

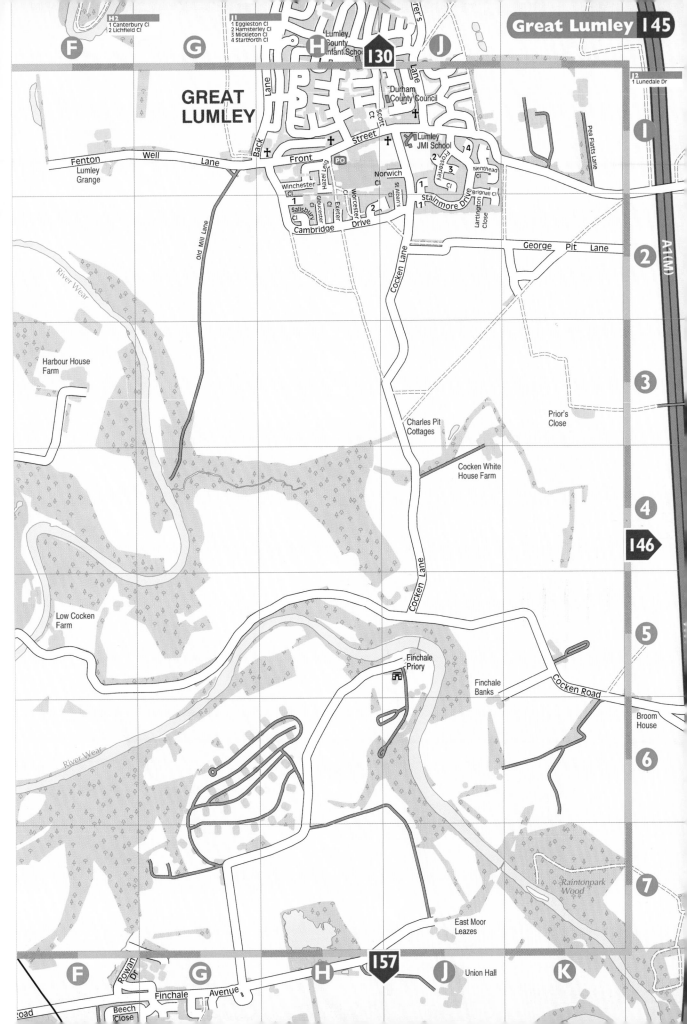

GREAT
LUMLEY

H2
1 Canterbury Cl
2 Lichfield Cl

J1
1 Eggleston Cl
2 Hamsterley Cl
3 Mickleton Cl
4 Startforth Cl

1 Lunedale Dr

130

Lumley
County
Infant School

Durham
County Council

Lumley
JMI School

Back Lane

Scott Ct

Front Street

PO

Hazel Field Ct

Winchester Cl

Salisbury Cl

Cambridge

Gloucester Cl

Exeter Cl

Worcester Drive

Norwich Cl

St Alban's Cl

Frosterley

Nenthead Cl

Brignall Cl

Stainmore Drive

Lartington Close

Fenton
Lumley
Grange

Well Lane

Old Mill Lane

Pea Flatts Lane

A1(M)

J2

George Pit Lane

River Wear

Harbour House
Farm

Cocken Lane

Charles Pit
Cottages

Cocken White
House Farm

Prior's
Close

146

Low Cocken
Farm

Cocken Lane

River Wear

Finchale
Priory

Finchale
Banks

Cocken Road

Broom
House

Raintonpark
Wood

East Moor
Leazes

157

Union Hall

Rowan Dr

Finchale Avenue

Beech
Close

Road

I

2

3

4

5

6

7

F G H J

F G H J K

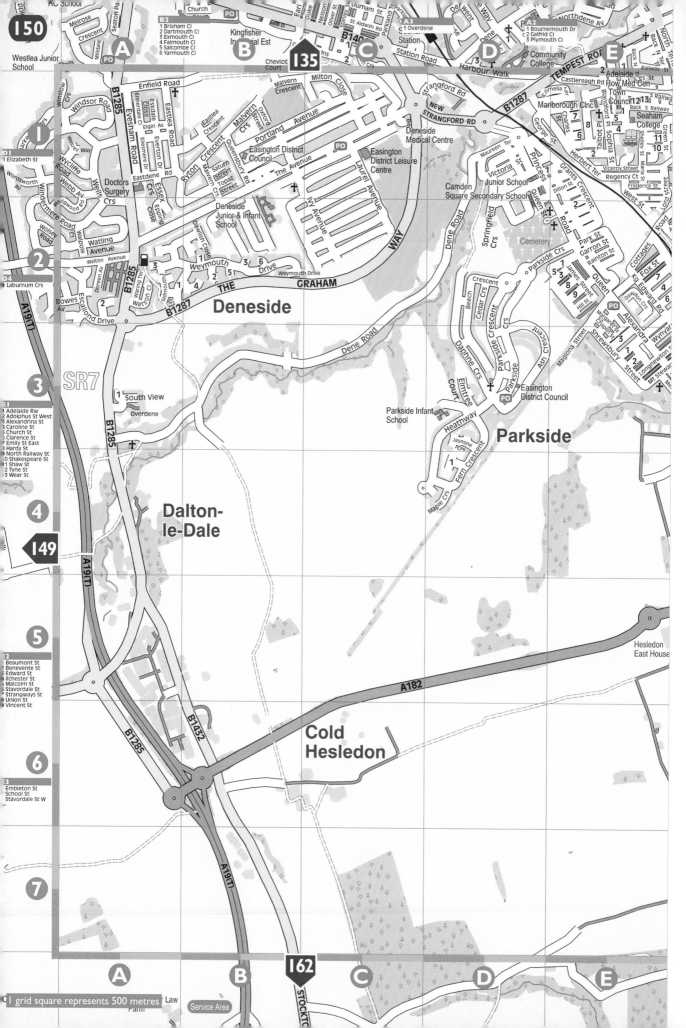

F1
1 Aline St
2 Mary St
3 South Ter

F2
1 Robert St
2 Ropery Wk

F3
1 Londonderry St
2 Seaham St

F G H J

Police Station

SEAHAM

PO

Foundry Road

Primary School

Bottle Works Rd

Gas Works Road

Albert St

Alfred St

Stewart St

Candlish Ter

Embankment

Hill Crs

Dawdon

Edith Street

LC

Nose's Point

A182

Kinley Hill

Chourdon Point

I

2

3

4

5

6

7

F G H J K

Hawthorn Hive

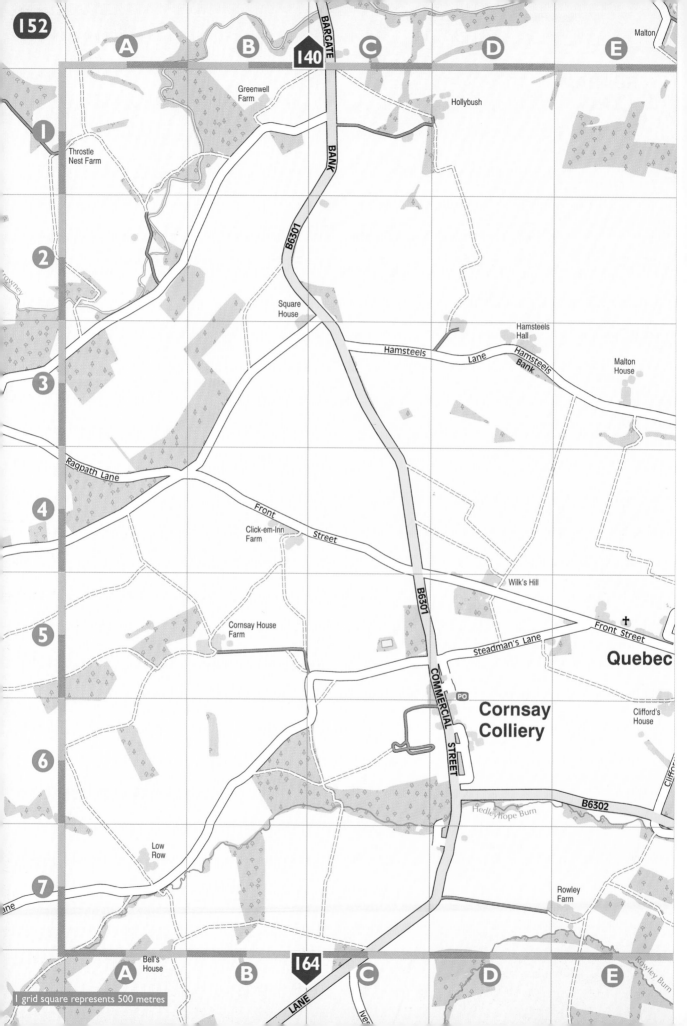

A   B   **140**   C   D   E

1

Throstle
Nest Farm

Greenwell
Farm

BARGATE

Hollybush

Malton

BANK

2

rowney

B6301

Square
House

Hamsteels
Hall

3

Hamsteels   Lane   Hamsteels
Bank

Malton
House

Ragpath Lane

4

Front
Street

Click-em-Inn
Farm

Wilk's Hill

5

Cornsay House
Farm

B6301

Steadman's Lane

Front Street

†

Quebec

6

PO

**Cornsay
Colliery**

COMMERCIAL   STREET

Clifford's
House

Hedley Hope Burn

B6302

Cliffor

7

Low
Row

Rowley
Farm

Lane

Rowley Burn

A   Bell's
House   B   **164**   C   D   E

LANE

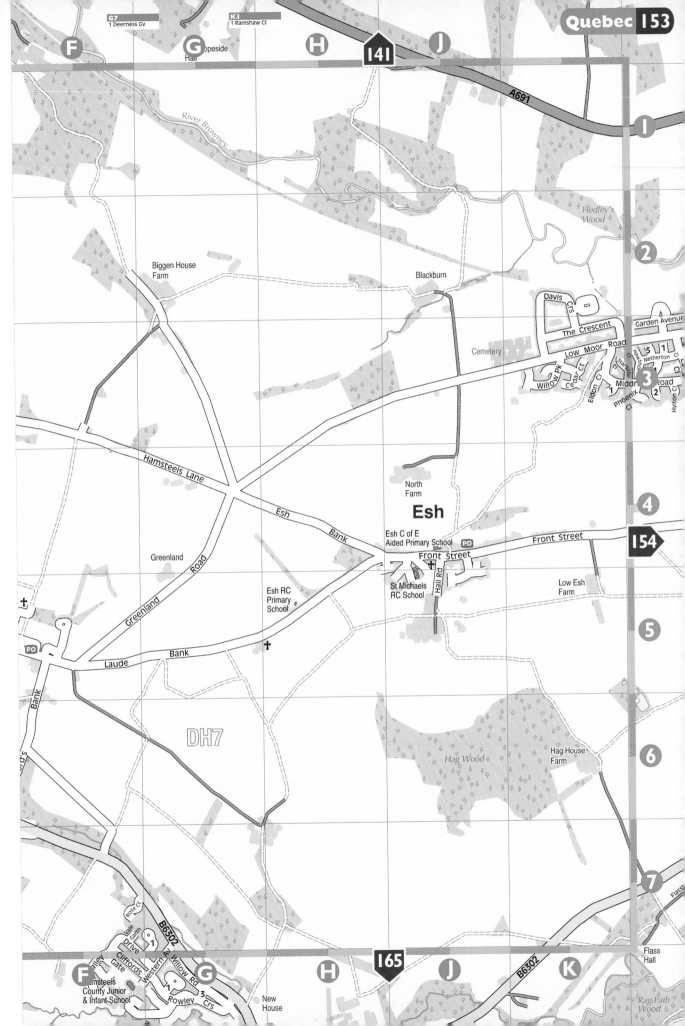

F
G
H
J
I

G7
1 Deerness Gv

K3
1 Ramshaw Cl

141

A691

Hopeside Hall

River Browney

Hedley's Wood

2

Biggen House Farm

Blackburn

Davis Crs

The Crescent

Garden Avenue

Cemetery

Low Moor Road

5 1

Netherton Cl

3

Willow Pk

Cedar Ct

Eldon Cl

Middr Road

Phoenix Cl

Hytton Cl

2

Hamsteels Lane

North Farm

Esh

4

Esh Bank

Esh C of E Aided Primary School

PO

Front Street

154

Greenland Road

Front Street

Greenland

St Michaels RC School

Hall Rd

Low Esh Farm

Esh RC Primary School

†

5

Laude Bank

Bank

†

Bank

DH7

Hag Wood

Hag House Farm

6

7

B6302

Flass

Rose Ct

Garth

Drive

Cliffords Gate

Western Av

Willow Rd

165

B6302

Flass Hall

F

Hamsteels County Junior & Infant School

G

Rowley Crs

1 3

New House

H

J

K

Rag-Path Wood

154

B3
1 Hazelwood Ct
2 Springwell Cl

B2
1 Brownney Ct
2 Oak St

A3
1 Beamish Cl
2 Elemore Cl
3 Meadowbank
4 Penshaw Cl
5 Whitburn Cl

A   B   **142**   C   D   E

Notburn Lane

I

A691   A691

Hedley's Wood

Stobbilee Farm

Wall Nook

Wallnook Lane

River Browney

2

Dale St

Hawthorne Ter

Bridge St

Palm St

Bridge Wy

1

Derwentside College

Garden Avenue

Wd Vw

Pine St

Elm St

PO

Park

Langley Park

w Moor Road

5 1

Netherton Cl

4

3 1

Cherrytree Drive

Maplewood Court

Beech Court

Park Close

Bridge Drive

Esh Hillside

3   Middridge Road

Phoenix Cl

2

Eppleton

Hylton Cl

Hospital Road

Kingsway

Eastern Av

Crossways

2

Hilltop View

Stangate

Eldo

Cedar Ct

Langley Park Primary School

Springwell Av

East Clere

Hill Top

Front Street

4

153

eet

Esh

5

College   Road

Ushaw Farm

Ushaw College

6

Broadgate Road

East Flass Farm

B6302

COCKHOUSE

Arthur St Surgery

7

Flasshall Lane

LANE

Temperance Ter

PO

Whitehouse

Sta Road

Flass Av

Ushaw Moor Infant School

Ushaw Moor

Ushaw Moor Cricket Club

Flass Hall

A   B   **166**   C   D   E

Rag Path Wood

1 grid square represents 500 metres

Hare Holme Farm

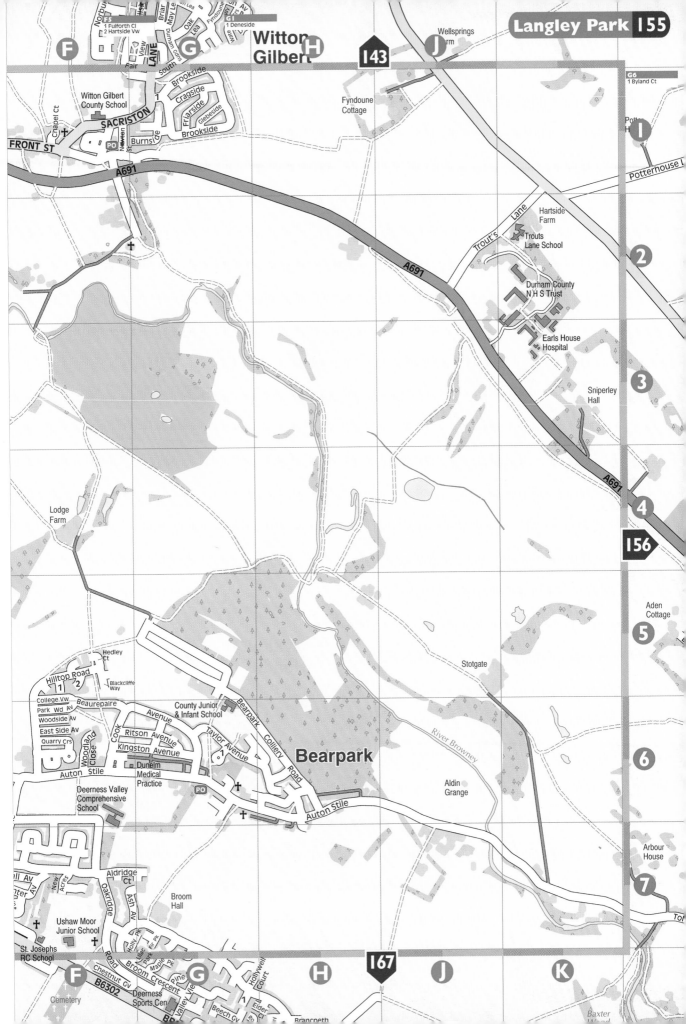

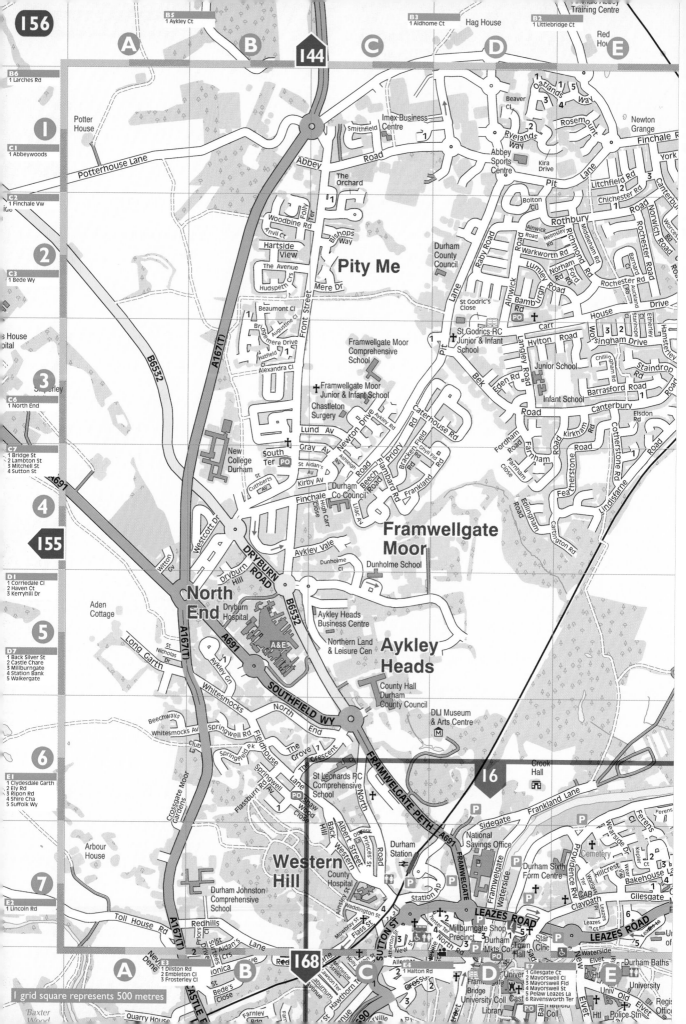

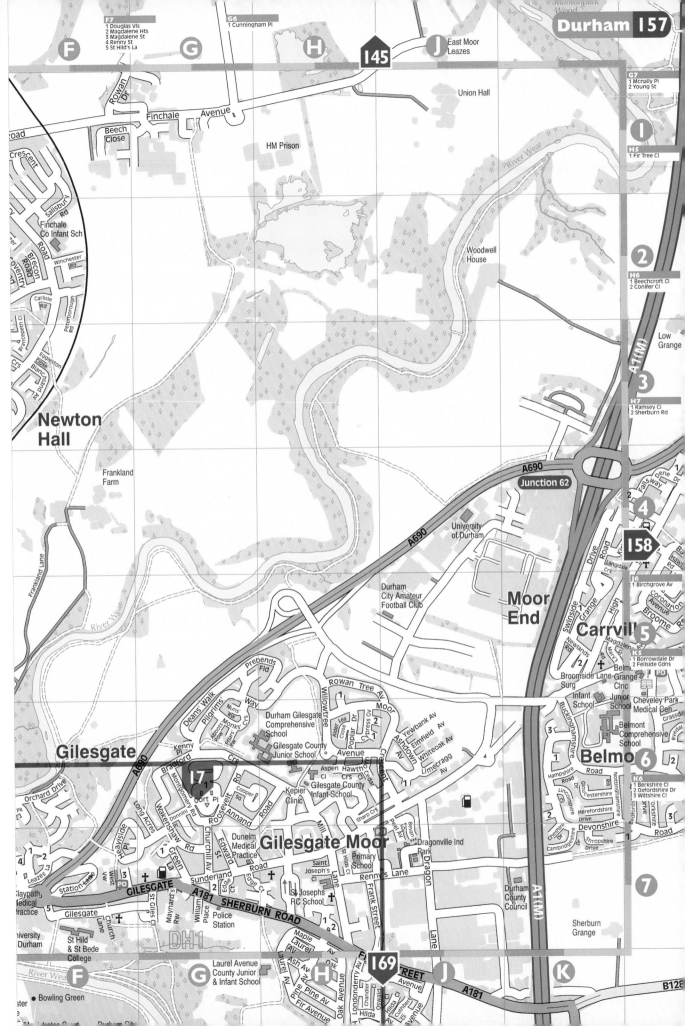

F7
1 Douglas Vls
2 Magdalene Hts
3 Magdalene St
4 Renny St
5 St Hild's La

G6
1 Cunningham Pl

F **G** **H** **145** **J** East Moor Leazes

G7
1 Mcnally Pl
2 Young St

Rowan Dr

Finchale Avenue

Beech Close

Union Hall

1

HM Prison

H5
1 Fir Tree Cl

Salisbury Rd

Finchale Co Infant Sch

Winchester

River Wear

Woodwell House

2

H6
1 Beechcroft Cl
2 Conifer Cl

Brecon Road

Carlisle Rd

Low Grange

Coventry

Peterborough Rd

Eggleston

Blanc

A1(M)

3

H7
1 Ramsey Cl
2 Sherburn Rd

Newton Hall

Frankland Farm

Gene

Fallsway

A690

Junction 62

4

University of Durham

Moor Road

Drive

158

Langdale Crs

J6
1 Birchgrove Av

Frankland Lane

Durham City Amateur Football Club

Moor End

Swinside Grange

High Grange

Magdalene

St Mark's

Carrvil

5

River Wear

Newlands Rd

Belm

Broomside Lane Grange Clnc

Surg

K5
1 Borrowdale Dr
2 Fellside Gdns

PO

Coronation Avenue

Broome

Buckinghamshire

Infant School

Junior School

Cheveley Park Medical Cen

Prebends Fld

Deans' Walk

Pilgrims Way

Rowan Tree Av

Willowtree

Moor

Yewbank Av

Elmfield Av

Gilesgate

Kenny

Nuns' Rw

Monks' Crs

Friars' Crs

Alder Lea Close

Poplar Dr

Cypress Gv

Ashdown Av

Whiteoak Av

Belmont Comprehensive School

Belmo

6

A690

Bradford

Montgomery Rd

Durham Gilesgate Comprehensive School

Gilesgate County Junior School

Aspen Cl

Cedar

Hawthn Crs

Limecragg Av

Hampshire Road

Gloucestershire

K6
1 Berkshire Cl
2 Oxfordshire Dr
3 Wiltshire Cl

Lincolnshire

7

Oort Pl

Roosevelt Road

Donnini

Road

Annand

Kepier Clinic

Gilesgate County Infant School

Sharp Crs

Cheshire Dr

Herefordshire Drive

Devonshire

Cambridgeshire Drive

Shropshire

Bedford

Yorkshire

Road

Long Acres

Heavyside Pl

Wakenshaw Rd

Green La

Churchill Av

Edward St

Dunelm Medical Practice

Gilesgate Moor

Mill Lane

Bevan

Peel Av

Saint Joseph's Cl

Dragonville Ind Park

Dragon

Durham County Council

A1(M)

Orchard Drive

Station Lane

West Vw

Leazes La

Sunderland

Edge

Edge

Road

Maynard's Rw

William Place

Police Station

Gilesgate Moor Primary School

St Hild's La

Renny's Lane

Frank Street

Sherburn Grange

Claypath Medical Practice

PO **GILESGATE**

St Giles Cl

Church Lane

A181 SHERBURN ROAD

St Josephs RC School

Lane

DH1

niversity Durham

St Hild & St Bede College

Maple Av

Laurel Av

Ash Av

Laurel Av

Pine Av

Fir Avenue

Oak Avenue

Londonderry Av

Chandler

Oswald

Hilda Cl

Cunningham

169

EET

A181

River Wear

F

G Laurel Avenue County Junior & Infant School

H

J

K

B12

Bowling Green

F G H 147 J

I Ele
Va

2 Hetton le Hill

3

4 160

5

6

7

F G H 171 J K

Front Street
York St

Moorsley Road

High Moorsley

Lorne St

Sunderland
Durham County

Elemore Lane

Hillside

St Lawrence
Newby Lane
PO

Church Vale

Elemore Hall
School

Elemore Grange

Littletown

Coalford Lane

Cross Street

Plantation Avenue

Hastings House Farm

Green Lane

Littletown House

Littleton Lane

Cook's Hold

Haswell Moor Farm

Kell Crs
Jub Crs
The Croft

Sherburn Hill

Local Avenue
al Av

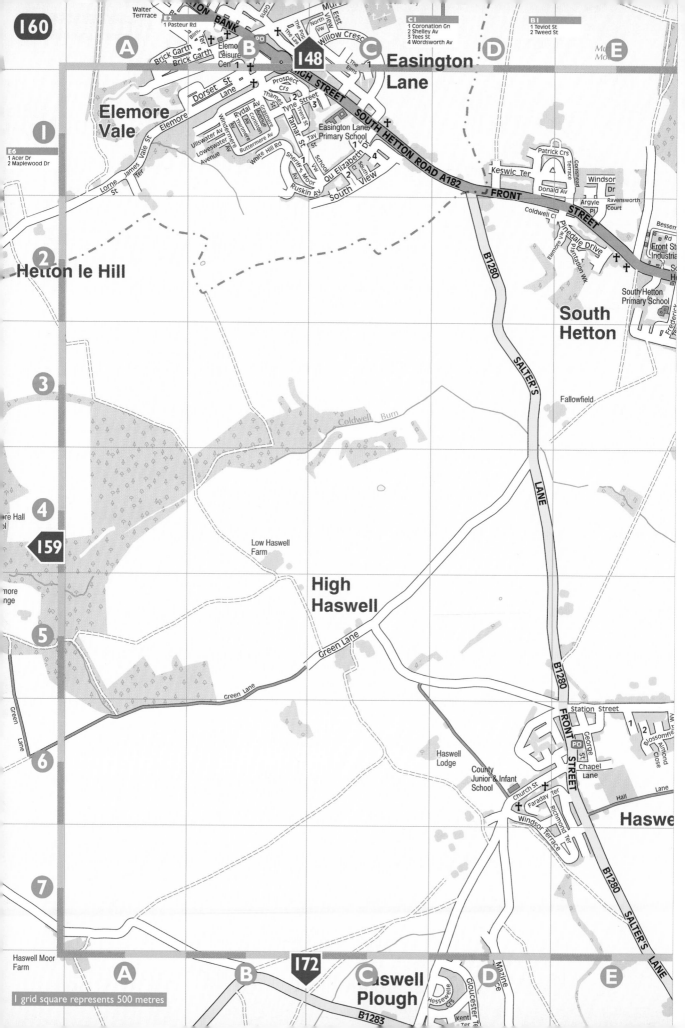

G2
1 Grasmere Ter

F

G

H

149

J

Little Coop House
Farm

I

West
Farm

2

Windermere Road

Street
l Estate

uth Hetton
ealth Centre

+

A182

PO

Terrace

Greencroft

Bevin
Sq

Hawthorn
Cottages

Coronation
Sq

1

West Lane

3

Great Coop House
Farm

Ashwood

Oakwood

Maythorne
Drive

Hallfield

West Moor House
Farm

4

Duncombe
Moor

162

A182

5

Holy
Cross

Pesspool Lane

Pesspool Lane

Chestnut
Drive

Low Ling
Close

6

Pesspool
Hall

ell

High Ling
Close

7

Moor House
Farm

B1283 DURHAM LANE

Durha

HA

F

G

H

173

J

K

162

150

D5
1 Comet Dr
2 Jupiter Ct
3 Saturn Cl

C6
1 Brampton Ct
2 Church Wk
3 East Grange Ct
4 Thorpe Rd

B6
1 St Mary's Cl
2 St Thomas Cl
3 Westcliff Cl

A   B   C   D   E

1   tle Coop House
rm

East Batter Law
Farm

Service Area

E4
1 Easington St
2 Oswald Ter

West Batter Law
Farm

Hawthorn

Barn Hollows

Belmont Av

2   West   Lane

Eagle
Hall

E5
1 St Nicholas Ter
2 Tennyson Rd
3 Whickham St

Thorpe Lea West

Hawthorn Burns

3   Hallfield Burn

Lea Lane

SUNDERLAND ROAD

STOCKTON ROAD

Letch Av

B1432

A19(T)

4   Hallfield

Holme Hill
Farm

Petwell Lane

Holmhill
Hawthorn St
James St
Cavell
Square

161

B1432

Crawlaw
2 1

PO

5   EASINGTON

A19(T)

Petwell Crs

Shakespeare Ter

Milton Lane

Wordsworth Road

SEASIDE LANE

Glebe Ter

Paradise Lane

Rydal Mount

Police
Station

3
7

Paradise Crs

Glenhurst Rd

HALL WALKS

The Spinney

Cadwell
Lane

Rosemary Lane PO

Easington
District
Council

Lauren
Court

1 3 1

Primary
School

2

Manisty Terrace

Moncrieff Terrace

The Grove

Glen Dene
School

ROSEMARY LANE

Sunderland Rd

Low Row

B1432

Burn Gdns

1 3 1
2

Davis Terrace

HALL WALKS

2

North Crescent

Oak Road

6   Hallfield Drive

School
1
3
Close
Rivers
2

Durham Lane

Claggersgate

South Side

Tudor
Grange

Cemetery

Durham

Lane

Stockton Road

Easington
Comprehensive
School

Nursery
Gdns

THORPE ROAD

Sea Vw
Gra Av

1
4
3

Thorpe Burn

Little Thorpe

7   DURH
LANE

A1086

Andrew's

Lane

THORPE RO

Cemetery

A   B   C   D   E

174

1 grid square represents 500 metres

F5
1 Vincent St

F

G

H

151

J

I

Hawthorn
Hive

2

Beacon
Point

Shippersea
Bay

3

White
Lea

4

Dene Av

East View

Raby Av

West Av

The Crs

Lane

John Street

Cem

**EASINGTON
COLLIERY**

Memorial Avenue

Noble Street

Thomas St

Thorpe St

Bell's Buildings

Road

Tower St

Abbot Street

Ashton St

School
Street

1

Welfare Close

B1283

PO

Bede Street

Office Street

STATION ROAD

5

Memorial Avenue

Paradise

Horden Burn

6

Horden
Point

SUNDERLAND ROAD

Maritime
Crs

7

F

G

175

H

J

K

AD

A1086

Thorpe Rd

Rd

Kilburn

Horden & Easington
RC Primary School

G1
1 Castle Vw
2 Priestburn Cl
3 Rowley Link

F · G · H · 153 · J

Flass Hall

I

Esh Winning

Vale Garth
Valley Drive
Cliffords Gate
Western Av
B6302
Willow Rd
Rowley
Crs
3

Hamsteels County Junior & Infant School

New House

New Houses

Swallow Close
Fir Terraces
Woodlands
Road
Newhouse Av
2
Esh Winning Child Hlth Clinic
Fair View
South Terrace
B6302
Castlefields

Osprey Cl
Falcon Wy
Osprey Cl
Dene Park
Birch Place
Arbourcourt Av
Arbourcourt Av
Road
Riding
Riding Ct
NEWHOUSE ROAD
Hill View
Evenwood Rd
STATION VW
DURHAM ROAD
Burtell Rd
Brandon Road
Acton Road
Coppice Hill
Pine View Villas

Raven Court
Cypress Park
Merlin Ct
The Oaks
The Larches
Redwood Road
Pinetree
Ridding
Cem
The Wynds
Mckennas Sports Club
Station Avenue
PO

Rowan Court
Ridding
College View
Waterhouses JMI School

Holburn Wood

2

3

Hill Hou

Station Street
Russell Street
River Deerness

4

166

Waterhouses Wood

Standalone

5

Brandon Lane
West Brandon

6

Baal Hill

7

Weather Hill Wood

Wolsingham Road

F · G · H · J · K

South Brandon

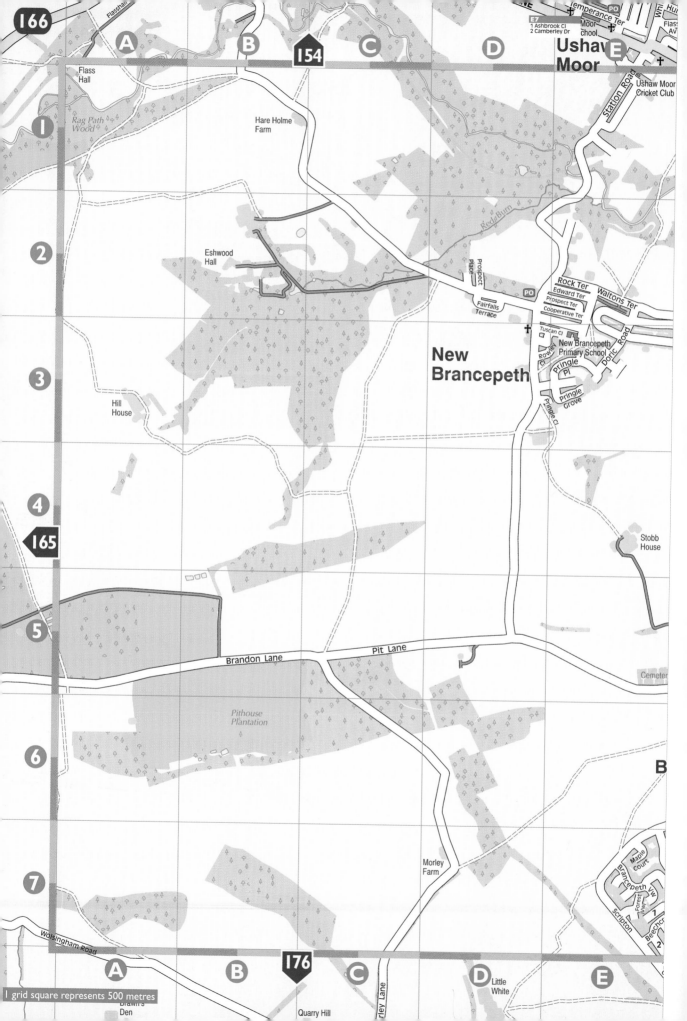

166

A B **154** C D **E**

Flass Hall

Flasshall

Ushaw Moor

E7
1 Ashbrook Cl
2 Camberley Dr

Moor School

Temperance Ter

PO

Whi Hu

Flass Av

1

Rag Path Wood

Hare Holme Farm

Ushaw Moor Cricket Club

Station Road

2

Eshwood Hall

Red Burn

Prospect place

Rock Ter

Waltons Ter

PO

Edward Ter

Prospect Ter

Cooperative Ter

Fairfalls Terrace

Tuscan Cl

Rowley Cl

New Brancepeth Primary School

Doric Road

New Brancepeth

3

Hill House

Pringle Pl

Pringle Cl

Pringle Grove

4

165

Stobb House

5

Brandon Lane

Pit Lane

Cemeter

6

Pithouse Plantation

B

7

Morley Farm

Maple Court

Brancepeth Vw

Forest Vi

Scripton

Beechc

Wolsingham Road

A B **176** C D Little White **E**

Drawn's Den

rley Lane

Quarry Hill

I grid square represents 500 metres

F6
1 Dove Cl
2 Palm Lea
3 Rushey Gill

F7
1 Laburnam Pk

Broom Hall

Usher Moor
Junior School

St. Josephs
RC School

F

Chestnut Gv

B6302

Cemetery

Broom Crescent

Pine Pk

Maple Pk

Lilac Pk

Hollywell Court

Valley View

Thornley Cl

Elm Gv

Beech Gv

Rowley Dr

Wooley

Elder Cl

Broom Hall Dr

Stockley Court

Brancpeth Close

Deerness Sports Cen

Deerness Valley Walk

River Deerness

Alum Waters

North End

Mill Lane

G1
1 Holburn Ct
2 Relley Cl

I

G6
1 Acorn Pl
2 Hawthorn Pk
3 Linden Pk
4 Vicarage Flats

Baxter Wood

155

Broompark

B6302

BROOM LANE

2

G7
1 Cypress Ct

Stone Brid

3

H1
1 Alderdene Cl
2 Castle Vw

Langley Hall Farm

GROVE TERRACE

Front Street

Langley Moor Primary School

4

Langley

168

Black Road

PO

Brandon Lane

Langley Crs

Lyne's Dr

Blair Ct

St Cuthberts Wk

High Street

High St S Back

Littleburn La

H5
1 Hemmel Cts

5

H6
1 Allendale Rd
2 Brecken Wy
3 Chalfont Wy
4 Frensham Wy
5 Stanhope Cl

Brandon United Football Club

Stack Garth

Tiree Cl

Brandon Cricket Club

Brandon & Byshottles Parish Council

St Patricks RC School

Durham Business Centre

A690

Mill Road

Littleburn Road

Rosebay Road

RANDON

High Mdw

Deerness Heights

Midhill Cl

Oakgreen Flats

Pear Lea

Pine Lea

Redwood

Rowan Lea

Lyme Pk

Holly

Red Firs

Meadowfield Sports Centre

Meadowfield

PO

Cemetery

St John's Road

6

H7
1 Leesfield Rd

Sawmill Lane

Scripton Gilln

St Brandon's Gv

White Ced

Silver Cts

Lowland Road

PO

Brandon Modern School

Victoria Avenue

Station Avenue

Carr Avenue

Leesfield Gardens

Leesfield Dr

Chalfont Way

Penny

Arundel

Perth

Aston Way

Chalfont Way

Meadowfield Clinic

Edwardson Road

Browney County Primary School

Littleb Farm

7

Beech Park

Cherry Pk

Alder Park

Alder Park

Alder Park

Willow Pk

Fir Av

Grove Road

Meadow

Bell

Briar

Elm Gv Rd

Moor Edge

Health Centre

West View

South View

Dorlonco Villas

Central Av

A690

Carvis Cl

Clover Laid

Hazel Rd

Dominion Road

Cft Rigg

Red Barns

A690

BROWNEY LANE

Murrayfield Drive

Shaftsbury Dr

Lexington Court

Cavendish Ct

Winchester Drive

Road

F

K5
1 St Bedes Wy

G

K4
1 N Brancepeth Cl

H

177

J

J5
1 Boyne Ct

K

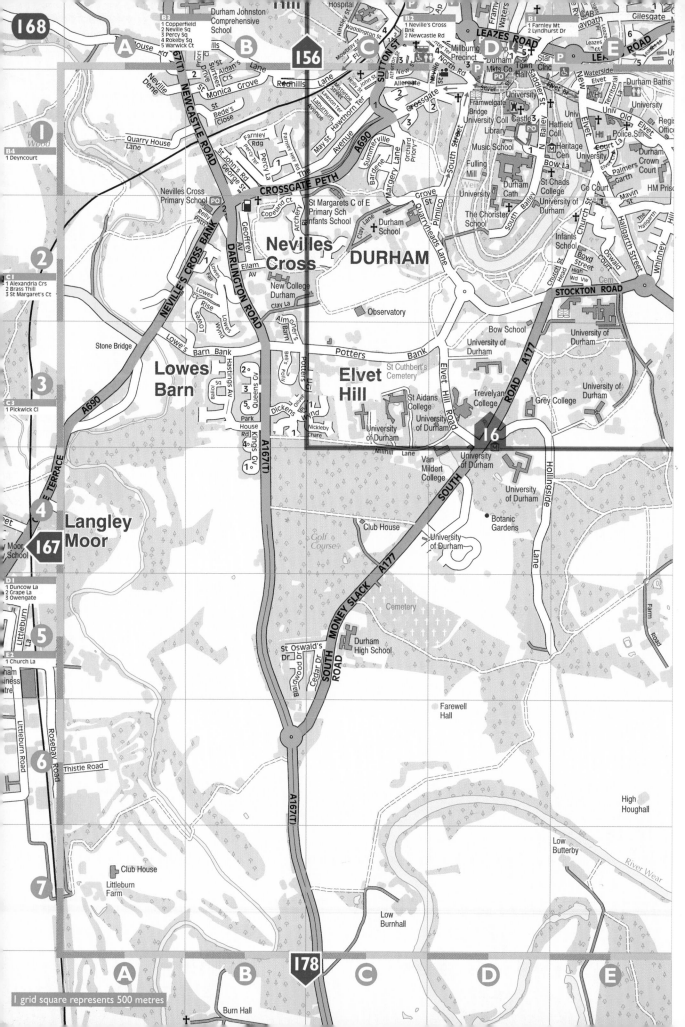

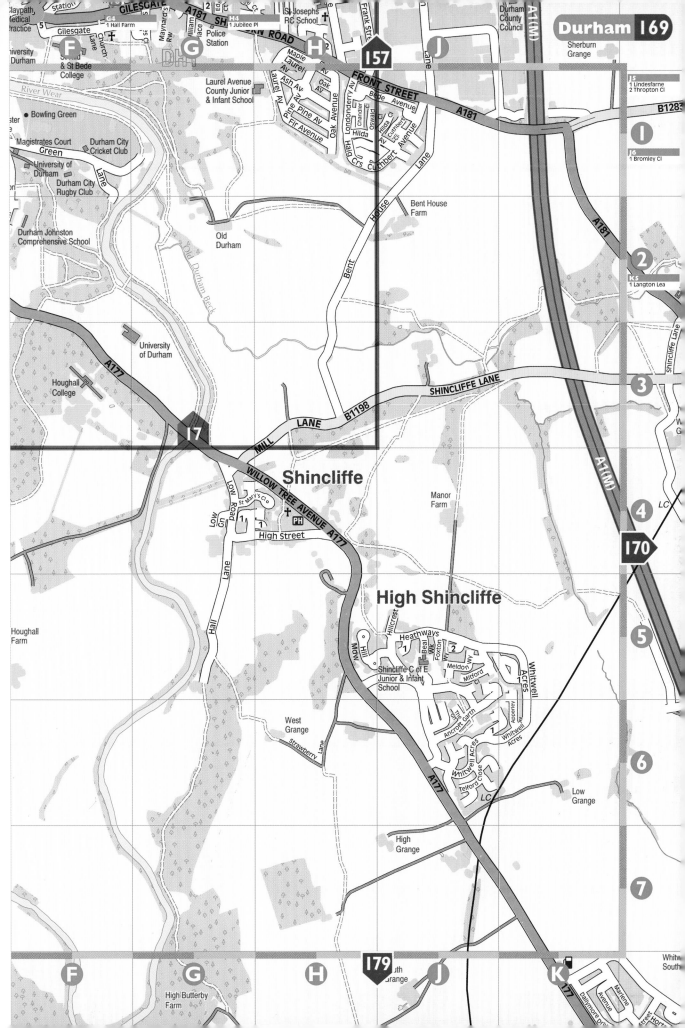

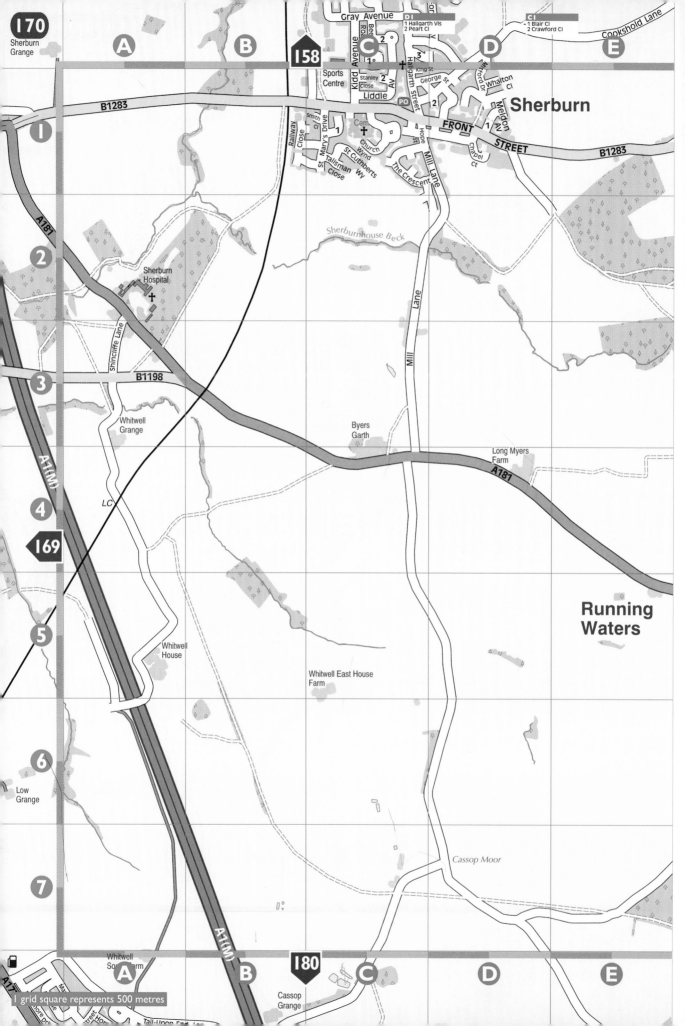

F G H **159** J

I

Sherburn Hill

Kell Crs
Jubilee Crs
The Croft
Local Avenue
Local Av
LOCAL AV
FRONT STREET
Pinders Wy

Haswell Moor Farm

B1283

2

DURHAM LANE

B1283

Crime Rigg

Crime Rigg
Woodside Bank
Church Lane

Hill House

3

Shadforth

Lu

Bridge Court
Chare
Dene Ct
Oliver Crs
George Square

4

172

Ox Close

5

A181

A181

SILENT BANK

Strawberry Hill

6

High Croft House

DH6

DUNELM ROAD

Old Cassop

7

D House

B6291

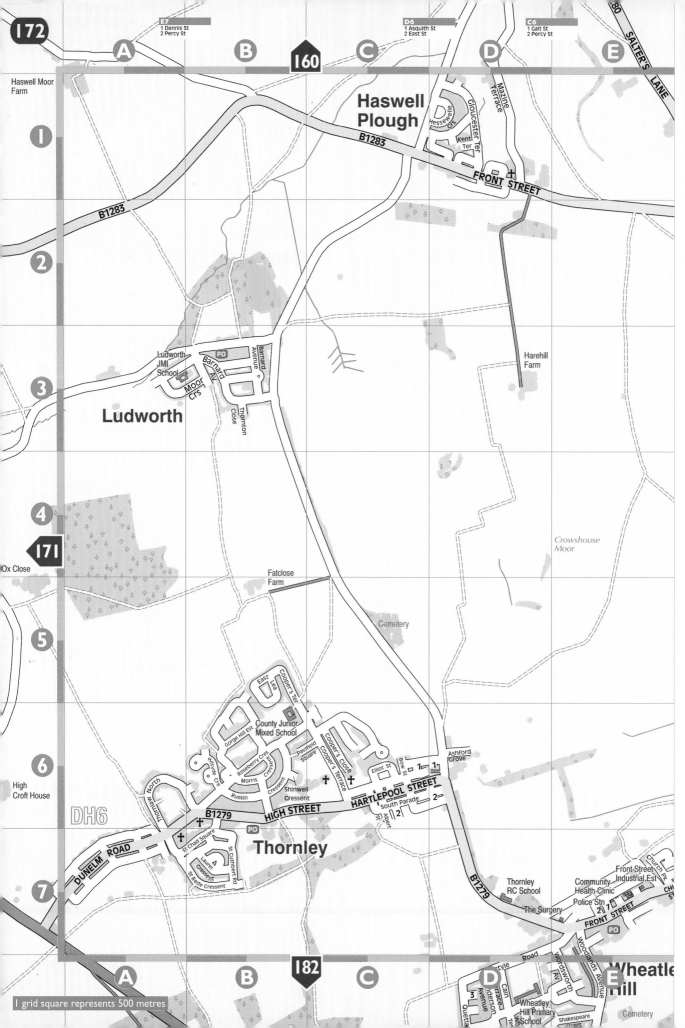

172

160

182

171

E7
1 Dennis St
2 Percy St

D6
1 Asquith St
2 East St

C6
1 Galt St
2 Percy St

SALTER'S LANE

A B C D E

1

Haswell Moor
Farm

B1283

**Haswell
Plough**

B1283

Hessewelle Crs
Gloucester Ter
Kent Ter
Mazine Terrace

FRONT STREET

2

Harehill
Farm

3

Ludworth
JMI
School

PO

Barnard Avenue
Barnard Av
Moor Crs
Thornton Close

Ludworth

4

Ox Close

Crowshouse
Moor

5

Fatclose
Farm

Cemetery

6

High
Croft House

East Lea
Cooper's Ter
Gorge Hill Est
Kilsyde Cres
Roseberry Cres
Morris
Ruskin
Russell Cressent
Shinwell Cressent
County Junior
Mixed School
Passfield
Square
Cooper's Close
Cooper's Terrace
Elliot St
Bow St
Ashford
Grove

Thornlaw North

B1279

HIGH STREET

HARTLEPOOL STREET

Albert St
South Parade

DH6

Thornley

7

DUNELM ROAD

St Chad Square
St Cuthbert Rd
Laurel Cressent
St Bede Cressent

PO

Thornley
RC School

The Surgery

Thornley
Community
Health Clinic

Police Stn

Front Street
Industrial Est

Church Pk

FRONT STREET

PO

A B C D E

Cain Terrace
Anderson Avenue
Quetland
Woodlands Avenue
Wordsworth Av
Wheatley
Hill Primary
School
Shakespeare
Street

**Wheatley
Hill**

Cemetery

F7
1 Greenwood Cl

H3
1 Jubilee Pl

High Ling
Close

161

J

Moor House
Farm

B1283

H4
1 Hamilton Ct

I

J4
1 Alcote Gv
2 Cowley St
3 Dunelm Pl
4 East Gn
5 Potto St

District Council

B1283

Sandy
Carrs

Westmoor
Farm

2

B1280

Mill Hill

COOK

Cem

Shotton
RC JMI
School

Fleming
Field

Worton
Close

Waverley Cl

Waverley

Station

Road

Modern Mixed
School

The
Surgery

Shotton Colliery
Primary School

Southdene
Medical
Centre

Burdon Drive

Shotton   Road

3

Belverdere
Gdns

Westgarth
Grove

Atkinson Gv

Thornhill Rd

Winhfield

Thornhill

Hawthorne

Arden
Street

Tudor
Ct

Windsor Pl

East St

Shotton

Eden
Vw

Lane

Shotton
Colliery

Lilac
Terrace

Hazel Terrace

Terrace

West St

The Surg

PO

3 2

1

King St

Victoria Street

4

Milton
Grove

4

Hooper
Ter

Milbank

Friar
St

5

7

Terrace

174

Whitwort

Grove
Court

Shotton
Parish
Council

Byron Ter

Burn's Ter

Shotton Lane

Brac

5

PO

Dixon Est

A J Cook
Ter

Bruce
Terrace

Glaser

Low Crow's
House

Dixon Est Bungalows

6

Edder
Acres

Thornley Station
Industrial Estate

B1279

Green Hills

7

Watson Cl

Dodds Cl

PATTON WALK

URCH
REET

Weardale
Park

ey

F

G

H

183

SALTER'S LANE

J

K

Edderacres
Plantation

B1280

SALTER'S LANE

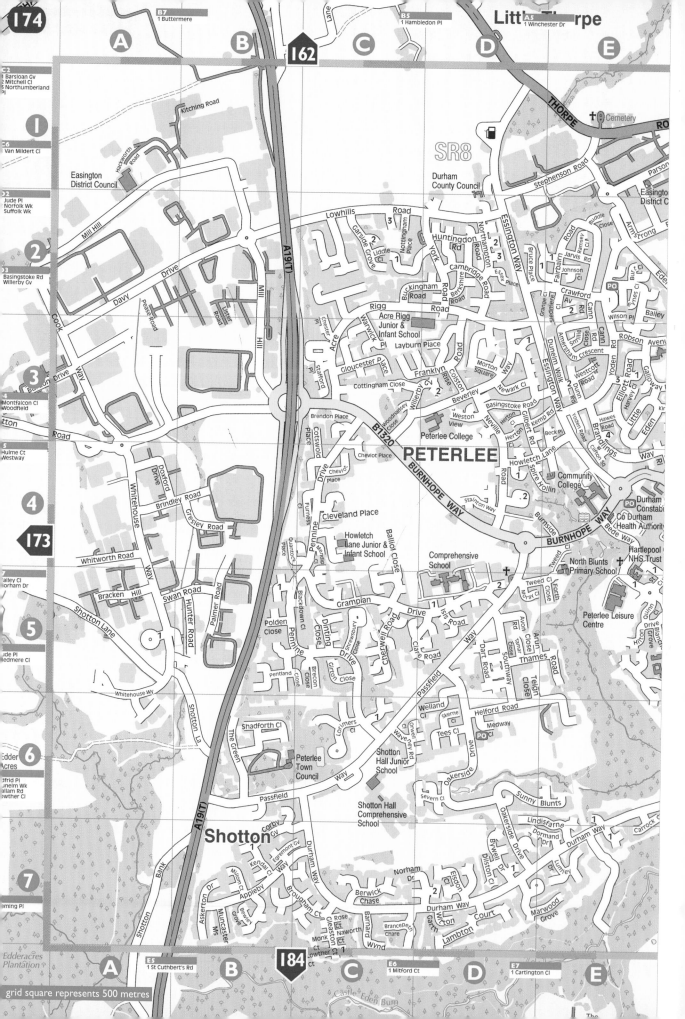

163

185

Primary School

Farm

Red Barns

A690

Dominion Road

West View

Villas

167

BROWNEY LANE

B6300

I

2

Burnig

Scripton Lane

Scripton

Holywell Beck

Nafferton

Holywell

River Wear

3

4

178

Brancepeth Park

Scripton Lane

5

Colds Farm

East Parks

6

Spring Wood

Weardale Way

7

Page Bank PO

Woodhouse Farm

Lane

Mill

F

G

H

J

K

3

4

5

Murrayfield Drive

Clover Laid

Cavendish Ct

Hazel Av

Winchester Drive

Shaftsbury Dr

Lexington Court

Cft Rigg

Road

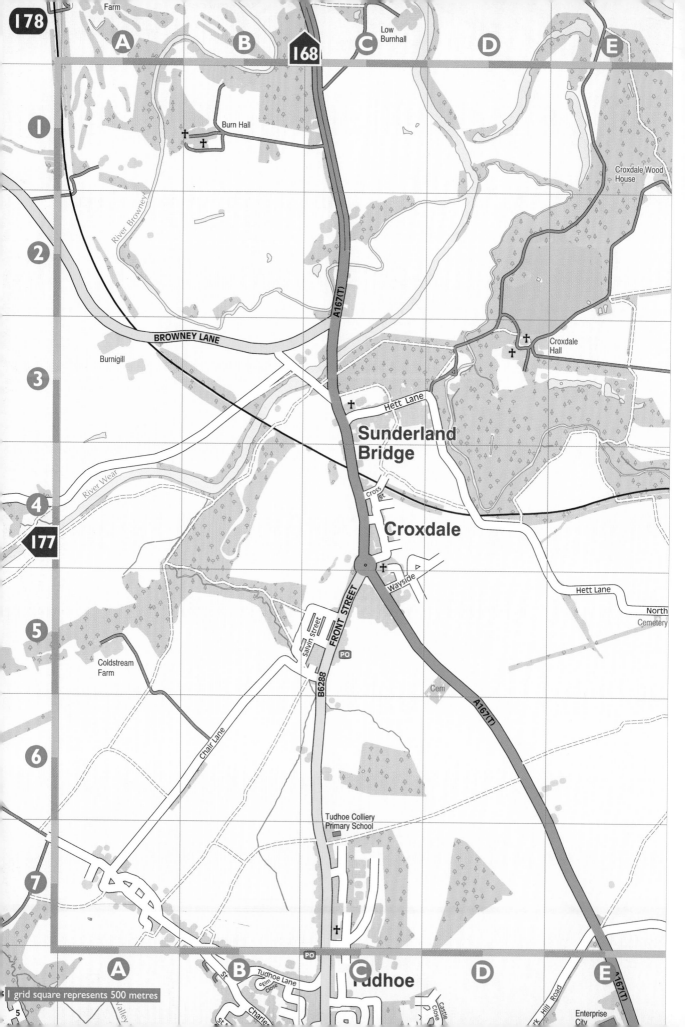

F G H **169** J

A177

Whitw
South

South
Grange

High Butterby
Farm

Dalymore drive

Marlene
Avenue
George

Horton Crs

I

Robson
Crs

Phillip

Pr Charles

Avenue Edward

Jr

2

Castle Av

Tweddle Ter

Beta

Burn Av

Burn St

Bow St

PO

Steavel

DURHAM Rd

3

High
Croxdale

Bowburn

4

Durham Service Area

180

Tursdale
House

LC

5

A688

Street

East Street

West St

Hett

Leeman's   Lane

6

Broom Hill
Farm

Ramsay St

School St

Tursdale

7

F G Hett Moor H J K

A   B   170   C   D   E

B2
1 Broadmeadows

A3
1 Carey Cl

A2
1 Margaret Ct
2 Norton Av
3 Runcie Rd
4 St John's Crs
5 William St
6 Wolseley Cl

Whitwell
South Farm

A177

B3
1 Landsdowne Crs

Dalbr

Avenue

Marlene

George Street

Horton Crs

Tail-Upon-End Lane

Cassop
Grange

Heugh
Hall Farm

A1(M)

Robson
Crs

Philip Avenue

Robert
Ter

David
Terrace

Leyland
Cl

Millford Way

Oakfield Crs

Pr Charles

Avenue

B5
1 Holmfield Vls

Castle Av

Bede Terrace

Edward Av

Tunstall Av

New Burn Av

Lawson Rd

Surtees   Avenue

Monteigne

Dr

Barrington Way

Burn St

Runcie Crs

Beaumont
Close

Bowburn County
Junior School

Grange Pk Crs

C7
1 Meadow Cl

DURHAM ROAD

Stevenson St

Walker St

Clarence St

Wyburn St

Crow Trees
Lane

Bowburn
County
Infant School

Bowburn

Old
Quarrington

Heugh
Hall Row

Cemetery

Junction 61

Durham Service Area

D7
1 Browns Cl

A1(M)

A688

B6291

Park Av

Park Av

Park Hill

B6291

Tursdale

Ramsay St

Beechfield Rise

Browning Hill

Coxhoe

Petterson Dale

PO

THE AVENUE

Grange Cres

Green Cres

Landsdowne Road

Coxhoe District
Sports Centre

Coxhoe
Medical
Practice

Linden Gv

Mulberry

Lane

East Pasture
House

Hadleigh
Ct

Featherstones

Oakwood

The Grove

Station Road

Belgrave
Av

Corngarth

Ashbourne Drive

A   B   C   D   E

THINFORD RD

1 grid square represents 500 metres

F   G   H   **171**   J

I

2

3

Dene House
Farm

Cassop

Luke Avenue

Dene View

PO

Cemetery

Church Street

Cassop
Primary
School

FRONT   STREET

B6291

PO

**Quarrington
Hill**

David Terrace

Malcolm
Av
Hazel
Avenue

Carr
House

4

182

Cemetery

Ann
AV
School
AV

Mary Crs

Kelloe
JMI School

Kelloe Beck

**Town
Kelloe**

5

Kelloe

6

Ramona
Avenue

Woodland

Tate Av

Crescent

Tate Avenue

Sharon Avenue

PO

Low Raisby

7

Coxhoe
East House

F   G   H   J   K

Garmondsway

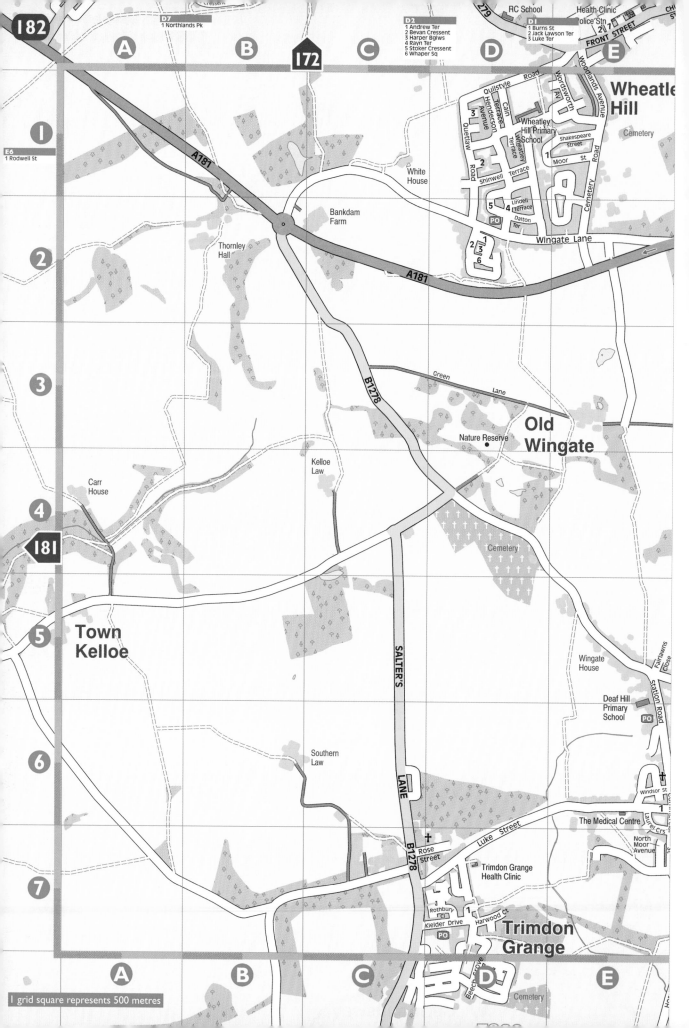

F
F6
1 Ash Gv
2 Cinnamon Dr

F7
1 Lawson's St

G

H

173

J

Edderacres Plantation

G6
1 Laburnum Cressent
2 Laburnum Sq
3 Lilac Cressent
4 Springdale Av
5 Watson Cressent

I

J2
1 Dobson Ter

A181

2

J3
1 Partridge Ter
2 Quin Crs

Durham Road

Taylor Grove

Wingrove

Greenhills Est

The Maltings

Wellfield Road

Walton Terrace

Dodds Ter

Coronation Road

Burdon Crs

NORTH ROAD

Wellfield Comprehensive Sch

Roxby Wynd

Martindale Wk

Stewart Dr

2

Oaklea Sch Clinic

King's Road

Snaith Ter

Vicarage Est

Vicarage Estate

3

K2
1 Fourway Ct
2 Goldsborough Ct
3 Granby Ter

B1280

Dawson Rd

Gray Sq

Gully Road

1 2

Wingate

Queen's Road

New Cross Rd

PO

Forest Gate

7

Woodland View

County Junior Mixed School

Moor Lane

4

Wingate Grange Farm

NORTH ROAD

Wingate RC Junior & Infant School

184

K3
1 Armstrong Av
2 Howden Gdns

Pickering St

FRONT ST

2

PO

5

STATION RD

Station

Lake VW

K4
1 Chapel St
2 Johnson's St

Lake Bank

Ter

Church St

Acclom St

2 Van

Deaf Hill

Wingate Road

Beech

Grove

Wood View

Russel Crs

Station Town

Malvern Crs

Rydale Ct

1

5

2

3

1

6

FRONT ST

MILBANK

Margaret Ter

4

Newholme Est

Trimdon Colliery

Commercial

West Woodburn

1

7

Low Dyke Street

Park Road

Woodlands Close

F

Close Lane

G

Hurworth Bryan Farm

H

J

K

A B 174 C D E

E6
1 Claypool Farm Cl

C1
1 Blenkinsopp Ct

A6
1 Brackendale Ct
2 East Ter

Askerton Dr
Appleby
Brougham Ct
Berwick Chase
Monk
Rose
Gleaston Ct
Lowther Ct
Na
Ct
Barnard Wynd
Brancepeth Chare
Lambt
Court

Edderacres
Plantation

1

Golf Course

The Castle

Castle Eden Burn

A181

The Maltings

2

Roxby Wynd
Martindale Wk
Stewart Dr

B1281

South Vw

Mill Hill

Castle Eden

Est

Vicarage Estate

Gray Sq

3

Road

A19(T)

Eden Val

Thacmyers

Lane

Heads Hope

4

183

PO

5

Rodridge Pk

Lane Vw
Lake Bank
Lake Ter

Church St

Acclom St

Vane St

Hutton Henry

Station Town

FRONT ST

MILBANK TER

Ferndale Cl

Beechdale Cl

Newholme Est

6

Cem

Rodridge Hall

Hutton Henry C of E School

The Oaks

Front Street

Hutton Crs

PO

7

B1280

Blakeley Hill

Rodridge Farm

Ashbrooke Ct

Leechmire

TS2 A B C D E

I grid square represents 500 metres

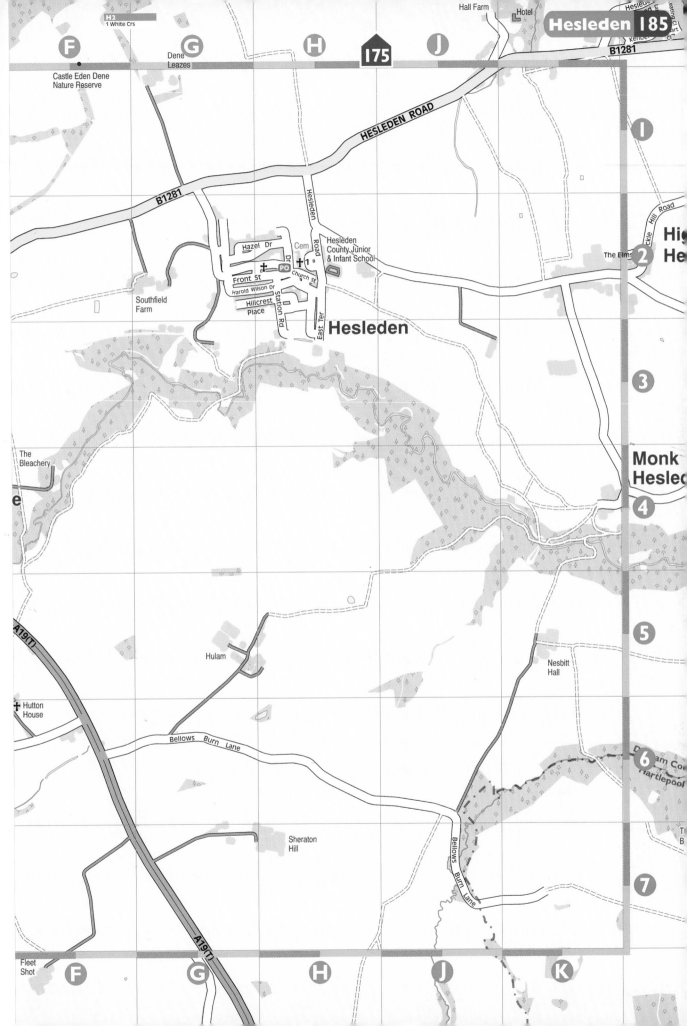

H2
1 White Crs

F

Dene
Leazes

G

H

175

J

Castle Eden Dene
Nature Reserve

HESLEDEN ROAD

B1281

I

B1281

Ckie Hill Road

Hall Farm

Hotel

Hig
He

The Elms

2

Hazel Dr
Dr
Hazel Dr
Cem
PO
Front St
Harold Wilson Dr
Hillcrest
Place
Station Rd
East Ter
Church St
Hesleden Road

Hesleden County Junior
& Infant School

Hesleden

Southfield
Farm

3

The
Bleachery

Monk
Hesle

e

4

Hulam

5

Nesbitt
Hall

Hutton
House

Bellows Burn Lane

am Co
artlepool

6

Sheraton
Hill

Bellows Burn Lane

T
B

7

A19(T)

Fleet
Shot

F

G

A19(T)

H

J

K

Albany 102 D6
Annfield Plain 125 J3
Annitsford 38 D7
Ashington 23 G2
Axwell Park 84 B4
Aykley Heads 156 C5
Ayres Quay 14 B2
Ayton 116 B3
Backworth 48 E5
Bank Top 66 D2
Barley Mow 115 J4
Barlow 83 F6
Bar Moor 66 C6
Barmston 117 H1
Battle Hill 58 E5
Beaconhill 37 K2
Beacon Lough 101 J1
Beamish 113 J7
Bearpark 155 H6
Bebside 30 A7
Bedlington 29 G4
Bedlington Station 29 H4
Bell's Close 68 C5
Belmont 157 K6
Benfieldside 122 C2
Bensham 10 C6
Benton Square 58 C1
Benwell 69 F5
Biddick 117 F2
Biddick Hall 91 F2
Bill Quay 13 L3
Billy Mill 60 B3
Birtley 101 K3
Bishopwearmouth 14 B4
Black Callerton 53 J2
Blackfell 102 C7
Blackhall Mill 95 H6
Blackhill 122 D4
Blakelaw 69 G1
Blaydon 84 B1
Blaydon Burn 83 G3
Blaydon Haughs 68 C7
Blyth 34 E1
Boldon Colliery 90 D2
Bomarsund 29 J1
Bothal 22 B3
Bournmoor 131 G4
Bowburn 179 K3
Brancepeth 176 C3
Branch End 79 H5
Brandon 166 E6
Brenkley 36 B5
Bridgehill 122 C3
Broom Hill 109 F4
Broom Hill 147 K2
Broomley 78 B7
Broompark 167 J2
Brunswick Village 45 K4
Burdon 134 B4
Burnhope 141 H4
Burnopfield 97 H7
Burnside 131 K5
Burradon 47 H4
Byermoor 98 B6
Byker 7 G6
Bywell 78 D4
Callerton 53 K4
Callerton Lane End 53 F3
Cambois 30 E1
Camperdown 47 J4
Carley Hill 106 B2
Carr Hill 87 H5
Carville 157 K5
Cassop 181 J2
Castle Eden 184 D3
Castleside 136 E1
Castletown 104 E4
Catchgate 125 F2
Causey 113 F1
Chester-le-Street 129 F4
Chester Moor 144 B1
Chilton Moor 146 E1
Chirton 2
Chirton 60 C4
Choppington 23 F7
Chopwell 95 J4
Chowdene 100 E3
Clara Vale 66 B5
Cleadon 92 A4
Cleadon Park 76 A6
Clifton 26 E4
Clough Dene 111 K3
Coalburns 81 J5
Cold Hesledon 150 C6
Colliery Row 132 A7
Collingwood 38 C4
Columbia 117 G2
Concord 102 E5
Consett 122 D5
Cornsay Colliery 152 D6
Cowpen 30 D6
Coxhoe 180 E7
Coxlodge 56 A5
Craghead 127 H5
Cramlington 37 K3
Crawcrook 66 C7
Crookgate Bank 98 A7
Crookhall 123 H6
Crookhill 67 G6
Croxdale 178 C4
Cullercoats 51 H7
Dalton-le-Dale 150 A4

Darras Hall 42 E4
Dawdon 151 F3
Deaf Hill 183 F6
Deckham 11 H8
Delves 138 D1
Deneside 150 B2
The Dene 109 G4
Denton Burn 68 C4
Deptford 14 A2
Deptford 106 A5
Dinnington 44 E2
Dipton 110 E6
Donwell 102 D4
Downhill 105 F1
Doxford Park 134 A3
Dudley 47 G2
Dunston 9 G6
Dunston Hill 8 E9
Durham 16 B4
Earsdon 49 J3
Easington 162 B5
Easington Colliery 163 G4
Easington Lane 148 C7
East Boldon 91 G4
East Cramlington 39 F3
East Denton 68 E3
East Gateshead 11 M2
East Hartford 33 H4
East Herrington 133 H1
East Holywell 49 F2
East Kyo 125 K1
East Law 108 D4
East Rainton 147 G4
East Sleekburn 30 C3
East Stanley 112 E7
Ebchester 109 F3
Eden Vale 184 E4
Edmondsley 143 F2
Eighton Banks 101 K3
Eland Green 43 H1
Elemore Vale 160 A1
Elswick 9 H1
Eltringham 79 K2
Elvet Hill 16 B9
Esh 153 J4
Esh Winning 165 F2
Farringdon 119 J7
Fatfield 116 E6
Fawdon 55 J3
Feligate 89 J3
Felling 12 D7
Felling Shore 12 D3
Fellside 84 D6
Fence Houses 131 J6
Fenham 69 H4
Fleming Field 173 F3
Flint Hill 111 H5
Follingsby 89 F7
Fordley 47 H2
Forest Hall 57 K1
Framwellgate Moor 156 C4
Fulbeck 20 C2
Fulwell 106 C1
Gateshead 11 H1
Gilesgate 17 H1
Gilesgate 157 F6
Gilesgate Moor 17 L2
Glebe 116 E1
Gosforth 56 B5
Grangetown 120 E5
Grange Villa 128 A2
Grasswell 132 B5
Great Eppleton 148 C3
Great Lumley 145 G1
Greencroft 125 F4
Greenhill 149 H4
Greenside 82 C3
Grindon 119 F3
The Grove 122 B6
Guide Post 23 F6
Hallgarth 158 D5
Hamsterley 109 H1
Harelaw 125 G1
Harlow Green 101 H3
Harperley 125 J1
Harraton 116 C5
Hartley 41 H4
Harton 75 J5
Hasting Hill 118 E4
Haswell 160 E6
Haswell Plough 172 C1
Hawthorn 162 C2
Hazlerigg 46 A5
Healeyfield 136 D3
Heaton 6 F1
Hebburn 73 G6
Hebburn Colliery 73 G3
Hebburn New Town 72 E5
Heddon-on-the-Wall 66 A2
Hedley Hill 164 A2
Hedworth 90 A2
Hendon 15 H7
Hepscott 27 K1
Hepscott Park 27 J5
Hesleden 185 H3
Hett 179 F5
Hetton Downs 148 A3
Hetton-le-Hill 159 K2
Hetton-le-Hole 148 A5
Heworth 13 G8
High Callerton 43 G7
High Church 20 C6

High Dubmire 131 K7
Highfield 96 E4
High Forge 113 J5
High Friarside 97 F7
High Handenhold 114 A7
High Haswell 160 C5
High Mickley 79 K5
High Moorsley 159 G1
High Shields 74 E3
High Shincliffe 169 H5
High Southwick 106 A2
High Spen 96 B1
High Urpeth 114 B6
High Westwood 109 H2
Hill Top 111 G4
Hill Top 154 C4
Hillview 120 C5
Hirst 24 A2
Hobson 111 K2
Holmside 142 C1
Holy Cross 58 E7
Holywell 40 C6
Hooker Gate 96 B2
Horden 175 F5
Horsley 64 D3
Horsley Hill 75 K3
Horsleyhope 136 A5
Houghton 65 J1
Houghton-le-Spring 132 B7
Howdon 59 J7
Howdon Pans 74 A2
Humbledon 119 K3
Hutton Henry 184 D6
Hylton Castle 104 E3
Hylton Red House 105 H1
Isabella Pit 35 F2
Iveston 124 B6
Jarrow 74 B5
Jesmond 71 F3
Kelloe 181 G6
Kenton 55 H6
Kenton Bankfoot 54 E4
Kenton Bar 55 H6
Kibblesworth 100 E7
Killingworth 47 K7
Killingworth Moor 48 C7
Killingworth Village 48 A5
Kimblesworth 143 K5
Kingston Park 55 H4
Kip Hill 112 E5
Knitsley 138 B2
Lady Park 100 D4
Lambton 116 C3
Lamesley 100 D4
Lanchester 140 A5
Langley Moor 168 A4
Langley Park 154 C3
The Lawe 3 J4
Leadgate 95 C1
Leadgate 123 K3
Leam Lane 88 C2
Leamside 146 B6
Lemington 68 C5
Lintz 111 H1
Lintzford 96 D6
Little Thorpe 162 D7
Littletown 159 H5
Loansdean 26 C1
Lobley Hill 86 B6
Longbenton 57 J2
Lowes Barn 168 A3
Low Fell 87 F7
Low Greenside 82 C2
Low Moorsley 147 J7
Low Prudhoe 64 B7
Low Thornley 83 J7
Low Westwood 109 G1
Ludworth 172 A3
Lumley Thicks 130 E6
Lynemouth 18 B2
Lyons 148 B6
Maiden Law 125 J7
Marden 50 E7
Marley Hill 99 F4
Marley Pots 105 K2
Marsden 76 C6
Mason 45 F1
Mayfield 38 D3
Meadowfield 167 J6
Medburn 42 A7
Medomsley 109 J5
Mickley Square 79 K3
Middle Herrington 119 F6
Middle Rainton 147 F5
The Middles 126 E4
Mill Dam 74 E2
Millfield 106 A6
Monkseaton 50 B3
Monkton 73 J7
Monkwearmouth 106 B4
Moor End 157 K5
Moorside 137 H1
Morpeth 20 D5
Mount Pleasant 11 K7
Murton 49 K7
Murton 149 C4
Nedderton 28 B6
Nelson Village 38 A1
Nettlesworth 143 K4
Nevilles Cross 168 B2
Newbiggin 139 J4

Newbiggin-by-the-Sea 19 F6
Newbiggin Hall Estate 54 D6
Newbottle 132 C4
New Brancepeth 166 D3
Newburn 67 J3
Newcastle upon Tyne 6 B7
New Delaval 34 D4
Newfield 128 C2
New Hartley 40 B2
New Herrington 132 C1
New Kyo 125 K3
Newlands 108 D3
Newsham 34 C2
Newsham 35 F3
New Silksworth 119 K7
Newton 62 A5
Newton Hall 62 B4
Newton Hall 157 F3
New Town 90 D3
New Town 132 E7
New York 60 A1
North Blyth 31 G4
North End 156 A5
North Hylton 104 C6
Northlea 135 H6
North Seaton 24 D4
North Seaton Colliery 24 B5
North Shields 2 A4
North Walbottle 53 J7
Offerton 118 C3
Old Burdon 134 A5
Old Cassop 171 G7
Old Fold 11 L4
Old Quarrington 180 D3
Old Wingate 182 D3
Ornsby Hill 140 C3
Ouston 115 G4
Ovingham 63 K7
Ovington 63 G7
Oxclose 116 C1
Oxhill 126 B1
Page Bank 177 F7
Painshawfield 79 G6
Pallion 105 H5
Palmersville 58 C1
Parkside 150 D3
Path Head 67 K7
Pegswood 21 J1
Pelaw 13 H5
Pelton 128 D1
Pelton Fell 129 F3
Pennywell 119 F2
Penshaw 118 A7
Percy Main 74 C1
Perkinsville 114 E6
Peterlee 174 C4
Philadelphia 131 J2
Pickering Nook 111 J2
Pittington 158 E3
Pity Me 156 C2
Plawsworth 144 B4
Ponteland 43 J2
Portobello 115 J2
Preston 60 E2
Preston Grange 50 D7
Prestwick 44 B4
Primrose 74 A7
Prudhoe 80 C1
Quaking Houses 126 B5
Quarrington Hill 181 G3
Quebec 152 E5
Rainton Bridge 147 H2
Rainton Gate 146 B7
Rickleton 116 B7
Roker 107 F3
Rosehill 73 G2
Rowlands Gill 97 G3
Rowley 137 G3
Running Waters 170 E5
Ryhope 135 F1
Ryhope Colliery 120 E7
Ryton 66 E6
Ryton Woodside 82 D2
Sacriston 143 G4
St Anthony's 13 G1
St Peter's 7 H9
Saltwell 10 F9
Scotland Gate 29 G1
Scotswood 68 E7
Seaham 151 F1
Seaton 40 D3
Seaton Burn 37 H7
Seaton Delaval 39 K4
Seaton Sluice 41 F3
Seghill 39 G7
Shadforth 171 H3
Shankhouse 33 J6
Sheep Hill 97 K6
Sheepwash 22 E5
Sherburn 170 D1
Sherburn Hill 171 H1
Sheriff Hill 87 H6
Shield Row 113 F6
Shincliffe 169 H4
Shiney Row 131 K2
Shiremoor 49 J6
Shotley Bridge 108 B7
Shotton 174 B7
Shotton Colliery 173 G4
Simonside 74 C7
South Beach 35 J3

South Bents 92 E6
Southfield 38 C5
South Gosforth 56 C6
South Hetton 160 E2
South Hylton 105 F7
South Moor 126 B3
South Newsham 34 E4
South Pelaw 129 H1
South Shields 3 L6
South Stanley 126 C2
Southwick 106 A4
Spital Tongues 4 C2
Springwell 102 C3
Springwell 119 J3
Stakeford 23 H6
Stanley 126 D1
Stargate 83 F1
Station Town 183 K6
Stella 67 J7
Stobhill 20 E7
Stobhillgate 21 F6
Stocksfield 79 F5
Stony Gate 132 E3
Stony Heap 124 C4
Street Gate 99 H3
Sulgrave 103 G5
Sunderland 14 C3
Sunderland 106 A5
Sunderland Brige 178 C3
Sunniside 98 E3
Sunniside 132 A4
Swalwell 84 E3
Tanfield 112 B2
Tanfield Lea 112 B5
Tan Hills 144 A4
Tantobie 111 J4
Teams 9 L6
Team Valley 86 D7
Templetown 122 E6
Thorney Close 119 G5
Thornley 172 B7
Throckley 53 G7
Town Kelloe 182 A5
Tranwell 26 A2
Trimdon Colliery 183 F6
Trimdon Grange 182 D7
Tunstall 120 C7
Tursdale 179 K7
Tyne Dock 74 E4
Tynemouth 61 F2
Urpeth 114 E4
Ushaw Moor 154 E7
Usworth 102 E4
Walbottle 67 G2
Waldridge 128 B6
Walker 72 B6
Wall Nook 154 C2
Wallsend 72 B1
Wardley 13 M7
Washington 103 J7
Washington Village 117 F1
Waterhouses 164 E4
West Allotment 59 G1
West Boldon 90 E4
West Chirton 59 J5
West Denton 68 C2
Westerhope 54 B6
Western Hill 156 B7
West Harton 74 E5
West Herrington 118 D7
West Holywell 49 F3
West Jesmond 70 B1
West Kyo 125 H2
Westlea 28 D6
West Lea 149 K2
West Monkseaton 50 A6
West Moor 57 H1
Westoe 75 J2
West Park 75 G4
West Pelton 113 K7
West Rainton 146 D5
West Sleekburn 23 K6
West Wylam 80 E1
Wheatley Hill 182 A1
Whickham 85 F5
Whitburn 93 F3
Whitburn Colliery 77 F7
Whitehills 87 K7
Whiteleas 91 G1
White-le-Head 111 J5
Whitley Bay 51 G4
Whitley Sands 50 E2
Wickham Fell 99 F1
Wide Open 46 C4
Willington 59 G6
Willington Quay 73 J2
Windy Nook 87 K6
Wingate 183 H3
Winlaton 83 J2
Winlaton Mill 83 K6
Witherwack 105 J1
Witton Gilbert 143 H7
Woodbridge 18 B6
Woodhorn 18 C6
Woolsington 54 B2
Woolsington Hall 44 C7
Wrekenton 101 H2
Wylam 65 H6

USING THE STREET INDEX

Street names are listed alphabetically. Each street name is followed by its postal town or area locality, the Postcode District, the page number, and the reference to the square in which the name is found.

Example: Abbey Dr WD/WHPE/BLK NE5.............53 K6 [1]

Some entries are followed by a number in a blue box. This number indicates the location of the street within the referenced grid square. The full street name is listed at the side of the map page.

GENERAL ABBREVIATIONS

ACC	ACCESS	BLDS	BUILDINGS	BVD	BOULEVARD	CHA	CHASE
ALY	ALLEY	BND	BEND	BY	BYPASS	CHYD	CHURCHYARD
AP	APPROACH	BNK	BANK	CATH	CATHEDRAL	CIR	CIRCLE
AR	ARCADE	BR	BRIDGE	CEM	CEMETERY	CIRC	CIRCUS
ASS	ASSOCIATION	BRK	BROOK	CEN	CENTRE	CL	CLOSE
AV	AVENUE	BTM	BOTTOM	CFT	CROFT	CLFS	CLIFFS
BCH	BEACH	BUS	BUSINESS	CH	CHURCH	CMP	CAMP

CNR	CORNER
CO	COUNTY
COLL	COLLEGE
COM	COMMON
COMM	COMMISSION
CON	CONVENT
COT	COTTAGE

187

COTS COTTAGES
CP CAPE
CPS COPSE
CR CREEK
CREM CREMATORIUM
CRS CRESCENT
CSWY CAUSEWAY
CT COURT
CTRL CENTRAL
CTS COURTS
CTYD COURTYARD
CUTT CUTTINGS
CV COVE
CYN CANYON
DEPT DEPARTMENT
DL DALE
DM DAM
DR DRIVE
DRO DROVE
DRY DRIVEWAY
DWGS DWELLINGS
E EAST
EMB EMBANKMENT
EMBY EMBASSY
ESP ESPLANADE
EST ESTATE
EX EXCHANGE
EXPY EXPRESSWAY
EXT EXTENSION
F/O FLYOVER
FC FOOTBALL CLUB
FK FORK
FLD FIELD
FLDS FIELDS
FLS FALLS
FLS FLATS
FM FARM
FT FORT
FWY FREEWAY
FY FERRY
GA GATE
GAL GALLERY
GDN GARDEN
GDNS GARDENS
GLD GLADE
GLN GLEN
GN GREEN
GND GROUND
GRA GRANGE
GRG GARAGE
GT GREAT
GTWY GATEWAY
GV GROVE
HGR HIGHER
HL HILL
HLS HILLS
HO HOUSE
HOL HOLLOW
HOSP HOSPITAL
HRB HARBOUR
HTH HEATH
HTS HEIGHTS
HVN HAVEN
HWY HIGHWAY
IMP IMPERIAL
IN INLET
IND EST INDUSTRIAL ESTATE
INF INFIRMARY
INFO INFORMATION
INT INTERCHANGE
IS ISLAND
JCT JUNCTION
JTY JETTY
KG KING
KNL KNOLL
L LAKE
LA LANE
LDG LODGE
LGT LIGHT
LK LOCK
LKS LAKES
LNDG LANDING
LTL LITTLE
LWR LOWER
MAG MAGISTRATE
MAN MANSIONS
MD MEAD
MDW MEADOWS
MEM MEMORIAL
MKT MARKET
MKTS MARKETS
ML MALL
ML MILL
MNR MANOR
MS MEWS
MSN MISSION
MT MOUNT
MTN MOUNTAIN
MTS MOUNTAINS
MUS MUSEUM
MWY MOTORWAY
N NORTH
NE NORTH EAST
NW NORTH WEST
O/P OVERPASS
OFF OFFICE
ORCH ORCHARD
OV OVAL
PAL PALACE
PAS PASSAGE
PAV PAVILION
PDE PARADE
PH PUBLIC HOUSE
PK PARK
PKWY PARKWAY
PL PLACE
PLN PLAIN
PLNS PLAINS
PLZ PLAZA
POL POLICE STATION
PR PRINCE
PREC PRECINCT
PREP PREPARATORY
PRIM PRIMARY
PROM PROMENADE
PRS PRINCESS
PRT PORT
PT POINT
PTH PATH
PZ PIAZZA
QD QUADRANT
QU QUEEN
QY QUAY
R RIVER
RBT ROUNDABOUT
RD ROAD
RDG RIDGE
REP REPUBLIC
RES RESERVOIR
RFC RUGBY FOOTBALL CLUB
RI RISE
RP RAMP
RW ROW
S SOUTH
SCH SCHOOL
SE SOUTH EAST
SER SERVICE AREA
SH SHORE
SHOP SHOPPING
SKWY SKYWAY
SMT SUMMIT
SOC SOCIETY
SP SPUR
SPR SPRING
SQ SQUARE
ST STREET
STN STATION
STR STREAM
STRD STRAND
SW SOUTH WEST
TDG TRADING
TER TERRACE
THWY THROUGHWAY
TNL TUNNEL
TOLL TOLLWAY
TPK TURNPIKE
TR TRACK
TRL TRAIL
TWR TOWER
U/P UNDERPASS
UNI UNIVERSITY
UPR UPPER
V VALE
VA VALLEY
VIAD VIADUCT
VIL VILLA
VIS VISTA
VLG VILLAGE
VLS VILLAS
VW VIEW
W WEST
WD WOOD
WHF WHARF
WK WALK
WKS WALKS
WLS WELLS
WY WAY
YD YARD
YHA YOUTH HOSTEL

POSTCODE TOWNS AND AREA ABBREVIATIONS

ASHBK/HED/RY Ashbrooke/Hedon/Ryhope
ASHGTN Ashington
BDLGTN Bedlington
BDN/LAN/SAC Brandon/Lanchester/Sacriston
BLAY Blaydon
BLYTH Blyth
BOL Boldon
BOLCOL Boldon Colliery
BW/LEM/TK/HW Benwell/Lemington/Throckley/Heddon-on-the-Wall
BYK/HTN/WLK Byker/Heaton/Walker
CHPW Chopwell
CLDN/WHIT/ROK Cleadon/Whitburn/Roker
CLS/BIR/GTL Chester-le-Street/Birtley/Great Lumley
CLSW/PEL Chester-le-Street west/Pelton
CNUT Central Newcastle upon Tyne
CON/LDGT Consett/Leadgate
CRAM Cramlington
CRK/WIL Crook/Willington
DHAM Durham
DIN/WO Dinnington/Wide Open
DUN/TMV Dunston/Team Valley
ELS/FEN Elswick/Fenham
FELL Felling
GATE Gateshead
GOS/KPK Gosforth/Kingston Park
HAR/WTLS Harton/Whiteleas
HEBB Hebburn
HLH Hetton-le-Hole
HLS Houghton-le-Spring
JES Jesmond
JRW Jarrow
LGB/HTN Longbenton/Heaton
LGB/KIL Longbenton/Killingworth
LWF/SPW/WRK Low Fell/Springwell/Wrekenton
MLFD/PNYW Millfield/Pennywell
MONK Monkseaton
MPTH Morpeth
NSHW North Shields west
NWBGN Newbiggin-by-the-Sea
PLEE/EAS Peterlee/Easington
PONT/DH Ponteland/Darras Hall
PRUD Prudhoe
PSHWF Painshawfield
RDHAMSE Rural Durham south & east
RHTLP Rural Hartlepool
ROWG Rowlands Gill
RYTON Ryton
SEA/MUR Seaham/Murton
SMOOR Shiremoor
SPEN Spennymoor
SSH South Shields
STKFD/GP Stakefold/Guide Post
STLY/ANP Stanley/Annfield Plain
STMFDH Stamfordham
SUND Sunderland
SUNDSW Sunderland southwest
SWCK/CAS Southwick/Castletown
TRIM Trimdon
TYNE/NSHE Tynemouth/North Shields east
WASHN Washington north
WASHS Washington south
WBAY Whitley Bay
WD/WHPE/BLK West Denton/Westerhope/Blakelaw
WEAR Weardale
WICK/BNPF Wickham/Burnopfield
WLSD/HOW Wallsend/Howdon
WNGT Wingate
WYLAM Wylam

Index - streets

Abb - All

A

Abbay St *SWCK/CAS* SR5 106 A4
Abbey Cl *MONK* NE25 50 B5
WASHS NE38 117 F1
Abbey Ct *GATE* NE8 11 H6
Abbey Dr *JRW* NE32 74 A4
TYNE/NSHE NE30 61 H2
WD/WHPE/BLK NE5 53 K6
Abbey Ga *MPTH* NE61 20 B6
Abbey Mdw *MPTH* NE61 20 B6
Abbey Rd *DHAM* DH1 156 B1
WASHS NE38 117 F1
Abbeywoods *DHAM* DH1 156 C1
Abbots Cl *STKFD/GP* NE62 23 H5
Abbotsfield Cl *SUNDSW* SR3 133 K2
Abbotsford Gv
ASHBK/HED/RY SR2 14 C7
Abbotsford Pk *MONK* NE25 50 D5
Abbotsford Rd *FELL* NE10 12 C5
Abbotsford Ter *JES* NE2 70 D3
Abbotside Cl *CLSW/PEL* DH2 114 D4
Abbotside Pl
WD/WHPE/BLK NE5 68 B2
Abbotsmeade Cl
WD/WHPE/BLK NE5 69 F3
Abbot's Rd *GATE* NE8 6 A9
Abbots' Rw *DHAM* DH1 157 G6
Abbot St *PLEE/EAS* SR8 163 G4
Abbots Wk *STLY/ANP* DH9 113 K6
Abbots Wy *MPTH* NE61 20 C5
NSHW NE29 60 B1
Abbs St *SWCK/CAS* SR5 106 D4
Abercorn Pl *WLSD/HOW* NE28 59 G4
Abercorn Rd
BW/LEM/TK/HW NE15 68 E6
SUNDSW SR3 119 H5
Abercrombie Pl
WD/WHPE/BLK NE5 69 F1
Aberdare Rd *SUNDSW* SR3 119 H7
Aberdeen *CLSW/PEL* DH2 115 F5
Aberdeen Ct *DIN/WO* NE13 55 H2
Aberdeen Dr *JRW* NE32 74 C7
Aberford Cl
WD/WHPE/BLK NE5 53 K7
Aberfoyle *CLSW/PEL* DH2 115 F5
Aberfoyle Ct *STLY/ANP* DH9 127 F1
Abernethy *CLSW/PEL* DH2 115 F4
Abingdon Rd *BYK/HTN/WLK* NE6 72 D4
Abingdon Sq *CRAM* NE23 33 J6
Abingdon St *MLFD/PNYW* SR4 119 K1
Abingdon Wy *BOL* NE36 90 C5
BOLCOL NE35 90 B3
Abinger St *ELS/FEN* NE4 4 F6
Aboyne Sq *SUNDSW* SR3 119 H5
Acacia Av *HLS* DH4 131 J6
PLEE/EAS SR8 175 J4
Acacia Gv *HAR/WTLS* NE34 75 J6
Acacia Rd *FELL* NE10 11 M4
Acacia St *DUN/TMV* NE11 86 C7
Acanthus Av *ELS/FEN* NE4 69 H4
Acclom St *WNGT* TS28 184 A6
Acer Ct *ASHBK/HED/RY* SR2 14 F9
Acer Dr *RDHAMSE* DH6 160 E6
Acklam Av *ASHBK/HED/RY* SR2 121 F5
Acomb Av *MONK* NE25 40 A6
WLSD/HOW NE28 59 F3
Acomb Ct
ASHBK/HED/RY SR2 121 F5
BDLGTN NE22 29 G5
Acomb Crs *GOS/KPK* NE3 55 K2
Acomb Dr *WYLAM* NE41 65 G4
Acomb Gdns
WD/WHPE/BLK NE5 69 G3
Acorn Av *BDLGTN* NE22 29 F6
GATE NE8 10 A7
Acorn Cl *BDN/LAN/SAC* DH7 143 G4
Acornclose La
BDN/LAN/SAC DH7 142 E4
Acorn Pl *BDN/LAN/SAC* DH7 167 G6
Acorn Rd *JES* NE2 70 E1
Acreford Ct *STKFD/GP* NE62 22 E7
Acre Rigg Rd *PLEE/EAS* SR8 174 C3
Acton Dene *STLY/ANP* DH9 127 G1
Acton Dr *NSHW* NE29 60 B2
Acton Pl *LGB/HTN* NE7 71 H1
Acton Rd *BDN/LAN/SAC* DH7 165 H2
WD/WHPE/BLK NE5 68 D3
Adair Av *BW/LEM/TK/HW* NE15 69 G5
Adam St *PLEE/EAS* SR8 175 J4
Ada St *BYK/HTN/WLK* NE6 7 L5
SSH NE33 75 H2
Adderlane Rd *PRUD* NE42 80 E1
Adderstone Av *CRAM* NE23 38 C3
Adderstone Crs *JES* NE2 71 F1
Adderstone Gdns *NSHW* NE29 59 K1
Addington Crs *NSHW* NE29 60 C4
Addington Dr *BLYTH* NE24 35 G2
WLSD/HOW NE28 59 F3
Addison Ct *WLSD/HOW* NE28 73 J2
Addison Gdns *FELL* NE10 13 M9
Addison Rd *BOL* NE36 90 E5
BW/LEM/TK/HW NE15 68 B4
Addison St *ASHBK/HED/RY* SR2 15 J7
NSHW NE29 2 D4
Addycombe Ter
BYK/HTN/WLK NE6 71 J2
Adelaide Cl *SUND* SR1 15 H4
Adelaide Pl *SUND* SR1 15 J4
Adelaide Rw *SEA/MUR* SR7 150 E1
Adelaide Ter *ELS/FEN* NE4 69 H6
Adeline Gdns *GOS/KPK* NE3 70 A1
Adelphi Cl *NSHW* NE29 60 A2
Adelphi Pl *BYK/HTN/WLK* NE6 7 L6
Adfrid Pl *PLEE/EAS* SR8 174 E3
Admington Ct
STKFD/GP NE62 23 F6
Admiral Wy *SUNDSW* SR3 133 G2
Adolphus St
CLDN/WHIT/ROK SR6 93 F4
Adolphus St West
SEA/MUR SR7 150 E1
Adventure La *HLS* DH4 146 C5
Affleck St *GATE* NE8 10 E4
Afton Ct *HAR/WTLS* NE34 75 G6
Afton Wy *GOS/KPK* NE3 55 J5
Agar Rd *SUNDSW* SR3 119 H6
Agincourt *HEBB* NE31 73 F4
LGB/KIL NE12 47 K5
Agnes Maria St *GOS/KPK* NE3 56 A5
Agnes St *STLY/ANP* DH9 112 D7
Agricola Gdns *WLSD/HOW* NE28 59 F4
Agricola Rd *ELS/FEN* NE4 4 A5
Aidan Av *WBAY* NE26 40 E2
Aidan Cl *DIN/WO* NE13 46 B3
STLY/ANP DH9 113 F7
Aidan Wk *GOS/KPK* NE3 56 D5
Aiden Wy *HLH* DH5 147 K3
Ailesbury St *MLFD/PNYW* SR4 106 A6
Ainderby Rd
BW/LEM/TK/HW NE15 66 D1
Ainsdale Gdns
WD/WHPE/BLK NE5 68 A1
Ainsley St *DHAM* DH1 16 A3
Ainslie Pl *WD/WHPE/BLK* NE5 69 F2
Ainsworth Av *HAR/WTLS* NE34 90 E1
Ainthorpe Cl *SUNDSW* SR3 120 B7
Ainthorpe Gdns *LGB/HTN* NE7 57 H6
Aintree Dr *CON/LDGT* DH8 108 D7
Aintree Gdns *GATE* NE8 10 B9
Aintree Rd *SUNDSW* SR3 119 H6
Airedale *WLSD/HOW* NE28 58 B5
Airedale Gdns *HLH* DH5 147 J6
Aireys Cl *HLS* DH4 132 A7
Airey Ter *BYK/HTN/WLK* NE6 72 C6
GATE NE8 10 D6
Airport Freightway
DIN/WO NE13 44 C7
Airville Mt *SUNDSW* SR3 134 A3
Aisgill Cl *CRAM* NE23 38 C2
Aisgill Dr *WD/WHPE/BLK* NE5 68 A2
Aiskell St *MLFD/PNYW* SR4 106 A7
Aj Cook Ter *RDHAMSE* DH6 173 H5
Akeld Cl *CRAM* NE23 38 C3
Akenside Hl *CNUT* NE1 5 L8
Alamein Av *HLH* DH5 132 D7
Alansway Gdns *SSH* NE33 75 H3
Albany Av *LGB/KIL* NE12 57 K2
Albany Ct *ELS/FEN* NE4 9 H2
Albany Rd *GATE* NE8 11 K1
Albany St East *SSH* NE33 75 H3
Albany St West *SSH* NE33 75 H3
Albany Wy *WASHN* NE37 102 E6
Albatross Wy *BLYTH* NE24 35 G4
Albemarle Av *JES* NE2 56 D7
Albemarle St *SSH* NE33 3 H7
Albert Av *WLSD/HOW* NE28 72 D1
Albert Dr *LWF/SPW/WRK* NE9 87 F7
Albert Pl *LWF/SPW/WRK* NE9 101 F1
WASHS NE38 117 H3
Albert Rd *BDLGTN* NE22 29 K4
CON/LDGT DH8 123 F5
JRW NE32 73 K4
MLFD/PNYW SR4 106 A6
WBAY NE26 41 G2
Albert St *CLS/BIR/GTL* DH3 129 J4
CLSW/PEL DH2 128 A2
DHAM DH1 16 A2
HEBB NE31 73 F4
JES NE2 6 A5
RDHAMSE DH6 172 C6
SEA/MUR SR7 150 E2
Albert Ter *LGB/KIL* NE12 57 J1
Albion Pl *SUND* SR1 14 D6
Albion Rd *TYNE/NSHE* NE30 2 E1
Albion Rd West *NSHW* NE29 2 C2
Albion Rw *BYK/HTN/WLK* NE6 6 E5
Albion St *FELL* NE10 87 K6
MLFD/PNYW SR4 104 E7
Albion Ter *MPTH* NE61 18 C1
NSHW NE29 2 D1
Albion Wy *BLYTH* NE24 30 E7
CRAM NE23 33 K6
Albury Park Rd
TYNE/NSHE NE30 61 G3
Albury Pl *WICK/BNPF* NE16 84 E7
Albury Rd *JES* NE2 56 D7
Albyn Gdns *SUNDSW* SR3 120 A3
Alcester Cl *STKFD/GP* NE62 23 F6
Alconbury Cl *BLYTH* NE24 35 G2
Alcote Gv *RDHAMSE* DH6 173 J4
Alcroft Cl *WD/WHPE/BLK* NE5 53 K7
Aldborough St *BLYTH* NE24 31 G7
Aldbrough Cl
ASHBK/HED/RY SR2 135 F1
Aldbrough St *HAR/WTLS* NE34 74 E6
Aldeburgh Av
BW/LEM/TK/HW NE15 68 A3
Aldenham Rd *SUNDSW* SR3 119 J6
Alder Av *ELS/FEN* NE4 69 H3
Alder Cl *HLH* DH5 147 J5
MPTH NE61 20 E5
Alder Crs *STLY/ANP* DH9 111 H4
Alderdene *BDN/LAN/SAC* DH7 140 B5
Alderdene Cl
BDN/LAN/SAC DH7 167 H1
Alder Gv *CON/LDGT* DH8 123 K4
MONK NE25 50 C3
Alder Lea Cl *DHAM* DH1 157 H6
Alderley Cl *ASHBK/HED/RY* SR2 121 F4
BOLCOL NE35 90 C3
Alderley Dr *LGB/KIL* NE12 48 B5
Alderley Rd *LWF/SPW/WRK* NE9 86 E7
Alderley Wy *CRAM* NE23 33 K6
Alderman Wood Rd
STLY/ANP DH9 112 C6
Alderney Gdns
WD/WHPE/BLK NE5 68 A1
Alder Pk *BDN/LAN/SAC* DH7 167 F7
Alder Rd *NSHW* NE29 59 J3
PLEE/EAS SR8 175 J4
WLSD/HOW NE28 59 G4
Aldershot Rd *SUNDSW* SR3 119 H7
Aldershot Sq *SUNDSW* SR3 119 H7
Alderside Crs
BDN/LAN/SAC DH7 140 B4
Alder St *SWCK/CAS* SR5 105 F4
Alder Wy *LGB/KIL* NE12 47 J5
Alderwood *ASHGTN* NE63 23 J3
WASHS NE38 116 D5
Alderwood Crs
BYK/HTN/WLK NE6 72 B2
Alderwyk *FELL* NE10 88 D6
Aldhome Ct *DHAM* DH1 156 B3
Aldridge Ct *BDN/LAN/SAC* DH7 155 F7
Aldsworth Cl
LWF/SPW/WRK NE9 102 B4
Aldwick Rd
BW/LEM/TK/HW NE15 68 D5
Aldwych Dr *NSHW* NE29 59 K3
Aldwych Rd *SUNDSW* SR3 119 H7
Aldwych Sq *SUNDSW* SR3 133 H1
Aldwych St *SSH* NE33 3 M9
Alexander Dr *HLH* DH5 147 J5
Alexander Ter
CLDN/WHIT/ROK SR6 106 D2
Alexandra Av *SWCK/CAS* SR5 105 K4
Alexandra Cl *DHAM* DH1 156 B3
Alexandra Dr *WICK/BNPF* NE16 8 A7
Alexandra Gdns *NSHW* NE29 60 C4
Alexandra Pk
ASHBK/HED/RY SR2 120 C2
SUNDSW SR3 120 B2
Alexandra Rd *ASHGTN* NE63 24 A1
BYK/HTN/WLK NE6 71 H2
GATE NE8 10 F6
MPTH NE61 20 E5
Alexandra St *CLSW/PEL* DH2 128 C1
CON/LDGT DH8 123 F5
WLSD/HOW NE28 72 E1
Alexandra Wy *CRAM* NE23 38 C3
Alexandria Crs *DHAM* DH1 16 B4
Alexandrina St
SEA/MUR SR7 150 E1
Alford *CLSW/PEL* DH2 115 F4
Alfred Av *BDLGTN* NE22 29 H5
Alfred St *BYK/HTN/WLK* NE6 7 L5
HEBB NE31 73 F6
SEA/MUR SR7 151 F2
Alfreton Cl *BDN/LAN/SAC* DH7 177 F1
Algernon *LGB/KIL* NE12 47 K4
Algernon Pl *WBAY* NE26 51 F5
Algernon Rd
BW/LEM/TK/HW NE15 68 A5
BYK/HTN/WLK NE6 7 G4
Algernon Ter *TYNE/NSHE* NE30 61 G2
WYLAM NE41 65 G5
Algiers Rd *SUNDSW* SR3 119 G7
Alice St *ASHBK/HED/RY* SR2 14 D7
BLAY NE21 83 K3
CLSW/PEL DH2 115 F6
SSH NE33 75 G3
Aline St *SEA/MUR* SR7 151 F1
SUNDSW SR3 120 B7
Alison Dr *BOL* NE36 91 H5
Allandale Av *LGB/KIL* NE12 57 K3
Allanville *LGB/KIL* NE12 47 J5
All Church
BW/LEM/TK/HW NE15 69 F5
Allchurch Dr *ASHGTN* NE63 24 C2
Allendale Av *WLSD/HOW* NE28 58 D6
Allendale Crs *HLS* DH4 117 J6
SMOOR NE27 49 J6
STKFD/GP NE62 23 G4
Allendale Dr *HAR/WTLS* NE34 76 A3
Allendale Pl *TYNE/NSHE* NE30 61 H3
Allendale Rd
BDN/LAN/SAC DH7 167 H6
BLYTH NE24 35 H1
BYK/HTN/WLK NE6 7 J7
SUNDSW SR3 119 H7
Allendale Sq *SUNDSW* SR3 119 J5

Allendale St *HLH* DH5 .... 147 K6 ⑥
Allendale Ter
  BYK/HTN/WLK NE6 .... 72 B5 ⑥
Allenheads *WASHS* NE38 ...... 117 G5
Allenheads *MONK* NE25........ 39 K4
  WD/WHPE/BLK NE5 .... 68 C2 ⑥
Allensford Bank
  CON/LDGT DH8................. 136 E1
Allensgreen *CRAM* NE23 .... 38 C2
Allerdean Cl
  BW/LEM/TK/HW NE15 .... 67 K4 ⑥
Allergate *DHAM* DH1 .... 16 B4
Allerhope *CRAM* NE23 .... 38 C3
Allerton Gdns
  BYK/HTN/WLK NE6 .... 71 K1 ⑥
Allerwash
  WD/WHPE/BLK NE5 .... 68 C2 ⑥
Allery Banks *MPTH* NE61 .... 20 E5
Allhusen Ter *GATE* NE8 .... 11 M5
Alliance St *MLFD/PNYW* SR4.. 14 B3
Allingham Ct *LGB/HTN* NE7 ... 58 A7 ⑥
Allison Gdns *CON/LDGT* DH8 .. 123 F3 ⑥
Allison St *CON/LDGT* DH8 ...... 123 F4
Alloa Rd *SUNDSW* SR3 .... 119 H6 ⑥
Allonby Wy
  WD/WHPE/BLK NE5 .... 69 F3 ⑥
All Saints Dr *HLH* DH5 .... 147 K2
Alma Pl *NSHW* NE29 .... 60 E4
  WBAY NE26 .... 51 F5
Alma St *MLFD/PNYW* SR4 ...... 104 E6
Alma Ter *RYTON* NE40 .... 82 E2
Almond *RDHAMSE* DH6 .... 160 E6
Almond Crs *GATE* NE8 .... 10 A7
Almond Dr *SWCK/CAS* SR5 .... 104 E5
Almond Pl *ELS/FEN* NE4 .... 69 H4 ⑥
Almoner's Barn *DHAM* DH1 .... 168 B2
Aln Av *GOS/KPK* NE3 .... 56 A4
Aln Ct *BW/LEM/TK/HW* NE15 .. 68 A5
Aln Crs *GOS/KPK* NE3 .... 56 A3
Aln Gv *BW/LEM/TK/HW* NE15 .. 68 A4
Alnham Ct *GOS/KPK* NE3 .... 55 J3 ⑥
Alnmouth Av *NSHW* NE29 ...... 60 B6
Alnmouth Dr *GOS/KPK* NE3 .... 56 E6 ⑥
Aln St *ASHGTN* NE63 .... 24 A1
  HEBB NE31 .... 73 F5
Aln Wk *GOS/KPK* NE3 .... 56 A4 ⑥
Alnwick Av *NSHW* NE29 .... 60 B6
Alnwick Cl *CLSW/PEL* DH2 ...... 129 C6
  WICK/BNPF NE16 .... 84 E5
Alnwick Gv *JRW* NE32 .... 89 K2 ⑥
Alnwick Rd *DHAM* DH1 .... 156 D2 ⑥
  SUNDSW SR3 .... 119 J6
Alnwick Sq *SUNDSW* SR3 ...... 119 J6
Alnwick St
  BW/LEM/TK/HW NE15 .... 67 H3 ⑥
  PLEE/EAS SR8.................. 175 G1 ⑥
  WLSD/HOW NE28 .... 72 E1 ⑥
Alnwick Ter *DIN/WO* NE13 ...... 46 C2 ⑥
Alpine Gv *BOL* NE36 .... 91 F5 ⑥
Alpine Wy *SUNDSW* SR3 .... 120 A3 ⑥
Alresford *LGB/KIL* NE12 .... 47 K5 ⑥
Alston Av *BYK/HTN/WLK* NE6 .. 7 M4
  CRAM NE23 .... 38 E3 ⑥
Alston Cl *NSHW* NE29 .... 60 A3 ⑥
  WLSD/HOW NE28 .... 59 J6
Alston Crs *CLDN/WHIT/ROK* SR6.. 92 C7
Alstone Ct *STKFD/GP* NE62 .... 23 F6 ⑥
Alston Gdns
  BW/LEM/TK/HW NE15 .... 53 F7
Alston Gv *WBAY* NE26 .... 40 E1 ⑥
Alston Rd *MONK* NE25 .... 40 A2
  WASHS NE38 .... 103 K7
Alston St *GATE* NE8 .... 10 B6
Alston Ter *CON/LDGT* DH8 ..... 122 C3
Alston Wk *PLEE/EAS* SR8 ...... 175 F3 ⑥
Alston Wy *BDN/LAN/SAC* DH7.. 167 H6 ⑥
Altan Pl *LGB/KIL* NE12 .... 57 H3
Alum Well Rd
  LWF/SPW/WRK NE9 .... 86 E7 ⑥
  LWF/SPW/WRK NE9 .... 87 F7 ⑥
Alverston Cl
  BW/LEM/TK/HW NE15 .... 68 A3
Alverstone Av
  LWF/SPW/WRK NE9 .... 100 E1
Alverthorpe St *SSH* NE33 ...... 75 H3
Alveston Cl *STKFD/GP* NE62 ... 23 F6
Alvin Gra *JRW* NE32 .... 73 H4 ⑥
Alwin *WASHS* NE38 .... 116 C5
Alwin Cl *HLS* DH4 .... 131 G4
Alwinton Av *NSHW* NE29 .... 60 B2
Alwinton Cl *BLYTH* NE24 .... 30 E6
  WD/WHPE/BLK NE5 .... 54 E6 ⑥
Alwinton Dr *CLSW/PEL* DH2 .... 129 C6
Alwinton Gdns *DUN/TMV* NE11 .. 86 A7
Alwinton Rd *SMOOR* NE27 ..... 49 J6
Alwinton Ter *GOS/KPK* NE3 .... 56 D5
Amara Sq *SUNDSW* SR3 .... 119 J6
Ambassadors Wy *NSHW* NE29 .. 59 K2
Amber Ct *BLYTH* NE24 .... 34 E1 ⑥
Ambergate Cl
  WD/WHPE/BLK NE5 .... 54 E7 ⑥
Amberley Cha *LGB/KIL* NE12 ... 48 A5 ⑥
Amberley Cl *WLSD/HOW* NE28 .. 59 J6 ⑥
Amberley Gdns *LGB/HTN* NE7 .. 71 J1 ⑥
Amberley St *ASHBK/HED/RY* SR2.. 15 G7
  GATE NE8 .... 9 M6
Amberley St South
  ASHBK/HED/RY SR2 .... 15 G8 ⑥
Amberley Wy *BLYTH* NE24 ...... 35 G2 ⑥
Amberly Gv *WICK/BNPF* NE16 .. 84 E7 ⑥
Amble Av *HAR/WTLS* NE34 ...... 76 B3
  MONK NE25 .... 51 F6
Amble Cl *BLYTH* NE24 .... 34 E2
Amble Gv *JES* NE2................ 6 B2
Amble Pl *LGB/KIL* NE12 .... 58 B1
Ambleside
  BW/LEM/TK/HW NE15 .... 53 G7
Ambleside Av *HAR/WTLS* NE34.. 75 J6
  SEA/MUR SR7................... 134 E7
Ambleside Cl *MONK* NE25 ...... 40 A5 ⑥
  PLEE/EAS SR8.................. 175 F3 ⑥
Ambleside Ms
  CON/LDGT DH8................. 123 K3 ⑥
Ambleside Ter
  CLDN/WHIT/ROK SR6 .... 106 C1

Amble Wy *GOS/KPK* NE3 .... 56 B4 ⑥
Ambridge Wy *GOS/KPK* NE3 ... 55 K5 ⑥
Ambrose Pl
  BYK/HTN/WLK NE6 .... 72 D5 ⑥
Ambrose Rd *SUNDSW* SR3 ..... 119 H6
Amec Wy *WLSD/HOW* NE28 ..... 73 G2
Amelia Cl *ELS/FEN* NE4 .... 8 F1
Amelia Gdns *SUNDSW* SR3 .... 119 F7
Amersham Crs *PLEE/EAS* SR8.. 174 E3 ⑥
Amersham Pl
  WD/WHPE/BLK NE5 .... 69 F1 ⑥
Amersham Rd *BLYTH* NE24 ..... 35 F3
Amesbury Cl
  WD/WHPE/BLK NE5 .... 53 K7 ⑥
Amethyst Rd *ELS/FEN* NE4 ...... 9 H2
Amethyst St
  MLFD/PNYW SR4 .... 105 K6 ⑥
Amherst Rd *GOS/KPK* NE3 ...... 55 J4
Amos Ayre Pl *HAR/WTLS* NE34.. 74 D6
Amos Dr *STLY/ANP* DH9 .... 125 H6
Amsterdam St *MLFD/PNYW* SR4.. 105 H3
Amy St *SWCK/CAS* SR5 .... 106 B3 ⑥
Ancaster Rd *LGB/KIL* NE12 ..... 57 H4
Ancaster Rd *WICK/BNPF* NE16.. 84 D7 ⑥
Ancona St *MLFD/PNYW* SR4 .... 105 K5
Ancroft Av *NSHW* NE29 .... 60 D3
Ancroft Garth *DHAM* DH1 ...... 169 J6 ⑥
Ancroft Pl *ASHGTN* NE63 .... 24 B4
  WD/WHPE/BLK NE5 .... 69 F3
Ancroft Rd *MONK* NE25......... 39 J5
Ancroft Wy *GOS/KPK* NE3 ...... 55 K2 ⑥
Ancrum St *JES* NE2............... 4 E2
Anderson St *SSH* NE33 .... 3 J7
Andover Pl *WLSD/HOW* NE28... 59 C4
Andrew Rd *SUNDSW* SR3 .... 119 G7
Andrew's La *PLEE/EAS* SR8 ..... 162 B7
Andrew Ter *RDHAMSE* DH6 ..... 182 D2 ⑥
Anfield Rd *GOS/KPK* NE3 .... 55 J5
Angerton Av *SMOOR* NE27 ..... 49 H7
  TYNE/NSHE NE30 .... 60 E1
Angerton Gdns
  WD/WHPE/BLK NE5 .... 69 H3
Anglesey Gdns
  WD/WHPE/BLK NE5 .... 68 A1 ⑥
Anglesey Pl *ELS/FEN* NE4 .... 4 D7
Anglesey Rd *SUNDSW* SR3 ..... 119 H7 ⑥
Angle Ter *WLSD/HOW* NE28..... 73 H1 ⑥
Angram Dr *ASHBK/HED/RY* SR2.. 121 C5 ⑥
Angrove Gdns
  MLFD/PNYW SR4 .... 105 K7
Angus *CLSW/PEL* DH2............ 115 F4
Angus Cl *LGB/KIL* NE12 .... 47 J6 ⑥
Angus Crs *NSHW* NE29.......... 60 B6
Angus Dr *GATE* NE8 .... 10 A7
Annand Rd *DHAM* DH1 .... 17 K1
Annaside Ms *CON/LDGT* DH8 .. 123 K3
Ann Av *RDHAMSE* DH6 .... 181 C5
Anne Dr *LGB/KIL* NE12 .... 58 C2
Annfield Pl *STLY/ANP* DH9 ...... 125 C3
Annfield Rd *DHAM* DH1 .... 33 H5
Annie St *CLDN/WHIT/ROK* SR6.. 106 D1
Ann's Rw *BLYTH* NE24 .... 31 G5
Ann St *BLAY* NE21 .... 84 A3
  CON/LDGT DH8.................. 123 F5 ⑥
  GATE NE8 .... 11 G3
  HEBB NE31 .... 72 E4
Annville Crs *BYK/HTN/WLK* NE6.. 72 C7
Anscomb Gdns *LGB/KIL* NE12 .. 57 F7
Anson Cl *SSH* NE33 .... 75 F3
Anson Pl *WD/WHPE/BLK* NE5 .. 54 D7 ⑥
Anstead Cl *CRAM* NE23.......... 38 C2
Anthony Rd *SUNDSW* SR3 ...... 119 H7 ⑥
Anthony St *STLY/ANP* DH9 ...... 112 C7 ⑥
Antonine Wk
  BW/LEM/TK/HW NE15 .... 66 B1
Anton Pl *CRAM* NE23 .... 38 C3
Antrim Cl *WD/WHPE/BLK* NE5 .. 55 G7
Antrim Gdns *SEA/MUR* SR7 .... 135 J7 ⑥
Antwerp Rd *SUNDSW* SR3 ...... 119 G7
Anvil Ct *DHAM* DH1 .... 156 B2 ⑥
Apperley *WD/WHPE/BLK* NE5 .. 68 C2
Apperley Av *DHAM* DH1 .... 169 K6 ⑥
Apperley Rd *GOS/KPK* NE3 ..... 55 G6
Apperley Rd *PSHWF* NE43 ...... 79 G5 ⑥
Appian Pl
  BW/LEM/TK/HW NE15 .... 67 C1 ⑥
  LWF/SPW/WRK NE9 .... 11 L9
Appleby Ct *NSHW* NE29 .... 2 B1
Appleby Gdns *WLSD/HOW* NE28.. 59 J6 ⑥
Appleby Pk *NSHW* NE29 .... 60 D4
Appleby Rd *SUNDSW* SR3 ...... 119 H6
Appleby Sq *SUNDSW* SR3 ...... 119 H7 ⑥
Appleby St *NSHW* NE29 .... 2 D5
Appleby Wy *PLEE/EAS* SR8 ..... 174 B7 ⑥
Apple Cl *BW/LEM/TK/HW* NE15.. 68 A3
Appledore Gdns
  CLS/BIR/GTL DH3 .... 129 K2
Appledore Rd *BLYTH* NE24 ..... 35 G2
Appleforth Av
  ASHBK/HED/RY SR2 .... 121 G5
Appletree Dr *PRUD* NE42 .... 80 C1
Appletree Gdns
  BYK/HTN/WLK NE6 .... 72 A3
  MONK NE25 .... 40 A4
Applewood *LGB/KIL* NE12 ...... 48 B6 ⑥
Appley Ter
  CLDN/WHIT/ROK SR6 .... 106 E4
Apsley Crs *GOS/KPK* NE3 .... 55 J5
Aqua Ter *NWBGN* NE64 .... 25 F1
Aquila Dr *BW/LEM/TK/HW* NE15.. 65 K1
Arbourcourt Av
  BDN/LAN/SAC DH7 .... 165 G2
Arbroath Rd *SUNDSW* SR3 ..... 119 H6
Arcadia *CLS/BIR/GTL* DH3 ...... 129 J2
Arcadia Ter *BLYTH* NE24 .... 35 G1
Archbold St *JES* NE2 .... 5 M2
Archer Rd *SUNDSW* SR3 .... 119 H6
Archer Sq *SUNDSW* SR3 .... 119 H6 ⑥
Archer St *WLSD/HOW* NE28 .... 59 G7
Archery Ri *DHAM* DH1 .... 168 B2 ⑥
Archibald St *GOS/KPK* NE3 ..... 56 C5
Arcot Av *CRAM* NE23 .... 32 E7
  MONK NE25 .... 50 C6
Arcot Dr *MONK* NE25 .... 50 C7
  WD/WHPE/BLK NE5 .... 68 D3 ⑥
Arden Av *GOS/KPK* NE3 .... 56 B1

Arden Cl *WLSD/HOW* NE28 ..... 59 F3
Arden Crs *WD/WHPE/BLK* NE5.. 69 H2
Arden Sq *SUNDSW* SR3 .... 119 J6
Arden St *RDHAMSE* DH6 .... 173 H3
Ardrossan Rd *SUNDSW* SR3 ... 119 H7
Ardrossan Rd *CLSW/PEL* DH2... 115 F5
Arena Wy *ELS/FEN* NE4 .... 10 A2
Argus Cl *DUN/TMV* NE11 .... 86 B5
Argyle Ct *STLY/ANP* DH9 .... 112 E6
Argyle Pl *NSHW* NE29 .... 60 E2 ⑥
  RDHAMSE DH6 .... 160 E2 ⑥
Argyle Sq *ASHBK/HED/RY* SR2.. 14 D7
Argyle St *ASHBK/HED/RY* SR2.. 14 D7
  CNUT NE1 .... 5 M6
  HEBB NE31 .... 73 G4
  TYNE/NSHE NE30 .... 61 H2 ⑥
Argyle Ter *NWBGN* NE64 .... 25 F1
Ariel St *ASHGTN* NE63 .... 24 A2
Arisaig *CLSW/PEL* DH2........... 115 F4
Arklecrag *WASHN* NE37 .... 102 E7
Arkleside Pl
  WD/WHPE/BLK NE5 .... 68 B2 ⑥
Arkle St *DIN/WO* NE13 .... 46 A5
  GATE NE8 .... 10 B8
Arkwright St *GATE* NE8 .... 86 D5
Arlington Av *GOS/KPK* NE3 ..... 55 K7
Arlington Gv *CRAM* NE23 .... 33 H5
  WICK/BNPF NE16 .... 84 E6
Arlington Rd *HEBB* NE31 .... 73 H7 ⑥
Arlington St
  MLFD/PNYW SR4 .... 105 K7 ⑥
Armondside Rd *CHPW* NE17 .... 95 J7
Armstrong Av
  BYK/HTN/WLK NE6 .... 71 H2
  HAR/WTLS NE34 .... 75 J4 ⑥
  WNGT TS28 .... 183 K3 ⑥
Armstrong Dr *LGB/KIL* NE12 .... 47 H7
Armstrong Rd
  BW/LEM/TK/HW NE15 .... 68 D6
  ELS/FEN NE4 .... 69 H7
  PLEE/EAS SR8.................. 174 E2 ⑥
  WASHN NE37 .... 102 B6
  WLSD/HOW NE28 .... 73 J2
Armstrong St *DUN/TMV* NE11 .. 86 C5
  GATE NE8 .... 10 B9
Armstrong Ter *SSH* NE33 .... 75 J2 ⑥
Arncliffe Av *MLFD/PNYW* SR4 .. 119 J2 ⑥
Arncliffe Gdns
  WD/WHPE/BLK NE5 .... 68 A1 ⑥
Arnham Gv *MLFD/PNYW* SR4 ... 118 D4
Arnold Cl *STLY/ANP* DH9 .... 126 E1
Arnold Rd *SUNDSW* SR3 .... 119 H6
Arnold St *BOLCOL* NE35 .... 90 D4
Arran Cl *SUNDSW* SR3 .... 134 A1 ⑥
Arran Dr *JRW* NE32 .... 90 C1
Arran Pl *NSHW* NE29 .... 60 A2
Arras La *SUND* SR1 .... 15 H4
Arrol Pk *MLFD/PNYW* SR4 ...... 14 A5
Arrow Cl *LGB/KIL* NE12 .... 47 H7
Arthur Av *ASHBK/HED/RY* SR2.. 135 C1
Arthur Cook Av
  WICK/BNPF NE16 .... 85 G5
Arthur St *BLYTH* NE24 .... 31 G6 ⑥
  CLDN/WHIT/ROK SR6 .... 77 F7 ⑥
  GATE NE8 .... 11 G4
  JRW NE32 .... 73 K5 ⑥
  STLY/ANP DH9 .... 114 A7
Arun Cl *PLEE/EAS* SR8 .... 174 D5
Arundel Cl *NE22* 29 J3
  DIN/WO NE13 .... 46 A4 ⑥
Arundel Dr
  BW/LEM/TK/HW NE15 .... 68 C4
  MONK NE25 .... 49 K5
Arundel Gdns
  LWF/SPW/WRK NE9 .... 87 G7
  SUNDSW SR3 .... 119 G2
Arundel Rd *SUNDSW* SR3 ...... 119 H6
Arundel Wy *BDN/LAN/SAC* DH7.. 167 H6 ⑥
Asama Ct *ELS/FEN* NE4 .... 9 J2
Ascot Cl *WLSD/HOW* NE28...... 59 F4
Ascot Ct *SUNDSW* SR3 .... 119 H7
Ascot Crs *GATE* NE8 .... 10 B9
Ascot Gdns *HAR/WTLS* NE34 ... 75 H5
Ascot Pl *CLSW/PEL* DH2 .... 115 F7
Ascot Rd *CON/LDGT* DH8 .... 108 E7
Ash Av *BDN/LAN/SAC* DH7 ..... 155 F7
  DHAM DH1 .... 17 L4
  DIN/WO NE13................... 45 F2
Ash Banks *MPTH* NE61 .... 20 E6 ⑥
Ashberry Gv
  CLDN/WHIT/ROK SR6 .... 106 D4
Ashbourne Av
  BYK/HTN/WLK NE6 .... 72 B5
Ashbourne Cl *SMOOR* NE27 .... 48 E4 ⑥
Ashbourne Crs *ASHGTN* NE63 .. 23 J2
Ashbourne Rd *JRW* NE32 .... 74 A6 ⑥
Ashbrook Cl
  BDN/LAN/SAC DH7 .... 166 E7 ⑥
Ashbrooke *MONK* NE25 .... 50 C4
Ashbrooke Cl *RHTLP* TS27 ..... 184 D7 ⑥
Ashbrooke Cross
  ASHBK/HED/RY SR2 .... 120 C3 ⑥
Ashbrooke Dr *PONT/DH* NE20.. 43 G2 ⑥
Ashbrooke Gdns
  WLSD/HOW NE28 .... 59 G7 ⑥
Ashbrooke Range
  ASHBK/HED/RY SR2 .... 120 C3 ⑥
Ashbrooke Rd
  ASHBK/HED/RY SR2 .... 120 C3 ⑥
Ashbrooke St
  WD/WHPE/BLK NE5 .... 55 G7 ⑥
Ashburne Ct
  ASHBK/HED/RY SR2 .... 14 F9
Ashburn Rd *WLSD/HOW* NE28.. 59 C7 ⑥
Ashburton Rd *GOS/KPK* NE3 ... 56 A6
Ashbury *MONK* NE25 .... 50 A3
Ashby Crs *CON/LDGT* DH8 ...... 122 D2
Ashby La *CON/LDGT* DH8 .... 122 D3 ⑥
Ashby St *ASHBK/HED/RY* SR2.. 121 F3
Ash Crs *SEA/MUR* SR7 .... 150 D3
Ashcroft Dr *LGB/KIL* NE12 ...... 58 A3
Ashdale *HLS* DH4................. 117 G6
Ashdale Crs *WD/WHPE/BLK* NE5.. 68 A2
Ashdale Rd *CON/LDGT* DH8 .... 123 F4
Ashdown Av *DHAM* DH1 .... 157 J6
Ashdown Cl *LGB/KIL* NE12 ...... 57 H3 ⑥
Ashdown Rd *SUNDSW* SR3 .... 119 H6

Ashdown Wy *LGB/KIL* NE12 .... 57 H3 ⑥
Asher St *GATE* NE8 .... 11 M6
Ashfield *CON/LDGT* DH8 .... 122 D1 ⑥
  JRW NE32 .... 90 B3
Ashfield Av *WICK/BNPF* NE16... 8 A8
Ashfield Cl *ELS/FEN* NE4 .... 4 D8 ⑥
Ashfield Ct *ROWG* NE39 .... 96 C1
Ashfield Gdns *WLSD/HOW* NE28.. 58 B7
Ashfield Gv *NSHW* NE29 .... 2 C1 ⑥
  WBAY NE26 .... 50 E3
Ashfield Pk *WICK/BNPF* NE16... 85 F7
Ashfield Ri *WICK/BNPF* NE16 ... 85 F7
Ashfield Rd *GOS/KPK* NE3 ...... 56 A6
  WICK/BNPF NE16 .... 85 F7
Ashford *WD/WHPE/BLK* NE5 ... 68 E3 ⑥
Ashford Cl *BLYTH* NE24 .... 35 C2 ⑤
Ashford Dr *BDN/LAN/SAC* DH7.. 143 G4
Ashford Gv *RDHAMSE* DH6 ..... 172 D6
  WD/WHPE/BLK NE5 .... 53 K6 ⑥
Ashford Rd *SUNDSW* SR3 ...... 119 H7 ⑥
Ash Gv *CLDN/WHIT/ROK* SR6 .. 93 G4 ⑥
  DUN/TMV NE11 .... 8 F6
  MPTH NE61 .... 20 C6
  RYTON NE40 .... 66 E5
  TRIM TS29 .... 183 F6 ⑥
  WLSD/HOW NE28 .... 73 F1
Ashgrove Av *HAR/WTLS* NE34 .. 75 K4
Ashington Dr *STKFD/GP* NE62 .. 23 F5
Ashkirk *CRAM* NE23 .... 47 G1
Ashkirk Cl *CLSW/PEL* DH2 ...... 129 C6
Ashkirk Wy *MONK* NE25 .... 40 A6
Ashleigh Av *DHAM* DH1 .... 156 C4
Ashleigh Cl *BLAY* NE21 .... 84 B3
Ashleigh Gdns
  WD/WHPE/BLK NE5 .... 68 E3 ⑥
Ashleigh Gv *BDN/LAN/SAC* DH7.. 140 A4
  CLDN/WHIT/ROK SR6 .... 106 E1
  JES NE2 .... 70 D1
  LGB/KIL NE12................... 57 K3
  TYNE/NSHE NE30 .... 61 G2
Ashleigh Rd *WD/WHPE/BLK* NE5.. 68 E3
  WASHS NE38 .... 117 F3
Ashley Cl *LGB/KIL* NE12 .... 48 B5
Ashley Gdns *STKFD/GP* NE62 .. 23 G3
Ashley Rd *HAR/WTLS* NE34 ..... 75 C5
Ashley Ter *CLS/BIR/GTL* DH3 ... 129 J3
Ashmead Cl *LGB/KIL* NE12 ..... 48 A5
Ash Mdw *CLS/BIR/GTL* DH3 .... 116 A7
Ashmore St *ASHBK/HED/RY* SR2.. 14 E8
Ashridge Cl *HAR/WTLS* NE34 ... 76 C3
Ashridge Ct *FELL* NE10 .... 88 D5 ⑥
Ash St *BLAY* NE21 .... 84 A3
  CON/LDGT DH8.................. 123 F5
Ash Tree Dr *BDLGTN* NE22 ..... 29 F4
Ashtree La *BLAY* NE21 .... 82 E7
Ashtrees Gdns
  LWF/SPW/WRK NE9 .... 11 H9
Ash Tree Ter *BDN/LAN/SAC* DH7.. 142 C1 ⑥
Ashvale Av *DUN/TMV* NE11 ..... 100 C7
Ashwell Rd *SUNDSW* SR3 ...... 119 H7 ⑥
Ashwood *RDHAMSE* DH6 .... 161 F3
Ashwood Av *SWCK/CAS* SR5 ... 105 K3
Ashwood Cl *CRAM* NE23 .... 33 H5
  LGB/KIL NE12................... 58 A2 ⑥
Ashwood Crs
  BYK/HTN/WLK NE6 .... 72 B3 ⑥
Ashwood Cft *HEBB* NE31 .... 73 F4 ⑥
Ashwood Gdns
  LWF/SPW/WRK NE9 .... 101 G3
Ashwood Gv *DIN/WO* NE13 .... 46 B4
  SWCK/CAS SR5 .... 105 F4 ⑥
Ashwood Ter
  ASHBK/HED/RY SR2 .... 14 B8
Askern Av
  ASHBK/HED/RY SR2 .... 121 C5 ⑥
Askerton Dr *PLEE/EAS* SR8 ..... 174 B7
Askew Rd *GATE* NE8 .... 10 D3
Askew Rd West *GATE* NE8 ...... 10 C4
Askrigg Av *ASHBK/HED/RY* SR2.. 121 F5 ⑥
  WLSD/HOW NE28 .... 59 F3
Aspen Cl *DHAM* DH1 .... 17 M1 ⑥
Aspen Ct *SUNDSW* SR3 .... 133 J1 ⑥
Aspley Cl *SUNDSW* SR3 .... 134 A1
Asquith St *RDHAMSE* DH6 ..... 172 D6 ⑥
Association Rd
  CLDN/WHIT/ROK SR6 .... 106 E3 ⑥
Aster Pl *ELS/FEN* NE4 .... 69 G4
Astley Dr *WBAY* NE26 .... 50 C1
Astley Gdns *MONK* NE25 .... 39 K5 ⑥
  WBAY NE26 .... 40 E1
Astley Gv *WBAY* NE26 .... 40 E1
Astley Rd *MONK* NE25 .... 39 K4
Aston Sq *SUNDSW* SR3 .... 119 H7 ⑥
Aston St *SSH* NE33 .... 75 H4
Athelhampton Rigg
  ASHBK/HED/RY SR2 .... 121 G2 ⑥
Athenaeum St *SUND* SR1 .... 14 F5
Atherton Dr *ELS/FEN* NE4 ...... 69 J7
  HLS DH4 .... 146 D1
Athlone Pl *CLS/BIR/GTL* DH3 ... 115 K5 ⑤
Athol Gdns *ASHBK/HED/RY* SR2.. 120 C3
  MONK NE25 .... 50 B6
Athol Gn *DUN/TMV* NE11 .... 9 H8
Athol Gv *SUNDSW* SR3 .... 120 A7 ⑤
Atholl Gdns *LWF/SPW/WRK* NE9.. 11 M9
Athol Rd *ASHBK/HED/RY* SR2 .. 120 C3
Athol St *DUN/TMV* NE11 .... 9 J5 ⑥
Athol Ter *ASHBK/HED/RY* SR2 .. 121 F3
Athull *CLSW/PEL* DH2............ 115 F4
Atkinson Gv *NSHW* NE29 .... 2 D7
Atkinson Gv *RDHAMSE* DH6 ... 173 G3
Atkinson Rd
  CLDN/WHIT/ROK SR6 .... 106 D1 ⑥
  CLS/BIR/GTL DH3 .... 129 K2
  ELS/FEN NE4 .... 69 H7
Atkinson St *WLSD/HOW* NE28 .. 72 D2 ⑥
Atkinson Ter *ELS/FEN* NE4 ...... 69 H6 ⑥

  WLSD/HOW NE28 .... 72 D2
Atkin St *LGB/KIL* NE12 .... 47 H4
Atlantis Rd *SUNDSW* SR3 ...... 119 G6
Atley Wy *CRAM* NE23 .... 32 E5
Attlee Cl *CRAM* NE23 .... 47 H4 ⑥
Attlee Gv *ASHBK/HED/RY* SR2 .. 120 E6
Attwood Gv *SWCK/CAS* SR5 ... 106 B4 ⑥
Aubone Av
  BW/LEM/TK/HW NE15 .... 69 G5 ⑥
Auburn Cl *WLSD/HOW* NE28 ... 73 J1
Auburn Gdns *ELS/FEN* NE4 ..... 69 J3
Auckland *CLSW/PEL* DH2 .... 129 F5
Auckland Av *HAR/WTLS* NE34 .. 76 B5
Auckland Rd *DHAM* DH1 .... 156 E2
  HEBB NE31 .... 73 H4
Auckland Ter *JRW* NE32 .... 74 C7
Auden Gv *ELS/FEN* NE4 .... 69 J5
Audley Gdns *SUNDSW* SR3 .... 120 B3
Audley Rd *GOS/KPK* NE3 .... 56 E6
Augusta Ct *WLSD/HOW* NE28 .. 59 G4
Augusta Sq *SUNDSW* SR3 ...... 119 H7
Augustine Cl *DHAM* DH1 .... 156 B3
August Pl *SSH* NE33 .... 3 K9
  SSH NE33........................ 75 J2 ⑥
Augustus Dr *BDLGTN* NE22 .... 28 E4
Austen Av *HAR/WTLS* NE34 .... 91 F1
Austen Pl *STLY/ANP* DH9 .... 126 E3
Austin Sq *SWCK/CAS* SR5 ...... 106 B3
Australia Gv *HAR/WTLS* NE34 .. 90 D1
Austral Pl *DIN/WO* NE13 .... 46 A4 ⑥
Auton Stile *BDN/LAN/SAC* DH7.. 155 F6
Autumn Cl *WASHS* NE38 .... 103 F7
Avalon Dr *BW/LEM/TK/HW* NE15.. 68 C3 ⑥
Avalon Rd *SUNDSW* SR3 .... 119 H6
Avebury Av *STKFD/GP* NE62 ... 23 G6
Avebury Pl *CRAM* NE23 .... 33 J6
Avenue Rd *GATE* NE8 .... 11 G8
  MONK NE25 .... 39 K6
Avenue Ter *ASHBK/HED/RY* SR2.. 14 D8
The Avenue *ASHBK/HED/RY* SR2.. 14 D8
  BDN/LAN/SAC DH7 .... 141 H3
  BLAY NE21 .... 84 C2
  CLS/BIR/GTL DH3 .... 115 J2
  CLS/BIR/GTL DH3 .... 131 G2
  CLSW/PEL DH2 .... 129 H4
  DHAM DH1 .... 16 A5
  DHAM DH1 .... 156 B2
  DHAM DH1 .... 168 B1
  HLH DH5 .... 148 A4
  LWF/SPW/WRK NE9 .... 87 G5
  MONK NE25 .... 40 A4
  MPTH NE61 .... 26 D1
  PONT/DH NE20 .... 52 A1
  RDHAMSE DH6 .... 180 D7
  ROWG NE39 .... 97 H4
  SEA/MUR SR7................... 150 B1
  STLY/ANP DH9 .... 125 G4
  WASHS NE38 .... 117 G1
  WBAY NE26 .... 50 D3
  WLSD/HOW NE28 .... 72 D2
Avenue Vivian *HLS* DH4 .... 131 H6
Aviemore Rd *BOL* NE36 .... 91 F5
Avis Av *NWBGN* NE64 .... 24 D7
Avison St *ELS/FEN* NE4 .... 4 E6
Avocet Cl *BLYTH* NE24 .... 35 G4
Avolon Pl *ELS/FEN* NE4 .... 4 E5
Avon Av *JRW* NE32 .... 90 A2
  NSHW NE29 .... 60 C6
Avon Cl *ROWG* NE39 .... 97 H2
  WLSD/HOW NE28 .... 59 F4
Avon Ct *MONK* NE25 .... 40 A3
Avon Crs *HLS* DH4 .... 131 J7
Avoncroft Cl *SEA/MUR* SR7 .... 134 D7
Avondale *MLFD/PNYW* SR4 .... 118 E1
Avondale Av *BLYTH* NE24 ...... 30 A6
  HLS DH4 .... 117 K7
  LGB/KIL NE12................... 57 K2
Avondale Cl *BLYTH* NE24 .... 30 B6
Avondale Gdns *ASHGTN* NE63 .. 24 C4
  BOL NE36 .... 90 E5 ⑥
Avondale Rd *BYK/HTN/WLK* NE6.. 7 H6
  CON/LDGT DH8.................. 123 F4
  PONT/DH NE20 .... 42 C6
Avondale Ter *CLSW/PEL* DH2 ... 129 J4
  GATE NE8 .... 10 E7
Avonlea Wy
  WD/WHPE/BLK NE5 .... 55 G7 ⑥
Avonmouth Rd *SUNDSW* SR3 .. 119 G7
Avonmouth Sq *SUNDSW* SR3 .. 119 H7
Avon Rd *HEBB* NE31 .... 73 G7
  PLEE/EAS SR8.................. 174 D5
  STLY/ANP DH9 .... 126 D2
Avon St *GATE* NE8 .... 11 K6
  SUND SR1 .... 15 J6
Awnless Ct *HAR/WTLS* NE34 ... 75 C6 ⑥
Axbridge Cl *STKFD/GP* NE62 ... 23 G6
Axbridge Gdns *ELS/FEN* NE4 ... 69 J7
Axminster Cl *CRAM* NE23 .... 33 J6
Axwell Dr *BLYTH* NE24 .... 30 D7
Axwell Park Rd *BLAY* NE21 ..... 84 C3
Axwell Park Vw
  BW/LEM/TK/HW NE15 .... 69 F6
Axwell Vw *BLAY* NE21 .... 84 A3
  WICK/BNPF NE16 .... 84 E5 ⑥
Aycliffe Av *LWF/SPW/WRK* NE9.. 101 K1
Aycliffe Crs
  LWF/SPW/WRK NE9 .... 101 K1
Aydon Gv *JRW* NE32............. 89 K1
Aykley Ct *DHAM* DH1 .... 156 B5 ⑥
Aykley Gn *DHAM* DH1 .... 156 B5
Aykley Rd *DHAM* DH1 .... 156 C3
Aykley V *DHAM* DH1 .... 156 B4
Aylesbury Dr *SUNDSW* SR3 .... 134 A2
Aylesbury Pl *LGB/KIL* NE12 ..... 57 H3 ⑥
Aylesford Sq *BLYTH* NE24 ...... 35 G2 ⑥
Aylsham Cl *WD/WHPE/BLK* NE5.. 53 K6
Aylsham Ct *SUNDSW* SR3 ...... 134 A3
Aylyth Pl *GOS/KPK* NE3 .... 55 K7 ⑥
Aynsley Ter *CON/LDGT* DH8 .... 123 F4
Ayr Dr *JRW* NE32 .... 90 B1
Ayre's Quay Rd *SUND* SR1 ..... 14 C4 ⑥
Ayre's Ter *NSHW* NE29 .... 2 C1 ⑥
Ayrey Av *HAR/WTLS* NE34 ...... 74 D7
Aysgarth Av
  ASHBK/HED/RY SR2 .... 121 F4
  WLSD/HOW NE28 .... 59 F3

Ayton Av ASHBK/HED/RY SR2 121 F5
Ayton Cl PSHWF NE43 79 H6
WD/WHPE/BLK NE5 54 C7
Ayton Ct BDLGTN NE22 28 D4
Ayton Rd WASHS NE38 116 B2
Ayton St BYK/HTN/WLK NE6 7 H7
Azalea Av ASHBK/HED/RY SR2 14 D8
Azalea Ter North
ASHBK/HED/RY SR2 14 D7
Azalea Ter South
ASHBK/HED/RY SR2 14 D8

B

Back Bridge St SUND SR1 14 E4
Back Croft Rd BLYTH NE24 31 G7 2
Back East Pde CON/LDGT DH8 123 G5
Back George St ELS/FEN NE4 5 G9
Back Goldspink La JES NE2 6 B1
Back Heaton Park Rd
BYK/HTN/WLK NE6 6 E4
Back La BLAY NE21 83 K2
CLS/BIR/GTL DH3 145 H1
CON/LDGT DH8 124 B5
HLS DH4 117 K6
MONK NE25 50 C4
Back Lodge Ter SUND SR1 15 K5
Back Mitford St ELS/FEN NE4 9 M2 1
Back New Bridge St CNUT NE1 6 A5
Back North Bridge St
SWCK/CAS SR5 14 E1
Back North Railway St
SEA/MUR SR7 135 K7
Back North Ter SEA/MUR SR7 135 K7
Back Palmerston St
CON/LDGT DH8 123 F5
Back Percy Gdns
TYNE/NSHE NE30 61 H2 2
Back Rw WICK/BNPF NE16 84 E5
Back Ryhope St
ASHBK/HED/RY SR2 120 E7
Back Silver St DHAM DH1 16 D4
Back South Railway St
SEA/MUR SR7 150 E1
Back Stephen St
BYK/HTN/WLK NE6 6 D5
Backstone Burn
CON/LDGT DH8 122 C2
Backstone Rd CON/LDGT DH8 122 B3
Back St BLAY NE21 83 K3 1
Back Walker Rd
BYK/HTN/WLK NE6 72 C7 1
Back Western Hl DHAM DH1 16 A2
Back Woodbine St GATE NE8 10 D5
Backworth La CRAM NE23 48 B1
Baden Crs SWCK/CAS SR5 104 E2
Baden Powell St
LWF/SPW/WRK NE9 11 J9
Baden St CLS/BIR/GTL DH3 129 J5
Badger Cl SUNDSW SR3 134 A2
Badgers Gn MPTH NE61 20 B3
Badminton Cl BOLCOL NE35 90 B3 1
Baffin Ct SUNDSW SR3 133 K1
Baildon Cl WLSD/HOW NE28 58 E6 1
Bailey Ri PLEE/EAS SR8 174 E2
Bailey Sq SWCK/CAS SR5 104 E1 1
Bailey Wy HLH DH5 148 A6
Bainbridge Av HAR/WTLS NE34 74 D7
SUNDSW SR3 120 B3
Bainbridge Holme Cl
SUNDSW SR3 120 B3
Bainbridge Holme Rd
SUNDSW SR3 120 C3
Bainbridge St DHAM DH1 158 A4
Bainford Av
BW/LEM/TK/HW NE15 68 E5
Baird Av WLSD/HOW NE28 74 A1
Baird Cl WASHN NE37 103 G3
Baird St SWCK/CAS SR5 104 E2 1
Bakehouse La DHAM DH1 16 F2
Baker Gdns FELL NE10 13 L7
Baker Rd CRAM NE23 32 D6
Baker St HLH DH5 132 C6
SWCK/CAS SR5 104 E2
Bakewell Ter BYK/HTN/WLK NE6 7 K9
Baldersdale Gdns SUNDSW SR3 120 B4
Baldwin Av BOL NE36 91 H5
ELS/FEN NE4 4 A3 1
Balfour Rd
BW/LEM/TK/HW NE15 68 E6
Balfour St BLYTH NE24 31 F5
CON/LDGT DH8 123 F3
GATE NE8 10 D7
HLH DH5 132 C6
Balgonie Cottages RYTON NE40 66 E6
Baliol Rd PSHWF NE43 79 G5
Baliol Sq DHAM DH1 168 B3
Balkwell Av NSHW NE29 60 B5
Balkwell Gn NSHW NE29 60 C4
Ballast Hl BLYTH NE24 31 H6 1
Ballast Hill Rd NSHW NE29 2 D7
Ballater Cl STLY/ANP DH9 127 F1
Balliol Av LGB/KIL NE12 57 J1
Balliol Cl PLEE/EAS SR8 174 C4
Balliol Gdns LGB/HTN NE7 57 H5 1
Balmain Rd GOS/KPK NE3 55 J6
Balmoral Av GOS/KPK NE3 56 E6 2
JRW NE32 90 C1 1
Balmoral Cl BDLGTN NE22 29 J4
Balmoral Ct SWCK/CAS SR5 104 E2 2
Balmoral Crs HLH DH5 147 J1
Balmoral Dr FELL NE10 12 A8
Balmoral Gdns NSHW NE29 60 D3
Balmoral St WLSD/HOW NE28 72 D1
Balmoral Ter
ASHBK/HED/RY SR2 121 F4
BYK/HTN/WLK NE6 6 F2
GOS/KPK NE3 56 E6
SUNDSW SR3 119 G7
Balmoral Wy FELL NE10 12 A9
Balroy Ct LGB/KIL NE12 58 A2
Baltic Millennium Br CNUT NE1 6 A8
Baltic Rd FELL NE10 12 C2
Baltimore Av SWCK/CAS SR5 104 C1
Baltimore Sq SWCK/CAS SR5 104 D2
Bamborough Ct CRAM NE23 47 F1 1
Bamborough Ter
TYNE/NSHE NE30 60 E3
Bambro' St
ASHBK/HED/RY SR2 15 H8 1
Bamburgh Av SSH NE33 75 K2
Bamburgh Cl BLYTH NE24 30 E7
WASHS NE38 116 C1
Bamburgh Ct DUN/TMV NE11 86 C6
Bamburgh Dr FELL NE10 13 M3
MPTH NE61 21 K2
WLSD/HOW NE28 73 H1
Bamburgh Gdns
SUNDSW SR3 120 B3 1
Bamburgh Gv HAR/WTLS NE34 76 B3
Bamburgh Rd DHAM DH1 156 D2
LGB/KIL NE12 58 B2
WD/WHPE/BLK NE5 54 C7 1
Bamburgh Ter ASHGTN NE63 23 J2
Bampton Av
CLDN/WHIT/ROK SR6 92 C7
Banbury WASHN NE37 103 G5
Banbury Gdns
WLSD/HOW NE28 59 F5 1
Banbury Rd GOS/KPK NE3 55 K4
Banbury Ter SSH NE33 75 H3
Banbury Wy BLYTH NE24 35 F2
NSHW NE29 60 B6
Bancroft Ter MLFD/PNYW SR4 105 K7
Banesley La DUN/TMV NE11 100 B4
Banff St SWCK/CAS SR5 104 E1
Bank Av WICK/BNPF NE16 84 E5
Bankdale Gdns BLYTH NE24 30 C7
Bankhead Rd
BW/LEM/TK/HW NE15 67 H2 1
Bankhead Ter HLS DH4 131 J6
Bank Rd GATE NE8 6 A9
Banks Holt CLSW/PEL DH2 129 F5 1
Bankside MPTH NE61 20 E5
Bankside Cl
ASHBK/HED/RY SR2 120 E7
Bankside La HAR/WTLS NE34 75 G6
Bankside Rd
BW/LEM/TK/HW NE15 68 D6
Bank Top RYTON NE40 82 A1
Bankwell La GATE NE8 5 M9
Bannister Dr LGB/KIL NE12 58 B2
Bannockburn LGB/KIL NE12 47 K5 1
Barbara St ASHBK/HED/RY SR2 121 F3
Barbary Cl CLSW/PEL DH2 114 E7
Barbary Dr
CLDN/WHIT/ROK SR6 107 F3
Barbondale Lonnen
WD/WHPE/BLK NE5 68 A2
Barbour Av HAR/WTLS NE34 76 A4
Barclay Pl WD/WHPE/BLK NE5 69 F2
Barclay St SWCK/CAS SR5 14 E2
Barcusclose La
WICK/BNPF NE16 98 A7
Bardolph Rd NSHW NE29 60 B4
Bardon Cl
WD/WHPE/BLK NE5 54 D6 1
Bardon Crs MONK NE25 40 C6 1
Barehirst St SSH NE33 75 F4
Barents Cl
WD/WHPE/BLK NE5 68 D1 1
Baret Rd BYK/HTN/WLK NE6 7 M1
Barford Dr CLSW/PEL DH2 129 G6
Bargate Bank
BDN/LAN/SAC DH7 140 C7
Baring St SSH NE33 3 H4
Barker St JES NE2 6 A4
Barking Crs SWCK/CAS SR5 104 D2
Barking Sq SWCK/CAS SR5 104 D2 1
Barkwood Rd ROWG NE39 97 F3
Barley Mill Crs CON/LDGT DH8 122 B3
Barley Mill Rd CON/LDGT DH8 122 B3
Barlow Crs BLAY NE21 82 E6 1
Barlow Fell Rd BLAY NE21 82 E7
Barlowfield Cl BLAY NE21 83 J4 1
Barlow La BLAY NE21 83 F6
Barmoor La RYTON NE40 66 D6
Barmouth Cl
WLSD/HOW NE28 59 F5 2
Barmouth Rd NSHW NE29 60 A5
Barmouth Wy NSHW NE29 60 B6
Barmston La WASHN NE37 104 A7
WASHS NE38 117 K1
Barmston Rd WASHS NE38 117 J2
Barmston Wy WASHS NE38 103 H7
Barnard Av RDHAMSE DH6 172 B3
Barnard Cl BDLGTN NE22 28 D5
DHAM DH1 156 E2
Barnard Crs HEBB NE31 73 G4
Barnard Gv JRW NE32 74 B7 1
Barnard St BLYTH NE24 31 G7 3
MLFD/PNYW SR4 119 K1
Barnard Wynd PLEE/EAS SR8 174 C7
Barnesbury Rd ELS/FEN NE4 69 J6
Barnes Park Rd
MLFD/PNYW SR4 120 A2
Barnes Rd SEA/MUR SR7 149 G5
SSH NE33 75 F3 1
Barnes St HLH DH5 147 K4 1
Barnes Vw MLFD/PNYW SR4 119 K2
Barn Hl STLY/ANP DH9 112 C7
Barn Hollows SEA/MUR SR7 162 D2
Barningham WASHS NE38 117 J2
Barningham Cl SUNDSW SR3 120 B4
Barns Cl JRW NE32 73 J7
Barnstaple Cl
WLSD/HOW NE28 59 F5 3
Barnstaple Rd NSHW NE29 60 A2
The Barns STLY/ANP DH9 112 C6
Barnston ASHGTN NE63 24 D2
Barnton Rd FELL NE10 88 A6
Barnwood Cl
WLSD/HOW NE28 58 E5 1
Baroness Dr
BW/LEM/TK/HW NE15 68 E4
Baron's Quay Rd
SWCK/CAS SR5 105 F5
Baronswood GOS/KPK NE3 56 B6
Barrack Rd ELS/FEN NE4 4 E3
Barrack St SUND SR1 15 J2
Barras Av BLYTH NE24 35 F2
CRAM NE23 38 C7
Barras Av West BLYTH NE24 34 E3
Barras Br CNUT NE1 5 K4
Barras Dr SUNDSW SR3 120 B4
Barrasford Cl ASHGTN NE63 23 G3
GOS/KPK NE3 56 A6
Barrasford Dr DIN/WO NE13 46 C4
Barrasford Rd CRAM NE23 38 D3 1
DHAM DH1 156 E3
Barrasford St
WLSD/HOW NE28 74 A2 1
Barrass Av CRAM NE23 39 F7
Barr Cl WLSD/HOW NE28 59 G5
Barr Hills CON/LDGT DH8 123 F4 1
Barr House Av
CON/LDGT DH8 123 F4 2
Barrie Sq SWCK/CAS SR5 106 B3
Barrington Av TYNE/NSHE NE30 50 D7
Barrington Ct BDLGTN NE22 29 G6 1
Barrington Dr WASHS NE38 117 F1
Barrington Pk BDLGTN NE22 30 B3
Barrington Rd BDLGTN NE22 29 J3
STKFD/GP NE62 29 F3
Barrington St SSH NE33 3 G7
Barrington Ter HLH DH5 147 K3 2
Barrington Wy RDHAMSE DH6 180 A2
Barron St South
SWCK/CAS SR5 105 G4 1
Barrowburn Pl CRAM NE23 39 H7
Barrow St SWCK/CAS SR5 104 E1 2
Barry St DUN/TMV NE11 9 H6
GATE NE8 86 D5
Barsloan Gv PLEE/EAS SR8 174 C2 1
Barton Cl TYNE/NSHE NE30 61 F1
WASHN NE37 103 G3
WLSD/HOW NE28 59 F5 4
Barton Ct
CLDN/WHIT/ROK SR6 92 C7 1
Bartram St SWCK/CAS SR5 106 C2
Barwell Cl WLSD/HOW NE28 59 F5
Barwell Ct LGB/HTN NE7 58 A7
Basildon Gdns
WLSD/HOW NE28 58 E5 2
Basil Wy HAR/WTLS NE34 91 J1
Basingstoke Pl LGB/KIL NE12 57 J3
Basingstoke Rd
PLEE/EAS SR8 174 D3 1
Baslow Gdns SUNDSW SR3 120 B3
Bassington Av CRAM NE23 37 K1
Bassington Dr CRAM NE23 32 D7
Bassington La CRAM NE23 32 D7
Bates La BLAY NE21 84 D2
Bath Cl WLSD/HOW NE28 59 G5
Bathgate Cl WLSD/HOW NE28 59 G5
Bathgate Sq SWCK/CAS SR5 104 D2 2
Bath La BLYTH NE24 31 H7
CNUT NE1 5 H7
CON/LDGT DH8 123 F4
Bath Lane Ter ELS/FEN NE4 4 F7
Bath Rd FELL NE10 12 C4
HEBB NE31 89 G1 1
Bath St BYK/HTN/WLK NE6 72 C6
Bath Ter BLYTH NE24 31 H7
GOS/KPK NE3 56 D5
TYNE/NSHE NE30 61 H3
Batley St SWCK/CAS SR5 104 D2 3
Batt House Rd PSHWF NE43 79 F7
Battle Hill Dr WLSD/HOW NE28 58 D6
WLSD/HOW NE28 59 H5
Baugh Cl WASHN NE37 102 C7
Baulkham Hills HLS DH4 131 K1
Bavington FELL NE10 88 C7 1
Bavington Dr
WD/WHPE/BLK NE5 69 G2
Bavington Gdns
TYNE/NSHE NE30 60 E1
Bavington Rd MONK NE25 40 A5
Bawtry Gv NSHW NE29 60 C5
Baxter Av ELS/FEN NE4 69 J5
Baxter Rd SWCK/CAS SR5 104 D1
Baxter Sq SWCK/CAS SR5 104 D1 1
Bay Av PLEE/EAS SR8 175 J4
Baybridge Rd
WD/WHPE/BLK NE5 54 C7 2
Baysdale HLS DH4 117 G6 1
Bayswater Av SWCK/CAS SR5 104 E2
Bayswater Rd GATE NE8 11 L7
JES NE2 70 E1
Bayswater Sq SWCK/CAS SR5 104 E2 3
Baytree Gdns MONK NE25 50 C6
Baytree Ter STLY/ANP DH9 114 B7
Baywood Gv
WLSD/HOW NE28 58 E5 3
Beach Av WBAY NE26 50 E4
Beach Croft Av
TYNE/NSHE NE30 51 F7
Beachcross Rd
MLFD/PNYW SR4 14 A7 1
Beachdale Cl WNGT TS28 184 A6
Beach Gv PLEE/EAS SR8 175 H4
Beach Rd NSHW NE29 60 C3
SSH NE33 3 K8
TYNE/NSHE NE30 60 E2
Beach St MLFD/PNYW SR4 14 B2
Beach Ter NWBGN NE64 25 F3
Beachville St
MLFD/PNYW SR4 14 A7 2
Beachway BLYTH NE24 35 H3
Beach Wy TYNE/NSHE NE30 60 E1
Beacon Dr
CLDN/WHIT/ROK SR6 107 F4
DIN/WO NE13 46 A4
Beacon Gld HAR/WTLS NE34 76 C5
Beacon La CRAM NE23 37 J2
Beacon Lough Rd
LWF/SPW/WRK NE9 101 G1
Beaconsfield Av
LWF/SPW/WRK NE9 87 G7
Beaconsfield Cl MONK NE25 50 B2
Beaconsfield Crs
LWF/SPW/WRK NE9 87 G7 1
Beaconsfield Rd
LWF/SPW/WRK NE9 87 F7
Beaconsfield St BLYTH NE24 31 H6 2
CON/LDGT DH8 123 F3
ELS/FEN NE4 4 D5
STLY/ANP DH9 112 D7 2
Beaconside HAR/WTLS NE34 76 C5
Beacon St LWF/SPW/WRK NE9 87 F7
SSH NE33 3 H3
TYNE/NSHE NE30 2 F1
Beadling Gdns ELS/FEN NE4 69 J5
Beadnell Av NSHW NE29 60 B6
Beadnell Cl BLAY NE21 83 J4
Beadnell Gdns SMOOR NE27 49 H6
Beadnell Pl JES NE2 6 A5
Beadnell Rd BLYTH NE24 34 D2
Beadnell Wy GOS/KPK NE3 56 A4 2
Beal Cl BLYTH NE24 30 E7
Beal Dr LGB/KIL NE12 58 B2
Beal Gdns WLSD/HOW NE28 59 H5
Beal Rd SMOOR NE27 49 H6
Beal Ter BYK/HTN/WLK NE6 72 B7
Beal Wk DHAM DH1 169 J5
Beal Wy GOS/KPK NE3 56 B5
Beaminster Wy GOS/KPK NE3 55 G5
WD/WHPE/BLK NE5 55 G5
Beamishburn Rd
STLY/ANP DH9 112 E5
Beamish Cl
BDN/LAN/SAC DH7 154 A3 1
WLSD/HOW NE28 58 E5 4
Beamish Gdns
LWF/SPW/WRK NE9 101 K1
Beamish Hills STLY/ANP DH9 113 H7
Beamish St STLY/ANP DH9 112 C7 1
Beamish Vw CLSW/PEL DH2 128 B4
STLY/ANP DH9 113 F7
Beaney La CLSW/PEL DH2 144 A2
Beanley Av HEBB NE31 73 F7
Beanley Crs TYNE/NSHE NE30 61 G3
Beanley Pl LGB/HTN NE7 57 G7
Bearpark Colliery Rd
BDN/LAN/SAC DH7 155 G6
Beatrice Av BLYTH NE24 34 D3 1
Beatrice Gdns BOL NE36 91 H5 1
HAR/WTLS NE34 75 J5
Beatrice St
CLDN/WHIT/ROK SR6 106 E4
Beatrice Ter HLS DH4 117 G5
Beattie St HAR/WTLS NE34 75 F6 1
Beatty Av JES NE2 56 E7
Beatty Rd BDLGTN NE22 29 H6
Beaufort Cl HLS DH4 131 K2 1
WD/WHPE/BLK NE5 55 H7 1
Beaufort Gdns
WLSD/HOW NE28 58 E5 5
Beaufront Cl FELL NE10 88 D6 2
Beaufront Gdns GATE NE8 11 L5
WD/WHPE/BLK NE5 69 G3
Beaufront Ter JRW NE32 89 K1
SSH NE33 75 G3 1
Beauly WASHS NE38 117 F3 1
Beaumaris Gdns SUNDSW SR3 119 G7
Beaumaris Wy
WD/WHPE/BLK NE5 55 F6
Beaumont Cl DHAM DH1 156 B2
RDHAMSE DH6 180 A3
Beaumont Crs PLEE/EAS SR8 175 F1
Beaumont Dr MONK NE25 50 A2
WASHS NE38 117 F2
Beaumont Mnr BLYTH NE24 30 B7
Beaumont Pl PLEE/EAS SR8 175 F5 1
Beaumont St
ASHBK/HED/RY SR2 15 G9
BLYTH NE24 31 F6
ELS/FEN NE4 9 G1
NSHW NE29 2 C2 1
SEA/MUR SR7 150 E2 1
SWCK/CAS SR5 106 A2
Beaumont Ter GOS/KPK NE3 56 D5
JRW NE32 73 J6
WD/WHPE/BLK NE5 68 D1
Beaumont Wy PRUD NE42 80 B3
Beaurepaire BDN/LAN/SAC DH7 155 F6
Beaver Cl DHAM DH1 156 D1
Bebdon Ct BLYTH NE24 34 E1 2
Bebside Furnace Rd
BLYTH NE24 29 K6
Bebside Rd BLYTH NE24 29 J7
Beckenham Av BOL NE36 91 H4
Beckenham Cl BOL NE36 91 J4 1
Beckenham Gdns
WLSD/HOW NE28 58 E6
Beckett St GATE NE8 6 D9
Beckfoot Cl WD/WHPE/BLK NE5 69 F2
Beckford WASHS NE38 117 J2
Beckford Cl WLSD/HOW NE28 58 E5 6
Beck Pl PLEE/EAS SR8 174 E3
Beckside Gdns
WD/WHPE/BLK NE5 67 K2
Beckwith Rd SUNDSW SR3 119 G6
Beda Hl BLAY NE21 84 A1
Bedale Cl DHAM DH1 158 A5
WLSD/HOW NE28 58 E5 7
Bedale Crs SWCK/CAS SR5 104 E2
Bedale Dr MONK NE25 50 D6
Bedale Gn WD/WHPE/BLK NE5 55 H7
Bedale St HLH DH5 147 K6
Bedburn WASHS NE38 116 B5
Bede Burn Rd JRW NE32 73 K5 2
Bedeburn Rd
WD/WHPE/BLK NE5 54 D5
Bede Burn Vw JRW NE32 73 K6
Bede Cl LGB/KIL NE12 58 D2
Bede Ct CLS/BIR/GTL DH3 129 J4
GATE NE8 11 J4 1
Bede Crs WASHS NE38 102 E7
WLSD/HOW NE28 59 F6
Bede St CLDN/WHIT/ROK SR6 106 E3
PLEE/EAS SR8 163 G5
Bedesway JRW NE32 74 B5
Bede Ter BOL NE36 91 J5 1
CLSW/PEL DH2 129 H4
JRW NE32 74 A6 2
RDHAMSE DH6 180 A2
Bede Wk HEBB NE31 73 H6
Bede Wy DHAM DH1 156 C3 1
PLEE/EAS SR8 174 E4
Bedford Av CLS/BIR/GTL DH3 115 K5
SSH NE33 75 G2
WLSD/HOW NE28 58 C7
Bedford Pl SUNDSW SR3 120 A6 1
WD/WHPE/BLK NE5 68 A2 1
Bedfordshire Dr DHAM DH1 158 A7
Bedford St NSHW NE29 2 D2 1
SUND SR1 14 F3
Bedford Wy NSHW NE29 2 D2
Bedlington Bank BDLGTN NE22 29 G6
Beech Av CLDN/WHIT/ROK SR6 93 G3
CRAM NE23 38 E3
DIN/WO NE13 45 F2
GOS/KPK NE3 55 K4
HLS DH4 132 B6
MPTH NE61 21 F6
WICK/BNPF NE16 8 A8
Beech Cl DHAM DH1 157 F1
GOS/KPK NE3 56 D1 1
Beech Ct BDN/LAN/SAC DH7 154 B3
BW/LEM/TK/HW NE15 52 C2
PONT/DH NE20 52 C1
Beech Crs SEA/MUR SR7 150 D2
Beechcroft Av
BDN/LAN/SAC DH7 166 E7
GOS/KPK NE3 56 A7
Beechcroft Cl DHAM DH1 157 H6 1
Beechdale Rd CON/LDGT DH8 123 G4
Beech Dr DUN/TMV NE11 8 F6
Beecher St BLYTH NE24 30 D5
The Beeches PONT/DH NE20 43 F3
Beechfield Gdns
WLSD/HOW NE28 58 C7 1
Beechfield Ri RDHAMSE DH6 180 D6
Beechfield Rd GOS/KPK NE3 56 B6
Beech Gv BDN/LAN/SAC DH7 141 G4
BDN/LAN/SAC DH7 167 G1
HAR/WTLS NE34 75 K7
LGB/KIL NE12 57 K4
LWF/SPW/WRK NE9 102 B4
TRIM TS29 183 F6
WBAY NE26 50 D4
WLSD/HOW NE28 72 D1
Beech Grove Ct RYTON NE40 66 B7
Beech Grove Rd ELS/FEN NE4 4 C8
Beech Pk BDN/LAN/SAC DH7 167 F7
Beech Rd CON/LDGT DH8 123 K4 1
DHAM DH1 156 C4
RDHAMSE DH6 158 C7
Beech Sq WASHS NE38 117 G2 1
Beech St ELS/FEN NE4 69 J7
GATE NE8 11 L5
JRW NE32 73 J4
PSHWF NE43 79 J4
Beech Ter BLAY NE21 84 A3 1
STLY/ANP DH9 127 F4
Beech Wy LGB/KIL NE12 47 J5 2
Beechways DHAM DH1 156 A6
Beechwood Av
LWF/SPW/WRK NE9 101 G2
MONK NE25 50 B5
RYTON NE40 66 E6
STKFD/GP NE62 23 G5
Beechwood Cl JRW NE32 74 B5 1
Beechwood Crs SWCK/CAS SR5 105 K3
Beechwood Gdns
DUN/TMV NE11 86 B7
Beechwood Pl PONT/DH NE20 43 G2
Beechwoods CLSW/PEL DH2 129 H2
Beechwood St
ASHBK/HED/RY SR2 14 B7
Beechwood Ter
ASHBK/HED/RY SR2 14 B7
HLS DH4 132 A5
Beeston Av SWCK/CAS SR5 104 D2 4
Beetham Crs
WD/WHPE/BLK NE5 68 E3
Beethoven St SSH NE33 3 K9
Begonia Cl HEBB NE31 89 G1 2
Bek Rd DHAM DH1 156 D3
Beldene Dr MLFD/PNYW SR4 119 J2
Belford Av SMOOR NE27 49 H6
Belford Cl ASHBK/HED/RY SR2 120 D3
WLSD/HOW NE28 58 E5 8
Belford Gdns DUN/TMV NE11 86 A7 1
Belford Rd ASHBK/HED/RY SR2 120 E3
Belford St PLEE/EAS SR8 175 G2
Belford Ter BYK/HTN/WLK NE6 7 M6
TYNE/NSHE NE30 60 E3
The Belfry HLS DH4 131 J3
Belgrade Crs SWCK/CAS SR5 104 D1
Belgrade Sq SWCK/CAS SR5 104 D2 5
Belgrave Crs BLYTH NE24 31 H7
Belgrave Gdns ASHGTN NE63 24 C3
Belgrave Pde ELS/FEN NE4 4 E9
Belgrave Ter FELL NE10 12 D9
SSH NE33 3 K7
Bellburn Ct CRAM NE23 33 K7 1
Belle Gv West JES NE2 4 E2
Bellerby Dr CLSW/PEL DH2 114 E4 1
Belle St STLY/ANP DH9 112 D7
Belle View Dr CON/LDGT DH8 137 F2 1
Belle Vue Av GOS/KPK NE3 56 D5
Belle Vue Bank
LWF/SPW/WRK NE9 86 E7
Bellevue Crs CRAM NE23 33 H5 1
Belle Vue Crs SSH NE33 75 F5 1
Belle Vue Gdns CON/LDGT DH8 123 F4
Belle Vue Gv
LWF/SPW/WRK NE9 87 F7 3
Belle Vue Pk ASHBK/HED/RY SR2 14 C9
Belle Vue Rd
ASHBK/HED/RY SR2 120 C2
Bellfield Av GOS/KPK NE3 55 K4 1
Bellgreen Av GOS/KPK NE3 56 D1
Bell Gv LGB/KIL NE12 47 H5 1
Bell House Rd SWCK/CAS SR5 92 A7
Bellingham Cl
WLSD/HOW NE28 59 F6 1
Bellingham Ct GOS/KPK NE3 55 H5 1
Bellingham Dr LGB/KIL NE12 58 B3
Bellister Gv WD/WHPE/BLK NE5 69 G3
Bellister Pk PLEE/EAS SR8 175 F6
Bellister Rd NSHW NE29 60 B4 1
Bell Meadow
BDN/LAN/SAC DH7 167 F7
Belloc Av HAR/WTLS NE34 91 F1
Bellows Burn La RHTLP TS27 185 G6
Bell Rd WYLAM NE41 65 H5
Bellsburn Ct ASHGTN NE63 23 H3 1
Bells Cl BLYTH NE24 30 B6
BW/LEM/TK/HW NE15 68 C6
Bell's Folly DHAM DH1 168 B3
Bellshill Cl WLSD/HOW NE28 59 G4
Bell's Pl BDLGTN NE22 29 G6
Bell St HEBB NE31 73 F5
HLS DH4 117 K6

MLFD/PNYW SR4 105 K7 2
WASHS NE38 117 H2 1
Bell Vw PRUD NE42 81 F1
Belmont FELL NE10 88 C7
Belmont Av MONK NE25 50 B5
SEA/MUR SR7 162 C1
Belmont Cl WLSD/HOW NE28 59 F5
Belmont Ri HLH DH5 147 K7
Belmont Rd MLFD/PNYW SR4 119 K1
Belmont St BYK/HTN/WLK NE6 13 G1
Belmount Av GOS/KPK NE3 56 D1
Belper Cl WLSD/HOW NE28 58 E5 5
Belsay WASHS NE38 116 B2
Belsay Av DIN/WO NE13 46 A5 1
HAR/WTLS NE34 76 A4
MONK NE25 51 F5
Belsay Cl MPTH NE61 21 K2
WLSD/HOW NE28 58 E5 10
Belsay Ct BLYTH NE24 30 E7 1
Belsay Gdns DUN/TMV NE11 86 A7 2
GOS/KPK NE3 55 K2
MLFD/PNYW SR4 119 K1
Belsay Pl ELS/FEN NE4 4 C5
Belsfield Gdns JRW NE32 73 K7
Belsize Pl BYK/HTN/WLK NE6 72 B3
Beltingham
WD/WHPE/BLK NE5 68 C2 2
Belvedere NSHW NE29 60 D3
Belvedere Av MONK NE25 50 D5
Belvedere Gdns LGB/KIL NE12 57 K4 1
Belvedere Pkwy
GOS/KPK NE3 55 G4 1
Belvedere Rd
ASHBK/HED/RY SR2 14 D8
Belverdere Gdns
RDHAMSE DH6 173 G3
Bemersyde Dr JES NE2 56 E7
Benbrake Av NSHW NE29 60 C1
Bendigo Av HAR/WTLS NE34 90 D1 1
Benedict Rd
CLDN/WHIT/ROK SR6 107 F3
Benevente St SEA/MUR SR7 150 E2 2
Benfield Cl CON/LDGT DH8 122 C1
Benfield Gv WBAY NE26 40 E1
Benfield Rd BYK/HTN/WLK NE6 71 K1
Benfieldside Rd CON/LDGT DH8 122 C2
Benjamin Rd WLSD/HOW NE28 59 J7
Bennett's Wk MPTH NE61 20 E5
Benridge Bank HLS DH4 146 C6
Bensham Av GATE NE8 10 D6
Bensham Ct HAR/WTLS NE34 75 G6 3
Bensham Crs GATE NE8 10 B6
Bensham Rd GATE NE8 10 E3
Benson Rd BYK/HTN/WLK NE6 7 K5
Benson St CLS/BIR/GTL DH3 129 J5
STLY/ANP DH9 112 C7
Bent House La DHAM DH1 17 M7
Bentinck Crs MPTH NE61 21 J2
Bentinck Rd ELS/FEN NE4 4 B8
Bentinck St ELS/FEN NE4 4 B8
Benton Bank BYK/HTN/WLK NE6 71 G2
JES NE2 71 G2
Benton Cl LGB/HTN NE7 57 H5 2
Benton Hall Wk LGB/HTN NE7 71 K1 2
Benton La LGB/KIL NE12 57 H3
Benton Lodge Av
LGB/HTN NE7 57 J5 1
Benton Park Rd LGB/HTN NE7 57 F5
Benton Rd HAR/WTLS NE34 91 G2
LGB/HTN NE7 57 J5
SMOOR NE27 49 F7
Benton Wy WLSD/HOW NE28 72 D2 2
Bents Park Rd SSH NE33 3 M7
Benwell Dene Ter
BW/LEM/TK/HW NE15 69 G6
Benwell Grange Av
BW/LEM/TK/HW NE15 69 H6 2
Benwell Grange Rd
BW/LEM/TK/HW NE15 69 G6
Benwell Grange Ter
BW/LEM/TK/HW NE15 69 G6
Benwell Gv ELS/FEN NE4 69 J6
Benwell Hall Dr
BW/LEM/TK/HW NE15 69 F5 2
Benwell Hill Gdns
WD/WHPE/BLK NE5 69 G4 1
Benwell Hill Rd
WD/WHPE/BLK NE5 69 F4
Benwell La
BW/LEM/TK/HW NE15 69 F6 1
Benwell Village
BW/LEM/TK/HW NE15 69 F5
Benwell Village Ms
BW/LEM/TK/HW NE15 69 G5 2
Beresford Av HEBB NE31 89 G1
Beresford Gdns
BYK/HTN/WLK NE6 7 G7
Beresford Pk
ASHBK/HED/RY SR2 14 B8 1
Beresford Rd TYNE/NSHE NE30 50 E6
WBAY NE26 41 G3
Bergen Cl NSHW NE29 59 K6
Bergen Sq SWCK/CAS SR5 104 D1 2
Bergen St SWCK/CAS SR5 104 D1
Berkdale Rd
LWF/SPW/WRK NE9 100 E3
Berkeley Cl BOLCOL NE35 90 C3
LGB/KIL NE12 48 A5
SUNDSW SR3 119 G7 2
Berkeley Sq GOS/KPK NE3 56 B3 1
Berkely St SSH NE33 3 J8
Berkhamstead Ct FELL NE10 88 E5 1
Berkley Av BLAY NE21 84 C2
Berkley Cl WLSD/HOW NE28 59 F5
Berkley Rd NSHW NE29 60 B4 2
Berkley St
BW/LEM/TK/HW NE15 67 H3 1
Berkley Wy HEBB NE31 73 H3
Berkshire Cl DHAM DH1 157 K6 1
WD/WHPE/BLK NE5 68 D1
Berkshire Rd PLEE/EAS SR8 174 D2
Bermondsey St JES NE2 6 B5
Bernard St BYK/HTN/WLK NE6 72 C7
HLS DH4 132 B7
Berrington Dr
WD/WHPE/BLK NE5 55 F7
Berrishill Gv MONK NE25 50 A3
Berry Cl BYK/HTN/WLK NE6 72 C6
WLSD/HOW NE28 58 E5 11
Berry Edge Rd CON/LDGT DH8 123 F5
Berry Edge Vw CON/LDGT DH8 122 E4
Berryfield Cl SUNDSW SR3 134 A2
Berry Hl RYTON NE40 82 D3
Berryhill Cl BLAY NE21 84 B3
Berrymoor ASHGTN NE63 24 A1
Bertha St CON/LDGT DH8 123 F4
Bertram Crs
BW/LEM/TK/HW NE15 69 G5
Bertram St SSH NE33 75 G3
Bertram Ter ASHGTN NE63 23 K2 1
Berwick WASHS NE38 116 B2
Berwick Av SWCK/CAS SR5 104 D1
Berwick Cha PLEE/EAS SR8 174 C7
Berwick Cl
BW/LEM/TK/HW NE15 67 J4 1
Berwick Ct PONT/DH NE20 43 H2 1
Berwick Dr WLSD/HOW NE28 59 F5
Berwick Hill Rd PONT/DH NE20 43 H2
Berwick Sq SWCK/CAS SR5 104 D2 2
Berwick Ter NSHW NE29 60 B6
Besford Gv SUND SR1 15 H5
Bessemer St CON/LDGT DH8 122 E4
Bethnell Av BYK/HTN/WLK NE6 7 J2 1
Betjeman Cl STLY/ANP DH9 126 E1
Bet's La MPTH NE61 26 B5
Betts Av BW/LEM/TK/HW NE15 69 F6
Beumaris HLS DH4 131 F4
Bevan Av ASHBK/HED/RY SR2 134 E1
Bevan Cressent
RDHAMSE DH6 182 D2 2
Bevan Gdns FELL NE10 13 K8
Bevan Gv DHAM DH1 157 J6
Bevan Sq SEA/MUR SR7 149 H4
Beverley Cl GOS/KPK NE3 46 B7 1
Beverley Crs
LWF/SPW/WRK NE9 87 G6 1
Beverley Dr BLAY NE21 83 H4
STKFD/GP NE62 23 G5
WICK/BNPF NE16 8 A6
Beverley Gdns
CLS/BIR/GTL DH3 129 K5
CON/LDGT DH8 122 D2
TYNE/NSHE NE30 51 G6
Beverley Pk MONK NE25 50 C5
Beverley Pl WLSD/HOW NE28 73 H1
Beverley Rd
ASHBK/HED/RY SR2 121 F4
LWF/SPW/WRK NE9 87 G6
MONK NE25 50 D5
Beverley Ter
BYK/HTN/WLK NE6 72 C6 1
TYNE/NSHE NE30 51 G6
Beverley Wy PLEE/EAS SR8 174 D3
Bevin Sq RDHAMSE DH6 161 G2
Beweshill Crs BLAY NE21 83 J3
Beweshill La BLAY NE21 83 J1 1
Bewick Cl CLSW/PEL DH2 129 G7
Bewick Crs
BW/LEM/TK/HW NE15 68 B4
Bewicke Rd WLSD/HOW NE28 73 J2
Bewicke St WLSD/HOW NE28 73 K2
Bewick Garth PSHWF NE43 79 J3
Bewick La PRUD NE42 64 B7
Bewick Pk WLSD/HOW NE28 59 H4
Bewick Rd GATE NE8 10 E6
Bewick St CNUT NE1 5 H8 1
SSH NE33 75 G3
Bewley Gdns
WLSD/HOW NE28 59 F5 8
Bewley Gv PLEE/EAS SR8 174 B7
Bexhill Rd SWCK/CAS SR5 104 D2
Bexhill Sq BLYTH NE24 35 G2 4
SWCK/CAS SR5 104 D2
Bexley Av BW/LEM/TK/HW NE15 68 E5
Bexley Pl WICK/BNPF NE16 84 E7
Bexley St MLFD/PNYW SR4 105 K7
Bickington Ct HLS DH4 132 A4 1
Biddick Hall Dr HAR/WTLS NE34 75 F7
Biddick La WASHS NE38 117 F3
Biddick Vw WASHS NE38 117 G3
Biddick Vls WASHS NE38 117 G3
Biddlestone Crs NSHW NE29 60 B5 1
Biddlestone Rd
BYK/HTN/WLK NE6 71 J2
Bideford Gdns
HAR/WTLS NE34 76 A2 1
JRW NE32 74 B6
LWF/SPW/WRK NE9 101 F2
WBAY NE26 50 D3
Bideford Gv WICK/BNPF NE16 84 E7
Bideford Rd GOS/KPK NE3 55 J6
Bideford St
ASHBK/HED/RY SR2 121 F4
Bigbury Cl HLS DH4 132 A3 1
Bigges Gdns WLSD/HOW NE28 58 B6
Bilbrough Gdns ELS/FEN NE4 69 H7
Billy Mill Av NSHW NE29 60 C4
Billy Mill La NSHW NE29 60 B3
Bilsdale CLDN/WHIT/ROK SR6 93 F5
Bilsdale Pl LGB/KIL NE12 57 F4 1
Bilsmoor Av LGB/HTN NE7 71 H1
Bilton Hall Rd JRW NE32 74 B5
Binchester St HAR/WTLS NE34 74 E7 1
Bingfield Gdns
WD/WHPE/BLK NE5 69 G3
Bingley Cl WLSD/HOW NE28 59 G5
Bingley St SWCK/CAS SR5 104 D2
Bink Moss WASHN NE37 102 C7
Binswood Av
WD/WHPE/BLK NE5 69 F2
Bircham Dr BLAY NE21 84 B2
Bircham St STLY/ANP DH9 126 B2
Birch Av CLDN/WHIT/ROK SR6 93 F3
FELL NE10 13 J9
Birch Ct SUNDSW SR3 133 J1
Birch Crs WICK/BNPF NE16 97 H7
Birches Nook Rd PSHWF NE43 79 F5
The Birches STLY/ANP DH9 112 D6 1
WICK/BNPF NE16 99 G2
Birchfield WICK/BNPF NE16 85 F7 1
Birchfield Gdns
BW/LEM/TK/HW NE15 68 C4
LWF/SPW/WRK NE9 101 G3
Birchfield Rd
ASHBK/HED/RY SR2 14 B9
Birchgate Cl BLAY NE21 83 J3 1
Birch Gv CON/LDGT DH8 138 D1
WLSD/HOW NE28 58 E5
Birchgrove Av DHAM DH1 157 J6 1
Birchington Av SSH NE33 75 G4
Birch Pl BDN/LAN/SAC DH7 165 G2
Birch Rd BLAY NE21 84 B2
Birch St CON/LDGT DH8 123 F5
JRW NE32 73 J4
Birch Ter BYK/HTN/WLK NE6 72 C6
Birchvale Av
WD/WHPE/BLK NE5 68 E1
Birchwood Av DIN/WO NE13 46 B4
LGB/HTN NE7 57 J7
WICK/BNPF NE16 84 E7
Birchwood Cl CRAM NE23 39 F7
STLY/ANP DH9 113 J6
Birdhill Pl HAR/WTLS NE34 75 G6
Birds Nest Rd
BYK/HTN/WLK NE6 7 K8 1
Bird St TYNE/NSHE NE30 3 G1
Birkdale MONK NE25 50 B4
SSH NE33 75 J2
Birkdale Av
CLDN/WHIT/ROK SR6 92 E5
Birkdale Cl LGB/HTN NE7 57 J6 1
WLSD/HOW NE28 58 D6 1
Birkdale Dr HLS DH4 131 J3
Birkdale Gdns DHAM DH1 158 A6
Birkdene PSHWF NE43 79 H6
Birkheads La DUN/TMV NE11 99 J7
Birkland La WICK/BNPF NE16 99 H5
Birling Pl WD/WHPE/BLK NE5 69 H1
Birnam Gv JRW NE32 90 C2 1
Birney Edge PONT/DH NE20 52 E1
Birnie Cl ELS/FEN NE4 69 J7
Birrell Sq SWCK/CAS SR5 104 D1 3
Birrell St SWCK/CAS SR5 104 D1
Birtley Av TYNE/NSHE NE30 61 H2 3
Birtley Cl GOS/KPK NE3 56 A6
Birtley La CLS/BIR/GTL DH3 115 J2 1
Birtwistle Av HEBB NE31 89 F1 1
Biscop Ter JRW NE32 73 K6
Bishops Crs JRW NE32 74 A3
Bishopdale HLS DH4 117 G6 2
WLSD/HOW NE28 58 B5
Bishopdale Av BLYTH NE24 34 C1
Bishop Morton Gv SUND SR1 15 H6 1
Bishop Ramsay Ct
HAR/WTLS NE34 76 A5 1
Bishop Rock Cl LGB/KIL NE12 57 G4
Bishop Rock Rd LGB/KIL NE12 57 G4 1
Bishop's Av ELS/FEN NE4 4 C6
Bishops Cl WLSD/HOW NE28 73 G1 1
Bishops Dr RYTON NE40 83 F1
Bishops Meadow
BDLGTN NE22 28 E5 1
Bishop's Rd ELS/FEN NE4 69 H7
Bishops Wy DHAM DH1 156 C2
SUNDSW SR3 133 K2
Bisley Dr HAR/WTLS NE34 75 H4
Bittern Cl WLSD/HOW NE28 59 J4
Biverfield Rd PRUD NE42 80 E1 1
Black Boy Rd HLS DH4 146 B1
Blackburn Gn FELL NE10 12 B9
Blackcliffe Wy
BDN/LAN/SAC DH7 155 F5
Blackclose Bank ASHGTN NE63 23 J5
Blackclose Est ASHGTN NE63 23 K5
Blackdene ASHGTN NE63 23 H3
Blackdown Cl LGB/KIL NE12 57 G4 2
PLEE/EAS SR8 174 C5
Black Dr CLS/BIR/GTL DH3 130 C2
Blackett St CNUT NE1 5 J6
HEBB NE31 73 H3
STLY/ANP DH9 125 G3
Blackfell Rd WASHN NE37 102 B6
Blackfriars Wy LGB/KIL NE12 57 G3
Blackheath Cl WASHN NE37 102 E3 1
Blackheath Ct
WD/WHPE/BLK NE5 55 F5
Blackhill Av WLSD/HOW NE28 59 G3
Blackhill Crs
LWF/SPW/WRK NE9 101 K1
Blackhills Rd PLEE/EAS SR8 175 H2
Black House La
BDN/LAN/SAC DH7 127 K7
Blackhouse La RYTON NE40 66 D6
Black La BLAY NE21 83 J2
LWF/SPW/WRK NE9 101 H4
Black Rd ASHBK/HED/RY SR2 121 F7
BDN/LAN/SAC DH7 167 K4
HEBB NE31 73 H4
Blackrow La
BW/LEM/TK/HW NE15 52 C6
Blackstone Ct BLAY NE21 83 J2
Blackthorn Dr WLSD/HOW NE28 58 E5
Blackthorn Wy ASHGTN NE63 23 H3
HLS DH4 131 J5
Blackwell Av BYK/HTN/WLK NE6 72 C5
Blackwood Rd
SWCK/CAS SR5 104 E1 3
Bladen St JRW NE32 73 J4
Blagdon Av HAR/WTLS NE34 75 J3
Blagdon Cl MPTH NE61 20 C5
Blagdon Ct BDLGTN NE22 29 J4
Blagdon Crs CRAM NE23 32 E7
Blagdon Dr BLYTH NE24 34 E5
Blaidwood Dr DHAM DH1 168 B5
Blair Cl RDHAMSE DH6 170 C1 1
Blair Ct BDN/LAN/SAC DH7 167 K5
Blake Av WICK/BNPF NE16 85 F5
Blakelaw Rd
WD/WHPE/BLK NE5 69 F1 3
Blakemoor Pl
WD/WHPE/BLK NE5 69 G2 1
Blakes Cl STLY/ANP DH9 126 E1
Blanche Gv PLEE/EAS SR8 174 E5
Blanchland WASHS NE38 117 G5
Blanchland Av
BW/LEM/TK/HW NE15 67 K4
DHAM DH1 157 F3
DIN/WO NE13 46 B3
Blanchland Cl
WLSD/HOW NE28 59 F6 2
Blanchland Dr MONK NE25 40 C6
SWCK/CAS SR5 106 C2
Blanchland Ter
TYNE/NSHE NE30 61 F3
Blandford Pl SEA/MUR SR7 150 E1
Blandford Rd NSHW NE29 60 B2
Blandford Sq CNUT NE1 5 G8
Blandford St CNUT NE1 5 G9
Blaxton Pl WICK/BNPF NE16 84 D7
Blaydon Bank BLAY NE21 83 K2
Blaydon Hwy BLAY NE21 84 A1
Blaykeston Cl SEA/MUR SR7 134 E6
Bleachfeld FELL NE10 88 B6 1
Bleasdale Crs HLS DH4 117 K7
Blencathra WASHN NE37 102 E6
Blenheim LGB/KIL NE12 47 K5 4
Blenheim Dr BDLGTN NE22 29 J3
Blenheim Gdns MPTH NE61 21 J1 1
Blenheim Pl DUN/TMV NE11 8 E5
Blenheim St CNUT NE1 5 G8
Blenkinsop Gv JRW NE32 89 J1
Blenkinsopp Ct
PLEE/EAS SR8 184 C1 1
Blenkinsop St WLSD/HOW NE28 72 C1
Blind La CLS/BIR/GTL DH3 129 K1
HLS DH4 131 K4
SUNDSW SR3 120 A6
Blindy La HLH DH5 148 B7
Bloomfield Dr HLH DH5 147 G5
Bloomsbury Ct GOS/KPK NE3 56 B6 1
Blossomfield Wy
RDHAMSE DH6 160 E6
Blossom Gv HLS DH4 131 K3
Blount St BYK/HTN/WLK NE6 7 K5
Blucher Rd LGB/KIL NE12 57 J1
NSHW NE29 2 B6
Bluebell Cl WYLAM NE41 65 G4
Bluebell Dene
WD/WHPE/BLK NE5 54 E5
Bluebell Wy HAR/WTLS NE34 75 F6
Blueburn Dr LGB/KIL NE12 48 B5
Bluehouse Bank STLY/ANP DH9 127 K4
Blue House Ct WASHN NE37 102 D5
Blue House La
CLDN/WHIT/ROK SR6 91 K5
WASHN NE37 102 D5
Blue House Rd HEBB NE31 89 F1
Blue Quarries Rd
LWF/SPW/WRK NE9 87 H6
Blyth Cl CRAM NE23 47 F1
Blyth Ct
BW/LEM/TK/HW NE15 68 A4 1
HAR/WTLS NE34 75 G6
Blyth Rd WBAY NE26 41 H5
Blyth Sq SWCK/CAS SR5 104 E2
Blyth St MONK NE25 39 K4
SWCK/CAS SR5 104 E2
Blyth Ter ASHGTN NE63 24 A1
Blyton Av ASHBK/HED/RY SR2 120 E7
HAR/WTLS NE34 74 D6
Bodlewell La SUND SR1 15 H3 1
Bodley Cl GOS/KPK NE3 55 H5 2
Bodmin Cl WLSD/HOW NE28 59 G5
Bodmin Rd NSHW NE29 60 A2 1
Bodmin Sq SWCK/CAS SR5 104 E2 4
Bodmin Wy GOS/KPK NE3 55 K4 2
Bognor St SWCK/CAS SR5 104 D1
Bohemia Ter BLYTH NE24 35 G1
Boker La BOL NE36 91 F4
Bolam Av BLYTH NE24 31 F7
TYNE/NSHE NE30 60 E1
Bolam Dr ASHGTN NE63 24 A3
Bolam Gdns WLSD/HOW NE28 59 K7
Bolam Gv TYNE/NSHE NE30 60 E1
Bolam Rd LGB/KIL NE12 47 K6 1
Bolam St BYK/HTN/WLK NE6 7 H7
GATE NE8 9 M7
Bolam Wy BYK/HTN/WLK NE6 7 G7
MONK NE25 39 K5
Boland Rd MPTH NE61 18 C1
Bolbec Rd ELS/FEN NE4 69 J4
Bolburn FELL NE10 13 K9
Boldon Cl WLSD/HOW NE28 59 F5
Boldon Dr BOL NE36 90 D5
Boldon Gdns
LWF/SPW/WRK NE9 101 J2
Boldon La CLDN/WHIT/ROK SR6 91 J3
HAR/WTLS NE34 75 G7
Boldon North Br BOL NE36 91 G4
Bolingbroke Rd NSHW NE29 60 B4
Bolingbroke St
BYK/HTN/WLK NE6 6 D4
SSH NE33 3 J8 1
Bollihope Dr SUNDSW SR3 120 B4
Bolsover St ASHGTN NE63 23 K2
Bolsover Ter ASHGTN NE63 23 K2 1
Bolton Cl DHAM DH1 156 D2
Bonchester Ct BDLGTN NE22 29 F4
Bond Cl SWCK/CAS SR5 106 C4
Bondene Av FELL NE10 12 E7
Bondene Av West FELL NE10 12 E7
Bondene Wy CRAM NE23 33 H5
Bondfield Gdns FELL NE10 13 K7
Bondicarr Pl
WD/WHPE/BLK NE5 69 H2 1
Bondicar Ter BLYTH NE24 31 F7
Bonemill La CLS/BIR/GTL DH3 116 A6
WASHS NE38 116 E6
Bonington Wy
WD/WHPE/BLK NE5 69 F1 4
Bonner's Fld
CLDN/WHIT/ROK SR6 14 E2
Bonnivard Gdns CRAM NE23 39 H7
Booths Rd ASHGTN NE63 23 G1
Booth St FELL NE10 12 C7
MLFD/PNYW SR4 106 A6
Bootle St SWCK/CAS SR5 104 E2 3
Bordeaux Cl SUNDSW SR3 133 J1 2
Border Rd WLSD/HOW NE28 72 D2 3
Boreham Cl WLSD/HOW NE28 59 F5 6
Borodin Av SWCK/CAS SR5 104 D1
Borough Rd HAR/WTLS NE34 75 K6
JRW NE32 73 K5
NSHW NE29 2 D3
SUND SR1 14 F5
SUND SR1 15 H5 1
Borrowdale CON/LDGT DH8 123 K3
WICK/BNPF NE16 8 C9
Borrowdale Av BLYTH NE24 30 C6
BYK/HTN/WLK NE6 72 B4
CLDN/WHIT/ROK SR6 92 C7
Borrowdale Cl BOL NE36 91 G4 1
DHAM DH1 158 B5 1
Borrowdale Crs BLAY NE21 83 K4
HLS DH4 117 J6
Borrowdale Dr DHAM DH1 157 K5 1
Borrowdale Gdns
LWF/SPW/WRK NE9 101 H2
Borrowdale St HLH DH5 147 K6
Boscombe Dr
WLSD/HOW NE28 58 E6 2
Boston Av LGB/HTN NE7 57 H5
WASHS NE38 102 E7
Boston Cl WLSD/HOW NE28 59 F5
Boston Crs BOL NE36 104 C1
SWCK/CAS SR5 104 C1
Boston St SWCK/CAS SR5 104 C1
Boswell Av HAR/WTLS NE34 91 F1
Bosworth LGB/KIL NE12 47 K5
Bosworth Gdns
BYK/HTN/WLK NE6 71 J1
Bothal Av STKFD/GP NE62 22 E6
Bothal Bank MPTH NE61 22 C3
Bothal Cl MPTH NE61 21 J2
Bothal St BYK/HTN/WLK NE6 7 J5
Bottle Bank GATE NE8 5 M9
Bottlehouse St
BYK/HTN/WLK NE6 7 G9
Bottle Works Rd SEA/MUR SR7 151 F1
Boulby Cl SUNDSW SR3 120 C7 1
Boulmer Av CRAM NE23 33 H5
Boulmer Cl GOS/KPK NE3 55 K2 2
Boulmer Ct CLSW/PEL DH2 129 J5
Boulmer Gdns DIN/WO NE13 46 B3
Boulsworth Rd NSHW NE29 60 C1
Boundary Dr MPTH NE61 20 E6
Boundary Gdns LGB/HTN NE7 57 G7
Boundary St SWCK/CAS SR5 106 C3 1
Bourne Av ELS/FEN NE4 69 J4
Bourne Ct STLY/ANP DH9 112 E7
Bournemouth Dr
SEA/MUR SR7 150 A2 1
Bournemouth Gdns WBAY NE26 50 D3
WD/WHPE/BLK NE5 54 D7 2
Bournemouth Rd NSHW NE29 60 A5 1
Bourn Lea HLS DH4 131 J2
Bourtree Cl WLSD/HOW NE28 58 E6
Bowbank Cl SUNDSW SR3 120 B3 2
Bowburn Av SWCK/CAS SR5 105 G3 1
Bowburn Cl FELL NE10 88 E5
Bower St
CLDN/WHIT/ROK SR6 106 D1 2
The Bower JRW NE32 89 K4 1
Bowes Av SEA/MUR SR7 149 K2
Bowes Cl WICK/BNPF NE16 99 F3
Bowes Lea HLS DH4 131 H3
Bowes Lyon Cl ROWG NE39 97 F5 1
Bowes St BLYTH NE24 31 F7
GOS/KPK NE3 56 E5 1
Bowfell Av WD/WHPE/BLK NE5 55 H7
Bowfell Cl
WD/WHPE/BLK NE5 55 H7 2
Bowfell Gdns STKFD/GP NE62 23 G5
Bowfield Av GOS/KPK NE3 56 C1
Bow La DHAM DH1 16 D5
Bowler's Hl PSHWF NE43 79 K5
Bowlynn Cl SUNDSW SR3 133 J1 3
Bowman Dr CRAM NE23 47 H1
Bowman St
CLDN/WHIT/ROK SR6 93 F3
Bowmont Dr CRAM NE23 33 K7 2
STLY/ANP DH9 112 A6
Bowness Av WLSD/HOW NE28 59 G4
Bowness Cl BOL NE36 91 G5 1
PLEE/EAS SR8 175 F3 3
Bowness Pl
LWF/SPW/WRK NE9 101 H1
Bowness Rd
WD/WHPE/BLK NE5 68 E2
WICK/BNPF NE16 8 B9
Bowness St SWCK/CAS SR5 104 E1
Bowsden Ct GOS/KPK NE3 56 E5 2
Bowsden Ter GOS/KPK NE3 56 E5
Bow St RDHAMSE DH6 172 C6
RDHAMSE DH6 180 A2
Boyd Crs WLSD/HOW NE28 72 E1
Boyd Rd WLSD/HOW NE28 72 E1
Boyd St BW/LEM/TK/HW NE15 67 G3
DHAM DH1 16 E7
JES NE2 6 B5
Boyne Ct BDN/LAN/SAC DH7 167 J5 1
BLYTH NE24 31 G6 2
Brabourne St HAR/WTLS NE34 75 G5
Bracken Av WLSD/HOW NE28 58 E5
Brackenbeds Cl CLSW/PEL DH2 114 E7
Bracken Cl DIN/WO NE13 44 E3
STLY/ANP DH9 126 B1
Brackendale Ct WNGT TS28 184 A6 1
Brackendale Rd DHAM DH1 158 A6
Brackendene Dr
LWF/SPW/WRK NE9 86 E7 2
Bracken Dr DUN/TMV NE11 85 K6
Bracken Field Rd DHAM DH1 156 C4
Brackenfield Rd GOS/KPK NE3 56 B6
Bracken Hl PLEE/EAS SR8 174 A5
Bracken Rdg MPTH NE61 20 A3
Brackenridge WICK/BNPF NE16 97 G7
Brackenside GOS/KPK NE3 56 C1
Bracken Wy RYTON NE40 82 C1
Brackenwood Gv
ASHBK/HED/RY SR2 120 C4 1
Brackley WASHN NE37 103 G4
Bracknell Cl SUNDSW SR3 120 C6
Bracknell Gdns
WD/WHPE/BLK NE5 67 K2
Brack Ter FELL NE10 13 L4
Bradbury Cl FELL NE10 88 E5 2
STLY/ANP DH9 112 A6
Bradbury Ct MONK NE25 40 A2
Bradford Av SWCK/CAS SR5 104 E1
WLSD/HOW NE28 59 F5
Bradley Av HAR/WTLS NE34 76 A6
HLH DH5 147 H2
Bradley Cl CLSW/PEL DH2 114 D4
Bradley Fell La WYLAM NE41 81 J2
Bradley Fell Rd PRUD NE42 81 H4
Bradley Lodge Dr
STLY/ANP DH9 111 G6 1
Bradley Rd PRUD NE42 81 F1
Bradley St CON/LDGT DH8 123 J3 1

Bradley Ter *HLH* DH5 .... 148 A7
Bradman Dr *CLS/BIR/GTL* DH3 .. 130 A5
Bradman Sq *SWCK/CAS* SR5 ...... 104 E1
Bradman St *SWCK/CAS* SR5 ...... 104 E2
Bradshaw St *SWCK/CAS* SR5 ..... 104 E2
Bradwell Rd *GOS/KPK* NE3 .... 55 J5
Bradwell Wy *HLS* DH4 .... 131 K3
Brady Sq *WASHS* NE38 .... 117 H2
Brady St *MLFD/PNYW* SR4 .... 105 K6
Braebridge Pl *GOS/KPK* NE3 ..... 55 K2
Braemar Ct *CON/LDGT* DH8 ...... 122 C4
   FELL NE10 .... 13 M4
Braemar Dr *HAR/WTLS* NE34 ..... 76 A3
Braemar Gdns *SUNDSW* SR3 ..... 120 B3
   SUNDSW SR3 .... 133 G1
Braeside *ASHBK/HED/RY* SR2 ..... 14 B9
   BDN/LAN/SAC DH7 .... 141 G4
   DUN/TMV NE11 .... 86 A6
Brahman Av *NSHW* NE29 .... 60 B6
Braintree Gdns *GOS/KPK* NE3 .... 55 K6
Braithwaite Rd *PLEE/EAS* SR8 ... 175 G4
Bramble Dykes
   BW/LEM/TK/HW NE15 .... 69 F6
Bramley Cl *MLFD/PNYW* SR4 ..... 118 E4
Bramley Ct *LGB/HTN* NE7 .... 58 A7
Brampton Av
   BYK/HTN/WLK NE6 .... 72 B7
Brampton Ct *PLEE/EAS* SR8 ...... 162 C6
Brampton Gdns
   BW/LEM/TK/HW NE15 .... 67 F1
   LWF/SPW/WRK NE9 .... 101 G2
   WLSD/HOW NE28 .... 59 J6
Brampton Pl *NSHW* NE29 .... 60 B5
Brampton Rd *HAR/WTLS* NE34 ... 74 E6
Bramwell Rd
   ASHBK/HED/RY SR2 .... 15 H7
   HLS DH4 .... 131 J6
Brancepeth Av *ELS/FEN* NE4 ..... 69 J7
Brancepeth Chare
   PLEE/EAS SR8 .... 174 C7
Brancepeth Cl
   BW/LEM/TK/HW NE15 .... 68 A3
   DHAM DH1 .... 157 F3
Brancepeth Rd *HEBB* NE31 .... 73 H3
   WASHS NE38 .... 116 C2
Brancepeth Ter *JRW* NE32 .... 89 K1
Brancepeth Vw
   BDN/LAN/SAC DH7 .... 166 E7
Branch St *BLAY* NE21 .... 83 K3
Brancpeth Cl
   BDN/LAN/SAC DH7 .... 167 H1
Brand Av *ELS/FEN* NE4 .... 69 J4
Brandling Ct *HAR/WTLS* NE34 .... 75 K7
Brandling Pk *JES* NE2 .... 5 K1
Brandling St
   CLDN/WHIT/ROK SR6 .... 106 E3
Brandling St South
   CLDN/WHIT/ROK SR6 .... 106 E4
Brandlings Wy *PLEE/EAS* SR8 .... 174 E3
Brandon Av *SMOOR* NE27 .... 49 G6
Brandon Cl *BLAY* NE21 .... 83 J4
   BLYTH NE24 .... 30 D6
   HLS DH4 .... 147 G1
Brandon Gdns
   LWF/SPW/WRK NE9 .... 101 K2
Brandon Gv *JES* NE2 .... 6 B2
Brandon La *BDN/LAN/SAC* DH7 .. 166 B5
   BDN/LAN/SAC DH7 .... 167 J5
   CRK/WIL DL15 .... 165 J6
Brandon Rd *BDN/LAN/SAC* DH7 .. 165 H2
   GOS/KPK NE3 .... 55 K4
   NSHW NE29 .... 60 B4
Brandy La *WASHN* NE37 .... 102 D6
Brannen St *NSHW* NE29 .... 2 C3
Bransdale *HLS* DH4 .... 117 G6
Bransdale Av
   CLDN/WHIT/ROK SR6 .... 92 E5
Branston St *SWCK/CAS* SR5 ..... 106 B3
Branton Av *HEBB* NE31 .... 89 F1
Brantwood *CLSW/PEL* DH2 ...... 129 F4
Brantwood Av *MONK* NE25 .... 50 B5
Branxton Crs
   BYK/HTN/WLK NE6 .... 72 B6
Brass Thill *DHAM* DH1 .... 16 B4
Bray Cl *WLSD/HOW* NE28 .... 59 F5
Braydon Dr *NSHW* NE29 .... 60 B7
Brayside *JRW* NE32 .... 90 B3
Breamish Dr *WASHS* NE38 .... 116 B6
Breamish St *CNUT* NE1 .... 6 B6
   JRW NE32 .... 73 J6
Brearley Wy *FELL* NE10 .... 12 A7
Breckenbeds Rd
   LWF/SPW/WRK NE9 .... 100 E1
Brecken Wy
   BDN/LAN/SAC DH7 .... 167 H6
Breckon Cl *ASHGTN* NE63 .... 24 A4
Brecon Cl *PLEE/EAS* SR8 .... 174 C5
   WD/WHPE/BLK NE5 .... 55 F6
Brecon Pl *CLSW/PEL* DH2 ...... 115 F6
Brecon Rd *DHAM* DH1 .... 157 F2
Bredon Cl *WASHS* NE38 .... 116 D3
Brendale Av *WD/WHPE/BLK* NE5.. 54 B7
Brendon Pl *PLEE/EAS* SR8 .... 174 C3
Brenkley Av *SMOOR* NE27 .... 49 G7
Brenkley Cl *DIN/WO* NE13 .... 45 F2
Brenkley Ct *DIN/WO* NE13 .... 46 B1
Brenkley Wy *DIN/WO* NE13 ...... 37 G7
Brenlynn Cl *SUNDSW* SR3 .... 133 J1
Brennan Cl *ASHGTN* NE63 .... 24 C2
   BW/LEM/TK/HW NE15 .... 68 E4
Brentford Av *SWCK/CAS* SR5 .... 104 E2
Brentford Sq *SWCK/CAS* SR5 ... 104 E2
Brentwood Av *JES* NE2 .... 70 D1
Brentwood Cl *MONK* NE25 .... 40 B7
Brentwood Ct *STLY/ANP* DH9.... 127 G1
Brentwood Gdns
   SUNDSW SR3 .... 120 B3
   WICK/BNPF NE16 .... 85 F7
Brentwood Gv
   WLSD/HOW NE28 .... 73 F2
Brentwood Rd *HLS* DH4 .... 131 J2
Brettanby Rd *FELL* NE10 .... 12 A9
Brett Cl *LGB/HTN* NE7 .... 57 K7
Brettonby Av *PSHWF* NE43...... 79 H5
Brewer's La *NSHW* NE29 .... 60 A7
Brewer Ter *ASHBK/HED/RY* SR2.. 135 G1

Brewery Bank
   WICK/BNPF NE16 .... 84 E3
Brewery La *FELL* NE10 .... 12 D5
   PONT/DH NE20 .... 43 G3
   SSH NE33 .... 2 E8
   WICK/BNPF NE16 .... 84 E3
Briar Av *BDN/LAN/SAC* DH7 ..... 167 F7
   HLS DH4 .... 132 B7
   WBAY NE26 .... 50 D2
Briar Cl *CLSW/PEL* DH2 .... 144 A5
   HLS DH4 .... 131 H3
   WLSD/HOW NE28 .... 58 E5
Briardale *BDLGTN* NE22 .... 28 E5
Briar Dl *CON/LDGT* DH8 .... 123 J7
Briardale Rd *BLYTH* NE24 .... 30 C7
Briardene *ASHGTN* NE63 .... 23 J3
   BDN/LAN/SAC DH7 .... 140 B5
   DHAM DH1 .... 16 B5
   WICK/BNPF NE16 .... 97 G7
Briardene Cl *SUNDSW* SR3 ..... 133 G1
Briardene Crs *GOS/KPK* NE3 .... 56 A7
Briardene Dr *FELL* NE10 .... 89 F5
Briar Edge *LGB/KIL* NE12 .... 57 K2
Briar Fld *WASHS* NE38 .... 117 F5
Briarfield Rd *GOS/KPK* NE3 ...... 56 B6
Briarhill *CLSW/PEL* DH2 .... 129 G2
Briar La
   BW/LEM/TK/HW NE15 .... 67 G2
Briar Lea *BDN/LAN/SAC* DH7 .... 143 G7
   HLS DH4 .... 131 H3
Briarlea *MPTH* NE61 .... 27 J2
Briar Ms *CON/LDGT* DH8 .... 122 D2
Briar Pl *BW/LEM/TK/HW* NE15 ... 66 E1
Briar Rd *DHAM* DH1 .... 158 A5
   ROWG NE39 .... 97 F3
Briarside *CON/LDGT* DH8 .... 122 D2
   WD/WHPE/BLK NE5 .... 54 B7
Briarsyde Cl *WICK/BNPF* NE16 ... 84 C7
Briarwood *CRAM* NE23 .... 47 H1
Briarwood Av *CLSW/PEL* DH2.... 128 E4
   GOS/KPK NE3 .... 56 A4
Briarwood Crs
   BYK/HTN/WLK NE6 .... 72 B2
Briarwood Rd *BLYTH* NE24 .... 35 H1
Briary Gdns *CON/LDGT* DH8 .... 122 C1
The Briary
   BW/LEM/TK/HW NE15 .... 66 E1
   CON/LDGT DH8 .... 122 D1
Brick Garth *HLH* DH5 .... 148 A7
Brick Rw *ASHBK/HED/RY* SR2.... 120 E7
Bridge Cottages *CRAM* NE23 .... 47 J1
Bridge Ct *RDHAMSE* DH6 .... 171 H3
Bridge Crs *SUND* SR1 .... 14 E3
Bridgemere Dr *DHAM* DH1 ...... 156 B3
Bridge Pk *GOS/KPK* NE3 .... 56 C2
Bridge Rd South *NSHW* NE29 .... 60 C6
Bridge St *BDN/LAN/SAC* DH7 .... 154 B2
   BLAY NE21 .... 67 K7
   BLYTH NE31 .... 31 H7
   CON/LDGT DH8 .... 122 D4
   DHAM DH1 .... 16 B3
   GATE NE8 .... 5 L9
   MPTH NE61 .... 20 D5
   NWBGN NE64 .... 25 C1
   STLY/ANP DH9 .... 126 B3
   SUND SR1 .... 14 E4
Bridgewater Cl
   BW/LEM/TK/HW NE15 .... 68 A4
   WLSD/HOW NE28 .... 58 E6
Bridgewater Rd *WASHN* NE37 ... 103 G6
Bridge Wy *BDN/LAN/SAC* DH7 ... 154 C2
Bridle Pth *BOL* NE36 .... 91 G5
   SUNDSW SR3 .... 119 G6
The Bridle *SMOOR* NE27 .... 49 K7
Bridlington Av
   LWF/SPW/WRK NE9 .... 101 F2
Bridport Rd *NSHW* NE29 .... 60 B1
Brier Dene Crs *WBAY* NE26 ...... 50 C1
Brierdene Rd *WBAY* NE26 .... 41 J7
Brierfield Gv *MLFD/PNYW* SR4 ... 119 H2
Brierley Rd *BLYTH* NE24 .... 30 D7
Briermede Av
   LWF/SPW/WRK NE9 .... 101 F1
Brieryside
   WD/WHPE/BLK NE5 .... 69 H1
Briery Vale Rd
   ASHBK/HED/RY SR2 .... 14 D8
Brigham Av *GOS/KPK* NE3 .... 55 J7
Brigham Pl *SSH* NE33 .... 3 H6
Brightlea *CLS/BIR/GTL* DH3 ..... 116 A1
Brightman Rd *NSHW* NE29 .... 2 C1
Brighton Cl *WLSD/HOW* NE28..... 59 G5
Brighton Gv *ELS/FEN* NE4 .... 4 C5
   NSHW NE29 .... 2 A1
   WBAY NE26 .... 50 D2
Brighton Rd *GATE* NE8............ 10 D6
Bright St *CLDN/WHIT/ROK* SR6... 106 E4
   CON/LDGT DH8 .... 123 F3
   SSH NE33 .... 3 K7
Brignall Cl *CLS/BIR/GTL* DH3 .... 145 J2
Brignall Gdns
   BW/LEM/TK/HW NE15 .... 68 E4
Brignall Ri *SUNDSW* SR3 .... 120 B4
Brindley Rd *PLEE/EAS* SR8 ...... 174 A4
   WASHN NE37 .... 103 G2
Brinkburn *CLSW/PEL* DH2 ...... 129 G4
   WASHS NE38 .... 117 G4
Brinkburn Av *BLYTH* NE24........ 35 H1
   CRAM NE23 .... 38 D2
   GATE NE8 .... 10 F7
   GOS/KPK NE3 .... 56 B4
   WICK/BNPF NE16 .... 84 E4
Brinkburn Cl *BLAY* NE21 .... 83 J4
   BYK/HTN/WLK NE6 .... 6 F5
Brinkburn Crs *ASHGTN* NE63 .... 24 A2
   HLS DH4 .... 147 F2
Brinkburn Gdns *STKFD/GP* NE62.. 23 F5
Brinkburn Pl *BYK/HTN/WLK* NE6 .. 6 F4
   HAR/WTLS NE34 .... 76 C4
   MLFD/PNYW SR4 .... 120 A1
   WLSD/HOW NE28 .... 74 A2
Brinkburn St South
   BYK/HTN/WLK NE6 .... 7 G7
Brisbane Av *HAR/WTLS* NE34 .... 90 D1

Brisbane St *SWCK/CAS* SR5 .... 104 E2
Bristlecone *SUNDSW* SR3 .... 133 J2
Bristol Av *WASHN* NE37 .... 102 D5
Bristol Dr *WLSD/HOW* NE28 ..... 59 F5
Bristol St *MONK* NE25 .... 39 K3
Bristol Ter *ELS/FEN* NE4 .... 4 C8
Britannia Pl *ELS/FEN* NE4 .... 4 C7
Britannia Rd *SUNDSW* SR3 ..... 120 A7
Brixham Av
   LWF/SPW/WRK NE9 .... 101 F2
Brixham Cl *SEA/MUR* SR7 ...... 150 B2
Brixham Crs *JRW* NE32 .... 74 B6
Brixham Gdns *SUNDSW* SR3 .... 120 B4
Broadbank *FELL* NE10 .... 13 L7
Broad Chare *CNUT* NE1 .... 5 M7
Broadfield Pl *HAR/WTLS* NE34 .. 75 H6
Broad Garth *CNUT* NE1 .... 5 M8
Broadgate Rd
   BDN/LAN/SAC DH7 .... 154 B6
Broad Landing *SSH* NE33 .... 2 F6
Broadlands
   CLDN/WHIT/ROK SR6 .... 92 A5
Broadlea *FELL* NE10 .... 13 L7
Broadmayne Av
   MLFD/PNYW SR4 .... 119 H2
Broadmayne Gdns
   MLFD/PNYW SR4 .... 119 H2
Broad Mdw *ASHBK/HED/RY* SR2 .. 14 B8
Broadmeadows
   RDHAMSE DH6 .... 180 B3
   SUNDSW SR3 .... 133 F1
   WASHS NE38 .... 117 G4
Broadmead Wy
   BW/LEM/TK/HW NE15 .... 68 E6
Broadoak *FELL* NE10 .... 13 L6
Broadoak Dr
   BDN/LAN/SAC DH7 .... 140 B5
Broadpark *FELL* NE10 .... 13 L7
Broadsheath Ter
   SWCK/CAS SR5 .... 105 K4
Broadside *FELL* NE10 .... 13 L7
Broadstairs Ct
   MLFD/PNYW SR4 .... 119 H2
Broadstone Gv
   WD/WHPE/BLK NE5 .... 68 A2
Broadwater *FELL* NE10 .... 13 L6
Broadway *BLYTH* NE24 .... 35 G1
   BW/LEM/TK/HW NE15 .... 68 B3
   CLS/BIR/GTL DH3 .... 129 K2
   CON/LDGT DH8 .... 138 C1
   LWF/SPW/WRK NE9 .... 11 L9
   PONT/DH NE20 .... 42 E6
   STKFD/GP NE62 .... 22 E6
   TYNE/NSHE NE30 .... 61 G2
   WICK/BNPF NE16 .... 84 D7
Broadway Cl *MONK* NE25 .... 51 F6
Broadway Crs *BLYTH* NE24 .... 35 G1
Broadway East *GOS/KPK* NE3 .... 56 C3
The Broadway *HLS* DH4 .... 132 C7
   MLFD/PNYW SR4 .... 119 G2
   TYNE/NSHE NE30 .... 51 F6
Broadway Vls
   BW/LEM/TK/HW NE15 .... 69 F6
Broadway West *GOS/KPK* NE3 ... 56 B3
Broadwell Ct *GOS/KPK* NE3 ..... 57 F6
Broadwood Rd
   BW/LEM/TK/HW NE15 .... 68 D4
Broadwood Vw *CON/LDGT* DH8.. 122 C2
Brockenhurst Dr
   MLFD/PNYW SR4 .... 118 A4
Brock Farm Ct *TYNE/NSHE* NE30.. 60 E4
Brockhampton Cl
   BOLCOL NE35 .... 90 C2
Brock La *BDLGTN* NE22 .... 30 B3
   STKFD/GP NE62 .... 24 B7
Brockley Av *HAR/WTLS* NE34 .... 74 E7
Brockley St *SWCK/CAS* SR5 .... 104 E2
Brockwell Cl *BLAY* NE21 .... 83 J3
Brockwell Rd *BLYTH* NE24 .... 34 E3
Brockwell Rd *WASHS* NE38 ..... 116 B1
Brockwood Cl *ASHGTN* NE63 .... 23 H4
Brodie Cl *HAR/WTLS* NE34 ...... 91 G1
Brodrick Cl *GOS/KPK* NE3 .... 55 H5
Brodrick St *SSH* NE33 .... 3 K7
Brokenheugh
   WD/WHPE/BLK NE5 .... 68 D2
Bromford Rd *GOS/KPK* NE3 ..... 55 H5
Bromley Av *MONK* NE25 .... 50 C6
Bromley Cl *DHAM* DH1 .... 169 J6
Bromley Gdns *BLYTH* NE24 ...... 35 G2
   WLSD/HOW NE28 .... 59 F5
Bromsgrove Cl
   WLSD/HOW NE28 .... 59 G5
Bronte Pl *STLY/ANP* DH9 .... 127 F3
Bronte St *GATE* NE8 .... 11 M5
Brookbank Cl *SUNDSW* SR3 .... 133 K2
Brook Cl *BDLGTN* NE22 .... 29 G6
Brookdale *DHAM* DH1 .... 158 B6
Brooke Av *BOLCOL* NE35 .... 91 F4
   WICK/BNPF NE16 .... 84 E4
Brooke St *SWCK/CAS* SR5 .... 14 D2
Brookfield Crs
   WD/WHPE/BLK NE5 .... 68 A2
Brookland Dr *LGB/KIL* NE12 ..... 48 A6
Brookland Rd
   MLFD/PNYW SR4 .... 105 K7
Brooklands *PONT/DH* NE20 ...... 42 C6
Brooklands Wy *BOLCOL* NE35 ... 90 B4
Brookside *BDN/LAN/SAC* DH7 .. 143 H4
   BDN/LAN/SAC DH7 .... 155 G1
   CRAM NE23 .... 47 G1
Brookside Av *BLYTH* NE24 .... 30 D7
   DIN/WO NE13 .... 46 A4
Brookside Crs
   WD/WHPE/BLK NE5 .... 69 H2
Brookside Gdns
   ASHBK/HED/RY SR2 .... 14 C9
Brookside Wd *WASHS* NE38 .... 117 F5
Brooksmead *WLSD/HOW* NE28 .. 58 B6
Brook St *WBAY* NE26 .... 51 F4
Brookvale *GOS/KPK* NE3 .... 55 K6
Brook Vw *BDN/LAN/SAC* DH7 ... 140 B5
Broom Cl *MPTH* NE61 .... 21 G6
   STLY/ANP DH9 .... 113 F7
   WICK/BNPF NE16 .... 97 G7
Broom Ct *LWF/SPW/WRK* NE9 ... 102 B4
Broom Crs *BDN/LAN/SAC* DH7 .. 167 F1
Broome Cl *GOS/KPK* NE3 .... 56 A4

Broome Rd *DHAM* DH1 .... 158 A5
Broomfield *JRW* NE32 .... 90 A3
Broomfield Av
   BYK/HTN/WLK NE6 .... 72 A2
   MONK NE25 .... 58 E5
Broomfield Crs *CHPW* NE17 ..... 95 H5
Broomfield Rd *GOS/KPK* NE3 .... 56 B6
Broom Hall Dr
   BDN/LAN/SAC DH7 .... 167 G1
Broomhill Gdns
   WD/WHPE/BLK NE5 .... 69 H2
Broomhill Rd *PRUD* NE42 .... 80 E1
Broomhill Ter *HLH* DH5 .... 147 J3
Broomhouse La *PRUD* NE42 ..... 80 D1
Broomhouse Rd *PRUD* NE42 .... 80 E1
Broom La *BDN/LAN/SAC* DH7 ... 167 G1
   WICK/BNPF NE16 .... 85 F7
Broomlea *NSHW* NE29 .... 59 K1
Broomlea Ct *LGB/KIL* NE12 ...... 47 K6
Broomley Wk *GOS/KPK* NE3 ..... 55 K3
Broomridge Av
   BW/LEM/TK/HW NE15 .... 69 H6
Broomshields Av
   SWCK/CAS SR5 .... 106 B2
Broomshields Cl *SWCK/CAS* SR5.. 106 B2
Broomside La *DHAM* DH1 .... 158 A5
Brooms La *CON/LDGT* DH8 ..... 124 C4
Broom Ter *WICK/BNPF* NE16 .... 98 A5
Broom Wood Ct *PRUD* NE42 .... 80 B2
Broomy Hill Rd
   BW/LEM/TK/HW NE15 .... 67 F1
Brotherlee Rd *GOS/KPK* NE3 .... 55 K3
Brougham Ct *PLEE/EAS* SR8 .... 174 B7
Brougham St *SUND* SR1 .... 14 D5
Brough Gdns *WLSD/HOW* NE28 .. 59 J6
Brough Park Wy
   BYK/HTN/WLK NE6 .... 7 K4
Brough St *BYK/HTN/WLK* NE6 .... 7 J2
Broughton Rd *SSH* NE33 .... 3 K8
Browbank *BDN/LAN/SAC* DH7 .. 143 J6
Browne Rd
   CLDN/WHIT/ROK SR6 .... 106 D2
Browney La *BDN/LAN/SAC* DH7 .. 167 J2
Browning Cl *HAR/WTLS* NE34.... 91 F2
   STLY/ANP DH9 .... 112 E7
Browning HI *RDHAMSE* DH6 .... 180 D7
Brownlow Cl *LGB/HTN* NE7 ...... 58 A7
Brownlow Rd *HAR/WTLS* NE34 .. 75 G5
Browney Ct
   BDN/LAN/SAC DH7 .... 154 B2
Brownrigg Dr *CRAM* NE23 .... 38 D3
Browns Ri *RDHAMSE* DH6 ...... 180 D7
Brownsea Pl
   LWF/SPW/WRK NE9 .... 11 K9
Browntop Pl *HAR/WTLS* NE34 ... 75 G6
Broxburn Cl *WLSD/HOW* NE28 ... 59 G5
Broxburn Ct
   WD/WHPE/BLK NE5 .... 55 G7
Broxholm Rd
   BYK/HTN/WLK NE6 .... 71 H2
Bruce Cl *HAR/WTLS* NE34 .... 75 C7
   WD/WHPE/BLK NE5 .... 68 D1
Bruce Gdns *WD/WHPE/BLK* NE5 .. 69 G4
Bruce Glasier Ter
   RDHAMSE DH6 .... 173 H5
Bruce Kirkup Rd *PLEE/EAS* SR8 .. 175 F2
Bruce Pl *PLEE/EAS* SR8 .... 174 D7
Bruce St *BDN/LAN/SAC* DH7 ... 143 G2
Brumell Dr *MPTH* NE61 .... 20 B4
Brumwell St *PSHWF* NE43 .... 79 F5
Brundon Av *WBAY* NE26 .... 50 D2
Brunel Dr *CLDN/WHIT/ROK* SR6 .. 107 F4
Brunel St *ELS/FEN* NE4 .... 9 M1
   GATE NE8 .... 10 C8
Brunel Ter *ELS/FEN* NE4 .... 9 J1
Brunel Wk *ELS/FEN* NE4 .... 9 H1
Brunswick Gv *DIN/WO* NE13 .... 46 A3
Brunswick Rd *SMOOR* NE27 ..... 49 H7
   SWCK/CAS SR5 .... 104 E1
Brunswick St *SSH* NE33 .... 75 C2
Brunton Av *HAR/WTLS* NE34 .... 55 K4
   WLSD/HOW NE28 .... 59 K7
Brunton Cl *SMOOR* NE27 .... 49 H7
Brunton Gv *GOS/KPK* NE3 ...... 55 K4
Brunton La *DIN/WO* NE13 .... 45 K7
   GOS/KPK NE3 .... 55 C5
Brunton Ms *NSHW* NE29 .... 60 B7
Brunton Rd *DIN/WO* NE13 ...... 55 C3
   GOS/KPK NE3 .... 55 G5
   NSHW NE29 .... 60 B7
Brunton Ter
   MLFD/PNYW SR4 .... 106 A7
Brunton Wy *CRAM* NE23 .... 33 H5
   FELL NE10 .... 13 M3
Brussels Rd *MLFD/PNYW* SR4.... 105 H6
   WLSD/HOW NE28 .... 72 D2
Bryden Ct *HAR/WTLS* NE34 ..... 75 H6
Bryers St *CLDN/WHIT/ROK* SR6 .. 93 F3
Buckham St *ELS/FEN* NE4 .... 4 F6
Buckingham *SUNDSW* SR3 ..... 119 J6
Buckingham Cl
   CLDN/WHIT/ROK SR6 .... 93 F3
Buckingham Ct *PLEE/EAS* SR8 .. 174 C7
Buckinghamshire Rd
   DHAM DH1 .... 157 K6
Buckingham St *ELS/FEN* NE4 ..... 4 F6
Buckland Cl *HLS* DH4 .... 132 A5
   WASHS NE38 .... 117 F3
Buck's Nook La *RYTON* NE40 .... 81 J5
Buckthorne Gv *LGB/HTN* NE7 ... 57 J2
Buddle Cl *ELS/FEN* NE4 .... 69 H7
   PLEE/EAS SR8 .... 174 E2
Buddle Ct *ELS/FEN* NE4 .... 69 J7
Buddle Rd *ELS/FEN* NE4 .... 69 H7
Buddle St *WLSD/HOW* NE28 .... 72 D3
Buddle Ter
   ASHBK/HED/RY SR2 .... 15 H8
Bude Gv *NSHW* NE29 .... 60 B1
Bude Sq *SEA/MUR* SR7 .... 149 J4
Budle Cl *BLYTH* NE24 .... 30 E7
Budleigh Rd *GOS/KPK* NE3 ...... 55 K3
Budworth Av *WBAY* NE26 .... 41 C3
Bullers Gn *MPTH* NE61 .... 20 C4
Bullfinch Dr *WICK/BNPF* NE16 .. 84 E6
Bullion La *CLSW/PEL* DH2 ...... 129 H4
Bulman's La *NSHW* NE29 .... 60 E2
Bulmer Rd *HAR/WTLS* NE34 .... 76 A4

The Bungalows *STLY/ANP* DH9 .. 112 A6
Bunyan Av *HAR/WTLS* NE34 ..... 90 E1
Burdale Av *WD/WHPE/BLK* NE5 ... 68 E2
Burdon Av *CRAM* NE23 .... 38 A1
   MONK NE25 .... 58 E5
Burdon Cl *CLDN/WHIT/ROK* SR6.. 91 J3
Burdon Crs *CLDN/WHIT/ROK* SR6.. 91 J3
   SEA/MUR SR7 .... 135 F6
   WNGT TS28 .... 183 J2
Burdon Dr *PLEE/EAS* SR8 ...... 173 K3
Burdon Gv *SUNDSW* SR3 ...... 120 B7
Burdon La *ASHBK/HED/RY* SR2 .. 134 E1
   SUNDSW SR3 .... 134 A3
Burdon Ldg *WICK/BNPF* NE16 ... 99 G3
Burdon Main Rw *NSHW* NE29 .... 2 C5
Burdon Pk *WICK/BNPF* NE16 .... 99 G3
Burdon Pl *PLEE/EAS* SR8 .... 175 F4
Burdon Pln *WICK/BNPF* NE16 .... 99 F6
Burdon Rd *ASHBK/HED/RY* SR2 .. 14 F7
   CLDN/WHIT/ROK SR6 .... 91 J3
   SUNDSW SR3 .... 134 B2
Burdon St *NSHW* NE29 .... 70 D3
Burdon Ter *JES* NE2 .... 70 D3
   SEA/MUR SR7 .... 57 G6
Burford Ct *LGB/HTN* NE7 .... 57 G6
Burford Gdns *SUNDSW* SR3 .... 120 B4
Burghley Rd *FELL* NE10 .... 87 J6
Burke St *SWCK/CAS* SR5 .... 104 E2
Burlawn Cl
   ASHBK/HED/RY SR2 .... 121 F6
Burleigh St *SSH* NE33 .... 3 K9
Burlington Cl
   ASHBK/HED/RY SR2 .... 15 J7
Burlington Ct
   WLSD/HOW NE28 .... 59 G3
Burlington Gdns
   BYK/HTN/WLK NE6 .... 71 H3
Burnaby Dr *RYTON* NE40 .... 66 D7
Burnaby St *MLFD/PNYW* SR4 ... 120 A1
Burn Av *LGB/KIL* NE12 .... 57 K2
Burnbank Av *MONK* NE25 .... 49 K4
Burnbridge *DIN/WO* NE13 .... 46 B1
Burn Crook *HLH* DH5 .... 147 G2
Burnden Gv *HLS* DH4 .... 131 H2
Burnell Rd *BDN/LAN/SAC* DH7 .. 165 H4
Burnet Cl *WLSD/HOW* NE28 ..... 58 E5
Burnet Ct *ASHGTN* NE63 .... 23 H4
Burney Vls *GATE* NE8 .... 11 J6
Burnfoot Wy *GOS/KPK* NE3 ..... 55 J7
Burn Gdns *PLEE/EAS* SR8 ...... 162 D5
Burnhall Dr *SEA/MUR* SR7 ..... 135 G6
Burnham Av
   BW/LEM/TK/HW NE15 .... 67 J4
Burnham Cl *BLYTH* NE24 .... 35 G2
Burnham Gv *BOL* NE36 .... 91 H5
   BYK/HTN/WLK NE6 .... 7 M8
Burnham St *HAR/WTLS* NE34 ... 75 G5
Burn Heads Rd *HEBB* NE31 ..... 73 F7
Burnhills Gdns *RYTON* NE40 .... 82 C3
Burnhills La *RYTON* NE40 .... 82 C3
Burnhope Dr *SWCK/CAS* SR5 ... 106 B2
Burnhope Rd *WASHS* NE38 .... 103 G7
Burnhopeside Av
   BDN/LAN/SAC DH7 .... 140 D5
Burnhope Wy *PLEE/EAS* SR8 ... 174 C4
Burnip Rd *SEA/MUR* SR7 .... 149 H4
Burn La *HLH* DH5 .... 147 K5
Burnlea Gdns *CRAM* NE23 ...... 39 H6
Burnley St *BLAY* NE21 .... 84 A2
Burnmill Bank *CON/LDGT* DH8 .. 122 A1
Burnmoor Gdns
   LWF/SPW/WRK NE9 .... 101 G2
Burnopfield Gdns
   BW/LEM/TK/HW NE15 .... 68 E5
Burnopfield Rd *ROWG* NE39 .... 97 H4
Burn Park Rd
   ASHBK/HED/RY SR2 .... 14 B7
   HLS DH4 .... 132 A7
Burn Prom *HLS* DH4 .... 132 B7
Burn Rd *BLAY* NE21 .... 83 H3
Burns Av *BLYTH* NE24 .... 34 E2
   BOLCOL NE35 .... 91 F4
Burns Av South *HLH* DH5 ...... 147 H1
Burns Cl *HAR/WTLS* NE34 ...... 91 F1
   HLS DH4 .... 146 D6
   STLY/ANP DH9 .... 126 C1
   WICK/BNPF NE16 .... 85 F7
Burns Crs *WICK/BNPF* NE16 .... 84 E4
Burnside *BDLGTN* NE22 .... 29 K3
   BDN/LAN/SAC DH7 .... 140 B4
   BDN/LAN/SAC DH7 .... 155 G1
   BOL NE36 .... 91 J3
   JRW NE32 .... 74 A7
   PLEE/EAS SR8 .... 174 D4
   PONT/DH NE20 .... 42 D6
Burnside Av *CRAM* NE23 .... 47 H1
   HLS DH4 .... 132 A6
   PLEE/EAS SR8 .... 175 H4
Burnside Cl *BLYTH* NE24 .... 30 D6
   PRUD NE42 .... 64 A7
   WICK/BNPF NE16 .... 98 E1
Burnside Rd *GOS/KPK* NE3 ...... 56 C3
   ROWG NE39 .... 97 F4
   TYNE/NSHE NE30 .... 51 F6
The Burnside
   WD/WHPE/BLK NE5 .... 68 C2
Burnside Vw *CRAM* NE23 .... 39 F7
Burns St *JRW* NE32 .... 73 K4
   RDHAMSE DH6 .... 182 D1
Burn's Ter *RDHAMSE* DH6 ...... 173 J5
Burnstones
   WD/WHPE/BLK NE5 .... 68 C2
Burn St *RDHAMSE* DH6 .... 180 A2
Burnthouse Bank
   CLSW/PEL DH2 .... 129 F3
Burnthouse Cl *BLAY* NE21 .... 83 J4
Burnthouse La *WICK/BNPF* NE16.. 84 E7
Burnt House Rd *MONK* NE25 .... 50 C6
Burntland Av *SWCK/CAS* SR5 ... 105 K3
Burn Vw *CRAM* NE23 .... 47 H3
Burnville Rd *MLFD/PNYW* SR4 ... 14 A7
Burnville Rd South
   MLFD/PNYW SR4 .... 14 A8
Burradon Rd *CRAM* NE23 .... 47 H3
Burrow St *SSH* NE33 .... 3 H7
Burscough Crs
   CLDN/WHIT/ROK SR6 .... 106 D3
Burstow Av *BYK/HTN/WLK* NE6 .. 12 F1
Burt Av *NSHW* NE29 .... 60 B7

Burt Cl *PLEE/EAS* SR8 — 174 E2
Burt Crs *CRAM* NE23 — 47 H1
Burt Rd *BDLGTN* NE22 — 30 A3
Burt St *BLYTH* NE24 — 31 G6
Burwell Av *WD/WHPE/BLK* NE5 — 68 D3
Burwood Rd *BYK/HTN/WLK* NE6 — 13 H1
  NSHW NE29 — 60 A2
Bushblades La *STLY/ANP* DH9 — 111 H7
Buston Ter *JES* NE2 — 71 F2
Busty Bank *WICK/BNPF* NE16 — 97 J5
Butcher's Bridge Rd *JRW* NE32 — 73 K7
Bute Dr *ROWG* NE39 — 96 B1
Buteland Rd
  BW/LEM/TK/HW NE15 — 68 D4
Buteland Ter *NWBGN* NE64 — 25 F1
Bute Rd North *ROWG* NE39 — 96 B1
Bute Rd South *ROWG* NE39 — 96 B2
Bute St *STLY/ANP* DH9 — 111 J4
Butsfield Gdns *SUNDSW* SR3 — 120 B4
Butsfield La *CON/LDGT* DH8 — 138 D2
Butterfield Cl *RYTON* NE40 — 66 B7
Buttermere
  CLDN/WHIT/ROK SR6 — 92 A3
  FELL NE10 — 13 J7
  PLEE/EAS SR8 — 174 B7
Buttermere Av *HLH* DH5 — 160 B1
  WICK/BNPF NE16 — 85 G5
Buttermere Cl
  WD/WHPE/BLK NE5 — 69 F2
Buttermere Crs *BLAY* NE21 — 83 K4
Buttermere Gdns
  HAR/WTLS NE34 — 75 J5
  LWF/SPW/WRK NE9 — 87 G7
Buttermere Rd
  TYNE/NSHE NE30 — 50 E7
Buttermere St
  ASHBK/HED/RY SR2 — 120 E4
Buttermere Wy *BLYTH* NE24 — 30 D5
Butterwell Dr *MPTH* NE61 — 21 H2
Button's Bank
  BDN/LAN/SAC DH7 — 164 E1
Buxton Cl *JRW* NE32 — 73 F5
  WLSD/HOW NE28 — 59 F5
Buxton Gdns *SUNDSW* SR3 — 120 B3
  WD/WHPE/BLK NE5 — 54 D7
Buxton Rd *JRW* NE32 — 74 A6
Byers Ct *SUNDSW* SR3 — 120 B6
Byer Sq *HLH* DH5 — 147 K2
Byer St *HLH* DH5 — 147 K2
The Bye *CON/LDGT* DH8 — 122 C7
The Byeways *LGB/KIL* NE12 — 57 H4
Bygate Cl *WD/WHPE/BLK* NE5 — 55 J7
Bygate Rd *MONK* NE25 — 50 C5
Byker Bank *BYK/HTN/WLK* NE6 — 6 B5
Byker Br *CNUT* NE1 — 6 B5
Byker Buildings
  BYK/HTN/WLK NE6 — 6 D5
Byker Ter *BYK/HTN/WLK* NE6 — 72 B5
Byland Cl *HLS* DH4 — 132 C6
Byland Ct *BDN/LAN/SAC* DH7 — 155 G6
  WASHS NE38 — 116 E1
Byland Rd *LGB/KIL* NE12 — 57 F4
Byony Toft *ASHBK/HED/RY* SR2 — 121 G7
Byrness *WD/WHPE/BLK* NE5 — 68 C2
Byrness Cl *GOS/KPK* NE3 — 55 G6
Byron Av *BLYTH* NE24 — 34 E2
  BOLCOL NE35 — 90 E4
  CLSW/PEL DH2 — 128 E4
  HEBB NE31 — 73 H5
Byron Cl *CLSW/PEL* DH2 — 115 G5
  STKFD/GP NE62 — 22 E6
Byron Pl *ASHGTN* NE63 — 24 B3
Byron Rd *SWCK/CAS* SR5 — 106 A3
Byron St *JES* NE2 — 5 M4
  SWCK/CAS SR5 — 106 B4
Byron Ter *RDHAMSE* DH6 — 173 J4
The By-way
  BW/LEM/TK/HW NE15 — 67 F2
Bywell Av *BW/LEM/TK/HW* NE15 — 68 C4
  GOS/KPK NE3 — 55 K2
  HAR/WTLS NE34 — 76 A4
  SWCK/CAS SR5 — 106 C2
Bywell Dr *PLEE/EAS* SR8 — 174 D7
Bywell Gdns *DUN/TMV* NE11 — 86 A7
  LWF/SPW/WRK NE9 — 87 H6
Bywell Rd *ASHGTN* NE63 — 23 K3
Bywell St *BYK/HTN/WLK* NE6 — 7 K6
  CLDN/WHIT/ROK SR6 — 91 K4
Bywell Ter *BYK/HTN/WLK* NE6 — 7 K6
Bywell Ter *JRW* NE32 — 89 K1

C

Cadehill Rd *PSHWF* NE43 — 79 F6
Cadger Bank
  BDN/LAN/SAC DH7 — 140 B5
Cadleston Ct *CRAM* NE23 — 33 K7
Cadwell La *PLEE/EAS* SR8 — 162 C5
Caernarvon Cl
  WD/WHPE/BLK NE5 — 55 F6
Caernarvon Dr *SUNDSW* SR3 — 133 G1
Caer Urfa Cl *SSH* NE33 — 3 H4
Cain Ter *RDHAMSE* DH6 — 182 D1
Cairncross *SWCK/CAS* SR5 — 104 E2
Cairnglass Gn *CRAM* NE23 — 33 K7
Cairngorm Av *WASHS* NE38 — 116 C3
Cairnmore CRAM NE23 — 38 C4
Cairnsmore Cl *CRAM* NE23 — 38 C4
Cairnsmore Dr *WASHS* NE38 — 116 D3
Cairns Rd *SEA/MUR* SR7 — 149 F5
  SWCK/CAS SR5 — 106 C1
Cairns Sq *SWCK/CAS* SR5 — 106 C1
Cairns Wy *GOS/KPK* NE3 — 55 K3
Cairo St *ASHBK/HED/RY* SR2 — 120 E2
Caithness Rd *SWCK/CAS* SR5 — 104 D3
Caithness Sq *SWCK/CAS* SR5 — 104 D4
Calais Rd *SWCK/CAS* SR5 — 104 D4
Caldbeck Av *BYK/HTN/WLK* NE6 — 13 G2
Caldbeck Cl *BYK/HTN/WLK* NE6 — 13 G2
Calderbourne Av
  CLDN/WHIT/ROK SR6 — 106 E1
Calderdale Av *WLSD/HOW* NE28 — 58 B5
Calderdale Av
  BYK/HTN/WLK NE6 — 72 B5
Calder Wk *WICK/BNPF* NE16 — 98 E3

Calderwood Crs
  LWF/SPW/WRK NE9 — 101 G2
Caldew Ct *HLH* DH5 — 148 A6
Caldew Crs *WD/WHPE/BLK* NE5 — 68 E3
Caldew La *WD/WHPE/BLK* NE5 — 55 K2
Caledonia St *HEBB* NE31 — 73 F4
Caledonian St
  BYK/HTN/WLK NE6 — 72 C7
Calf Close Dr *JRW* NE32 — 89 K2
Calfclose La *JRW* NE32 — 90 A2
Calf Close Wk *JRW* NE32 — 89 K1
California *BLAY* NE21 — 83 K3
Callalley Av *WICK/BNPF* NE16 — 84 D6
Callaly Av *CRAM* NE23 — 38 D2
Callaly Cl *MPTH* NE61 — 21 K2
Callaly Wy *BYK/HTN/WLK* NE6 — 7 K9
Callander *CLSW/PEL* DH2 — 115 G4
Callerdale Rd *BLYTH* NE24 — 30 C7
Callerton Av *NSHW* NE29 — 60 A3
Callerton Ct *PONT/DH* NE20 — 43 G5
Callerton La *PONT/DH* NE20 — 43 G4
  WD/WHPE/BLK NE5 — 53 G2
Callerton Pl *ELS/FEN* NE4 — 4 C6
Callerton Rd
  BW/LEM/TK/HW NE15 — 67 G1
Callerton Vw
  WD/WHPE/BLK NE5 — 53 K6
Calley Cl *PLEE/EAS* SR8 — 174 D7
Callington Dr
  ASHBK/HED/RY SR2 — 121 F7
Calvert Ter *SEA/MUR* SR7 — 149 G5
Calvus Dr
  BW/LEM/TK/HW NE15 — 66 B1
Camberley Cl *SUNDSW* SR3 — 120 C6
Camberley Dr
  BDN/LAN/SAC DH7 — 166 E7
Camberley Rd *WLSD/HOW* NE28 — 59 J6
Camberwell Wy *SUNDSW* SR3 — 133 H2
Cambo Av *BDLGTN* NE22 — 29 J5
  MONK NE25 — 50 B6
Cambo Cl *BLYTH* NE24 — 30 E7
  GOS/KPK NE3 — 56 D5
  WLSD/HOW NE28 — 59 F4
Cambo Dr *CRAM* NE23 — 38 D3
Cambo Gn *WD/WHPE/BLK* NE5 — 69 G1
Cambo Pl *TYNE/NSHE* NE30 — 60 E1
Camborne Gv *GATE* NE8 — 11 G6
Camborne Pl *GATE* NE8 — 11 G6
Cambourne Av
  CLDN/WHIT/ROK SR6 — 106 E1
Cambria Pl
  MLFD/PNYW SR4 — 104 E7
Cambrian St *JRW* NE32 — 73 K4
Cambrian Wy *WASHS* NE38 — 116 D2
Cambria St *MLFD/PNYW* SR4 — 104 E7
Cambridge Av
  CON/LDGT DH8 — 137 F2
  HEBB NE31 — 73 H6
  LGB/KIL NE12 — 57 K2
  WASHN NE37 — 102 D5
  WLSD/HOW NE28 — 58 C7
Cambridge Dr
  CLS/BIR/GTL DH3 — 145 H2
Cambridge Pl *CLS/BIR/GTL* DH3 — 115 J5
Cambridge Rd *PLEE/EAS* SR8 — 174 D2
  STKFD/GP NE62 — 23 G6
  SUNDSW SR3 — 120 A7
Cambridgeshire Dr *DHAM* DH1 — 157 K7
Cambridge St *ELS/FEN* NE4 — 9 K1
Camden St
  SWCK/CAS SR5 — 106 A4
  TYNE/NSHE NE30 — 2 E2
Camelford Ct
  BW/LEM/TK/HW NE15 — 68 A3
Camelot Cl *SEA/MUR* SR7 — 135 J7
Cameron Cl *HAR/WTLS* NE34 — 91 G1
Cameron Rd *PRUD* NE42 — 80 D2
Camerton Pl *WLSD/HOW* NE28 — 59 G3
Camilla Rd
  BW/LEM/TK/HW NE15 — 66 B1
Camilla St *GATE* NE8 — 11 H5
Campbell Park Rd *HEBB* NE31 — 73 G5
Campbell Pl *ELS/FEN* NE4 — 4 D6
Campbell Rd *SWCK/CAS* SR5 — 104 D3
Campbell St *HEBB* NE31 — 73 F4
Camperdown
  WD/WHPE/BLK NE5 — 68 D2
Camperdown Av
  CLS/BIR/GTL DH3 — 129 K2
Campion Dr *STLY/ANP* DH9 — 112 B6
Campion Gdns *FELL* NE10 — 87 K7
Campion Wy *ASHGTN* NE63 — 23 J5
Camp Rd *WLSD/HOW* NE28 — 72 D3
Campsie Crs *TYNE/NSHE* NE30 — 60 E1
Camp Ter *NSHW* NE29 — 60 E4

Capulet Ter
  ASHBK/HED/RY SR2 — 15 H9
Caradoc Cl *WASHS* NE38 — 116 D3
Caragh Rd *CLSW/PEL* DH2 — 129 J6
Caraway Wk *HAR/WTLS* NE34 — 91 J1
Carden Av *HAR/WTLS* NE34 — 76 B6
Cardiff Sq *SWCK/CAS* SR5 — 104 D4
Cardigan Gv *MONK* NE25 — 50 E6
Cardigan Ter *BYK/HTN/WLK* NE6 — 6 E3
Cardinal Cl *LGB/KIL* NE12 — 57 G4
  WD/WHPE/BLK NE5 — 53 K7
Cardinals Cl *SUNDSW* SR3 — 133 K2
Cardonnel St *NSHW* NE29 — 2 C4
Cardwell St — 106 E4
Careen Crs *SUNDSW* SR3 — 119 F7
Carey Cl *RDHAMSE* DH6 — 180 A3
Carham Av *CRAM* NE23 — 38 D2
Carham Ct *GOS/KPK* NE3 — 56 D4
Carisbrooke *BDLGTN* NE22 — 29 F4
Caris St *GATE* NE8 — 11 J8
Carlby Wy *CRAM* NE23 — 33 F5
Carlcroft Pl *CRAM* NE23 — 38 D3
Carley Hill Rd *SWCK/CAS* SR5 — 106 B2
Carley Rd *SWCK/CAS* SR5 — 106 B2
Carlingford Rd *CLSW/PEL* DH2 — 129 H6
Carliol Sq *CNUT* NE1 — 5 L6
Carliol St *CNUT* NE1 — 5 L6
Carlisle Crs *HLS* DH4 — 117 J7
Carlisle Lea *MPTH* NE61 — 20 E6
Carlisle Rd *DHAM* DH1 — 157 F2
Carlisle St *FELL* NE10 — 12 C6
Carlisle Vw *MPTH* NE61 — 20 D5
Carlow Dr *STKFD/GP* NE62 — 23 K5
Carlton Av *BLYTH* NE24 — 34 E4
Carlton Cl *CLSW/PEL* DH2 — 114 E4
  GOS/KPK NE3 — 56 A7
Carlton Ct *DUN/TMV* NE11 — 86 D7
Carlton Crs *SUNDSW* SR3 — 119 G7
Carlton Gdns
  BW/LEM/TK/HW NE15 — 68 C4
Carlton Gv *WICK/BNPF* NE16 — 24 B4
Carlton Rd *LGB/KIL* NE12 — 57 K4
Carlton St *BLYTH* NE24 — 31 H7
Carlton Ter *LWF/SPW/WRK* NE9 — 86 E7
  NSHW NE29 — 2 A2
Carlyle Ct *WLSD/HOW* NE28 — 73 J2
Carlyle Crs *WICK/BNPF* NE16 — 84 E4
Carlyle St *WLSD/HOW* NE28 — 73 J2
Carlyon St
  ASHBK/HED/RY SR2 — 14 E8
Carmel Gv *CRAM* NE23 — 33 G6
Carmel Rd *STLY/ANP* DH9 — 126 B1
Carnaby Rd
  BYK/HTN/WLK NE6 — 72 B7
Carnation Av *HLS* DH4 — 131 F4
Carnegie Cl *HAR/WTLS* NE34 — 75 G7
Carnegie St
  ASHBK/HED/RY SR2 — 121 F4
Carnforth Cl *WLSD/HOW* NE28 — 59 F3
Carnforth Gdns
  LWF/SPW/WRK NE9 — 101 H1
  ROWG NE39 — 97 G2
Carnforth Gn *GOS/KPK* NE3 — 55 J6
Carnoustie *CLSW/PEL* DH2 — 115 F5
  HAR/WTLS NE34 — 91 K1
  WASHN NE37 — 102 E3
Carnoustie Cl *MONK* NE25 — 50 A4
Carnoustie Ct
  HAR/WTLS NE34 — 91 K1
Carol Gdns *LGB/HTN* NE7 — 57 H7
Caroline Gdns *WLSD/HOW* NE28 — 59 J3
Caroline St *ELS/FEN* NE4 — 69 J7
  HLH DH5 — 147 K4
  JRW NE32 — 73 J4
  SEA/MUR SR7 — 150 E1
Carol St *MLFD/PNYW* SR4 — 14 A3
Carolyn Cl *LGB/KIL* NE12 — 57 J4
Carolyn Crs *WBAY* NE26 — 50 C2
Carolyn Wy *WBAY* NE26 — 50 C2
Carpenter St *SSH* NE33 — 2 F9
Carr Av *BDN/LAN/SAC* DH7 — 167 G6
Carr Fld *PONT/DH* NE20 — 43 H2
Carrfield Rd *GOS/KPK* NE3 — 55 K5
Carr Hill Rd *LWF/SPW/WRK* NE9 — 11 J8
Carr House La *HLH* DH5 — 156 D3
Carrhouse La *HLH* DH5 — 148 D3
Carrick Dr *BLYTH* NE24 — 35 F3
Carrigill Pl *LGB/KIL* NE12 — 57 G4
Carrington Cl *CRAM* NE23 — 39 G7
Carrmere Rd
  ASHBK/HED/RY SR2 — 120 E5
Carrmyers *STLY/ANP* DH9 — 125 C1
Carrock Cl *PLEE/EAS* SR8 — 174 E7
Carrowmore Rd
  CLSW/PEL DH2 — 129 J6
Carrs Cl *PRUD* NE42 — 81 F4
Carrsdale *DHAM* DH1 — 158 A4
Carr St *BLYTH* NE24 — 34 E3
  HEBB NE31 — 73 F4
Carrsway *DHAM* DH1 — 158 A4
Carrsyde Cl *WICK/BNPF* NE16 — 84 D7
Carsdale Rd *GOS/KPK* NE3 — 55 H5
Carter Av *HAR/WTLS* NE34 — 74 C7
Cartington Av *SMOOR* NE27 — 49 G7
Cartington Cl *PLEE/EAS* SR8 — 174 E7
Cartington Ct *GOS/KPK* NE3 — 55 J3
Cartington Rd *DHAM* DH1 — 156 D4
  NSHW NE29 — 60 C5
Cartington Ter
  BYK/HTN/WLK NE6 — 71 J2
Cartmel Ct *CLSW/PEL* DH2 — 129 C5
Cartmel Gv *GATE* NE8 — 10 C9
Cartmel Pk *FELL* NE10 — 13 K6
Cartwright Rd *SWCK/CAS* SR5 — 105 G4
Carville Rd *WLSD/HOW* NE28 — 72 D2
Carville St *FELL* NE10 — 11 M3
Carvill Gdns *WLSD/HOW* NE28 — 72 D3
Carvis Cl *BDN/LAN/SAC* DH7 — 167 F5
Carwarding Pl
  WD/WHPE/BLK NE5 — 69 G2
Caseton Cl *MONK* NE25 — 50 A3
Caspian Cl *JRW* NE32 — 74 A6
Caspian Rd *SWCK/CAS* SR5 — 104 D4
Caspian Sq *SWCK/CAS* SR5 — 104 D4
Castellian Rd *SWCK/CAS* SR5 — 105 G4

Casterton Gv
  WD/WHPE/BLK NE5 — 53 K7
Castle Av *RDHAMSE* DH6 — 179 K2
Castle Bank *MPTH* NE61 — 20 C5
Castle Chare *DHAM* DH1 — 16 C3
Castle Cl *CLS/BIR/GTL* DH3 — 129 K5
  GOS/KPK NE3 — 55 H5
  HLH DH5 — 148 A6
  MPTH NE61 — 20 D5
  WICK/BNPF NE16 — 84 E5
Castledale Av *BLYTH* NE24 — 34 C1
Castledene Ct *GOS/KPK* NE3 — 57 F6
Castle Dene Gv *HLS* DH4 — 132 B7
Castledene Rd *CON/LDGT* DH8 — 123 H6
Castlefields *BDN/LAN/SAC* DH7 — 165 J1
Castleford Rd *SWCK/CAS* SR5 — 104 D3
Castlegate Gdns *GATE* NE8 — 9 K6
Castle Hills *MPTH* NE61 — 20 C6
Castle Mdw *MPTH* NE61 — 20 C6
Castlenook Pl
  BW/LEM/TK/HW NE15 — 68 D4
Castlereagh Cl *SEA/MUR* SR7 — 135 J7
Castlereagh Rd *SEA/MUR* SR7 — 150 E1
Castlereagh St *SUNDSW* SR3 — 120 A7
Castlereigh Cl *HLS* DH4 — 131 F4
Castle Riggs *CLSW/PEL* DH2 — 129 H4
Castles Farm Rd *LGB/HTN* NE7 — 56 E6
Castles Gn *LGB/KIL* NE12 — 48 A6
Castleside Rd
  BW/LEM/TK/HW NE15 — 68 E5
Castle Sq *SMOOR* NE27 — 48 D5
Castle St *DIN/WO* NE13 — 46 A5
  SUND SR1 — 14 D4
Castle St South
  SWCK/CAS SR5 — 105 G4
Castleton Cl *CRAM* NE23 — 33 G6
  JES NE2 — 71 F1
Castleton Gv *JES* NE2 — 71 F1
Castletown Rd *SWCK/CAS* SR5 — 105 H3
Castletown Wy *SWCK/CAS* SR5 — 105 H3
Castle Vw *BDN/LAN/SAC* DH7 — 165 J1
  BDN/LAN/SAC DH7 — 167 H1
  CLS/BIR/GTL DH3 — 129 J2
  PRUD NE42 — 64 B7
  SWCK/CAS SR5 — 105 F4
Castle Wk *MPTH* NE61 — 20 D6
Castleway *DIN/WO* NE13 — 45 F3
  MPTH NE61 — 21 K2
Castlewood Cl
  WD/WHPE/BLK NE5 — 68 B1
Catchside Cl *WICK/BNPF* NE16 — 84 E7
Catchwell Rd *STLY/ANP* DH9 — 111 F6
Cateran Wy *CRAM* NE23 — 38 D4
Caterhouse Rd *DHAM* DH1 — 156 C3
Catharine St West
  MLFD/PNYW SR4 — 106 A7
Cathedral Vw
  BDN/LAN/SAC DH7 — 143 J6
  HLS DH4 — 132 B4
Catherine Cookson Ct
  SSH NE33 — 75 J2
Catherine Rd *HLS* DH4 — 132 B1
Catherine St *SSH* NE33 — 3 J7
Catherine Ter *STLY/ANP* DH9 — 112 D6
Catholic Rw *BDLGTN* NE22 — 28 E6
Catkin Wk *RYTON* NE40 — 66 C7
Cato Sq *SWCK/CAS* SR5 — 106 A3
Cato St *SWCK/CAS* SR5 — 106 A3
Catton Gv *WICK/BNPF* NE16 — 99 F2
Catton Pl *WLSD/HOW* NE28 — 59 G4
Cauldwell Av *HAR/WTLS* NE34 — 75 J4
  MONK NE25 — 50 B6
Cauldwell Cl *MONK* NE25 — 50 B5
Cauldwell La *MONK* NE25 — 50 B5
Cauldwell Pl *HAR/WTLS* NE34 — 75 J4
Cauldwell Vls *HAR/WTLS* NE34 — 75 J4
Causeway
  CLDN/WHIT/ROK SR6 — 14 F1
  LWF/SPW/WRK NE9 — 87 H6
The Causeway
  BW/LEM/TK/HW NE15 — 67 F2
  LWF/SPW/WRK NE9 — 11 K8
Causey Bank *CNUT* NE1 — 5 M7
Causey Dr *STLY/ANP* DH9 — 112 E6
Causey Rd *STLY/ANP* DH9 — 112 E4
Causey St *GOS/KPK* NE3 — 56 C6
Cavalier Vw *HEBB* NE31 — 73 F4
Cavalier Wy *SUNDSW* SR3 — 119 K7
Cavell Sq *PLEE/EAS* SR8 — 162 E4
Cavendish Ct
  BDN/LAN/SAC DH7 — 167 F7
Cavendish Pl *JES* NE2 — 71 F2
  SUNDSW SR3 — 133 K2
Cavendish Rd *JES* NE2 — 71 F2
Cavendish Sq *MPTH* NE61 — 21 J2
Cavendish Ter *ASHGTN* NE63 — 23 K2
Caversham Rd
  WD/WHPE/BLK NE5 — 53 K7
Cawnpore Sq *MLFD/PNYW* SR4 — 105 J7
Caynham Cl *NSHW* NE29 — 2 C2
Cayton Gv *WD/WHPE/BLK* NE5 — 67 K1
Cecil Cl *PONT/DH* NE20 — 43 H3
Cecil St *NSHW* NE29 — 2 C2
Cedar Av *CLSW/PEL* DH2 — 144 A4
Cedar Cl *BDLGTN* NE22 — 29 F4
  DHAM DH1 — 17 M1
Cedar Ct *BDN/LAN/SAC* DH7 — 153 K3
  DHAM DH1 — 17 M1
Cedar Crs *SEA/MUR* SR7 — 149 J5
Cedars Ct *ASHBK/HED/RY* SR2 — 14 F9
Cedar Crs *CLSW/PEL* DH2 — 144 A4
Cedar Dr *DHAM* DH1 — 168 C5
Cedar Gdns *CON/LDGT* DH8 — 122 C6
Cedar Gv *CLDN/WHIT/ROK* SR6 — 93 F2
  HAR/WTLS NE34 — 75 K6
  RYTON NE40 — 66 E6
  WASHS NE38 — 116 D2
Cedar Rd *BLAY* NE21 — 84 A2
  ELS/FEN NE4 — 69 H4
Cedars Crs *ASHBK/HED/RY* SR2 — 120 E3
Cedars Gn *LWF/SPW/WRK* NE9 — 101 G2
Cedars Pk *ASHBK/HED/RY* SR2 — 120 E3
The Cedars *ASHBK/HED/RY* SR2 — 120 D2

  WICK/BNPF NE16 — 99 F1
Cedar St *PLEE/EAS* SR8 — 175 J4
Cedartree Gdns *MONK* NE25 — 50 C6
Cedarway *FELL* NE10 — 88 A7
Cedar Wy *LGB/KIL* NE12 — 58 A2
Cedarwood Av
  BYK/HTN/WLK NE6 — 72 C2
Cedarwood Gv
  ASHBK/HED/RY SR2 — 120 C4
Cedric Crs *ASHBK/HED/RY* SR2 — 14 A9
Celadon Cl
  BW/LEM/TK/HW NE15 — 68 A3
Celandine Cl *GOS/KPK* NE3 — 56 D3
Celandine Ct *ASHGTN* NE63 — 23 H4
Celandine Wy *FELL* NE10 — 87 K6
Celtic Cl *CLDN/WHIT/ROK* SR6 — 91 J3
Celtic Crs
  CLDN/WHIT/ROK SR6 — 91 J3
Cemetery Ap *HAR/WTLS* NE34 — 75 J3
Cemetery Rd *GATE* NE8 — 11 H5
  JRW NE32 — 74 A6
  RDHAMSE DH6 — 182 E2
  STLY/ANP DH9 — 112 D7
Centenary Av *HAR/WTLS* NE34 — 76 A5
Central Av *BDN/LAN/SAC* DH7 — 167 H7
  CLDN/WHIT/ROK SR6 — 92 A4
  HAR/WTLS NE34 — 75 K5
  NSHW NE29 — 60 C5
  STKFD/GP NE62 — 22 E6
Central Gdns *HAR/WTLS* NE34 — 75 K5
Centurion Wy *BDLGTN* NE22 — 28 E4
Centurion Rd
  BW/LEM/TK/HW NE15 — 68 C3
Centurion Wy
  BW/LEM/TK/HW NE15 — 66 A1
  LWF/SPW/WRK NE9 — 87 H6
Ceolfrid Ter *STLY/ANP* DH9 — 74 A7
Chacombe *WASHS* NE38 — 116 E3
Chadderton Dr
  WD/WHPE/BLK NE5 — 53 K7
Chadwick Cl
  WLSD/HOW NE28 — 72 D2
Chaffinch Ct *ASHGTN* NE63 — 23 H3
Chaffinch Wy *LGB/KIL* NE12 — 47 J5
Chain Bridge Rd *BLAY* NE21 — 84 D1
Chainbridge Rd *BLAY* NE21 — 84 B1
Chair La *SPEN* DL16 — 178 B6
Chalfont Gv *MLFD/PNYW* SR4 — 14 A9
Chalfont Rd *BYK/HTN/WLK* NE6 — 72 B7
Chalfont Wy
  BDN/LAN/SAC DH7 — 167 H6
Chalford Rd *SWCK/CAS* SR5 — 106 B3
Challoner's Gdns *MPTH* NE61 — 20 C4
Chamberlain St *BLYTH* NE24 — 35 H1
  RYTON NE40 — 66 B7
Chandler Cl *DHAM* DH1 — 17 M4
Chandlers Ford *HLS* DH4 — 117 H6
Chandlers Quay
  BYK/HTN/WLK NE6 — 12 B1
Chandos *SUNDSW* SR3 — 134 A3
Chandos St *GATE* NE8 — 11 H7
Chandra Pl
  WD/WHPE/BLK NE5 — 69 F1
Chantry Cl *SUNDSW* SR3 — 133 J2
Chantry Dr *DIN/WO* NE13 — 46 B2
Chantry Pl *MPTH* NE61 — 20 D5
Chapel Av *WICK/BNPF* NE16 — 97 K7
Chapel Cl *GOS/KPK* NE3 — 56 D1
Chapel Ct *BDN/LAN/SAC* DH7 — 155 F1
  RDHAMSE DH6 — 170 D1
Chapel Hill Rd *PLEE/EAS* SR8 — 175 F3
Chapel House Dr
  WD/WHPE/BLK NE5 — 68 A2
Chapel House Gv
  BW/LEM/TK/HW NE15 — 68 A2
Chapel La *RDHAMSE* DH6 — 160 E6
  WYLAM NE41 — 65 G5
Chapel Rd *JRW* NE32 — 73 K4
Chapel Rw *HLS* DH4 — 132 K4
  PSHWF NE43 — 79 J3
Chapel St *HLH* DH5 — 147 K4
  NSHW NE29 — 60 C5
  STLY/ANP DH9 — 111 J4
  WNGT TS28 — 183 K5
Chapel Vw *HLS* DH4 — 146 C7
  ROWG NE39 — 97 G2
Chaplin St *SEA/MUR* SR7 — 150 E2
Chapman St
  CLDN/WHIT/ROK SR6 — 106 E1
Chapter Rw *SSH* NE33 — 3 G7
Chare La *RDHAMSE* DH6 — 171 H3
Charlaw Cl *BDN/LAN/SAC* DH7 — 143 G4
Charlaw La *BDN/LAN/SAC* DH7 — 142 D3
Charlbury Cl
  LWF/SPW/WRK NE9 — 102 B4
Charlcote Crs *BOL* NE36 — 91 H5
Charles Av *GOS/KPK* NE3 — 55 J4
  LGB/KIL NE12 — 57 K2
Charles Baker Wk
  HAR/WTLS NE34 — 76 B5
Charles Dr *CRAM* NE23 — 47 H1
Charles St *BOLCOL* NE35 — 90 D4
  CLDN/WHIT/ROK SR6 — 14 C7
  DIN/WO NE13 — 46 A4
  GATE NE8 — 11 G3
  MPTH NE61 — 21 K2
  SEA/MUR SR7 — 150 E1
  STLY/ANP DH9 — 126 C3
  SUND SR1 — 15 G3
Charleswood *GOS/KPK* NE3 — 56 D2
Charlotte Cl *ELS/FEN* NE4 — 9 L1
Charlotte Sq *CNUT* NE1 — 5 H7
Charlotte St *SSH* NE33 — 3 H7
  STLY/ANP DH9 — 126 C3
  TYNE/NSHE NE30 — 2 F2
  WLSD/HOW NE28 — 72 E1
Charlton Gdns *MPTH* NE61 — 21 F6
Charlton Gv
  CLDN/WHIT/ROK SR6 — 92 A4
Charlton Rd *SWCK/CAS* SR5 — 106 C2
Charlton St
  BW/LEM/TK/HW NE15 — 68 B5
Charman St *SUND* SR1 — 14 E4
Charminster Gdns
  BYK/HTN/WLK NE6 — 71 J1
Charnwood *STLY/ANP* DH9 — 112 C6
Charnwood Av *LGB/KIL* NE12 — 57 G4
Charter Dr *SUNDSW* SR3 — 119 G7

Chartwell Pl CON/LDGT DH8 ..... 123 F3 🔲
Chasedale Crs BLYTH NE24 .... 30 C7
Chase Farm Dr BLYTH NE24 .... 30 B6
Chase Ms BLYTH NE24 .... 30 B7 🔲
The Chase LGB/KIL NE12 .... 47 C7
  NSHW NE29 .... 2 B1
  WASHS NE38 .... 116 B5
Chatham Cl MONK NE25 .... 40 A7
Chatham Rd SWCK/CAS SR5 ...... 104 E3
Chathill Cl MONK NE25 .... 50 A4
  MPTH NE61 .... 26 E1 🔲
Chathill Ter BYK/HTN/WLK NE6 ... 72 B6
Chatsworth Crs
  MLFD/PNYW SR4 .... 120 A2 🔲
Chatsworth Gdns
  BYK/HTN/WLK NE6 .... 7 K9
  WD/WHPE/BLK NE5 .... 54 D7 🔲
Chatsworth Pl HAR/WTLS NE16 .. 84 E7
Chatsworth Rd JRW NE32 .... 74 A6 🔲
Chatsworth St
  MLFD/PNYW SR4 .... 120 A1
Chatsworth St South
  MLFD/PNYW SR4 .... 120 A2 🔲
Chatterton St SWCK/CAS SR5 .... 106 A3
Chatton Av CRAM NE23 .... 38 D3
  HAR/WTLS NE34 .... 76 B3
Chatton Cl CLSW/PEL DH2 .... 129 C6
Chatton St WLSD/HOW NE28 ...... 74 A2
Chatton Wynd GOS/KPK NE3 ..... 56 A3 🔲
Chaucer Av HAR/WTLS NE34 ...... 90 E1
Chaucer Cl GATE NE8 .... 11 J3
  STLY/ANP DH9 .... 126 E1
Chaucer Rd WICK/BNPF NE16 ..... 84 E4
Chaytor Rd CON/LDGT DH8 .... 122 C3
Chaytor St JRW NE32 .... 73 K3
Cheadle Av CRAM NE23 .... 33 G6 🔲
  WLSD/HOW NE28 .... 59 F4
Cheadle Rd SWCK/CAS SR5 ...... 104 E3
Cheam Cl WICK/BNPF NE16 .... 85 F7 🔲
Cheam Rd SWCK/CAS SR5 .... 104 E3
Cheeseburn Gdns
  WD/WHPE/BLK NE5 .... 69 G3
Cheldon Cl MONK NE25 .... 50 A3
Chelford Cl WLSD/HOW NE28 ...... 59 C3
Chelmsford Gv JES NE2 .... 6 C3
Chelmsford Rd SWCK/CAS SR5 .. 104 E3
Chelmsford Sq
  SWCK/CAS SR5 .... 104 E2 🔲
Chelsea Gdns GATE NE8 .... 11 L7
Chelsea Gv ELS/FEN NE4 .... 4 C6
Cheltenham Dr BOLCOL NE35 ..... 90 C2
Cheltenham Rd
  SWCK/CAS SR5 .... 104 E3 🔲
Cheltenham Sq
  SWCK/CAS SR5 .... 104 E3 🔲
Cheltenham Ter
  BYK/HTN/WLK NE6 .... 6 F2
Chelton Cl DIN/WO NE13 .... 46 B5 🔲
Chepstow Cl CON/LDGT DH8 ..... 108 D7 🔲
Chepstow Gdns GATE NE8 .... 10 C9
Chepstow Rd
  BW/LEM/TK/HW NE15 .... 68 D5
Chepstow St
  MLFD/PNYW SR4 .... 14 A6 🔲
Cherry Banks CLS/BIR/GTL DH3 .. 129 K2
Cherry Blossom Wy
  WASHN NE37 .... 103 K5
Cherry Gv LGB/KIL NE12 .... 47 J5
  PRUD NE42 .... 80 B1
Cherry Pk BDN/LAN/SAC DH7 .... 167 F7
Cherrytree Cl LGB/KIL NE12 .... 48 D7
Cherrytree Ct BDLGTN NE22 .... 29 K4 🔲
Cherry Tree Dr BDLGTN NE22 ...... 29 F5
Cherrytree Dr
  BDN/LAN/SAC DH7 .... 154 A3
  WICK/BNPF NE16 .... 8 B8
Cherry Tree Gdns
  BW/LEM/TK/HW NE15 .... 64 C3
Cherrytree Gdns
  LWF/SPW/WRK NE9 .... 101 G1
  MONK NE25 .... 50 D6
Cherry Tree La WYLAM NE41 .... 65 C5
Cherry Trees BLYTH NE24 .... 35 F1 🔲
Cherry Wy HLS DH4 .... 131 K6
Cherwell WASHN NE37 .... 103 H5
Cherwell Rd PLEE/EAS SR8 .... 174 C5
Chesham Gdns
  WD/WHPE/BLK NE5 .... 67 K1
Cheshire Av CLS/BIR/GTL DH3 ... 115 J5
Cheshire Cl ASHGTN NE63 .... 23 G1 🔲
Cheshire Dr DHAM DH1 .... 157 K7
Cheshire Gdns WLSD/HOW NE28 .. 58 C7
Cheshire Gv HAR/WTLS NE34 ...... 76 B4
The Chesils LGB/KIL NE12 .... 57 G5
Chesmond Dr BLAY NE21 .... 83 K1
Chessar Av WD/WHPE/BLK NE5 .. 68 E2
Chester Cl PONT/DH NE20 .... 42 D5
Chester Ct LGB/KIL NE12 .... 57 H4
Chester Gdns
  CON/LDGT DH8 .... 137 F1
  HLS DH4 .... 131 F4
  MLFD/PNYW SR4 .... 118 C4
  STLY/ANP DH9 .... 112 E7
Chester Road Est
  STLY/ANP DH9 .... 112 E7
Chesters Av LGB/KIL NE12 .... 57 C4
Chesters Dene CON/LDGT DH8 .. 108 E3
Chesters Pk
  LWF/SPW/WRK NE9 .... 87 F6 🔲
The Chesters CON/LDGT DH8 ..... 108 E3
  MONK NE25 .... 50 B3
  WD/WHPE/BLK NE5 .... 68 A2
Chester St HLS DH4 .... 132 B5
  JES NE2 .... 6 A3
  MLFD/PNYW SR4 .... 106 A7
Chester St East
  MLFD/PNYW SR4 .... 14 A5
Chester St West
  MLFD/PNYW SR4 .... 106 A7 🔲

Chester Ter SUND SR1 .... 14 B5
Chester Ter North
  MLFD/PNYW SR4 .... 14 A5
Chesterton Rd HAR/WTLS NE34 .. 75 F7
Chesterwood Dr
  WLSD/HOW NE28 .... 72 C1
Chestnut Av BLYTH NE24 .... 31 F5
  MONK NE25 .... 50 D5
  WD/WHPE/BLK NE5 .... 69 J1
  WICK/BNPF NE16 .... 85 F7
Chestnut Cl JRW NE32 .... 90 B3
  LGB/KIL NE12 .... 47 H5 🔲
Chestnut Crs SWCK/CAS SR5 .... 105 K2
Chestnut Dr RDHAMSE DH6 ...... 161 F6
Chestnut Gdns GATE NE8 .... 10 A7
Chestnut Gv BDN/LAN/SAC DH7 .. 167 F1
  HAR/WTLS NE34 .... 75 K7
Chestnut St WLSD/HOW NE28 ..... 72 E2 🔲
Cheswick Dr GOS/KPK NE3 .... 56 D4
Cheveley Wk DHAM DH1 .... 158 A6
Chevin Cl BYK/HTN/WLK NE6 ...... 72 C2
Chevington FELL NE10 .... 88 C6 🔲
Chevington Cl MPTH NE61 .... 21 H2
Chevington Gdns
  WD/WHPE/BLK NE5 .... 69 H2 🔲
Cheviot Cl WASHN NE37 .... 102 C7
Cheviot Gdns DUN/TMV NE11 ..... 86 A5 🔲
  SEA/MUR SR7 .... 135 G7
Cheviot Gra CRAM NE23 .... 47 J3
Cheviot Gv MPTH NE61 .... 21 H2
Cheviot La ASHBK/HED/RY SR2 .. 120 D7
Cheviot Pl PLEE/EAS SR8 .... 174 C4
Cheviot Rd BLAY NE21 .... 84 A3
  HAR/WTLS NE34 .... 76 A3
  JRW NE32 .... 73 H7 🔲
Cheviot St MLFD/PNYW SR4 ...... 105 K6
Cheviot Vw ASHGTN NE63 .... 18 A7
  CLSW/PEL DH2 .... 129 C7
  DIN/WO NE13 .... 46 A3
  PRUD NE42 .... 80 E2
Cheyne Rd PRUD NE42 .... 80 C1
The Cheyne SUNDSW SR3 .... 134 A2
Chichester Av CRAM NE23 .... 33 F7
Chichester Cl ASHGTN NE63 .... 24 C3
  GOS/KPK NE3 .... 55 G3
Chichester Gv BDLGTN NE22 .... 29 F4
Chichester Pl SSH NE33 .... 75 C3 🔲
Chichester Rd
  CLDN/WHIT/ROK SR6 .... 106 E1
  DHAM DH1 .... 156 E1
  SSH NE33 .... 75 H2 🔲
Chichester Rd East SSH NE33 ...... 75 H2
Chicken Rd WLSD/HOW NE28 ...... 58 C7
Chigwell Cl HLS DH4 .... 117 K7
Chilcrosse FELL NE10 .... 88 B5 🔲
Chilham Ct NSHW NE29 .... 59 K2
Chillingham Cl BLYTH NE24 .... 34 D2
Chillingham Crs ASHGTN NE63 ..... 23 J2
Chillingham Dr
  CLSW/PEL DH2 .... 129 G7 🔲
  NSHW NE29 .... 60 B6 🔲
Chillingham Rd
  BYK/HTN/WLK NE6 .... 71 J2
  DHAM DH1 .... 156 E1
Chillingham Ter JRW NE32 .... 74 B7
Chilside Rd FELL NE10 .... 12 C9
Chiltern Cl ASHGTN NE63 .... 24 A4
  WASHS NE38 .... 116 D3
Chiltern Dr LGB/KIL NE12 .... 57 H1
Chiltern Gdns DUN/TMV NE11 ..... 86 A5
Chiltern Rd NSHW NE29 .... 50 D7
Chilton Gdns HLS DH4 .... 131 J7 🔲
Chilton Garth PLEE/EAS SR8 .... 175 C5
Chilton St SWCK/CAS SR5 .... 106 A4 🔲
China St ASHBK/HED/RY SR2 ..... 120 E2
Chingford Cl HLS DH4 .... 118 A7 🔲
Chipchase WASHS NE38 .... 116 B2
Chipchase Av CRAM NE23 .... 33 H4
Chipchase Cl BDLGTN NE22 .... 28 D5 🔲
  MPTH NE61 .... 21 K2 🔲
Chipchase Ct MONK NE25 .... 39 K2
Chipchase Crs
  WD/WHPE/BLK NE5 .... 54 C7
Chipchase Ter JRW NE32 .... 89 K1
The Chip MPTH NE61 .... 26 D1
Chirton Av HAR/WTLS NE34 .... 76 C5
  NSHW NE29 .... 2 D1 🔲
Chirton Dene Quays NSHW NE29 . 2 B8
Chirton Dene Wy NSHW NE29 ...... 2 B7
Chirton Gn NSHW NE29 .... 2 A2
Chirton Gv HAR/WTLS NE34 .... 76 C5
Chirton Hill Dr NSHW NE29 .... 60 A3
Chirton La NSHW NE29 .... 60 C4
Chirton West Vw NSHW NE29 .... 2 B2
Chirton Wynd BYK/HTN/WLK NE6 . 7 H6
Chislehurst Rd HLS DH4 .... 117 K7
Chiswick Gdns GATE NE8 .... 11 K8
Chiswick Rd MONK NE25 .... 40 A6
  SWCK/CAS SR5 .... 104 E3
Chollerford Av MONK NE25 .... 50 B5 🔲
  NSHW NE29 .... 60 A4
Chollerford Cl GOS/KPK NE3 .... 56 A6
Chollerford Ms MONK NE25 .... 40 C6
Chollerton Dr BDLGTN NE22 .... 29 G5
  LGB/KIL NE12 .... 58 C3
Choppington Rd MPTH NE61 .... 21 F7
  STKFD/GP NE62 .... 29 F3
Chopwell Rd CHPW NE17 .... 95 J7
Chorley Pl BYK/HTN/WLK NE6 ...... 7 L6
Chowdene Bank
  DUN/TMV NE11 .... 100 E3
  LWF/SPW/WRK NE9 .... 101 F2
Christal Ter
  CLDN/WHIT/ROK SR6 .... 106 D2
Christie Ter BYK/HTN/WLK NE6 .... 72 B6
Christon Cl GOS/KPK NE3 .... 56 E5 🔲
Christon Rd GOS/KPK NE3 .... 56 C5
Christon Wy FELL NE10 .... 13 M4
Chudleigh Gdns
  WD/WHPE/BLK NE5 .... 67 K1
Church Av GOS/KPK NE3 .... 56 D5
  STKFD/GP NE62 .... 23 K6
Church Bank
  BW/LEM/TK/HW NE15 .... 67 H4 🔲

  CON/LDGT DH8 .... 122 C1
  JRW NE32 .... 74 B4
  STLY/ANP DH9 .... 112 D7
  SWCK/CAS SR5 .... 106 A4 🔲
  WLSD/HOW NE28 .... 73 F1
Churchburn Dr MPTH NE61 .... 20 D7
Church Chare PONT/DH NE20 ...... 43 H2
  WICK/BNPF NE16 .... 85 F5
Church Cl BDLGTN NE22 .... 29 F6 🔲
  CON/LDGT DH8 .... 108 E3
  DIN/WO NE13 .... 45 F7
  MONK NE25 .... 50 A5
  PLEE/EAS SR8 .... 175 F5
  SEA/MUR SR7 .... 135 J7
Church Ct BDLGTN NE22 .... 29 F6
  SEA/MUR SR7 .... 135 G7
Churchdown Cl BOLCOL NE35 ..... 90 C2 🔲
Church Dr
  LWF/SPW/WRK NE9 .... 87 G6 🔲
Churcher Gdns
  WLSD/HOW NE28 .... 58 C6 🔲
Church Flatt PONT/DH NE20 .... 43 H2
Church Gn SEA/MUR SR7 .... 135 J7 🔲
Churchill Av DHAM DH1 .... 17 K1
  MONK NE25 .... 50 C5
  SWCK/CAS SR5 .... 106 A3 🔲
Churchill Cl CON/LDGT DH8 .... 122 C1
Churchill Gdns JES NE2 .... 71 G2 🔲
Churchill Sq HLS DH4 .... 131 K7 🔲
Churchill St SUND SR1 .... 15 G6
  WLSD/HOW NE28 .... 59 H6
Church La BDLGTN NE22 .... 29 G6
  CLDN/WHIT/ROK SR6 .... 93 F4
  DHAM DH1 .... 16 E6
  DHAM DH1 .... 17 H3 🔲
  GOS/KPK NE3 .... 56 D5
  LWF/SPW/WRK NE9 .... 87 H6 🔲
  RDHAMSE DH6 .... 171 H3
  SEA/MUR SR7 .... 149 G5
Church Pk RDHAMSE DH6 .... 172 E7
Church Pl FELL NE10 .... 12 C5
Church Ri RYTON NE40 .... 67 G6
  WICK/BNPF NE16 .... 85 F5
Church Rd
  BW/LEM/TK/HW NE15 .... 67 H4 🔲
  CON/LDGT DH8 .... 122 D3
  GOS/KPK NE3 .... 56 D5
  HLH DH5 .... 147 K2
  LWF/SPW/WRK NE9 .... 101 H1
  SMOOR NE27 .... 48 E4
  WYLAM NE41 .... 65 G5
Church St BDN/LAN/SAC DH7 .... 143 G5
  BLAY NE21 .... 83 J3
  BYK/HTN/WLK NE6 .... 72 C7
  CON/LDGT DH8 .... 123 J3
  CON/LDGT DH8 .... 123 F5 🔲
  CON/LDGT DH8 .... 136 E3
  DHAM DH1 .... 16 E6
  DUN/TMV NE11 .... 9 J5
  GATE NE8 .... 5 M9
  HEBB NE31 .... 73 F4
  HLH DH5 .... 132 C7 🔲
  HLS DH4 .... 132 C7
  HLS DH4 .... 146 D6
  MLFD/PNYW SR4 .... 104 E7
  RDHAMSE DH6 .... 160 D6
  RDHAMSE DH6 .... 172 E7
  RDHAMSE DH6 .... 181 G3
  RHTLP TS27 .... 185 H2
  SEA/MUR SR7 .... 149 J6
  SEA/MUR SR7 .... 150 E1 🔲
  STLY/ANP DH9 .... 112 D7
  SWCK/CAS SR5 .... 106 B3 🔲
  TYNE/NSHE NE30 .... 2 F1 🔲
  WICK/BNPF NE16 .... 98 E5
  WNGT TS28 .... 184 A5
Church St East SUND SR1 .... 15 H3
Church Street Head DHAM DH1 .... 16 E7
Church St North
  CLDN/WHIT/ROK SR6 .... 106 D4
Church V RDHAMSE DH6 .... 159 F5
Church Vw BOLCOL NE35 .... 90 C3
  CLSW/PEL DH2 .... 144 B5
  SUNDSW SR3 .... 120 A7
  WLSD/HOW NE28 .... 73 F1
Church Wk MPTH NE61 .... 162 C6 🔲
  PLEE/EAS SR8 .... 162 C6 🔲
Church Wy MONK NE25 .... 49 J3
  NSHW NE29 .... 2 D1 🔲
  SSH NE33 .... 3 G7
Church Wynd RDHAMSE DH6 .... 170 C1
Chyll Edge MPTH NE61 .... 20 A4
Cinderford Cl BOLCOL NE35 .... 90 B2
Cinnamon Dr TRIM TS29 .... 183 F6 🔲
Cirencester St MLFD/PNYW SR4 .. 14 A3
Citadel East LGB/KIL NE12 .... 47 K6
Citadel West LGB/KIL NE12 .... 47 K6
City Rd CNUT NE1 .... 5 L7 🔲
City Wy SUNDSW SR3 .... 133 G1
Civic Ct HEBB NE31 .... 73 H6
Clacton Rd SWCK/CAS SR5 .... 104 D4 🔲
Clanfield Ct LGB/HTN NE7 .... 57 F6
Clanny St SUND SR1 .... 14 B6
Clanton Ct FELL NE10 .... 88 C5
Clapham Av BYK/HTN/WLK NE6 .... 7 K7
Clappersgate PLEE/EAS SR8 ..... 162 B6
Clara St ELS/FEN NE4 .... 69 H7
  SEA/MUR SR7 .... 135 H7 🔲
Claremont Av
  BW/LEM/TK/HW NE15 .... 68 B3
  CLDN/WHIT/ROK SR6 .... 106 E2 🔲
Claremont Crs WBAY NE26 .... 50 C1
Claremont Dr HLS DH4 .... 131 J1
Claremont Gdns BOL NE36 .... 91 H5
  WBAY NE26 .... 50 D3
Claremont Rd
  CLDN/WHIT/ROK SR6 .... 106 E2
  JES NE2 .... 70 A3
  WBAY NE26 .... 50 C1
Claremont St JES NE2 .... 5 G2
Claremount Ct BOL NE36 .... 91 F5 🔲
Clarence St JES NE2 .... 6 A5
  RDHAMSE DH6 .... 180 A3 🔲
  SEA/MUR SR7 .... 150 E1 🔲
  SWCK/CAS SR5 .... 106 A3 🔲
  WBAY NE26 .... 41 G3
Clarence Ter CLS/BIR/GTL DH3 .. 129 J4

Clarendon Sq SWCK/CAS SR5 ... 106 B2 🔲
Clarendon St CON/LDGT DH8 ..... 123 F2 🔲
Clare Rd PLEE/EAS SR8 .... 174 C5
Clarewood Av HAR/WTLS NE34 ... 76 A3
Clarewood Pl
  WD/WHPE/BLK NE5 .... 69 G3
Clarke Ter FELL NE10 .... 12 B8
  SEA/MUR SR7 .... 149 H4
Clarks Fld MPTH NE61 .... 20 C5
Clasper St
  CON/LDGT DH8 .... 108 E3
  DIN/WO NE13 .... 45 F7
  MONK NE25 .... 50 A5
  PLEE/EAS SR8 .... 175 F5
  SEA/MUR SR7 .... 135 J7
Claude St HLH DH5 .... 147 K5
Claude Ter SEA/MUR SR7 .... 149 J5
Claverdon St
  WD/WHPE/BLK NE5 .... 53 K6 🔲
Clavering Pl CNUT NE1 .... 5 K8 🔲
Clavering Rd
  WICK/BNPF NE16 .... 85 F3 🔲
  WLSD/HOW NE28 .... 73 K3 🔲
Clavering Wy BLYTH NE21 .... 84 C3
Claverley Dr SMOOR NE27 .... 48 E4
Claxheugh Rd
  MLFD/PNYW SR4 .... 105 F6 🔲
Claxton St PLEE/EAS SR8 .... 175 H3
Clay La DHAM DH1 .... 168 B2
Claymere Rd
  ASHBK/HED/RY SR2 .... 120 E5
Claypath DHAM DH1 .... 16 E3
Claypath La SSH NE33 .... 3 H9
Claypath Rd HLH DH5 .... 147 K6
Claypool Ct HAR/WTLS NE34 ...... 75 G6 🔲
Claypool Farm Cl
  RHTLP TS27 .... 184 E6 🔲
Clayton Park Sq JES NE2 .... 5 L1
Clayton Rd JES NE2 .... 5 K1
Clayton St BDLGTN NE22 .... 29 K4
  CNUT NE1 .... 5 J7
  JRW NE32 .... 73 K4 🔲
Clayton St West CNUT NE1 .... 5 H8
Clayton Terrace Rd CHPW NE17 ... 95 J3
Clayworth Rd GOS/KPK NE3 .... 56 B1
Cleadon Hill Dr HAR/WTLS NE34 . 92 A1
Cleadon Hill Rd HAR/WTLS NE34 . 76 B7
Cleadon La BOL NE36 .... 91 J4
  CLDN/WHIT/ROK SR6 .... 92 C3
Cleadon Mdw
  CLDN/WHIT/ROK SR6 .... 92 A3
Cleadon St BYK/HTN/WLK NE6 ...... 7 J5
  CLDN/WHIT/ROK SR6 .... 92 C3
Cleasby Gdns
  LWF/SPW/WRK NE9 .... 87 F6
Cleaside Av HAR/WTLS NE34 ...... 76 A7
Cleaswell HI STKFD/GP NE62 ...... 22 E6 🔲
Cleehill Dr NSHW NE29 .... 60 C2
Cleeve Ct WASHS NE38 .... 116 E1 🔲
Clement Av BDLGTN NE22 .... 29 J5 🔲
Clementina Cl
  ASHBK/HED/RY SR2 .... 15 H7 🔲
Clement St
  LWF/SPW/WRK NE9 .... 87 F7 🔲
Clennel Av HEBB NE31 .... 73 F6
Clent Wy LGB/KIL NE12 .... 57 G4
Clephan St DUN/TMV NE11 .... 9 H7
Clervaux Ter JRW NE32 .... 74 A5
Cleveland Av CLSW/PEL DH2 ..... 129 H5
  NSHW NE29 .... 60 D3
  NWBGN NE64 .... 25 F1
Cleveland Crs NSHW NE29 .... 60 E4 🔲
Cleveland Dr WASHS NE38 .... 116 D3
Cleveland Gdns LGB/HTN NE7 ..... 57 J7 🔲
  WLSD/HOW NE28 .... 59 K7 🔲
Cleveland Pl PLEE/EAS SR8 .... 174 C4
Cleveland Rd MLFD/PNYW SR4 .. 119 K2
Cleveland St SSH NE33 .... 3 J7
Cleveland Ter NSHW NE29 .... 60 E4 🔲
Cleveland Vw
  CLDN/WHIT/ROK SR6 .... 92 E6
Clickemin PONT/DH NE20 .... 43 J3
Clifford Rd BW/LEM/TK/HW NE15 .. 7 J7
Clifford's Bank
  BDN/LAN/SAC DH7 .... 152 E6
Cliffords Ga BDN/LAN/SAC DH7 .. 165 F1
Clifford St BLAY NE21 .... 84 A1
  BYK/HTN/WLK NE6 .... 6 E5
  CLS/BIR/GTL DH3 .... 129 J6
  MLFD/PNYW SR4 .... 106 A7
  TYNE/NSHE NE30 .... 3 H1
Clifford Ter CLS/BIR/GTL DH3 .... 129 J6
  RYTON NE40 .... 66 B7
Cliff Rd ASHBK/HED/RY SR2 ...... 135 G1
Cliff Rw WBAY NE26 .... 51 G5
Clifton Av HAR/WTLS NE34 .... 75 J4
  WLSD/HOW NE28 .... 72 D1 🔲
Cliftonbourne Av
  CLDN/WHIT/ROK SR6 .... 106 E2
Clifton Cl RYTON NE40 .... 67 C7 🔲
  STKFD/GP NE62 .... 23 C5
Clifton Gdns BLYTH NE24 .... 35 F3 🔲
  LWF/SPW/WRK NE9 .... 87 F5
  NSHW NE29 .... 60 C7
Clifton Gv MONK NE25 .... 50 C3
Clifton La MPTH NE61 .... 27 F5
Clifton Rd CLDN/WHIT/ROK SR6 .. 106 D2
  CRAM NE23 .... 38 D3
  ELS/FEN NE4 .... 69 J6
  PLEE/EAS SR8 .... 174 E5
Clifton Ter LGB/KIL NE12 .... 57 K3
  SSH NE33 .... 75 G4 🔲
  WBAY NE26 .... 51 F4
Cliftonville Av ELS/FEN NE4 .... 69 J6
Cliftonville Gdns WBAY NE26 .... 50 E3
Clinton Pl GOS/KPK NE3 .... 46 B7 🔲
Clipsham Cl LGB/KIL NE12 .... 57 H7 🔲
Clipstone Av BYK/HTN/WLK NE6 . 12 F1
Clipstone Cl
  BW/LEM/TK/HW NE15 .... 66 E1 🔲
Clive Pl BYK/HTN/WLK NE6 .... 7 H1
Clive St HAR/WTLS NE34 .... 74 E7
  NSHW NE29 .... 2 E4
Clockburn Lonnen
  WICK/BNPF NE16 .... 84 B7
Clockburnsyde Cl
  WICK/BNPF NE16 .... 84 C7 🔲
Clockmill Rd GATE NE8 .... 9 K5
Clockstand Cl
  CLDN/WHIT/ROK SR6 .... 93 G1
Clockwell St SWCK/CAS SR5 ..... 105 K4 🔲
Cloister Av HAR/WTLS NE34 .... 74 E6
Cloister Garth LGB/HTN NE7 .... 57 F5 🔲

The Cloisters
  ASHBK/HED/RY SR2 .... 14 E9
  LGB/HTN NE7 .... 57 F5 🔲
Cloister Wk JRW NE32 .... 74 A4
Close CNUT NE1 .... 5 K9
Closeburn Sq SUNDSW SR3 ...... 134 B1 🔲
Closefield Gv MONK NE25 .... 50 C5
Close St MLFD/PNYW SR4 .... 106 A6
  SWCK/CAS SR5 .... 106 A5
The Close BDN/LAN/SAC DH7 ... 140 B4
  BLAY NE21 .... 83 J3
  CLDN/WHIT/ROK SR6 .... 91 K3
  CON/LDGT DH8 .... 122 D1
  CRAM NE23 .... 39 G7
  HLH DH5 .... 132 D7 🔲
  PONT/DH NE20 .... 43 G4
  PRUD NE42 .... 80 E1 🔲
  WD/WHPE/BLK NE5 .... 68 C3 🔲
  WICK/BNPF NE16 .... 98 A6
Cloth Market CNUT NE1 .... 5 K7
Clousden Dr LGB/KIL NE12 .... 58 A1
Clousden Gra LGB/KIL NE12 .... 58 A1 🔲
Clovelly Av ELS/FEN NE4 .... 69 J6
Clovelly Gdns BDLGTN NE22 .... 50 E3
  WBAY NE26 .... 50 E3
Clovelly Pl JRW NE32 .... 74 C6
  PONT/DH NE20 .... 42 E7
Clovelly Rd SWCK/CAS SR5 .... 104 D2
Clover Av BLAY NE21 .... 84 A6
  FELL NE10 .... 11 M4
Cloverdale BDLGTN NE22 .... 28 E5 🔲
Cloverdale Gdns LGB/HTN NE7 ... 57 H7
  WICK/BNPF NE16 .... 85 F7 🔲
Cloverfield Av GOS/KPK NE3 .... 55 K4
Clover HI WICK/BNPF NE16 .... 98 E5
Cloverhill Av HEBB NE31 .... 89 F1
Cloverhill Cl CRAM NE23 .... 38 B7
Cloverhill Dr RYTON NE40 .... 66 C7
Clover Laid BDN/LAN/SAC DH7 .. 167 F7
Club La DHAM DH1 .... 156 B6
Clumber St ELS/FEN NE4 .... 9 J1
Clumber St North ELS/FEN NE4 ..... 4 C9
Clyde Av HEBB NE31 .... 89 G1
Clydedale Av LGB/KIL NE12 .... 57 J3
Clydedale Av HLS DH4 .... 117 K7
Clydedale Garth DHAM DH1 ..... 156 E1 🔲
Clydedale Rd BYK/HTN/WLK NE6 . 7 H6
Clydesdale St HLH DH5 .... 147 K6
Clyde St CHPW NE17 .... 95 J4
  GATE NE8 .... 11 K7
Clyvedon Ri HAR/WTLS NE34 ..... 92 A1
Coach La DIN/WO NE13 .... 45 J5
  LGB/HTN NE7 .... 57 J5
  NSHW NE29 .... 2 C3
Coach Open WLSD/HOW NE28 .... 73 K2
Coach Rd BW/LEM/TK/HW NE15 .. 66 E1 🔲
  DUN/TMV NE11 .... 86 B7
  WASHN NE37 .... 102 E3
  WLSD/HOW NE28 .... 72 E2
Coach Road Gn FELL NE10 .... 12 B4
Coalbank Rd HLH DH5 .... 147 F5
Coaley La HLS DH4 .... 132 A4
Coalford La RDHAMSE DH6 .... 158 E3
Coalford Rd RDHAMSE DH6 .... 158 C7
Coal La PRUD NE42 .... 63 H7
Coalway Dr WICK/BNPF NE16 ..... 85 F4
Coalway La WICK/BNPF NE16 ..... 85 F4
Coalway La North
  WICK/BNPF NE16 .... 85 F3 🔲
Coanwood Dr CRAM NE23 .... 38 C3
Coanwood Gdns
  DUN/TMV NE11 .... 86 B7 🔲
Coanwood Rd
  BW/LEM/TK/HW NE15 .... 69 F7
Coanwood Wy WICK/BNPF NE16 . 99 F2
Coast Rd BYK/HTN/WLK NE6 ...... 71 J1
  HAR/WTLS NE34 .... 76 D4
  NSHW NE29 .... 60 B4
  PLEE/EAS SR8 .... 175 J4
  SSH NE33 .... 75 J5
  WLSD/HOW NE28 .... 59 F6
Coates Cl STLY/ANP DH9 .... 126 E1
Coatsworth Ct GATE NE8 .... 10 E3
Coatsworth Rd GATE NE8 .... 10 E3
Cobalt Cl
  BW/LEM/TK/HW NE15 .... 68 A3 🔲
Cobbett Crs HAR/WTLS NE34 ..... 91 F1
Cobbler's La PSHWF NE43 .... 63 F2
Cobden Rd CRAM NE23 .... 38 D4 🔲
Cobden St CON/LDGT DH8 .... 123 C4
  GATE NE8 .... 11 K6
  WLSD/HOW NE28 .... 72 C1 🔲
Cobden Ter GATE NE8 .... 11 J6
Cobham Pl
  BYK/HTN/WLK NE6 .... 72 C7 🔲
Cobham Sq SWCK/CAS SR5 ...... 106 B3
Coble Dene NSHW NE29 .... 74 C1
Coburg St BLYTH NE24 .... 31 H7 🔲
  GATE NE8 .... 10 F4
  TYNE/NSHE NE30 .... 61 F4
Cochrane Park Av LGB/HTN NE7 .. 71 J1
Cochrane St ELS/FEN NE4 .... 69 J6
Cochran St BLAY NE21 .... 68 A7
Cockburn Ter NSHW NE29 .... 60 B7 🔲
Cocken La CLS/BIR/GTL DH3 ...... 145 J2
  DHAM DH1 .... 145 J1
Cocken Rd CLS/BIR/GTL DH3 .... 144 E5
  DHAM DH1 .... 145 K1
Cockermouth Rd
  SWCK/CAS SR5 .... 104 D2
Cockhouse La
  BDN/LAN/SAC DH7 .... 154 C7
Cockshott Dean PRUD NE42 .... 80 C1 🔲
Cohort Cl CON/LDGT DH8 .... 108 E3
Colbeck Av WICK/BNPF NE16 ..... 85 F5
Colbourne Av CRAM NE23 .... 32 C6
Colbury Cl CRAM NE23 .... 33 G5 🔲
Colby Ct ELS/FEN NE4 .... 4 E8
Colchester St HAR/WTLS NE34 ... 74 E7
Colchester Ter
  MLFD/PNYW SR4 .... 119 K1
Coldbeck Ct CRAM NE23 .... 38 D3 🔲
Coldingham Ct
  BDN/LAN/SAC DH7 .... 143 G5
Coldingham Gdns
  WD/WHPE/BLK NE5 .... 69 H1 🔲
Coldside Gdns
  WD/WHPE/BLK NE5 .... 67 K1

Coldstream *CLSW/PEL* DH2 .... 115 F4
Coldstream Av
  SWCK/CAS SR5 .... 106 B3 ⬚
Coldstream CI *HLS* DH4 .... 131 K2 ⬚
Coldstream Dr *BLAY* NE21 .... 83 J4
Coldstream Gdns
  WLSD/HOW NE28 .... 59 H7
Coldstream Rd
  BW/LEM/TK/HW NE15 .... 67 F2 ⬚
Coldwell CI *RDHAMSE* DH6 .... 160 D2
Coldwell Dr *FELL* NE10 .... 87 J5
Coldwell Park Av *FELL* NE10 .... 12 B9
Coldwell Park Dr *FELL* NE10 .... 12 B9
Coldwell Rd *PRUD* NE42 .... 81 F1
Coldwell St *FELL* NE10 .... 12 C8
Colebridge CI *WD/WHPE/BLK* NE5 .... 55 G7 ⬚
Colebrooke *CLS/BIR/GTL* DH3 .... 115 K4
Cole Gdns *FELL* NE10 .... 13 K8
Colegate *FELL* NE10 .... 88 B5
Colegate West *FELL* NE10 .... 88 A5
Colepike Rd *BDN/LAN/SAC* DH7 .... 140 B5
Coleridge Av
  LWF/SPW/WRK NE9 .... 100 E1
  SSH NE33 .... 75 J2
Coleridge Dr *STKFD/GP* NE62 .... 23 G6
Coleridge Sq *SWCK/CAS* SR5 .... 105 F3 ⬚
Coleridge Sq *HEBB* NE31 .... 73 G5 ⬚
Coley Hill CI
  WD/WHPE/BLK NE5 .... 54 A6 ⬚
Coley Ter *CLDN/WHIT/ROK* SR6 .... 106 E1
Colgrove Wy *GOS/KPK* NE3 .... 55 K5 ⬚
Colin PI *BLAY* NE21 .... 72 C3 ⬚
Colin Ter *ASHBK/HED/RY* SR2 .... 135 K1
College Burn Rd *SUNDSW* SR3 .... 133 J2
College Dr *SSH* NE33 .... 75 J3 ⬚
College Dr *FELL* NE10 .... 87 K6 ⬚
College La *LGB/HTN* NE7 .... 57 J4
College Rd *ASHGTN* NE63 .... 24 A3
  HEBB NE31 .... 89 F1
College St *CNUT* NE1 .... 5 L4
College Vw *BDN/LAN/SAC* DH7 .... 155 F6 ⬚
  BDN/LAN/SAC DH7 .... 165 G3
  CON/LDGT DH8 .... 123 J7
Collier CI
  BW/LEM/TK/HW NE15 .... 67 F2 ⬚
Collierley La *STLY/ANP* DH9 .... 110 E5
Colliery La *HLH* DH5 .... 148 A6
Colliery Rd *DUN/TMV* NE11 .... 9 H4
Collin Av *HAR/WTLS* NE34 .... 76 B6
Collingdon Gn *ROWG* NE39 .... 82 B7
Collingdon Rd *ROWG* NE39 .... 96 C1
Collingwood Av
  WLSD/HOW NE28 .... 58 D6
Collingwood Crs *PONT/DH* NE20 .... 43 F5
Collingwood Dr *HLS* DH4 .... 131 J1
Collingwood Gdns *FELL* NE10 .... 12 D4
Collingwood PI *STKFD/GP* NE62 .... 23 H6
Collingwood St *MONK* NE25 .... 49 J4
Collingwood St *CNUT* NE1 .... 5 K8
  HEBB NE31 .... 73 J5 ⬚
  HLH DH5 .... 147 K2 ⬚
  SSH NE33 .... 75 G3
  SWCK/CAS SR5 .... 106 B3 ⬚
Collingwood Ter *BLYTH* NE24 .... 31 G7
  TYNE/NSHE NE30 .... 61 J3
Collingwood Vw *NSHW* NE29 .... 2 B3
Collison St *CON/LDGT* DH8 .... 123 F4 ⬚
Collywell Bay Rd *WBAY* NE26 .... 41 G2
Collywell Ct *WBAY* NE26 .... 41 G2 ⬚
Colman Av *HAR/WTLS* NE34 .... 74 E6
Colnbrook CI *GOS/KPK* NE3 .... 55 H3
Colombo Rd *SWCK/CAS* SR5 .... 104 D4
Colston PI *ELS/FEN* NE4 .... 174 D3 ⬚
Colston St *ELS/FEN* NE4 .... 69 H6
Colston Wy *MONK* NE25 .... 50 B2
Coltere Av *BOL* NE36 .... 91 J5
Colton Gdns
  LWF/SPW/WRK NE9 .... 101 G2
Coltpark *WD/WHPE/BLK* NE5 .... 68 D2 ⬚
Coltsfoot Gdns *FELL* NE10 .... 87 J6 ⬚
Coltspool *DUN/TMV* NE11 .... 100 D7
Columba St *SWCK/CAS* SR5 .... 106 B3 ⬚
Columba Wk *GOS/KPK* NE3 .... 55 J5 ⬚
Columbia Gra *GOS/KPK* NE3 .... 55 J5 ⬚
Columbia Ter *BLYTH* NE24 .... 35 G1 ⬚
Colville Ct *STLY/ANP* DH9 .... 127 F1
Colwell PI *WD/WHPE/BLK* NE5 .... 69 G4 ⬚
Colwell Rd *ASHGTN* NE63 .... 24 B4
  SMOOR NE27 .... 49 H7
Colwyne PI *WD/WHPE/BLK* NE5 .... 69 F7 ⬚
Combe Dr
  BW/LEM/TK/HW NE15 .... 67 K4
Comet Dr *PLEE/EAS* SR8 .... 162 D5 ⬚
Comet Rw *LGB/KIL* NE12 .... 47 J7
Comet Sq *SUNDSW* SR3 .... 120 A7 ⬚
Comical Cnr *SSH* NE33 .... 2 F5
Comma Ct *DUN/TMV* NE11 .... 86 D7
Commercial Rd
  ASHBK/HED/RY SR2 .... 121 F2
  BYK/HTN/WLK NE6 .... 7 G7
  GOS/KPK NE3 .... 56 E5 ⬚
  JRW NE32 .... 74 A3 ⬚
  SSH NE33 .... 75 F2
Commercial St
  BDN/LAN/SAC DH7 .... 152 D5
  BLAY NE21 .... 83 K3
  TRIM TS29 .... 182 E6
Commissioners' Whf *NSHW* NE29 .... 2 B8
Compton Av *HAR/WTLS* NE34 .... 75 H4
Compton Rd *NSHW* NE29 .... 2 A3
Concorde Wy *JRW* NE32 .... 73 K5
Condercum Ct
  BW/LEM/TK/HW NE15 .... 69 G6 ⬚
Condercum Rd *ELS/FEN* NE4 .... 69 H6
Cone St *SSH* NE33 .... 2 F9
Congburn Bank
  BDN/LAN/SAC DH7 .... 128 B7
Conhope La
  BW/LEM/TK/HW NE15 .... 69 H6
Conifer CI *DHAM* DH1 .... 157 H6 ⬚
Coniscliffe Av *GOS/KPK* NE3 .... 55 K7
Coniscliffe Rd *STLY/ANP* DH9 .... 126 B2
Conishead Ter *RDHAMSE* DH6 .... 160 E1
Coniston *CLS/BIR/GTL* DH3 .... 115 K5
  FELL NE10 .... 13 J7

Coniston Av *HEBB* NE31 .... 73 H6
  HLH DH5 .... 160 B1
  JES NE2 .... 70 E1
  NWBGN NE64 .... 24 E2 ⬚
  SWCK/CAS SR5 .... 106 C1
  WICK/BNPF NE16 .... 8 C9
Coniston CI *DHAM* DH1 .... 158 B5
  LGB/KIL NE12 .... 47 J6 ⬚
  PLEE/EAS SR8 .... 175 H4 ⬚
Coniston Crs *BLAY* NE21 .... 83 K4 ⬚
Coniston Dr *BDN/LAN/SAC* DH7 .... 143 G4
  JRW NE32 .... 90 B1
Coniston Gdns
  LWF/SPW/WRK NE9 .... 87 H7
Coniston PI
  LWF/SPW/WRK NE9 .... 87 H7 ⬚
Coniston Rd *BLYTH* NE24 .... 30 B5
  TYNE/NSHE NE30 .... 50 D7
  WLSD/HOW NE28 .... 59 H6
Coniston Wy *WD/WHPE/BLK* NE5 .... 54 A6 ⬚
Connaught CI *HLS* DH4 .... 132 A3 ⬚
Connaught Ter *JRW* NE32 .... 73 K5
Conningsby CI *GOS/KPK* NE3 .... 56 D2
Connolly Ter *CHPW* NE17 .... 95 J7
Consett La *CON/LDGT* DH8 .... 122 B5
Consett Rd *CON/LDGT* DH8 .... 136 C2
  DUN/TMV NE11 .... 85 K7
Constable CI *RYTON* NE40 .... 66 E7
  STLY/ANP DH9 .... 126 C1
Constable Gdns *HAR/WTLS* NE34 .... 91 G1
Constance St *CLSW/PEL* DH2 .... 114 E7
  CON/LDGT DH8 .... 123 F5
Content St *BLAY* NE21 .... 84 A3
Conway CI *BDLGTN* NE22 .... 28 D5
  RYTON NE40 .... 83 F1
Conway Dr *LGB/HTN* NE7 .... 57 G6
Conway Gdns *SUNDSW* SR3 .... 119 H7 ⬚
  WLSD/HOW NE28. .... 58 C6
Conway Gv *WBAY* NE26 .... 40 E1
Conway Rd *CLSW/PEL* DH2 .... 115 F6
  SWCK/CAS SR5 .... 104 D3
Conway Sq *LWF/SPW/WRK* NE9 .... 11 J8
  SWCK/CAS SR5 .... 104 D3 ⬚
Conyers Av *CLSW/PEL* DH2 .... 129 H2
Conyers Gdns *CLSW/PEL* DH2 .... 129 H2
Conyers PI *CLSW/PEL* DH2 .... 129 H2
Conyers Rd *BYK/HTN/WLK* NE6 .... 6 F5
  CLSW/PEL DH2 .... 129 H2
Cook Av *BDN/LAN/SAC* DH7 .... 155 F6
Cook CI *SSH* NE33 .... 75 F3
Cook Crs *SEA/MUR* SR7 .... 149 G5
Cooke's Wd *BDN/LAN/SAC* DH7 .... 167 H2
Cook Gdns *FELL* NE10 .... 13 L8
Cookshold La *RDHAMSE* DH6 .... 158 E7
Cookson CI *ELS/FEN* NE4 .... 4 E6
Cookson's La *CNUT* NE1 .... 5 J9
Cookson Ter *CLSW/PEL* DH2 .... 129 H4
Cook Sq *SWCK/CAS* SR5 .... 104 E3 ⬚
Cooks Wd *WASHS* NE38 .... 117 F3
Cook Wy *PLEE/EAS* SR8 .... 173 K3 ⬚
Coomassie Rd *BLYTH* NE24 .... 31 F7 ⬚
Coomside *CRAM* NE23 .... 38 D4 ⬚
Co-operative Ter
  BDN/LAN/SAC DH7 .... 141 H3 ⬚
  BDN/LAN/SAC DH7 .... 166 D2
  MLFD/PNYW SR4 .... 120 A1 ⬚
  ROWG NE39 .... 82 B7
  STLY/ANP DH9 .... 110 E6
Cooper's CI *RDHAMSE* DH6 .... 172 C6
Cooper Sq *DHAM* DH1 .... 17 K1
Cooper's Ter *RDHAMSE* DH6 .... 172 C6
Cooper St
  CLDN/WHIT/ROK SR6 .... 106 E4 ⬚
Coopies Fld *MPTH* NE61 .... 21 F6
Coopies Haugh *MPTH* NE61 .... 21 G6 ⬚
Coopie's La *MPTH* NE61 .... 21 F5
Coopies Wy *MPTH* NE61 .... 21 G6
Copeland Ct *DHAM* DH1 .... 168 B2
Copland Ter *JES* NE2 .... 6 E5
Copley Av *HAR/WTLS* NE34 .... 91 G2
Copley Dr *SUNDSW* SR3 .... 120 B4
Copperas La
  BW/LEM/TK/HW NE15 .... 68 D4 ⬚
Copper Chare *MPTH* NE61 .... 20 D4
Copperfield *DHAM* DH1 .... 168 B3 ⬚
Coppergate Ct *HEBB* NE31 .... 73 H4
Coppice HI *BDN/LAN/SAC* DH7 .... 165 J2 ⬚
Coppice Wy *JES* NE2 .... 6 A4
Coppy La *STLY/ANP* DH9 .... 113 G3
  WICK/BNPF NE16 .... 113 F1
The Copse *BLAY* NE21 .... 84 D2 ⬚
  PRUD NE42 .... 81 F2
  WICK/BNPF NE16 .... 97 H7
Coquet *WASHS* NE38 .... 116 B6
Coquet Av *BLYTH* NE24 .... 35 G2 ⬚
  GOS/KPK NE3 .... 56 B4
  HAR/WTLS NE34. .... 76 A3
  WBAY NE26. .... 50 E4
Coquetdale Av
  BYK/HTN/WLK NE6 .... 72 C5
Coquetdale CI *MPTH* NE61 .... 21 H2
Coquet Dr *CLSW/PEL* DH2 .... 114 E6
Coquet Gdns *STLY/ANP* DH9 .... 126 C3 ⬚
Coquet Gv
  BW/LEM/TK/HW NE15 .... 66 E2
Coquet St *CNUT* NE1 .... 6 B6 ⬚
  HEBB NE31 .... 73 F5 ⬚
  JRW NE32 .... 73 J6
Coquet Ter *BYK/HTN/WLK* NE6 .... 71 H2
  CRAM NE23 .... 47 F1
Corbiere CI *SUNDSW* SR3 .... 133 J1
Corbitt St *GATE* NE8 .... 10 B6
Corbridge Ct *WLSD/HOW* NE28 .... 59 G4
Corbridge Rd *BYK/HTN/WLK* NE6 .... 7 G4
Corbridge St *BYK/HTN/WLK* NE6 .... 6 F5
Corby Ga
  ASHBK/HED/RY SR2 .... 120 D2 ⬚
Corby Gv *PLEE/EAS* SR8 .... 174 B7 ⬚
Corby Hall Dr
  ASHBK/HED/RY SR2 .... 120 D2 ⬚
Corchester Rd *BDLGTN* NE22 .... 28 E4 ⬚
Corchester Wk *LGB/HTN* NE7 .... 57 H6 ⬚
Corinthian Sq *SWCK/CAS* SR5 .... 104 E3 ⬚
Cork St *SUND* SR1 .... 15 G4 ⬚
Cormorant CI *ASHGTN* NE63 .... 24 A5 ⬚
  BLYTH NE24 .... 35 H3
Cornbank CI *SUNDSW* SR3 .... 134 A2

Corndean *WASHS* NE38 .... 117 J2
Cornelia Ter *SEA/MUR* SR7 .... 150 D1
Cornel Rd *LGB/HTN* NE7 .... 57 H7
Corney St *SSH* NE33 .... 75 H4
The Cornfields *HEBB* NE31 .... 73 G5
Cornforth CI *ASHGTN* NE63 .... 23 H5
  FELL NE10 .... 88 E6
Cornhill Av *GOS/KPK* NE3 .... 55 K3 ⬚
Cornhill Crs *NSHW* NE29 .... 60 B3
Cornhill Rd *CRAM* NE23 .... 38 C2
  SWCK/CAS SR5 .... 106 B3 ⬚
Corn Mill Dr *HLH* DH5 .... 147 G2
Cornmoor Gdns
  WICK/BNPF NE16 .... 85 F6
Cornmoor Rd *WICK/BNPF* NE16 .... 85 F6
Cornthwaite Dr
  CLDN/WHIT/ROK SR6 .... 93 F4 ⬚
Cornwallis Sq *SSH* NE33 .... 75 F2 ⬚
Cornwall Rd *HEBB* NE31 .... 89 H1 ⬚
Cornwell Ct *LGB/HTN* NE7 .... 57 F6 ⬚
Cornwell Crs *BDLGTN* NE22 .... 29 H6 ⬚
Coronation Av *DHAM* DH1 .... 158 A5 ⬚
Coronation Gn *HLH* DH5 .... 160 C1 ⬚
Coronation Rd
  WD/WHPE/BLK NE5 .... 53 K7
  WICK/BNPF NE16 .... 99 F3
  WNGT TS28 .... 183 J2
Coronation Sq *RDHAMSE* DH6 .... 161 G2
Coronation St
  CLS/BIR/GTL DH3 .... 129 K5 ⬚
  NSHW NE29 .... 2 D4
  SSH NE33 .... 2 F8
  SUND SR1 .... 15 G4 ⬚
  WLSD/HOW NE28 .... 72 E1
Coronation Ter
  MLFD/PNYW SR4 .... 105 F7 ⬚
Corporation Rd
  ASHBK/HED/RY SR2 .... 121 F2
Corporation St *ELS/FEN* NE4 .... 5 F7 ⬚
Corporation Yd *MPTH* NE61 .... 20 D5
Corriedale CI *DHAM* DH1 .... 156 D1 ⬚
Corrofell Gdns *FELL* NE10 .... 13 G4
Corry Ct *MLFD/PNYW* SR4 .... 119 J2 ⬚
Corsair *WICK/BNPF* NE16 .... 84 D6
Corsenside *WD/WHPE/BLK* NE5 .... 68 D2
Corstorphine Town *SSH* NE33 .... 75 F3
Cortina Av *MLFD/PNYW* SR4 .... 119 H2
Cortland Rd *CON/LDGT* DH8 .... 122 C3
Cort St *CON/LDGT* DH8 .... 122 E4
Cossack Ter *MLFD/PNYW* SR4 .... 105 J6
Cosserat PI *HEBB* NE31 .... 73 F4 ⬚
Cosser St *BLYTH* NE24 .... 34 D3 ⬚
Coston Dr *SSH* NE33 .... 3 H6
Cosyn St *BYK/HTN/WLK* NE6 .... 6 F6 ⬚
Cotehill Dr *PONT/DH* NE20 .... 42 D5
Cotehill Rd
  WD/WHPE/BLK NE5 .... 69 F2 ⬚
Cotemede *FELL* NE10 .... 88 C7
Cotherstone Ct *SUNDSW* SR3 .... 120 B4 ⬚
Cotherstone Rd *DHAM* DH1 .... 156 E3
Cotman Gdns *HAR/WTLS* NE34. .... 91 H2
Cotsford La *PLEE/EAS* SR8 .... 175 J4
Cotswold Av *LGB/KIL* NE12 .... 57 H1 ⬚
Cotswold CI *WASHS* NE38 .... 116 D2
Cotswold Dr *ASHGTN* NE63 .... 24 A4
  MONK NE25 .... 50 D6
Cotswold Gdns *DUN/TMV* NE11 .... 86 A5
  LGB/HTN NE7 .... 57 G7
Cotswold La *BOLCOL* NE35 .... 90 C2
Cotswold Rd *NSHW* NE29 .... 50 C7
  SWCK/CAS SR5 .... 104 E3
Cotswold Sq *SWCK/CAS* SR5 .... 104 E2 ⬚
Cotswold Ter *STLY/ANP* DH9 .... 126 C3 ⬚
Cottage La *WD/WHPE/BLK* NE5 .... 69 H2
Cottages Rd *SEA/MUR* SR7 .... 150 E2
Cottenham St *ELS/FEN* NE4 .... 4 F7
Cotterdale *WLSD/HOW* NE28 .... 58 B5 ⬚
Cotter Riggs PI
  WD/WHPE/BLK NE5 .... 67 K1
Cottersdale Gdns
  WD/WHPE/BLK NE5 .... 53 K7
Cottingham CI *PLEE/EAS* SR8 .... 174 C3 ⬚
Cottinglea *MPTH* NE61 .... 20 D3 ⬚
Cottingvale *MPTH* NE61 .... 20 D3
Cottingwood Gn *BLYTH* NE24 .... 34 D4
Cottingwood La *MPTH* NE61 .... 20 D3
Cottonwood *SUNDSW* SR3 .... 133 J2 ⬚
Coulthards La *GATE* NE8 .... 11 H1
Coulthards PI *GATE* NE8 .... 6 C9
Coulton Dr *BOL* NE36 .... 91 H5 ⬚
Council Av *HLS* DH4 .... 131 K1 ⬚
Counden Rd
  WD/WHPE/BLK NE5 .... 54 C7 ⬚
Countess Av *WBAY* NE26 .... 50 E4
Countess Dr
  BW/LEM/TK/HW NE15 .... 68 E4
Coupland Gv *JRW* NE32 .... 89 J1
Coupland Rd *ASHGTN* NE63 .... 23 J2
Courtfield Rd
  BYK/HTN/WLK NE6 .... 72 B3
Court La *DHAM* DH1 .... 16 E5
Courtney Dr *SUNDSW* SR3 .... 119 K6
Court Rd *BDLGTN* NE22 .... 29 F5
The Court *WICK/BNPF* NE16 .... 85 G6
The Courtyard *STLY/ANP* DH9 .... 112 A5
Cousin St *SUND* SR1 .... 15 H4
Coutts Rd *BYK/HTN/WLK* NE6 .... 7 M1
Coventry Gdns *ELS/FEN* NE4 .... 69 J7 ⬚
  NSHW NE29 .... 60 C5 ⬚
Coventry Rd *DHAM* DH1 .... 156 E2
Coverdale *FELL* NE10 .... 88 C6
  WLSD/HOW NE28. .... 58 B5 ⬚
Coverdale Av *BLYTH* NE24 .... 30 C7 ⬚
Coverley Rd *SWCK/CAS* SR5 .... 104 E2
The Covers *LGB/KIL* NE12 .... 58 A4
  MPTH NE61 .... 20 E6 ⬚
The Cove *HLS* DH4 .... 131 K1
Cowan CI *BLAY* NE21 .... 67 J7
Cowans Av *LGB/KIL* NE12 .... 47 J5 ⬚
Cowan Ter *ASHBK/HED/RY* SR2 .... 14 D6
Cowdray Rd *SWCK/CAS* SR5 .... 105 F3
Cowell Gv *ROWG* NE39 .... 96 E3
Cowell St *PLEE/EAS* SR8 .... 175 G3 ⬚
Cowen Gdns
  LWF/SPW/WRK NE9 .... 101 G4

Cowen Rd *BLAY* NE21 .... 84 B1
Cowen St *BYK/HTN/WLK* NE6 .... 72 B5 ⬚
Cowley PI *BLYTH* NE24. .... 30 C6
Cowley Rd *BLYTH* NE24 .... 30 D5
Cowley St *DHAMSE* DH6 .... 173 J4 ⬚
Cowpen Hall Rd *BLYTH* NE24 .... 30 C6 ⬚
Cowpen Rd *BLYTH* NE24 .... 30 C6 ⬚
Coxfoot CI *HAR/WTLS* NE34 .... 75 G6 ⬚
Coxgreen Rd *HLS* DH4 .... 117 J6
Coxlodge Rd *GOS/KPK* NE3 .... 56 A5
Coxlodge Ter *GOS/KPK* NE3 .... 56 A5
Coxon St *ASHBK/HED/RY* SR2 .... 15 G6
Crabtree Rd *PSHWF* NE43 .... 79 G5
Cradock Av *HEBB* NE31 .... 73 F7 ⬚
Craggyknowe *WASHN* NE37 .... 102 B7
Craghall Dene *JES* NE2 .... 56 E6 ⬚
Craghall Dene Av *JES* NE2 .... 56 E6 ⬚
Craghead La *STLY/ANP* DH9 .... 127 J4
Cragleas *WICK/BNPF* NE16 .... 111 J2
Cragside *BDN/LAN/SAC* DH7 .... 155 G1
  CLSW/PEL DH2 .... 129 C3
  CRAM NE23. .... 38 C4
  HAR/WTLS NE34 .... 76 B6
  LGB/HTN NE7 .... 57 H7
  WBAY NE26 .... 50 C2
Cragside Av *NSHW* NE29 .... 60 B2
Cragside Gdns *DUN/TMV* NE11 .... 86 A7
  LGB/KIL NE12 .... 48 B5 ⬚
  WLSD/HOW NE28 .... 59 H7 ⬚
Cragside Rd *WASHN* NE37 .... 102 C6
Cragston Av *WD/WHPE/BLK* NE5. .... 55 G7
Cragston CI
  WD/WHPE/BLK NE5 .... 69 G1 ⬚
Cragton Gdns *BLYTH* NE24 .... 30 D7 ⬚
Craigavon Rd *SWCK/CAS* SR5 .... 105 F4
Craig Crs *CRAM* NE23 .... 47 G1
Craighill *HLS* DH4 .... 131 J1 ⬚
Craigmillar Av
  WD/WHPE/BLK NE5 .... 55 G7
Craigmillar CI
  WD/WHPE/BLK NE5 .... 55 F7
Craigmill Pk *BLYTH* NE24 .... 30 C6
Craigshaw Rd
  SWCK/CAS SR5 .... 104 D2 ⬚
Craigweit Dr *SUNDSW* SR3 .... 134 A3
Craik Av *HAR/WTLS* NE34 .... 75 F6
Crake Wy *WASHS* NE38 .... 116 B4
Cramer St *GATE* NE8. .... 11 H6
Cramlington Rd *SWCK/CAS* SR5 .... 104 D4
Cramlington Sq
  SWCK/CAS SR5 .... 104 D3 ⬚
Cramlington Ter *BLYTH* NE24 .... 34 E3 ⬚
Cramond Ct
  LWF/SPW/WRK NE9 .... 100 E2
Cramond Wy *CRAM* NE23 .... 38 C4
Cranberry Rd *SWCK/CAS* SR5 .... 104 E3
Cranberry Sq *SWCK/CAS* SR5 .... 104 E3 ⬚
Cranborne *SUNDSW* SR3 .... 133 G1
Cranbourne Gv
  TYNE/NSHE NE30 .... 51 F6 ⬚
Cranbrook Av *GOS/KPK* NE3 .... 56 C3
Cranbrook Ct *GOS/KPK* NE3 .... 55 J3
Cranbrook Dr *PRUD* NE42 .... 80 B2
Cranbrook PI
  BW/LEM/TK/HW NE15 .... 69 F7 ⬚
Cranbrook Rd
  BW/LEM/TK/HW NE15 .... 69 F7
Cranemarsh CI *ASHGTN* NE63 .... 23 H4 ⬚
Craneswater Av *WBAY* NE26 .... 41 J7
Cranfield PI
  BW/LEM/TK/HW NE15 .... 68 A4 ⬚
Cranford St *HAR/WTLS* NE34 .... 75 G5
Cranford Ter
  MLFD/PNYW SR4 .... 120 A1 ⬚
Cranham CI *LGB/KIL* NE12 .... 48 B5 ⬚
Cranleigh Av *DIN/WO* NE13 .... 55 F3
Cranleigh Gv *PRUD* NE42 .... 80 C1
Cranleigh PI *MONK* NE25 .... 50 B2
Cranleigh Rd *SWCK/CAS* SR5 .... 104 E3
Cranshaw PI *CRAM* NE23 .... 38 D3 ⬚
Crantock Rd *GOS/KPK* NE3 .... 55 K5 ⬚
Cranwell Dr *DIN/WO* NE13 .... 46 B3
Craster Av *HAR/WTLS* NE34 .... 76 B3 ⬚
  LGB/KIL NE12 .... 58 B1
  SMOOR NE27 .... 49 G6
Craster CI *BLYTH* NE24 .... 30 E7
  CLSW/PEL DH2 .... 129 F6
  MONK NE25 .... 50 B3
Craster Gdns
  WLSD/HOW NE28 .... 59 H7 ⬚
Craster Ms *NSHW* NE29 .... 60 B5 ⬚
Craster Sq *GOS/KPK* NE3 .... 56 A4
Craster Ter *LGB/HTN* NE7 .... 71 H1
Crawcrook La *WYLAM* NE41 .... 65 J6
Crawford Av *PLEE/EAS* SR8 .... 174 E2
Crawford CI *RDHAMSE* DH6 .... 170 C1 ⬚
Crawford PI *MONK* NE25 .... 50 C5
Crawford St *BLYTH* NE24 .... 31 F5
Crawford Ter
  BYK/HTN/WLK NE6 .... 72 B6
Crawhall Crs *MPTH* NE61 .... 20 C6
Crawhall Rd *CNUT* NE1 .... 6 B6
Crawlaw Rd *PLEE/EAS* SR8 .... 162 E4
Crawley Av *HEBB* NE31 .... 89 F1
Crawley Gdns
  WICK/BNPF NE16 .... 8 B9 ⬚
Crawley Rd *WLSD/HOW* NE28 .... 72 D2
Crawley Sq *HEBB* NE31 .... 89 F1 ⬚
Craythorne Gdns
  BYK/HTN/WLK NE6 .... 71 J1
Creeverlea *WASHS* NE38 .... 116 E3
Creighton Av *GOS/KPK* NE3 .... 55 J7
Creland Wy
  WD/WHPE/BLK NE5 .... 55 G7 ⬚
The Crescent
  BDN/LAN/SAC DH7 .... 125 J7
  BDN/LAN/SAC DH7 .... 143 G7
  BDN/LAN/SAC DH7 .... 153 K3
  BW/LEM/TK/HW NE15 .... 67 J4
  CLDN/WHIT/ROK SR6 .... 91 K4
  CLSW/PEL DH2 .... 129 H4
  CLSW/PEL DH2 .... 144 B1
  CON/LDGT DH8 .... 122 B3
  CON/LDGT DH8 .... 123 F3
  CRAM NE23. .... 39 G7
  DHAM DH1 .... 156 B6
  DIN/WO NE13. .... 55 F4

HAR/WTLS NE34 .... 75 K7
  HLS DH4 .... 131 J2
  HLS DH4 .... 132 B3
  HLS DH4 .... 146 C6
  JRW NE32 .... 73 J7
  LGB/HTN NE7 .... 57 H5
  MPTH NE61 .... 20 D7
  PLEE/EAS SR8 .... 163 F4
  PONT/DH NE20 .... 42 C6
  RDHAMSE DH6 .... 170 C1
  ROWG NE39 .... 96 B3
  ROWG NE39 .... 97 H3
  RYTON NE40 .... 67 F6
  STLY/ANP DH9 .... 112 B6
  SUNDSW SR3 .... 120 A5
  TYNE/NSHE NE30. .... 61 G2
  WICK/BNPF NE16 .... 85 G6
  WLSD/HOW NE28 .... 58 D7
  WYLAM NE41 .... 65 H6
Crescent Wy North
  LGB/KIL NE12 .... 58 A2
Crescent Wy South
  LGB/KIL NE12 .... 58 A2
Cressbourne Av
  CLDN/WHIT/ROK SR6 .... 106 E1 ⬚
Cresswell Av *LGB/KIL* NE12 .... 58 A1
  NSHW NE29 .... 60 D3
  PLEE/EAS SR8. .... 175 H4
  WBAY NE26 .... 41 F2
Cresswell CI *BLAY* NE21 .... 83 J4 ⬚
  MONK NE25 .... 50 C6
Cresswell Dr *BLYTH* NE24 .... 34 D2
  GOS/KPK NE3 .... 55 J5
Cresswell Rd *WLSD/HOW* NE28 .... 72 C2
Cresswell St *BYK/HTN/WLK* NE6 .... 7 K5
The Crest *BDLGTN* NE22 .... 28 E5
  DIN/WO NE13 .... 45 F2
  WBAY NE26 .... 41 G4
Crichton Av *CLS/BIR/GTL* DH3 .... 129 K6
Cricklewood Dr *HLS* DH4 .... 117 K7 ⬚
  HLS DH4 .... 132 A1 ⬚
Cricklewood Rd *SWCK/CAS* SR5 .... 104 D4
Criddle St *GATE* NE8 .... 6 C9
Crieff Gv *JRW* NE32 .... 90 B1
Crieff Sq *SWCK/CAS* SR5 .... 104 D3 ⬚
Crigdon HI *WD/WHPE/BLK* NE5 .... 68 B2
Crighton *WASHS* NE38 .... 116 C1
Crimdon Gv *HLS* DH4 .... 147 F1 ⬚
Crime Rigg Bank
  RDHAMSE DH6 .... 171 G2
Crindledykes *WASHS* NE38 .... 117 G4
Cripps Av *FELL* NE10 .... 13 M8
  WLSD/HOW NE28 .... 72 E1 ⬚
Croft Av *LGB/KIL* NE12 .... 58 A3
  WLSD/HOW NE28 .... 72 E1 ⬚
Croft CI *RYTON* NE40 .... 67 F7
Croftdale Rd *BLAY* NE21 .... 83 K2
Crofter CI *CRAM* NE23 .... 38 B7
Crofthead Dr *CRAM* NE23 .... 38 C4
Crofton St *BLYTH* NE24 .... 31 G7 ⬚
  HAR/WTLS NE34. .... 75 G5
Crofton Wy
  BW/LEM/TK/HW NE15 .... 67 K4
Croft Rigg *BDN/LAN/SAC* DH7 .... 167 F7
Croft Rd *BLYTH* NE24 .... 31 G7
Croftside Av
  CLDN/WHIT/ROK SR6 .... 93 F4
Croft's La *BW/LEM/TK/HW* NE15. .... 64 C3
Crofts Pk *MPTH* NE61 .... 27 J1
Croft St *CNUT* NE1 .... 5 L6
Croftsway *ELS/FEN* NE4 .... 4 A8
Croft Ter *JRW* NE32 .... 73 K5
The Croft *GOS/KPK* NE3. .... 56 A6
  LGB/KIL NE12 .... 48 A5
  RDHAMSE DH6 .... 171 G1
Cromarty *CLSW/PEL* DH2 .... 115 F4
Cromarty St
  CLDN/WHIT/ROK SR6 .... 106 D3
Cromdale PI *WD/WHPE/BLK* NE5.. .... 69 F2
Cromer Av *LWF/SPW/WRK* NE9 .... 101 F2
Cromer Gdns *WBAY* NE26 .... 50 E3
Crompton Rd
  BYK/HTN/WLK NE6 .... 71 J3
Cromwell Av *BLAY* NE21 .... 83 K2
Cromwell CI *BLAY* NE21 .... 67 J7
Cromwell Rd *FELL* NE10 .... 13 L3
  WICK/BNPF NE16 .... 8 A8
Cromwell St *GATE* NE8 .... 11 J6
  MLFD/PNYW SR4 .... 106 A6
Cromwell Ter *GATE* NE8 .... 10 D6
Crondall St *SSH* NE33 .... 75 H4
Cronin Av *HAR/WTLS* NE34 .... 74 E7
Crookhall La *CON/LDGT* DH8. .... 123 J4
Crookhall Rd *CON/LDGT* DH8 .... 123 G4
Crookham Gv *MPTH* NE61 .... 27 F1
Crookham Wy *CRAM* NE23 .... 38 D4
Cropthorne *FELL* NE10 .... 88 D3 ⬚
Cross Av *WLSD/HOW* NE28 .... 58 B6
Crossbank Rd
  WD/WHPE/BLK NE5 .... 55 H7
Crossbrook Rd
  WD/WHPE/BLK NE5 .... 69 H1 ⬚
Crosby Ct *ASHBK/HED/RY* SR2 .... 15 J7
Crossfell *PONT/DH* NE20 .... 42 E6
Crossfell Gdns *STKFD/GP* NE62 .... 23 G5
Crossfield Pk *FELL* NE10 .... 87 J6
Crossfield Ter
  BYK/HTN/WLK NE6 .... 72 C7 ⬚
Crossgate *DHAM* DH1 .... 16 C4
  SSH NE33 .... 3 H9
Crossgate Moor Gdns
  DHAM DH1 .... 156 A7
Crossgate Peth *DHAM* DH1 .... 16 A5
Crossgate Rd *HLH* DH5 .... 147 K6 ⬚
Crosshill Rd
  BW/LEM/TK/HW NE15 .... 69 F7
Cross Keys La
  LWF/SPW/WRK NE9 .... 87 H7 ⬚
Cross La *BDN/LAN/SAC* DH7 .... 143 H2 ⬚
  DUN/TMV NE11 .... 8 A5
  DUN/TMV NE11 .... 100 A2
  WICK/BNPF NE16. .... 8 B7
Crosslaw *WD/WHPE/BLK* NE5 .... 68 C2
Crosslea Av *SUNDSW* SR3 .... 120 B3
Crossley Ter *ELS/FEN* NE4 .... 4 B5
  LGB/KIL NE12 .... 58 B1
Cross Pde *ELS/FEN* NE4 .... 4 E8
Cross PI *SUND* SR1 .... 15 G4 ⬚

Cross Rigg Cl *HLS* DH4 .... 117 J7 🔲
Cross Rw *GATE* NE8 .... 11 M5
Cross St *CNUT* NE1 .... 5 H7
CON/LDGT DH8 .... 122 D3 🔲
GATE NE8 .... 11 H6
HLS DH4 .... 131 J7
HLS DH4 .... 132 B6 🔲
RDHAMSE DH6 .... 159 G6
RDHAMSE DH6 .... 178 C4
Cross Ter *ROWG* NE39 .... 97 F4 🔲
Cross Vale Rd
ASHBK/HED/RY SR2 .... 14 D9
Crossway *HAR/WTLS* NE34 .... 76 A6 🔲
JES NE2 .... 56 E7
LWF/SPW/WRK NE9 .... 87 G6
STKFD/GP NE62 .... 23 F6 🔲
TYNE/NSHE NE30 .... 61 G2
Crossways *BDN/LAN/SAC* DH7 ...... 154 B3 🔲
BOL NE36 .... 91 J5 🔲
SUNDSW SR3 .... 119 K7
The Crossway
BW/LEM/TK/HW NE15 .... 68 B4 🔲
The Cross Wy *GOS/KPK* NE3 .... 55 K6
MPTH NE61 .... 20 D7
Croudace Rw *FELL* NE10 .... 12 C7
Crow Bank *WLSD/HOW* NE28 .... 72 E1
Crow Hall La *CRAM* NE23 .... 38 A1
Crow Hall Rd *CRAM* NE23 .... 33 F6
Crow La *SUNDSW* SR3 .... 119 F7
Crowley Av *WICK/BNPF* NE16 .... 8 F8 🔲
Crowley Gdns *BLAY* NE21 .... 84 A2 🔲
Crowley Rd *WICK/BNPF* NE16 .... 84 E3
Crown Rd *SWCK/CAS* SR5 .... 106 A5
Crown St *BLYTH* NE24 .... 31 H7 🔲
Crowther Rd *WASHS* NE38 .... 116 B1
Crowtree Rd *SUND* SR1 .... 14 D4
Crow Trees La *RDHAMSE* DH6 .... 180 A3 🔲
Crowtree Ter *SUND* SR1 .... 14 D5
Croydon St *ELS/FEN* NE4 .... 4 C5
Crozier St *SWCK/CAS* SR5 .... 106 C4 🔲
Crudwell Cl *BOLCOL* NE35 .... 90 C2 🔲
Crummock Av
CLDN/WHIT/ROK SR6 .... 106 C1
Crummock Rd
WD/WHPE/BLK NE5 .... 69 F3
Crumstone Ct *LGB/KIL* NE12 .... 48 A5
Cuba St *ASHBK/HED/RY* SR2 .... 120 E2 🔲
Cuillin Cl *WASHS* NE38 .... 116 D3
Culford Pl *WLSD/HOW* NE28 .... 59 G4
Cullercoats Rd
SWCK/CAS SR5 .... 104 D4 🔲
Cullercoats St *BYK/HTN/WLK* NE6 .... 7 L5
Culloden St *LGB/KIL* NE12 .... 47 K5 🔲
Culzean Ct *CON/LDGT* DH8 .... 122 D3 🔲
Cumberland Av *BDLGTN* NE22 .... 28 E5 🔲
NWBGN NE64 .... 25 F1
Cumberland Pl
CLS/BIR/GTL DH3 .... 115 K5
HAR/WTLS NE34 .... 76 B4
Cumberland Rd *CON/LDGT* DH8.... 137 F2 🔲
NSHW NE29 .... 59 K3
SUNDSW SR3 .... 120 A6
Cumberland St *SUND* SR1 .... 14 E3 🔲
WLSD/HOW NE28 .... 72 E1
WLSD/HOW NE28 .... 73 K2 🔲
Cumberland Wk
LGB/HTN NE7 .... 57 H6 🔲
Cumberland Wy
WASHN NE37 .... 103 F3 🔲
Cumbrian Av
CLDN/WHIT/ROK SR6 .... 92 C7 🔲
Cumbrian Wy *PLEE/EAS* SR8.... 175 F4
Cumbria Pl *STLY/ANP* DH9 .... 112 E7
Cummings Av *RDHAMSE* DH6.... 158 C7
Cummings St *BLYTH* NE24 .... 31 G6 🔲
Cunningham Pl *DHAM* DH1 .... 17 J1
Curlew Cl *ASHGTN* NE63 .... 23 K5
LGB/KIL NE12 .... 57 G3 🔲
RYTON NE40 .... 67 G7
WASHS NE38 .... 116 C4
Curlew Hl *MPTH* NE61 .... 20 B3
Curlew Rd *JRW* NE32 .... 74 A3
Curlew Wy *BLYTH* NE24 .... 35 G3
Curly Kews *MPTH* NE61 .... 20 D5
Curtis Rd *ELS/FEN* NE4 .... 4 A3
Curzon Pl *WD/WHPE/BLK* NE5 .... 69 F1 🔲
Curzon Rd West
WLSD/HOW NE28 .... 72 D2 🔲
Curzon St *GATE* NE8 .... 10 E7
Cushat Cl *BYK/HTN/WLK* NE6 .... 7 G7
Cushy Cow La *RYTON* NE40 .... 67 F7
Cut Bank *CNUT* NE1 .... 6 C6
Cuthbert Cl *DHAM* DH1 .... 169 J1
Cuthbert St *JRW* NE32 .... 74 C5
Cuthbertson Cl
CLDN/WHIT/ROK SR6 .... 92 E7 🔲
Cuthbert St *GATE* NE8 .... 10 C4
WICK/BNPF NE16 .... 98 E4
Cutler's Av *CON/LDGT* DH8 .... 122 C2
Cutlers' Hall Rd *CON/LDGT* DH8.. 122 C2
Cut Throat La *CHPW* NE17 .... 109 H2
Cygnet Cl *ASHGTN* NE63 .... 23 K5
WD/WHPE/BLK NE5 .... 54 B6
Cyncopa Wy
WD/WHPE/BLK NE5 .... 69 H1
Cypress Av *ELS/FEN* NE4 .... 69 H3
Cypress Ct
BDN/LAN/SAC DH7 .... 167 G7 🔲
Cypress Crs *BLYTH* NE24 .... 31 G7 🔲
DUN/TMV NE11 .... 9 H8
Cypress Dr *BLYTH* NE24 .... 31 G7
Cypress Gdns *BLYTH* NE24 .... 31 G7
Cypress Gv *DHAM* DH1 .... 157 H6
RYTON NE40 .... 66 E5 🔲
Cypress Pk *BDN/LAN/SAC* DH7 ... 165 C2 🔲
Cypress Rd *BLAY* NE21 .... 84 A2
LWF/SPW/WRK NE9 .... 101 K3 🔲
Cypress Sq *SUNDSW* SR3 .... 120 A6 🔲
Cyprus Gdns
LWF/SPW/WRK NE9 .... 87 G6
Cyril St *CON/LDGT* DH8 .... 123 F3

D

Dachet Rd *MONK* NE25 .... 50 B2

Dacre Rd *CLDN/WHIT/ROK* SR6 .... 106 D1
Dacre St *MPTH* NE61 .... 20 D4
SSH NE33 .... 75 G3
Dahlia Ct *MLFD/PNYW* SR4 .... 14 B4 🔲
Dahlia Pl *ELS/FEN* NE4 .... 69 H3
Dainton Cl *HLS* DH4 .... 132 A3
Dairy La *HLS* DH4 .... 132 B7
Dalden Gv *SEA/MUR* SR7 .... 135 K7
Dalegarth *CLDN/WHIT/ROK* SR6 .... 92 C7 🔲
Dale Rd *MONK* NE25 .... 50 B5
Daleside *BDN/LAN/SAC* DH7 .... 143 H4
Dale St *BDN/LAN/SAC* DH7 .... 154 B2
BLYTH NE24 .... 31 G5
CON/LDGT DH8 .... 122 D4
RYTON NE40 .... 66 B7
SSH NE33 .... 3 J6
Dale Ter *CLDN/WHIT/ROK* SR6 .... 106 E3
Dale Top *MONK* NE25 .... 40 B7
Dale View Gdns *RYTON* NE40 .... 82 A1
Dalla St *MLFD/PNYW* SR4 .... 104 E6 🔲
Dallymore Dr *RDHAMSE* DH6 .... 179 K1
Dalmahoy *WASHN* NE37 .... 103 F2
Dalmatia Ter *BLYTH* NE24 .... 35 G1
Dalston Pl *BLYTH* NE24 .... 35 G3 🔲
Dalton Cl *CRAM* NE23 .... 38 C2 🔲
Dalton Cl *WLSD/HOW* NE28 .... 58 B5
Dalton Pl *WD/WHPE/BLK* NE5 .... 54 A7
Daltons La *SSH* NE33 .... 3 H3
Dalton St *BYK/HTN/WLK* NE6 .... 6 F5 🔲
Dalton Ter *RDHAMSE* DH6 .... 182 D2
Dame Dorothy St
CLDN/WHIT/ROK SR6 .... 14 E2
Dame Flora Robson Av
HAR/WTLS NE34 .... 74 D7
WASHS NE38 .... 116 B6
Danby Cl *SUNDSW* SR3 .... 134 B1 🔲
Danby Gdns
BYK/HTN/WLK NE6 .... 71 K2 🔲
Danville Rd
CLDN/WHIT/ROK SR6 .... 106 E1
Daphne Crs *SEA/MUR* SR7 .... 150 D3
Darden Cl *LGB/KIL* NE12 .... 48 B5 🔲
Darden Lough
WD/WHPE/BLK NE5 .... 68 D2
Darien Av *CLDN/WHIT/ROK* SR6 .. 106 D1
Dark La *MPTH* NE61 .... 20 E4
Darley Ct *CLSW/PEL* DH2 .... 144 B3
Darley Pl *BW/LEM/TK/HW* NE15 .. 68 E6
Darlington Rd *DHAM* DH1 .... 168 B2
Darnley Rd *ASHGTN* NE63 .... 23 J2
Darras Ct *SSH* NE33 .... 75 H2
Darras Dr *NSHW* NE29 .... 60 A3
Darras Rd *PONT/DH* NE20 .... 42 D6
Darrell St *DIN/WO* NE13 .... 46 A3
Dartford Rd
CLDN/WHIT/ROK SR6 .... 106 D1
SSH NE33 .... 75 K1
Dartmouth Av
LWF/SPW/WRK NE9 .... 101 F2
Dartmouth Cl *SEA/MUR* SR7 ...... 150 B2 🔲
Dart Rd *PLEE/EAS* SR8 .... 174 D5
Darvall Cl *MONK* NE25 .... 50 B2
Darwin Crs *GOS/KPK* NE3 .... 55 K7
Darwin St *SWCK/CAS* SR5 .... 105 K4
Daryl Cl *BLAY* NE21 .... 83 J3 🔲
Daryl Wy *FELL* NE10 .... 89 F5 🔲
Davenport Dr *GOS/KPK* NE3 .... 56 B1
David Gdns
CLDN/WHIT/ROK SR6 .... 107 F2
Davidson Rd *FELL* NE10 .... 13 M4
Davidson St *FELL* NE10 .... 12 C7
David Ter *RDHAMSE* DH6 .... 180 A1
RDHAMSE DH6 .... 181 G4
Davis Cl *BDN/LAN/SAC* DH7 .... 153 K2
Davison Av *SUNDSW* SR3 .... 120 B7
WBAY NE26 .... 50 D3
Davison Crs *SEA/MUR* SR7 .... 149 G4
Davison St *BLYTH* NE24 .... 31 G6 🔲
BOLCOL NE35 .... 90 C3
BW/LEM/TK/HW NE15 .... 67 G3
Davis Ter *PLEE/EAS* SR8 .... 162 E6
Davy Bank *WLSD/HOW* NE28 .... 73 F2
Davy Dr *PLEE/EAS* SR8 .... 174 A2
Dawdon Crs *SEA/MUR* SR7 .... 150 E2
Dawlish Cl *SEA/MUR* SR7 .... 150 B2
Dawlish Gdns
LWF/SPW/WRK NE9 .... 101 F2
Dawlish Pl *WD/WHPE/BLK* NE5 .... 54 A7
Dawson Pl *MPTH* NE61 .... 20 D4
Dawson St *WNGT* TS28 .... 183 K3
Dawson Ter *MLFD/PNYW* SR4 ...... 104 E6
Daylesford Dr *LGB/HTN* NE7 .... 57 F6
Daylesford Rd *CRAM* NE23 .... 33 G5
Dayshield *WD/WHPE/BLK* NE5 .... 68 D2
Deacon Cl
WD/WHPE/BLK NE5 .... 67 K1 🔲
Deaconsfield Cl
SUNDSW SR3 .... 133 K2 🔲
Deal Cl *BLYTH* NE24 .... 35 G3
Dean Cl *PLEE/EAS* SR8 .... 175 G5 🔲
Deanery St *BDLGTN* NE22 .... 28 E5
Deanham Gdns
WD/WHPE/BLK NE5 .... 69 G3
Dean Rd *SSH* NE33 .... 75 F4 🔲
Deans Av *NWBGN* NE64 .... 18 E7
Deansfield Cl *SUNDSW* SR3 ...... 133 K2 🔲
Dean St *CNUT* NE1 .... 5 L7
LWF/SPW/WRK NE9 .... 87 F7
Deans' Wk *DHAM* DH1 .... 157 G6
Dean Ter *SSH* NE33 .... 75 F4
SWCK/CAS SR5 .... 105 K4
Dean View Dr *BLYTH* NE24 .... 30 D6
Dearham Gv *CRAM* NE23 .... 33 G5
Debdon Gdns
BYK/HTN/WLK NE6 .... 71 J2
Debdon Pl *CRAM* NE23 .... 38 C2 🔲
Debdon Rd *ASHGTN* NE63 .... 24 A3
Deckham Ter *GATE* NE8 .... 11 J7
Deepbrook Rd
WD/WHPE/BLK NE5 .... 69 G2 🔲
Deepdale *WLSD/HOW* NE28 .... 58 B5
Deepdale Cl *WICK/BNPF* NE16 .... 98 D1
Deepdale Crs
WD/WHPE/BLK NE5 .... 69 H1

Deepdale Gdns *LGB/KIL* NE12 .... 47 J6
Deepdale Rd *TYNE/NSHE* NE30 .... 51 F7
Deepdale St *HLS* DH4 .... 147 K7
Deepdene Gv
CLDN/WHIT/ROK SR6 .... 92 D7
Deepdene Rd
CLDN/WHIT/ROK SR6 .... 92 D7
Deerbolt Pl *LGB/KIL* NE12 .... 57 J3 🔲
Deer Bush *WD/WHPE/BLK* NE5 .... 68 D2
Deerfell Cl *ASHGTN* NE63 .... 23 H3 🔲
Deerness Gv
BDN/LAN/SAC DH7 .... 153 G7 🔲
Deerness Hts
BDN/LAN/SAC DH7 .... 167 G5
Dee Rd *HEBB* NE31 .... 89 H1 🔲
Deer Park Wy *BLYTH* NE24 .... 84 C3
Dees St *JRW* NE32 .... 74 A4 🔲
Dee St *JRW* NE32 .... 74 A4
Defender Cl *SWCK/CAS* SR5 ...... 105 G5 🔲
Defoe Av *HAR/WTLS* NE34 .... 91 F1
Deighton Wk
WD/WHPE/BLK NE5 .... 68 D2 🔲
Delacour Rd *BLAY* NE21 .... 84 A1
Delamere Ct *SUNDSW* SR3 ...... 134 A1 🔲
Delamere Crs *CRAM* NE23 .... 33 G5
Delamere Rd *GOS/KPK* NE3 .... 55 K5
Delaval Av *NSHW* NE29 .... 60 C4
Delaval Ct *BDLGTN* NE22 .... 29 J4
SSH NE33 .... 75 H2
Delaval Crs *BLYTH* NE24 .... 34 E3 🔲
Delavale Cl *PLEE/EAS* SR8 .... 175 G5 🔲
Delaval Gdns
BW/LEM/TK/HW NE15 .... 69 F7
Delaval Rd
BW/LEM/TK/HW NE15 .... 69 F7
CLDN/WHIT/ROK SR6 .... 106 D1
Delaval St *BLYTH* NE24 .... 34 D3
Delaval Ter *BLYTH* NE24 .... 31 F6 🔲
GOS/KPK NE3 .... 56 A6 🔲
Delight Bank *STLY/ANP* DH9 ...... 111 F7
Dellfield Dr *MLFD/PNYW* SR4 ...... 118 E2 🔲
The Dell *HLS* DH4 .... 132 B4
MPTH NE61 .... 20 C7
Delta Bank Rd *WICK/BNPF* NE16 .... 8 B2
Delvedene *CON/LDGT* DH8 ...... 123 H6 🔲
Delves La *CON/LDGT* DH8 .... 123 H7
De Merley Rd *MPTH* NE61 .... 20 D3
Demesne Dr *BDLGTN* NE22 .... 29 F6
The Demesne *ASHGTN* NE63 .... 24 D3
De Mowbray Wy *MPTH* NE61 ...... 20 D3
Dempsey Rd *DIN/WO* NE13 .... 46 B4 🔲
Denbeigh Pl *LGB/KIL* NE12 .... 57 J3
Denbigh Av
CLDN/WHIT/ROK SR6 .... 106 E1
WLSD/HOW NE28 .... 59 J6
Denby Cl *CRAM* NE23 .... 33 G5
Dene Av *BW/LEM/TK/HW* NE15 .... 68 B5
DIN/WO NE13 .... 46 A3
GOS/KPK NE3 .... 56 E6
HLH DH5 .... 132 E7
LGB/KIL NE12 .... 47 G7 🔲
PLEE/EAS SR8 .... 163 F4
ROWG NE39 .... 97 F4
Denebank *MONK* NE25 .... 50 D3
Dene Bank Av *PLEE/EAS* SR8 .. 175 H4 🔲
Dene Bank Vw *GOS/KPK* NE3 .... 55 J7 🔲
Dene Cl *LGB/HTN* NE7 .... 71 G1
PRUD NE42 .... 64 B6
RYTON NE40 .... 67 F6
Dene Ct *BDN/LAN/SAC* DH7 ...... 143 G7
CHPW NE17 .... 95 H7
CLS/BIR/GTL DH3 .... 101 J7
RDHAMSE DH6 .... 171 H4
WASHS NE38 .... 102 E7
Dene Crs *GOS/KPK* NE3 .... 56 E6
ROWG NE39 .... 97 F4
RYTON NE40 .... 67 F6
WBAY NE26 .... 50 D3
WLSD/HOW NE28 .... 73 F1
Denecroft *WYLAM* NE41 .... 65 G5
Dene Dr *DHAM* DH1 .... 158 A4
Denefold *LWF/SPW/WRK* NE9 .... 101 G4
Dene Gdns *FELL* NE10 .... 13 L5
HLH DH5 .... 147 J1
Dene Garth *PRUD* NE42 .... 64 A6
Dene Gv *CRAM* NE23 .... 39 F6
GOS/KPK NE3 .... 56 E6
PRUD NE42 .... 80 B1
Deneholm *MONK* NE25 .... 50 C3
WLSD/HOW NE28 .... 59 F7
Dene House Rd *SEA/MUR* SR7 .... 135 J7
Dene La
CLDN/WHIT/ROK SR6 .... 106 D1 🔲
Dene Pk *BDN/LAN/SAC* DH7 ...... 165 G2
PONT/DH NE20 .... 42 D6
SWCK/CAS SR5 .... 105 G3
Dene Rd *BLAY* NE21 .... 84 A1
ROWG NE39 .... 97 F4
SEA/MUR SR7 .... 150 D3
STKFD/GP NE62 .... 22 E6
SWCK/CAS SR5 .... 105 G4
TYNE/NSHE NE30 .... 61 G2
WYLAM NE41 .... 65 H5
Deneside Av
LWF/SPW/WRK NE9 .... 100 E1
Dene St *HLH* DH5 .... 147 K2
MLFD/PNYW SR4 .... 105 K6
PLEE/EAS SR8 .... 175 H3
PRUD NE42 .... 80 C1
SUNDSW SR3 .... 120 A5
Dene Ter *JRW* NE32 .... 73 J7
The Dene *CLSW/PEL* DH2 .... 129 H7
HLS DH4 .... 146 D5
MONK NE25 .... 50 C4
WYLAM NE41 .... 65 H5
Dene Vw *ASHGTN* NE63 .... 23 G2
BDLGTN NE22 .... 29 J5
GOS/KPK NE3 .... 56 E6
RDHAMSE DH6 .... 181 J2
ROWG NE39 .... 96 C2 🔲

Dene View Crs
MLFD/PNYW SR4 .... 105 F7
Dene Vw East *BDLGTN* NE22 .... 29 J6
Dene Vw West *BDLGTN* NE22 .... 29 H6
Dene Vls *PLEE/EAS* SR8 .... 175 H4
Deneway *ROWG* NE39 .... 97 J1
Dene Wy *SEA/MUR* SR7 .... 135 J7
Denewell Av *LGB/HTN* NE7 .... 57 G7
LWF/SPW/WRK NE9 .... 87 F7
Denewood *LGB/KIL* NE12 .... 48 A7
Denham Av
CLDN/WHIT/ROK SR6 .... 106 D1
Denham Dr *MONK* NE25 .... 40 A6
Denham Gv *BLAY* NE21 .... 83 H4
Denhill Pk
BW/LEM/TK/HW NE15 .... 69 H5
Denholm Av *CRAM* NE23 .... 33 G5 🔲
Denmark St
BYK/HTN/WLK NE6 .... 7 G4 🔲
GATE NE8 .... 11 C5
Dennis St *RDHAMSE* DH6 .... 172 E7 🔲
Denshaw Cl *CRAM* NE23 .... 33 G5
Dentdale *HLS* DH4 .... 117 G7
Denton Av
BW/LEM/TK/HW NE15 .... 68 B5
NSHW NE29 .... 60 A4
Denton Ga
WD/WHPE/BLK NE5 .... 54 E7 🔲
Denton Gv
WD/WHPE/BLK NE5 .... 54 E7 🔲
Denton Rd
BW/LEM/TK/HW NE15 .... 68 D6
Denton Vw *BLAY* NE21 .... 83 K2
Dent St *BLYTH* NE24 .... 35 H1
Denver Gdns *BYK/HTN/WLK* NE6 ... 7 M6
Denway Gv *WBAY* NE26 .... 40 E1
Denwick Cl *CLSW/PEL* DH2 ...... 129 C7
Denwick Ter *TYNE/NSHE* NE30.... 61 G3
Depot Rd *BYK/HTN/WLK* NE6 .... 7 J2
Deptford Rd *GATE* NE8 .... 6 D8
MLFD/PNYW SR4 .... 14 A3
Deptford Ter *MLFD/PNYW* SR4 .... 106 A5
Derby Crs *CON/LDGT* DH8 .... 137 F1
HEBB NE31 .... 73 F6
Derby Dr *CON/LDGT* DH8 .... 137 F1
Derby Gdns *WLSD/HOW* NE28 .... 58 C7 🔲
Derby St *STLY/ANP* DH9 .... 126 C2
Derbyshire Dr *DHAM* DH1 .... 158 A7
Derby St *ASHBK/HED/RY* SR2 .... 14 C6
ELS/FEN NE4 .... 4 F5
JRW NE32 .... 74 A4
SSH NE33 .... 3 H9
Dereham Cl *WBAY* NE26 .... 41 G3
Dereham Ct
WD/WHPE/BLK NE5 .... 55 F6 🔲
Dereham Rd *WBAY* NE26 .... 41 G4
Dereham Ter *STKFD/GP* NE62 ...... 23 J5
Dereham Wy *NSHW* NE29 .... 59 K2
Dere Pk *CON/LDGT* DH8 .... 123 J3
Dere Rd *CON/LDGT* DH8 .... 123 H6
Derry Av *CLDN/WHIT/ROK* SR6 .... 106 E1
Derwent Av *DUN/TMV* NE11 .... 86 D7
HEBB NE31 .... 89 G1 🔲
ROWG NE39 .... 97 G4
Derwent Cl *BDN/LAN/SAC* DH7 .. 143 G5
SEA/MUR SR7 .... 135 J7
Derwent Crs *CHPW* NE17 .... 95 H7
CON/LDGT DH8 .... 123 K2
WICK/BNPF NE16 .... 84 E4
Derwentdale Gdns
LGB/HTN NE7 .... 57 H7
Derwent Gdns *WLSD/HOW* NE28 ... 59 J6
Derwenthaugh Rd *BLAY* NE21 .... 84 C2
Derwent Ms *CON/LDGT* DH8 ...... 123 K2 🔲
Derwent Pl *CON/LDGT* DH8 ...... 122 C1 🔲
Derwent Rd *PLEE/EAS* SR8 .... 175 F3
TYNE/NSHE NE30 .... 51 F7
WBAY NE26 .... 40 E2
Derwent St *CHPW* NE17 .... 95 H7
CHPW NE17 .... 95 H4
CON/LDGT DH8 .... 122 D3
HLH DH5 .... 148 A6
SUND SR1 .... 14 D6
Derwent Vw *BLAY* NE21 .... 83 K3
Derwent Wk *WICK/BNPF* NE16 .... 84 D4
Derwentwater Rd *GATE* NE8 .... 9 K7
NWBGN NE64 .... 24 E1
Derwent Wy *BLAY* NE21 .... 84 C3
LGB/KIL NE12 .... 47 J6
Deuchar St *JES* NE2 .... 71 F3
Devon Cl *ASHGTN* NE63 .... 23 F1 🔲
Devon Crs *CLS/BIR/GTL* DH3 ...... 101 H7
CON/LDGT DH8 .... 137 C1
Devon Dr *SUNDSW* SR3 .... 120 A6
Devon Gdns *HAR/WTLS* NE34 ...... 76 B4
Devonport *HLS* DH4 .... 132 A4
Devon Rd *HEBB* NE31 .... 89 H1
NSHW NE29 .... 60 B1
Devonshire Dr *LGB/KIL* NE12 ...... 58 D1
Devonshire Gdns
WLSD/HOW NE28 .... 58 B7
Devonshire Pl *JES* NE2 .... 71 F2
Devonshire Rd *DHAM* DH1 ...... 157 K7
Devonshire St *SSH* NE33 .... 75 F4
SWCK/CAS SR5 .... 106 C4
Devonworth Pl *BLYTH* NE24 .... 30 C7
De Walden Sq *MPTH* NE61 .... 21 J2
Dewberry Cl *BLYTH* NE24 .... 34 E3
Dewley *CRAM* NE23 .... 38 C3
Dewley Pl
WD/WHPE/BLK NE5 .... 54 C6 🔲
Dewley Rd *WD/WHPE/BLK* NE5 .. 68 E2
Dewsgreen *CRAM* NE23 .... 38 C2
Dexter Wy *FELL* NE10 .... 12 B7
Deyncourt *DHAM* DH1 .... 168 B4 🔲
PONT/DH NE20 .... 43 H6
Deyncourt Cl *PONT/DH* NE20 ...... 53 F1
Diamond Ct *GOS/KPK* NE3 .... 55 J4
Diamond St *WLSD/HOW* NE28 .. 72 D1 🔲
Diana St *ELS/FEN* NE4 .... 4 F6
Dickens Av *HAR/WTLS* NE34 .... 91 F1
WICK/BNPF NE16 .... 84 E4
Dickens St *HLS* DH4 .... 132 B7
SWCK/CAS SR5 .... 106 A4 🔲
Dickens Wynd *DHAM* DH1 .... 168 B3
Didcot Av *NSHW* NE29 .... 60 C6 🔲

Didcot Wy *BOL* NE36 .... 90 D5
BOLCOL NE35 .... 90 D5
Dillon St *JRW* NE32 .... 73 J6
SEA/MUR SR7 .... 150 E1
Dilston Av *NSHW* NE25 .... 51 F5
Dilston Cl *MPTH* NE61 .... 22 A2
PLEE/EAS SR8 .... 174 D7
SMOOR NE27 .... 49 H7
WASHS NE38 .... 116 C2
Dilston Dr *ASHGTN* NE63 .... 23 K3
WD/WHPE/BLK NE5 .... 54 C7
Dilston Gdns
MLFD/PNYW SR4 .... 119 K1
Dilston Rd *DHAM* DH1 .... 156 E3 🔲
ELS/FEN NE4 .... 4 C5
Dilston Ter *JRW* NE32 .... 89 K1
Dimbula Gdns *LGB/HTN* NE7 .... 71 K1
Dinsdale Av *WLSD/HOW* NE28 .... 58 E5
Dinsdale Dr *DHAM* DH1 .... 158 A5
Dinsdale Pl *JES* NE2 .... 6 B3
Dinsdale Rd
CLDN/WHIT/ROK SR6 .... 106 E3
JES NE2 .... 6 B3
Dinsdale St *ASHBK/HED/RY* SR2.. 135 F1
Dinting Cl *PLEE/EAS* SR8 .... 174 C5
Dipe La *BOL* NE36 .... 90 E6
Dipton Gdns *SUNDSW* SR3 ...... 120 B4 🔲
Dipton Gv *CRAM* NE23 .... 38 C2
Dipton Rd *MONK* NE25 .... 50 B2
Dipwood Rd *ROWG* NE39 .... 97 F4
Dipwood Wy *ROWG* NE39 .... 97 F5
Disraeli St *BLYTH* NE24 .... 31 F6
HLS DH4 .... 131 K7
Dissington Pl
WD/WHPE/BLK NE5 .... 69 G3
WICK/BNPF NE16 .... 84 E7
Ditchburn Ter *MLFD/PNYW* SR4.. 105 K5
Dixon Av *CON/LDGT* DH8 .... 109 F3
Dixon Est *RDHAMSE* DH6 .... 173 H5
Dixon Estate Bungalows
RDHAMSE DH6 .... 173 H6
Dixon Pl *DUN/TMV* NE11 .... 9 H7
Dixon Ri *PLEE/EAS* SR8 .... 175 J4
Dixon Rd *HLH* DH5 .... 147 G2
Dixon's Sq
CLDN/WHIT/ROK SR6 .... 106 D4 🔲
Dixon St *CON/LDGT* DH8 .... 122 E3 🔲
GATE NE8 .... 10 B6
SSH NE33 .... 75 G2 🔲
Dobson Cl *ELS/FEN* NE4 .... 9 L1
Dobson Crs *BYK/HTN/WLK* NE6 .... 7 H9
Dobson Ter *SEA/MUR* SR7 ...... 149 H5 🔲
WNGT TS28 .... 183 J2 🔲
Dock Rd *NSHW* NE29 .... 2 C5
Dock Rd South *NSHW* NE29 ...... 2 D6
Dock St *CLDN/WHIT/ROK* SR6 .... 15 G1
Dockwray Cl *TYNE/NSHE* NE30 ...... 2 F7
Dockwray Sq *TYNE/NSHE* NE30.... 2 F7
Doddfell Cl *WASHN* NE37 .... 102 C7
Doddington Cl
BW/LEM/TK/HW NE15 .... 67 K4
Doddington Dr *CRAM* NE23 .... 38 B2
Dodds Cl *RDHAMSE* DH6 .... 173 F7
Dodds Ter *WNGT* TS28 .... 183 J2
Dogger Bank *MPTH* NE61 .... 20 C4
Dolphin St *ELS/FEN* NE4 .... 69 H6
Dominies Cl *ROWG* NE39 .... 97 J1
Dominion Rd
BDN/LAN/SAC DH7 .... 167 G7
Donald Av *RDHAMSE* DH6 .... 160 D1
Donald St *GOS/KPK* NE3 .... 56 E5 🔲
Doncaster Rd *JES* NE2 .... 6 B2
Doncrest Rd *WASHN* NE37 .... 102 D4
Don Dixon Dr *JRW* NE32 .... 89 K3 🔲
Don Gdns *BOL* NE36 .... 90 D5
Donkin Rd *WASHN* NE37 .... 102 D4
Donkin Ter *TYNE/NSHE* NE30 ...... 61 G3
Donnington Cl
SWCK/CAS SR5 .... 104 C4 🔲
Donnington Ct *GOS/KPK* NE3 ...... 57 F6
Donnini Pl *DHAM* DH1 .... 17 J1
Donnison Gdns *SUND* SR1 ...... 15 H4 🔲
Donridge *WASHN* NE37 .... 102 D4
Don Rd *JRW* NE32 .... 74 B4
Don St *DUN/TMV* NE11 .... 100 C1
Donvale Rd *WASHN* NE37 .... 102 C4
Don Vw *BOL* NE36 .... 90 D5
Dorcas Av
BW/LEM/TK/HW NE15 .... 69 G6
Dorchester Cl
WD/WHPE/BLK NE5 .... 53 K7 🔲
Dorchester Ct *MONK* NE25 .... 39 K2
Dorchester Gdns
LWF/SPW/WRK NE9 .... 101 F3
Doreen Av *SEA/MUR* SR7 .... 150 A2
Doric Rd *BDN/LAN/SAC* DH7 ...... 166 E3
Dorking Av *NSHW* NE29 .... 60 C6
Dorking Cl *BLYTH* NE24 .... 35 G3
Dorking Rd
CLDN/WHIT/ROK SR6 .... 106 D1
Dorlonco Vls
BDN/LAN/SAC DH7 .... 167 H7
Dormand Dr *PLEE/EAS* SR8 ...... 174 D7
Dornoch Crs *FELL* NE10 .... 88 A6 🔲
Dorrington Rd *GOS/KPK* NE3 ...... 55 J4
Dorset Av *CLDN/WHIT/ROK* SR6 .. 106 E1
CLS/BIR/GTL DH3 .... 115 J5
HAR/WTLS NE34 .... 76 B4
HEBB NE31 .... 73 H6
WLSD/HOW NE28 .... 72 C1
Dorset Cl *ASHGTN* NE63 .... 23 F1 🔲
Dorset Gv *NSHW* NE29 .... 60 B1
Dorset La *SUNDSW* SR3 .... 120 B7
Dorset Rd
BW/LEM/TK/HW NE15 .... 68 D5
GATE NE8 .... 6 C8
Dorset St *HLH* DH5 .... 160 B1
Douai Dr *CON/LDGT* DH8 .... 123 J7
Double Rw *MONK* NE25 .... 39 J4
Douglas Cl *HAR/WTLS* NE34 ...... 75 G7 🔲
Douglas Ct *STLY/ANP* DH9 .... 125 G4
Douglas Gdns *DUN/TMV* NE11 .... 86 A5
Douglas Rd
CLDN/WHIT/ROK SR6 .... 106 E1
Douglass St *WLSD/HOW* NE28 .... 72 C1
Douglas St *WLSD/HOW* NE28 .... 73 J2 🔲
Douglas Ter *ELS/FEN* NE4 .... 4 F6
HLS DH4 .... 117 K6

Douglas Vls *DHAM* DH1 .... 17 G2
Doulting Cl *LGB/KIL* NE12 .... 57 H4 🔲
Dove Av *JRW* NE32 .... 90 A1
Dove Cl *BDN/LAN/SAC* DH7 .. 167 F6 🔲
Dovecote Cl *MONK* NE25 .... 50 A3 🔲
Dovecote Rd *LGB/KIL* NE12 .... 58 A5 🔲
Dovedale Av *BLYTH* NE24 .... 30 C7
Dovedale Gdns *LGB/HTN* NE7 .. 57 G7
LWF/SPW/WRK NE9 .... 101 G1
Dovedale Rd
CLDN/WHIT/ROK SR6 .... 92 C7
Dover Cl *BDLGTN* NE22 .... 28 D5
WD/WHPE/BLK NE5 .... 54 A7
Dovercourt Rd
BYK/HTN/WLK NE6 .... 72 C7
Dowling Av *MONK* NE25 .... 50 D5
Downe Cl *BLYTH* NE24 .... 35 G3
Downend Rd
WD/WHPE/BLK NE5 .... 54 C7
Downfield *WASHN* NE37 .... 103 F2 🔲
Downhill Cl *WD/WHPE/BLK* NE5 .. 68 D2
Downhill La *BOL* NE36 .... 104 C1 🔲
WASHN NE37 .... 104 B1
Downing Dr *MPTH* NE61 .... 20 B6
Downs La *HLH* DH5 .... 148 A3
Downs Pit La *HLH* DH5 .... 148 A3
Downswood *LGB/KIL* NE12 .... 48 B6 🔲
Dowsey Rd *RDHAMSE* DH6 .. 158 C7 🔲
Dowson Sq *SEA/MUR* SR7 .... 149 F5
Doxford Av *HLH* DH5 .... 147 J2
Doxford Dr *PLEE/EAS* SR8 .... 174 A4
Doxford Gdns
WD/WHPE/BLK NE5 .... 69 H2 🔲
Doxford Park Wy *SUNDSW* SR3 .. 133 J1
Doxford Pl *CRAM* NE23 .... 38 C3 🔲
Doxford Ter *DHAM* DH1 .... 157 J7
Dragon La *DHAM* DH1 .... 157 J7
Drake Cl *SSH* NE33 .... 75 F3
Drawback Cl *PRUD* NE42 .... 80 D2 🔲
The Dray *PONT/DH* NE20 .... 42 D6
Drayton Rd
CLDN/WHIT/ROK SR6 .... 106 D1
GOS/KPK NE3 .... 55 J6
The Drive *CLS/BIR/GTL* DH3 .. 115 K5
CON/LDGT DH8 .... 122 D1
FELL NE10 .... 12 E8
GOS/KPK NE3 .... 56 C7
LGB/HTN NE7 .... 57 H6
LWF/SPW/WRK NE9 .... 87 F6
MPTH NE61 .... 26 B5
TYNE/NSHE NE30 .... 61 H1
WASHN NE37 .... 102 E4
WD/WHPE/BLK NE5 .... 68 D3
WICK/BNPF NE16 .... 85 C6
WLSD/HOW NE28 .... 72 D1
Dronfield Cl *CLSW/PEL* DH2 .. 129 F6
Drove Rd *BW/LEM/TK/HW* NE15 .. 52 E7
Drover Rd *CON/LDGT* DH8 .... 137 F2
Drover Ter *CON/LDGT* DH8 .... 137 F2
Drummond Cres *HAR/WTLS* NE34 .. 74 D6
Drummond Rd *GOS/KPK* NE3.. 55 K7
Drummond Ter
TYNE/NSHE NE30 .... 61 F3
Drumoyne Cl *SUNDSW* SR3 .. 133 F1
Drumoyne Gdns *MONK* NE25 .. 50 B6
Drum Rd *CLSW/PEL* DH2 .... 115 H7 🔲
Drumsheugh Pl
WD/WHPE/BLK NE5 .... 69 F1
Druridge Av
CLDN/WHIT/ROK SR6 .... 92 D7
Druridge Crs *BLYTH* NE24 .... 34 D2
HAR/WTLS NE34 .... 76 B3
Druridge Dr *BLYTH* NE24 .... 34 D2
WD/WHPE/BLK NE5 .... 69 H2
Drury La *NSHW* NE29 .... 60 A3
SUND SR1 .... 15 G4
Drybeck Ct *CRAM* NE23 .... 33 K7
Drybeck Sq *SUNDSW* SR3 .. 134 B1 🔲
Drybeck Wk *CRAM* NE23 .... 33 K7 🔲
Dryborough St
MLFD/PNYW SR4 .... 14 A3 🔲
Dryburgh *WASHS* NE38 .... 116 E1
Dryburgh Cl *NSHW* NE29 .... 60 C2
Dryburn Hl *DHAM* DH1 .... 156 B5
Dryburn Rd *DHAM* DH1 .... 156 B4
Dryden Cl *HAR/WTLS* NE34 .. 91 F2
STLY/ANP DH9 .... 126 E1
Dryden Rd *LWF/SPW/WRK* NE9 .. 11 H8
Dryden St *SWCK/CAS* SR5 .. 106 A4
Drysdale Cl *DIN/WO* NE13 .... 46 A3
Drysdale Crs *DIN/WO* NE13 .... 46 A3
Dubmire Cottages *HLS* DH4 .. 131 H7
Dubmire Ct *HLS* DH4 .... 131 J7
Duchess Crs *JRW* NE32 .... 89 K1
Duchess Crs East *JRW* NE32 .. 89 K1 🔲
Duchess Dr
BW/LEM/TK/HW NE15 .... 68 C4
Duchess St *WBAY* NE26 .... 50 E4
Duckets *PRUD* NE42 .... 80 D1
Duckpool La *WICK/BNPF* NE16.. 85 C5
Duddon Cl *PLEE/EAS* SR8 .. 175 F4 🔲
Duddon Pl *LWF/SPW/WRK* NE9 .. 101 H1
Dudley Av
CLDN/WHIT/ROK SR6 .... 106 D1 🔲
Dudley Dr *CRAM* NE23 .... 47 C1
Dudley Gdns *SUNDSW* SR3 .. 133 C1
Dudley La *CRAM* NE23 .... 38 B3
DIN/WO NE13 .... 46 C1
Dugdale Rd *GOS/KPK* NE3.... 55 H5
Duke's Av *HEBB* NE31 .... 73 F7
Dukes Dr *GOS/KPK* NE3 .... 56 B1
Dukesfield *CRAM* NE23 .... 38 C3 🔲
Dukes Meadow *DIN/WO* NE13 .. 54 C2
Duke St *FELL* NE10 .... 13 J5
MLFD/PNYW SR4 .... 106 A7 🔲
SEA/MUR SR7 .... 135 H7
WBAY NE26 .... 50 E4
Duke St North
CLDN/WHIT/ROK SR6 .... 106 D3
Dukesway *DUN/TMV* NE11 .... 86 B7
Dukes Wy *PRUD* NE42 .... 64 E7
Dulverston Cl
WD/WHPE/BLK NE5 .... 54 A7 🔲

Dunblane Crs
WD/WHPE/BLK NE5 .... 68 D3
Dunblane Dr *BLYTH* NE24 .... 35 C3
Dunblane Rd
CLDN/WHIT/ROK SR6 .... 92 C7
Dunbreck Gv *MLFD/PNYW* SR4 .. 120 A2
Duncan St *BYK/HTN/WLK* NE6 .. 72 C5
GATE NE8 .... 11 L6
MLFD/PNYW SR4 .... 105 K6
Duncombe Crs *STLY/ANP* DH9 .. 112 D6
Dun Cow La *DHAM* DH1 .... 16 F5
Dundas St *CLDN/WHIT/ROK* SR6 .. 14 E1
Dundee Cl *WD/WHPE/BLK* NE5 .. 54 A7
Dundrennan *WASHS* NE38 .... 116 E3
Dunelm Cl *CON/LDGT* DH8 .. 123 K4
Dunelm Dr *BOL* NE36 .... 91 F5
HLS DH4 .... 132 A7
Dunelm Pl *RDHAMSE* DH6 .. 173 J4 🔲
Dunelm Rd *CON/LDGT* DH8 .. 122 B7
HLH DH5 .... 147 J4
RDHAMSE DH6 .... 172 A7
Dunelm St *SSH* NE33 .... 3 J9
Dunelm Wk *CON/LDGT* DH8 .. 123 K4
PLEE/EAS SR8 .... 174 E3 🔲
Dunelm Wy *CON/LDGT* DH8 .. 123 K3
Dunford Gdns
WD/WHPE/BLK NE5 .... 54 B6 🔲
Dunholm Cl *HLH* DH5 .... 147 H1
Dunholm Cl *DHAM* DH1 .... 156 C4
Dunholme Rd *ELS/FEN* NE4 .... 4 A7
Dunira Cl *JES* NE2 .... 71 F1 🔲
Dunkeld Cl *BLYTH* NE24 .... 35 G3
Dunkirk Av *HLH* DH5 .... 147 J1
Dunlin Cl *RYTON* NE40 .... 67 G7 🔲
Dunlin Dr *BLYTH* NE24 .... 35 G3
WASHS NE38 .... 116 B3
Dunlop Cl *LGB/HTN* NE7 .... 57 J6 🔲
Dunmore Crs *HAR/WTLS* NE34.. 76 A5
Dunmoor Cl *GOS/KPK* NE3 .. 56 A6 🔲
Dunmore Av
CLDN/WHIT/ROK SR6 .... 92 E7
Dunmorlie St *BYK/HTN/WLK* NE6 .. 7 J5
Dunn Av *SUNDSW* SR3 .... 120 A5
Dunning St *SUND* SR1 .... 14 D3
Dunnlynn Cl *SUNDSW* SR3 .. 133 J1 🔲
Dunnock Dr *WASHS* NE38 .... 116 B4
WICK/BNPF NE16 .... 98 C2
Dunn Rd *PLEE/EAS* SR8 .... 174 E3
Dunn's Ter *JES* NE2 .... 4 E1 🔲
Dunn St *ELS/FEN* NE4 .... 9 L1
Dunnykirk Av *GOS/KPK* NE3 .. 55 H5 🔲
Dunsdale Dr *CRAM* NE23 .... 33 K7
Dunsdale Rd *MONK* NE25 .... 40 B6
Dunsgreen *PONT/DH* NE20........ 43 G4
Dunsley Gdns *DIN/WO* NE13...... 45 F2
Dunsmuir Gv *GATE* NE8 .... 10 D8
Dunstable Pl
WD/WHPE/BLK NE5 .... 53 K7 🔲
Dunstanburgh Cl *BDLGTN* NE22.. 28 D5
Dunstanburgh Cl *BDLGTN* NE22.. 28 D5
WASHS NE38 .... 116 D2
Dunstanburgh Rd
BYK/HTN/WLK NE6 .... 7 K7
Dunstan Cl *CLSW/PEL* DH2 .. 129 D8
Dunston Bank *DUN/TMV* NE11 .. 85 J5
Dunston Pl *BLYTH* NE24 .... 30 D7
Dunston Rd *DUN/TMV* NE11...... 9 G5
Dunvegan *CLS/BIR/GTL* DH3.. 116 A4
Dunvegan Av *CLSW/PEL* DH2.. 129 H5
Durant Rd *CNUT* NE1 .... 5 L5
Durban St *BLYTH* NE24 .... 31 F5
Durham Av *PLEE/EAS* SR8........ 175 G2
WASHN NE37 .... 102 C5
Durham Cl *BDLGTN* NE22 .... 28 D5 🔲
Durham Dr *BOLCOL* NE35........ 89 K4
JRW NE32 .... 89 K2
Durham Gdns
BDN/LAN/SAC DH7 .... 143 G7
Durham Gv *JRW* NE32 .... 89 J2
Durham La *PLEE/EAS* SR8 .... 162 A6
RDHAMSE DH6 .... 171 J2
RDHAMSE DH6 .... 172 C1
RDHAMSE DH6 .... 173 G1
Durham Pl *CLS/BIR/GTL* DH3 .. 115 J5
GATE NE8 .... 11 H6 🔲
Durham Rd *ASHBK/HED/RY* SR2 .. 14 B6
BDN/LAN/SAC DH7 .... 140 C5
BDN/LAN/SAC DH7 .... 143 H6
BDN/LAN/SAC DH7 .... 165 H2
CLS/BIR/GTL DH3 .... 115 J1
CON/LDGT DH8 .... 122 C3
CRAM NE23 .... 33 J6
GATE NE8 .... 11 G6
HLH DH5 .... 132 D4
HLS DH4 .... 132 C7
LWF/SPW/WRK NE9 .... 101 F1
RDHAMSE DH6 .... 180 A3
STLY/ANP DH9 .... 125 J4
SUNDSW SR3 .... 120 A3
WNGT TS28 .... 183 J2
Durham St *ELS/FEN* NE4 .... 4 B8
HLS DH4 .... 131 J7
SEA/MUR SR7 .... 135 H7
WLSD/HOW NE28 .... 72 E1
Durham St West
WLSD/HOW NE28 .... 72 E1 🔲
Durham Ter *SUNDSW* SR3 .... 120 A5
Durham Wy *PLEE/EAS* SR8 .... 174 D2
Duxfield Rd *LGB/HTN* NE7 .... 57 H7
Dwyer Crs *ASHBK/HED/RY* SR2 .. 135 F1
Dyer Sq *SWCK/CAS* SR5 .... 106 B3
Dykefield Cl *GOS/KPK* NE3...... 55 J3
Dyke Heads La *RYTON* NE40...... 82 D2
Dykelands Rd
LDN/WHIT/ROK SR6 .... 106 D1
Dykelands Wy *HAR/WTLS* NE34 .. 90 A1
Dykenook Cl *WICK/BNPF* NE16 .. 98 E1
Dykes Wy *FELL* NE10 .... 87 K7
Dymock Ct *WD/WHPE/BLK* NE5.. 55 F5

E

Eaglescliffe Dr *LGB/HTN* NE7 .. 57 K7
Eaglesdene *HLH* DH5 .... 147 K4 🔲
Eagle St *DUN/TMV* NE11 .... 86 B6

Ealing Dr *TYNE/NSHE* NE30.... 61 G1
Eardulph Av *CLS/BIR/GTL* DH3 .. 129 K4
Earls Ct *PRUD* NE42 .... 64 E7 🔲
Earl's Dr *BW/LEM/TK/HW* NE15 .. 68 E4
Earl's Gdns *BLYTH* NE24 .... 30 E6 🔲
Earl St *MLFD/PNYW* SR4 .... 14 A5
SEA/MUR SR7 .... 135 G7
Earlsway *DUN/TMV* NE11 .... 86 C5
Earlswood Av
LWF/SPW/WRK NE9 .... 101 F1
Earlswood Gn *MONK* NE25 .... 50 B5
Earnshaw Wy *MONK* NE25 .... 50 B2
Earsdon Cl *WD/WHPE/BLK* NE5 .. 68 E1
Earsdon Rd *GOS/KPK* NE3 .... 55 J7
HLH DH5 .... 132 D7 🔲
MONK NE25 .... 50 B5
SMOOR NE27 .... 49 G6
Earsdon Vw *SMOOR* NE27 .... 49 H5
Easby Cl *GOS/KPK* NE3 .... 56 D2
Easby Rd *WASHS* NE38 .... 117 F2
Easdale Av *GOS/KPK* NE3 .... 56 C1
Easedale *WBAY* NE26 .... 41 F2
Easedale Gdns
LWF/SPW/WRK NE9 .... 101 G1
Easington Av *CRAM* NE23 .... 33 J5
LWF/SPW/WRK NE9 .... 101 J2
Easington St *PLEE/EAS* SR8 .. 162 E4 🔲
Easington St North
SWCK/CAS SR5 .... 14 D2
East Acre *BLAY* NE21 .... 84 B2
East Acres *DIN/WO* NE13 .... 45 F1
East Av *HAR/WTLS* NE34 .... 76 A5
LGB/KIL NE12 .... 57 K4
WASHS NE38 .... 116 E5
East Back Pde
ASHBK/HED/RY SR2 .... 15 K7
East Bailey *LGB/KIL* NE12 .... 47 K5 🔲
LGB/KIL NE12 .... 47 K6 🔲
East Boldon Rd
CLDN/WHIT/ROK SR6 .... 91 K3 🔲
Eastbourne Av
BYK/HTN/WLK NE6 .... 72 C4
GATE NE8 .... 10 F7
Eastbourne Gdns
BYK/HTN/WLK NE6 .... 72 C4
WBAY NE26 .... 50 D3
Eastbourne Gv *SSH* NE33 ...... 3 K7 🔲
Eastcheap *BYK/HTN/WLK* NE6 .. 71 J2 🔲
East Cleft Rd
ASHBK/HED/RY SR2 .... 14 A8
East Clere *BDN/LAN/SAC* DH7 .. 154 B3
Eastcliffe Av *GOS/KPK* NE3 .... 56 A7
East Ct *HAR/WTLS* NE34 .... 76 A5
Eastcombe Cl *BOLCOL* NE35.... 90 C2 🔲
Eastcote Ter *BYK/HTN/WLK* NE6 .. 3 H1
East Cros BDLGTN NE22 .... 29 K4
East Cross St *SUND* SR1 .... 14 F3
Eastdene Rd *SEA/MUR* SR7 .... 150 A1
Eastdene Wy *PLEE/EAS* SR8 .. 175 G5
East Dr *BLYTH* NE24 .... 34 E3 🔲
CLDN/WHIT/ROK SR6 .... 91 J4
East End *WBAY* NE26 .... 41 H4
Easterfield Ct *MPTH* NE61 .... 20 E4
Eastern Av *BDN/LAN/SAC* DH7 .. 154 B3
DUN/TMV NE11 .... 100 D1
Eastern Wy *PONT/DH* NE20 .. 43 F6
WD/WHPE/BLK NE5 .... 69 H1
Eastfield *PLEE/EAS* SR8 .... 175 H5
Eastfield Av *BYK/HTN/WLK* NE6 .. 72 C3
MONK NE25 .... 50 B5
Eastfield Rd *HAR/WTLS* NE34 .. 75 K3 🔲
LGB/KIL NE12 .... 57 K4
Eastfield Ter *LGB/KIL* NE12 .. 57 K4 🔲
East Ford Rd *STKFD/GP* NE62 .. 23 J5
East Forest Hall Rd
LGB/KIL NE12 .... 58 A2 🔲
East Front *JES* NE2 .... 5 L1
Eastgarth *WD/WHPE/BLK* NE5 .. 54 E5
Eastgate Cl *LGB/KIL* NE12 .... 58 A1 🔲
Eastgate Bank *PSHWF* NE43 .. 79 K4
East Ga *GATE* NE8 .... 11 G1
East George Potts St
SSH NE33 .... 75 H2 🔲
East Gra *MONK* NE25 .... 40 C6
SWCK/CAS SR5 .... 106 C2
East Grange Ct
PLEE/EAS SR8 .... 162 C6 🔲
East Gn *RDHAMSE* DH6 .... 173 J4 🔲
Eastgreen *STKFD/GP* NE62 .... 29 F1
East Gv *MLFD/PNYW* SR4 .... 119 F1
East Hill Rd *GATE* NE8 .... 11 M5
Eastlands *BLAY* NE21 .... 83 K3
LGB/HTN NE7 .... 57 G7
East Lea *BLAY* NE21 .... 84 A4
East Pastures *ASHGTN* NE63...... 23 H3
East Percy St *TYNE/NSHE* NE30.. 61 G4
East Riggs *BDLGTN* NE22 .... 29 F5
East Side Av *BDN/LAN/SAC* DH7.. 155 F4
East Stevenson St *SSH* NE33 .. 75 H2 🔲
East Stoneycroft
LGB/KIL NE12 .... 48 A7 🔲
East St *CLDN/WHIT/ROK* SR6.. 93 F4
CLSW/PEL DH2 .... 128 A2
GATE NE8 .... 11 G1
RDHAMSE DH6 .... 172 D6 🔲
RDHAMSE DH6 .... 173 J4
ROWG NE39 .... 96 B1
SSH NE33 .... 3 G7
STLY/ANP DH9 .... 113 J7

TYNE/NSHE NE30.............. 61 J2
East Ter *RHTLP* TS27 .... 185 H3
WNGT TS28 .... 184 A6 🔲
East Thorp *WD/WHPE/BLK* NE5.. 54 D5
East Vw *CON/LDGT* DH8 .... 123 F3
HEBB NE31 .... 73 F7
MPTH NE61 .... 20 E5
PLEE/EAS SR8 .... 163 F3
SWCK/CAS SR5 .... 105 G4 🔲
East View Ter
WICK/BNPF NE16 .... 85 F4 🔲
East Vines *SUND* SR1 .... 15 J3
Eastward Gn *MONK* NE25 .... 50 B5
Eastway *HAR/WTLS* NE34 .... 76 B6
Eastwood Av *BLYTH* NE24 .... 35 F4
Eastwood Cl *BDN/LAN/SAC* DH7.. 143 H6
Eastwood Gdns *FELL* NE10 .... 12 A5
GOS/KPK NE3 .... 55 K6
LWF/SPW/WRK NE9 .... 87 G6
Eastwood Pl *CRAM* NE23 .... 33 J5 🔲
Eastwoods Rd *PRUD* NE42 .... 81 F1
Eaton Pl *ELS/FEN* NE4 .... 4 B6
Eavers Ct *HAR/WTLS* NE34 .... 75 G6 🔲
Ebba Wk *GOS/KPK* NE3 .... 56 D5
Ebchester Ct *GOS/KPK* NE3 .. 55 G5
Ebchester Hl *CON/LDGT* DH8 .. 109 F4 🔲
Ebchester St *HAR/WTLS* NE34 .. 74 E6
Ebdon La *CLDN/WHIT/ROK* SR6 .. 106 D1
Ebor St *BYK/HTN/WLK* NE6 .... 71 J3
HAR/WTLS NE34 .... 74 E7
Eccleston Cl *SMOOR* NE27 .... 48 E5
Eccleston Rd *SSH* NE33 .... 3 M9
Ecgfrid Ter *JRW* NE32 .... 74 A6
Eddison Rd *WASHS* NE38 .... 117 H3
Eddleston Av *GOS/KPK* NE3 .. 56 A7
Eddrington Gv
WD/WHPE/BLK NE5 .... 54 A7
Ede Av *DUN/TMV* NE11 .... 9 G8
HAR/WTLS NE34 .... 76 B5
Eden Av *CON/LDGT* DH8 .... 123 K2
Edenbridge Crs *LGB/KIL* NE12 .. 57 H3
Eden Cl *WD/WHPE/BLK* NE5 .. 68 A1
Edendale Av *BLYTH* NE24 .... 30 D6
BYK/HTN/WLK NE6 .... 72 C5
Edendale Ter *GATE* NE8 .... 11 G8
PLEE/EAS SR8 .... 175 G4 🔲
Eden Gv *MPTH* NE61 .... 20 E7
Edenhill Rd *PLEE/EAS* SR8 .. 175 F5
Eden House Rd
MLFD/PNYW SR4 .... 14 A8
Eden La *PLEE/EAS* SR8 .... 174 E2
Eden Pl *TYNE/NSHE* NE30 .... 60 E1
Eden Rd *DHAM* DH1 .... 156 D3
Eden St *PLEE/EAS* SR8 .... 175 H4
WLSD/HOW NE28 .... 72 D2 🔲
Eden St West *CLS/BIR/GTL* DH3 .. 130 E7
SUND SR1 .... 14 C4
Eden Vw *RDHAMSE* DH6 .... 173 J4
Edgar St *GOS/KPK* NE3 .... 57 F5
Edgecote *WASHN* NE37 .... 103 H5
Edge Ct *DHAM* DH1 .... 17 K3
Edgefield Av *GOS/KPK* NE3 .. 55 K5
Edgefield Dr *CRAM* NE23 .... 33 J5
Edgehill *MPTH* NE61 .... 21 F7
Edge Hl *PONT/DH* NE20 .... 42 E1
Edgehill Cl *PONT/DH* NE20 .... 52 E1
Edge La *BDN/LAN/SAC* DH7.. 140 E1
Edge Mt *LGB/KIL* NE12 .... 47 K5
Edgewell Gra *PRUD* NE42 .... 80 C2 🔲
Edgewell House Rd
PSHWF NE43 .... 80 A5
Edgewell Rd *PRUD* NE42 .... 80 B5
Edgewood *PONT/DH* NE20 .... 43 F7
Edgeworth Cl *BOLCOL* NE35.... 90 C2 🔲
Edgeworth Crs
CLDN/WHIT/ROK SR6 .... 106 D3 🔲
Edgmond Ct *ASHBK/HED/RY* SR2 .. 120 E6
Edgware Rd *GATE* NE8 .... 11 K7
Edhill Av *HAR/WTLS* NE34 .... 74 D6
Edinburgh Rd *JRW* NE32 .... 74 C7
Edington Gv *TYNE/NSHE* NE30 .. 60 E1
Edington Rd *TYNE/NSHE* NE30 .. 60 E1
Edison Gdns *GATE* NE8 .... 10 E9
Edison St *SEA/MUR* SR7 .... 149 H5
Edith Av *BLAY* NE21 .... 84 A2
Edith St *ASHBK/HED/RY* SR2.... 15 H9
CON/LDGT DH8 .... 123 F7
JRW NE32 .... 73 J4
SEA/MUR SR7 .... 151 F3
SWCK/CAS SR5 .... 106 C3 🔲
TYNE/NSHE NE30 .... 61 G2
Edlingham Cl *GOS/KPK* NE3 .. 57 F6
Edlingham Ct *HLH* DH5 .... 132 D7 🔲
Edlingham Rd *DHAM* DH1 .... 156 D4
Edmondsley La
BDN/LAN/SAC DH7 .... 143 G3
Edmund Pl
LWF/SPW/WRK NE9 .... 87 F7 🔲
Edna St *WD/WHPE/BLK* NE5...... 54 E7
Edward Av *PLEE/EAS* SR8 .... 175 G2
RDHAMSE DH6 .... 180 A2
Edward Burdis St
SWCK/CAS SR5 .... 106 B3 🔲
Edward Cain Ct
PLEE/EAS SR8 .... 175 H3 🔲
Edwardia Ct *CON/LDGT* DH8 .. 122 E5 🔲
Edward Pl *ELS/FEN* NE4 .... 4 E6
Edward Rd *BDLGTN* NE22 .... 29 K4 🔲
CLS/BIR/GTL DH3 .... 115 H1
WLSD/HOW NE28 .... 59 H7
Edwardson Rd
BDN/LAN/SAC DH7 .... 140 E5
Edwards Rd *WBAY* NE26 .... 51 G5
Edward St *BLYTH* NE24 .... 31 F6
DHAM DH1 .... 17 K2
GOS/KPK NE3 .... 56 C5 🔲
HEBB NE31 .... 72 E4 🔲
HLH DH5 .... 147 K4
SEA/MUR SR7 .... 150 E2 🔲
STLY/ANP DH9 .... 127 G5
SUNDSW SR3 .... 120 A7
Edward's Wk *CNUT* NE1 .... 5 J4

Edward Ter *BDN/LAN/SAC* DH7 .. 166 E2
Edwin Gv *WLSD/HOW* NE28 .... 59 J7
Edwins Av *LGB/KIL* NE12 .... 58 A2
Edwins Av South *LGB/KIL* NE12 .. 58 A2
Edwin St *HLH* DH5 .... 132 C6
MPTH NE61 .... 20 E5
BW/LEM/TK/HW NE15 .... 69 G7
Eggleston Cl
CLS/BIR/GTL DH3 .... 145 J1 🔲
DHAM DH1 .... 157 F3
Eggleston Dr *SUNDSW* SR3.... 120 A4
Egham Rd *WD/WHPE/BLK* NE5 .. 68 A1
Eglesfield Rd *SSH* NE33 .... 75 G5
Eglingham Wy *MPTH* NE61...... 21 F7
Eglinton St SWCK/CAS SR5 .. 106 C4
Eglinton St North
SWCK/CAS SR5 .... 106 C4
Egremont Dr
LWF/SPW/WRK NE9 .... 87 H6 🔲
Egremont Gdns
LWF/SPW/WRK NE9 .... 87 G6 🔲
Egremont Gv *PLEE/EAS* SR8 .. 174 B7
Egremont Pl *WBAY* NE26 .... 51 F5
Eider Cl *BLYTH* NE24 .... 35 G4
Eighteenth Av *BLYTH* NE24 .... 34 E2 🔲
Eighth Av *ASHGTN* NE63 .... 24 A4
BLYTH NE24 .... 35 F2 🔲
BYK/HTN/WLK NE6 .... 7 G1
CLSW/PEL DH2 .... 129 H4
MPTH NE61 .... 21 F6 🔲
Eighth St *PLEE/EAS* SR8 .... 175 H3
Eighton Ter
LWF/SPW/WRK NE9 .... 101 K2
Eishort Wy *LGB/KIL* NE12 .... 57 H4
Eland Cl *GOS/KPK* NE3 .... 55 H5
Eland Edge *PONT/DH* NE20 .... 43 H3
Eland La *PONT/DH* NE20 .... 43 H2
Elberfeld Ct *JRW* NE32 .... 73 K5
Elder Cl *BDN/LAN/SAC* DH7 .. 167 G1
Elder Gv *HAR/WTLS* NE34 .... 75 K6
LWF/SPW/WRK NE9 .... 87 F7 🔲
Elderwood Gdns
DUN/TMV NE11 .... 86 B7
Eldon Cl *BDN/LAN/SAC* DH7.. 153 K3
Eldon La *CNUT* NE1 .... 5 K6
Eldon Pl *BW/LEM/TK/HW* NE15 .... 68 B4
Eldon Rd *BW/LEM/TK/HW* NE15 .. 68 B4
Eldon St *GATE* NE8 .... 11 J3
MLFD/PNYW SR4 .... 106 A7
SSH NE33 .... 75 F2
WLSD/HOW NE28 .... 73 J1
Eleanor St *SSH* NE33 .... 3 K6
TYNE/NSHE NE30 .... 51 G5
Elemore Cl
BDN/LAN/SAC DH7 .... 154 A3 🔲
Elemore La *HLH* DH5 .... 160 A1
RDHAMSE DH6 .... 159 H3
Elemore St *RDHAMSE* DH6 .. 158 E4
Elemore Vw *RDHAMSE* DH6 .. 160 D2
Elenbel Av *BDLGTN* NE22 .... 29 J5
Eleventh Av *BLYTH* NE24 .... 35 G1 🔲
MPTH NE61 .... 21 F6
Eleventh St *PLEE/EAS* SR8 .... 175 G3
RHTLP TS27 .... 175 K6
Elford Cl *MONK* NE25 .... 50 B4
Elfordleigh *HLS* DH4 .... 132 A3 🔲
Elgar Av *WD/WHPE/BLK* NE5 .. 68 A1 🔲
Elgar Cl *STLY/ANP* DH9 .... 126 E2
Elgin Av *SEA/MUR* SR7 .... 150 A1
WLSD/HOW NE28 .... 59 H6
Elgin Cl *NSHW* NE29 .... 60 A2 🔲
Elgin Gdns *STLY/ANP* DH9 .... 127 F1
Elgin Rd *LWF/SPW/WRK* NE9 .. 11 L8
Elgin St *JRW* NE32 .... 74 C7
Elgy Rd *GOS/KPK* NE3 .... 56 B7
Elisabeth Av *CLS/BIR/GTL* DH3 .. 101 H7
Elizabeth Ct *LGB/KIL* NE12 .... 58 C2
Elizabeth Crs *CRAM* NE23 .... 47 G1
Elizabeth Diamond Gdns
SSH NE33 .... 75 F3 🔲
Elizabeth Dr *LGB/KIL* NE12 .... 58 C2
Elizabeth Rd *WLSD/HOW* NE28 .. 58 C6
Elizabeth St *BYK/HTN/WLK* NE6.. 6 D4
HLH DH5 .... 132 C6
SEA/MUR SR7 .... 150 D1 🔲
SWCK/CAS SR5 .... 105 F4 🔲
SWCK/CAS SR5 .... 106 C2 🔲
Eliza La *CON/LDGT* DH8 .... 138 B6
Ellam Av *DHAM* DH1 .... 168 B2
Ell-dene Crs *FELL* NE10 .... 12 E9
Ellersmere Gdns
TYNE/NSHE NE30 .... 51 F7 🔲
Ellerton Wy *CRAM* NE23 .... 33 J5 🔲
FELL NE10 .... 12 A8
Ellesmere *HLS* DH4 .... 131 F4
Ellesmere Av *BYK/HTN/WLK* NE6.. 7 M2
WD/WHPE/BLK NE5 .... 68 E1
Ellesmere Ct
ASHBK/HED/RY SR2 .... 120 E5
Ellesmere Dr *SEA/MUR* SR7 .. 150 A1
Ellesmere Rd *ELS/FEN* NE4 .... 69 J6
Ellington Cl
ASHBK/HED/RY SR2 .... 135 F2 🔲
BW/LEM/TK/HW NE15 .... 67 K4
Elliot Cl *HLS* DH4 .... 117 K7
Elliot Rd *FELL* NE10 .... 11 M5
Elliot St *RDHAMSE* DH6 .... 172 C6
Elliott Dr *FELL* NE10 .... 12 D7
Elliott Gdns *WLSD/HOW* NE28 .. 58 C6
Elliott Rd *FELL* NE10 .... 11 M5
Elliott St *BLYTH* NE24 .... 34 D3
Elliott Ter *ELS/FEN* NE4 .... 4 C6
Ellison Pl *CNUT* NE1 .... 5 L5
JRW NE32 .... 73 K3
LWF/SPW/WRK NE9 .... 101 K1
Ellison Rd *DUN/TMV* NE11 .... 9 G8
PLEE/EAS SR8 .... 175 J3
Ellison St *GATE* NE8 .... 11 G1
HEBB NE31 .... 73 F5
JRW NE32 .... 73 K4 🔲
Ellis Rd *SWCK/CAS* SR5 .... 106 A4 🔲
Ellis Sq *SWCK/CAS* SR5 .... 106 B2
Elm Av *BDN/LAN/SAC* DH7 .... 167 G2
CLSW/PEL DH2 .... 128 C1
DIN/WO NE13 .... 45 F2

Elm - Fie 197

DUN/TMV NE11 9 H9
HAR/WTLS NE34 75 K7
WICK/BNPF NE16 8 A8
Elm Bank Rd WYLAM NE41 65 H6
Elm Cl CRAM NE23 33 J5
Elm Ct WICK/BNPF NE16 85 F7
Elm Crs CLSW/PEL DH2 144 A5
Elm Croft Rd LGB/KIL NE12 58 A3
Elmdale Rd CON/LDGT DH8 123 G4
Elm Dr BDLGTN NE22 29 F7
CLDN/WHIT/ROK SR6 93 G3
Elmfield BDN/LAN/SAC DH7 140 B4
Elmfield Av DHAM DH1 157 J6
Elmfield Cl SUNDSW SR3 133 F1
Elmfield Gdns WLSD/HOW NE28 58 B6
Elmfield Gv GOS/KPK NE3 56 B7
Elmfield Pk GOS/KPK NE3 56 B7
Elmfield Rd
BW/LEM/TK/HW NE15 67 G1 2
CON/LDGT DH8 123 F3
GOS/KPK NE3 56 B7
HEBB NE31 89 H1
Elmfield Ter HEBB NE31 73 H7
Elm Gv BDN/LAN/SAC DH7 167 G1
GOS/KPK NE3 55 K3
HAR/WTLS NE34 75 K7
LGB/KIL NE12 57 K1
WICK/BNPF NE16 97 H7
Elm Park Rd CON/LDGT DH8 109 F7
Elm Rd BLAY NE21 84 B2
NSHW NE29 59 K3
PONT/DH NE20 43 J4
Elmsford Gv LGB/KIL NE12 57 J4
Elmsleigh Gdns
CLDN/WHIT/ROK SR6 92 A1
The Elms HLH DH5 148 C7
RHTLP TS27 185 K2
Elm St BDN/LAN/SAC DH7 154 B3
CLS/BIR/GTL DH3 129 J4
CON/LDGT DH8 123 F3
DUN/TMV NE11 86 B6
JRW NE32 73 J4
STLY/ANP DH9 126 B3
WICK/BNPF NE16 99 F3
Elm St West WICK/BNPF NE16 99 F3
Elmtree Ct SEA/MUR SR7 150 D3
Elmtree Gdns MONK NE25 50 C6
Elmtree Gv GOS/KPK NE3 56 B6
Elm Trees BLYTH NE24 35 F1 2
Elmway CLSW/PEL DH2 129 G2
Elmwood Av DIN/WO NE13 46 B4
SWCK/CAS SR5 105 K2
Elmwood Crs
BYK/HTN/WLK NE6 72 B2 1
Elmwood Dr PONT/DH NE20 43 G2
Elmwood Gdns DUN/TMV NE11 86 B6
Elmwood Gv WBAY NE26 50 E3
Elmwood Rd MONK NE25 50 C5
Elmwood St ASHBK/HED/RY SR2 14 B7
HLS DH4 131 G6
Elrick Cl WD/WHPE/BLK NE5 68 A1 3
Elrington Gdns
WD/WHPE/BLK NE5 69 F3 2
Elsdon Av MONK NE25 40 A5
Elsdonburn Rd SUNDSW SR3 133 J2 3
Elsdon Cl BLYTH NE24 30 E7
PLEE/EAS SR8 174 D7
Elsdon Ct WICK/BNPF NE16 84 E7
Elsdon Dr ASHGTN NE63 23 J2
LGB/KIL NE12 58 B2
Elsdon Gdns CON/LDGT DH8 123 F3
DUN/TMV NE11 9 J8
Elsdon Pl NSHW NE29 2 C4
Elsdon Rd DHAM DH1 156 E3
GOS/KPK NE3 56 C5
WICK/BNPF NE16 84 E6
Elsdon St NSHW NE29 2 C4
Elsdon Ter NSHW NE29 60 B6
Elsing Cl WD/WHPE/BLK NE5 55 F6
Elstob Pl BYK/HTN/WLK NE6 7 M9
SUNDSW SR3 120 A4
Elston Cl WD/WHPE/BLK NE5 68 A1 2
Elstree Ct DIN/WO NE13 55 F3 1
Elstree Gdns BLYTH NE24 35 F4 1
Elswick East Ter ELS/FEN NE4 4 F8
Elswick Rd ELS/FEN NE4 69 J7
Elswick Rw ELS/FEN NE4 4 E7
Elswick Wy HAR/WTLS NE34 74 E5
Elterwater Rd CLSW/PEL DH2 129 H6
Elton St East WLSD/HOW NE28 72 D2
Elton St West WLSD/HOW NE28 72 C2
Eltringham Cl
WLSD/HOW NE28 72 C1 2
Eltringham Rd PRUD NE42 80 A2
Elvaston Rd RYTON NE40 66 E5
Elvet Br DHAM DH1 16 D4
Elvet Cl DIN/WO NE13 46 B3 2
Elvet Crs DHAM DH1 16 E5
Elvet Gn CLSW/PEL DH2 129 J5
HLH DH5 147 K7 1
Elvet Hill Rd DHAM DH1 16 C8
Elvet Waterside DHAM DH1 16 E4
Elvington St
CLDN/WHIT/ROK SR6 106 E2
Elwin Cl WBAY NE26 41 G3
Elwin Pl CLSW/PEL DH2 128 E1
Elwin Ter ASHBK/HED/RY SR2 14 C6
Elwyn Cl WBAY NE26 41 G3
Ely Cl LGB/KIL NE12 57 K6
Ely Rd DHAM DH1 156 E1 2
Elysium La GATE NE8 10 B6
Ely St GATE NE8 11 H5
Embankment Rd SEA/MUR SR7 135 H6
Embassy Gdns
BW/LEM/TK/HW NE15 69 F5
Emblehope WASHN NE37 102 C7
Emblehope Dr GOS/KPK NE3 56 A6
Embleton Av GOS/KPK NE3 56 A4 1
HAR/WTLS NE34 76 B3
WLSD/HOW NE28 59 G5
Embleton Cl DHAM DH1 156 E3 2
Embleton Crs NSHW NE29 60 A2
Embleton Dr BLYTH NE24 34 E2 1
Embleton Gdns
WD/WHPE/BLK NE5 69 H2 5
Embleton Rd FELL NE10 13 M3
NSHW NE29 60 A2
Embleton St SEA/MUR SR7 150 E3 1
Emden Rd GOS/KPK NE3 55 J4
Emily Davison Av MPTH NE61 20 C5 1
Emily St BYK/HTN/WLK NE6 7 L5
GATE NE8 11 M5
Emily St East SEA/MUR SR7 150 E1 2
Emlyn Rd HAR/WTLS NE34 75 G5
Emmbrook Cl HLH DH5 147 G4 1
Emmerson Pl SMOOR NE27 49 G6
Empress Rd BYK/HTN/WLK NE6 72 D7
Empress St SWCK/CAS SR5 106 C4 3
Emsworth Rd SWCK/CAS SR5 106 A2
Enderby Rd MLFD/PNYW SR4 14 A3
Enfield Av WICK/BNPF NE16 85 F3
Enfield Gdns WICK/BNPF NE16 85 F7
Enfield Rd LWF/SPW/WRK NE9 11 G8
SEA/MUR SR7 150 A1
Enfield St MLFD/PNYW SR4 105 K6 2
Engine Inn Rd WLSD/HOW NE28 59 H6
Engine La LWF/SPW/WRK NE9 101 F1
Engine Rd CHPW NE17 94 E1
PRUD NE42 81 F7
Englemann Wy SUNDSW SR3 133 J3
Enid Av CLDN/WHIT/ROK SR6 106 D2
Enid St DIN/WO NE13 46 A5 2
Ennerdale ASHBK/HED/RY SR2 14 D9
CLS/BIR/GTL DH3 115 K4
Ennerdale Cl DHAM DH1 158 B5 2
SEA/MUR SR7 150 A1
Ennerdale Crs BLAY NE21 83 K4 3
HLS DH4 117 J6 1
Ennerdale Gdns
LWF/SPW/WRK NE9 87 G7
WLSD/HOW NE28 59 J6 2
Ennerdale Rd BLYTH NE24 30 B5
BYK/HTN/WLK NE6 72 B5
TYNE/NSHE NE30 50 E7
Ennerdale St HLH DH5 147 H6
Ennis Cl STKFD/GP NE62 23 K5 1
Enslin St BYK/HTN/WLK NE6 13 G1
Epping Cl SEA/MUR SR7 150 A2
Eppleton Cl BDN/LAN/SAC DH7 154 A3
Eppleton Hall Cl SEA/MUR SR7 134 E7
Eppleton Rw HLH DH5 148 A4 1
Epsom Cl CON/LDGT DH8 108 E7 1
NSHW NE29 2 A5
Epsom Ct GOS/KPK NE3 55 G3
Epsom Wy BLYTH NE24 35 F4
Epworth STLY/ANP DH9 112 A6
Equitable St
WLSD/HOW NE28 72 D2 1
Erick St CNUT NE1 5 L6 1
Erith Ter MLFD/PNYW SR4 105 K7
Ernest St ASHBK/HED/RY SR2 15 H9
BOLCOL NE35 90 E4
CLSW/PEL DH2 114 E7
Ernest Ter STLY/ANP DH9 112 D6 3
Ernwill Av SWCK/CAS SR5 105 F4
Errington Cl PONT/DH NE20 42 E7
Errington Dr STLY/ANP DH9 112 A6
Errington Rd PONT/DH NE20 42 E6
Errington Ter LGB/KIL NE12 58 A1 3
Errol Pl CLS/BIR/GTL DH3 115 K4
Erskine Rd SSH NE33 3 J9
Erskine Wy SSH NE33 3 K8
Escallond Dr SEA/MUR SR7 150 A2
Esdale ASHBK/HED/RY SR2 134 E1
Esh Bank BDN/LAN/SAC DH7 153 H4
Esher Gdns BLYTH NE24 35 F4
Esh Hillside BDN/LAN/SAC DH7 154 C3
Eshmere Crs
WD/WHPE/BLK NE5 68 A1
Eshott Cl GOS/KPK NE3 56 A4
WD/WHPE/BLK NE5 68 E2
Eskdale CLS/BIR/GTL DH3 116 A5
HLS DH4 117 J6 2
Eskdale Av BLYTH NE24 30 C6
WLSD/HOW NE28 58 E6
Eskdale Cl SEA/MUR SR7 150 A1
Eskdale Ct HAR/WTLS NE34 75 G5
Eskdale Dr JRW NE32 90 B1
Eskdale Gdns
LWF/SPW/WRK NE9 101 G1
Eskdale Rd CLDN/WHIT/ROK SR6 93 F6
Eskdale St HAR/WTLS NE34 75 G6 3
HLH DH5 147 J6
Eskdale Ter JES NE2 5 L1
WBAY NE26 51 G5
Eskdale Wk PLEE/EAS SR8 175 F4 4
Esk St LWF/SPW/WRK NE9 11 M9
Eslington Rd JES NE2 5 M2 1
Eslington Ter JES NE2 70 E3
Esmaralda Gdns CRAM NE23 39 H7 1
Esplanade WBAY NE26 51 F4
Espley Cl LGB/KIL NE12 58 C2
Espley Ct GOS/KPK NE3 55 J3 3
Essen Wy SUNDSW SR3 120 B3
Essex Av CON/LDGT DH8 137 F2
Essex Cl ASHGTN NE63 23 G1 2
ELS/FEN NE4 9 L1
Essex Crs SEA/MUR SR7 150 A1
Essex Dr WASHN NE37 103 F4 1
Essex Gdns HAR/WTLS NE34 76 C4
WLSD/HOW NE28 59 G7
Essex Gv SUNDSW SR3 120 A6
Essex Pl PLEE/EAS SR8 174 D2
Essington Wy PLEE/EAS SR8 174 D2
Esst Vw HLH DH5 148 C7
Esther Sq WASHS NE38 117 G2
Esthwaite Av CLSW/PEL DH2 129 H6
Eston Ct BLYTH NE24 30 D6
WLSD/HOW NE28 58 B5 2
Eston Gv SWCK/CAS SR5 106 C2
Estuary Wy MLFD/PNYW SR4 105 F6
Etal Av MONK NE25 51 F5
NSHW NE29 60 B6
Etal Crs JRW NE32 74 B7
SMOOR NE27 49 H6
Etal La WD/WHPE/BLK NE5 54 E7
Etal Pl GOS/KPK NE3 56 A3 2
Etal Rd BLYTH NE24 34 D4 1
Etal Wy WD/WHPE/BLK NE5 55 F6
Ethel Av ASHBK/HED/RY SR2 135 G1
BLAY NE21 84 A2 3
Ethel St CRAM NE23 47 G3
ELS/FEN NE4 69 H7
Ethel Ter HAR/WTLS NE34 75 F6
SWCK/CAS SR5 105 F4
Etherley Cl DHAM DH1 156 E2
Etherley Rd BYK/HTN/WLK NE6 7 J2
Etherstone Av LGB/HTN NE7 71 J1
Eton Cl CRAM NE23 33 J5 3
Eton Sq HEBB NE31 73 H5
Ettrick Cl LGB/KIL NE12 47 J5 4
Ettrick Gdns GATE NE8 11 M7
MLFD/PNYW SR4 119 J2
Ettrick Gv MLFD/PNYW SR4 119 K2
SUNDSW SR3 119 K3 1
Ettrick Rd JRW NE32 73 J6
European Wy MLFD/PNYW SR4 105 H5
Euryalus Ct SSH NE33 75 K2
Eustace Av NSHW NE29 2 A2
Evanlade FELL NE10 88 D6
Evansleigh Rd CON/LDGT DH8 122 C7
Eva St BW/LEM/TK/HW NE15 68 A5
Evelyn St ASHBK/HED/RY SR2 14 A8
Evenwood Gdns
LWF/SPW/WRK NE9 87 H7
Evenwood Rd
BDN/LAN/SAC DH7 165 H2
Everard St CRAM NE23 33 H4
Everest Gv BOL NE36 91 F5 3
Eversleigh Pl
BW/LEM/TK/HW NE15 67 G1 3
Eversley Pl WLSD/HOW NE28 59 H7 3
Everton Dr SEA/MUR SR7 150 A1
Everton La SWCK/CAS SR5 106 A2
Evesham MLFD/PNYW SR4 104 E7
Evesham Av WBAY NE26 50 D3
Evesham Cl BOLCOL NE35 90 D3
Evesham Garth GOS/KPK NE3 55 J7
Evesham Rd SEA/MUR SR7 150 A1
Eve St PLEE/EAS SR8 175 J4 2
Evistones Gdns
BYK/HTN/WLK NE6 12 E1
Evistones Rd
LWF/SPW/WRK NE9 87 F6 2
Ewart Crs HAR/WTLS NE34 74 C7
Ewbank Av ELS/FEN NE4 69 J4
Ewehurst Crs STLY/ANP DH9 111 G5
Ewehurst Pde STLY/ANP DH9 111 G5
Ewehurst Rd STLY/ANP DH9 111 G5
WICK/BNPF NE16 111 H4
Ewen Ct NSHW NE29 59 K2
Ewesley WASHS NE38 116 C6
Ewesley Cl WD/WHPE/BLK NE5 68 E1
Ewesley Gdns DIN/WO NE13 46 B3
Ewesley Rd MLFD/PNYW SR4 119 K1
Ewing Rd MLFD/PNYW SR4 14 A8 1
Exebly Cl GOS/KPK NE3 56 D2
Exeter Cl ASHGTN NE63 24 C3 1
CLS/BIR/GTL DH3 145 H2
Exeter Rd WLSD/HOW NE28 58 C5
Exeter St BYK/HTN/WLK NE6 72 C7
GATE NE8 10 F6
MLFD/PNYW SR4 105 K6
Exmouth Cl SEA/MUR SR7 150 B2 3
Exmouth Rd NSHW NE29 60 A5
Exmouth Sq SWCK/CAS SR5 106 A2
Extension Rd SUND SR1 15 K5
Eyemouth La SWCK/CAS SR5 106 A2
Eyemouth Rd NSHW NE29 60 A5 2
Eyre St STLY/ANP DH9 126 B2

F

Faber Rd SWCK/CAS SR5 106 A2
Factory Rd BLAY NE21 68 B7
Fairbairn Rd PLEE/EAS SR8 174 E2
Fairburn Av HLH DH5 147 H2
LGB/HTN NE7 57 J6
Fairdale Av LGB/HTN NE7 57 J6
Fairfalls Ter BDN/LAN/SAC DH7 166 D2
Fairfield CLSW/PEL DH2 114 D7
CON/LDGT DH8 123 H6
LGB/KIL NE12 57 F4
STLY/ANP DH9 125 H2
Fairfield Av BLYTH NE24 35 F3
WICK/BNPF NE16 84 E7
Fairfield Cl DUN/TMV NE11 9 G6
Fairfield Dr ASHGTN NE63 24 C3
CLDN/WHIT/ROK SR6 92 E2
MONK NE25 50 A5
TYNE/NSHE NE30 51 F7
Fairfield Gn MONK NE25 50 A5
Fairfield Rd JES NE2 70 D2
Fairfields RYTON NE40 66 D7
Fair Gn MONK NE25 50 A5
Fairgreen Cl SUNDSW SR3 134 A2 1
Fairhaven LWF/SPW/WRK NE9 102 B3
Fairhaven Av
BYK/HTN/WLK NE6 72 C5
Fairhill Cl LGB/HTN NE7 57 J6
Fairholme Av HAR/WTLS NE34 75 H5
Fairholme Rd SUNDSW SR3 120 C3 3
Fairholm Rd ELS/FEN NE4 69 J6
Fairlands East
CLDN/WHIT/ROK SR6 106 D3 3
Fairlands West SWCK/CAS SR5 106 D3
Fairlawn Gdns
MLFD/PNYW SR4 119 J2
Fairlawns Cl TRIM TS29 182 E5
Fairles St SSH NE33 3 J5
Fairmead Wy MLFD/PNYW SR4 118 E1
Fairmile Dr SUNDSW SR3 134 A2
Fairmont Wy LGB/HTN NE7 57 J6 3
Fairney Cl PONT/DH NE20 43 H3
Fairney Edge PONT/DH NE20 43 H3
Fairspring WD/WHPE/BLK NE5 68 E1
Fair Vw BDN/LAN/SAC DH7 143 F7
BDN/LAN/SAC DH7 165 H1
Fairview Av HAR/WTLS NE34 75 K4
Fairview Dr CON/LDGT DH8 109 G6
Fairview Gn LGB/HTN NE7 57 J6 3
Fairville Cl CRAM NE23 33 H5
Fairville Crs LGB/HTN NE7 57 J6
Fairway MPTH NE61 26 D1
STKFD/GP NE62 23 G5
Fairway Cl GOS/KPK NE3 55 H6
Fairways CON/LDGT DH8 123 F2
MONK NE25 50 A4
SUNDSW SR3 120 B7 2
Fairways Av LGB/HTN NE7 57 J5 2
The Fairways BOL NE36 90 E5 2
BOL NE36 91 G5 2
STLY/ANP DH9 126 B5
The Fairway BLAY NE21 67 J7
GOS/KPK NE3 56 B2
WASHN NE37 103 F2
Falconar's Ct CNUT NE1 5 J7
Falconar St JES NE2 5 M5
Falcon Ct ASHGTN NE63 23 H4
Falcon Hl MPTH NE61 20 B6
Falcon Pl LGB/KIL NE12 57 G3
Falcon Ter WYLAM NE41 65 H5
Falcon Wy BDN/LAN/SAC DH7 165 F1
HAR/WTLS NE34 75 F7
Faldonside
BYK/HTN/WLK NE6 71 K1 3
Falkirk LGB/KIL NE12 47 K5 2
Falkland Av GOS/KPK NE3 55 K7
HEBB NE31 73 G5
Falkland Rd MLFD/PNYW SR4 105 J7
Falla Park Crs FELL NE10 12 B8
Falla Park Rd FELL NE10 12 B8
Falloden Av GOS/KPK NE3 55 K2
Fallodon Gdns
WD/WHPE/BLK NE5 69 H1 4
Fallodon Rd NSHW NE29 60 B5
Fallowfeld FELL NE10 88 C5
Fallowfield WASHS NE38 117 G5
Fallowfield Av GOS/KPK NE3 55 K4
Fallowfield Wy ASHGTN NE63 23 H3
WASHS NE38 117 F4
Fallow Park Av BLYTH NE24 34 E1 3
Fallow Rd HAR/WTLS NE34 76 D5
Fallsway DHAM DH1 158 A4
Falmouth Cl SEA/MUR SR7 150 B2 4
Falmouth Dr JRW NE32 74 B6
Falmouth Rd BYK/HTN/WLK NE6 6 E3
MLFD/PNYW SR4 105 J6
NSHW NE29 60 B1
Falmouth Sq MLFD/PNYW SR4 105 J7
Falsgrave Pl WICK/BNPF NE16 84 D7
Falstaff Rd NSHW NE29 60 B4
Falstone FELL NE10 88 B7
WASHS NE38 117 G4
Falstone Av
BW/LEM/TK/HW NE15 68 C3
HAR/WTLS NE34 76 A5
Falstone Cl LGB/KIL NE12 58 C2
Falstone Crs ASHGTN NE63 24 A4
Falstone Dr CLSW/PEL DH2 129 F6
Falstone Sq GOS/KPK NE3 56 A4 1
Falston Rd BLYTH NE24 34 E2
Faraday Cl WASHS NE38 117 K1
Faraday Gv GATE NE8 10 D9
MLFD/PNYW SR4 105 J7
Faraday Rd PLEE/EAS SR8 175 F1
Faraday St SEA/MUR SR7 149 H5 2
Faraday Ter RDHAMSE DH6 160 D6
Farbridge Crs CON/LDGT DH8 109 F3
Fareham Gv BOLCOL NE35 90 B4
Farlam Av TYNE/NSHE NE30 60 E1
Farlam Rd
WD/WHPE/BLK NE5 69 F3 3
Farleigh Ct NSHW NE29 59 K2
Farm Cl WASHN NE37 102 D4
WICK/BNPF NE16 99 F3
Farm Ct BLAY NE21 84 D2
Farmer Crs SEA/MUR SR7 149 G5
Farm Hill Rd
CLDN/WHIT/ROK SR6 92 A2
Farm Rd DHAM DH1 168 E5
Farm St SWCK/CAS SR5 106 B4
Farnborough Cl CRAM NE23 33 H7
Farnborough Dr SUNDSW SR3 120 B6
Farn Ct DIN/WO NE13 55 H2
Farndale WLSD/HOW NE28 58 B5
Farndale Av
CLDN/WHIT/ROK SR6 93 F6
STKFD/GP NE62 23 G4
Farndale Cl BLAY NE21 83 H4 1
DIN/WO NE13 45 F2 2
Farndale Rd ELS/FEN NE4 69 J6
Farne Av ASHGTN NE63 23 K3
GOS/KPK NE3 56 A2
HAR/WTLS NE34 76 B4
Farne Rd LGB/KIL NE12 58 A2
SMOOR NE27 49 H6
Farne Sq MLFD/PNYW SR4 105 H6
Farne Ter BYK/HTN/WLK NE6 7 M5
Farnham Cl DHAM DH1 156 D4
Farnham Gv BLYTH NE24 35 F3
Farnham Rd DHAM DH1 156 D3
HAR/WTLS NE34 75 G5 2
Farnham St
BW/LEM/TK/HW NE15 68 B5
Farnham Ter MLFD/PNYW SR4 119 K1
Farnley Hey Rd DHAM DH1 168 B1
Farnley Mt DHAM DH1 168 B1 1
Farnley Rdg DHAM DH1 168 B1
Farnley Rd BYK/HTN/WLK NE6 71 J2 2
Farnon Rd GOS/KPK NE3 56 A5
Farquhar St JES NE2 71 F3
Farrier Cl WASHS NE38 117 G4
Farriers Ct STKFD/GP NE62 29 H1
Farringdon Rd TYNE/NSHE NE30 50 E7
Farringdon Rw
MLFD/PNYW SR4 14 B2
Farrington Av SUNDSW SR3 119 G6
Farrow Dr CLDN/WHIT/ROK SR6 92 E3
The Farthings WASHN NE37 102 D3
Fatfield Pk WASHS NE38 117 F5
Fatfield Rd WASHS NE38 117 G2
Faversham Ct GOS/KPK NE3 55 H3 1
Faversham Pl CRAM NE23 33 H7
Fawcett St SUND SR1 14 E4
Fawcett Ter
ASHBK/HED/RY SR2 135 G1 1
Fawdon Cl GOS/KPK NE3 55 J2
Fawdon Gv MPTH NE61 21 H2 1
Fawdon La GOS/KPK NE3 55 H3
Fawdon Park Rd
GOS/KPK NE3 55 J3 4
Fawdon Pl NSHW NE29 60 A4
Fawley Cl BOLCOL NE35 90 C3 2
Fawn Rd MLFD/PNYW SR4 105 G7
Feather Bed La
ASHBK/HED/RY SR2 135 G1
Featherstone Gv BDLGTN NE22 28 D4
JRW NE32 89 J1
Featherstone Rd DHAM DH1 156 E4
Featherstone St
CLDN/WHIT/ROK SR6 107 F3
Federation Sq SEA/MUR SR7 149 H6
Federation Wy DUN/TMV NE11 8 E6
Feetham Av LGB/KIL NE12 58 B2
Felixstowe Dr LGB/HTN NE7 57 J7
Fell Bank CLS/BIR/GTL DH3 115 K2
Fell Cl CLS/BIR/GTL DH3 116 A3
WICK/BNPF NE16 99 F3
Felldyke FELL NE10 88 B7 1
Fellgate Av JRW NE32 90 A3
Fellgate Gdns FELL NE10 88 E4 1
Felling House Gdns FELL NE10 12 C5
Felling Vw BYK/HTN/WLK NE6 13 G2
Fellmere Av FELL NE10 13 H7
Fell Rd CLSW/PEL DH2 128 E4
LWF/SPW/WRK NE9 102 B4
MLFD/PNYW SR4 105 H6
Fellside HAR/WTLS NE34 76 B6
PONT/DH NE20 52 D1
Fellside Av WICK/BNPF NE16 99 F2
Fellside Cl PONT/DH NE20 52 D1
Fellside Ct WICK/BNPF NE16 84 E5 3
Fellside Gdns DHAM DH1 157 K5 2
Fellside Rd WICK/BNPF NE16 84 D7
WICK/BNPF NE16 98 A6
The Fell Side GOS/KPK NE3 55 K6
Fells Rd DUN/TMV NE11 86 D5
Fell Vw CON/LDGT DH8 122 C6
ROWG NE39 96 C2
The Fell Wy
WD/WHPE/BLK NE5 68 B2 3
Felsham Sq MLFD/PNYW SR4 105 J7
Felstead Crs MLFD/PNYW SR4 105 H6
Felstead Pl BLYTH NE24 35 F3
Felstead Sq MLFD/PNYW SR4 105 H7
Felton Av GOS/KPK NE3 56 A4
HAR/WTLS NE34 76 A5
MONK NE25 51 F5
Felton Cl MPTH NE61 21 F7
SMOOR NE27 49 H6
Felton Crs GATE NE8 86 E5
Felton Dr LGB/KIL NE12 58 B1
Fencer Ct GOS/KPK NE3 56 C2
Fence Rd CLS/BIR/GTL DH3 131 G1
Fenhall Pk BDN/LAN/SAC DH7 140 B4
Fenham Cha ELS/FEN NE4 69 H3
Fenham Hall Dr ELS/FEN NE4 69 H3
Fenham Rd ELS/FEN NE4 4 B4
MPTH NE61 18 B2
Fenkle St CNUT NE1 5 H7
Fennel Gv HAR/WTLS NE34 91 J1
Fenside Rd ASHBK/HED/RY SR2 121 F6
Fenton Cl CLSW/PEL DH2 129 G6
Fenton Sq MLFD/PNYW SR4 105 H7 1
Fenton Well La
CLS/BIR/GTL DH3 145 F1
Fenwick Av BLYTH NE24 35 F2 2
HAR/WTLS NE34 74 E6
Fenwick Cl CLSW/PEL DH2 129 F6
HLS DH4 117 K6 1
Fenwick Gv MPTH NE61 20 E4
Fenwick St HLS DH4 117 K6
Ferens Cl DHAM DH1 16 F1
Ferens Pk DHAM DH1 16 F1
Ferguson Crs DIN/WO NE13 46 A5
Ferguson's La
BW/LEM/TK/HW NE15 68 E5
Ferguson St ASHBK/HED/RY SR2 15 K6
Fern Av CLDN/WHIT/ROK SR6 93 F2
CRAM NE23 33 H5
GOS/KPK NE3 56 A3 3
JES NE2 70 E2
NSHW NE29 2 A1
SWCK/CAS SR5 106 A3
Fern Ct STKFD/GP NE62 22 E6 3
Fern Crs SEA/MUR SR7 150 D4
Ferndale DHAM DH1 158 A6
Ferndale Av BOL NE36 91 H5
GOS/KPK NE3 56 D1
WLSD/HOW NE28 72 E1
Ferndale Cl BLYTH NE24 30 C6 2
WNGT TS28 184 A6
Ferndale Gv BOL NE36 91 H5
Ferndale La BOL NE36 91 H5
Ferndale Rd HLS DH4 117 J6
Ferndale Ter MLFD/PNYW SR4 105 J5
Ferndene Crs MLFD/PNYW SR4 105 K7
Ferndene Gv LGB/HTN NE7 57 H7
Fern Dene Rd GATE NE8 10 E8
Ferndown Ct RYTON NE40 67 F7 1
Fern Dr CLDN/WHIT/ROK SR6 91 K3
CRAM NE23 47 G1
Fernhill Av WICK/BNPF NE16 84 E5
Fernlea Cl WASHS NE38 117 G4
Fernlea Gdns RYTON NE40 66 C7 1
Fernley Vls CRAM NE23 38 E2
Fern Rd BDN/LAN/SAC DH7 143 J5
Fern St CON/LDGT DH8 123 F4 1
MLFD/PNYW SR4 14 B3
Fernsway SUNDSW SR3 120 B3 3
Fernville Av WICK/BNPF NE16 99 F3
Fernville Rd GOS/KPK NE3 56 B7
Fernville St MLFD/PNYW SR4 14 A7 3
Fernway MPTH NE61 21 F5
Fernwood Av GOS/KPK NE3 56 D4
Fernwood Cl SUNDSW SR3 134 A2 2
Fernwood Rd
BW/LEM/TK/HW NE15 68 B5
JES NE2 5 M1
Ferrand Dr HLS DH4 132 B7
Ferriby Cl GOS/KPK NE3 56 D2 2
Ferrisdale Wy GOS/KPK NE3 55 K3
Ferryboat La SWCK/CAS SR5 104 D4
Ferrydene Av GOS/KPK NE3 55 K6
Ferry St JRW NE32 73 K3
SSH NE33 2 F7
Festival Park Dr DUN/TMV NE11 9 M9
Festival Wy DUN/TMV NE11 9 J6
Field Cl JES NE2 6 B5
Field Fare Ct WICK/BNPF NE16 112 A1
Fieldhouse Cl MPTH NE61 27 J1
Fieldhouse La DHAM DH1 156 B6
MPTH NE61 27 J1
Field House Rd GATE NE8 10 E9
Fielding Ct
WD/WHPE/BLK NE5 54 E6 2
Fielding Pl LWF/SPW/WRK NE9 11 M8

Field La *FELL* NE10 .... 13 H8
Fieldside *CLDN/WHIT/ROK* SR6... 92 E3
 CLSW/PEL DH2 .... 114 E7
 HLH DH5 .... 147 F5
Field Sq *MLFD/PNYW* SR4 .... 105 G7
 GOS/KPK NE3 .... 56 E5
Field St *FELL* NE10 .... 12 C6
Field Ter *JRW* NE32 .... 73 K6
Fieldway *BOLCOL* NE35 .... 90 A4
 JRW NE32 .... 90 B3 ▣
Fife Av *JRW* NE32 .... 90 C1
Fife St *GATE* NE8 .... 11 H6
 SEA/MUR SR7 .... 149 J6
Fifteenth Av *BLYTH* NE24 .... 35 F1
Fifth Av *ASHGTN* NE63 .... 23 K3
 BYK/HTN/WLK NE6 .... 7 G2
 DUN/TMV NE11 .... 86 D7
 MPTH NE61 .... 21 F6
Fifth St *PLEE/EAS* SR8 .... 175 H3
Filby Dr *DHAM* DH1 .... 158 A4
Filey Cl *CRAM* NE23 .... 33 H7
Filton Cl *CRAM* NE23 .... 33 H7
Finchale *WASHS* NE38 .... 116 E3
Finchale Av *DHAM* DH1 .... 157 G1
Finchale Cl *ASHBK/HED/RY* NE29... 15 H7
 DUN/TMV NE11 .... 85 K6 ▣
 HLS DH4 .... 132 B7
Finchale Gdns
 BW/LEM/TK/HW NE15 .... 53 F7
Finchale Rd *DHAM* DH1 .... 156 E1
 HEBB NE31 .... 89 G1
Finchale Ter *JRW* NE32 .... 74 B7
 MLFD/PNYW SR4 .... 105 H6
Finchale Vw *DHAM* DH1 .... 156 C2 ▣
 HLS DH4 .... 146 B6
Finchdale Cl *NSHW* NE29 .... 2 B4
Finchley Crs *BYK/HTN/WLK* NE6... 72 C3
Findon Av *BDN/LAN/SAC* DH7 .... 143 C7
Findon Gv *NSHW* NE29 .... 60 C6
Findon Hl *BDN/LAN/SAC* DH7 .... 143 H6
Fine La *CON/LDGT* DH8 .... 108 B3
Fines Rd *CON/LDGT* DH8 .... 109 H6
Finsbury Av *BYK/HTN/WLK* NE6... 7 M5
Finsbury St *SWCK/CAS* SR5 .... 106 C4 ▣
Finsmere Av
 WD/WHPE/BLK NE5 .... 69 F2 ▣
Finsmere Pl
 WD/WHPE/BLK NE5 .... 69 F2 ▣
Finstock Ct *LGB/HTN* NE7 .... 57 F6
Fir Av *BDN/LAN/SAC* DH7 .... 167 G7
 DHAM DH1 .... 17 L4
Firbank Av *TYNE/NSHE* NE30 .... 51 F7
Firbanks *JRW* NE32 .... 90 B3
Firfield Rd *WD/WHPE/BLK* NE5 .... 69 H1
Fir Gv *HAR/WTLS* NE34 .... 75 K6
Fir Pk *BDN/LAN/SAC* DH7 .... 155 C7
First Av *ASHGTN* NE63 .... 23 K1
 BLYTH NE24 .... 35 F1
 BYK/HTN/WLK NE6 .... 7 G2
 CLSW/PEL DH2 .... 115 H6
 DUN/TMV NE11 .... 86 C6
 MPTH NE61 .... 21 F6
 NSHW NE29 .... 59 K6
The Firs *GOS/KPK* NE3 .... 56 B6 ▣
Fir St *JRW* NE32 .... 73 J4
First St *GATE* NE8 .... 10 C6
 PLEE/EAS SR8 .... 175 H3
Fir Terraces *BDN/LAN/SAC* DH7... 165 C1
Firth Sq *MLFD/PNYW* SR4 .... 105 H7
Firtree Av *BYK/HTN/WLK* NE6... 72 C2
 LGB/KIL NE12 .... 57 K1
 WASHS NE38 .... 116 E5
Fir Tree Cl *DHAM* DH1 .... 157 H5 ▣
Firtree Crs *LGB/KIL* NE12 .... 57 J1
Firtree Gdns *MONK* NE25 .... 50 D6
Firtree Rd *WICK/BNPF* NE16 .... 84 E6
Firtrees *CLSW/PEL* DH2 .... 129 H2
 FELL NE10 .... 88 A7
Firtrees Av *WLSD/HOW* NE28 .... 59 K7
Firwood Crs *ROWG* NE39 .... 96 C2
Firwood Gdns *DUN/TMV* NE11... 86 B7
Fisher La *CRAM* NE23 .... 32 C7
 DIN/WO NE13 .... 37 G5
Fisher Rd *SMOOR* NE27 .... 48 D3
Fisher St *BYK/HTN/WLK* NE6 .... 72 D4
 WLSD/HOW NE28 .... 72 D4
Fisherwell Rd *HLS* DH4 .... 13 K4
Fitzpatrick Pl *SSH* NE33 .... 3 L9
Fitzsimmons Av
 WLSD/HOW NE28 .... 58 D7
Flambard Rd *DHAM* DH1 .... 156 D4
Flass Av *BDN/LAN/SAC* DH7 .... 154 E7
Flassburn Rd *DHAM* DH1 .... 156 B6
Flasshall La *BDN/LAN/SAC* DH7... 154 A7
Flass St *DHAM* DH1 .... 16 A3
Flaunden Cl *HAR/WTLS* NE34 ... 76 B6 ▣
Flaxby Cl *GOS/KPK* NE3 .... 56 D2
Flax Sq *MLFD/PNYW* SR4 .... 105 G6 ▣
Fleet St *SUND* SR1 .... 15 K5
Fleming Gdns *FELL* NE10 .... 87 J5
Fleming Pl *PLEE/EAS* SR8 .... 174 E4 ▣
Fletcher Crs *HLS* DH4 .... 132 C1
Flexbury Gdns
 BW/LEM/TK/HW NE15 .... 68 C4 ▣
 FELL NE10 .... 12 B7
 LWF/SPW/WRK NE9 .... 101 G3
Flint Hill Bank *STLY/ANP* DH9 ... 111 G5
Flodden *LGB/KIL* NE12 .... 47 K5
Flodden Cl *CLSW/PEL* DH2 .... 129 F6
Flodden Rd *MLFD/PNYW* SR4 .... 105 H7
Flodden St *BYK/HTN/WLK* NE6... 7 K6
Floral Dene *MLFD/PNYW* SR4 .... 104 E7
Florence Av
 LWF/SPW/WRK NE9 .... 87 G6 ▣
Florence Crs *SWCK/CAS* SR5 .... 105 K4
Florence St *BLAY* NE21 .... 83 K3
Florida St *MLFD/PNYW* SR4 .... 105 K5
Flotterton Gdns
 WD/WHPE/BLK NE5 .... 69 G4
Flour Mill Rd *DUN/TMV* NE11 ... 9 H4
The Fold *MONK* NE25 .... 50 C4
 WICK/BNPF NE16 .... 97 J6
Folldon Av
 CLDN/WHIT/ROK SR6 .... 106 D2 ▣
Follingsby Av *FELL* NE10 .... 89 G6
Follingsby Dr *FELL* NE10 .... 88 E5
Follingsby La *FELL* NE10 .... 89 G7
Follingsby Wy *FELL* NE10 .... 89 F6
Folly La *RYTON* NE40 .... 82 D2

Folly Ter *DHAM* DH1 .... 156 B2
The Folly *BOL* NE36 .... 90 E5
Fondlyset La *STLY/ANP* DH9 ... 111 F7
Fontaine Rd *SUND* SR1 .... 14 C3
Fontburn Cl *SWCK/CAS* SR5 ... 105 K1 ▣
Fontburn Pl *LGB/HTN* NE7 .... 57 G5
Fontburn Rd *MONK* NE25 .... 40 A5
Fontburn Ter *TYNE/NSHE* NE30... 61 F4
Fonteyn Pl *CRAM* NE23 .... 33 H5
 STLY/ANP DH9 .... 127 F2
Fontwell Dr *GATE* NE8 .... 10 C9
Forbeck Rd *MLFD/PNYW* SR4 ... 105 H7
Forber Av *HAR/WTLS* NE34 .... 76 B5
Ford Av *ASHGTN* NE63 .... 23 K3
 MLFD/PNYW SR4 .... 104 E7
 NSHW NE29 .... 60 B6
Ford Crs *BDN/LAN/SAC* DH7 ... 140 C6
 JRW NE32 .... 89 K1
 MLFD/PNYW SR4 .... 104 E7
 SMOOR NE27 .... 49 C6
Ford Dr *BLYTH* NE24 .... 30 E7
Fordenbridge Crs
 MLFD/PNYW SR4 .... 105 H7
Fordenbridge Rd
 MLFD/PNYW SR4 .... 105 H7 ▣
Fordenbridge Sq
 MLFD/PNYW SR4 .... 105 J7 ▣
Fordfield Rd *MLFD/PNYW* SR4... 105 G7
Fordham Dr *MLFD/PNYW* SR4 ... 105 J7 ▣
Fordham Rd *DHAM* DH1 .... 156 D4
 MLFD/PNYW SR4 .... 105 H6
Fordham Sq *MLFD/PNYW* SR4 ... 105 J7
Fordland Pl *MLFD/PNYW* SR4 ... 105 K7
Fordley Ov *MLFD/PNYW* SR4 ... 105 F6
Ford Ov *BDN/LAN/SAC* DH7 ... 140 C5
 DHAM DH1 .... 156 C5
Ford St *BDN/LAN/SAC* DH7 ... 140 C5 ▣
 BYK/HTN/WLK NE6 .... 6 D6
 GATE NE8 .... 11 M5
Ford Ter *STKFD/GP* NE62 .... 23 F6
 WLSD/HOW NE28 .... 73 G1
The Ford *PRUD* NE42 .... 80 C1
Ford Vw *CRAM* NE23 .... 38 B7
Forest Av *LGB/KIL* NE12 .... 58 A2
Forest Dr *WASHS* NE38 .... 116 B6
Forest Gra *WNGT* TS28 .... 183 J3
Forest Hall Rd *LGB/KIL* NE12 ... 58 A1
Fore St *JES* NE2 .... 6 D1
Forest Rd *BW/LEM/TK/HW* NE15... 69 F7
 MLFD/PNYW SR4 .... 105 H6
 SSH NE33 .... 3 H8
Forest Vw *BDN/LAN/SAC* DH7... 166 E1
Forest Wy *CRAM* NE23 .... 39 G7
Forfar St *MLFD/PNYW* SR4 .... 106 D3
Forge Cl *CHPW* NE17 .... 95 H7 ▣
Forge La *CHPW* NE17 .... 110 A1
 CLS/BIR/GTL DH3 .... 130 C4
Forge Rd *DUN/TMV* NE11 .... 9 K8
Forres St *STLY/ANP* DH9 .... 127 F1 ▣
Forres Pl *CRAM* NE23 .... 33 H7
Forrest Rd *WLSD/HOW* NE28 ... 72 C2 ▣
Forster Av *BDLGTN* NE22 .... 28 E5
 HAR/WTLS NE34 .... 75 J4 ▣
 RDHAMSE DH6 .... 158 C7
Forster St *BLYTH* NE24 .... 31 H7
 CLDN/WHIT/ROK SR6 .... 106 E4
Forsyth Rd *JES* NE2 .... 70 D2
Forth Banks *CNUT* NE1 .... 5 J9
Forth Cl *PLEE/EAS* SR8 .... 174 E5
Forth Ct *HAR/WTLS* NE34 .... 75 G6
Forth Pl *CNUT* NE1 .... 5 H8
Forth St *CNUT* NE1 .... 5 H9
Fortrose Av *SUNDSW* SR3 .... 120 A3
Fort St *SSH* NE33 .... 3 L4
Forum Ct *BDLGTN* NE22 .... 29 F5
The Forum
 BW/LEM/TK/HW NE15 .... 68 D4
Forum Wy *CRAM* NE23 .... 38 B2
Fossdyke *FELL* NE10 .... 88 B7 ▣
Fossefeld *FELL* NE10 .... 88 C5
Fosse Law
 BW/LEM/TK/HW NE15 .... 67 G2
Fosse Ter *LWF/SPW/WRK* NE9... 87 H6 ▣
Fossway *BYK/HTN/WLK* NE6 .... 7 K3
Foss Wy *CON/LDGT* DH8 .... 108 E3
Foster Av *BYK/HTN/WLK* NE6... 72 D6
Foundry La *BYK/HTN/WLK* NE6... 6 D5
Foundry Rd *SEA/MUR* SR7 .... 151 F1 ▣
Fountain Cl *BDLGTN* NE22 .... 29 F5 ▣
Fountain Gv *HAR/WTLS* NE34 ... 75 K3
Fountain Head Bank
 WBAY NE26 .... 40 E2
Fountain La *BLAY* NE21 .... 67 K7
Fountain Rw *JES* NE2 .... 4 E2
Fountains Cl *DUN/TMV* NE11 ... 86 A3
 WASHS NE38 .... 117 F2
Fountains Crs *HEBB* NE31 .... 89 G1
 HLS DH4 .... 132 A5
Fouracres Rd
 WD/WHPE/BLK NE5 .... 69 J1
Four Lane Ends *HLH* DH5 .... 148 A6
Fourstones *WD/WHPE/BLK* NE5 ... 68 D1
Fourstones Cl *GOS/KPK* NE3 ... 55 H5
Fourstones Rd
 MLFD/PNYW SR4 .... 105 J6
Fourth Av *ASHGTN* NE63 .... 23 K2
 BLYTH NE24 .... 35 F1 ▣
 BYK/HTN/WLK NE6 .... 7 G2
 CLSW/PEL DH2 .... 129 H4
 DUN/TMV NE11 .... 86 C7
 MPTH NE61 .... 21 F6
Fourth St *GATE* NE8 .... 10 C6
 PLEE/EAS SR8 .... 175 H3
Fourway Ct *WNGT* TS28 .... 183 K2 ▣
Fowberry Crs *ELS/FEN* NE4 .... 69 J4
Fowberry Rd
 BW/LEM/TK/HW NE15 .... 68 D5
Fowler Cl *HLS* DH4 .... 132 A3 ▣
Fowler St *SSH* NE33 .... 3 H7
Fox And Hounds La
 BW/LEM/TK/HW NE15 .... 69 G5
Fox And Hounds Rd
 WD/WHPE/BLK NE5 .... 69 G4
Fox Av *HAR/WTLS* NE34 .... 74 D7
Foxcover La *SUNDSW* SR3 .... 119 F7
Foxcover Rd *MLFD/PNYW* SR4... 118 D4
Fox Covert La *PONT/DH* NE20... 43 F3

Foxglove Ct *HAR/WTLS* NE34 ... 74 E7
Foxhall Cl *ASHGTN* NE63 .... 23 H4
Foxhills Cl *WASHS* NE38 .... 117 G4
Foxhills Covert
 WICK/BNPF NE16 .... 84 C7
Fox Hills Crs *BDN/LAN/SAC* DH7... 140 A4
Foxhunters Rd *MONK* NE25 .... 50 B6
Foxlair Cl *SUNDSW* SR3 .... 134 A3
Fox Lea Wk *CRAM* NE23 .... 39 F7
Foxley *WASHN* NE37 .... 103 G5
Foxley Cl *LGB/KIL* NE12 .... 48 B5
Fox St *ASHBK/HED/RY* NE8 .... 14 A8
 SEA/MUR SR7 .... 150 E2
Foxton Av *NSHW* NE3 .... 55 K3
 TYNE/NSHE NE30 .... 51 F6
Foxton Cl *NSHW* NE29 .... 60 C7
Foxton Hall *WASHN* NE37 .... 103 F7
Foxton Wy *DHAM* DH1 .... 169 J5 ▣
 FELL NE10 .... 13 M3
Foyle St *SUND* SR1 .... 14 F5
Framwelgate *DHAM* DH1 .... 16 C3
Framwelgate Br *DHAM* DH1 .... 16 C2
Framwelgate Peth *DHAM* DH1.. 156 C6
Framwelgate Waterside
 DHAM DH1 .... 16 D3
Frances St *BLAY* NE21 .... 83 J2
Francis St *CLDN/WHIT/ROK* SR6.. 106 D3
Frankham St
 WD/WHPE/BLK NE5 .... 68 D1 ▣
Frankland Dr *MONK* NE25 .... 50 C6
Frankland La *DHAM* DH1 .... 16 D1
Frankland Rd *DHAM* DH1 .... 156 C4
Franklin St *MLFD/PNYW* SR4 ... 106 A6
Franklyn Av *WBAY* NE26 .... 40 E1
Franklyn Rd *PLEE/EAS* SR8 .... 174 C3
Frank Pl *NSHW* NE29 .... 2 D1
Frank St *DHAM* DH1 .... 17 M3
 SWCK/CAS SR5 .... 106 B3 ▣
 WLSD/HOW NE28 .... 72 D2
Fraser Cl *SSH* NE33 .... 75 F3
Freda St *SWCK/CAS* SR5 .... 105 K4
Frederick Rd *SUND* SR1 .... 14 F4
Frederick St
 MLFD/PNYW SR4 .... 104 E7 ▣
 SEA/MUR SR7 .... 150 E1
 SSH NE33 .... 75 G3
 SUND SR1 .... 14 F5 ▣
Frederick Ter *RDHAMSE* DH6 ... 160 E3
Freehold Av *STKFD/GP* NE62 ... 23 F3
Freeman Rd *GOS/KPK* NE3 .... 57 F6
 LGB/HTN NE7 .... 57 F6
Freeman Wy *ASHGTN* NE63 .... 24 B4
Freesia Gra *WASHS* NE38 .... 117 G3 ▣
Freezemoor Rd *HLS* DH4 .... 132 B1
Fremantle Rd *HAR/WTLS* NE34... 76 B6
Frenchman's Wy
 HAR/WTLS NE34 .... 76 B4
French St *BLYTH* NE24 .... 31 G6 ▣
Frensham *WASHS* NE38 .... 117 J2 ▣
Frensham Wy
 BDN/LAN/SAC DH7 .... 167 H6 ▣
Frenton Cl
 WD/WHPE/BLK NE5 .... 68 A1 ▣
Friarage Av
 CLDN/WHIT/ROK SR6 .... 106 D2 ▣
Friar Rd *MLFD/PNYW* SR4 .... 105 H7
Friars Dene Rd *FELL* NE10 .... 12 A4
Friarsfield Cl *SUNDSW* SR3 .... 133 J2
Friars Ga *ASHGTN* NE63 .... 20 B6
Friarside *BDN/LAN/SAC* DH7 ... 155 C1
Friarside Crs *ROWG* NE39 .... 97 F5
Friarside Gdns *WICK/BNPF* NE16.. 84 E6
Friarside Rd *ELS/FEN* NE4 .... 69 J3
Friar Sq *MLFD/PNYW* SR4 .... 105 H7
Friars' Rw *DHAM* DH1 .... 157 G6
Friars St *CNUT* NE1 .... 5 H7
Friar St *RDHAMSE* DH6 .... 173 J4
Friars Wy *WD/WHPE/BLK* NE5 ... 69 G3 ▣
Friar Wy *JRW* NE32 .... 74 A4
Friary Gdns *FELL* NE10 .... 12 A5
Frobisher Ct *SUNDSW* SR3 .... 133 K2
Frobisher St *HEBB* NE31 .... 73 H5
Frome Gdns
 LWF/SPW/WRK NE9 .... 101 F3
Frome Pl *CRAM* NE23 .... 33 H7
Frome Sq *MLFD/PNYW* SR4 ... 105 G7 ▣
Front Rd *MLFD/PNYW* SR4 .... 105 H7
Front St *BDN/LAN/SAC* DH7 ... 140 B4
 BDN/LAN/SAC DH7 .... 143 C5
 BDN/LAN/SAC DH7 .... 152 E5
 BDN/LAN/SAC DH7 .... 152 B4
 BDN/LAN/SAC DH7 .... 153 J4
 BDN/LAN/SAC DH7 .... 155 F1
 BDN/LAN/SAC DH7 .... 167 K4
 BLAY NE21 .... 83 K3
 BLYTH NE24 .... 29 K7
 BOL NE36 .... 91 G5
 BOLCOL NE35 .... 90 C3
 CLDN/WHIT/ROK SR6 .... 92 A3
 CLDN/WHIT/ROK SR6 .... 92 E4
 CLS/BIR/GTL DH3 .... 129 J4
 CLS/BIR/GTL DH3 .... 145 H1
 CLSW/PEL DH2 .... 114 D7
 CON/LDGT DH8 .... 122 C1
 CON/LDGT DH8 .... 123 J4
 CON/LDGT DH8 .... 123 F5
 CON/LDGT DH8 .... 136 C1
 CRAM NE23 .... 38 C7
 CRAM NE23 .... 39 H7
 DHAM DH1 .... 17 M4
 DHAM DH1 .... 156 B3
 DIN/WO NE13 .... 37 G7
 DIN/WO NE13 .... 45 F2
 HLH DH5 .... 147 H7
 HLS DH4 .... 131 J7
 HLS DH4 .... 132 B4
 LGB/HTN NE7 .... 57 J5
 LGB/KIL NE12 .... 47 H4 ▣
 MONK NE25 .... 49 J4
 MONK NE25 .... 50 C5
 NSHW NE29 .... 60 C5
 NSHW NE29 .... 60 D2
 NWBGN NE64 .... 25 F1
 PRUD NE42 .... 80 D2
 RDHAMSE DH6 .... 158 D3
 RDHAMSE DH6 .... 160 E6

 RDHAMSE DH6 .... 160 D1
 RDHAMSE DH6 .... 170 D1
 RDHAMSE DH6 .... 171 H2
 RDHAMSE DH6 .... 171 F1
 RDHAMSE DH6 .... 172 E7
 RDHAMSE DH6 .... 172 D1
 RDHAMSE DH6 .... 178 C5
 RDHAMSE DH6 .... 181 J3
 RHTLP TS27 .... 184 D6
 RHTLP TS27 .... 185 G2
 STKFD/GP NE62 .... 22 E6
 STLY/ANP DH9 .... 110 E7
 STLY/ANP DH9 .... 111 G5
 STLY/ANP DH9 .... 111 K4
 STLY/ANP DH9 .... 112 B3
 STLY/ANP DH9 .... 112 D7 ▣
 STLY/ANP DH9 .... 112 E7
 STLY/ANP DH9 .... 127 G4
 TYNE/NSHE NE30 .... 51 G6
 TYNE/NSHE NE30 .... 61 H3
 WASHN NE37 .... 103 G5 ▣
 WICK/BNPF NE16 .... 84 E5
 WICK/BNPF NE16 .... 97 G7
 WICK/BNPF NE16 .... 97 J7
 WICK/BNPF NE16 .... 111 J2
 WNGT TS28 .... 183 K5
 WYLAM NE41 .... 65 F6
Front St East *BDLGTN* NE22 .... 29 G6
Frosterley Cl *CLS/BIR/GTL* DH3 ... 145 J1
 DHAM DH1 .... 156 E3 ▣
 HLH DH5 .... 148 C7 ▣
Frosterley Gdns
 SUNDSW SR3 .... 120 B4 ▣
Frosterley Pl *ELS/FEN* NE4 .... 4 D5
Froude Av *HAR/WTLS* NE34 .... 91 F1
Fuchsia Pl
 WD/WHPE/BLK NE5 .... 69 H1 ▣
Fulbrook Rd *GOS/KPK* NE3 .... 55 K5
Fulforth Cl
 BDN/LAN/SAC DH7 .... 155 F5 ▣
Fullerton Pl *LWF/SPW/WRK* NE9 ... 11 J8
Fulmar Dr *BLYTH* NE24 .... 35 G3
 WASHS NE38 .... 116 B3
Fulmar Wk *CLDN/WHIT/ROK* SR6.. 93 F2
Fulwell Av *HAR/WTLS* NE34 .... 76 B4
Fulwell Gn
 WD/WHPE/BLK NE5 .... 69 F2 ▣
Fulwell Rd
 CLDN/WHIT/ROK SR6 .... 106 D4 ▣
 PLEE/EAS SR8 .... 175 G5
Furnace Bank *BDLGTN* NE22 ... 29 K5
Furness Cl *PLEE/EAS* SR8 .... 174 C4
Furrowfield *FELL* NE10 .... 87 J6 ▣
Furzefield Rd *GOS/KPK* NE3 .... 56 B6
Fylingdale Dr *SUNDSW* SR3 ... 120 C7
Fyndoune Wy
 BDN/LAN/SAC DH7 .... 143 G7
Fynes Cl *PLEE/EAS* SR8 .... 174 E2
Fynway *BDN/LAN/SAC* DH7 ... 143 H6 ▣

G

The Gables
 BDN/LAN/SAC DH7 .... 141 G4 ▣
 DIN/WO NE13 .... 55 F4
Gainers Ter *WLSD/HOW* NE28 ... 72 E3
Gainford *CLSW/PEL* DH2 .... 129 G4
Gainsborough Av
 HAR/WTLS NE34 .... 91 H1
 WASHS NE38 .... 116 E6
Gainsborough Cl *MONK* NE25 ... 50 A2
Gainsborough Crs *HLS* DH4 .... 131 H2
Gainsborough Pl *CRAM* NE23 ... 38 C5
Gainsborough Rd
 MLFD/PNYW SR4 .... 119 G4
 STLY/ANP DH9 .... 126 D2
Gainsbro Gv *ELS/FEN* NE4 .... 4 B5
Gairloch Dr *CLSW/PEL* DH2 ... 115 F7
Gairloch Rd *MLFD/PNYW* SR4 ... 119 G3
Galashiels Gv *HLS* DH4 .... 131 K2 ▣
Galashiels Rd *MLFD/PNYW* SR4 ... 119 F3 ▣
Galashiels Sq
 MLFD/PNYW SR4 .... 119 G3 ▣
Gale St *STLY/ANP* DH9 .... 126 B2
Galfrid Cl *SEA/MUR* SR7 .... 150 A2 ▣
Gallalaw Ter *GOS/KPK* NE3 .... 57 F5 ▣
Galley's Gill Rd *SUND* SR1 .... 14 C4
Galloping Green Rd
 LWF/SPW/WRK NE9 .... 101 K3
Galloway Rd *PLEE/EAS* SR8 ... 174 E3
Gallowgate *CNUT* NE1 .... 5 H6
Gallowhill La *PRUD* NE42 .... 64 B5
Galsworthy Rd *HAR/WTLS* NE34 ... 90 E1
 MLFD/PNYW SR4 .... 119 G3
Galt St *RDHAMSE* DH6 .... 172 C6 ▣
Galway Rd *MLFD/PNYW* SR4 ... 119 F3 ▣
Gambia Rd *MLFD/PNYW* SR4 ... 119 F4 ▣
Gambia Sq *MLFD/PNYW* SR4 ... 119 F4 ▣
Ganton Av *CRAM* NE23 .... 38 C4
Ganton Cl *WASHN* NE37 .... 102 E3 ▣
Ganton Ct *HAR/WTLS* NE34 .... 91 K1 ▣
Garasdale Cl *BLYTH* NE24 .... 35 F4
Garden Av *BDN/LAN/SAC* DH7... 154 A3
Garden Cl *DIN/WO* NE13 .... 37 G7 ▣
Garden Crs *CON/LDGT* DH8 .... 108 E2
Garden Cft *LGB/KIL* NE12 .... 58 A2
Garden Dr *HEBB* NE31 .... 73 F7 ▣
Garden House Est *RYTON* NE40... 66 B7
Garden La *SSH* NE33 .... 3 H7
Garden Pk *WLSD/HOW* NE28 ... 59 H6 ▣
Garden Pl *HLS* DH4 .... 117 K7
 SUND SR1 .... 14 D4 ▣
The Gardens *CLSW/PEL* DH2 ... 114 D7
 MONK NE25 .... 50 D5
Garden St *BLAY* NE21 .... 84 A1 ▣
 HLS DH4 .... 132 B4 ▣
Garden Ter *CON/LDGT* DH8 .... 123 J3
 MONK NE25 .... 49 J4
 RYTON NE40 .... 66 B7
Gardiner Rd *MLFD/PNYW* SR4... 118 E3
Gardiner Sq
 MLFD/PNYW SR4 .... 119 F3 ▣
Gardner Pk *NSHW* NE29 .... 2 B3
Gardner Pl *NSHW* NE29 .... 2 D3 ▣

Garesfield Gdns *ROWG* NE39 ... 97 G2 ▣
Garesfield La *BLAY* NE21 .... 83 H5
Gareston Cl *BLYTH* NE24 .... 30 D7
Garforth Cl *CRAM* NE23 .... 38 B4
Garleigh Cl *LGB/KIL* NE12 .... 48 B6 ▣
Garner Cl *WD/WHPE/BLK* NE5 ... 54 B7
Garnet St *MLFD/PNYW* SR4 .... 105 K6
Garrick Cl *NSHW* NE29 .... 60 A3
Garrick St *SSH* NE33 .... 75 G3
Garrigill *WASHS* NE38 .... 117 H5
Garron St *SEA/MUR* SR7 .... 150 E2
Garsdale Av *WASHN* NE37 .... 102 D5
Garsdale Rd *WBAY* NE26 .... 41 H7
Garside Av *CLS/BIR/GTL* DH3 ... 115 J1
Garside Gv *PLEE/EAS* SR8 .... 174 C2
Garsin Cl *LGB/HTN* NE7 .... 58 A7
Garth Cornfield *PLEE/EAS* SR8... 175 G5
Garth Crs *BLAY* NE21 .... 83 K3
 HAR/WTLS NE34 .... 76 A2
Garth Farm Rd *BLAY* NE21 .... 83 K3
Garthfield Crs
 WD/WHPE/BLK NE5 .... 68 E1
Garth Heads *CNUT* NE1 .... 6 A7
Garth Six *LGB/KIL* NE12 .... 47 J6
Garth Sixteen *LGB/KIL* NE12 ... 47 J5 ▣
The Garth *GOS/KPK* NE3 .... 55 K6
 WD/WHPE/BLK NE5 .... 68 C2 ▣
Garth Thirteen *LGB/KIL* NE12 ... 47 H5 ▣
Garth Thirty Three
 LGB/KIL NE12 .... 47 K6
Garth Thirty Two *LGB/KIL* NE12.. 48 A6
Garth Twelve *LGB/KIL* NE12 ... 47 J5 ▣
Garth Twenty *LGB/KIL* NE12 ... 48 A6
Garth Twenty Five
 LGB/KIL NE12 .... 48 B6 ▣
Garth Twenty Four
 LGB/KIL NE12 .... 48 B6 ▣
Garth Twenty Seven
 LGB/KIL NE12 .... 48 B6
Garth Twenty Two *LGB/KIL* NE12.. 48 A6
Gartland Rd *MLFD/PNYW* SR4 ... 118 E3
Garvey Vls *LWF/SPW/WRK* NE9 ... 87 J6
Garwood St *SSH* NE33 .... 75 F3
Gas House La *HLS* DH4 .... 132 B6
 MPTH NE61 .... 20 E5
Gaskell Av *HAR/WTLS* NE34 .... 91 F1
Gas La *BLAY* NE21 .... 68 A7
Gas Works Rd *SEA/MUR* SR7 ... 151 F2
Gatacre St *BLYTH* NE24 .... 31 G6 ▣
Gateley Av *BLYTH* NE24 .... 35 F3
Gatesgarth *LWF/SPW/WRK* NE9.. 87 G7
Gatesgarth Gv
 CLDN/WHIT/ROK SR6 .... 92 C7 ▣
Gateshead Hwy *GATE* NE8 .... 11 H1
Gateshead Rd *WICK/BNPF* NE16 ... 99 G2
Gatwick Rd *MLFD/PNYW* SR4 ... 119 F3
Gayhurst Crs *SUNDSW* SR3 .... 134 A1
Gayton Rd *WASHN* NE37 .... 103 G4
Geddes Rd *MLFD/PNYW* SR4 ... 119 F3
Gelt Crs *HLH* DH5 .... 148 A6 ▣
General Graham St
 MLFD/PNYW SR4 .... 119 K1 ▣
General Havelock Rd
 MLFD/PNYW SR4 .... 105 J7
The General's Wd *WASHS* NE38 ... 116 E6
Genesis Wy *CON/LDGT* DH8 .... 122 E5
Geneva Rd *MLFD/PNYW* SR4 ... 119 F3 ▣
Genister Pl *ELS/FEN* NE4 .... 69 H3 ▣
Geoffrey Av *DHAM* DH1 .... 168 B2
Geoffrey St
 CLDN/WHIT/ROK SR6 .... 93 F3
Geoffrey Ter *STLY/ANP* DH9 .... 126 B2
George Pit La *CLS/BIR/GTL* DH3.. 145 K2
George Rd *BDLGTN* NE22 .... 29 K4 ▣
 WLSD/HOW NE28 .... 72 D3
George Scott St *SSH* NE33 .... 3 K5
George Smith Gdns
 FELL NE10 .... 12 B4 ▣
George Sq *RDHAMSE* DH6 .... 171 H4
George Stephenson Wy
 NSHW NE29 .... 2 B6
George St *ASHBK/HED/RY* SR2... 135 G1
 BLAY NE21 .... 84 B1 ▣
 BLYTH NE24 .... 35 G1 ▣
 CLS/BIR/GTL DH3 .... 115 H2
 CLS/BIR/GTL DH3 .... 129 K5
 CON/LDGT DH8 .... 122 D2
 CON/LDGT DH8 .... 123 F4
 DHAM DH1 .... 168 B1
 ELS/FEN NE4 .... 5 G9
 GOS/KPK NE3 .... 56 A5
 HLH DH5 .... 147 K3
 RDHAMSE DH6 .... 160 E6
 RDHAMSE DH6 .... 170 C1
 RDHAMSE DH6 .... 179 K1
 SEA/MUR SR7 .... 149 K6
 SEA/MUR SR7 .... 150 D1
 TYNE/NSHE NE30 .... 2 F1
 WD/WHPE/BLK NE5 .... 67 H1
 WICK/BNPF NE16 .... 84 E5 ▣
 WLSD/HOW NE28 .... 73 K2
George St North
 CLDN/WHIT/ROK SR6 .... 14 F1
Georgia Ct *CON/LDGT* DH8 .... 122 E5 ▣
Georgian Ct *LGB/KIL* NE12 .... 57 H1
 MLFD/PNYW SR4 .... 120 A2 ▣
Gerald St *ELS/FEN* NE4 .... 69 H7
 HAR/WTLS NE34 .... 91 G1
Gerrard Cl *CRAM* NE23 .... 38 C4
 WBAY NE26 .... 41 H7
Gerrard Rd *MLFD/PNYW* SR4 ... 119 F3 ▣
 WBAY NE26 .... 41 H7
Gertrude St *HLS* DH4 .... 132 B5 ▣
Ghyll Field Rd *DHAM* DH1 .... 156 D4
Gibside *CLSW/PEL* DH2 .... 129 G4
Gibside Cl *STLY/ANP* DH9 .... 113 F7
Gibside Ct *DUN/TMV* NE11 .... 85 K6 ▣
Gibside Gdns
 BW/LEM/TK/HW NE15 .... 69 F5
Gibside Vw *BLAY* NE21 .... 83 K4 ▣
Gibside Wy *WICK/BNPF* NE16 ... 85 F6 ▣
Gibson Ct *BOLCOL* NE35 .... 90 D4 ▣
Gibson St *CNUT* NE1 .... 6 B6
 CON/LDGT DH8 .... 123 F4
 NWBGN NE64 .... 25 F1
 WLSD/HOW NE28 .... 59 G6

Gifford Sq MLFD/PNYW SR4 119 G2
Gilbert Rd MLFD/PNYW SR4 119 F3
PLEE/EAS SR8 174 D3
Gilbert St SSH NE33 75 G3 3
Gilderdale HLS DH4 117 G6
Gilderdale Wy CRAM NE23 38 B5 1
CRAM NE23 38 C5 1
Gilesgate DHAM DH1 16 F3
Gilesgate Ct DHAM DH1 16 F3 1
Gilesgate Rd HLH DH5 148 A6
Gilhurst Gra SUND SR1 14 B5
Gillas La HLH DH5 147 K1
Gillas La East HLH DH5 147 J1
Gillas La West HLH DH5 147 H2
Gillies St BYK/HTN/WLK NE6 7 J5
Gillingham Rd
MLFD/PNYW SR4 119 G3
Gill Rd SUND SR1 14 D3
Gill Side Gv
CLDN/WHIT/ROK SR6 106 E3
Gill Side Vw CON/LDGT DH8 122 C3
Gill St CON/LDGT DH8 123 G6
ELS/FEN NE4 69 J6
Gilmore Cl WD/WHPE/BLK NE5 54 B7
Gilpin St HLS DH4 132 B7
Gilsland Av WLSD/HOW NE28 59 H7
Gilsland Gv CRAM NE23 33 H6 1
Gilsland St MLFD/PNYW SR4 106 A6 1
Gilwell Wy GOS/KPK NE3 56 B1
Gingler La RYTON NE40 82 C2
Girtin Rd HAR/WTLS NE34 91 H2
Girton Cl PLEE/EAS SR8 174 C5
Girvan Cl STLY/ANP DH9 127 F1
Gishford Wy
WD/WHPE/BLK NE5 69 F1
Givens St CLDN/WHIT/ROK SR6 106 E3
Gladeley Wy WICK/BNPF NE16 98 E3
The Glade JRW NE32 89 K3
WD/WHPE/BLK NE5 67 J1
Gladewell Ct STKFD/GP NE62 22 E7 1
Gladstonbury Pl LGB/KIL NE12 57 J4
Gladstone St BLYTH NE24 31 F6
BW/LEM/TK/HW NE15 68 A5 1
CLDN/WHIT/ROK SR6 106 D4
CON/LDGT DH8 123 G4 1
HEBB NE31 73 H5
HLS DH4 131 K7
STLY/ANP DH9 113 H7
STLY/ANP DH9 126 B2
WLSD/HOW NE28 73 K2 3
Gladstone Ter GATE NE8 11 G5
JES NE2 5 M3
Gladstone Ter West GATE NE8 10 F5
Gladwyn Rd
MLFD/PNYW SR4 119 F4 3
Glaholm Rd ASHBK/HED/RY SR2 15 J6
Glaisdale Dr
CLDN/WHIT/ROK SR6 92 E6
Glaisdale Rd LGB/HTN NE7 57 G5 1
Glamis Av GOS/KPK NE3 46 C7
MLFD/PNYW SR4 119 G2
Glamis Ct HAR/WTLS NE34 91 K1
Glamis Crs ROWG NE39 97 J1
Glamis Vls CLS/BIR/GTL DH3 101 J7
Glanmore Rd
MLFD/PNYW SR4 119 F3 3
Glantlees WD/WHPE/BLK NE5 68 E1
Glanton Av MONK NE25 39 K5
Glanton Cl CLSW/PEL DH2 129 G5
MPTH NE61 27 F1
Glanton Rd NSHW NE29 60 B3
Glanton Sq MLFD/PNYW SR4 119 G3 2
Glanton Wynd GOS/KPK NE3 56 B3
Glanville Cl DUN/TMV NE11 86 B5
Glanville Rd SUNDSW SR3 133 H2
Glasbury Av
MLFD/PNYW SR4 119 G2 1
Glasgow Rd JRW NE32 90 C1
Glasshouse St BYK/HTN/WLK NE6 7 G9
Glastonbury WASHS NE38 117 F2 1
Glastonbury Gv JES NE2 71 F1
Gleaston Ct PLEE/EAS SR8 174 C7
Glebe Av LGB/KIL NE12 57 K3
WICK/BNPF NE16 85 F5
Glebe Cl WD/WHPE/BLK NE5 54 B7 1
Glebe Crs LGB/KIL NE12 57 K1
WASHS NE38 103 G7
Glebe Farm MPTH NE61 22 E5
Glebe Ms BDLGTN NE22 29 F5 2
Glebe Ri WICK/BNPF NE16 84 E5
Glebe Rd BDLGTN NE22 29 F5
LGB/KIL NE12 57 K1
Glebeside BDN/LAN/SAC DH7 155 G1
Glebe St ELS/FEN NE4 69 H5
Glebe Ter LGB/KIL NE12 57 K1
PLEE/EAS SR8 162 D5
Glebe Vls LGB/KIL NE12 57 J1
Glenallen Gdns
TYNE/NSHE NE30 61 G1
Glen Barr CLSW/PEL DH2 129 H3
Glenbrooke Ter
LWF/SPW/WRK NE9 101 F1
Glenburn Cl WASHS NE38 116 B3
Glencarron Cl WASHS NE38 116 C2
Glen Cl ROWG NE39 97 G2
Glencoe LGB/KIL NE12 47 K5
Glencoe Av CLSW/PEL DH2 129 H3
CRAM NE23 38 C5
Glencoe Rd MLFD/PNYW SR4 119 F4
Glencourse BOL NE36 91 J5
Glendale Av BLYTH NE24 30 A6
GOS/KPK NE3 56 A6
NSHW NE29 60 C4
STKFD/GP NE62 23 G5
WBAY NE26 50 E2
WICK/BNPF NE16 84 E6
WLSD/HOW NE28 58 D6 2
Glendale Cl BLAY NE21 83 H4
SUNDSW SR3 133 G1
WD/WHPE/BLK NE5 54 B6
Glendale Gdns
LWF/SPW/WRK NE9 87 H7
STKFD/GP NE62 23 G5 2
Glendale Gv NSHW NE29 2 A1
Glendale Rd ASHGTN NE63 24 C3
SMOOR NE27 49 J6
Glendale Ter BYK/HTN/WLK NE6 7 G4
Glendford Pl BLYTH NE24 35 F3 2
Glendower Av NSHW NE29 60 B4 3
Glendyn Cl LGB/HTN NE7 71 G2
Gleneagle Cl
WD/WHPE/BLK NE5 54 B7 2
Gleneagles SSH NE33 75 J2 3
Gleneagles Cl LGB/HTN NE7 57 J5 3
Gleneagles Dr WASHN NE37 102 D3
Gleneagles Rd
LWF/SPW/WRK NE9 100 E2
MLFD/PNYW SR4 119 G3 3
Gleneagles Sq
MLFD/PNYW SR4 119 F4 4
Glenesk Gdns
ASHBK/HED/RY SR2 120 C4 2
Glenesk Rd ASHBK/HED/RY SR2 120 C3
Glenfield Av CRAM NE23 33 H6
Glenfield Rd LGB/KIL NE12 57 J3
Glengarvan Cl WASHS NE38 116 C3
Glenhurst Dr
WD/WHPE/BLK NE5 54 B7
WICK/BNPF NE16 98 D1
Glenhurst Gv HAR/WTLS NE34 75 K5
Glenhurst Rd PLEE/EAS SR8 162 E5
Glenleigh Dr MLFD/PNYW SR4 119 G3
Glen Luce Dr
ASHBK/HED/RY SR2 121 F4
Glenluce Dr CRAM NE23 38 B5
Glenmoor HEBB NE31 73 F4
Glenmore CON/LDGT DH8 123 J7
Glenmore Av CLSW/PEL DH2 129 H3
Glenmuir Av CRAM NE23 38 B5 2
Glenorrin Cl WASHS NE38 116 C3
Glen Pth ASHBK/HED/RY SR2 120 D3
Glenridge Av BYK/HTN/WLK NE6 71 H2
Glenroy Gdns CLSW/PEL DH2 129 H3
Glenshiel Cl WASHS NE38 116 C3
Glenside CON/LDGT DH8 122 D1
Glen St HEBB NE31 73 F6
Glen Ter CLSW/PEL DH2 129 G3
The Glen ASHBK/HED/RY SR2 120 D3 1
Glenthorn Rd JES NE2 70 E1
Glenuce CLS/BIR/GTL DH3 116 A3
Glenwood ASHGTN NE63 23 J3
Gloria Av MONK NE25 40 A2
Glossop St ROWG NE39 96 B1
Gloucester Av
CLDN/WHIT/ROK SR6 106 E1
Gloucester Cl CLS/BIR/GTL DH3 145 H2
Gloucester Pl HAR/WTLS NE34 76 A6 2
PLEE/EAS SR8 174 C3
Gloucester Rd CON/LDGT DH8 123 G6
ELS/FEN NE4 4 D6
NSHW NE29 59 K3
Gloucestershire Dr DHAM DH1 157 K6
Gloucester Ter ELS/FEN NE4 4 D8
RDHAMSE DH6 172 D1
Gloucester Wy ELS/FEN NE4 4 E9
Glover Rd MLFD/PNYW SR4 119 F4
WASHN NE37 103 H5
Glynfellis FELL NE10 88 B7
Glynwood Cl CRAM NE23 33 H6 2
Glynwood Gdns
LWF/SPW/WRK NE9 87 G7
Goathland Av LGB/KIL NE12 57 J3
Goathland Cl SUNDSW SR3 120 C7
Goathland Dr SUNDSW SR3 120 B7
Godfrey Rd MLFD/PNYW SR4 118 E3
Goldcrest Rd WASHS NE38 116 B3
Golden Acre CON/LDGT DH8 122 D2
Goldlynn Dr SUNDSW SR3 133 H1
Goldsborough Ct WNGT TS28 183 K2 2
Goldsmith Rd MLFD/PNYW SR4 119 F4
Goldspink La JES NE2 6 B2
Golf Course Rd HLS DH4 131 H3
Gompertz Gdns SSH NE33 75 F3
Goodrich Cl HLS DH4 132 A2 2
Good St STLY/ANP DH9 112 C6
Goodwell Lea
BDN/LAN/SAC DH7 176 D2
Goodwood LGB/KIL NE12 48 B6 6
Goodwood Av GATE NE8 10 B8
Goodwood Cl CON/LDGT DH8 122 E1
WD/WHPE/BLK NE5 54 B7 3
Goodwood Rd
MLFD/PNYW SR4 118 E3 1
Goole Rd MLFD/PNYW SR4 119 G3
Goose Hl MPTH NE61 20 E5 1
Gordon Av GOS/KPK NE3 56 C6 1
SWCK/CAS SR5 104 E5
Gordon Dr BOL NE36 91 H5
Gordon Rd HAR/WTLS NE34 75 G5
MLFD/PNYW SR4 118 E4
Gordon Sq BYK/HTN/WLK NE6 6 F6
WBAY NE26 51 G5
Gordon St GATE NE8 10 D4
SSH NE33 75 G3
Gordon Ter SWCK/CAS SR5 106 A3
Gorecock La STLY/ANP DH9 124 E6
Gore Hill Est RDHAMSE DH6 172 B6
Gorleston Wy SUNDSW SR3 133 K3
Gorse Av HAR/WTLS NE34 76 A6
Gorsdale Gv DHAM DH1 158 A6 1
Gorsedene Rd WBAY NE26 41 J7
Gorse Rd ASHBK/HED/RY SR2 14 E8
Gorseway MPTH NE61 20 B6
Gort Pl DHAM DH1 17 J1
Goschen St BLYTH NE24 31 F6 1
BLYTH NE24 31 G5 1
GATE NE8 10 D7
SWCK/CAS SR5 106 A3
Gosforth Av HAR/WTLS NE34 91 G1
Gosforth Park Wy LGB/KIL NE12 57 F3
Gosforth St JES NE2 6 A4
Gosforth Ter FELL NE10 13 H5
Gosport Wy BLYTH NE24 35 F3
Gossington WASHS NE38 117 J1
Goswick Av LGB/HTN NE7 71 H1
Goswick Dr GOS/KPK NE3 55 K2
Goundry Av
ASHBK/HED/RY SR2 135 G1
Gowanburn CRAM NE23 38 B5 3
WASHS NE38 117 G4
Gowan Ter JES NE2 71 F2
Gower Rd SWCK/CAS SR5 106 A3
Gower St BYK/HTN/WLK NE6 72 C7
Gower Wk FELL NE10 12 A7
Gowland Av ELS/FEN NE4 69 J4
Gracefield Cl
WD/WHPE/BLK NE5 54 B7 4
Grace Gdns WLSD/HOW NE28 58 C6
Grace St BYK/HTN/WLK NE6 7 H5
DUN/TMV NE11 9 G8
Grafton Rd WBAY NE26 51 G5
Grafton St MLFD/PNYW SR4 14 A3
Graham Av WICK/BNPF NE16 84 E4
Graham Ct
BDN/LAN/SAC DH7 143 H5 1
Graham Park Rd GOS/KPK NE3 56 C7
Grahamsley St GATE NE8 11 G3
Graham St SSH NE33 3 K9
The Graham Wy SEA/MUR SR7 150 B2
Grainger Park Rd ELS/FEN NE4 4 A8
Grainger St CNUT NE1 5 J7
Grampian Dr PLEE/EAS SR8 174 C5
Grampian Gv BOL NE36 91 F5 4
Grampian Pl LGB/KIL NE12 57 H1 2
The Granaries ROWG NE39 96 B1
Granby Cl SUNDSW SR3 120 B3
WICK/BNPF NE16 99 F2
Granby Ter WNGT TS28 183 K2 3
Grand Pde TYNE/NSHE NE30 61 H2
Grandstand Rd JES NE2 69 K3
Grange Av BDLGTN NE22 29 K3
HLS DH4 131 J6
LGB/KIL NE12 58 A4
PLEE/EAS SR8 162 C6
SMOOR NE27 49 H5
Grange Cl BLYTH NE24 35 F3
MONK NE25 50 B5
PLEE/EAS SR8 174 D2
TYNE/NSHE NE30 51 F7 2
WLSD/HOW NE28 72 E1
Grange Ct PRUD NE42 80 D2 2
Grange Crs FELL NE10 13 J9
RYTON NE40 66 E7
Grange Cressent
RDHAMSE DH6 180 D7
Grange Dr RYTON NE40 66 E7
Grange Est DUN/TMV NE11 100 C7
Grange Farm Dr
WICK/BNPF NE16 84 E7
Grange La WICK/BNPF NE16 84 E7
Grange Lonnen RYTON NE40 66 D6
Grangemere Cl
ASHBK/HED/RY SR2 121 F4
Grange Nook WICK/BNPF NE16 84 E7
Grange Pk MONK NE25 50 A6
Grange Park Av BDLGTN NE22 29 K3
SWCK/CAS SR5 106 C2
Grange Park Crs
RDHAMSE DH6 180 B3
Grange Pl JRW NE32 73 K4
Grange Rd
BW/LEM/TK/HW NE15 67 G3
DHAM DH1 157 K5
ELS/FEN NE4 69 H5
FELL NE10 13 J9
GOS/KPK NE3 56 C3
JRW NE32 73 K4
MPTH NE61 20 E6
PONT/DH NE20 43 G2
RYTON NE40 66 E6
STLY/ANP DH9 126 B1
SWCK/CAS SR5 104 E6
Grange Rd West JRW NE32 73 J4
Grange St CLSW/PEL DH2 128 E1
Grange St South
ASHBK/HED/RY SR2 121 F4
Grange Ter BOL NE36 91 H5 4
LWF/SPW/WRK NE9 11 K8
SWCK/CAS SR5 106 B3
The Grange BDLGTN NE22 28 A6
STLY/ANP DH9 112 A6
Grange Vw HLH DH5 147 G3
HLS DH4 132 B4
RYTON NE40 66 E7
SWCK/CAS SR5 106 C2
Grange Vls WLSD/HOW NE28 72 E1
Grantham Dr
LWF/SPW/WRK NE9 100 E1
Grantham Pl CRAM NE23 38 B4 1
Grantham Rd
CLDN/WHIT/ROK SR6 106 E3
JES NE2 6 A3
Grantham St BLYTH NE24 35 H1
Grants Crs SEA/MUR SR7 150 E1
Grant St JRW NE32 73 J4
PLEE/EAS SR8 175 H3 2
Granville Av LGB/KIL NE12 58 A1
WBAY NE26 41 G3
Granville Crs LGB/KIL NE12 58 A4
Granville Dr HLS DH4 132 A2
LGB/KIL NE12 58 A2
WD/WHPE/BLK NE5 54 B7
Granville Gdns JES NE2 71 G3 1
STKFD/GP NE62 23 G5
Granville Rd GOS/KPK NE3 56 C3
JES NE2 6 A1
PLEE/EAS SR8 175 G5
Granville St GATE NE8 11 G5
MLFD/PNYW SR4 14 A4
Grape La DHAM DH1 16 B4
Grasmere CLDN/WHIT/ROK SR6 92 A3
Grasmere Av BYK/HTN/WLK NE6 7 M6
FELL NE10 13 H7
HLH DH5 160 B1
JRW NE32 90 B1
Grasmere Ct LGB/KIL NE12 47 J6 2
Grasmere Crs BLAY NE21 83 K4 4
SWCK/CAS SR5 106 C2
WBAY NE26 50 D2
Grasmere Gdns
HAR/WTLS NE34 75 J5 2
Grasmere Pl GOS/KPK NE3 56 B3
Grasmere Rd CLSW/PEL DH2 129 H6
HEBB NE31 73 H6
PLEE/EAS SR8 175 F3
WICK/BNPF NE16 8 B9
WLSD/HOW NE28 72 C2
Grasmere St GATE NE8 10 E6
Grasmere St West GATE NE8 10 E6 1
Grasmere Ter RDHAMSE DH6 161 G2 1
SEA/MUR SR7 149 J6
Grasmoor Pl
BW/LEM/TK/HW NE15 67 K4 2
Grassdale DHAM DH1 158 A6
Grassholme Mdw SUNDSW SR3 120 B4
Grassholm Pl LGB/KIL NE12 57 G3
Grassington Dr CRAM NE23 38 B4
Grasslees WASHS NE38 116 B6
Grassmere Ms CON/LDGT DH8 123 K3
Grasswell Dr
WD/WHPE/BLK NE5 55 H7
Gravel Wks HLH DH5 132 C6
Gravesend Rd
MLFD/PNYW SR4 119 F4 3
Gravesend Sq
MLFD/PNYW SR4 119 G4 1
Gray Av DHAM DH1 156 B4
DIN/WO NE13 46 C2
RDHAMSE DH6 158 C7
SEA/MUR SR7 149 H5
Grayling Ct SUNDSW SR3 133 G2 1
Gray Rd ASHBK/HED/RY SR2 14 F9
ASHBK/HED/RY SR2 15 K7
Gray Sq WNGT TS28 183 K3
Grays Ter BOLCOL NE35 90 C3 3
Graystones FELL NE10 88 D5
Gray St BLYTH NE24 31 G5
Graythwaite CLSW/PEL DH2 129 F4
Greathead St SSH NE33 75 F4 2
Great Lime Rd DIN/WO NE13 47 G4
LGB/KIL NE12 47 F6
Great North Forest Trail
HAR/WTLS NE34 76 D4
Great North Rd GOS/KPK NE3 56 C3
Grebe Cl ASHGTN NE63 24 A4
BLYTH NE24 35 G2
Greely Rd WD/WHPE/BLK NE5 68 D1
Greenacres CLSW/PEL DH2 114 D7
Green Acres MPTH NE61 20 C6
PONT/DH NE20 42 E7
Greenacres Cl RYTON NE40 82 C1 1
Greenacres Rd CON/LDGT DH8 122 D2
Green Av HLS DH4 132 B3 1
Greenbank BLAY NE21 84 A2
JRW NE32 73 K4
Greenbank Dr
MLFD/PNYW SR4 118 E1
Greenbourne Gdns FELL NE10 87 J5 2
Green Cl TYNE/NSHE NE30 61 F1
Green Crs CRAM NE23 47 F1 2
Green Cressent RDHAMSE DH6 180 D7
Greencroft ASHGTN NE63 23 J3
RDHAMSE DH6 161 G2
Greencroft Av
BYK/HTN/WLK NE6 72 C3
Greencroft Pkwy
STLY/ANP DH9 125 H6
Greencroft Rd CON/LDGT DH8 123 J7
Greendale Cl BLYTH NE24 30 C6 3
Greendale Gdns HLH DH5 147 J6
Greener Ct PRUD NE42 80 B3 1
Greenfield Av
WD/WHPE/BLK NE5 68 E1
Greenfield Dr STKFD/GP NE62 22 E7 2
Greenfield Rd DIN/WO NE13 46 B7
GOS/KPK NE3 56 B1
Greenfinch Cl WASHS NE38 116 B3
Greenford DUN/TMV NE11 100 D7
Greenford La DUN/TMV NE11 100 E6
Greenford Rd
BYK/HTN/WLK NE6 13 J1
Greenhaugh LGB/KIL NE12 57 H1
Greenhead WASHS NE38 116 B2
Greenhead Rd CHPW NE17 95 H2
Greenhills LGB/KIL NE12 47 K4
Greenhills Est WNGT TS28 183 K2
Greenhill Vw
WD/WHPE/BLK NE5 69 J1
Green Hill Wk HAR/WTLS NE34 76 C5
Greenholme Cl CRAM NE23 33 H5 2
Greenhow Cl
ASHBK/HED/RY SR2 135 F2 2
Greenland Rd
BDN/LAN/SAC DH7 153 F5
Greenlands STLY/ANP DH9 126 B3 1
Greenlands Ct MONK NE25 40 A4
Green La ASHGTN NE63 23 J2
BDN/LAN/SAC DH7 141 K2
BOL NE36 91 H6
DHAM DH1 17 J2
DHAM DH1 17 G5
DIN/WO NE13 54 D2
FELL NE10 12 C4
FELL NE10 13 J6
HAR/WTLS NE34 75 F7
LGB/KIL NE12 48 A6 1
MPTH NE61 21 F6
MPTH NE61 26 A7
RDHAMSE DH6 159 K6
RDHAMSE DH6 160 C5
SEA/MUR SR7 148 D2
STLY/ANP DH9 126 C7
TRIM TS29 182 D3
Greenlaw WD/WHPE/BLK NE5 68 C3
Greenlaw Rd CRAM NE23 38 B5
Green Lea BDN/LAN/SAC DH7 143 G7
Greenlea NSHW NE29 59 K1
Greenlea Cl MLFD/PNYW SR4 119 G3
ROWG NE39 96 C1
Greenlee ASHGTN NE63 24 A3
Greenlee Dr LGB/HTN NE7 57 K7
Greenock Rd
MLFD/PNYW SR4 119 F4 6
Green Pk WLSD/HOW NE28 58 A7
Greenrigg Gdns
SUNDSW SR3 120 B3 6
Green's Bank STLY/ANP DH9 114 A7
Greenshields Rd
MLFD/PNYW SR4 119 F4
Greenside Av PLEE/EAS SR8 175 G3
WLSD/HOW NE28 59 H7
Greenside Crs
BW/LEM/TK/HW NE15 68 E4
Greenside Rd RYTON NE40 82 B1
Green's Pl SSH NE33 3 H4
Green St CON/LDGT DH8 108 C7
CON/LDGT DH8 123 J3 2
SEA/MUR SR7 150 E1
SUND SR1 14 E4
Green Ter SUND SR1 14 D5
The Green
BW/LEM/TK/HW NE15 67 H2
DHAM DH1 169 J6
GOS/KPK NE3 55 K7
HLH DH5 132 D6
MONK NE25 50 C3
PLEE/EAS SR8 174 B6
PONT/DH NE20 43 H1
SWCK/CAS SR5 106 A4
Green Va RYTON NE40 82 B2
Greenway ELS/FEN NE4 69 H3
WD/WHPE/BLK NE5 54 A6
Greenways CON/LDGT DH8 123 J7
The Greenway
MLFD/PNYW SR4 119 G2 2
Greenwell Cl BLAY NE21 83 J3 5
Greenwell Dr PRUD NE42 80 D1
Greenwell Pk
BDN/LAN/SAC DH7 140 C5
Greenwich Pl GATE NE8 6 D9
Greenwood LGB/KIL NE12 48 B6 7
Greenwood Av BDLGTN NE22 29 K3 1
BDN/LAN/SAC DH7 141 G5
BYK/HTN/WLK NE6 72 C2 3
HLS DH4 132 A7
Greenwood Cl
RDHAMSE DH6 173 F7 1
Greenwood Gdns
DUN/TMV NE11 86 A7 3
FELL NE10 12 D4 1
Greenwood Rd
MLFD/PNYW SR4 119 F3
Greetlands Rd
ASHBK/HED/RY SR2 120 C3
Gregson St BDN/LAN/SAC DH7 143 H5
Gregson Ter SEA/MUR SR7 135 F6
Grenada Cl WBAY NE26 50 D1 1
Grenada Dr WBAY NE26 50 D1
Grenada Pl WBAY NE26 50 D1 2
Grenfell Sq MLFD/PNYW SR4 119 F4 7
Grenville Ct PONT/DH NE20 42 C5
Grenville Dr GOS/KPK NE3 56 B1
Grenville Wy WBAY NE26 50 C2
Gresford St SSH NE33 75 G5
Gresham Cl CRAM NE23 38 C4
Gresley Rd PLEE/EAS SR8 174 B4
Greta Gdns SSH NE33 75 H3
Greta Ter MLFD/PNYW SR4 120 A1
Gretna Dr HAR/WTLS NE34 90 D2 1
Gretna Rd
BW/LEM/TK/HW NE15 69 F4
Gretton Pl LGB/HTN NE7 57 G7 1
Grey Av CRAM NE23 38 B5
Greybourne Gdns
ASHBK/HED/RY SR2 120 C4 3
Greyfriars La LGB/KIL NE12 57 G4 4
Grey Lady Wk PRUD NE42 80 D1 1
Greystead Cl
WD/WHPE/BLK NE5 54 B7
Greystead Rd MONK NE25 49 K4
Greystoke Av
ASHBK/HED/RY SR2 120 C4
JES NE2 6 C2
WICK/BNPF NE16 85 F6
Greystoke Gdns
ASHBK/HED/RY SR2 120 C3 4
JES NE2 6 C1
LWF/SPW/WRK NE9 101 H3
WICK/BNPF NE16 85 F7
Greystoke Pk GOS/KPK NE3 56 C2
Greystoke Wk
WICK/BNPF NE16 85 F6 1
Grey St CNUT NE1 5 K6
DIN/WO NE13 46 A3 2
HLS DH4 132 B6
TYNE/NSHE NE30 61 F4
WLSD/HOW NE28 72 E1
Greywood Av ELS/FEN NE4 69 J4
Grieves' Rw CRAM NE23 47 G1
Grieve St BLYTH NE24 31 F5 1
Grimsby St BLYTH NE24 35 G1
Grindon Av MLFD/PNYW SR4 119 F1 1
Grindon Cl CRAM NE23 38 B5
MONK NE25 50 C7
Grindon Ct MLFD/PNYW SR4 119 G3
Grindon Gdns MLFD/PNYW SR4 119 G3
Grindon La MLFD/PNYW SR4 119 F1
SUNDSW SR3 119 J4 1
Grindon Pk MLFD/PNYW SR4 119 G3 4
Grindon Ter MLFD/PNYW SR4 120 A1
Grinstead Cl HAR/WTLS NE34 75 K4 1
Grinstead Wy DHAM DH1 158 A4
Grisedale Gdns
LWF/SPW/WRK NE9 101 G1
Grisedale Rd PLEE/EAS SR8 175 F4 5
Grizedale WASHN NE37 102 D7
Grizedale Ct
CLDN/WHIT/ROK SR6 92 C6
Grosvenor Av JES NE2 71 F2
WICK/BNPF NE16 85 F4
Grosvenor Cl CRAM NE23 38 B5 4
Grosvenor Ct
WD/WHPE/BLK NE5 54 B7 5
Grosvenor Crs HEBB NE31 89 H1
Grosvenor Dr
CLDN/WHIT/ROK SR6 91 J3
HAR/WTLS NE34 75 K3
MONK NE25 50 E5
Grosvenor Gdns
HAR/WTLS NE34 75 K5 2
JES NE2 71 G3 2
WLSD/HOW NE28 59 J7
Grosvenor Pl JES NE2 71 F2
NSHW NE29 60 E4
Grosvenor Rd HAR/WTLS NE34 75 J3
JES NE2 71 F2
Grosvenor St SWCK/CAS SR5 105 K3
Grosvenor Wy
WD/WHPE/BLK NE5 68 B1
Grotto Gdns HAR/WTLS NE34 76 D5
Grotto Rd HAR/WTLS NE34 76 D5
Grousemoor Dr ASHGTN NE63 23 J3
Grove Av GOS/KPK NE3 56 D6 1
Grove Ct RDHAMSE DH6 173 H5
RDHAMSE DH6 179 F6
Grove Rd BDN/LAN/SAC DH7 167 G7
BW/LEM/TK/HW NE15 67 J2
LWF/SPW/WRK NE9 87 G6

Grove St *DHAM* DH1 ...... 16 B6
Grove Ter *BDN/LAN/SAC* DH7 ...... 167 K4
The Grove *ASHBK/HED/RY* SR2 ... 14 D9
 ASHBK/HED/RY SR2 ...... 121 F7
 BDN/LAN/SAC DH7 ...... 141 G4
 DHAM DH1 ...... 156 B6
 GOS/KPK NE3 ...... 56 D6
 HLH DH5 ...... 147 H2
 JES NE2 ...... 71 F1 8
 JES NE2 ...... 71 F2 11
 JRW NE32 ...... 89 K3
 LGB/KIL NE12 ...... 57 K4
 MONK NE25 ...... 50 D5
 PLEE/EAS SR8 ...... 162 B5
 PONT/DH NE20 ...... 43 F4
 ROWG NE39 ...... 97 H4
 SWCK/CAS SR5 ...... 105 F4 4
 WD/WHPE/BLK NE5 ...... 68 B2
 WICK/BNPF NE16 ...... 85 G6
Guardians Ct *PONT/DH* NE20 ... 43 H2 11
Guelder Rd *LGB/HTN* NE7 ...... 57 J7
Guernsey Rd *MLFD/PNYW* SR4 ... 119 F4
Guernsey Sq *MLFD/PNYW* SR4 ... 119 F4
Guessburn *PSHWF* NE43 ...... 79 F6
Guildford PI *BYK/HTN/WLK* NE6 ... 6 F3
Guildford St *ASHBK/HED/RY* SR2 ... 15 H9
Guillemot CI *BLYTH* NE24 ...... 35 G2 3
Guisborough Dr *NSHW* NE29 ...... 59 K2
Guisborough St
 MLFD/PNYW SR4 ...... 119 K1
Gullane *WASHN* NE37 ...... 103 F2
Gullane *LGB/HTN* NE10 ...... 88 E2
 STLY/ANP DH9 ...... 127 F1
Gully Rd *WNGT* TS28 ...... 183 K3
Gunnerton Gv *GOS/KPK* NE3 ... 55 H5 5
Gunnerton CI *CRAM* NE23 ...... 38 C4
Gunnerton PI *NSHW* NE29 ...... 60 B4 3
Gunn St *DUN/TMV* NE11 ...... 9 G8
Gut Rd *WLSD/HOW* NE28 ...... 73 H1
Guyzance Av *GOS/KPK* NE3 ... 56 A4

H

Hackworth Gdns *WYLAM* NE41 ... 65 H5
Hackworth Rd *PLEE/EAS* SR8... 174 A1
Hackworth Wy *NSHW* NE29 ...... 2 B6
Haddington Rd *MONK* NE25... 50 A2
Haddon CI *MONK* NE25 ...... 49 K4
Haddon Gn *MONK* NE25 ...... 49 K4
Haddricksmill Rd *GOS/KPK* NE3... 56 C6
Hadleigh Rd *MLFD/PNYW* SR4 ... 119 F4
Hadrian Av *CLS/BIR/GTL* DH3 ... 129 K2
Hadrian Ct *PONT/DH* NE20 ...... 52 D1
Hadrian Gdns *BLAY* NE21 ...... 84 B3
Hadrian PI
 BW/LEM/TK/HW NE15 ...... 67 F1
 LWF/SPW/WRK NE9 ...... 87 H5 3
Hadrian Rd *BLYTH* NE24 ...... 34 E4
 ELS/FEN NE4 ...... 69 J3
 JRW NE32 ...... 74 B7
 WLSD/HOW NE28 ...... 72 C2
Hadrians Ct *DUN/TMV* NE11 ... 100 J1
Hadrian St *MLFD/PNYW* SR4... 106 A6
Hadrians Wy *CON/LDGT* DH8 ... 108 E3
Hadstone PI
 WD/WHPE/BLK NE5 ...... 69 G2 8
Haggerston CI
 WD/WHPE/BLK NE5 ...... 55 F6 10
Haggerston Ct
 WD/WHPE/BLK NE5 ...... 55 F6 9
Haggerston Crs
 WD/WHPE/BLK NE5 ...... 55 F6
Haggerston Dr
 SWCK/CAS SR5 ...... 104 E5 1
Haggerston Ter *JRW* NE32 ...... 74 C7
Haggie Av *WLSD/HOW* NE28 ... 59 F7 8
Haig Av *MONK* NE25 ...... 50 D5
Haig Crs *BW/LEM/TK/HW* NE15 ... 68 E6
 DHAM DH1 ...... 17 M5
Haig Rd *BDLGTN* NE22 ...... 29 H6
Hailsham Av *LGB/KIL* NE12 ...... 57 J3
Haininghead Meadow *WASHS* NE38 ... 117 G4
Hainingwood Ter *FELL* NE10 ... 13 L4 11
Haldane St *ASHGTN* NE63 ...... 23 J1
Haldane Ter *JES* NE2 ...... 70 E3
Hale Ri *PLEE/EAS* SR8 ...... 174 E4
Halewood Av *GOS/KPK* NE3 ... 55 J6
Half Fields Rd *BLAY* NE21 ...... 83 K3
Half Moon La *GATE* NE8 ...... 5 M9 3
Half Moon St *STKFD/GP* NE62 ... 23 H5
Halfway House La
 ASHBK/HED/RY SR2 ...... 121 G3
Halidon Rd *ASHBK/HED/RY* SR2... 120 D5
Halidon Sq
 ASHBK/HED/RY SR2 ...... 120 D5 8
Halifax Rd *DUN/TMV* NE11 ...... 8 E5
Halkirk Wy *CRAM* NE23 ...... 33 C6
Hallam Rd *PLEE/EAS* SR8 ...... 174 E3 3
Hall Av *BDN/LAN/SAC* DH7...... 141 G4
 SEA/MUR SR7 ...... 134 D7
Hall CI *HLS* DH4 ...... 146 D6
Hall Dr *LGB/KIL* NE12 ...... 47 J4 8
Halleypike CI *LGB/HTN* NE7 ... 57 H7 2
Hallfield CI *BOL* NE36 ...... 90 E5
Hall Farm *DHAM* DH1 ...... 169 G4 8
Hall Farm CI *PSHWF* NE43 ...... 79 F5
Hall Farm Rd *SUNDSW* SR3 ... 133 K2
Hallfield CI *SUNDSW* SR3 ...... 134 A2
Hallfield Dr *PLEE/EAS* SR8 ...... 174 E4
Hall Gdns *BOL* NE36 ...... 90 E5
 FELL NE10 ...... 87 K5
Hallgarth La *RDHAMSE* DH6 ... 170 J1 1
Hallgarth Rd *BLAY* NE21 ...... 83 K2
Hallgarth St *DHAM* DH1 ...... 16 F6
 RDHAMSE DH6 ...... 158 C7
The Hallgarth *DHAM* DH1 ...... 16 F6
Hall Gn *BLYTH* NE24 ...... 30 D7
Halling CI *BYK/HTN/WLK* NE6 ... 7 G2
Hallington Dr *MONK* NE25 ...... 40 A5
Halliwell St *HLS* DH4...... 132 B6
Hall La *DHAM* DH1 ...... 169 G5
 HLH DH5 ...... 147 H1
 HLS DH4 ...... 146 D6
 RDHAMSE DH6 ...... 160 E6
Hall Pk *BLAY* NE21 ...... 67 J7

Hall Rd *BDN/LAN/SAC* DH7 ...... 153 J5
 CHPW NE17 ...... 95 J3
 CON/LDGT DH8 ...... 122 C6
 HEBB NE31 ...... 73 G6
 WASHN NE37 ...... 103 G5 3
Hallside Rd *BLYTH* NE24 ...... 34 D1
Hall Ter *FELL* NE10 ...... 13 M4
Hall Vw *CLDN/WHIT/ROK* SR6 ... 93 F4
Hall Wks *PLEE/EAS* SR8 ...... 162 B6
Hallwood CI *BDLGTN* NE22 ...... 28 A6
Halstead Sq *MLFD/PNYW* SR4 ... 119 H1
Halterburn CI *GOS/KPK* NE3 ... 56 B6
Halton CI *PSHWF* NE43 ...... 79 C6
Halton Rd *DHAM* DH1 ...... 156 E4 8
Hamar CI *NSHW* NE29 ...... 60 A6
Hambard Wy *WASHS* NE38 ...... 117 F2
Hambledon Av
 TYNE/NSHE NE30 ...... 50 E6
Hambledon CI *BOLCOL* NE35 ... 90 C4 3
Hambledon Gdns *LGB/HTN* NE7 ... 57 G7
Hambledon PI *PLEE/EAS* SR8 ... 174 B5 6
Hambledon St *BLYTH* NE24 ...... 31 F6 6
Hambleton Ct *ASHGTN* NE63 ... 24 B4 6
Hambleton Dr *SEA/MUR* SR7 ... 135 H7 2
Hambleton Rd *WASHS* NE38 ... 116 D3
Hamilton Crs *ELS/FEN* NE4 ...... 4 E5
 NSHW NE29 ...... 60 A2
Hamilton Dr *WBAY* NE26 ...... 50 D1
Hamilton Rw
 BDN/LAN/SAC DH7 ...... 164 E4
Hamilton St *PLEE/EAS* SR8 ... 175 G3 8
Hamilton Ter
 BDN/LAN/SAC DH7 ...... 143 G2
 BOL NE36 ...... 90 E5 9
Hammer Square Bank
 STLY/ANP DH9 ...... 113 K5
Hampden Rd
 CLDN/WHIT/ROK SR6 ...... 106 E3
Hampden St *SSH* NE33 ...... 75 G3 8
Hampshire Ct *ELS/FEN* NE4 ...... 9 K2
Hampshire PI *WASHN* NE37 ... 103 F4 8
Hampshire Rd *DHAM* DH1 ...... 157 K6
Hampshire Wy
 HAR/WTLS NE34 ...... 76 C4 8
Hampstead CI *BLYTH* NE24 ...... 34 E4
Hampstead Rd *ELS/FEN* NE4 ... 69 J6
 MLFD/PNYW SR4 ...... 119 H2
Hampstead Sq
 MLFD/PNYW SR4 ...... 119 G2 5
Hampton CI *CRAM* NE23 ...... 38 E1 6
Hampton Ct *CLS/BIR/GTL* DH3 ... 115 K7
Hampton Dr *FELL* NE10 ...... 12 A7
Hampton Rd *TYNE/NSHE* NE30 ... 50 E7
Hamsteels Bank
 BDN/LAN/SAC DH7 ...... 152 D3
Hamsteels La
 BDN/LAN/SAC DH7 ...... 152 C3
 BDN/LAN/SAC DH7 ...... 153 G4
Hamsterley CI
 CLS/BIR/GTL DH3 ...... 145 J1 8
Hamsterley Crs
 BW/LEM/TK/HW NE15 ...... 67 K4 3
 DHAM DH1 ...... 156 B3
 LWF/SPW/WRK NE9 ...... 101 J2
Hamsterley Dr *LGB/KIL* NE12 ... 47 J5
Hamsterley Gdns
 STLY/ANP DH9 ...... 125 H3
Hanby Gdns *SUNDSW* SR3 ... 120 A3 8
Hancock St *CNUT* NE1 ...... 5 K3
 SSH NE33 ...... 3 K9
Handel St *MLFD/PNYW* SR4 ... 106 A6
Handley Cross *CON/LDGT* DH8 ... 109 J5
Handley St *PLEE/EAS* SR8 ...... 175 G3 8
Handy Dr *DUN/TMV* NE11 ...... 8 D4
Hangingstone La
 STLY/ANP DH9 ...... 124 E5
Hangmans La *HLH* DH5 ...... 133 J4
Hanlon Ct *JRW* NE32 ...... 73 H4
Hannington St
 BYK/HTN/WLK NE6 ...... 6 C5
Hanover Ct *CRAM* NE23 ...... 38 C7 1
Hanover Dr *BLAY* NE21 ...... 83 J4
Hanover PI *CRAM* NE23 ...... 33 G5 8
 MLFD/PNYW SR4 ...... 14 B1
Hanover St *CNUT* NE1 ...... 5 K9
Harbottle Av *GOS/KPK* NE3 ... 56 A4
 SMOOR NE27 ...... 49 H7
Harbottle Ct *BYK/HTN/WLK* NE6 ... 7 H8
Harbottle Crs *JRW* NE32 ...... 89 K2
Harbour Dr *SSH* NE33 ...... 3 K3
The Harbour *HLS* DH4 ...... 131 K1 8
Harbour Vw
 CLDN/WHIT/ROK SR6 ...... 107 F4
 SSH NE33 ...... 3 H3
Harbour Wk *SEA/MUR* SR7 ... 135 J7
Harcourt Rd
 ASHBK/HED/RY SR2 ...... 120 D5 8
Harcourt St
 LWF/SPW/WRK NE9 ...... 87 G7 3
Hardgate Rd
 ASHBK/HED/RY SR2 ...... 120 E5 8
Hardie Av *WICK/BNPF* NE16 ... 84 E4
Hardie Dr *BOL* NE36 ...... 90 E5
Hardwick Ct *GATE* NE8 ...... 11 K5 9
Hardwick PI *GOS/KPK* NE3 ... 56 A7 8
Hardwick Ri
 CLDN/WHIT/ROK SR6 ...... 15 H1 8
Hardwick St *PLEE/EAS* SR8 ... 175 H4
 RHTLP TS27...... 175 K7
Hardyards Ct *HAR/WTLS* NE34... 75 C6 8
Hardy Av *HAR/WTLS* NE34 ...... 91 F1
Hardy Gv *WLSD/HOW* NE28 ... 58 C5
Hardy Sq *SWCK/CAS* SR5 ...... 106 A2
Hardy St *SEA/MUR* SR7 ...... 150 E1 8
Harebell Rd
 LWF/SPW/WRK NE9 ...... 101 J1
Harehills Av *WD/WHPE/BLK* NE5... 55 H7
Harelaw Dr *ASHGTN* NE63 ...... 23 H4
Harelaw Gdns *STLY/ANP* DH9 ... 125 F1
Harelaw Gv
 WD/WHPE/BLK NE5 ...... 68 B2 4
Hareside *CRAM* NE23 ...... 38 B3
Harewood CI *WICK/BNPF* NE16 ... 98 E1
Harewood Crs *MONK* NE25 ... 49 K5 3
Harewood Gdns *MPTH* NE61 ... 21 J1 8

Harewood Rd *GOS/KPK* NE3... 56 C4
Hareydene *WD/WHPE/BLK* NE5... 54 D5
Hargill Dr *WASHS* NE38 ...... 116 C5
Hargrave Ct *BLYTH* NE24 ...... 34 E1 8
Harland Wy *WASHS* NE38 ...... 117 F1
Harle CI *WD/WHPE/BLK* NE5... 68 C2 8
Harleston Wy *FELL* NE10 ...... 88 A4
Harle Rd *SMOOR* NE27 ...... 49 F5
Harle St *WLSD/HOW* NE28 ...... 72 D1 8
Harley Ter *GOS/KPK* NE3 ...... 56 D5
 SMOOR NE27 ...... 49 F6
Harlow Av *GOS/KPK* NE3 ...... 55 K3
Harlow Green La
 LWF/SPW/WRK NE9 ...... 101 G3
Harlow PI *LGB/HTN* NE7 ...... 57 H7
Harnham Av *NSHW* NE29 ...... 60 A5
Harnham Gdns
 WD/WHPE/BLK NE5 ...... 69 G3
Harnham Gv *CRAM* NE23 ...... 38 B3
Harold St *JRW* NE32 ...... 74 A4
Harold Wilson Dr *RHTLP* TS27 ... 185 G2
Harper Bglws
 RDHAMSE DH6 ...... 182 D2 8
Harperley St *SUNDSW* SR3 ... 120 B4
Harperley La *STLY/ANP* DH9 ... 111 J5
Harperley Rd *STLY/ANP* DH9 ... 125 H2
Harper St *BLYTH* NE24 ...... 31 F6
Harras Bank *CLS/BIR/GTL* DH3 ... 115 J3
Harriet St *BLAY* NE21 ...... 84 A2
 BYK/HTN/WLK NE6 ...... 7 J5
Harrington St
 WLSD/HOW NE28 ...... 72 D1 8
Harriot Dr *LGB/KIL* NE12 ...... 47 G7
Harrison CI *PLEE/EAS* SR8 ...... 175 F5
Harrison Gdns *GATE* NE8 ...... 86 D5 8
Harrison Garth
 RDHAMSE DH6 ...... 158 C7 8
Harrison PI *JES* NE2 ...... 5 M3
Harrison Rd *WLSD/HOW* NE28 ... 59 J7
Harrogate St
 ASHBK/HED/RY SR2 ...... 15 G7
Harrogate Ter *SEA/MUR* SR7 ... 149 H5 8
Harrow Gdns *DIN/WO* NE13 ... 46 C4
Harrow Sq *MLFD/PNYW* SR4 ... 119 H1
Harrow St *GOS/KPK* NE3 ...... 55 H5
Hartburn CI *FELL* NE10 ...... 88 C7
Hartburn Dr *WD/WHPE/BLK* NE5... 54 B7
Hartburn PI *ELS/FEN* NE4 ...... 4 A7
Hartburn Rd *TYNE/NSHE* NE30 ... 60 D1
Hartburn Wk *GOS/KPK* NE3 ... 55 H5
Hartford Bank *CRAM* NE23 ...... 32 C3
Hartford Crs *BDLGTN* NE22 ...... 28 E6
Hartford Crs *ASHGTN* NE63 ...... 23 K3
Hartford Dr *BDLGTN* NE22 ...... 28 E6
Hartford Rd *BDLGTN* NE22 ...... 32 C2
 GOS/KPK NE3 ...... 56 D3
 HAR/WTLS NE34 ...... 74 E6
 MLFD/PNYW SR4 ...... 119 H1
Harthope Av *SWCK/CAS* SR5 ... 105 G2 5
Harthope CI *WASHS* NE38 ...... 116 B6
Harthope Dr *NSHW* NE29 ...... 60 B2 8
Hartington Rd *TYNE/NSHE* NE30... 60 E1
Hartington St
 CLDN/WHIT/ROK SR6 ...... 106 E3
 CON/LDGT DH8 ...... 123 F4
 ELS/FEN NE4 ...... 4 C7
 GATE NE8 ...... 11 G6
Hartington Ter *SSH* NE33 ...... 75 H4
Hartlands *BDLGTN* NE22 ...... 28 E6
Hartleigh PI *BLYTH* NE24 ...... 30 D7 2
Hartlepool St *RDHAMSE* DH6 ... 172 C6
Hartley Av *WBAY* NE26 ...... 50 C4
Hartleyburn Av *HEBB* NE31 ... 89 F1 1
Hartley La *MONK* NE25 ...... 49 K3
Hartley St *MONK* NE25 ...... 39 K5
 SUND SR1 ...... 15 J3
Hartley Ter *BLYTH* NE24 ...... 34 E1
Hartoft CI *HLS* DH4 ...... 132 B4 8
Harton Gv *HAR/WTLS* NE34 ...... 75 J4
Harton House Rd
 HAR/WTLS NE34 ...... 75 K4
Harton House Rd East
 HAR/WTLS NE34 ...... 76 A4
Harton La *HAR/WTLS* NE34 ...... 75 C6
Harton Ri *HAR/WTLS* NE34 ...... 75 K4
Hartside *BW/LEM/TK/HW* NE15 ... 68 A4
 CLS/BIR/GTL DH3 ...... 115 K5
Hartside Crs *BLAY* NE21 ...... 83 J5
 CRAM NE23 ...... 33 G5 8
 SMOOR NE27 ...... 49 F5
Hartside Gdns *HLH* DH5...... 148 B7
 JES NE2 ...... 71 F2 8
Hartside PI *GOS/KPK* NE3 ...... 56 C1 8
Hartside Vw
 BDN/LAN/SAC DH7 ...... 155 F5 8
 DHAM DH1 ...... 156 B2
Hart Sq *MLFD/PNYW* SR4 ...... 119 H1
Hart Ter *CLDN/WHIT/ROK* SR6 ... 93 F6 8
Harvard Rd *DIN/WO* NE13 ...... 46 A1
Harvest CI *SUNDSW* SR3 ...... 133 K2 8
Harvey CI *ASHGTN* NE63 ...... 24 C2
 PLEE/EAS SR8...... 174 E3 8
 WASHS NE38 ...... 116 B1
Harvey Combe *LGB/KIL* NE12 ... 47 H6
Harvey Crs *FELL* NE10 ...... 13 M8
Harwick Ct *STLY/ANP* DH9 ...... 127 C1
Harwood Ct *CRAM* NE23 ...... 38 B3
 WASHS NE38 ...... 116 C5 1
Harwood Dr *LGB/KIL* NE12 ...... 48 B6
Hascombe CI *MONK* NE25 ...... 50 B3
Haslemere Dr *SUNDSW* SR3 ... 120 A3 8
Hassop Wy *BDLGTN* NE22 ...... 29 F4
Hastings Av *DHAM* DH1 ...... 168 B3
 GOS/KPK NE3 ...... 55 H3
 LGB/KIL NE12 ...... 57 K3 8
 WBAY NE26 ...... 40 E1 8
Hastings Ct *BDLGTN* NE22 ...... 29 J4
 CRAM NE23 ...... 38 D3

Harewood Rd *GOS/KPK* NE3... 56 C4
SUNDSW SR3 ...... 120 A3 8
Hastings Ter
 ASHBK/HED/RY SR2 ...... 121 F3
 CRAM NE23 ...... 33 K5
 MONK NE25 ...... 40 A1
Haswell CI *FELL* NE10 ...... 89 F5
Haswell Gdns *TYNE/NSHE* NE30... 60 E4
Hatfield CI *DHAM* DH1 ...... 156 B3
Hatfield Dr *CRAM* NE23 ...... 39 G6
Hatfield Gdns *MONK* NE25 ...... 49 K5
 SUNDSW SR3 ...... 120 A3 8
Hathaway Gdns
 SUNDSW SR3 ...... 120 A3 8
Hatherton Av *TYNE/NSHE* NE30... 51 F6
Hathery La *BLYTH* NE24 ...... 33 K4
Haugh La *RYTON* NE40 ...... 67 D1 8
The Haughs *PRUD* NE42 ...... 80 D1 8
Haughton Ct *MLFD/PNYW* SR4 ... 14 C1
 WD/WHPE/BLK NE5 ...... 68 C2
Haughton Ter *BLYTH* NE24 ...... 31 G7
Hautmont Rd *HEBB* NE31 ...... 73 H7
Hauxley CI *LGB/KIL* NE12 ...... 47 K4 8
Hauxley Dr *CLSW/PEL* DH2 ... 129 F7
 CRAM NE23 ...... 33 G5
 GOS/KPK NE3 ...... 55 J3
Hawes Av *CLSW/PEL* DH2 ... 129 J6
Hawes Ct *CLDN/WHIT/ROK* SR6 ... 92 C7
Hawes Rd *PLEE/EAS* SR8 ...... 174 E3
Haweswater CI
 HAR/WTLS NE34 ...... 75 H5 8
Haweswater Crs *NWBGN* NE64 ... 24 E1
Hawick St *STLY/ANP* DH9 ...... 127 F1
Hawick Crs *BYK/HTN/WLK* NE6 ... 6 F8
Hawkey's La *NSHW* NE29 ...... 2 B1
Hawkhill CI *CLSW/PEL* DH2 ... 129 C7
Hawkhurst *WASHS* NE38 ...... 117 C4 1
Hawkins St *SUNDSW* SR3 ...... 133 K1 8
Hawksbury *WICK/BNPF* NE16 ... 84 E5 8
Hawkshead Ct *DIN/WO* NE13 ... 55 H3 8
Hawkshead PI
 LWF/SPW/WRK NE9 ...... 87 H7
Hawksley *WD/WHPE/BLK* NE5 ... 68 D1
Hawksmoor CI *ASHGTN* NE63 ... 23 J4
Hawks Rd *GATE* NE8 ...... 6 B9
Hawks St *GATE* NE8 ...... 6 B9
Hawkwell Ri
 BW/LEM/TK/HW NE15 ...... 67 F2 5
Hawksker CI *SUNDSW* SR3 ... 120 C7 8
Hawthorn Av *DIN/WO* NE13 ... 46 A4
 SUNDSW SR3 ...... 120 B6
Hawthorn Ct *CLSW/PEL* DH2 ... 144 A5
 WICK/BNPF NE16 ...... 99 F1
Hawthorn Cottages
 RDHAMSE DH6 ...... 161 G2
Hawthorn Crs *DHAM* DH1 ...... 17 M1
Hawthorn Dr *DUN/TMV* NE11 ... 9 G8
 JRW NE32 ...... 90 B2
Hawthorne Av *HAR/WTLS* NE34... 75 K7 8
 HEBB NE31 ...... 73 H5
Hawthorne CI
 BDN/LAN/SAC DH7 ...... 154 B2
 SMOOR NE27 ...... 49 F5
Hawthorne Gdns *GOS/KPK* NE3... 55 K6
 NSHW NE29 ...... 60 D3 8
 WBAY NE26 ...... 50 D4
Hawthorn Gdns *GOS/KPK* NE3... 55 K6
 NSHW NE29 ...... 60 D3 8
 WBAY NE26 ...... 50 D4
Hawthorn Pk
 BDN/LAN/SAC DH7 ...... 167 G6 8
Hawthorn Rd *ELS/FEN* NE4 ...... 9 K1
 LGB/KIL NE12 ...... 47 J5 8
Hawthorn Rd West
 GOS/KPK NE3 ...... 56 C6
The Hawthorns *BOL* NE36 ...... 91 H5
Hawthorn St *CON/LDGT* DH8 ... 122 D3
 JRW NE32 ...... 73 J4 8
 MLFD/PNYW SR4 ...... 106 A7
 PLEE/EAS SR8...... 162 E4
Hawthorn Ter
 CLDN/WHIT/ROK SR6 ...... 92 E6 8
 CON/LDGT DH8 ...... 122 D3
 DHAM DH1 ...... 16 A4
 ELS/FEN NE4 ...... 4 D8
Hawthorn Vls *CRAM* NE23 ...... 38 D2
Hawthorn Wy *PONT/DH* NE20 ... 43 F6
Haydock Dr *FELL* NE10 ...... 88 D5
Haydon *WASHS* NE38 ...... 117 G5
Haydon Rd *ASHGTN* NE63 ...... 23 K3 8
Haydon Sq *MLFD/PNYW* SR4 ... 119 H1
Hayes Wk *DIN/WO* NE13 ...... 46 B3
Hayfield La *WICK/BNPF* NE16... 85 F6

Hayhole Rd *NSHW* NE29 ...... 74 C1
Hayleazes Rd
 WD/WHPE/BLK NE5 ...... 68 A4
The Hayricks *STLY/ANP* DH9 ... 112 B2
Hay St *SWCK/CAS* SR5 ...... 14 D1
Hayton Av *HAR/WTLS* NE34 ...... 76 A6
Hayton CI *CRAM* NE23 ...... 38 D1
Hayton Rd *TYNE/NSHE* NE30 ... 60 D1
Hazard La *HLH* DH5 ...... 147 H5
Hazel Av *BDN/LAN/SAC* DH7 ... 167 F7
 NSHW NE29 ...... 60 D3
 RDHAMSE DH6 ...... 181 G4
 SUNDSW SR3 ...... 120 B6 8
Hazeldene *MONK* NE25 ...... 50 B4
Hazeldene Av *GOS/KPK* NE3 ... 55 G6
Hazeldene Ct *TYNE/NSHE* NE30... 61 G3
Hazel Dr *RHTLP* TS27 ...... 185 H2
Hazeley Gv *GOS/KPK* NE3 ...... 55 H5 8
Hazeley Wy *GOS/KPK* NE3 ...... 55 H5 8
Hazel Gv *CLSW/PEL* DH2 ...... 129 C2
Hazelgrove *FELL* NE10 ...... 88 D5
Hazel Gv *HAR/WTLS* NE34 ...... 75 K7
 LGB/KIL NE12 ...... 47 H7
Hazel Leigh *CLS/BIR/GTL* DH3 ... 145 H1
Hazelmere Av *BDLGTN* NE22 ... 28 E5
Hazelmere Crs *CRAM* NE23 ...... 33 J7
Hazelmere Dene *CRAM* NE23 ... 39 F7 2
Hazelmoor *HEBB* NE31 ...... 73 F4 3
 GATE NE8 ...... 10 A7
Hazel St *JRW* NE32 ...... 73 J4
Hazel Ter *RDHAMSE* DH6 ...... 173 H4
 STLY/ANP DH9 ...... 125 F4
Hazelwood *LGB/KIL* NE12 ...... 48 B6 8
Hazelwood Av *JES* NE2 ...... 70 E1
 NWBGN NE64 ...... 19 F7 3
 SWCK/CAS SR5 ...... 105 K3
Hazelwood CI
 LWF/SPW/WRK NE9 ...... 101 K3
Hazelwood Ct
 BDN/LAN/SAC DH7 ...... 154 B3 8
Hazelwood Ter
 WLSD/HOW NE28 ...... 73 J1
Hazledine Ter
 MLFD/PNYW SR4 ...... 105 K7 3
Hazlitt Av *HAR/WTLS* NE34 ...... 91 F1
Hazlitt PI *CRAM* NE23 ...... 39 H7 8
Headlam St *BYK/HTN/WLK* NE6 ... 7 G5
Headlam Vw *WLSD/HOW* NE28 ... 73 J1
Healey Dr *SUNDSW* SR3 ...... 120 B4
Healeyfield La *CON/LDGT* DH8 ... 136 A5
Heartsbourne Dr
 HAR/WTLS NE34 ...... 91 K1 8
Heath CI *DUN/TMV* NE11 ...... 9 M9
 PLEE/EAS SR8...... 174 E4
Heath Crs *BW/LEM/TK/HW* NE15... 68 E7
Heathdale Gdns *LGB/HTN* NE7 ... 57 H7
Heather CI
 CLDN/WHIT/ROK SR6 ...... 92 A2 8
Heatherdale Crs *DHAM* DH1 ... 158 A6
Heather Dr *HLH* DH5 ...... 147 K3
Heather Gv *FELL* NE10 ...... 11 L3
Heather Lea *STLY/ANP* DH9 ... 111 G4 8
Heatherlea Gdns
 SUNDSW SR3 ...... 120 B3 7
Heatherlee Gdns
 STKFD/GP NE62 ...... 23 G5 8
Heather PI *ELS/FEN* NE4 ...... 69 J3
 RYTON NE40 ...... 66 C7
Heatherslaw Rd
 WD/WHPE/BLK NE5 ...... 69 G3
Heather Wy *STLY/ANP* DH9 ... 126 B1
Heatherwell Gn *FELL* NE10 ... 12 A9
Heathery La *GOS/KPK* NE3 ... 56 E3
Heathfield *ASHBK/HED/RY* SR2 ... 120 C4
 MPTH NE61 ...... 20 E7
Heathfield Crs
 WD/WHPE/BLK NE5 ...... 55 H7
Heathfield Gdns *RYTON* NE40 ... 82 C3
Heathfield PI *GOS/KPK* NE3 ... 56 D1 8
Heathfield Rd
 LWF/SPW/WRK NE9 ...... 87 F6
Heath Gra *HLH* DH5 ...... 132 C6
Heathmeads *CLSW/PEL* DH2 ... 128 C1
Heath Sq *MLFD/PNYW* SR4 ... 119 J1
Heathway *JRW* NE32 ...... 90 A2
 SEA/MUR SR7 ...... 150 D3
Heathways *DHAM* DH1 ...... 169 J5
Heathwell Gdns
 WICK/BNPF NE16 ...... 85 F4 8
Heathwell Rd
 BW/LEM/TK/HW NE15 ...... 68 D4
Heathwood Av
 WICK/BNPF NE16 ...... 84 E5 8
Heaton Gdns *HAR/WTLS* NE34... 91 G2
Heaton Hall Rd
 BYK/HTN/WLK NE6 ...... 6 E2
Heaton Park Rd
 BYK/HTN/WLK NE6 ...... 6 E3
Heaton Park Vw
 BYK/HTN/WLK NE6 ...... 6 E2
Heaton PI *BYK/HTN/WLK* NE6 ... 6 F3
Heaton Rd *BYK/HTN/WLK* NE6 ... 6 E3
Heaton Ter *BYK/HTN/WLK* NE6 ... 6 D4
 NSHW NE29 ...... 60 C4
Heaviside PI *DHAM* DH1 ...... 17 J2
Heber St *ELS/FEN* NE4 ...... 5 G6
Hebron Av *MPTH* NE61 ...... 21 J1
Hebron PI *ASHGTN* NE63 ...... 24 A2
Hebron Wy *CRAM* NE23 ...... 38 B3
Hector St *SMOOR* NE27 ...... 49 H5
Heddon Banks
 BW/LEM/TK/HW NE15 ...... 66 A2
Heddon Ct *GOS/KPK* NE3 ...... 56 A4 8
Heddon Vw *BLAY* NE21 ...... 83 K2
Heddon Wy *HAR/WTLS* NE34 ... 75 F5
Hedgefield Gv *BLYTH* NE24 ...... 34 E4
Hedgefield Vw *CRAM* NE23 ...... 38 B7
Hedgehope Rd
 WD/WHPE/BLK NE5 ...... 54 E6
Hedgelea *RYTON* NE40 ...... 66 D6
Hedgelea Rd *HLH* DH5 ...... 147 F5
Hedgeley Rd *HEBB* NE31 ...... 73 G5
 NSHW NE29 ...... 60 B3 8
 WD/WHPE/BLK NE5 ...... 68 C3 8
Hedgeley Ter
 BYK/HTN/WLK NE6 ...... 72 B5 8

Hedgerow Ms ASHGTN NE63 ..... 23 H3 ⑥
Hedley Ct BDN/LAN/SAC DH7 ..... 155 F5
Hedleyhill La
  BDN/LAN/SAC DH7 ..... 164 A1
Hedley Pl WLSD/HOW NE28 ..... 72 D2 ⑤
Hedley Rd MONK NE25 ..... 40 B6
  NSHW NE29 ..... 2 B7
  WYLAM NE41 ..... 65 H5
Hedley St GATE NE8 ..... 10 C8
  GOS/KPK NE3 ..... 56 C5
  SSH NE33 ..... 3 H5
Hedley Ter
  ASHBK/HED/RY SR2 ..... 135 G1 ③
  GOS/KPK NE3 ..... 56 C4
Hedworth Av HAR/WTLS NE34 ... 74 E7 ⑤
Hedworth La BOLCOL NE35 ..... 90 B3
  JRW NE32 ..... 90 B2
Hedworth Ter SUND SR1 ..... 15 H5
Heighley St
  BW/LEM/TK/HW NE15 ..... 68 D6
Helen St BLAY NE21 ..... 83 J2
  CLDN/WHIT/ROK SR6 ..... 106 E1
Helford Rd PLEE/EAS SR8 ..... 174 D6
Helmdon WASHN NE37 ..... 103 C1
Helmsdale Av MLFD/PNYW NE10 ... 12 C6 ③
Helmsdale Rd MLFD/PNYW NE4 ... 119 H1
Helmsley Cl HLS DH4 ..... 131 J1
Helmsley Ct SWCK/CAS SR5 ..... 105 J2
Helmsley Dr WLSD/HOW NE28 ..... 73 H1
Helmsley Rd DHAM DH1 ..... 156 D2
  JES NE2 ..... 6 B3
Helston Ct
  BW/LEM/TK/HW NE15 ..... 67 K4 ⑥
Helvellyn Av WASHS NE38 ..... 116 C3
Helvellyn Rd
  ASHBK/HED/RY SR2 ..... 120 D5
Hemlington Cl
  ASHBK/HED/RY SR2 ..... 135 F1 ③
Hemmel Cts
  BDN/LAN/SAC DH7 ..... 167 H5 ②
Hemming St
  ASHBK/HED/RY SR2 ..... 121 F4 ③
Hemsley Rd HAR/WTLS NE34 ..... 75 K2
  WICK/BNPF NE16 ..... 84 E4 ③
Henderson Gdns FELL NE10 ..... 13 L9
Henderson Rd HAR/WTLS NE34 ... 74 D6
  MLFD/PNYW NE4 ..... 119 K1
  WLSD/HOW NE28 ..... 58 D7 ⑥
Hendersyde Cl
  WD/WHPE/BLK NE5 ..... 55 F7 ⑥
Hendon Burn Av
  ASHBK/HED/RY SR2 ..... 15 H8
Hendon Burn Av West
  ASHBK/HED/RY SR2 ..... 15 H9 ③
Hendon Cl NSHW NE29 ..... 2 D6 ⑥
Hendon Gdns JRW NE32 ..... 90 B2
Hendon Rd LWF/SPW/WRK NE9 ... 11 L8
  SUND SR1 ..... 15 H4
Hendon Rd East SUND SR1 ..... 15 K5
Hendon St SUND SR1 ..... 15 J6
Hendon Valley Rd
  ASHBK/HED/RY SR2 ..... 15 G8
Henley Av CLSW/PEL DH2 ..... 128 C4
Henley Cl CRAM NE23 ..... 38 E1
Henley Gdns WLSD/HOW NE28 ... 58 K6 ③
Henley Rd MLFD/PNYW NE4 ..... 119 H1
  TYNE/NSHE NE30 ..... 61 F1
Henley Wy BOLCOL NE35 ..... 90 C4
Henlow Rd
  BW/LEM/TK/HW NE15 ..... 68 A4 ③
Henry Nelson St SSH NE33 ..... 3 K5
Henry Sq JES NE2 ..... 6 A5 ③
Henry St CON/LDGT DH8 ..... 122 E4 ③
  GOS/KPK NE3 ..... 56 C5
  HLH DH5 ..... 132 C6
  NSHW NE29 ..... 2 C4 ⑤
  SEA/MUR SR7 ..... 135 K7 ②
  SSH NE33 ..... 3 J4
Henry St East
  ASHBK/HED/RY SR2 ..... 15 J6
Hensby Ct
  WD/WHPE/BLK NE5 ..... 55 F6 ⑥
Henshaw Ct ASHGTN NE63 ..... 23 H3 ③
Henshaw Gv MONK NE25 ..... 40 C6
Henshaw Pl WD/WHPE/BLK NE5.. 68 C4 ③
Henshelwood Ter JES NE2 ..... 70 E2 ③
Henson Cl WASHS NE38 ..... 117 F2
Hepburn Gdns FELL NE10 ..... 12 A5
Hepburn Gv SWCK/CAS SR5 ..... 104 D4 ③
Hepple Ct BLYTH NE24 ..... 34 E1 ③
Hepple Rd NWBGN NE64 ..... 24 E2 ②
Hepple Wy GOS/KPK NE3 ..... 56 A4 ③
Hepscott Dr MONK NE25 ..... 50 B3
Hepscott Ter HAR/WTLS NE34 ... 75 H4
Herbert St CON/LDGT DH8 ..... 123 F4 ③
  GATE NE8 ..... 11 K5
Herbert Ter SEA/MUR SR7 ..... 150 E1
Herd Cl BLAY NE21 ..... 83 J3 ③
Herd House La BLAY NE21 ..... 83 H2
Herdinghill WASHN NE37 ..... 102 B7
Herdlaw CRAM NE23 ..... 38 B2
Hereford Ct
  ASHBK/HED/RY SR2 ..... 120 D5 ③
  DIN/WO NE13 ..... 45 G4
Hereford Rd
  ASHBK/HED/RY SR2 ..... 120 D5
Herefordshire Dr DHAM DH1 .... 157 K6
Hereford Sq
  ASHBK/HED/RY SR2 ..... 120 D5 ②
Hermiston MONK NE25 ..... 50 C4
Heron Cl ASHGTN NE63 ..... 24 A4
  BLYTH NE24 ..... 35 G4
  WASHS NE38 ..... 116 C4
Heron Dr SSH NE33 ..... 3 G5
Heron Pl LGB/KIL NE12 ..... 57 G3 ②
Herrick St WD/WHPE/BLK NE5 ... 54 E7
Herring Gull Cl BLYTH NE24 ..... 35 G4
Herrington Rd HLS DH4 ..... 132 D1
  SUNDSW SR3 ..... 119 F7
Hersham Cl DIN/WO NE13 ..... 55 H2 ③
  DIN/WO NE13 ..... 55 G2 ③
  GOS/KPK NE3 ..... 55 H5
Hertford LWF/SPW/WRK NE9 ... 101 F3 ③
Hertford Av HAR/WTLS NE34 ... 76 B4
Hertford Cl MONK NE25 ..... 50 A3
Hertford Crs HLH DH5 ..... 147 J4

Hertford Gv CRAM NE23 ..... 38 D1
Herton Cl PLEE/EAS SR8 ..... 174 D3
Hesket Ct GOS/KPK NE3 ..... 55 J3 ②
Hesleden Rd RHTLP TS27 ..... 185 H1
Hesleyside ASHGTN NE63 ..... 24 B3 ②
Hesleyside Dr
  WD/WHPE/BLK NE5 ..... 69 F3
Hesleyside Rd MONK NE25 ..... 49 K4
Hessewelle Crs RDHAMSE DH6... 172 C1 ③
Hester Av MONK NE25 ..... 40 A2
Hett La RDHAMSE DH6 ..... 178 C3
Hetton Rd HLH DH5 ..... 147 H1
Heugh Hl LWF/SPW/WRK NE9 ... 102 C3
Hewison Pl
  LWF/SPW/WRK NE9 ..... 87 H6 ③
Heworth Burn Crs FELL NE10 ... 12 F7
Heworth Gv WASHN NE37 ..... 102 E5 ③
Heworth Rd WASHN NE37 ..... 103 F3
Heworth Wy FELL NE10 ..... 13 J7
Hewley Crs
  BW/LEM/TK/HW NE15 ..... 67 F2
Hewson Pl
  LWF/SPW/WRK NE9 ..... 87 H6 ③
Hexham WASHS NE38 ..... 116 B2 ③
Hexham Av BYK/HTN/WLK NE6 .. 72 B6
  CRAM NE23 ..... 38 E1
  HEBB NE31 ..... 89 G2
Hexham Cl NSHW NE29 ..... 60 A3 ③
Hexham Ct DUN/TMV NE11 ..... 85 K6 ③
Hexham Dr STLY/ANP DH9 ..... 125 H2
Hexham Old Rd RYTON NE40 ... 66 E6
Hexham Rd
  BW/LEM/TK/HW NE15 ..... 65 K1
  MLFD/PNYW NE4 ..... 119 H1
  WICK/BNPF NE16 ..... 84 E3
Hextol Gdns
  BW/LEM/TK/HW NE15 ..... 68 D4 ③
Heybrook Av NSHW NE29 ..... 60 D2
Heyburn Gdns
  BW/LEM/TK/HW NE15 ..... 69 H6
Hibernian Rd JRW NE32 ..... 73 K4 ③
Hibernia Rd
  BYK/HTN/WLK NE6 ..... 72 C7 ③
Hickling Ct WD/WHPE/BLK NE5.. 55 F6
Hickstead Cl
  WLSD/HOW NE28 ..... 59 G3 ③
Hickstead Gv CRAM NE23 ..... 38 E1
Hiddleston Av LGB/HTN NE7 ... 57 H5
Higgins Ter SUNDSW SR3 ..... 120 B7
Higham Pl CNUT NE1 ..... 5 L5 ③
High Back Cl JRW NE32 ..... 73 J7
High Barnes Ter
  MLFD/PNYW SR4 ..... 120 A1 ③
High Br CNUT NE1 ..... 5 K7
Highbury FELL NE10 ..... 12 E8
  MONK NE25 ..... 50 C4 ③
Highbury Av
  LWF/SPW/WRK NE9 ..... 102 C3
Highbury Cl
  LWF/SPW/WRK NE9 ..... 102 C3
High Carr Cl DHAM DH1 ..... 156 C4
High Chare CLS/BIR/GTL DH3 .... 129 J4
Highcliffe Gdns GATE NE8 ..... 11 K7
High Cl PRUD NE42 ..... 81 F1 ③
High Cft CLDN/WHIT/ROK SR6 ... 93 F3
  WASHN NE37 ..... 102 D4
High Croft Cl HEBB NE31 ..... 73 F7 ③
Highcroft Dr
  CLDN/WHIT/ROK SR6 ..... 92 E3 ③
Highcross Rd TYNE/NSHE NE30 .. 50 E6
High Dene GATE NE8 ..... 71 G2
Highfield BDN/LAN/SAC DH7 ... 143 H5
  PRUD NE42 ..... 80 C2
  WICK/BNPF NE16 ..... 99 F7
Highfield Cl
  WD/WHPE/BLK NE5 ..... 54 D7 ③
Highfield Ct FELL NE10 ..... 88 A5 ③
Highfield Crs CLS/BIR/GTL DH3 .. 129 J2
Highfield Dr ASHGTN NE63 ..... 24 B3
  HAR/WTLS NE34 ..... 75 K3
  HLS DH4 ..... 131 K7
Highfield Gra HLS DH4 ..... 146 E1 ③
Highfield La PRUD NE42 ..... 80 C3
Highfield Pl DIN/WO NE13 ..... 46 A4 ③
Highfield Ri CLS/BIR/GTL DH3 ... 129 J3
Highfield Rd GATE NE8 ..... 11 K6
  HAR/WTLS NE34 ..... 75 K3
  HLS DH4 ..... 131 J1
  ROWG NE39 ..... 96 E4
  WD/WHPE/BLK NE5 ..... 68 D1
Highfield Ter
  BYK/HTN/WLK NE6 ..... 72 C7
High Flatworth NSHW NE29 ..... 59 K5
Highgate Gdns JRW NE32 ..... 90 B2 ③
Highgate Rd MLFD/PNYW SR4 .. 119 H1
The High Ga SUND SR1 ..... 55 J6
Highgreen Cha
  WICK/BNPF NE16 ..... 98 E4 ③
High Gv RYTON NE40 ..... 67 F7
Highgrove WD/WHPE/BLK NE5 .. 68 D1
High Hamsterley Rd
  ROWG NE39 ..... 110 C1
Highheath WASHN NE37 ..... 102 C7 ③
High Heworth La FELL NE10 ..... 13 G8
High Horse Cl ROWG NE39 ..... 97 J1
High Horse Close Wd
  ROWG NE39 ..... 97 J1
High House Gdns FELL NE10 ... 12 F6
High House La CON/LDGT DH8 .. 137 K5
Highland Rd
  WD/WHPE/BLK NE5 ..... 55 H7
High La HLS DH4 ..... 132 D3
High Lane Rw HEBB NE31 ..... 73 H3
High La FELL NE10 ..... 13 H9
High Laws GOS/KPK NE3 ..... 57 F6
High Level Br CNUT NE1 ..... 5 L8
High Market ASHGTN NE63 ..... 23 F1
High Meadow HAR/WTLS NE34 ... 75 H5
High Mdw BDN/LAN/SAC DH7 .. 167 F5
High Mill Rd ROWG NE39 ..... 110 C1
Highmoor MPTH NE61 ..... 20 B6
High Moor Pl
  HAR/WTLS NE34 ..... 75 G6 ③
High Pk MPTH NE61 ..... 20 E6
High Pasture WASHS NE38 ..... 117 C5 ③
Highridge CON/LDGT DH8 ..... 122 C4
High Rdg DIN/WO NE13 ..... 46 B4 ③
The High Rd HAR/WTLS NE34 ... 75 K5

High Rw BW/LEM/TK/HW NE15 .. 68 A5
High Sandgrove
  CLDN/WHIT/ROK SR6 ..... 92 A3
High Shaw PRUD NE42 ..... 80 B3
Highside Dr SUNDSW SR3 ..... 120 A3
High Spen Ct ROWG NE39 ..... 96 C1
Highstead Av CRAM NE23 ..... 33 G6
Highsteads CON/LDGT DH8 ..... 109 H5
High Stobhill MPTH NE61 ..... 20 E7
High St BDN/LAN/SAC DH7 ..... 167 K5
  BLYTH NE24 ..... 31 F7 ③
  BW/LEM/TK/HW NE15 ..... 67 H4
  DHAM DH1 ..... 157 K5
  DHAM DH1 ..... 169 H4
  FELL NE10 ..... 12 C7
  GATE NE8 ..... 5 M9
  GOS/KPK NE3 ..... 56 C5
  HLH DH5 ..... 148 B7
  JRW NE32 ..... 74 A4
  MLFD/PNYW SR4 ..... 104 C7
  NWBGN NE64 ..... 19 G7
  RDHAMSE DH6 ..... 158 E3
  RDHAMSE DH6 ..... 172 B6
  STKFD/GP NE62 ..... 22 E7
  STLY/ANP DH9 ..... 112 D7
High St East SUND SR1 ..... 15 H3
  WLSD/HOW NE28 ..... 72 E2 ③
High Street South Back
  BDN/LAN/SAC DH7 ..... 167 K5
High St West BYK/HTN/WLK NE6.. 72 C7
  SUND SR1 ..... 14 E4
Hightree Cl SUNDSW SR3 ..... 133 K2 ③
  SUNDSW SR3 ..... 134 A2 ③
High Vw PONT/DH NE20 ..... 43 F7
  WLSD/HOW NE28 ..... 58 D7
High Vw North
  WLSD/HOW NE28 ..... 58 D6
Highwell La
  WD/WHPE/BLK NE5 ..... 68 C2 ③
High West St GATE NE8 ..... 10 C6
Highwood Rd
  BW/LEM/TK/HW NE15 ..... 68 D4
High Wood Vw DHAM DH1 ..... 16 E7
Highworth Dr WASHS NE38 ..... 58 A7 ③
  LWF/SPW/WRK NE9 ..... 102 B3
Hilda Av DHAM DH1 ..... 17 M5
Hilda Cl DHAM DH1 ..... 169 J1
Hilda Pk CLSW/PEL DH2 ..... 129 H2
Hilda St
  CLDN/WHIT/ROK SR6 ..... 106 D2 ③
  GATE NE8 ..... 10 D6
Hilden Gdns LGB/HTN NE7 ..... 71 J1
Hillary Av LGB/KIL NE12 ..... 58 A2
Hillary Pl WD/WHPE/BLK NE5 ... 54 E7 ③
Hill Av CRAM NE23 ..... 39 H6
Hill Crs SEA/MUR SR7 ..... 149 H5
  SEA/MUR SR7 ..... 151 F3
Hill Crest BDN/LAN/SAC DH7 ... 143 H6
  WICK/BNPF NE16 ..... 97 K7
Hillcrest ASHGTN NE63 ..... 24 C3
  CON/LDGT DH8 ..... 136 E2
  DHAM DH1 ..... 16 E2
  DHAM DH1 ..... 169 J5
  HAR/WTLS NE34 ..... 76 B7
  JRW NE32 ..... 90 A2
  MONK NE25 ..... 50 C4
  PRUD NE42 ..... 80 D2
  SUNDSW SR3 ..... 119 F7
Hillcrest Dr DUN/TMV NE11 ..... 85 J5
Hill Crest Gdns JES NE2 ..... 56 E6 ③
Hillcrest Pl RHTLP TS27 ..... 185 G2
Hillcroft LWF/SPW/WRK NE9 ... 87 G6
Hill Dyke LWF/SPW/WRK NE9.... 101 J3
Hillfield CON/LDGT DH8 ..... 122 D4
  MONK NE25 ..... 50 B4
Hillfield Gdns SUNDSW SR3 ..... 120 B3
Hillfield St GATE NE8 ..... 10 E4
Hillgarth CON/LDGT DH8 ..... 137 G2
Hillgate GATE NE8 ..... 5 M9
Hill Ga MPTH NE61 ..... 20 E5
Hill Head Dr WD/WHPE/BLK NE5.. 68 B2
Hillhead Gdns DUN/TMV NE11 .. 86 A6 ③
Hillhead La WICK/BNPF NE16 .... 98 B4
Hillhead Pkwy
  WD/WHPE/BLK NE5 ..... 54 A7
Hill Head Rd WD/WHPE/BLK NE5.. 68 B1
Hillheads Rd MONK NE25 ..... 50 D6
Hillhead Wy WD/WHPE/BLK NE5.. 54 C7
Hill House Rd
  BW/LEM/TK/HW NE15 ..... 66 D1
Hillingdon Gv MLFD/PNYW SR4 .. 118 E4
Hill La HLS DH4 ..... 118 A5
Hill Mdw DHAM DH1 ..... 169 H5
Hillmeads CLSW/PEL DH2 ..... 144 A4
Hill Pk PONT/DH NE20 ..... 43 F7
Hill Park Rd JRW NE32 ..... 74 A6
Hill Ri RYTON NE40 ..... 82 B1
  WASHS NE38 ..... 103 C7
Hillrise Crs SEA/MUR SR7 ..... 134 D7
Hillsden Rd MONK NE25 ..... 50 B2
Hillside BDN/LAN/SAC DH7 ..... 143 G7
  BLAY NE21 ..... 83 K2
  BOL NE36 ..... 90 B5
  CLS/BIR/GTL DH3 ..... 115 K2
  CLS/BIR/GTL DH3 ..... 129 J3
  DUN/TMV NE11 ..... 85 J5
  HAR/WTLS NE34 ..... 76 B7
  MPTH NE61 ..... 20 D6
  PONT/DH NE20 ..... 52 E1
  SUNDSW SR3 ..... 120 C3
Hillside Av
  BW/LEM/TK/HW NE15 ..... 68 D4 ③
Hillside Cl ROWG NE39 ..... 97 G3 ③
Hillside Crs
  BW/LEM/TK/HW NE15 ..... 68 E7
Hillside Dr CLDN/WHIT/ROK SR6... 92 E3
Hillside Gdns STLY/ANP DH9 ... 112 A4 ③
  SUNDSW SR3 ..... 120 C3 ③
Hillside Pl LWF/SPW/WRK NE9 ... 87 G2
Hillside Wy HLS DH4 ..... 132 C6
Hillsleigh Rd
  WD/WHPE/BLK NE5 ..... 55 H7
Hill St NSHW NE29 ..... 73 J4
  SEA/MUR SR7 ..... 150 E2
  SSH NE33 ..... 2 E9
  SUNDSW SR3 ..... 120 A7
Hillsview Av GOS/KPK NE3 ..... 55 K5 ③

Hill Ter HLS DH4 ..... 132 C1 ③
Hillthorne Cl WASHS NE38 ..... 117 H2 ③
Hill Top BLAY NE21 ..... 83 K3
  CLS/BIR/GTL DH3 ..... 115 K2
  STLY/ANP DH9 ..... 113 F7
Hill Top Av LWF/SPW/WRK NE9... 87 G7
Hill Top Cl STKFD/GP NE62 ..... 23 C7 ③
Hill Top Gdns
  LWF/SPW/WRK NE9 ..... 87 G7 ③
Hilltop Gdns SUNDSW SR3 ..... 120 C7 ③
Hilltop Rd BDN/LAN/SAC DH7 ... 155 F5
Hilltop Vw BDN/LAN/SAC DH7 .. 154 C3
Hill Vw BDN/LAN/SAC DH7 ..... 165 H2
Hillview SUNDSW SR3 ..... 119 F7
Hillview Crs HLS DH4 ..... 132 B4 ③
Hill View Gdns SUNDSW SR3 .... 120 B3
Hillview Gv HLS DH4 ..... 132 B4 ③
Hill View Rd
  ASHBK/HED/RY SR2 ..... 120 C3
Hillview Rd HLS DH4 ..... 132 B4 ③
Hill View Sq
  ASHBK/HED/RY SR2 ..... 120 C3
Hilsyde Cres RDHAMSE DH6 .... 172 B6
Hilton Av WD/WHPE/BLK NE5 ... 69 F1
Hilton Cl CRAM NE23 ..... 33 G5
Hilton Dr PLEE/EAS SR8 ..... 174 C1
Hindley Cl RYTON NE40 ..... 82 A1 ③
Hindley Gdns ELS/FEN NE4 ..... 69 H4
Hindmarch Dr BOL NE36 ..... 90 E5
Hind St SUND SR1 ..... 14 C5 ③
Hinkley Cl SUNDSW SR3 ..... 134 A1
Hipsburn Dr SUNDSW SR3 ..... 120 A3
Hiram Dr BOL NE36 ..... 91 H5
Histon Wy WD/WHPE/BLK NE5 .. 55 F7
Hither Gn JRW NE32 ..... 90 B2 ③
Hobart Av HAR/WTLS NE34 ..... 74 D7
Hobart WBAY NE26 ..... 50 D2
Hobart Rd HAR/WTLS NE34 ..... 74 D7
Hodgkin Park Crs
  BW/LEM/TK/HW NE15 ..... 69 G6
Hodgkin Park Rd
  BW/LEM/TK/HW NE15 ..... 69 G6
Hodgson's Rd BLYTH NE24 ..... 31 F6
Hodkin Gdns
  LWF/SPW/WRK NE9 ..... 87 H6
Hogarth Dr WASHS NE38 ..... 117 G3
Hogarth Rd HAR/WTLS NE34 ... 91 C3
Holbein Rd HAR/WTLS NE34 ... 91 C1
Holborn Pl
  WD/WHPE/BLK NE5 ..... 68 C2 ③
Holborn Rd MLFD/PNYW NE4 ... 119 H2
Holborn Sq MLFD/PNYW NE4 ... 119 H2 ③
Holburn Cl RYTON NE40 ..... 67 F6 ③
Holburn Ct
  BDN/LAN/SAC DH7 ..... 167 G1 ③
  RYTON NE40 ..... 67 F6 ③
Holburn Crs RYTON NE40 ..... 67 G6
Holburn Gdns RYTON NE40 ..... 67 G6
Holburn La RYTON NE40 ..... 67 F6
Holburn Wk RYTON NE40 ..... 67 F6
Holden Pl WD/WHPE/BLK NE5 .. 69 H1 ③
Holder House La
  HAR/WTLS NE34 ..... 91 J1
Holderness Rd
  BYK/HTN/WLK NE6 ..... 71 H2
  WLSD/HOW NE28 ..... 59 J7
Hole La WICK/BNPF NE16 ..... 98 D1
Holeyn Hall Rd WYLAM NE41 ... 65 G4
Holeyn Rd
  BW/LEM/TK/HW NE15 ..... 66 E2 ③
Holland Dr JES NE2 ..... 4 E3
Holland Pk WLSD/HOW NE28 ... 58 A7
Holland Park Dr JRW NE32 ..... 90 B2
Hollinghill Rd MONK NE25 ..... 40 B6
Hollings Crs WLSD/HOW NE28 .. 58 D6 ③
Hollingside La DHAM DH1 ..... 16 D9
Hollington Av LGB/KIL NE12 ... 57 H4
Hollinhill ROWG NE39 ..... 83 J7
Hollinside Cl WICK/BNPF NE16.. 84 E7
Hollinside Gdns
  BW/LEM/TK/HW NE15 ..... 69 F5
Hollinside Rd MLFD/PNYW NE4 .. 85 F2
  WICK/BNPF NE16 ..... 85 F2
Hollinside Sq MLFD/PNYW NE4.. 119 G1
Hollinside Ter ROWG NE39 ..... 97 F3 ③
Hollon St MPTH NE61 ..... 20 C4
Hollowdene HLS DH4 ..... 147 K5
The Hollows ASHGTN NE63 ..... 24 D3 ③
Holly Av BLAY NE21 ..... 84 A6
  CLDN/WHIT/ROK SR6 ..... 93 F4
  DUN/TMV NE11 ..... 9 H9
  GOS/KPK NE3 ..... 55 K4
  HAR/WTLS NE34 ..... 76 A6
  HLH DH5 ..... 132 C7
  JES NE2 ..... 70 E2
  LGB/KIL NE12 ..... 57 K1
  MONK NE25 ..... 49 K4
  MPTH NE61 ..... 20 D6
  RYTON NE40 ..... 66 E5 ③
  SUNDSW SR3 ..... 120 B6
  WBAY NE26 ..... 50 E4
  WLSD/HOW NE28 ..... 72 E2 ③
Holly Av West JES NE2 ..... 70 E2 ③
Hollybush Rd FELL NE10 ..... 12 A8
Hollycarrside Rd
  ASHBK/HED/RY SR2 ..... 120 E3
Holly Crs BDN/LAN/SAC DH7 ... 143 H6
Hollydene DUN/TMV NE11 ..... 100 H7 ③
  ROWG NE39 ..... 97 H3
Holly Gdns CON/LDGT DH8 ..... 122 C7 ③
Holly Gv PRUD NE42 ..... 80 B1
Holly Hvn HLH DH5 ..... 147 G4
Holly Hl FELL NE10 ..... 12 C7
Holly Hill Gdns East
  STLY/ANP DH9 ..... 126 D3
Holly Hill Gdns West
  STLY/ANP DH9 ..... 126 D3
Hollymount Sq BDLGTN NE22 ... 29 G6
Holly Pk BDN/LAN/SAC DH7 ... 167 G6
  BDN/LAN/SAC DH7 ..... 167 G6
Holly Park Vw FELL NE10 ..... 12 D7
Holly Rd NSHW NE29 ..... 60 D3
The Hollys CLS/BIR/GTL DH3 .... 101 H6 ③
Holly St DHAM DH1 ..... 16 A4
  JRW NE32 ..... 73 J4
Hollywell Ct BDN/LAN/SAC DH7.. 167 G1

Hollywell Gv DIN/WO NE13 ..... 54 D2
Hollywood Av NSHW NE29 ..... 60 B4
  GOS/KPK NE3 ..... 56 C4
  SWCK/CAS SR5 ..... 105 K3
Hollywood Crs GOS/KPK NE3 ... 56 D4
Hollywood Gdns
  DUN/TMV NE11 ..... 86 B7 ③
Holmdale ASHGTN NE63 ..... 23 J3
Holme Av BYK/HTN/WLK NE6 ... 72 B2
  WICK/BNPF NE16 ..... 85 F5
Holme Ri WICK/BNPF NE16 ..... 85 F5
Holmeside Rd
  DUN/TMV NE11 ..... 86 B7 ③
Holme Ri WICK/BNPF NE16 ..... 85 F5
Holmeside SUND SR1 ..... 14 E5
Holmewood Dr ROWG NE39 .... 97 F5
Holmfield Av HAR/WTLS NE34 .. 75 J4
Holmfield Vls RDHAMSE DH6 .. 180 B5 ③
Holm Gn MONK NE25 ..... 50 B5
Holmhill La CLS/BIR/GTL DH3 .... 144 D1
  PLEE/EAS SR8 ..... 162 E4
Holmland BW/LEM/TK/HW NE15.. 69 G7
Holmlands MONK NE25 ..... 50 C4 ③
Holmlands Pk North
  ASHBK/HED/RY SR2 ..... 120 C2 ③
Holmlands Pk South
  ASHBK/HED/RY SR2 ..... 120 C2 ③
Holmlea BDN/LAN/SAC DH7 ..... 141 G4
  DUN/TMV NE11 ..... 9 H8
Holmside Av
  BDN/LAN/SAC DH7 ..... 140 C5
  DUN/TMV NE11 ..... 9 H8
Holmside Hall Rd
  BDN/LAN/SAC DH7 ..... 127 F7
Holmside La BDN/LAN/SAC DH7.. 141 G4
  BDN/LAN/SAC DH7 ..... 141 K2
Holmwood Av MONK NE25 ..... 50 B5
Holmwood Gv JES NE2 ..... 70 D1 ③
Holyfields SMOOR NE27 ..... 49 F7
Holylake Sq MLFD/PNYW NE4 ... 119 H1
Holyoake Gdns
  CLS/BIR/GTL DH3 ..... 115 J2 ③
  LWF/SPW/WRK NE9 ..... 11 H8
Holyoake St CLSW/PEL DH2 ... 128 C1
  PRUD NE42 ..... 80 D1 ③
Holystone Av GOS/KPK NE3 ... 56 B4
  MONK NE25 ..... 51 F5
Holystone Cl BLYTH NE24 ..... 34 E2
  HLS DH4 ..... 131 K5 ③
Holystone Crs LGB/HTN NE7 ... 57 G7
Holystone Dr SMOOR NE27 ..... 48 E7
Holystone Gdns NSHW NE29 ... 60 D3
Holystone St HEBB NE31 ..... 73 F5
Holywell Av BYK/HTN/WLK NE6.. 72 C1
  MONK NE25 ..... 50 C3
  WBAY NE26 ..... 50 C3
Holywell Cl ELS/FEN NE4 ..... 4 F4 ③
  RYTON NE40 ..... 40 C6
Holywell Dene Rd MONK NE25.. 40 C7
Home Av LWF/SPW/WRK NE9.... 101 F1
Homedale PRUD NE42 ..... 80 E2
Homedale Pl PRUD NE42 ..... 80 E3 ③
Home Farm ASHGTN NE63 ..... 23 F1
Home Pk WLSD/HOW NE28 ..... 58 A7
Homestall HAR/WTLS NE34 ..... 75 H6 ③
Honeycomb Cl SUNDSW SR3 ... 133 K2 ②
Honeysuckle Av
  HAR/WTLS NE34 ..... 75 F7
Honeysuckle Cl SUNDSW SR3 .. 134 A2
Honister Av JES NE2 ..... 56 E7
Honister Cl
  BW/LEM/TK/HW NE15 ..... 68 B3 ③
Honister Dr SWCK/CAS SR5 .... 106 C2 ③
Honister Pl
  BW/LEM/TK/HW NE15 ..... 68 B3
Honister Rd TYNE/NSHE NE30 .. 51 F7
Honister Wy BLYTH NE24 ..... 34 E4
Honiton Cl HLS DH4 ..... 132 A3 ③
Honiton Ct
  WD/WHPE/BLK NE5 ..... 55 F4 ③
Honiton Wy NSHW NE29 ..... 59 K2
Hood Cl SWCK/CAS SR5 ..... 106 C4 ③
Hood St CNUT NE1 ..... 5 K6
  MPTH NE61 ..... 20 D4
  WICK/BNPF NE16 ..... 84 E3 ③
Hookergate La ROWG NE39 ..... 96 C3
Hooper Ter RDHAMSE DH6 ..... 173 H4
Hopedene FELL NE10 ..... 88 C7
Hope Shield WASHS NE38 ..... 116 B5
Hope St CON/LDGT DH8 ..... 122 E5
  HAR/WTLS NE34 ..... 75 F6 ③
  JRW NE32 ..... 74 A4
  RDHAMSE DH6 ..... 170 C1
  SUND SR1 ..... 14 C5
Hopgarth Gdns
  CLS/BIR/GTL DH3 ..... 129 K3
Hopkins Ct MLFD/PNYW SR4 ... 105 K6
Hopper Pl GATE NE8 ..... 11 G2
Hopper Rd FELL NE10 ..... 12 A9
Hopper St GATE NE8 ..... 11 G2
  NSHW NE29 ..... 2 B2
  WLSD/HOW NE28 ..... 72 D1 ③
Horatio St
  CLDN/WHIT/ROK SR6 ..... 106 E4
Hornbeam Pl ELS/FEN NE4 ..... 9 L1
Horncliffe Gdns WICK/BNPF NE16.. 8 A7
Horncliffe Pl
  BW/LEM/TK/HW NE15 ..... 66 D1
Hornsea Cl DIN/WO NE13 ..... 46 B3 ③
Hornsey Ter HLH DH5 ..... 148 A7 ③
Horse Crofts BLAY NE21 ..... 84 A1 ③
Horsegate Bank CHPW NE17 ... 81 K7 ③
Horsham Gdns SUNDSW SR3 ... 120 A3 ③
Horsham Gv NSHW NE29 ..... 60 D3
Horsley Av RYTON NE40 ..... 82 A1
  SMOOR NE27 ..... 49 H7
Horsley Cl STKFD/GP NE62 ..... 23 F5
Horsley Ct GOS/KPK NE3 ..... 55 J4 ③
Horsley Gdns DUN/TMV NE11 ... 9 H8 ③
  MONK NE25 ..... 40 C6 ③
Horsley Gv SUNDSW SR3 ..... 120 A3
Horsley Hill Rd SSH NE33 ..... 3 L5
Horsley Hill Sq
  HAR/WTLS NE34 ..... 76 B4 ③
Horsley Rd LGB/HTN NE7 ..... 71 H2
  PRUD NE42 ..... 64 A6
  WASHS NE38 ..... 103 J7

Horsley Ter
BYK/HTN/WLK NE6 .... 72 B6 🖪
Horsley V *HAR/WTLS* NE34 ...... 75 K4
Horsley Vw *PRUD* NE42............ 81 F1
Horton Av *BDLGTN* NE22 .... 29 F6
HAR/WTLS NE34.................. 91 H1
SMOOR NE27............................. 49 H7
Horton Crs *DIN/WO* NE13 .... 45 F2 🖪
RDHAMSE DH6 .... 180 A1
Hortondale Gv *BLYTH* NE24 ...... 30 D7
Horton Dr *CRAM* NE23.............. 38 A8
Horton Pl *BLYTH* NE24 .... 34 D3 🖪
Horton Rd *BLYTH* NE24 .... 33 J1
Horwood Av
WD/WHPE/BLK NE5 .... 68 B1
Hospital Dr *HEBB* NE31 .... 73 F7 🖪
Hospital La
BW/LEM/TK/HW NE15 .... 67 K4
Hospital Rd *BDN/LAN/SAC* DH7 .. 154 A3
Hotch Pudding Pl
WD/WHPE/BLK NE5 .... 68 D3
Hotspur Av *BDLGTN* NE22 .... 29 F6
MONK NE25 .... 50 E5
Hotspur Rd *WLSD/HOW* NE28 .... 58 C5
Hotspur St *BYK/HTN/WLK* NE6.... 6 C3
TYNE/NSHE NE30................... 61 H2
Houghton Av *TYNE/NSHE* NE30.. 51 F6
WD/WHPE/BLK NE5 .... 55 H7
Houghton Cut *HLH* DH5 .... 132 C6
Houghton Rd *HLH* DH5 .... 147 J2
HLS DH4 .... 132 B4
Houghton St *MLFD/PNYW* SR4.. 106 A7
Houlskye Cl *SUNDSW* SR3 .... 120 C7 🖪
Houndelee Pl
WD/WHPE/BLK NE5 .... 69 G2 🖪
Houndslow Dr *ASHGTN* NE63 .... 23 H3 🖪
Hounslow Gdns *JRW* NE32 .... 90 B2 🖪
House Ter *WASHN* NE37 .... 103 F5
Housing La *CON/LDGT* DH8 ..... 109 K5
Houston Ct *ELS/FEN* NE4 .... 4 F8
Houston St *ELS/FEN* NE4 .... 4 F8
Houxty Rd *MONK* NE25 .... 49 K4
Hovingham Cl *PLEE/EAS* SR8 ... 175 F5 🖪
Hovingham Gdns
SUNDSW SR3........................ 120 A3 🖪
Howard Gv *MPTH* NE61 .... 21 J2
Howardian Cl *WASHS* NE38 ..... 116 D5
Howard Rd *MPTH* NE61 .... 20 E4
Howard St *CNUT* NE1 .... 6 B6
FELL NE10 .... 87 J6
GATE NE8 .... 11 M6
JRW NE32 .... 74 A5
MPTH NE61 .... 21 J2 🖪
SWCK/CAS SR5 .... 106 D4 🖪
TYNE/NSHE NE30 .... 2 E2
Howarth St *MLFD/PNYW* SR4.... 106 A7
Howat Av *WD/WHPE/BLK* NE5 ... 69 J2 🖪
Howburn Crs *MPTH* NE61 .... 21 J2 🖪
Howden Bank
BDN/LAN/SAC DH7 .... 140 D1
Howdene Rd
BW/LEM/TK/HW NE15 .... 68 D5
Howden Gdns *WNGT* TS28 ..... 183 K3 🖪
Howdon La *WLSD/HOW* NE28 .... 59 J7
Howdon Rd *NSHW* NE29 .... 2 A6
WLSD/HOW NE28...................... 74 A1
Howe Sq *MLFD/PNYW* SR4 ...... 119 G1
Howe St *GATE* NE8 .... 11 L6
HEBB NE31 .... 73 J5 🖪
Howick Av *GOS/KPK* NE3 .... 56 A3
Howletch La *PLEE/EAS* SR8 ..... 174 D1
Howlett Hall Rd
BW/LEM/TK/HW NE15 .... 68 D5
Howley Av *SWCK/CAS* SR5 ...... 105 G3 🖪
Hownam Cl *GOS/KPK* NE3 ...... 56 A6 🖪
Hownsgill Dr *CON/LDGT* DH8 ... 138 D2
Hoy Crs *SEA/MUR* SR7 .... 135 F6
Hoylake Av *LGB/HTN* NE7 .... 57 J5
Hoyle Av *ELS/FEN* NE4.............. 69 J5
Hoyle Fold *SUNDSW* SR3 .... 134 A3
Hubert St *BOLCOL* NE35 .... 90 D4
Huddlestone Ri
CLDN/WHIT/ROK SR6 .... 15 H1 🖪
Huddleston Rd
BYK/HTN/WLK NE6 .... 7 J3
Hudson Av *BDLGTN* NE22 .... 29 H5
Hudson Rd *SUND* SR1 .... 15 G5
Hudson St *GATE* NE8 .... 10 F1 🖪
HAR/WTLS NE34 .... 75 F5
TYNE/NSHE NE30 .... 3 G1
Hudspeth Crs *DHAM* DH1 ...... 156 B2
Hugh St *CLDN/WHIT/ROK* SR6 .. 106 E2
WASHS NE38 .... 117 H2 🖪
WLSD/HOW NE28...................... 72 D2
Hull St *ELS/FEN* NE4 .... 4 B8
Hulme Ct *PLEE/EAS* SR8 .... 174 D5 🖪
Hulne Av *TYNE/NSHE* NE30 ...... 61 G3
Humber Gdns *GATE* NE8 .... 11 L6
Humber Hl *STLY/ANP* DH9....... 126 E2
Humberhill Dr
BDN/LAN/SAC DH7 .... 140 B5
Humberhill La
BDN/LAN/SAC DH7 .... 139 F3
Humber St *CHPW* NE17 .... 95 J4 🖪
Humbert St *JRW* NE32 .... 73 K5 🖪
Humbleburn La
BDN/LAN/SAC DH7 .... 127 J6
Hume St *BYK/HTN/WLK* NE6....... 6 A6
MLFD/PNYW SR4 .... 106 A6
Humford Gn *BLYTH* NE24 .... 30 B7
Humford Wy *BDLGTN* NE22 ..... 29 G7
Humsford Gv *CRAM* NE23........ 33 J7
Humshaugh Cl *LGB/KIL* NE12 ... 47 K5
Humshaugh Rd *NSHW* NE29 .... 60 A4 🖪
Hunstanton Ct
LWF/SPW/WRK NE9 .... 100 E2
Huntcliffe Av
CLDN/WHIT/ROK SR6 .... 92 E6
Huntcliffe Gdns
BYK/HTN/WLK NE6 .... 71 J3 🖪
BLYTH NE24............................ 35 H1
Hunter Cl *BOL* NE36 .... 91 H6
Hunter Ct *PLEE/EAS* SR8 .... 174 B5 🖪
Hunters Ct *NSHW* NE29 .... 60 B7
Hunters Ct *WLSD/HOW* NE28 ... 72 E1 🖪

Hunters Hall Rd
MLFD/PNYW SR4 .... 14 A8 🖪
Hunters Ldg *WLSD/HOW* NE28... 72 D1
Hunter's Moor Cl *JES* NE2......... 4 E1
Hunter's Pl *JES* NE2................... 4 E1
Hunter's Rd *GOS/KPK* NE3 .... 57 F5
JES NE2 .... 4 D2
Hunter St *HLS* DH4 .... 131 J2
SSH NE33 .... 75 H2
Hunter Ter *ASHBK/HED/RY* SR2 . 120 E3
Huntingdon Cl *DIN/WO* NE13 .... 55 G2
Huntingdon Gdns
SUNDSW SR3 .... 120 A3 🖪
Huntingdon Pl *TYNE/NSHE* NE30.. 61 H3
Huntingdon Rd *PLEE/EAS* SR8 .. 174 D2
Huntingdonshire Dr
DHAM DH1 .... 158 A6 🖪
Huntington Dr *CRAM* NE23....... 38 D1
Hunt Lea *WICK/BNPF* NE16 ..... 84 C7 🖪
Huntley Av *SEA/MUR* SR7 .... 149 G5 🖪
Huntley Crs *BLAY* NE21 .... 83 J4
Huntley Sq *MLFD/PNYW* SR4 ... 119 H1 🖪
Huntly Rd *MONK* NE25 .... 50 A2
Hurst Ter *BYK/HTN/WLK* NE6 ..... 7 M5
Hurstwood Rd
MLFD/PNYW SR4 .... 120 A2
Hurworth Av *HAR/WTLS* NE34 .. 76 A5
Hurworth Pl *JRW* NE32 .... 73 K5
Hustledown Gdns
STLY/ANP DH9 .... 126 D3 🖪
Hustledown Rd *STLY/ANP* DH9 .. 126 C3
Hutchinson Av
CON/LDGT DH8 .... 123 F4 🖪
Hutton Cl *HLS* DH4 .... 132 A7 🖪
WASHS NE38 .... 116 B1
Hutton Crs *RHTLP* TS27 .... 184 E6
Hutton St *BOLCOL* NE35 .... 90 C3
MLFD/PNYW SR4 .... 14 A7
Hutton Ter *JES* NE2 .... 6 A2
LWF/SPW/WRK NE9 .... 101 F1
Huxley Crs *GATE* NE8 .... 10 D9
Hyacinth Ct *MLFD/PNYW* SR4 .. 14 A3 🖪
Hydeside Gv *CON/LDGT* DH8 .. 122 C6
Hyde Pk *WLSD/HOW* NE28 .... 58 B7
Hydepark St *GATE* NE8 .... 10 D8
Hyde St *ASHBK/HED/RY* SR2 ... 121 F2 🖪
GOS/KPK NE3 .... 3 K9
Hyde Ter *GOS/KPK* NE3 .... 56 D5
Hylton Av *HAR/WTLS* NE34 ..... 76 B5
Hylton Bank *MLFD/PNYW* SR4 .. 105 J6
Hylton Castle Rd
SWCK/CAS SR5 .... 105 F4
Hylton Cl *BDLGTN* NE22 .... 28 D5
BDN/LAN/SAC DH7 .... 154 A3
Hylton Gra *SWCK/CAS* SR5 ..... 104 D6
Hylton La *BOL* NE36 .... 90 E6
SWCK/CAS SR5 .... 104 E2
Hylton Park Rd *SWCK/CAS* SR5 .. 105 J4
Hylton Rd *DHAM* DH1 .... 156 D3 🖪
JRW NE32 .... 73 K7
MLFD/PNYW SR4 .... 14 A4
Hylton St *GATE* NE8 .... 11 L5
HLS DH4 .... 132 B5 🖪
MLFD/PNYW SR4 .... 106 A7
NSHW NE29 ....
Hylton Wk *MLFD/PNYW* SR4 ... 118 E1 🖪
Hymers Av *HAR/WTLS* NE34 .... 74 D7
Hyperion Av *HAR/WTLS* NE34.... 74 E6

Ilchester St *SEA/MUR* SR7 ...... 150 E2 🖪
Ilderton Pl
WD/WHPE/BLK NE5 .... 68 C3 🖪
Ilex St *DUN/TMV* NE11 .... 86 C6
Ilford Av *CRAM* NE23 .... 33 G6 🖪
Ilford Pl *GATE* NE8 .... 11 K8
Ilford Rd *JES* NE2 .... 56 D7
WLSD/HOW NE28...................... 59 H7
Ilfracombe Av *ELS/FEN* NE4 ..... 69 J6
Ilminster Ct *GOS/KPK* NE3 .... 55 G4 🖪
Imeary Gv *SSH* NE33 .... 75 H2 🖪
Imeary St *SSH* NE33 .... 75 H2
Inchberry Cl *ELS/FEN* NE4 .... 69 J7
Inchbury Cl *ELS/FEN* NE4 .... 69 J7 🖪
Inchcliffe Crs
WD/WHPE/BLK NE5 .... 69 G1
Indigo St *DUN/TMV* NE11 .... 86 C6
Industrial Rd *WASHN* NE37 ..... 103 G6
Industrial St *CLSW/PEL* DH2 ... 128 C1
Industry Rd *BYK/HTN/WLK* NE6.. 71 K1
Ingham Gra *SSH* NE33 .... 75 J2 🖪
Ingham Gv *CRAM* NE23 .... 33 G6 🖪
Ingleby Ter *MLFD/PNYW* SR4 ... 120 A1 🖪
Ingleby Wy *BLYTH* NE24 .... 35 F4
Inglemere Pl
BW/LEM/TK/HW NE15 .... 68 E5 🖪
Ingleside *WICK/BNPF* NE16 ..... 84 D6
Ingleside Rd *NSHW* NE29 .... 60 D3
Ingleton Dr
BW/LEM/TK/HW NE15 .... 66 D1
Ingleton Gdns *BLYTH* NE24 ..... 34 E4
Inglewood Cl *BLYTH* NE24 .... 30 B7
Inglewood Pl *GOS/KPK* NE3 .... 56 C1 🖪
Ingoe Av *GOS/KPK* NE3 .... 55 K3 🖪
Ingoe Cl *BLYTH* NE24 .... 30 E7
Ingoe St *BW/LEM/TK/HW* NE15 .. 68 A5 🖪
WLSD/HOW NE28...................... 74 A1
Ingoldsby Ct
MLFD/PNYW SR4 .... 119 J2 🖪
Ingram Cl *CLSW/PEL* DH2 ...... 129 G6
WD/WHPE/BLK NE5 .... 54 B6
Ingram Dr *BLYTH* NE24 .... 30 D7 🖪
Ingram Ter
BYK/HTN/WLK NE6 .... 72 C5 🖪
Inkerman Rd *WASHN* NE37 ..... 103 F4
Inkerman St *SWCK/CAS* SR5 ... 106 A4
Inleborough Dr *RYTON* NE40 .... 67 F7
Innesmoor *HEBB* NE31 .... 73 F4
Inskip Ter *GATE* NE8 .... 11 H8
Institute Rd *ASHGTN* NE63 ..... 23 H1
Institute Ter West
CLSW/PEL DH2 .... 115 F6

Inverness Rd *JRW* NE32 .... 90 C1
Inverness St
CLDN/WHIT/ROK SR6 .... 106 D3
Invincible Dr *ELS/FEN* NE4 .... 9 K2
Iolanthe Cr *BYK/HTN/WLK* NE6 .. 7 L2
Iolanthe Ter *SSH* NE33 .... 3 L9
Iona Pl *BYK/HTN/WLK* NE6 ...... 72 C5 🖪
Iona Rd *FELL* NE10 .... 87 H5
JRW NE32 .... 90 C1
Irene Av *ASHBK/HED/RY* SR2 .. 121 F5
Iris Cl *DUN/TMV* NE11 .... 115 F4
Iris Pl *ELS/FEN* NE4 .... 69 H4
Iris St *DUN/TMV* NE11 .... 86 C6
Iris Ter *RYTON* NE40 .... 82 B1
Iroko St *DUN/TMV* NE11 .... 86 C6
Irton St *GOS/KPK* NE3 .... 56 C5
Irthing Av *BYK/HTN/WLK* NE6 ... 7 K8
Irwin Av *WLSD/HOW* NE28 ...... 58 D7
Isabella Rd *BLYTH* NE24 .... 34 E1
Isabella Wk
BW/LEM/TK/HW NE15 .... 67 F2 🖪
Isis Rd *PLEE/EAS* SR8 .... 174 D5
Ivanhoe *MONK* NE25 .... 50 C4
Ivanhoe Vw
LWF/SPW/WRK NE9 .... 101 H3
Iveagh Cl *ELS/FEN* NE4 .... 69 H7
Ivesley La *BDN/LAN/SAC* DH7 . 164 C1
Iveston St *BDN/LAN/SAC* DH7 . 143 G5
Iveston La *CON/LDGT* DH8 ...... 124 B6
Iveston Rd *CON/LDGT* DH8 ...... 123 F5
Iveston Ter *STLY/ANP* DH9 ...... 112 D7
Ivor St *ASHBK/HED/RY* SR2 .... 121 G4
Ivy Av *RYTON* NE40 .... 66 E5 🖪
SEA/MUR SR7 .... 150 C1
Ivy Cl *ELS/FEN* NE4 .... 9 M1
Ivy La *LWF/SPW/WRK* NE9 ...... 101 G2
Ivymount Rd *BYK/HTN/WLK* NE6.. 71 H2
Ivy Rd *BYK/HTN/WLK* NE6 .... 72 B3
GOS/KPK NE3 .... 56 C6
Ivy St *DUN/TMV* NE11 .... 86 C6
Ivyway *CLSW/PEL* DH2 .... 114 E7
Ixia St *DUN/TMV* NE11 .... 86 C6

Jack Lawson Ter
RDHAMSE DH6 .... 182 D1 🖪
Jackson Av *PONT/DH* NE20....... 43 H7
Jackson Cl *WYLAM* NE41 .... 65 H5 🖪
Jackson St *BYK/HTN/WLK* NE6 .. 72 B5 🖪
GATE NE8 .... 11 G2
MLFD/PNYW SR4 .... 120 A1
TYNE/NSHE NE30 .... 61 F4
Jackson St West
TYNE/NSHE NE30.................... 61 F4
Jack's Ter *HAR/WTLS* NE34 ...... 75 G6
Jacques St *MLFD/PNYW* SR4 .. 105 K6 🖪
Jacques Ter *CLSW/PEL* DH2 .... 129 H4
Jade Cl *BW/LEM/TK/HW* NE15 .. 68 A3
James Armitage St
SWCK/CAS SR5 .... 106 B3 🖪
James Mather St *SSH* NE33 ...... 3 J6
Jameson St *CON/LDGT* DH8 ... 123 F4 🖪
James St *ELS/FEN* NE4.............. 4 A9
PLEE/EAS SR8 .... 162 E4
SEA/MUR SR7 .... 150 E4
SWCK/CAS SR5 .... 106 A3 🖪
WD/WHPE/BLK NE5 .... 68 D1 🖪
WICK/BNPF NE16 .... 84 E5 🖪
James Ter *HLH* DH5 .... 160 A1
HLS DH4 .... 131 J7
SUNDSW SR3 .... 120 B7
WLSD/HOW NE28 .... 72 D2 🖪
James Williams St *SUND* SR1 .... 15 H3
Jane Eyre Ter *GATE* NE8 .... 11 L5
Jane Ter *BYK/HTN/WLK* NE6 .... 72 C6
Janet St *BYK/HTN/WLK* NE6 ...... 7 H8
Janus Cl *WD/WHPE/BLK* NE5 ... 54 A6 🖪
Jarrow Rd *HAR/WTLS* NE34 ..... 74 E5
JRW NE32 .... 74 D5
Jarvis Rd *PLEE/EAS* SR8 .... 174 E2
Jasmin Av *WD/WHPE/BLK* NE5 .. 54 A6
Jasmine Cl *BYK/HTN/WLK* NE6 .. 72 A2
Jasmine Ct *ASHGTN* NE63 .... 23 J4 🖪
MLFD/PNYW SR4 .... 14 B4 🖪
Jasmine Crs *SEA/MUR* SR7 .... 150 D3
Jasper Av *RYTON* NE40 .... 82 D3
Jedburgh Cl *GATE* NE8 .... 11 H6 🖪
NSHW NE29 .... 60 C2
WD/WHPE/BLK NE5 .... 54 A6
Jedburgh Gdns
BW/LEM/TK/HW NE15 .... 69 F5
Jedburgh Rd *HLS* DH4 .... 131 K1 🖪
Jedmoor *HEBB* NE31 .... 73 F4
Jefferson Pl *ELS/FEN* NE4 .... 4 A5
Jellicoe Rd *BYK/HTN/WLK* NE6 .. 12 E1
Jenifer Gv *LGB/HTN* NE7 .... 57 G7
Jenison Av
BW/LEM/TK/HW NE15 .... 69 G6
Jennifer Av *SWCK/CAS* SR5 .... 105 F4 🖪
Jervis St *HEBB* NE31 .... 73 H5
Jesmond Dene Rd *JES* NE2 ...... 70 D1
Jesmond Pk East *LGB/HTN* NE7.. 71 H1
Jesmond Pk West
LGB/HTN NE7 .... 71 H2 🖪
Jesmond Rd *JES* NE2 .... 5 K3
JES NE2 .... 71 G3 🖪
Jesmond Ter *WBAY* NE26 .... 50 E5
Jesmond V *BYK/HTN/WLK* NE6 .. 6 D2
Jesmond Vale La
BYK/HTN/WLK NE6 .... 6 E1
Jessel St *LWF/SPW/WRK* NE9 .. 101 H1
Joan Av *ASHBK/HED/RY* SR2 ... 121 F5
Joannah St *SWCK/CAS* SR5 .... 106 C2 🖪
Joan St *ELS/FEN* NE4 .... 69 H7
Jobling Av *BLAY* NE21 .... 83 J2
Jobling Crs *MPTH* NE61 .... 21 F6
Joel Ter *FELL* NE10 .... 13 L3
John Av *RYTON* NE40 .... 82 D3
John Brown Ct *BDLGTN* NE22 ... 29 F5 🖪
John Candlish Rd
MLFD/PNYW SR4 .... 106 A6
John Clay St *SSH* NE33 .... 75 H2 🖪

John Dobson St *CNUT* NE1......... 5 K4
John Reid Rd *HAR/WTLS* NE34 .. 74 D7
Johnson Cl *PLEE/EAS* SR8 .... 174 E2
Johnson's St *WNGT* TS28 .... 183 K5 🖪
Johnson St
BW/LEM/TK/HW NE15 .... 68 A5 🖪
DUN/TMV NE11 .... 9 H5
GATE NE8 .... 9 M5
SSH NE33 .... 75 G4
SUND SR1 .... 14 B4
Johnston Av *HEBB* NE31 .... 89 F1
John St *ASHGTN* NE63 .... 23 J1
BDN/LAN/SAC DH7 .... 143 H5
BLYTH NE24 .... 30 D6
CON/LDGT DH8 .... 122 D3
CON/LDGT DH8 .... 123 F5
DHAM DH1 .... 16 A4
FELL NE10 .... 13 H6
GATE NE8 .... 11 L5
GOS/KPK NE3 .... 56 A5
HLH DH5 .... 132 D1
HLH DH5 .... 147 K5
HLH DH5 .... 148 A5 🖪
HLS DH4 .... 131 J7
MLFD/PNYW SR4 .... 104 E6 🖪
MONK NE25 .... 49 J4
MPTH NE61 .... 21 K2
PLEE/EAS SR8 .... 163 F4
STLY/ANP DH9 .... 113 H7
STLY/ANP DH9 .... 126 B3
STLY/ANP DH9 .... 127 G5
SUND SR1 .... 14 F4 🖪
TYNE/NSHE NE30 .... 51 G5
WLSD/HOW NE28.................... 72 D1
John Street Sq
CON/LDGT DH8 .... 123 F5 🖪
SWCK/CAS SR5 .... 106 A2 🖪
John Taylor Ct
SWCK/CAS SR5 .... 106 A2 🖪
John Wesley Ct *PRUD* NE42 ..... 80 D2
John Williamson St *SSH* NE33 ... 75 F1
John Wilson Ct
PLEE/EAS SR8 .... 175 H3 🖪
Joicey Gdns *STLY/ANP* DH9 ... 112 D7 🖪
Joicey Rd *LWF/SPW/WRK* NE9 .. 87 F6
Joicey St *FELL* NE10 .... 13 J5 🖪
Jolliffe St *CLS/BIR/GTL* DH3 ... 129 K6
Jonadab Rd *FELL* NE10 .... 13 K3
Jonadab St *FELL* NE10 .... 13 J5
Jones St *CLS/BIR/GTL* DH3 ..... 115 H2
Jonquil Cl *WD/WHPE/BLK* NE5 .. 54 A6 🖪
Joseph Cl *ELS/FEN* NE4 .... 69 J7
Joseph St *STLY/ANP* DH9 .... 126 C2 🖪
Jowett Sq *SWCK/CAS* SR5 ...... 106 A3 🖪
Joyce Ter *SWCK/CAS* SR5 .... 105 F4 🖪
Jubilee Av *BDN/LAN/SAC* DH7 . 143 G1
Jubilee Crs *GOS/KPK* NE3 .... 56 A7
RDHAMSE DH6 .... 171 G1
Jubilee Est *ASHGTN* NE63 .... 23 K4
RDHAMSE DH6 .... 173 H3 🖪
Jubilee Pl *DHAM* DH1 .... 169 H4 🖪
CNUT NE1 .... 6 A6
GOS/KPK NE3 .... 56 A5
Jubilee Rd *BLYTH* NE24 .... 35 G1
Jubilee Sq *HLH* DH5 .... 148 B7 🖪
GOS/KPK NE3 .... 56 C1 🖪
Jubilee Ter *WICK/BNPF* NE16 .. 84 E3 🖪
Jude Pl *PLEE/EAS* SR8 .... 174 D2 🖪
PLEE/EAS SR8 .... 174 E2 🖪
Julian Av *BYK/HTN/WLK* NE6 .... 7 L2
SSH NE33 .... 3 J5
Julian Rd *FELL* NE10 .... 89 F4
Julian St *SSH* NE33 .... 3 J5
Juliet Av *NSHW* NE29 .... 60 B4 🖪
Julius Caesar St
SWCK/CAS SR5 .... 106 A3 🖪
June Av *BLAY* NE21 .... 84 A6
Juniper Cl *BLYTH* NE24 .... 34 E3
GOS/KPK NE3 .... 56 D1 🖪
Jupiter Ct *PLEE/EAS* SR8 .... 162 D5 🖪
Jutland Av *HEBB* NE31 .... 73 G5
Jutland Ter *STLY/ANP* DH9 ..... 112 B6

Kalmia St *DUN/TMV* NE11 .... 86 C7
Kane Gdns *FELL* NE10 .... 87 J6
Katrine Cl *CLSW/PEL* DH2 ...... 129 H5
Katrine Ct *SUNDSW* SR3 .... 134 A2 🖪
Kayll Rd *STLY/ANP* DH9 .... 112 D7
Kearsley Cl *MONK* NE25 .... 40 A5 🖪
Kearton Av *WD/WHPE/BLK* NE5 . 54 A7
Keats Av *BLYTH* NE24 .... 34 E2 🖪
BOLCOL NE35 .... 91 F4
SWCK/CAS SR5 .... 106 A3 🖪
Keats Cl *STLY/ANP* DH9 .... 126 E1
Keats Rd *BW/LEM/TK/HW* NE15 . 67 J5
Keeble Ct *ASHGTN* NE63 .... 24 D2
Keebledale Av
BYK/HTN/WLK NE6 .... 72 B4 🖪
Keelman's La *MLFD/PNYW* SR4.. 105 F6
Keelmans Rd *MLFD/PNYW* SR4 . 105 F6
Keir Hardie Av *FELL* NE10 .... 13 K8
STLY/ANP DH9 .... 126 D3
Keir Hardie St *HLS* DH4 .... 131 K7
Keir Hardie Wy *SWCK/CAS* SR5.. 106 B4
Keith Cl *ELS/FEN* NE4 .... 69 J7
Keldane Gdns *ELS/FEN* NE4 .... 69 H5
Kelfield Gv *CRAM* NE23 .... 33 H5 🖪
Kell Crs *RDHAMSE* DH6 .... 171 C1
Kellfield Av *LWF/SPW/WRK* NE9.. 87 G6
Kellfield Rd *LWF/SPW/WRK* NE9 . 87 G6
Kell Rd *PLEE/EAS* SR8 .... 175 G4 🖪
Kells La *LWF/SPW/WRK* NE9 .... 87 F7
Kellsway *FELL* NE10 .... 88 B7 🖪
Kell's Wy *ROWG* NE39 .... 97 G4
Kelly Rd *HEBB* NE31 .... 89 G1
Kelsey Wy *CRAM* NE23............ 33 H5
Kelso Cl *WD/WHPE/BLK* NE5 .... 54 A6 🖪
Kelso Dr *NSHW* NE29 .... 60 C2
Kelso Gdns
BW/LEM/TK/HW NE15 .... 69 F5
WLSD/HOW NE28.................... 59 J6
Kelso Gv *HLS* DH4 .... 131 J1 🖪
Kelson Wy
WD/WHPE/BLK NE5 .... 54 A6 🖪

Kelso Pl *GATE* NE8 .... 9 M6
Kelston Wy *WD/WHPE/BLK* NE5 . 69 G1
Kelvin Gv
CLDN/WHIT/ROK SR6 .... 91 J3 🖪
CLDN/WHIT/ROK SR6 .... 106 E3
GATE NE8 .... 10 D8
HAR/WTLS NE34 .... 75 K2
JES NE2 .... 6 B2
NSHW NE29 .... 60 E2
Kemble Cl *CRAM* NE23 .... 33 H5 🖪
Kemp Rd *PLEE/EAS* SR8 .... 174 D3
Kempton Cl *CON/LDGT* DH8 ... 108 D7 🖪
Kempton Gdns *GATE* NE8 .... 10 B9
Kendal Av *BLYTH* NE24 .... 35 F1 🖪
TYNE/NSHE NE30 .... 51 F7
Kendal Crs *LWF/SPW/WRK* NE9 . 101 H1
Kendal Dr *BOL* NE36 .... 91 H6 🖪
CRAM NE23............................ 33 J7
Kendale Wk
WD/WHPE/BLK NE5 .... 54 C7 🖪
Kendal Gdns *WLSD/HOW* NE28 . 59 J5
Kendor Gv *MPTH* NE61 .... 20 D7
Kenilworth *LGB/KIL* NE12 .... 47 K5
ELS/FEN NE4 .... 4 C8
MONK NE25 .... 50 C5
Kenilworth Rd *ASHGTN* NE63 ... 23 J1
MONK NE25 .... 50 C5
Kenilworth Sq *SWCK/CAS* SR5.. 105 G1
Kenilworth Vw
LWF/SPW/WRK NE9 .... 101 G3
Kenley Rd *WD/WHPE/BLK* NE5 .. 68 E3
Kenmoor Wy
WD/WHPE/BLK NE5 .... 54 A7
Kenmore Crs *RYTON* NE40 ...... 82 D2
Kennersdene *TYNE/NSHE* NE30.. 61 G2
Kennet Av *JRW* NE32 .... 90 A1
Kennington Gv
BYK/HTN/WLK NE6 .... 7 L6
Kenny Pl *DHAM* DH1 .... 157 G6
Kensington Av *GOS/KPK* NE3 ... 56 C3
Kensington Gdns
TYNE/NSHE NE30 .... 61 F3 🖪
WLSD/HOW NE28.................... 58 A7
Kensington Gv
TYNE/NSHE NE30 .... 61 F3 🖪
Kensington Ter *JES* NE2 .... 5 J2
HEBB NE31 .... 73 F6
WLSD/HOW NE28.................... 73 H1
Kentchester Rd *SWCK/CAS* SR5 . 105 F1
Kent Cl *ASHGTN* NE63 .... 23 G1 🖪
Kent Gdns *HLH* DH5 .... 147 J4
Kentmere Av *BYK/HTN/WLK* NE6.. 72 B5
CLDN/WHIT/ROK SR6 .... 92 C7
Kentmere Cl *CRAM* NE23 .... 39 H6
Kentmere Pl *PLEE/EAS* SR8 ..... 175 F4 🖪
Kenton Av *GOS/KPK* NE3 .... 56 A7
Kenton Ct *SSH* NE33 .... 75 H2
Kenton Crs *GOS/KPK* NE3 .... 55 K6
Kenton Gv
CLDN/WHIT/ROK SR6 .... 106 D4
Kenton La *GOS/KPK* NE3 .... 55 H6
WD/WHPE/BLK NE5 .... 55 J6
Kenton Rd *GOS/KPK* NE3 .... 56 A5
NSHW NE29 .... 60 A3
Kent Pl *HAR/WTLS* NE34 .... 75 K5
Kent Rd *CON/LDGT* DH8 .... 122 C7
Kent St *JRW* NE32 .... 73 J5
Kent Ter *RDHAMSE* DH6 .... 172 D1
Kentucky Rd *SWCK/CAS* SR5 ... 104 E1
Kenya Rd *SWCK/CAS* SR5 .... 105 F1
Kepier Chare *RYTON* NE40 .... 66 B7
Kepier Ct *DHAM* DH1 .... 16 F2
Kepier Gdns
MLFD/PNYW SR4 .... 104 E7 🖪
Keppel St *SSH* NE33 .... 3 H7
Kepwell Bank Top *PRUD* NE42 .. 80 D2
Kepwell Ct *PRUD* NE42 .... 80 C1
Kepwell Rd *PRUD* NE42 .... 80 C2
Kerry Cl *BLYTH* NE24 .... 31 G6 🖪
Kerryhill Dr *DHAM* DH1 .... 156 D1 🖪
Keston Dr *CRAM* NE23............. 33 H5
Kestrel Cl *WASHS* NE38 .... 116 C4
Kestrel Dr *ASHGTN* NE63 .... 23 H4
Kestrel Ms *WICK/BNPF* NE16 ... 84 E5 🖪
Kestrel Pl *LGB/KIL* NE12 .... 57 H3
Kestrel St *DUN/TMV* NE11 .... 86 C6
Kestrel Wy *HAR/WTLS* NE34 .... 75 F7
NSHW NE29 .... 2 B6
Keswick Av
CLDN/WHIT/ROK SR6 .... 106 C1
Keswick Dr *TYNE/NSHE* NE30.... 51 F7
Keswick Gdns *WLSD/HOW* NE28 . 59 J7
Keswick Gv *WD/WHPE/BLK* NE5 . 68 E3
Keswick Rd *PLEE/EAS* SR8 ...... 175 F4
STLY/ANP DH9 .... 126 B3
Keswick St *GATE* NE8 .... 10 E6
Keswic Ter *RDHAMSE* DH6 ...... 160 D1
Kettering Pl *CRAM* NE23 .... 33 J7 🖪
Kettlewell Ter *TYNE/NSHE* NE30 .. 2 F1
Ketton Cl *LGB/KIL* NE12 .... 57 H4 🖪
Kew Gdns *WBAY* NE26 .... 50 D3
Keyes Gdns *JES* NE2 .... 56 E7
Kibblesworth Bank
DUN/TMV NE11 .... 100 B7
Kidd Av *RDHAMSE* DH6 .... 170 C1
Kidderminster Dr
WD/WHPE/BLK NE5 .... 54 A7 🖪
Kidderminster Rd
SWCK/CAS SR5 .... 105 F2
Kidland Cl *ASHGTN* NE63 .... 24 B1
Kidlandlee Gn
WD/WHPE/BLK NE5 .... 54 E6 🖪
Kidlandlee Pl
WD/WHPE/BLK NE5 .... 54 E6
Kielder Av *CRAM* NE23 .... 37 J2
LGB/KIL NE12 .... 47 J5
WD/WHPE/BLK NE5 .... 54 E6 🖪
Kielder Dr *ASHGTN* NE63 .... 23 J2
TRIM TS29 .... 182 D7
Kielder Gdns *JRW* NE32 .... 89 J1
STKFD/GP NE62 .... 23 G4
Kielder Pl *MONK* NE25 .... 49 K4
Kielder Rd
BW/LEM/TK/HW NE15 .... 67 K4
MONK NE25 .... 49 K4
Kielder Ter *TYNE/NSHE* NE30 ... 61 F4 🖪

Kielder Wy GOS/KPK NE3 ... 56 B3 2
Kier Hardie Av STLY/ANP DH9 ... 126 D2
Kilburn Dr PLEE/EAS SR8 ... 175 G1
Kilburne Cl LGB/HTN NE7 ... 58 A7 3
Kilburn Gdns NSHW NE29 ... 60 B7
Kilchurn CON/LDGT DH8 ... 122 D4
Kildale HLS DH4 ... 117 G6 3
Killiebrigs BW/LEM/TK/HW NE15 .. 65 K1
Killin Cl WD/WHPE/BLK NE5 ... 54 A6 3
Killingworth Av SMOOR NE27 ... 48 C5
Killingworth Dr LGB/KIL NE12 ... 47 H7
SUNDSW SR3 ... 119 H2
Killingworth La LGB/KIL NE12 ... 48 C6
Killingworth Pl CNUT NE1 ... 5 J5
Killingworth Rd GOS/KPK NE3 ... 57 F5
LGB/KIL NE12 ... 58 A1
Killingworth Wy CRAM NE23 ... 48 A4
LGB/KIL NE12 ... 47 G5
Kiln Ri WICK/BNPF NE16 ... 98 E1
Kilnshaw Pl GOS/KPK NE3 ... 56 D1 3
Kimberley WASHS NE38 ... 117 J1
Kimberley Av NSHW NE29 ... 60 C4
Kimberley Gdns JES NE2 ... 71 G3 3
Kimberley St BLYTH NE24 ... 31 F6
MLFD/PNYW SR4 ... 105 K7 5
Kingarth Av
CLDN/WHIT/ROK SR6 ... 92 E7
Kingdom Pl NSHW NE29 ... 2 C7
King Edward Pl GATE NE8 ... 11 L5
King Edward Rd
BYK/HTN/WLK NE6 ... 71 H2
MLFD/PNYW SR4 ... 105 F7 2
RYTON NE40 ... 67 G7
SEA/MUR SR7 ... 150 E2
TYNE/NSHE NE30 ... 61 G3
King Edward St GATE NE8 ... 11 L6
Kingfisher Cl ASHGTN NE63 ... 24 A5
Kingfisher Rd LGB/KIL NE12 ... 57 G3
Kingfisher Wy BLYTH NE24 ... 35 G3
WLSD/HOW NE28 ... 59 J4
King George Av DUN/TMV NE11 ... 9 G9
King George Rd GOS/KPK NE3 ... 55 J4
HAR/WTLS NE34 ... 75 J4
King George's Rd NWBGN NE64 ... 19 F7
Kingham Ct LGB/HTN NE7 ... 57 F6 2
King John's Ct PONT/DH NE20 ... 42 C5
King John St BYK/HTN/WLK NE6 ... 6 F1
King John Ter BYK/HTN/WLK NE6 .. 6 F1
Kings Av CLDN/WHIT/ROK SR6 ... 92 E7
HEBB NE31 ... 73 H6
MPTH NE61 ... 20 D3
Kingsbridge LGB/KIL NE12 ... 57 F3 1
Kings Cl GATE NE8 ... 11 L5
Kingsdale Av BLYTH NE24 ... 30 C7
Kingsdale Rd LGB/KIL NE12 ... 57 F3
King's Dr WBAY NE26 ... 50 E4
King's Gdns BLYTH NE24 ... 30 E6
Kings Gv DHAM DH1 ... 168 B3
Kingsland JES NE2 ... 70 E3 2
King's La CLSW/PEL DH2 ... 114 D7
Kingsley Av GOS/KPK NE3 ... 56 D1
HAR/WTLS NE34 ... 90 E1
MONK NE25 ... 50 D5
Kingsley Cl SWCK/CAS SR5 ... 106 A4 1
Kingsley Pl DUN/TMV NE11 ... 9 H6 1
WICK/BNPF NE16 ... 85 F4
WLSD/HOW NE28 ... 59 H7 4
Kingsley Rd MPTH NE61 ... 18 C2 1
Kingsley Ter ELS/FEN NE4 ... 4 C7
Kingsmere CLS/BIR/GTL DH3 ... 115 J7
Kingsmere Gdns
BYK/HTN/WLK NE6 ... 72 C7 3
Kings Pk STKFD/GP NE62 ... 29 F1
King's Pl MLFD/PNYW SR4 ... 106 A6
King's Rd BDLGTN NE22 ... 29 K4
CNUT NE1 ... 5 J4
CON/LDGT DH8 ... 122 D2
LGB/KIL NE12 ... 57 J1
WBAY NE26 ... 50 D3
WNGT TS28 ... 183 J2
Kings Rd North
WLSD/HOW NE28 ... 58 D6
Kings Rd South
WLSD/HOW NE28 ... 58 D7
The King's Rd SWCK/CAS SR5 ... 106 A3
King's Ter MLFD/PNYW SR4 ... 105 K6
Kingston Av BDN/LAN/SAC DH7 .. 155 F6
BYK/HTN/WLK NE6 ... 7 K7
Kingston Cl WBAY NE26 ... 50 D1
Kingston Dr WBAY NE26 ... 50 D2
Kingston Park Av GOS/KPK NE3 .. 55 G4
Kingston Park Rd DIN/WO NE13 .. 55 H2
GOS/KPK NE3 ... 55 K3
Kingston Rd GATE NE8 ... 11 K7
Kingston Ter
CLDN/WHIT/ROK SR6 ... 106 D3
King St BLYTH NE24 ... 31 G6
CLDN/WHIT/ROK SR6 ... 106 D1
CLS/BIR/GTL DH3 ... 115 H2
CNUT NE1 ... 5 M8
FELL NE10 ... 13 K5
GATE NE8 ... 10 B7
RDHAMSE DH6 ... 170 C1
RDHAMSE DH6 ... 173 J4
SSH NE33 ... 3 G7
SUND SR1 ... 14 E4
TYNE/NSHE NE30 ... 61 F4
Kingsway BDN/LAN/SAC DH7 ... 154 B3
BLYTH NE24 ... 35 G1 1
ELS/FEN NE4 ... 69 J3
HLH DH5 ... 132 D7
PONT/DH NE20 ... 43 G3
SSH NE33 ... 75 K1
TYNE/NSHE NE30 ... 61 G2
WICK/BNPF NE16 ... 98 E2
Kingsway Av GOS/KPK NE3 ... 56 C3
Kingsway North DUN/TMV NE11 .. 86 C6
Kingsway Rd SWCK/CAS SR5 ... 104 E1
Kingsway South
DUN/TMV NE11 ... 100 D1
Kingswood Av JES NE2 ... 56 D7 2
Kingswood Cl BOLCOL NE35 ... 90 C3
Kingswood Dr PONT/DH NE20 ... 42 E5
Kingswood Gv
MLFD/PNYW SR4 ... 118 D4
Kingswood Rd CRAM NE23 ... 33 J7
King Ter STLY/ANP DH9 ... 126 B2
Kinlett WASHS NE38 ... 117 J1 2
Kinley Rd DHAM DH1 ... 158 A4
Kinloch Ct CLSW/PEL DH2 ... 129 H6
Kinloss Sq CRAM NE23 ... 33 J7 2
Kinnaird Av
BW/LEM/TK/HW NE15 ... 68 E5
Kinross Ct FELL NE10 ... 13 M4
Kinross Dr GOS/KPK NE3 ... 55 J5
STLY/ANP DH9 ... 127 F1
Kinver Dr WD/WHPE/BLK NE5 ... 54 A7
Kiphill Ct STLY/ANP DH9 ... 112 E6
Kipling Av BOLCOL NE35 ... 91 F4
HEBB NE31 ... 73 H5
WICK/BNPF NE16 ... 85 F4
Kipling Cl STLY/ANP DH9 ... 126 E1
Kipling Ct WICK/BNPF NE16 ... 85 F4 3
Kipling St SWCK/CAS SR5 ... 106 A4 5
Kira Dr DHAM DH1 ... 156 D1
Kirby Av DHAM DH1 ... 156 B4
Kirby Cl HAR/WTLS NE34 ... 74 D7
Kirkbride Pl CRAM NE23 ... 33 J7 3
Kirkdale Gn ELS/FEN NE4 ... 4 E8
Kirkdale St HLH DH5 ... 147 J6
Kirkham Av GOS/KPK NE3 ... 55 G3 1
Kirkham Rd DHAM DH1 ... 156 E3
Kirkharle Dr MPTH NE61 ... 21 J2
Kirkheaton Pl
WD/WHPE/BLK NE5 ... 69 G3
Kirkland Hl PLEE/EAS SR8 ... 174 E3
Kirklands CRAM NE23 ... 47 J4
Kirkland Wk SMOOR NE27 ... 49 G6
Kirklea Rd HLH DH5 ... 132 D7
Kirkleatham Gdns
BYK/HTN/WLK NE6 ... 71 K1 4
Kirkley Av HAR/WTLS NE34 ... 76 A5
Kirkley Cl GOS/KPK NE3 ... 56 B3
Kirkley Dr PONT/DH NE20 ... 43 G2
Kirkley Rd SMOOR NE27 ... 49 H7
Kirklinton Rd TYNE/NSHE NE30 ... 50 E7
Kirknewton Cl HLH DH5 ... 132 D7 5
Kirkside HLS DH4 ... 132 C1
Kirkston Av
BW/LEM/TK/HW NE15 ... 68 B4
Kirkstone CLS/BIR/GTL DH3 ... 115 K4
Kirkstone Av JRW NE32 ... 90 B1
PLEE/EAS SR8 ... 175 F4
SWCK/CAS SR5 ... 106 C2
TYNE/NSHE NE30 ... 50 E7
Kirkstone Cl HLH DH5 ... 132 D7
Kirkstone Dr DHAM DH1 ... 157 K4
Kirkstone Gdns LGB/HTN NE7 ... 57 G7 2
Kirkstone Rd FELL NE10 ... 13 H6
Kirk St CON/LDGT DH8 ... 122 E4 2
Kirk Vw HLS DH4 ... 132 B4 3
Kirkwall Cl SWCK/CAS SR5 ... 104 E4
Kirkwood CRAM NE23 ... 47 J4
Kirkwood Av MLFD/PNYW SR4 .. 118 E4
Kirkwood Cl CRAM NE23 ... 39 H6
Kirkwood Dr GOS/KPK NE3 ... 55 K5 3
Kirkwood Gdns FELL NE10 ... 13 L7
Kirton Av ELS/FEN NE4 ... 69 J5
Kirton Wy CRAM NE23 ... 33 J7
Kismet St SWCK/CAS SR5 ... 106 A3
Kitchener Rd
CLDN/WHIT/ROK SR6 ... 76 E7
Kitchener St
LWF/SPW/WRK NE9 ... 11 J9
MLFD/PNYW SR4 ... 119 K2
Kitchener Ter
ASHBK/HED/RY SR2 ... 121 F4
JRW NE32 ... 73 K6
TYNE/NSHE NE30 ... 61 G3
Kitching Rd PLEE/EAS SR8 ... 174 B1
Kitswell Rd BDN/LAN/SAC DH7 ... 140 A3
Kittiwake Cl BLYTH NE24 ... 35 G4
NSHW NE29 ... 59 J3
Kittiwake Dr WASHS NE38 ... 116 B3
Kittiwake St DUN/TMV NE11 ... 86 C7
Kitty Brewster Rd BLYTH NE24 ... 30 B6
Knaresborough Cl BDLGTN NE22 .. 28 D4
Knaresborough Rd
SEA/MUR SR7 ... 149 H5
Knaresdale CLS/BIR/GTL DH3 ... 115 K5
Knarsdale Av NSHW NE29 ... 60 B4
Knarsdale Pl
WD/WHPE/BLK NE5 ... 68 C2 3
Kneller Cl STLY/ANP DH9 ... 126 D1
Knightsbridge GOS/KPK NE3 ... 56 C4
SUNDSW SR3 ... 119 J6 2
Knightside Gdns
DUN/TMV NE11 ... 85 K6 4
Knitsley La CON/LDGT DH8 ... 123 F7
CON/LDGT DH8 ... 137 J4
CON/LDGT DH8 ... 138 C7
Knivestone Ct LGB/KIL NE12 ... 48 A5
Knobbyends La BLAY NE21 ... 83 H4
Knoll Ri DUN/TMV NE11 ... 85 K5
Knollside Cl SUNDSW SR3 ... 133 K2
Knott Pl BW/LEM/TK/HW NE15 ... 68 E6
Knoulberry WASHN NE37 ... 102 C7
Knoulberry Rd WASHN NE37 ... 102 C7
Knowledge Hl BLAY NE21 ... 83 K3
Knowle Pl LGB/KIL NE12 ... 57 H5
Knowsley Ct
WD/WHPE/BLK NE5 ... 55 F5 1
Knox Cl BDLGTN NE22 ... 29 K4 4
Knox Rd BDLGTN NE22 ... 29 H6
Knox Sq SWCK/CAS SR5 ... 106 A2
Kristin Av JRW NE32 ... 74 A7
Kyffin Vw HAR/WTLS NE34 ... 76 B6
Kyle Cl ELS/FEN NE4 ... 4 F9
Kyle Rd GATE NE8 ... 10 B7
Kyloe Av MONK NE25 ... 40 A6
Kyloe Cl GOS/KPK NE3 ... 55 J3
Kyloe Pl WD/WHPE/BLK NE5 ... 54 E7
Kyloe Vls WD/WHPE/BLK NE5 ... 54 E7 5
Kyo Bog La WYLAM NE41 ... 81 H3
Kyo Heugh Rd STLY/ANP DH9 ... 125 J1
Kyo La RYTON NE40 ... 81 K5
STLY/ANP DH9 ... 125 K2
Kyo Rd STLY/ANP DH9 ... 125 H2

L

Laburnam Pk
BDN/LAN/SAC DH7 ... 167 F7 1
Laburnam Rd
CLDN/WHIT/ROK SR6 ... 106 D2 5
Laburnum Av BLYTH NE24 ... 31 F6
BYK/HTN/WLK NE6 ... 72 B3
CON/LDGT DH8 ... 122 E3
DHAM DH1 ... 16 A4
FELL NE10 ... 13 J9
WLSD/HOW NE28 ... 72 D1
Laburnum Ct LGB/KIL NE12 ... 47 J5 9
Laburnum Crs DUN/TMV NE11 ... 100 C7
SEA/MUR SR7 ... 150 D4 1
Laburnum Cressent
TRIM TS29 ... 183 G6 1
Laburnum Gdns JRW NE32 ... 73 J7
Laburnum Gv
CLDN/WHIT/ROK SR6 ... 92 A3
HAR/WTLS NE34 ... 75 K6
SWCK/CAS SR5 ... 104 E5
WICK/BNPF NE16 ... 84 E5 9
WICK/BNPF NE16 ... 99 F2
Laburnum Rd BLAY NE21 ... 84 A2
CLDN/WHIT/ROK SR6 ... 106 D2 3
Laburnum Sq TRIM TS29 ... 183 G6 2
Laburnun Ct STKFD/GP NE62 ... 22 E6 4
Lacebark SUNDSW SR3 ... 133 J3
Ladock Cl
ASHBK/HED/RY SR2 ... 121 G6 1
Lady Anne Rd RDHAMSE DH6 ... 158 C7
Ladybank WD/WHPE/BLK NE5 ... 53 K7
Ladyhaugh Dr
WICK/BNPF NE16 ... 98 E1 1
Ladykirk Rd ELS/FEN NE4 ... 69 J6
Ladykirk Wy CRAM NE23 ... 37 K2 1
Ladyrigg PONT/DH NE20 ... 43 F5
Ladysmith Ct STLY/ANP DH9 ... 126 E2
Lady's Piece La RDHAMSE DH6 .. 158 D3
Lady's Wk MPTH NE61 ... 20 D5 1
SSH NE33 ... 3 G5
Ladywell Rd BLAY NE21 ... 84 A2
CON/LDGT DH8 ... 123 J7
Ladywell Wy PONT/DH NE20 ... 43 F2
Ladywood Pk HLS DH4 ... 117 H6 2
Laet St NSHW NE29 ... 2 E3
Laindon Av
CLDN/WHIT/ROK SR6 ... 106 D1
Laing Gv WLSD/HOW NE28 ... 59 J7
Laing St CON/LDGT DH8 ... 123 F3
Laith Rd GOS/KPK NE3 ... 55 J5
Lake Ap BLAY NE21 ... 84 D3 1
Lake Av HAR/WTLS NE34 ... 76 C5
Lake Bank Ter WNGT TS28 ... 183 K5
Lake Ct SUNDSW SR3 ... 134 A1 4
Lakeland Dr PLEE/EAS SR8 ... 175 F3
Lake Rd HLH DH5 ... 132 C7
Lakeside BLAY NE21 ... 84 D3
HAR/WTLS NE34 ... 76 D5
Lake Vw HEBB NE31 ... 73 F7
WNGT TS28 ... 183 K5
Lambden Cl NSHW NE29 ... 60 C7
Lambert Rd WASHN NE37 ... 102 B6
Lambeth Pl GATE NE8 ... 11 K7 1
Lambley Av TYNE/NSHE NE30 ... 51 F7
Lambley Cl WICK/BNPF NE16 ... 98 E3
Lambley Crs HEBB NE31 ... 89 F1
Lambourn Av LGB/KIL NE12 ... 57 J3
NSHW NE29 ... 60 B6
Lambourne Cl HLS DH4 ... 131 G4
Lambourne Rd
ASHBK/HED/RY SR2 ... 120 C3
Lamb St BYK/HTN/WLK NE6 ... 72 C6 2
Lambton Av CON/LDGT DH8 ... 123 H7
WICK/BNPF NE16 ... 8 A8
Lambton Cl RYTON NE40 ... 66 B7
Lambton Ct PLEE/EAS SR8 ... 174 D7
SUNDSW SR3 ... 119 G7 3
WASHS NE38 ... 116 A6
Lambton Dr HLH DH5 ... 147 K6
Lambton Rd HEBB NE31 ... 73 H4 2
JES NE2 ... 5 L1
Lambton St SUND SR1 ... 14 F3
Lambton Ter JRW NE32 ... 89 K1
Lampeter Cl
WD/WHPE/BLK NE5 ... 55 F6 7
Lamport St HEBB NE31 ... 72 E4 2
Lampton Ct BDLGTN NE22 ... 29 J4 1
Lanark Cl NSHW NE29 ... 60 A2
Lanark Dr JRW NE32 ... 90 C1
Lancashire Dr DHAM DH1 ... 158 A6
Lancaster Ct GOS/KPK NE3 ... 55 H3 3
Lancaster Dr WLSD/HOW NE28 ... 59 F3
Lancaster Rd CON/LDGT DH8 ... 137 F1
DUN/TMV NE11 ... 8 E6
Lancaster Ter CLS/BIR/GTL DH3 .. 129 K5
Lancastrian Rd CRAM NE23 ... 38 B3
Lancefield Av
BYK/HTN/WLK NE6 ... 72 B7
Lanchester Av
LWF/SPW/WRK NE9 ... 101 K2
Lanchester Cl FELL NE10 ... 88 E6 1
Lanchester Gn BDLGTN NE22 ... 29 F4 1
Lanchester Pk WASHS NE38 ... 117 G4 2
Lanchester Rd
BDN/LAN/SAC DH7 ... 125 J7
Lancing Ct GOS/KPK NE3 ... 55 G3
Landsdowne Crs
RDHAMSE DH6 ... 180 B3 1
Landsdowne Gdns
STKFD/GP NE62 ... 23 G5 4
Landsdowne Rd
RDHAMSE DH6 ... 180 C7
Landseer Cl STLY/ANP DH9 ... 126 D1
Landseer Gdns HAR/WTLS NE34 .. 91 H2
LWF/SPW/WRK NE9 ... 11 M9 1
Lane Cnr HAR/WTLS NE34 ... 75 G6
Lanercost WASHS NE38 ... 116 E1
Lanercost Av BLAY NE21 ... 83 K2 1
Lanercost Dr
WD/WHPE/BLK NE5 ... 69 F3
Lanercost Gdns
BW/LEM/TK/HW NE15 ... 53 F7
FELL NE10 ... 87 J6 2
Lanercost Rd NSHW NE29 ... 60 C5
Langdale MONK NE25 ... 50 C4
Langdale Cl CON/LDGT DH8 ... 123 K3 2
LGB/KIL NE12 ... 57 G4
Langdale Crs DHAM DH1 ... 157 K4
Langdale Dr CRAM NE23 ... 37 K2
Langdale Gdns
BYK/HTN/WLK NE6 ... 72 C5 3
WLSD/HOW NE28 ... 59 J6
Langdale Pl PLEE/EAS SR8 ... 175 F4 7
Langdale Rd HLS DH4 ... 117 J6
LWF/SPW/WRK NE9 ... 87 G7
Langdale St HLH DH5 ... 147 J6
Langdale Wy BOL NE36 ... 91 G4
Langdon Cl NSHW NE29 ... 60 D1 1
Langdon Rd WD/WHPE/BLK NE5 .. 68 B1
Langford Dr BOLCOL NE35 ... 90 C2
Langham Av NSHW NE29 ... 60 A2
Langham Rd
BW/LEM/TK/HW NE15 ... 68 D6 1
Langholm Rd BOL NE36 ... 91 H4
GOS/KPK NE3 ... 56 C3 1
Langhurst ASHBK/HED/RY SR2 .. 120 E6
Langleeford Rd
WD/WHPE/BLK NE5 ... 54 E7
Langley Av BDN/LAN/SAC DH7 ... 141 G3
BLYTH NE24 ... 30 D6
FELL NE10 ... 88 D6
MONK NE25 ... 50 B6
SMOOR NE27 ... 49 J7
Langley Cl WASHS NE38 ... 116 D2
Langley Crs BDN/LAN/SAC DH7 .. 167 J5
Langley La BDN/LAN/SAC DH7 ... 141 G4
BDN/LAN/SAC DH7 ... 141 K6
Langley Rd ASHGTN NE63 ... 23 J2
BYK/HTN/WLK NE6 ... 72 B5
DHAM DH1 ... 156 D3
NSHW NE29 ... 60 B4
SUNDSW SR3 ... 120 B4
WD/WHPE/BLK NE5 ... 68 D3
Langley St HLS DH4 ... 132 B1
Langley Ter JRW NE32 ... 89 K1
Langport Rd
ASHBK/HED/RY SR2 ... 120 D3 2
Langton Cl MLFD/PNYW SR4 ... 14 A5 1
Langton Ct PONT/DH NE20 ... 42 D5
Langton Dr CRAM NE23 ... 33 J5
Langton Lea DHAM DH1 ... 169 K5 1
Langton Ter LGB/HTN NE7 ... 71 H1 1
Langwell Ter MPTH NE61 ... 21 K1
Lanivet Cl ASHBK/HED/RY SR2 ... 121 F6
Lansbury Cl CLS/BIR/GTL DH3 ... 101 H7
Lansbury Dr CLS/BIR/GTL DH3 ... 101 H7
SEA/MUR SR7 ... 149 H5 3
Lansbury Gdns FELL NE10 ... 13 K8
Lansbury Rd WICK/BNPF NE16 ... 85 G6
Lansbury Wy SWCK/CAS SR5 ... 105 F4
Lansdowne
ASHBK/HED/RY SR2 ... 120 E7
Lansdowne Gdns JES NE2 ... 6 D1
Lansdowne Rd LGB/KIL NE12 ... 57 K2
Lansdowne St MLFD/PNYW SR4 .. 14 A3
Lansdowne Ter NSHW NE29 ... 2 B1
Lansdowne Ter West NSHW NE29 .. 2 A1
Lanthwaite Rd
LWF/SPW/WRK NE9 ... 87 G7
Lanton St HLS DH4 ... 132 B1
Lapford Dr CRAM NE23 ... 33 J6
Lapwing Cl BLYTH NE24 ... 35 G3
WASHS NE38 ... 116 B3
Lapwing Ct WICK/BNPF NE16 ... 112 A1
L'arbre Crs WICK/BNPF NE16 ... 84 D5
Larch Av CLDN/WHIT/ROK SR6 ... 93 G3
HAR/WTLS NE34 ... 76 A6
HLS DH4 ... 132 B6
Larch Cl LWF/SPW/WRK NE9 ... 101 K3
Larches Rd DHAM DH1 ... 156 B6 1
The Larches BDN/LAN/SAC DH7 .. 165 G2
WICK/BNPF NE16 ... 97 K6 1
Larchlea PONT/DH NE20 ... 42 E7
Larchlea South PONT/DH NE20 ... 42 E7
Larch Rd BLAY NE21 ... 84 B1
Larch St CON/LDGT DH8 ... 123 F4
Larch Ter STLY/ANP DH9 ... 111 J5
Larchwood WASHS NE38 ... 116 D5
Larchwood Av
BYK/HTN/WLK NE6 ... 72 A3
DIN/WO NE13 ... 46 C4
GOS/KPK NE3 ... 55 K3 3
Larchwood Gdns
DUN/TMV NE11 ... 86 B7
Larchwood Gv
ASHBK/HED/RY SR2 ... 120 C4 4
Larkfield Crs HLS DH4 ... 131 J2 1
Larkfield Rd
ASHBK/HED/RY SR2 ... 120 C3
Lark Rise Cl LGB/HTN NE7 ... 57 K7 3
Larkspur Cl STLY/ANP DH9 ... 112 B6
Larkspur Rd WICK/BNPF NE16 ... 84 E6
Larkspur Ter JES NE2 ... 70 E2
Larne Crs LWF/SPW/WRK NE9 ... 87 G7
Larriston Pl CRAM NE23 ... 38 A2 1
Lartington Cl CLS/BIR/GTL DH3 .. 145 J2
Lartington Gdns
GOS/KPK NE3 ... 57 F5 4
Larwood Cl CLS/BIR/GTL DH3 ... 130 A6
Larwood Ct STLY/ANP DH9 ... 125 G4
Lascelles Av HAR/WTLS NE34 ... 75 J6
Laski Gdns FELL NE10 ... 13 L7
Lassells Rigg PRUD NE42 ... 80 D1
Latimer St TYNE/NSHE NE30 ... 61 H2
Laude Bank BDN/LAN/SAC DH7 .. 153 F5
Lauderdale Av WLSD/HOW NE28 .. 58 D6
Launceston Cl DIN/WO NE13 ... 55 H2
Launceston Dr SUNDSW SR3 ... 119 G7
Laura St SUND SR1 ... 14 F6
Laurel Av DHAM DH1 ... 17 L3
GOS/KPK NE3 ... 56 A4
LGB/KIL NE12 ... 58 C1
SEA/MUR SR7 ... 150 C1
Laurel Ct CLSW/PEL DH2 ... 129 H2
Laurel Crs BYK/HTN/WLK NE6 ... 72 B2
STLY/ANP DH9 ... 114 B7
TRIM TS29 ... 182 E6
Laurel Cressent RDHAMSE DH6 .. 172 B7
Laurel Dr ASHGTN NE63 ... 23 J4
CON/LDGT DH8 ... 123 K4
Laurel Gv ASHBK/HED/RY SR2 ... 120 C4
Laurel Rd BLAY NE21 ... 84 B2
Laurel St BW/LEM/TK/HW NE15 ... 53 F7
WLSD/HOW NE28 ... 72 E2
Laurel Wy RYTON NE40 ... 82 C1
Laurelwood Gdns
DUN/TMV NE11 ... 86 B7
Lauren Ct PLEE/EAS SR8 ... 162 D5
Laurens Ct WASHN NE37 ... 103 F5 1
Lavender Ct ASHGTN NE63 ... 23 J4 2
Lavender Gdns
BDN/LAN/SAC DH7 ... 143 J5
JES NE2 ... 70 D2
Lavender Gv SWCK/CAS SR5 ... 104 E4
Lavender La HAR/WTLS NE34 ... 75 F6
Lavender Rd WICK/BNPF NE16 ... 84 E6
Laverock Hall Rd BLYTH NE24 ... 34 C4
Laverock Pl BLYTH NE24 ... 34 D4 2
GOS/KPK NE3 ... 55 H5 7
Lavington Rd HAR/WTLS NE34 ... 75 J3
Lawe Rd SSH NE33 ... 3 J4
Lawmill Wy
WD/WHPE/BLK NE5 ... 69 F1 7
Lawn Dr BOL NE36 ... 90 D6
The Lawns HLH DH5 ... 148 B7
Lawnswood HLH DH5 ... 147 J1
Lawrence Av BLAY NE21 ... 84 A1
HAR/WTLS NE34 ... 91 H1
Lawrence Ct BLAY NE21 ... 84 A1 4
Lawrence St SUND SR1 ... 15 H5
Lawson Av JRW NE32 ... 74 A7
Lawson Crs
CLDN/WHIT/ROK SR6 ... 106 D1
Lawson Rd RDHAMSE DH6 ... 180 A2
Lawson's St TRIM TS29 ... 183 F7 1
Lawson St NSHW NE29 ... 2 D5
WLSD/HOW NE28 ... 72 E2
Lawson Ter DHAM DH1 ... 16 A4
ELS/FEN NE4 ... 69 J7 2
HLH DH5 ... 148 A7
Laws St CLDN/WHIT/ROK SR6 ... 106 D1
Laxford Ct SUNDSW SR3 ... 133 K2
Laybourn Gdns
HAR/WTLS NE34 ... 74 E7 3
Layburn Gdns
BW/LEM/TK/HW NE15 ... 68 C3 4
Layburn Pl PLEE/EAS SR8 ... 174 C3
Layfield Rd GOS/KPK NE3 ... 56 C1
Laygate SSH NE33 ... 75 G3 1
Laygate Pl SSH NE33 ... 75 G2
Laygate St SSH NE33 ... 75 F2
Lea Av JRW NE32 ... 90 A2
Leabank BW/LEM/TK/HW NE15 ... 68 B3
Lead Ga BW/LEM/TK/HW NE15 ... 64 C2
Leadgate Rd CON/LDGT DH8 ... 123 H4
Lead La CON/LDGT DH8 ... 108 C1
Lead Rd CHPW NE17 ... 95 G1
RYTON NE40 ... 81 K6
RYTON NE40 ... 82 C3
Leafield Crs HAR/WTLS NE34 ... 76 A3
Lea Gn CLS/BIR/GTL DH3 ... 116 A5
Leagreen Ct GOS/KPK NE3 ... 56 A5 1
Leaholme Crs BLYTH NE24 ... 34 E1
Lea La PLEE/EAS SR8 ... 162 C3
Lealholm Rd LGB/HTN NE7 ... 57 G5 2
Leam Gdns FELL NE10 ... 88 E4
Leamington St MLFD/PNYW SR4 .. 14 A6
Leam La FELL NE10 ... 88 C7
JRW NE32 ... 74 B7
JRW NE32 ... 89 J3
LWF/SPW/WRK NE9 ... 102 B1
Leamside FELL NE10 ... 88 B6
JRW NE32 ... 74 A7
Leander Av CLS/BIR/GTL DH3 ... 115 K7
STKFD/GP NE62 ... 23 G5
Leander Ct STKFD/GP NE62 ... 23 H5 2
Leander Dr BOLCOL NE35 ... 90 C4
Leaplish WASHS NE38 ... 117 H4
Lea Riggs HLS DH4 ... 146 D6 1
The Leas HLS DH4 ... 132 B4
Leaway PRUD NE42 ... 80 B2
Leazes Ct DHAM DH1 ... 16 E3
Leazes Crs CNUT NE1 ... 5 H5
Leazes La CNUT NE1 ... 5 J5
DHAM DH1 ... 16 F3
Leazes Pde JES NE2 ... 4 F4
Leazes Park Rd CNUT NE1 ... 5 H5
Leazes Pkwy
BW/LEM/TK/HW NE15 ... 66 E2
Leazes Pl DHAM DH1 ... 16 E3
Leazes Ri PLEE/EAS SR8 ... 175 G4
Leazes Rd DHAM DH1 ... 16 E3
Leazes Ter CNUT NE1 ... 5 H4
The Leazes HAR/WTLS NE34 ... 75 K5
SUND SR1 ... 14 B5
Leazes Vw ROWG NE39 ... 97 F3
Lecondale FELL NE10 ... 88 B7
Ledbury Rd
ASHBK/HED/RY SR2 ... 120 D3
Leechmere Rd
ASHBK/HED/RY SR2 ... 120 C4
Leechmere Wy
ASHBK/HED/RY SR2 ... 120 E6
Lee Cl WASHS NE38 ... 117 K1
Leeds St
CLDN/WHIT/ROK SR6 ... 106 D3 4
Lee Hill Ct BDN/LAN/SAC DH7 ... 140 B4
Leeholme HLH DH5 ... 147 J1
Leeholme Ct STLY/ANP DH9 ... 125 J4 1
Leeman's La RDHAMSE DH6 ... 179 F6
Leeming Gdns
LWF/SPW/WRK NE9 ... 87 H6
Leesfield Dr BDN/LAN/SAC DH7 .. 167 H7
Leesfield Gdns
BDN/LAN/SAC DH7 ... 167 G7
Leesfield Rd
BDN/LAN/SAC DH7 ... 167 H7 1
Lees St STLY/ANP DH9 ... 112 D7
Lee St CLDN/WHIT/ROK SR6 ... 106 D1
SWCK/CAS SR5 ... 106 B4 3
Legg Av BDLGTN NE22 ... 30 A3
Legges Dr DIN/WO NE13 ... 36 C2
Legion Gv
BW/LEM/TK/HW NE15 ... 68 D4 4
Legion Rd
BW/LEM/TK/HW NE15 ... 68 D4 5
Leicester Cl WLSD/HOW NE28 ... 58 C5
Leicestershire Dr DHAM DH1 ... 158 A6 3
Leicester St BYK/HTN/WLK NE6 ... 7 L6
Leighton Rd
ASHBK/HED/RY SR2 ... 120 D4
Leighton St BYK/HTN/WLK NE6 ... 6 D5
SSH NE33 ... 3 L9
Leith Ct HAR/WTLS NE34 ... 75 G6
Leith Gdns STLY/ANP DH9 ... 112 B5

Leland Pl MPTH NE61 20 B6
Lemington Gdns
WD/WHPE/BLK NE5 69 G4
Lemington Rd
BW/LEM/TK/HW NE15 67 J4
Lemon St SSH NE33 75 F5
Lena Av MONK NE25 50 C5
Lenin Ter STLY/ANP DH9 126 E2
Leominster Rd
ASHBK/HED/RY SR2 120 D4
Leopold St JRW NE32 73 K5 1
Lesbury Av ASHGTN NE63 23 K3
SMOOR NE27 49 G6
STKFD/GP NE62 23 F4
WLSD/HOW NE28 59 H7
Lesbury Cha GOS/KPK NE3 56 B4
Lesbury Cl CLSW/PEL DH2 129 F6
Lesbury Rd BYK/HTN/WLK NE6 71 H2
Lesbury St
BW/LEM/TK/HW NE15 68 B5
WLSD/HOW NE28 74 A2 2
Leslie Av HEBB NE31 73 G6
Leslie Cl RYTON NE40 67 G7
Leslie Crs GOS/KPK NE3 56 C7 1
Leslies Vw MPTH NE61 20 C3
Letch Av SEA/MUR SR7 162 B1
Leven Av CLSW/PEL DH2 129 H6
Levisham Cl SUNDSW SR3 120 C7 5
Lewis Crs ASHBK/HED/RY SR2 15 J8
Lewis Dr ELS/FEN NE4 4 A5
Lexington Ct
BDN/LAN/SAC DH7 167 F7
Leybourne Av LGB/KIL NE12 57 K1
Leyburn Cl CLSW/PEL DH2 114 D5
HLS DH4 132 A6
Leyburn Dr LGB/HTN NE7 57 G7
Leyburn Gv HLS DH4 132 A6
Leyburn Pl CLS/BIR/GTL DH3 101 H7
Leyfield Cl SUNDSW SR3 134 B2 1
Leyland Cl RDHAMSE DH6 180 B1
Leyton Pl GATE NE8 11 K8
Liburn Cl BOL NE36 91 F4
Lichfield Av BYK/HTN/WLK NE6 7 M8
Lichfield Cl ASHGTN NE63 24 B3
CLS/BIR/GTL DH3 145 H2 2
GOS/KPK NE3 55 H3
Lichfield Rd SWCK/CAS SR5 106 A2
Lidcombe Cl SUNDSW SR3 120 B7
Liddell St CLDN/WHIT/ROK SR6 14 F1
TYNE/NSHE NE30 2 F3
Liddell Ter GATE NE8 10 C6
Liddle Av RDHAMSE DH6 158 C7 2
Liddle Cl PLEE/EAS SR8 174 C2
Liddle Rd ELS/FEN NE4 4 D6
Lieven St DIN/WO NE13 46 A5 3
Liffey Rd HEBB NE31 89 H1
Lightbourne Rd
BYK/HTN/WLK NE6 72 C5
Lightwood Av
BW/LEM/TK/HW NE15 68 E7 1
Lilac Av BDN/LAN/SAC DH7 143 H5
BLYTH NE24 31 F6
CLDN/WHIT/ROK SR6 93 F1
DHAM DH1 156 C4
HAR/WTLS NE34 75 K6
LGB/KIL NE12 58 B2
SUNDSW SR3 120 B6
Lilac Cl WD/WHPE/BLK NE5 53 K6 5
Lilac Ct ASHGTN NE63 23 J4
Lilac Cressent TRIM TS29 183 G6 3
Lilac Gdns LWF/SPW/WRK NE9 87 F6
WICK/BNPF NE16 84 E6
Lilac Gv CLSW/PEL DH2 129 G2
Lilac Pk BDN/LAN/SAC DH7 167 G1
Lilac Pl CON/LDGT DH8 123 K4
Lilac Rd BYK/HTN/WLK NE6 72 C2
Lilac Sq HLS DH4 131 G4
Lilac St MLFD/PNYW SR4 104 E7
Lilac Ter RDHAMSE DH6 173 H4
Lilburn Cl CLSW/PEL DH2 129 G7
Lilburn Gdns GOS/KPK NE3 57 F6
Lilburn Pl SWCK/CAS SR5 106 A4 6
Lilburn Rd SMOOR NE27 49 G7
Lilburn St NSHW NE29 2 A2
Lilian Av ASHBK/HED/RY SR2 120 E6
WLSD/HOW NE28 72 C2
Lilley Gv SWCK/CAS SR5 105 F4
Lily Av BDLGTN NE22 29 H6
JES NE2 70 E2
Lily Bank WLSD/HOW NE28 72 D1
Lily Crs CLDN/WHIT/ROK SR6 93 F1
JES NE2 70 E2
Lily Gdns STLY/ANP DH9 111 G6
Lily St MLFD/PNYW SR4 14 B3
Lily Ter WD/WHPE/BLK NE5 54 E7
Lilywhite Ter HLH DH5 148 A6
Lime Av HLS DH4 132 A7
Limecragg Av DHAM DH1 157 J6
Limecroft JRW NE32 90 A3
Lime Gv PRUD NE42 80 B1
RYTON NE40 66 E6
Limekiln Rd WLSD/HOW NE28 73 F1
Lime Pk BDN/LAN/SAC DH7 167 G6
The Limes HLS DH4 117 K6
Limestone La PONT/DH NE20 42 B3
Lime St BLAY NE21 84 B3
CNUT NE1 6 C5
MLFD/PNYW SR4 14 A4
Limetrees Gdns
LWF/SPW/WRK NE9 87 F5
Limewood Gv DIN/WO NE13 46 B4
Linacre Cl DIN/WO NE13 55 F4
Linbridge Dr
WD/WHPE/BLK NE5 68 C2 5
Linburn WASHS NE38 116 C5
Lincoln Av SUNDSW SR3 120 A6
WLSD/HOW NE28 58 C7
Lincoln Gn GOS/KPK NE3 56 B1
Lincoln Pl CON/LDGT DH8 137 F1 1
Lincoln Rd CRAM NE23 33 J6 1
DHAM DH1 156 E2 1
HAR/WTLS NE34 76 B4
Lincolnshire Cl DHAM DH1 157 K6
Lincoln St GATE NE8 10 F6
MLFD/PNYW SR4 105 K6 5
Lindale Av WICK/BNPF NE16 84 E7
Lindale Rd ELS/FEN NE4 69 J3
Lindean Pl CRAM NE23 38 A2 2
Lindell Ter RDHAMSE DH6 182 D2
Linden Av ELS/FEN NE4 69 H4
GOS/KPK NE3 56 C6 2
Linden Cl STKFD/GP NE62 23 G5
Linden Gdns
ASHBK/HED/RY SR2 120 C3 6
Linden Gv DUN/TMV NE11 9 J7
HLS DH4 132 B7 1
RDHAMSE DH6 180 C7
Linden Pk BDN/LAN/SAC DH7 167 G6 3
Linden Rd
ASHBK/HED/RY SR2 120 C3 7
BLAY NE21 84 B2
GOS/KPK NE3 56 C6
LGB/KIL NE12 57 K3
MONK NE25 39 J5
Linden Wy PONT/DH NE20 42 E7
Lindesfarne DHAM DH1 169 J5 1
Lindfield Av WD/WHPE/BLK NE5 69 F2
Lindisfarne PLEE/EAS SR8 174 D6
WASHS NE38 116 E2
Lindisfarne Av
CLS/BIR/GTL DH3 129 K4
Lindisfarne Cl HLS DH4 131 K6
JES NE2 57 F7
MPTH NE61 20 E7 1
MPTH NE61 21 K1
WD/WHPE/BLK NE5 68 D2 4
Lindisfarne Ct JRW NE32 74 D5
Lindisfarne Dr GATE NE8 11 H3
Lindisfarne La MPTH NE61 20 E7
Lindisfarne Pl WLSD/HOW NE28 59 F7
Lindisfarne Recess JRW NE32 74 B7
Lindisfarne Rd DHAM DH1 156 E4
HEBB NE31 89 G1
JES NE2 71 F1
Lindisfarne Ter
TYNE/NSHE NE30 60 E3
Lindom Av CLS/BIR/GTL DH3 129 K4
Lindon Rd STLY/ANP DH9 126 C2
Lindrick Ct FELL NE10 88 E5
Lindsay Av BLYTH NE24 30 E6
Lindsay Cl ASHBK/HED/RY SR2 15 G7
Lindsay Rd
ASHBK/HED/RY SR2 15 H7 2
Lindsay St HLH DH5 148 A2
Lindsey Cl CRAM NE23 37 K2
Lindum Rd LWF/SPW/WRK NE9 11 H8
Lingdale DHAM DH1 158 A6
Lingdale Av
CLDN/WHIT/ROK SR6 92 E6
Lingey Gdns FELL NE10 88 E4
Lingey La FELL NE10 88 D5
Lingfield Rd CON/LDGT DH8 122 E4 3
Lingholme CLSW/PEL DH2 129 G3
Lingmell WASHN NE37 102 D7
Lingshaw FELL NE10 13 L9
Linhope Av GOS/KPK NE3 55 K3
Linhope Rd WD/WHPE/BLK NE5 68 D1
Link Av BDLGTN NE22 28 D5
Link Rd WD/WHPE/BLK NE5 69 J1 1
Links Av TYNE/NSHE NE30 51 G7
WBAY NE26 50 D2
Links Dr CON/LDGT DH8 122 E2
Links Gn GOS/KPK NE3 56 D4
Links Rd BLYTH NE24 35 H4
TYNE/NSHE NE30 51 G7
WBAY NE26 35 K7
The Links DHAM DH1 158 A5 1
WBAY NE26 41 F2
Links Vw ASHGTN NE63 24 C5
BLYTH NE24 34 E3
Linkway JRW NE32 90 B3
Linley Hl WICK/BNPF NE16 98 C1
Linnel Dr BW/LEM/TK/HW NE15 68 C4
Linnet Ct ASHGTN NE63 23 H3
Linnet Gv SWCK/CAS SR5 105 G4
Linnheads PRUD NE42 80 B3 2
Linskell ASHBK/HED/RY SR2 120 E6
Linskill Pl TYNE/NSHE NE30 61 F3
Linskill St TYNE/NSHE NE30 2 F2
Linskill Ter TYNE/NSHE NE30 61 F4
Lintfort CLS/BIR/GTL DH3 115 K7
Linthorpe Rd GOS/KPK NE3 56 C3
TYNE/NSHE NE30 61 F1
Linton Rd LWF/SPW/WRK NE9 101 F2
WBAY NE26 41 H7
Lintonville Rd ASHGTN NE63 23 J1
Lintzford Gdns
BW/LEM/TK/HW NE15 68 C5 1
ROWG NE39 97 F5
Lintzford La ROWG NE39 96 D5
Lintzford Rd ROWG NE39 96 C7
Lintz Green La ROWG NE39 96 D6
Lintz La WICK/BNPF NE16 111 F2
Linum Pl ELS/FEN NE4 69 J3
Linwood Pl GOS/KPK NE3 56 C1 3
Lisa Av MLFD/PNYW SR4 118 E1
Lisburn Ter MLFD/PNYW SR4 106 A6
Lisle Gv WLSD/HOW NE28 59 J7
Lisle Rd HAR/WTLS NE34 75 K4
Lisle St WLSD/HOW NE28 72 D1
Lismore Av SSH NE33 75 H4 1
Lismore Pl
BW/LEM/TK/HW NE15 69 G5
Lister Av DUN/TMV NE11 9 G6
RYTON NE40 82 B4
Lister Cl HLH DH5 147 G2
Lister Rd PLEE/EAS SR8 174 B2
Litchfield La BLAY NE21 83 K3
Litchfield Rd DHAM DH1 156 E1
Little Bedford St NSHW NE29 2 E3
Littlebridge Ct DHAM DH1 156 B2 1
Littleburn Cl HLS DH4 132 A5 2
Littleburn La
BDN/LAN/SAC DH7 167 K5
Littleburn Rd
BDN/LAN/SAC DH7 167 K6
Littledene LWF/SPW/WRK NE9 87 F5
Little Eden PLEE/EAS SR8 174 E3
Littleton La RDHAMSE DH6 159 G7
Little Villiers St SUND SR1 14 F4 2
Little Wy BW/LEM/TK/HW NE15 69 F7
Littondale WLSD/HOW NE28 58 B6
Livingstone Rd SUND SR1 14 C4
Livingstone St
CON/LDGT DH8 123 F4 5
Lizard La CLDN/WHIT/ROK SR6 92 E2
HAR/WTLS NE34 76 D5
Lloyd Av HLH DH5 147 F4
Lobban Av HEBB NE31 89 F1
Lobelia Av FELL NE10 11 M4
Lobelia Cl WD/WHPE/BLK NE5 54 A7 3
Lobley Gdns DUN/TMV NE11 86 A6
Lobley Hill Rd DUN/TMV NE11 86 A6
Lobleyhill Rd WICK/BNPF NE16 98 B5
Local Av RDHAMSE DH6 171 F1
Lochcraig Pl CRAM NE23 38 A2 3
Lochmaben Ter SWCK/CAS SR5 106 D3
Lockerbie Rd CRAM NE23 38 A2
Lockhaugh Rd ROWG NE39 97 H2
Locksley Cl NSHW NE29 59 K1
Locomotion Wy LGB/KIL NE12 47 H4
NSHW NE29 2 C6
Lodge Cl ROWG NE39 110 C1
Lodgeside Meadow
SUNDSW SR3 134 B2
The Lodges Rd
LWF/SPW/WRK NE9 100 E2
Lodore Gv JRW NE32 90 B1
Lodore Rd JES NE2 56 D7
Logan Rd BYK/HTN/WLK NE6 72 B2
Logan St HLH DH5 147 K5
Lola St DIN/WO NE13 45 K4 1
Lombard Dr CLS/BIR/GTL DH3 115 J7
Lombard St SUND SR1 15 H4
Lomond Ct SUNDSW SR3 134 A1 5
Lomond Pl CLSW/PEL DH2 129 H6
London Av WASHN NE37 102 D4
Londonderry Av DHAM DH1 17 M4
Londonderry St
SEA/MUR SR7 151 F3 1
SUNDSW SR3 120 A7
Londonderry Ter SUNDSW SR3 120 B7
Longacre HLS DH4 132 A7
WASHS NE38 117 G5 2
Long Acres DHAM DH1 17 J1
Long Bank CLS/BIR/GTL DH3 101 J6
LWF/SPW/WRK NE9 101 J4
Longborough Ct
LGB/HTN NE7 57 G6 2
Long Burn Dr CLSW/PEL DH2 129 F5
Longclose Bank STLY/ANP DH9 109 K4
Long Close Rd ROWG NE39 110 B1
Long Dl CLSW/PEL DH2 129 F5
Longdean Cl HEBB NE31 72 E6 1
Longdean Pk CLS/BIR/GTL DH3 129 J1
Long Dr MPTH NE61 26 D1
Long Edge BDN/LAN/SAC DH7 141 J5
Longedge La CON/LDGT DH8 137 H5
Longfield Rd
CLDN/WHIT/ROK SR6 106 D2
Longfield Ter BYK/HTN/WLK NE6 72 B7
Long Gair BLAY NE21 83 J4
Long Garth DHAM DH1 156 A5
Longhirst FELL NE10 88 C5
LGB/KIL NE12 47 K5
WD/WHPE/BLK NE5 68 D1
Longhirst Dr DIN/WO NE13 46 B4
Longhirst Rd MPTH NE61 21 K1
Longlands Dr HLH DH5 147 H1
Longleat Gdns MPTH NE61 21 J1
Longley St ELS/FEN NE4 4 D5
Long Meadow Cl RYTON NE40 82 B1 1
Longmeadows PONT/DH NE20 42 D6
SUNDSW SR3 133 G1
Longnewton St SEA/MUR SR7 150 E3
Longniddry WASHN NE37 102 E2
Longniddry Ct
LWF/SPW/WRK NE9 100 E2
Longridge Av LGB/HTN NE7 57 K7
WASHS NE38 116 C4
Longridge Dr WBAY NE26 50 C2
Long Ridge Rd RYTON NE40 82 E2
Longridge Sq
ASHBK/HED/RY SR2 120 D4 1
Longridge Wy CRAM NE23 38 A2
STKFD/GP NE62 29 G3
Longrigg FELL NE10 88 B5 2
Long Rigg WICK/BNPF NE16 84 E3 5
Longrigg Rd WICK/BNPF NE16 84 E3
Long Rw SSH NE33 2 F6
Longsdale Av BLYTH NE24 30 A6
Longshank La
CLS/BIR/GTL DH3 101 G7
Longston Av TYNE/NSHE NE30 51 F6
Longstone Ct LGB/KIL NE12 48 A5
Longstone Sq
WD/WHPE/BLK NE5 68 B2
Longwood Cl WICK/BNPF NE16 99 F2
Lonnen Av ELS/FEN NE4 69 H4
Lonnen Dr WICK/BNPF NE16 84 E4
The Lonnen HAR/WTLS NE34 76 B7
Lonsdale CLS/BIR/GTL DH3 116 A5
Lonsdale Av
CLDN/WHIT/ROK SR6 92 E6
Lonsdale Gdns WLSD/HOW NE28 59 J6
Lonsdale Rd
CLDN/WHIT/ROK SR6 106 E3
Lonsdale Ter JES NE2 70 E1
Loraine Ter
BW/LEM/TK/HW NE15 68 A5 3
Lord Byrons Wk SEA/MUR SR7 135 F6
Lordenshaw
WD/WHPE/BLK NE5 68 D1 5
Lord Nelson St HAR/WTLS NE34 75 F5
Lord St SEA/MUR SR7 150 E2
SSH NE33 75 J2
SUNDSW SR3 120 B7
Lorimers Cl PLEE/EAS SR8 174 C6
Lorne St HLH DH5 160 A1
Lorne Ter ASHBK/HED/RY SR2 14 D8
Lorrain Rd HAR/WTLS NE34 91 H2
Lorton Av TYNE/NSHE NE30 50 E7
Lorton Rd LWF/SPW/WRK NE9 101 G1
Losh Ter BYK/HTN/WLK NE6 72 B6
Lossiemouth Rd NSHW NE29 59 K5
Lothian Ct
WD/WHPE/BLK NE5 55 G7 5
Lotus Cl WD/WHPE/BLK NE5 53 K7
Lotus Pl ELS/FEN NE4 69 H4 2
Loudon St HAR/WTLS NE34 75 G6 11
Loughborough Av
ASHBK/HED/RY SR2 120 C3
Loughrigg Av CRAM NE23 37 K2
Louie Ter LWF/SPW/WRK NE9 87 G7
Louis Av CLDN/WHIT/ROK SR6 106 D2
Loup St BLAY NE21 84 A1 5
Louvain Ter STKFD/GP NE62 23 F6 5
Lovaine Av MONK NE25 50 E5
Lovaine Pl NSHW NE29 2 C3
Lovaine Pl West NSHW NE29 2 B3 1
Lovaine Rw TYNE/NSHE NE30 61 H2
Lovaine St
BW/LEM/TK/HW NE15 67 G3
CLSW/PEL DH2 128 C1
Lovaine Ter NSHW NE29 2 C1
Love Av CRAM NE23 47 H2
Loveless Gdns FELL NE10 13 L9
Lowbiggin WD/WHPE/BLK NE5 54 C4
Low Chare CLS/BIR/GTL DH3 129 K4
Low Cl PRUD NE42 80 E1 3
Lowdham Av NSHW NE29 60 C6
Low Downs Rd HLH DH5 147 K2
Low Dyke St TRIM TS29 183 F7
Lower Dundas St
CLDN/WHIT/ROK SR6 14 F1 2
Lower Rudyerd St NSHW NE29 2 E3 1
Lowerson Av HLS DH4 131 J2
Lowery La STLY/ANP DH9 127 H5
Lowe's Barn Bank DHAM DH1 168 A3
Lowes Ct DHAM DH1 168 B2
Lowes Fall DHAM DH1 168 B2
Lowes Ri DHAM DH1 168 B3
Loweswater Av HLH DH5 160 B1
Loweswater Cl BLYTH NE24 30 B5
Loweswater Rd
WD/WHPE/BLK NE5 69 F2 6
Lowewood Cl LGB/HTN NE7 71 G2
Lowes Wynd DHAM DH1 168 B2
Lowfield Ter BYK/HTN/WLK NE6 72 B7
Low Flatts Rd CLSW/PEL DH2 129 H1
Low Friar St CNUT NE1 5 J7
Lowgate BW/LEM/TK/HW NE15 67 F2
Low Gosforth Ct GOS/KPK NE3 56 D1 6
Low Gn DHAM DH1 169 G4
Low Haugh PONT/DH NE20 43 H2
Low Heworth La FELL NE10 13 G5
Low Heyworth La FELL NE10 13 G5
Lowhills Rd PLEE/EAS SR8 174 C2
Lowland Cl SUNDSW SR3 134 A2
Lowland Rd BDN/LAN/SAC DH7 167 G6
Low La HAR/WTLS NE34 75 G7
Low Meadow
CLDN/WHIT/ROK SR6 92 A3 1
Low Moor Rd
BDN/LAN/SAC DH7 153 K3
Lownds Ter BYK/HTN/WLK NE6 7 M4
Low Quay BLYTH NE24 31 H7
Lowrey's La
LWF/SPW/WRK NE9 87 F7 7
Low Rd DHAM DH1 169 G4
Low Rw PLEE/EAS SR8 162 C5
Lowry Gdns HAR/WTLS NE34 91 H2
Lowry Rd CLDN/WHIT/ROK SR6 92 E7
Low Station Rd HLS DH4 146 B6
Low Stobhill MPTH NE61 20 E6
Low St SUND SR1 15 H3
Lowther Cl ASHGTN NE63 24 B4
PLEE/EAS SR8 174 E3 1
Lowther Ct PLEE/EAS SR8 184 C1
Lowthian Crs BYK/HTN/WLK NE6 7 M6
Low West Av ROWG NE39 96 E4
Lucknow St SUND SR1 15 J3
Lucock St HAR/WTLS NE34 75 F6 5
Ludlow Av NSHW NE29 60 C2
Ludlow Ct GOS/KPK NE3 55 J3 1
Ludlow Dr MONK NE25 49 K5
Ludlow Rd ASHBK/HED/RY SR2 120 D4
Luffness Dr HAR/WTLS NE34 91 K1
Luke Av RDHAMSE DH6 181 H2
Luke Crs SEA/MUR SR7 149 G5
Luke's La HEBB NE31 89 H2
Luke St TRIM TS29 182 D7
Luke Ter RDHAMSE DH6 182 D1 3
Lulsgate SWCK/CAS SR5 104 E4
Lulworth Av JRW NE32 74 B6
Lulworth Ct SUNDSW SR3 119 G7 4
Lulworth Gdns
ASHBK/HED/RY SR2 120 C3 8
Lumley Av HAR/WTLS NE34 76 B5
WICK/BNPF NE16 85 F3
Lumley Cl WASHS NE38 116 D1
Lumley Ct BDLGTN NE22 29 J4 2
SUNDSW SR3 119 G7 5
Lumley Dr CON/LDGT DH8 123 J7
PLEE/EAS SR8 174 E7
Lumley Gdns GATE NE8 11 L6
Lumley New Rd
CLS/BIR/GTL DH3 130 B5
HLS DH4 131 F6
Lumley Rd DHAM DH1 156 D2
Lumley's La PSHWF NE43 80 A6
Lumley St HLS DH4 132 B5
MLFD/PNYW SR4 106 A7
Lumley Ter CLS/BIR/GTL DH3 129 K5
JRW NE32 89 K1
Lumsden's La MPTH NE61 20 D4
Lumsden Sq SEA/MUR SR7 149 G5 2
Lund Av DHAM DH1 156 B3
Lund's La CON/LDGT DH8 124 D7
Lunedale Av
CLDN/WHIT/ROK SR6 92 C7
Lunedale Dr
CLS/BIR/GTL DH3 145 J2 1
Lunesdale St HLH DH5 147 K6
Lupin Cl WD/WHPE/BLK NE5 54 A6 7
Luss Av JRW NE32 90 C1
Lutterworth Cl LGB/KIL NE12 57 H4 5
Lutterworth Dr LGB/KIL NE12 57 G4
Lutterworth Rd
ASHBK/HED/RY SR2 120 C3
LGB/KIL NE12 57 H5 3
Luxembourg Rd
MLFD/PNYW SR4 105 H6
Lydbury Cl CRAM NE23 33 J6 2
Lydcott WASHS NE38 117 K2
Lydford Ct HLS DH4 132 A4 2
WD/WHPE/BLK NE5 55 G4
Lydford Wy CLS/BIR/GTL DH3 115 K3
Lyncroft ASHGTN NE63 23 J3
Lyncroft Rd NSHW NE29 60 C4
Lyndale CRAM NE23 33 J6
Lyndhurst Av CLS/BIR/GTL DH3 129 J1
JES NE2 70 D1
LWF/SPW/WRK NE9 101 F1
Lyndhurst Cl BLAY NE21 83 J4 5
Lyndhurst Crs
LWF/SPW/WRK NE9 101 G1
Lyndhurst Dr DHAM DH1 168 B1 2
LWF/SPW/WRK NE9 101 G1
Lyndhurst Gdns JES NE2 70 D1 2
Lyndhurst Gv
LWF/SPW/WRK NE9 101 G1
Lyndhurst Rd ASHGTN NE63 24 B4
LGB/KIL NE12 57 K3
STLY/ANP DH9 126 B1 1
Lyndhurst St SSH NE33 3 K8
Lyndhurst Ter
MLFD/PNYW SR4 105 J5 1
Lyndon Cl BOL NE36 91 F5
Lyndon Dr BOL NE36 91 F5
Lyndon Gv BOL NE36 91 F5
Lyndon Wk BLYTH NE24 30 B6
Lyne Cl CLSW/PEL DH2 115 F6
Lyne's Dr BDN/LAN/SAC DH7 167 J5
Lyne Ter MPTH NE61 18 B1
Lynfield WBAY NE26 50 C1
Lynfield Ct
WD/WHPE/BLK NE5 55 F7 2
Lynfield Pl
WD/WHPE/BLK NE5 55 F7 3
Lynford Gdns
ASHBK/HED/RY SR2 120 C3 9
Lynholm Gv LGB/KIL NE12 57 K2 4
Lynmouth Pl LGB/HTN NE7 57 H7 1
Lynmouth Rd NSHW NE29 60 A5 3
Lynndale Av BLYTH NE24 30 C7
Lynnholme Gdns
LWF/SPW/WRK NE9 11 J8
Lynn Rd NSHW NE29 60 B3 2
WLSD/HOW NE28 72 C2
Lynn St BLYTH NE24 31 F7
Lynnwood Av ELS/FEN NE4 4 B6
Lynnwood Ter ELS/FEN NE4 4 B6
Lynthorpe ASHBK/HED/RY SR2 121 F6
Lyn-thorpe Gv
CLDN/WHIT/ROK SR6 106 E2 2
Lynton Av JRW NE32 74 C6
Lynton Ct HLS DH4 132 A4
Lynton Pl WD/WHPE/BLK NE5 55 F7
Lynton Wy WD/WHPE/BLK NE5 55 F7
Lynwood Av BLAY NE21 84 A1 6
MLFD/PNYW SR4 118 E4
Lynwood Cl PONT/DH NE20 42 E7
Lyons Av HLH DH5 148 A6
Lyons La HLH DH5 148 B7
Lyon St HEBB NE31 73 F5
Lyric Cl NSHW NE29 59 K2
Lysdon Av MONK NE25 40 A2
Lyster Cl SEA/MUR SR7 134 E6
Lytham Cl CRAM NE23 37 K2 2
WASHN NE37 102 E3 3
WLSD/HOW NE28 59 G3
Lytham Dr MONK NE25 50 B4
Lytham Gra HLS DH4 131 J3
Lytham Pl BYK/HTN/WLK NE6 7 L7
Lythe Wy LGB/KIL NE12 57 J4

M

Mabel St BLAY NE21 84 A1
Macadam St GATE NE8 10 C9
Maclynn Cl SUNDSW SR3 133 J1
Macmerry Cl SWCK/CAS SR5 104 D5 1
Macmillan Gdns FELL NE10 13 K7
Maddison St BLYTH NE24 31 G6
Maddox Rd LGB/KIL NE12 57 K4
Madeira Av WBAY NE26 50 D2
Madeira Cl WD/WHPE/BLK NE5 54 A6
Madeira Ter SSH NE33 75 H2
Madras St HAR/WTLS NE34 74 E7
Mafeking Pl NSHW NE29 59 K1
Mafeking St LWF/SPW/WRK NE9 11 J8
MLFD/PNYW SR4 105 K7
Magdalene Av DHAM DH1 157 K5
Magdalene Hts DHAM DH1 17 G2
Magdalene St DHAM DH1 17 H2
Magdelene Pl MLFD/PNYW SR4 105 K6
Magenta Crs
WD/WHPE/BLK NE5 54 A6
Maglona St SEA/MUR SR7 150 E3
Magnolia Dr ASHGTN NE63 23 J4
Magpie Ct ASHGTN NE63 23 H3
Maiden La RYTON NE40 82 B2
Maiden Law HLS DH4 146 D1 1
Maiden St ELS/FEN NE4 9 M1 1
Maidstone Cl SUNDSW SR3 133 H1 1
Main Crs WLSD/HOW NE28 58 B6
Main Rd DIN/WO NE13 45 F2
DIN/WO NE13 55 F3
RYTON NE40 66 D6
WYLAM NE41 65 H5
Mainsforth Ter West
ASHBK/HED/RY SR2 15 H9
Mains Park Rd
CLS/BIR/GTL DH3 129 K5
Mainstone Cl CRAM NE23 38 B2 1
Main St CON/LDGT DH8 123 H5
PONT/DH NE20 43 G3
RYTON NE40 66 B7
Main St North CRAM NE23 48 A1
Makendon St HEBB NE31 73 G4
Malaga Wy SWCK/CAS SR5 106 A4 7
Malaga Cl WD/WHPE/BLK NE5 53 K6
Malaya Dr BYK/HTN/WLK NE6 72 C6
Malcolm Av RDHAMSE DH6 181 G4
Malcolm St BYK/HTN/WLK NE6 6 D4
SEA/MUR SR7 150 E2 5
Malden Cl CRAM NE23 38 A2
Maling Pk MLFD/PNYW SR4 105 F6 2
Malings Cl SUND SR1 15 J5
Maling St BYK/HTN/WLK NE6 6 D6 2
Mallard Cl ASHGTN NE63 23 K5 2
WASHS NE38 116 B2
Mallard Wy BLYTH NE24 35 H4
WLSD/HOW NE28 59 J4
Mallowburn Crs GOS/KPK NE3 55 G6
Malmo Cl NSHW NE29 59 K5
Malone Gdns CLS/BIR/GTL DH3 101 K7

Maltby Cl *WASHS* NE38 .... 117 F2
The Maltings *WNGT* TS28 .... 183 K2
Malton Cl *BLYTH* NE24 .... 30 D7
BW/LEM/TK/HW NE15 .... 68 C5 ▣
Malton Crs *NSHW* NE29 .... 60 C6
Malton Gdns *WLSD/HOW* NE28 .... 58 D7
Malvern *ASHGTN* NE63 .... 24 B4 ▣
Malvern Ct
BW/LEM/TK/HW NE15 .... 67 K4
Malvern Crs *SEA/MUR* SR7 .... 150 E2
TRIM TS29 .... 183 F6
Malvern Gdns
CLDN/WHIT/ROK SR6 .... 106 E2
DUN/TMV NE11 .... 86 A6 ▣
DUN/TMV NE11 .... 86 A5 ▣
Malvern Rd *NSHW* NE29 .... 60 C2
WBAY NE26 .... 41 G3
WLSD/HOW NE28 .... 59 H7
Malvern St *ELS/FEN* NE4 .... 4 C8
SSH NE33 .... 75 G4
Malvern Ter *STLY/ANP* DH9 .... 126 E2
Malvins Close Rd *BLYTH* NE24 ..... 30 E7
Malvins Rd *BLYTH* NE24 .... 30 D6
Manchester St *MPTH* NE61 .... 20 D4 ▣
Mandale Crs *TYNE/NSHE* 50 E6
Mandarin Cl *WD/WHPE/BLK* NE5 .. 53 K6
Mandela Cl *CRAM* NE23 .... 38 B3 ▣
Mandela Wy *DUN/TMV* NE11 .... 8 C3
Mandeville *WASHN* NE37 .... 103 C5
Manet Gdns *HAR/WTLS* NE34 ...... 75 H7
Mangrove Cl
WD/WHPE/BLK NE5 .... 53 K6
Manila St *ASHBK/HED/RY* SR2 ... 120 E2
Manisty Ter *PLEE/EAS* SR8 .... 162 D5
Manley Vw *ASHGTN* NE63 .... 24 C3
Mann Crs *SEA/MUR* SR7 .... 149 J4 ▣
Manningford Cl *CRAM* NE23 .... 38 B3 ▣
Manningford Dr *SUNDSW* SR3 .... 133 J2
Manor Av *LGB/HTN* NE7 .... 57 J5
Manor Chare *CNUT* 5 M7
Manor Cl *GOS/KPK* NE3 .... 56 D5 ▣
Manor Ct *BDN/LAN/SAC* DH7 ...... 140 D6
Manor Dr *LGB/HTN* NE7 .... 57 J5
NWBGN 19 G7
STLY/ANP DH9 .... 125 H2
Manorfields *LGB/KIL* NE12 .... 57 K4
Manor Gdns *FELL* NE10 .... 13 M8
LGB/HTN NE7 .... 57 J5
Manor Gra *BDN/LAN/SAC* DH7 .... 140 D5
Manor Gv *BW/LEM/TK/HW* NE15 ... 67 H4
HLS 118 D7
LGB/HTN NE7 .... 57 J5
Manor Hall Cl *SEA/MUR* SR7 ...... 134 E7
Manor House Rd *JES* NE2 .... 71 F2
Manor Pl *LGB/HTN* NE7 .... 57 J5
Manor Rd *CON/LDGT* DH8 .... 109 J5
LGB/HTN NE7 .... 57 J6
STLY/ANP DH9 .... 112 D7 ▣
TYNE/NSHE NE30 .... 61 H2
WASHN NE37 .... 103 F5
Manor Ter *BLAY* NE21 .... 84 A5
Manor Vw *NWBGN* NE64 .... 19 G7
WASHN NE37 .... 103 F5
Manor Vw East *WASHN* NE37 .... 103 C5
Manor Wk *LGB/HTN* NE7 .... 57 J5 ▣
Manor Wy *PLEE/EAS* SR8 .... 175 F4
Manorway *TYNE/NSHE* NE30 ...... 61 H2 ▣
Mansell Crs *PLEE/EAS* SR8 .... 175 F3
Mansell Pl *GOS/KPK* NE3 .... 55 J7
Manse St *CON/LDGT* DH8 .... 122 E4
Mansfield Crs
CLDN/WHIT/ROK SR6 .... 106 E2
Mansfield St *ELS/FEN* NE4 .... 4 E6
Manston Cl *SUNDSW* SR3 .... 133 H2
Manx Sq *SWCK/CAS* SR5 .... 106 B2
Maple Av *DHAM* DH1 .... 17 L3
DUN/TMV NE11 .... 9 J9
MONK NE25 .... 50 D6
SUNDSW SR3 .... 120 B6
Maplebeck Cl *SUNDSW* SR3 ...... 133 H2 ▣
Maple Cl
BW/LEM/TK/HW NE15 .... 68 C5 ▣
Maple Ct *BDN/LAN/SAC* DH7 ...... 166 E7
MONK NE25 .... 40 A2 ▣
Maple Crs *BLYTH* NE24 .... 30 B6
SEA/MUR SR7 .... 150 C4
Mapledene Rd *GOS/KPK* NE3 ...... 55 K4
Maple Gdns *CON/LDGT* DH8 ...... 122 C3
Maple Gv *CLDN/WHIT/ROK* SR6 .... 93 F3
FELL NE10 .... 12 E8
GATE NE8 .... 86 E5
HAR/WTLS NE34 .... 75 K6
PRUD NE42 .... 80 B7
Maple Pk *BDN/LAN/SAC* DH7 .... 167 G1
Maple Rd *BLAY* NE21 .... 84 A2
Maple Rw *WICK/BNPF* NE16 .... 85 F2
Maple St *CON/LDGT* DH8 .... 123 F4 ▣
ELS/FEN NE4 .... 4 F9
JRW NE32 .... 73 J4
STLY/ANP DH9 .... 126 B3
Maple Ter *ELS/FEN* NE4 .... 4 F9
HLS 131 J2
Maplewood *CLSW/PEL* DH2 ...... 129 H5
Maplewood Av *SWCK/CAS* SR5 .. 105 K2
Maplewood Dr
BDN/LAN/SAC DH7 .... 154 A3
Maplewood St *HLS* DH4 .... 131 G6
Mapperley Dr
BW/LEM/TK/HW NE15 .... 68 C4
Marblet Ct *DUN/TMV* NE11 .... 86 B5 ▣
Marbury Cl *SUNDSW* SR3 .... 133 H1 ▣
March Rd *CRAM* NE23 .... 47 H2 ▣
Marcia Cl
CLDN/WHIT/ROK SR6 .... 106 D2 ▣
Marconi Wy *WICK/BNPF* NE16 .... 85 F3
Marcross Cl
WD/WHPE/BLK NE5 .... 67 K1 ▣
Marcross Dr *SUNDSW* SR3 .... 133 H2 ▣
Mardale *WASHN* NE37 .... 102 D6
Mardale Gdns
LWF/SPW/WRK NE9 .... 101 G2
Mardale Rd *CLDN/WHIT/ROK* SR6 .. 69 F2
Mardale St *HLS* DH4 .... 147 K6
Marden Av *TYNE/NSHE* NE30 ...... 51 G6
Marden Cl *MPTH* NE61 .... 20 B6

Marden Ct *WBAY* NE26 .... 40 E1 ▣
Marden Crs *WBAY* NE26 .... 51 G5
Marden Rd South *MONK* NE25 .... 50 E5
Marden Ter *TYNE/NSHE* 51 G6
Mareburn Crs *FELL* NE10 .... 12 F7
Maree Cl *SUNDSW* SR3 .... 133 J2
Margaret Alice St
MLFD/PNYW SR4 .... 105 J6 ▣
Margaret Ct *RDHAMSE* DH6 ...... 180 A2 ▣
Margaret Dr *LGB/KIL* NE12 .... 58 C2 ▣
Margaret St *HAR/WTLS* NE34 ...... 74 E6 ▣
Margaret Rd *WBAY* NE26 .... 51 G5
Margaret Ter *ROWG* NE39 .... 96 E4
Margery La *DHAM* DH1 .... 16 E5
Marguerite Ct
MLFD/PNYW SR4 .... 14 B4 ▣
Marian Ct *GATE* NE8 .... 10 C5
Marian Dr *FELL* NE10 .... 13 M3
Marian Wy *HAR/WTLS* NE34 .... 91 K1
PONT/DH NE20 .... 42 D7
Maria St *ELS/FEN* NE4 .... 69 J7
SEA/MUR SR7 .... 150 E2
SUNDSW SR3 .... 120 A7
Marie Curie Dr *ELS/FEN* NE4 .... 4 B8
Marigold Av *FELL* NE10 .... 11 M3
Marigold Crs *HAR/WTLS* NE34 ..... 14 A3
Marigold Crs *HLS* DH4 .... 131 G4
Marigold Wk *HAR/WTLS* NE34 ..... 75 F6
Marina Av *CLDN/WHIT/ROK* SR6 .. 106 C1
Marina Ct
CLDN/WHIT/ROK SR6 .... 106 D2 ▣
SSH NE33 .... 3 L7
Marina Gv
CLDN/WHIT/ROK SR6 .... 106 D2 ▣
Marina Ter
CLDN/WHIT/ROK SR6 .... 93 F3 ▣
Marina Veiw *WLSD/HOW* NE28 ..... 73 H1
Marina Vw *HEBB* NE31 .... 73 F5
Marine Ap *SSH* NE33 .... 3 L8
Marine Av *WBAY* NE26 .... 50 E3
Marine Dr *ASHBK/HED/RY* SR2 .. 121 F6
HEBB NE31 .... 89 J1
JRW NE32 .... 89 J2
Marine Gdns *WBAY* NE26 .... 50 E4
Mariners' La *TYNE/NSHE* NE30 .... 61 G3
Marine St *NWBGN* NE64 .... 19 G7
Marine Ter *BLYTH* NE24 .... 31 F7
Marine Wk
CLDN/WHIT/ROK SR6 .... 107 F3
Marion St *ASHBK/HED/RY* SR2 ... 15 H9
Maritime Crs *PLEE/EAS* SR8 ...... 163 G7
Maritime St *SUND* SR1 .... 14 E5 ▣
Marius Av *BW/LEM/TK/HW* NE15 .. 66 B1
Mariville East
ASHBK/HED/RY SR2 .... 135 G2
Mariville West
ASHBK/HED/RY SR2 .... 135 G2
Markby Cl *SUNDSW* SR3 .... 133 J2 ▣
Market La *CNUT* NE1 .... 5 K7
WICK/BNPF NE16 .... 84 E3
Market Pl *HLH* DH5 .... 132 D7
Market Sq *JRW* NE32 .... 73 K4 ▣
Market St *CNUT* NE1 .... 5 K6
CON/LDGT DH8 .... 122 D3 ▣
CRAM NE23 .... 47 G1
HLH DH5 .... 148 A4
Market Wy *DUN/TMV* NE11 .... 86 D6
Markham Av
CLDN/WHIT/ROK SR6 .... 93 G4
Markham St
ASHBK/HED/RY SR2 .... 121 F4 ▣
Markington Dr
ASHBK/HED/RY SR2 .... 135 F1
Markle Gv *HLH* DH5 .... 147 G3
Mark Ri *HLH* DH5 .... 147 K3
Mark's La *HLS* DH4 .... 146 C4
Marlboro Av *WICK/BNPF* NE16 .... 85 F4
Marlborough Ap
GOS/KPK NE3 .... 56 C3 ▣
Marlborough Av *GOS/KPK* NE3 .... 56 B4
Marlborough Ct *GOS/KPK* NE3 .... 55 H3
HLH DH5 .... 147 H2 ▣
Marlborough Rd
MLFD/PNYW SR4 .... 118 D3
WASHN NE37 .... 103 G4
Marlborough St North
SSH NE33 .... 75 H3 ▣
Marlborough St South
SSH NE33 .... 75 H3 ▣
Marleen Av *BYK/HTN/WLK* NE6 ..... 7 H1
Marleen Ct *BYK/HTN/WLK* NE6 ..... 7 H1
Marlene Av *RDHAMSE* DH6 ...... 179 K1
Marley Crs *SWCK/CAS* SR5 ...... 105 K2
Marfield Ct
WD/WHPE/BLK NE5 .... 55 F7 ▣
Marlow Dr *SUNDSW* SR3 .... 133 H2
Marlowe Gdns *GATE* NE8 .... 11 H5
Marlowe Pl *HLH* DH5 .... 147 H1
Marlow Pl *LGB/KIL* NE12 .... 57 J4
Marlow St *BLYTH* NE24 .... 31 F7
Marmion Rd *BYK/HTN/WLK* NE6 .. 72 B3
Marmion Ter *MONK* NE25 .... 50 D4
Marne St *HLS* DH4 .... 131 K1
Marondale Av
BYK/HTN/WLK NE6 .... 72 B4
Marquis Av *WD/WHPE/BLK* NE5 .. 54 A5
Marr Rd *HEBB* NE31 .... 73 H6
Marsden Av
CLDN/WHIT/ROK SR6 .... 93 F2
Marsden Cl *HLS* DH4 .... 132 A1
Marsden Gv
LWF/SPW/WRK NE9 .... 101 K2 ▣
Marsden La *HAR/WTLS* NE34 ...... 76 B4
WD/WHPE/BLK NE5 .... 54 E7
Marsden Rd
CLDN/WHIT/ROK SR6 .... 91 K4
HAR/WTLS NE34 .... 75 K4
Marshall St
CLDN/WHIT/ROK SR6 .... 106 D1
Marshall Wallis Rd *SSH* NE33 ..... 75 G3
Marsham Cl
BW/LEM/TK/HW NE15 .... 68 C4
CRAM NE23 .... 92 A2

Marsham Rd
WD/WHPE/BLK NE5 .... 54 C7 ▣
Marsh Ct *DUN/TMV* NE11 .... 9 M9
Marske Ter *BYK/HTN/WLK* NE6 ..... 7 M5
Marston *LGB/KIL* NE12 .... 47 K5 ▣
Martello Gdns *LGB/HTN* NE7 ...... 71 K1
Martin Crs *RDHAMSE* DH6 .... 181 G6
Martin St *WASHN* NE38 .... 116 B4
Martindale Av
CLDN/WHIT/ROK SR6 .... 92 C7
Martindale Pk *HLH* DH5 .... 147 H1
Martindale Wy *WNGT* TS28 .... 183 K2
Martin Rd *WLSD/HOW* NE28 .... 73 H1
Marwell Dr *WASHN* NE37 .... 103 G5 ▣
Marwood Gv *PLEE/EAS* SR8 ...... 174 D7
Mary Agnes St *GOS/KPK* NE3 ..... 56 A5 ▣
Mary Av *CLS/BIR/GTL* DH3 .... 101 H7
Mary Crs *RDHAMSE* DH6 .... 181 G6
Maryhill Cl *ELS/FEN* NE4 .... 69 J7 ▣
Mary's Pl *BYK/HTN/WLK* NE6 ..... 72 D5
Mary St *BLAY* NE21 .... 83 J2
SEA/MUR SR7 .... 151 F1 ▣
SUND SR1 .... 14 D6 ▣
SUNDSW SR3 .... 120 A6
Mary Ter *WD/WHPE/BLK* NE5 ..... 68 C1
Masefield Av
WICK/BNPF NE16 .... 85 F3 ▣
Masefield Cl *STLY/ANP* DH9 ...... 113 G7
Masefield Dr *HAR/WTLS* NE34 .... 90 E2
Mason Rd *WLSD/HOW* NE28 ...... 58 C6
Mason St *BYK/HTN/WLK* NE6 .... 7 G6
CON/LDGT DH8 .... 123 F5
Master's Crs *PRUD* NE42 .... 80 B2
Mast La *TYNE/NSHE* NE30 .... 51 F6
Matamba Ter *MLFD/PNYW* SR4 ... 14 A5
Matanzas St
ASHBK/HED/RY SR2 .... 120 E3
Matfen Av *SMOOR* NE27 .... 49 H6
Matfen Cl *BLYTH* NE24 .... 30 E7
BW/LEM/TK/HW NE15 .... 68 B6 ▣
Matfen Dr *SUNDSW* SR3 .... 133 H1 ▣
Matfen Gdns *WLSD/HOW* NE28 ... 59 H5
Matfen Pl *ELS/FEN* NE4 .... 4 A2
GOS/KPK NE3 .... 56 A4 ▣
Mather Rd *ELS/FEN* NE4 .... 4 E9
Mathesons Gdns *MPTH* NE61 ..... 20 E3 ▣
Matlock Gdns
WD/WHPE/BLK NE5 .... 54 D7 ▣
Matlock Rd *JRW* NE32 .... 74 A6 ▣
Matlock St *SUND* SR1 .... 14 E3
Matterdale Rd *PLEE/EAS* SR8 .... 175 G4
Matthew Bank *JES* NE2 .... 56 E7
Matthew Rd *BLYTH* NE24 .... 35 H2
Maudlin Pl
WD/WHPE/BLK NE5 .... 69 H2 ▣
Maudlin St *HLH* DH5 .... 148 A2
Mauds La *SUND* SR1 .... 15 H4
Maud St
BW/LEM/TK/HW NE15 .... 68 A5 ▣
CLDN/WHIT/ROK SR6 .... 106 E1
Maughan St *BLYTH* NE24 .... 31 H7
Maureen Ter *SEA/MUR* SR7 .... 150 D1
Maurice Rd *WLSD/HOW* NE28 .... 72 D3 ▣
Mautland St *HLS* DH4 .... 132 C6 ▣
Mavin St *DHAM* DH1 .... 16 F6
Maxton Cl *SUNDSW* SR3 .... 133 H2 ▣
Maxwell St *GATE* NE8 .... 10 D9
MLFD/PNYW SR4 .... 105 K6 ▣
SSH NE33 .... 3 H9
May Av *BLAY* NE21 .... 84 A5
RYTON NE40 .... 66 E5 ▣
Maydown Cl *SWCK/CAS* SR5 ..... 104 D5 ▣
Mayfair Gdns *GATE* NE8 .... 11 K7
HAR/WTLS NE34 .... 75 J4
PONT/DH NE20 .... 43 H3
Mayfair Rd *JES* NE2 .... 70 D1 ▣
Mayfield Av
BW/LEM/TK/HW NE15 .... 67 G2 ▣
Mayfield Ct
CLDN/WHIT/ROK SR6 .... 106 D2
Mayfield Dr
CLDN/WHIT/ROK SR6 .... 92 B4 ▣
Mayfield Gdns
BW/LEM/TK/HW NE15 .... 67 G2 ▣
JRW NE32 .... 73 J5
WLSD/HOW NE28 .... 58 B7
Mayfield Gv *MLFD/PNYW* SR4 ... 118 E4
Mayfield Pl *DIN/WO* NE13 .... 46 A4
Mayfield Rd *GOS/KPK* NE3 .... 56 B6
MLFD/PNYW SR4 .... 104 D7
Mayfield Ter
WD/WHPE/BLK NE5 .... 69 J2 ▣
May Gv *CLDN/WHIT/ROK* SR6 .... 93 F1
May Lea *BDN/LAN/SAC* DH7 ...... 143 G7
Maynard's Rw *DHAM* DH1 .... 17 J3
Mayo Dr *SUNDSW* SR3 .... 133 J2 ▣
Mayoral Wy *DUN/TMV* NE11 ...... 100 D3
Mayorswell Cl *DHAM* DH1 .... 16 F2
Mayorswell Fld *DHAM* DH1 .... 16 F2 ▣
Mayorswell St *DHAM* DH1 .... 16 F2 ▣
Maypole Cl *SWCK/CAS* SR5 ...... 106 B4 ▣
May St *BLAY* NE21 .... 83 J2
CLS/BIR/GTL DH3 .... 115 J1
DHAM DH1 .... 16 A5
MLFD/PNYW SR4 .... 14 B4
SSH NE33 .... 75 H2
Mayswood Rd
CLDN/WHIT/ROK SR6 .... 106 D2
Maythorne Dr *RDHAMSE* DH6 ... 161 G3
Maywood Cl *GOS/KPK* NE3 .... 55 J6
Mazine Ter *RDHAMSE* DH6 .... 172 D1
Mcanany Av *HAR/WTLS* NE34 .... 75 H6
Mcclaren Wy *HLS* DH4 .... 118 D3
Mccracken Cl *GOS/KPK* NE3 ...... 56 C2
Mccracken Dr *DIN/WO* NE13 ...... 46 C2
Mcewan Gdns *ELS/FEN* NE4 .... 4 B7
Mcintyre Rd *HEBB* NE31 .... 73 H4 ▣
Mckendrick Vls
WD/WHPE/BLK NE5 .... 69 H2
Mcnally Pl *DHAM* DH1 .... 16 F2 ▣
Mcnamara Rd *WLSD/HOW* NE28 .. 59 G7
Meacham Wy *WICK/BNPF* NE16 ... 84 E7
Mead Av *LGB/KIL* NE12 .... 58 A2 ▣
Mead Crs *LGB/KIL* NE12 .... 58 A2 ▣
Meadowbank
BDN/LAN/SAC DH7 .... 154 A3 ▣

Meadow Bank Dr
STKFD/GP NE62 .... 22 E7
Meadow Brook Dr *CHPW* NE17 ... 95 J3
Meadowbrook Dr *FELL* NE10 ...... 88 E5 ▣
Meadow Cl *BLAY* NE21 .... 83 H3
CRAM NE23 .... 39 G6 ▣
DUN/TMV NE11 .... 8 F6
HLH DH5 .... 147 J1
LGB/KIL NE12 .... 57 H4 ▣
RDHAMSE DH6 .... 180 C2 ▣
RYTON NE40 .... 67 F6
Meadow Ct *BDLGTN* NE22 .... 28 E5
PONT/DH NE20 .... 43 C4
Meadowdale Crs *BDLGTN* NE22 ... 28 D5
WD/WHPE/BLK NE5 .... 55 H7
Meadow Dr *CLSW/PEL* DH2 ...... 129 F5
DIN/WO NE13 .... 46 C1
SUNDSW SR3 .... 133 F2
Meadowfield *ASHGTN* NE63 .... 24 C3
CON/LDGT DH8 .... 122 D4
MONK NE25 .... 50 B4
PONT/DH NE20 .... 43 G2
Meadowfield Av *GOS/KPK* NE3 .... 56 A4
Meadowfield Crs
RYTON NE40 .... 66 C7 ▣
Meadowfield Dr
CLDN/WHIT/ROK SR6 .... 92 A3
Meadowfield Gdns
BYK/HTN/WLK NE6 .... 72 C2 ▣
Meadowfield Pk South
PSHWF NE43 .... 79 C7
Meadowfield Rd
GOS/KPK NE3 .... 56 B6 ▣
PSHWF NE43 .... 79 C7
Meadowfield Wy
STLY/ANP DH9 .... 112 A6
Meadow Gdns *SUNDSW* SR3 .... 120 B3 ▣
Meadow Gra *HLS* DH4 .... 131 C5
Meadow Gv *MLFD/PNYW* SR4 ... 118 E1
Meadow La *DUN/TMV* NE11 .... 8 F5
RYTON NE40 .... 66 C7 ▣
Meadow Laws *HAR/WTLS* NE34 .. 76 A7
Meadow Ri *CON/LDGT* DH8 ...... 123 C5
WD/WHPE/BLK NE5 .... 55 F6
Meadow Rd
BW/LEM/TK/HW NE15 .... 68 B4
MONK NE25 .... 50 B5
WBAY NE26 .... 40 E2
WLSD/HOW NE28 .... 73 H2 ▣
Meadowside
ASHBK/HED/RY SR2 .... 120 B2
Meadows La *HLS* DH4 .... 146 E4
The Meadows *GOS/KPK* NE3 ..... 55 K4
HLH DH4 .... 131 F4
HLS DH4 .... 146 D5
RYTON NE40 .... 67 F6
Meadow Vw *HLH* DH5 .... 147 F4
Meadowvale *PONT/DH* NE20 ...... 42 C7
Meadow Vw *CON/LDGT* DH8 ..... 138 D1
MONK NE25 .... 40 A2
STLY/ANP DH9 .... 111 G5 ▣
SUNDSW SR3 .... 133 F2
Meadow Wy
BDN/LAN/SAC DH7 .... 140 B5
Meadow Well *NSHW* NE29 .... 60 C6 ▣
Mead Wk *BYK/HTN/WLK* NE6 ..... 72 B5
Meadway Dr *LGB/KIL* NE12 .... 58 B2
Means Dr *CRAM* NE23 .... 47 H4
Medburn Av *TYNE/NSHE* NE30 ... 51 G7
Medburn Rd
BW/LEM/TK/HW NE15 .... 67 K4
MONK NE25 .... 40 B6
Medham Cl *FELL* NE10 .... 88 A6 ▣
Medina Cl *SUNDSW* SR3 .... 133 J2 ▣
Medomsley Gdns
LWF/SPW/WRK NE9 .... 102 A1 ▣
Medomsley Rd *CON/LDGT* DH8 .. 122 C1 ▣
Medomsly St *MLFD/PNYW* SR4 .. 106 A6
Medway *JRW* NE32 .... 90 A2
Medway Cl *HEBB* NE31 .... 89 G1
Medway Crs *PLEE/EAS* SR8 ...... 174 D6
Medway Gdns *GATE* NE8 .... 11 L7
Medway Gdns
MLFD/PNYW SR4 .... 119 H2 ▣
TYNE/NSHE NE30 .... 60 E3 ▣
Medway Pl *CRAM* NE23 .... 33 J6
Medway Rd *LGB/KIL* NE12 .... 48 A5
Melbourne Crs *MONK* NE25 .... 50 C6
Melbourne Gdns
HAR/WTLS NE34 .... 90 D1
Melbourne Pl *MLFD/PNYW* SR4 . 119 J2
Melbourne St *CNUT* NE1 .... 5 M7
Melbury *MONK* NE25 .... 50 A3
Melbury Ct
CLDN/WHIT/ROK SR6 .... 106 D2 ▣
Melbury Rd *LGB/HTN* NE7 .... 71 G2
Melbury St *SEA/MUR* SR7 .... 150 E3
Meldon Av *GOS/KPK* NE3 .... 55 K3 ▣
HAR/WTLS NE34 .... 75 J5
RDHAMSE DH6 .... 170 D1
Meldon Ct *RYTON* NE40 .... 82 A1 ▣
Meldon Gdns *DUN/TMV* NE11 ..... 86 A7
STKFD/GP NE62 .... 23 F5 ▣
Meldon Rd *MLFD/PNYW* SR4 ..... 105 K6 ▣
Meldon St *WLSD/HOW* NE28 ...... 74 A2
Meldon Ter *BYK/HTN/WLK* NE6 ..... 6 F1
Meldon Wy *BLAY* NE21 .... 83 H4
DHAM DH1 .... 169 J5
STLY/ANP DH9 .... 125 K3
Melgarve Dr *SUNDSW* SR3 .... 133 J2
Melkington Ct
WD/WHPE/BLK NE5 .... 55 F7 ▣
Melkridge Pl *CRAM* NE23 .... 38 A3
Mellendean Cl
WD/WHPE/BLK NE5 .... 55 F7 ▣
Melling Rd *CRAM* NE23 .... 38 A2
Melmerby Cl *GOS/KPK* NE3 .... 56 D3
Melness Rd *DIN/WO* NE13 .... 46 A4
Melrose *WASHS* NE38 .... 117 F3
Melrose Av *BDLGTN* NE22 .... 29 K5
HEBB NE31 .... 89 G1
SEA/MUR SR7 .... 149 F6
SMOOR NE27 .... 48 E4
TYNE/NSHE NE30 .... 50 E7

Melrose Cl
BW/LEM/TK/HW NE15 .... 68 C5
GOS/KPK NE3 .... 46 B7 ▣
Melrose Ct *BDLGTN* NE22 .... 29 J4
Melrose Crs *SEA/MUR* SR7 ...... 135 F7
Melrose Gdns
CLDN/WHIT/ROK SR6 .... 106 E2
WLSD/HOW NE28 .... 59 J6
Melrose Gv *JRW* NE32 .... 74 C7 ▣
Melrose Ter *NWBGN* NE64 .... 25 F2
Melsonby Cl *SUNDSW* SR3 ...... 133 H1 ▣
Meltham Ct
WD/WHPE/BLK NE5 .... 67 K1 ▣
Meltham Dr *SUNDSW* SR3 .... 133 J2 ▣
Melton Av *BYK/HTN/WLK* NE6 .... 72 B6 ▣
Melton Crs *WBAY* NE26 .... 41 G4
Melton Dr *MONK* NE25 .... 40 A2
Melvaig Cl *SUNDSW* SR3 .... 133 J2
Melville Av *BLYTH* NE24 .... 30 E4
Melville Gdns *MONK* NE25 .... 50 A5
Melville Gv *LGB/HTN* NE7 .... 57 K4
Melville St *CLS/BIR/GTL* DH3 .... 129 J5
Melvin Pl *WD/WHPE/BLK* NE5 .... 69 F1
Melvyn Gdns
CLDN/WHIT/ROK SR6 .... 106 E2
Membury Cl *SUNDSW* SR3 .... 133 J2 ▣
Memorial Av *PLEE/EAS* SR8 ...... 163 F4
Mendip Av *CLSW/PEL* DH2 ...... 129 H5
Mendip Cl *ASHGTN* NE63 .... 24 A4 ▣
PLEE/EAS SR8 .... 174 C4
Mendip Dr *WASHS* NE38 .... 116 D3
Mendip Gdns *DUN/TMV* NE11 .... 86 B6 ▣
Mendip Ter *STLY/ANP* DH9 .... 126 C2
Mendip Wy *LGB/KIL* NE12 .... 57 K3 ▣
Menvill Pl *SUND* SR1 .... 15 H5
Mercantile Rd *HLS* DH4 .... 147 F1
Mercia Wy
BW/LEM/TK/HW NE15 .... 68 C6
Mere Dr *DHAM* DH1 .... 156 C2
Mere Knolls Rd
CLDN/WHIT/ROK SR6 .... 92 C7
Meresyde *FELL* NE10 .... 88 C5
Merevale Cl *WASHN* NE37 .... 103 G3
Meridan Wy *LGB/HTN* NE7 .... 57 K7
Merlay Dr *DIN/WO* NE13 .... 45 F3 ▣
Merle Gdns *MPTH* NE61 .... 20 B3
Merle Ter *MLFD/PNYW* SR4 ...... 105 K5 ▣
Merley Ga *MPTH* NE61 .... 20 E7
Merlin Cl *SEA/MUR* SR7 .... 135 J7
Merlin Ct *BDN/LAN/SAC* DH7 .... 165 F2
Merlin Crs *WLSD/HOW* NE28 ..... 59 H7
Merlin Dr *CLS/BIR/GTL* DH3 ...... 115 K7
Merlin Pl *LGB/KIL* NE12 .... 57 G3
Merlin Wy *SMOOR* NE27 .... 59 J1
Merrington Cl *SUNDSW* SR3 ..... 133 H1 ▣
Merrion Cl *SUNDSW* SR3 .... 133 H1 ▣
Merryfield Gdns
CLDN/WHIT/ROK SR6 .... 106 E2 ▣
Mersey Pl *GATE* NE8 .... 11 M6
Mersey Rd *GATE* NE8 .... 11 M7
HEBB NE31 .... 89 G1
Mersey St *CHPW* NE17 .... 95 J4
CON/LDGT DH8 .... 123 K2
Merton Ct *ELS/FEN* NE4 .... 69 H7
PONT/DH NE20 .... 43 G3 ▣
Merton Sq *BLYTH* NE24 .... 31 G6 ▣
Messenger Bank
CON/LDGT DH8 .... 122 C1 ▣
Metcalfe Crs *SEA/MUR* SR7 ...... 149 G5
Metcalfe Rd *CON/LDGT* DH8 ..... 123 H6
Methven Wy *CRAM* NE23 .... 33 J5
The Mews *BLAY* NE21 .... 84 C2
HLS DH4 .... 146 D1 ▣
SUNDSW SR3 .... 119 F7
TYNE/NSHE NE30 .... 60 E4
Michaelgate *BYK/HTN/WLK* NE6 ... 7 G6
Mickle Cl *WASHN* NE37 .... 102 C7
Mickleton Cl
CLS/BIR/GTL DH3 .... 145 J1 ▣
Mickleton Gdns
SUNDSW SR3 .... 120 B4 ▣
Middle Cl *WASHS* NE38 .... 116 D5
Middle Dr *DIN/WO* NE13 .... 54 D1
PONT/DH NE20 .... 42 D7
Middle Engine La *SMOOR* NE27 ... 59 H5
WLSD/HOW NE28 .... 59 H5
Middlefield *CLSW/PEL* DH2 .... 114 E7
Middlegarth
WD/WHPE/BLK NE5 .... 69 H1 ▣
Middle Ga *MPTH* NE61 .... 20 D7
WD/WHPE/BLK NE5 .... 68 B2
Middle Gn *MONK* NE25 .... 50 A5
Middleham Cl *CLSW/PEL* DH2 ... 114 E5
Middleham Ct *MLFD/PNYW* SR4 .. 14 C5
Middleham Rd *DHAM* DH1 .... 156 E2
Middles Rd *STLY/ANP* DH9 .... 126 E4
Middle St *BYK/HTN/WLK* NE6 ..... 72 B5
CON/LDGT DH8 .... 123 F5 ▣
SUND SR1 .... 14 D4 ▣
TYNE/NSHE NE30 .... 61 H3
Middle St East
BYK/HTN/WLK NE6 .... 72 C5
ROWG NE39 .... 97 H4 ▣
Middleton Av *ELS/FEN* NE4 .... 69 J3
Middleton Cl *SEA/MUR* SR7 ...... 134 E6
Middleton St *BLYTH* NE24 .... 31 G7
Middlewood Pk *ELS/FEN* NE4 .... 69 J3
Middlewood Rd
BDN/LAN/SAC DH7 .... 140 B5 ▣
Middridge Rd
BDN/LAN/SAC DH7 .... 153 K3
Midfield Dr
CLDN/WHIT/ROK SR6 .... 106 E3
Midgley Dr *SUNDSW* SR3 .... 133 J2
Midhill Cl *BDN/LAN/SAC* DH7 .... 167 G5
Midhurst Av *HAR/WTLS* NE34 .... 75 K3
Midhurst Cl *SUNDSW* SR3 .... 133 H1
Midhurst Rd *LGB/KIL* NE12 .... 57 K3
Midmoor Rd *MLFD/PNYW* SR4 ... 14 B5
Midsomer Cl *SUNDSW* SR3 ...... 133 H2 ▣
Midway *BYK/HTN/WLK* NE6 .... 72 C5
Milbanke Cl *CLSW/PEL* DH2 ...... 115 F5
Milbank Ter *RDHAMSE* DH6 ...... 173 H4
WNGT TS28 .... 184 A6
Milburn Dr
BW/LEM/TK/HW NE15 .... 69 F5
Milburn Rd *ASHGTN* NE63 .... 23 K2

Mildmay Rd JES NE2 ..... 70 D1
Milecastle Ct
  WD/WHPE/BLK NE5 ..... 68 B1
Mile End Rd SSH NE33 ..... 3 G4
Milfield Av SMOOR NE27 ..... 49 H6
  WLSD/HOW NE28 ..... 58 E6
Milford Gdns GOS/KPK NE3 ..... 56 B1
Milford Rd
  BW/LEM/TK/HW NE15 ..... 69 G6
Military Rd TYNE/NSHE NE30 ..... 61 F4
Milk Market CNUT NE1 ..... 6 A7
Millais Av HAR/WTLS NE34 ..... 91 G2
Mill Bank SWCK/CAS SR5 ..... 106 C1
Millbank Ct DHAM DH1 ..... 16 A1
Millbank Pl BDLGTN NE22 ..... 29 H6
Millbank Rd BDLGTN NE22 ..... 29 H5
  BYK/HTN/WLK NE6 ..... 7 G6
Millbeck Gv HLH DH5 ..... 147 G2
Millbrook NSHW NE29 ..... 60 C5
Millbrook Rd CRAM NE23 ..... 33 J6
Millburngate DHAM DH1 ..... 16 C4
Millburn St MLFD/PNYW SR4 ..... 14 A3
Mill Cl NSHW NE29 ..... 60 C5
Mill Ct HLS DH4 ..... 131 G5
Mill Crs HEBB NE31 ..... 88 E2
Milldale SEA/MUR SR7 ..... 135 F7
Milldale Av BLYTH NE24 ..... 30 C7
Mill Dam SSH NE33 ..... 2 F8
Milldene Av TYNE/NSHE NE30 ..... 61 G2
Mill Dene Vw JRW NE32 ..... 73 K6
Mill Dyke Cl MONK NE25 ..... 50 A3
Millenium Wy SWCK/CAS SR5 ..... 14 D1
Miller Gdns CLSW/PEL DH2 ..... 128 D3
Millershill La CON/LDGT DH8 ..... 137 K7
Miller's La WICK/BNPF NE16 ..... 85 F3
Miller St GATE NE8 ..... 10 C7
Miller Ter SUNDSW SR3 ..... 120 A6
Mill Farm Rd ROWG NE39 ..... 96 C7
Millfield BDLGTN NE22 ..... 29 G7
  BDN/LAN/SAC DH7 ..... 140 B4
  WBAY NE26 ..... 41 G3
Millfield Av GOS/KPK NE3 ..... 55 J7
Millfield Cl
  BW/LEM/TK/HW NE15 ..... 67 H3
  CLSW/PEL DH2 ..... 129 G6
Millfield Ct BDLGTN NE22 ..... 29 G6
Millfield East BDLGTN NE22 ..... 29 G6
Millfield Gdns BLYTH NE24 ..... 31 F5
  FELL NE10 ..... 12 B8
  TYNE/NSHE NE30 ..... 61 G2
Millfield Gv TYNE/NSHE NE30 ..... 61 G2
Millfield La
  BW/LEM/TK/HW NE15 ..... 67 H3
Millfield North BDLGTN NE22 ..... 29 G6
Millfield North WICK/BNPF NE16 ..... 85 F6
Millfield South BDLGTN NE22 ..... 29 G7
Millfield West BDLGTN NE22 ..... 29 G6
Millford FELL NE10 ..... 88 C7
Millford Wy RDHAMSE DH6 ..... 180 B2
Mill Gv HAR/WTLS NE34 ..... 76 B7
  TYNE/NSHE NE30 ..... 61 G2
Millgrove Vw GOS/KPK NE3 ..... 55 K7
Mill HI HLH DH5 ..... 147 G2
  PLEE/EAS SR8 ..... 174 B2
Mill Hill Rd SUNDSW SR3 ..... 133 K1
  WD/WHPE/BLK NE5 ..... 68 D3
Mill La BDN/LAN/SAC DH7 ..... 167 F2
  BLAY NE21 ..... 83 K5
  BW/LEM/TK/HW NE15 ..... 52 B7
  CLDN/WHIT/ROK SR6 ..... 93 F1
  CLSW/PEL DH2 ..... 144 C4
  CON/LDGT DH8 ..... 108 C2
  CRAM NE23 ..... 38 D7
  DHAM DH1 ..... 17 M2
  DHAM DH1 ..... 17 L9
  ELS/FEN NE4 ..... 4 C8
  HEBB NE31 ..... 89 F2
  NSHW NE29 ..... 2 E4
  RDHAMSE DH6 ..... 170 C1
  SPEN DL16 ..... 177 K7
  STLY/ANP DH9 ..... 114 D4
Millne Ct BDLGTN NE22 ..... 29 F5
Millom Ct PLEE/EAS SR8 ..... 174 B7
Millom Pl LWF/SPW/WRK NE9 ..... 87 H7
Mill Pit HLS DH4 ..... 131 K1
Mill Race CHPW NE17 ..... 95 H7
Mill Ri GOS/KPK NE3 ..... 56 E6
Mill Rd BDN/LAN/SAC DH7 ..... 167 K5
  CHPW NE17 ..... 95 H5
  GATE NE8 ..... 6 B9
  SEA/MUR SR7 ..... 135 F7
Mills Gdns WLSD/HOW NE28 ..... 58 D7
Millside MPTH NE61 ..... 20 D5
Mill St MLFD/PNYW SR4 ..... 14 A5
Millthorp Cl
  ASHBK/HED/RY SR2 ..... 121 G5
  FELL NE10 ..... 87 J5
Mill Vw BOL NE36 ..... 90 E5
  FELL NE10 ..... 87 J5
Mill View Av
  CLDN/WHIT/ROK SR6 ..... 106 D2
Millview Dr TYNE/NSHE NE30 ..... 61 G2
Mill Wy BW/LEM/TK/HW NE15 ..... 64 D3
Millway LWF/SPW/WRK NE9 ..... 11 K9
  WBAY NE26 ..... 41 G3
Milner Crs BLAY NE21 ..... 83 J3
Milner St SSH NE33 ..... 3 L9
Milne Wy GOS/KPK NE3 ..... 55 K4
Milrig Cl SUNDSW SR3 ..... 133 J2
Milsted Cl SUNDSW SR3 ..... 133 H2
Milsted Ct
  WD/WHPE/BLK NE5 ..... 67 K1
Milton Av HEBB NE31 ..... 73 G5
  HLH DH5 ..... 147 J1
Milton Cl JES NE2 ..... 6 A3
  SEA/MUR SR7 ..... 150 C1
  STLY/ANP DH9 ..... 127 F1
Milton Gv ASHGTN NE63 ..... 24 B3
  NSHW NE29 ..... 60 D4
  PRUD NE42 ..... 80 B2
  RDHAMSE DH6 ..... 173 J4
Milton La PLEE/EAS SR8 ..... 162 D5
Milton Pl JES NE2 ..... 6 A3
  LWF/SPW/WRK NE9 ..... 102 A4
  NSHW NE29 ..... 60 D4
Milton Rd WICK/BNPF NE16 ..... 85 F4
Milton St JRW NE32 ..... 73 K3
  MLFD/PNYW SR4 ..... 106 A6
RYTON NE40 ..... 82 A3
  NE33 ..... 75 H2
Milton Ter NSHW NE29 ..... 60 D4
Milvain Av ELS/FEN NE4 ..... 69 J5
Milvain St GATE NE8 ..... 11 H6
Milverton Ct GOS/KPK NE3 ..... 55 G4
Mimosa Dr WASHN NE31 ..... 89 G1
Mimosa Pl ELS/FEN NE4 ..... 69 H3
Mindrum Ter BYK/HTN/WLK NE6 ..... 72 B7
  NSHW NE29 ..... 60 B6
Mindrum Wy MONK NE25 ..... 40 A5
Minehead Gdns
  SUNDSW SR3 ..... 120 A6
Minerva Cl WD/WHPE/BLK NE5 ..... 54 A6
Mingary Cl HLH DH5 ..... 147 F4
Minorca Cl SUND SR1 ..... 15 H5
Minorca Pl GOS/KPK NE3 ..... 55 K7
Minskip Cl SUNDSW SR3 ..... 133 H2
Minster Gv WD/WHPE/BLK NE5 ..... 53 K2
Minster Pde JRW NE32 ..... 74 A4
Minting Pl CRAM NE23 ..... 38 A2
Minton Ct NSHW NE29 ..... 2 B4
Minton La NSHW NE29 ..... 2 B5
Minton Sq MLFD/PNYW SR4 ..... 105 J6
Mirk La GATE NE8 ..... 5 M9
Mirlaw Rd CRAM NE23 ..... 38 A3
Mistletoe Rd JES NE2 ..... 70 E2
Mistletoe St DHAM DH1 ..... 16 A4
Mitcham Crs LGB/HTN NE7 ..... 57 H7
Mitchell Av JES NE2 ..... 70 E1
  MONK NE25 ..... 50 B5
Mitchell Cl PLEE/EAS SR8 ..... 174 C2
Mitchell Dr ASHGTN NE63 ..... 24 D2
Mitchell Gdns HAR/WTLS NE34 ..... 75 K4
Mitchell St BYK/HTN/WLK NE6 ..... 72 D6
  DHAM DH1 ..... 16 B3
  STLY/ANP DH9 ..... 126 B3
Mitford Av BLYTH NE24 ..... 34 E1
  MONK NE25 ..... 39 K5
  MPTH NE61 ..... 21 J1
Mitford Cl DHAM DH1 ..... 169 J5
  WASHS NE38 ..... 116 D2
Mitford Ct PLEE/EAS SR8 ..... 174 E6
Mitford Dr ASHGTN NE63 ..... 23 K3
  RDHAMSE DH6 ..... 158 D7
  WD/WHPE/BLK NE5 ..... 54 C7
Mitford Gdns DUN/TMV NE11 ..... 86 A7
  STKFD/GP NE62 ..... 23 F5
  WLSD/HOW NE28 ..... 59 H5
Mitford Pl GOS/KPK NE3 ..... 56 A4
Mitford Rd HAR/WTLS NE34 ..... 75 J5
  MPTH NE61 ..... 20 A5
Mitford St
  CLDN/WHIT/ROK SR6 ..... 106 E1
  WLSD/HOW NE28 ..... 74 A1
Mitford Ter JRW NE32 ..... 89 K2
Mitford Wy DIN/WO NE13 ..... 45 F3
Mithras Gdns
  BW/LEM/TK/HW NE15 ..... 66 A1
Mitre Pl SSH NE33 ..... 75 F3
Moat Gdns FELL NE10 ..... 88 E4
Moffat Av JRW NE32 ..... 74 C7
Moffat Cl NSHW NE29 ..... 60 A2
Moine Gdns
  CLDN/WHIT/ROK SR6 ..... 106 E2
Molineux St BYK/HTN/WLK NE6 ..... 6 E4
Mollyfair Cl RYTON NE40 ..... 66 B7
Monarch Ter ELS/FEN NE4 ..... 9 J2
Monarch Wy SUNDSW SR3 ..... 133 J2
Mona St STLY/ANP DH9 ..... 112 D7
Moncreiff Ter PLEE/EAS SR8 ..... 162 D5
Monday Crs ELS/FEN NE4 ..... 4 E4
Monday Pl ELS/FEN NE4 ..... 4 E4
Money Slack DHAM DH1 ..... 168 C5
Monkchester Rd
  BYK/HTN/WLK NE6 ..... 7 L8
Monk Ct PLEE/EAS SR8 ..... 174 C7
Monkdale Av BLYTH NE24 ..... 34 C1
Monkhouse Av
  TYNE/NSHE NE30 ..... 60 E1
Monkridge WBAY NE26 ..... 50 C2
  WD/WHPE/BLK NE5 ..... 40 C1
Monkridge Gdns DUN/TMV NE11 ..... 9 H9
Monks Av MONK NE25 ..... 50 B6
Monks' Crs DHAM DH1 ..... 157 G6
Monkseaton Dr MONK NE25 ..... 50 A4
Monkseaton Rd MONK NE25 ..... 49 K4
Monksfeld FELL NE10 ..... 12 E9
Monksfield Cl SUNDSW SR3 ..... 133 K2
Monkside CRAM NE23 ..... 38 D1
Monkside Cl WASHS NE38 ..... 116 C4
Monks Park Wy LGB/KIL NE12 ..... 57 G4
Monks Rdg MPTH NE61 ..... 20 B6
Monks Rd MONK NE25 ..... 50 A6
Monkstone Av
  TYNE/NSHE NE30 ..... 61 G2
Monkstone Cl
  TYNE/NSHE NE30 ..... 61 G2
Monkstone Crs
  TYNE/NSHE NE30 ..... 61 G2
Monk St
  CLDN/WHIT/ROK SR6 ..... 106 D4
Monksway JRW NE32 ..... 74 C5
Monks Wy TYNE/NSHE NE30 ..... 61 G1
Monks Wd NSHW NE29 ..... 60 C2
Monkswood Sq
  SUNDSW SR3 ..... 134 B1
Monkton FELL NE10 ..... 88 B6
Monkton Av HAR/WTLS NE34 ..... 74 D7
Monkton La HEBB NE31 ..... 89 G2
  JRW NE32 ..... 89 F3
Monkton Rd JRW NE32 ..... 73 K4
Monkton Ter JRW NE32 ..... 73 K5
Monmouth Gdns
  WLSD/HOW NE28 ..... 59 J6
Monroe Pl
  WD/WHPE/BLK NE5 ..... 69 H1
Mons Av HEBB NE31 ..... 73 G6
Montagu Av WD/WHPE/BLK NE5 ..... 70 A1
Montagu Ct GOS/KPK NE3 ..... 70 A1
Montague St
  BW/LEM/TK/HW NE15 ..... 68 B5
  CLDN/WHIT/ROK SR6 ..... 106 D2
Monteigne Dr RDHAMSE DH6 ..... 180 A2
Monterey SUNDSW SR3 ..... 133 J2
  WASHN NE37 ..... 102 A1
Montfalcon Cl PLEE/EAS SR8 ..... 174 D4
Montford Cl SUNDSW SR3 ..... 133 H2
Montgomery Rd DHAM DH1 ..... 17 J1
Montpellier Pl GOS/KPK NE3 ..... 55 K7
Montpellier Ter
  ASHBK/HED/RY SR2 ..... 120 E2
Montrose Cl MONK NE25 ..... 40 A2
Montrose Crs
  LWF/SPW/WRK NE9 ..... 11 M9
Montrose Dr FELL NE10 ..... 88 E5
Montrose Gdns SUNDSW SR3 ..... 120 A3
Monument Vw HLS DH4 ..... 117 J6
Moor Cl NSHW NE29 ..... 60 A2
Moor Crs DHAM DH1 ..... 17 M1
  GOS/KPK NE3 ..... 56 C7
  RDHAMSE DH6 ..... 172 B3
Moorcroft Cl
  BW/LEM/TK/HW NE15 ..... 68 B4
Moorcroft Rd
  BW/LEM/TK/HW NE15 ..... 68 C4
Moordale Av BLYTH NE24 ..... 34 C1
Moore Av HAR/WTLS NE34 ..... 75 J5
Moore Crs South HLH DH5 ..... 147 H1
Moor Edge BDN/LAN/SAC DH7 ..... 167 G7
Moor Edge Rd SMOOR NE27 ..... 49 C5
Moore St GATE NE8 ..... 11 K5
  STLY/ANP DH9 ..... 126 C3
Moorfield JES NE2 ..... 56 D7
Moorfield Gdns
  CLDN/WHIT/ROK SR6 ..... 92 A5
Moorfields MPTH NE61 ..... 20 E7
Moorfoot Av CLSW/PEL DH2 ..... 129 J5
Moorfoot Gdns DUN/TMV NE11 ..... 86 A5
Moorhead WD/WHPE/BLK NE5 ..... 69 J2
Moorhill DUN/TMV NE11 ..... 100 C7
Moorhouse Cl
  HAR/WTLS NE34 ..... 75 H6
Moorhouse Est ASHGTN NE63 ..... 24 B1
Moorhouse La ASHGTN NE63 ..... 24 B2
Moorhouses Rd NSHW NE29 ..... 60 A3
Moorland Av BDLGTN NE22 ..... 30 A3
Moorland Ct BDLGTN NE22 ..... 30 A3
Moorland Crs BDLGTN NE22 ..... 30 A3
  BYK/HTN/WLK NE6 ..... 7 L3
  CON/LDGT DH8 ..... 136 E2
Moorland Dr BDLGTN NE22 ..... 30 A4
Moorlands CON/LDGT DH8 ..... 122 C2
  JRW NE32 ..... 90 B3
  PRUD NE42 ..... 80 E3
Moorlands Crs
  CON/LDGT DH8 ..... 122 D3
The Moorlands
  STLY/ANP DH9 ..... 111 G5
Moorland Vw CHPW NE17 ..... 95 H5
Moorland Vls BDLGTN NE22 ..... 30 A3
Moorland Wy CRAM NE23 ..... 32 E6
Moor La BOL NE36 ..... 91 J4
  CLDN/WHIT/ROK SR6 ..... 92 C4
  HAR/WTLS NE34 ..... 75 J5
  PONT/DH NE20 ..... 42 E5
  WD/WHPE/BLK NE5 ..... 55 H6
  WNGT TS28 ..... 183 K4
Moor La East HAR/WTLS NE34 ..... 75 J5
Moormill La DUN/TMV NE11 ..... 100 E7
Moor Park Ct NSHW NE29 ..... 60 A3
Moor Park Rd NSHW NE29 ..... 59 K3
Moor Pl GOS/KPK NE3 ..... 56 C7
Moor Rd PRUD NE42 ..... 80 E4
Moor Rd North GOS/KPK NE3 ..... 56 D7
Moor Rd South JES NE2 ..... 56 D7
Moorsburn Dr HLS DH4 ..... 132 A6
Moors HLS DH4 ..... 131 K7
Moorsfield HLS DH4 ..... 131 K7
Moorside WASHN NE37 ..... 102 D6
Moorside North ELS/FEN NE4 ..... 69 J2
Moorside Rd SUNDSW SR3 ..... 133 K2
Moorside South ELS/FEN NE4 ..... 4 A1
Moorsley Rd HLH DH5 ..... 147 J6
Moor St RDHAMSE DH6 ..... 182 E1
  SUND SR1 ..... 15 H4
Moor Ter SUND SR1 ..... 15 J5
Moorvale La
  WD/WHPE/BLK NE5 ..... 69 J1
Moor Vw
  CLDN/WHIT/ROK SR6 ..... 92 E4
Moorview CON/LDGT DH8 ..... 122 E5
Moor Vw LGB/KIL NE12 ..... 47 J5
Moor View Cl MPTH NE61 ..... 21 H2
Moorview Crs
  WD/WHPE/BLK NE5 ..... 69 J1
Moorway WASHN NE37 ..... 102 D7
Moorway Dr
  BW/LEM/TK/HW NE15 ..... 68 C4
Moraine Crs CHPW NE17 ..... 95 H7
Moralee Cl LGB/HTN NE7 ..... 57 K7
Moran St
  CLDN/WHIT/ROK SR6 ..... 106 D1
Moray Cl CLS/BIR/GTL DH3 ..... 115 K5
  PLEE/EAS SR8 ..... 174 D5
Moray St CLDN/WHIT/ROK SR6 ..... 106 D3
Morcott Gdns WLSD/HOW NE28 ..... 2 A5
Morden St CNUT NE1 ..... 5 J5
Mordey Cl ASHBK/HED/RY SR2 ..... 15 H7
Moreland Rd HAR/WTLS NE34 ..... 91 H7
Moreland St
  CLDN/WHIT/ROK SR6 ..... 106 D3
Morgan St SWCK/CAS SR5 ..... 106 B3
Morgans Wy BLAY NE21 ..... 83 J2
Morland Av WASHS NE38 ..... 117 G3
Morland Gdns
  LWF/SPW/WRK NE9 ..... 11 M9
Morley Av FELL NE10 ..... 13 L4
Morley Hill Rd
  WD/WHPE/BLK NE5 ..... 68 D3
Morley La BDN/LAN/SAC DH7 ..... 176 C1
Morley Ter HLS DH4 ..... 131 J7
Morningside
  BDN/LAN/SAC DH7 ..... 143 H4
  WASHS NE38 ..... 116 A4
Mornington Av HAR/WTLS NE34 ..... 55 K7
Morpeth Av DIN/WO NE13 ..... 46 C2
  HAR/WTLS NE34 ..... 75 J4
  JRW NE32 ..... 89 K1
  MPTH NE61 ..... 21 H1
Morpeth Cl STKFD/GP NE62 ..... 22 E7
  WASHS NE38 ..... 116 C2
Morpeth Dr SUNDSW SR3 ..... 133 H1
Morpeth Rd ASHGTN NE63 ..... 23 H1
  STKFD/GP NE62 ..... 22 E6
Morpeth St JES NE2 ..... 4 F1
PLEE/EAS SR8 ..... 175 G2
Morpeth Ter NSHW NE29 ..... 60 B6
Morris Av HAR/WTLS NE34 ..... 91 F1
Morris Crs BOLCOL NE35 ..... 90 E4
Morris Cressent DH6 ..... 172 B6
Morris Gdns FELL NE10 ..... 13 M8
Morrison Rd MPTH NE61 ..... 20 D4
Morrison St GATE NE8 ..... 10 A4
Morris Rd WICK/BNPF NE16 ..... 85 F4
Morris St CLS/BIR/GTL DH3 ..... 115 H2
  GATE NE8 ..... 10 A7
Morston Dr
  BW/LEM/TK/HW NE15 ..... 68 C5
Mortimer Av NSHW NE29 ..... 60 B4
  WD/WHPE/BLK NE5 ..... 54 E7
Mortimer Cha CRAM NE23 ..... 33 H4
Mortimer Rd HAR/WTLS NE34 ..... 75 J4
  SSH NE33 ..... 75 H3
Mortimer St CON/LDGT DH8 ..... 122 D4
  MLFD/PNYW SR4 ..... 105 K6
Morton Cl WASHS NE38 ..... 117 F2
Morton Sq PLEE/EAS SR8 ..... 174 D3
Morton St BYK/HTN/WLK NE6 ..... 7 J5
  SSH NE33 ..... 3 J5
Morval Cl SUNDSW SR3 ..... 133 H2
Morwick Cl CRAM NE23 ..... 38 A3
Morwick Pl
  WD/WHPE/BLK NE5 ..... 69 H2
Morwick Rd NSHW NE29 ..... 60 B2
Mosley St CNUT NE1 ..... 5 K7
Moss Bank LWF/SPW/WRK NE9 ..... 101 H2
Moss Cl BW/LEM/TK/HW NE15 ..... 68 A3
Moss Crs RYTON NE40 ..... 66 C7
Mossdale DHAM DH1 ..... 158 A5
Moss Side LWF/SPW/WRK NE9 ..... 101 H2
Mossway CLSW/PEL DH2 ..... 114 D7
Moulton Pl WD/WHPE/BLK NE5 ..... 69 G1
Mountbatten Av HEBB NE31 ..... 73 G7
Mount Cl LGB/KIL NE12 ..... 47 K5
  MLFD/PNYW SR4 ..... 105 F7
  MONK NE25 ..... 50 B6
Mountfield Rd MONK NE25 ..... 55 K6
Mountford Rd MONK NE25 ..... 40 A1
Mount Gv MLFD/PNYW SR4 ..... 120 A2
Mount La LWF/SPW/WRK NE9 ..... 102 A5
Mount Park Dr
  BDN/LAN/SAC DH7 ..... 140 B4
Mount Pleasant
  BDN/LAN/SAC DH7 ..... 141 G4
  BLAY NE21 ..... 83 K3
  CLS/BIR/GTL DH3 ..... 115 J1
  HLH DH5 ..... 132 D7
  STLY/ANP DH9 ..... 111 G5
  SWCK/CAS SR5 ..... 106 A4
Mount Pleasant Ct
  BW/LEM/TK/HW NE15 ..... 67 F1
Mount Rd CLS/BIR/GTL DH3 ..... 115 K1
  LWF/SPW/WRK NE9 ..... 102 A5
  MLFD/PNYW SR4 ..... 119 K2
Mountside CON/LDGT DH8 ..... 122 D1
Mountside Gdns DUN/TMV NE11 ..... 85 K5
Mount Stewart St
  SEA/MUR SR7 ..... 150 E3
Mount Ter SSH NE33 ..... 3 H4
The Mount
  BW/LEM/TK/HW NE15 ..... 66 E1
  CON/LDGT DH8 ..... 122 D1
  RYTON NE40 ..... 66 E6
Mount Vw
  BDN/LAN/SAC DH7 ..... 140 B4
  WICK/BNPF NE16 ..... 85 F4
Mourne Gdns DUN/TMV NE11 ..... 86 A6
Moutter Cl PLEE/EAS SR8 ..... 175 F2
Mowbray Cl ASHBK/HED/RY SR2 ..... 14 F8
Mowbray Rd
  ASHBK/HED/RY SR2 ..... 15 G3
  LGB/KIL NE12 ..... 57 K2
  NSHW NE29 ..... 60 B4
  SSH NE33 ..... 75 J2
Mowbray St BYK/HTN/WLK NE6 ..... 6 C4
  DHAM DH1 ..... 16 A3
Mozart St SSH NE33 ..... 3 K9
Muirfield MONK NE25 ..... 50 B4
  SSH NE33 ..... 75 K2
Muirfield Cl CON/LDGT DH8 ..... 122 E2
Muirfield Dr FELL NE10 ..... 87 K6
  WASHN NE37 ..... 102 E3
Muirfield Rd LGB/HTN NE7 ..... 57 J5
Mulben Cl ELS/FEN NE4 ..... 69 J2
Mulberry RDHAMSE DH6 ..... 180 D1
Mulberry St FELL NE10 ..... 12 B6
Mulcaster Gdns
  WLSD/HOW NE28 ..... 58 C7
Mulgrave Dr
  CLDN/WHIT/ROK SR6 ..... 15 H1
Mulgrave Ter GATE NE8 ..... 10 F2
Mullen Dr RYTON NE40 ..... 66 E7
Mullen Gdns WLSD/HOW NE28 ..... 58 C6
Mullen Rd WLSD/HOW NE28 ..... 58 C6
Mull Gv JRW NE32 ..... 90 C1
Muncaster Ms PLEE/EAS SR8 ..... 174 B7
Mundella Ter BYK/HTN/WLK NE6 ..... 6 F2
Mundell St STLY/ANP DH9 ..... 126 B3
Mundle Av BLAY NE21 ..... 84 A6
Mundles La BOL NE36 ..... 91 J5
Munslow Rd SUNDSW SR3 ..... 133 H2
Muriel St STLY/ANP DH9 ..... 126 C4
Murphy Gv
  ASHBK/HED/RY SR2 ..... 120 E7
Murray Av HLS DH4 ..... 131 J6
Murray Ct CON/LDGT DH8 ..... 122 D2
Murrayfield CRAM NE23 ..... 39 G6
Murrayfield Dr
  BDN/LAN/SAC DH7 ..... 167 F7
Murrayfield Rd
  WD/WHPE/BLK NE5 ..... 55 H7
Murray Gdns DUN/TMV NE11 ..... 9 J8
Murray Rd CLSW/PEL DH2 ..... 129 H4
  WLSD/HOW NE28 ..... 59 H7
Murray St BLAY NE21 ..... 84 A1
  PLEE/EAS SR8 ..... 175 H4
Murton La HLH DH5 ..... 148 C7
  NSHW NE29 ..... 59 J1
Murton St SUND SR1 ..... 15 G4
Muscott Gv
  BW/LEM/TK/HW NE15 ..... 68 E5

Musgrave Rd
  LWF/SPW/WRK NE9 ..... 87 F6
Musgrave Ter BYK/HTN/WLK NE6 ..... 7 M4
Muswell HI
  BW/LEM/TK/HW NE15 ..... 68 C6
Mutual St WLSD/HOW NE28 ..... 72 D1
Mylord Crs LGB/KIL NE12 ..... 47 H4
Myrella Crs ASHBK/HED/RY SR2 ..... 120 C4
Myreside Pl LGB/KIL NE12 ..... 57 H3
Myrtle Av CLDN/WHIT/ROK SR6 ..... 93 F3
  DUN/TMV NE11 ..... 9 H9
Myrtle Crs LGB/KIL NE12 ..... 57 K1
Myrtle Gv HAR/WTLS NE34 ..... 75 K7
  JES NE2 ..... 70 E1
  LWF/SPW/WRK NE9 ..... 101 F1
  SUNDSW SR3 ..... 120 B7
  WLSD/HOW NE28 ..... 73 F2
Myrtle Rd BLAY NE21 ..... 84 A3
Myrtles CLSW/PEL DH2 ..... 129 H2

N

Nafferton Pl
  WD/WHPE/BLK NE5 ..... 69 G3
Nailsworth Cl BOLCOL NE35 ..... 90 C2
Nairn Cl CLS/BIR/GTL DH3 ..... 115 K4
  WASHN NE37 ..... 102 E3
Nairn Rd CRAM NE23 ..... 38 C1
Nairn St JRW NE32 ..... 90 C1
Naisbitt Av PLEE/EAS SR8 ..... 175 F2
Nansen Cl
  WD/WHPE/BLK NE5 ..... 68 D1
Nansen St CON/LDGT DH8 ..... 123 G4
Napier Rd SEA/MUR SR7 ..... 135 G7
  WICK/BNPF NE16 ..... 84 E3
Napier St HAR/WTLS NE34 ..... 75 F5
  JES NE2 ..... 6 A4
  JRW NE32 ..... 73 K4
Napier Wy BLAY NE21 ..... 84 C2
Narvik Wy NSHW NE29 ..... 59 K5
Nash Av HAR/WTLS NE34 ..... 91 H1
Naters St WBAY NE26 ..... 51 G5
Natley Av BOL NE36 ..... 91 J5
Nattress Ter WNGT TS28 ..... 183 J3
Navan Cl STKFD/GP NE62 ..... 23 K5
Navenby Cl CRAM NE23 ..... 56 D2
Naworth Av TYNE/NSHE NE30 ..... 60 E1
Naworth Ct PLEE/EAS SR8 ..... 174 C7
Naworth Dr WD/WHPE/BLK NE5 ..... 54 C7
Naworth Ter JRW NE32 ..... 74 B7
Nayland Rd CRAM NE23 ..... 38 B1
Naylor Av BLAY NE21 ..... 84 A6
Naylor Pl WBAY NE26 ..... 40 E1
Neale St CLDN/WHIT/ROK SR6 ..... 106 D2
  PRUD NE42 ..... 80 D1
Nearlane Cl DIN/WO NE13 ..... 46 C1
Neasdon Crs TYNE/NSHE NE30 ..... 61 F1
Neasham Rd SEA/MUR SR7 ..... 135 G6
Nedderton Cl
  WD/WHPE/BLK NE5 ..... 53 K6
Needham Pl CRAM NE23 ..... 38 C1
Neill Dr WICK/BNPF NE16 ..... 99 F3
Neilson Rd FELL NE10 ..... 11 M3
Neil St HLH DH5 ..... 148 B7
Nelson Av CRAM NE23 ..... 32 E7
  GOS/KPK NE3 ..... 56 A5
  SSH NE33 ..... 3 L7
Nelson Cl PLEE/EAS SR8 ..... 175 H3
Nelson Crs NSHW NE29 ..... 60 B7
Nelson Dr CRAM NE23 ..... 32 E7
Nelson Rd BYK/HTN/WLK NE6 ..... 72 D7
  CRAM NE23 ..... 32 E6
  MONK NE25 ..... 49 K4
  STKFD/GP NE62 ..... 23 G4
Nelson St
  ASHBK/HED/RY SR2 ..... 121 F7
  CLS/BIR/GTL DH3 ..... 129 J5
  CNUT NE1 ..... 5 J6
  CON/LDGT DH8 ..... 123 J3
  CON/LDGT DH8 ..... 123 F5
  DUN/TMV NE11 ..... 9 G5
  GATE NE8 ..... 10 F1
  HLH DH5 ..... 147 K5
  SEA/MUR SR7 ..... 135 H7
  SSH NE33 ..... 3 G7
  WASHS NE38 ..... 117 G2
Nelson Ter NSHW NE29 ..... 60 B7
Nelson Wy CRAM NE23 ..... 32 D5
Nenthead Cl CLS/BIR/GTL DH3 ..... 145 J1
Neptune Rd
  BW/LEM/TK/HW NE15 ..... 68 B5
  WLSD/HOW NE28 ..... 72 D3
Nesbit Rd PLEE/EAS SR8 ..... 175 F5
Nesburn Rd MLFD/PNYW SR4 ..... 120 A2
Nesham Pl HLH DH5 ..... 132 C7
Ness Ct BLAY NE21 ..... 83 J2
Nest Rd FELL NE10 ..... 12 D3
Netherburn Rd SWCK/CAS SR5 ..... 106 C3
Netherby Dr
  WD/WHPE/BLK NE5 ..... 69 G3
Netherdale BDLGTN NE22 ..... 28 D5
Nether Farm Rd FELL NE10 ..... 13 H6
Nether Riggs BDLGTN NE22 ..... 29 F6
Netherton LGB/KIL NE12 ..... 47 J4
Netherton Av NSHW NE29 ..... 60 B3
Netherton Cl
  BDN/LAN/SAC DH7 ..... 154 A3
  CLSW/PEL DH2 ..... 129 F5
Netherton Gdns
  DIN/WO NE13 ..... 46 B3
Netherton Gv NSHW NE29 ..... 60 B3
Netherton La BDLGTN NE22 ..... 28 E5
Nettles La SUNDSW SR3 ..... 134 B1
Nettleham Rd SWCK/CAS SR5 ..... 106 C3
Neville Dene DHAM DH1 ..... 168 A1
Neville Rd
  BW/LEM/TK/HW NE15 ..... 68 B4
  MLFD/PNYW SR4 ..... 105 K6
  PLEE/EAS SR8 ..... 174 D3
Neville's Cross Bank
  DHAM DH1 ..... 168 B2
Neville's Cross Rd HEBB NE31 ..... 73 H6
Neville Sq DHAM DH1 ..... 168 B3
Neville St CNUT NE1 ..... 5 H8
  DHAM DH1 ..... 16 C4

Nevill Rd *PSHWF* NE43 .... 79 H5
Nevinson Av *HAR/WTLS* NE34.. 91 H1
Nevis CI *WBAY* NE26 .... 50 B1
Nevis Gv *BOL* NE36 .... 91 F5
New Acres *BDN/LAN/SAC* DH7 ... 155 F7
Newacres Rd *STLY/ANP* DH9 .... 126 C5
Newark CI *PLEE/EAS* SR8 .... 174 D3
Newark Crs *SEA/MUR* SR7 ...... 135 F4
Newark Dr *CLDN/WHIT/ROK* SR6 .. 93 F4
Newarth CI
  BW/LEM/TK/HW NE15 .... 68 B4
Newbiggin La
  BDN/LAN/SAC DH7 .... 139 H4
  CON/LDGT DH8 .... 138 E4
  WD/WHPE/BLK NE5 .... 54 D7 ⊞
Newbold Av *SWCK/CAS* SR5 .... 106 C3 ⊞
Newbold St *BYK/HTN/WLK* NE6 .. 7 K6
Newbottle La *HLS* DH4 .... 146 C1
Newbottle St *HLS* DH4 .... 132 B5
Newbridge Av
  SWCK/CAS SR5 .... 106 C3 ⊡
Newbridge Bank
  CLS/BIR/GTL DH3 .... 130 A2
Newbridge Banks
  CLSW/PEL DH2 .... 128 A3
New Bridge St *CNUT* NE1 .... 5 M5
New Bridge St West *CNUT* NE1 .. 5 L5 ⊡
Newbrough Crs *JES* NE2 .... 70 E1 ⊡
Newburgh Av *MONK* NE25 ...... 39 K6
New Burn Rd *RDHAMSE* DH6 ... 180 A2
Newburn Av *SWCK/CAS* SR5 .... 106 C3
Newburn Bridge Rd *BLAY* NE21 .. 67 G5
Newburn Crs *HLS* DH4 .... 132 B5
Newburn Rd
  BW/LEM/TK/HW NE15 .... 67 G2
  STLY/ANP DH9 .... 112 E6
Newbury CI *LGB/KIL* NE12 ...... 47 K5
Newbury Gv *GATE* NE8 .... 10 C8
Newbury CI
  BW/LEM/TK/HW NE15 .... 68 B4
Newbury Dr *CON/LDGT* DH8 .... 108 E7 ⊡
Newbury St *SSH* NE33 .... 75 H4 ⊡
  SWCK/CAS SR5 .... 106 C2
Newby La *RDHAMSE* DH6 ...... 159 F4
Newby PI *LWF/SPW/WRK* NE9 .. 101 H1
Newcastle Av *PLEE/EAS* SR8... 175 G2
Newcastle Bank
  CLS/BIR/GTL DH3 .... 101 H6
Newcastle Rd *BLYTH* NE24 ..... 34 E3
  BOL NE36 .... 89 J5
  CLS/BIR/GTL DH3 .... 101 J1 ⊡
  CLS/BIR/GTL DH3 .... 101 J1 ⊡
  DHAM DH1 .... 168 B2 ⊡
  HAR/WTLS NE34 .... 74 D6
  SWCK/CAS SR5 .... 92 A7
Newcastle St *NSHW* NE29 .... 2 C2
New Cross Rd *WNGT* TS28 ...... 183 J3
New Dr *SEA/MUR* SR7 .... 135 H6
New Durham Rd
  ASHBK/HED/RY SR2 .... 14 B7
New Elvet *DHAM* DH1 .... 16 E4
New Front *STLY/ANP* DH9 ...... 125 H7
New Front St *STLY/ANP* DH9 ... 112 B5
Newgate St *MPTH* NE61 .... 20 D4
New George St *SSH* NE33 ...... 75 G3
New Grange Ter
  CLSW/PEL DH2 .... 128 D3
New Green St *SSH* NE33 .... 75 G2 ⊡
Newham Av *DIN/WO* NE13 ...... 46 A5
Newhaven Av *SWCK/CAS* SR5... 106 C3
Newholme Est *WNGT* TS28 ..... 184 A6
Newhouse Av
  BDN/LAN/SAC DH7 .... 165 G1
Newhouse Rd
  BDN/LAN/SAC DH7 .... 165 G2
Newington Ct *SWCK/CAS* SR5... 106 C3
Newington Rd
  BYK/HTN/WLK NE6 .... 6 C4
  JES NE2 .... 6 B3
New King St *NWBGN* NE64 ...... 19 G7
Newland Ct *HAR/WTLS* NE34 ... 75 G6 ⊡
Newlands *CON/LDGT* DH8 ...... 122 D2
Newlands Av *BLYTH* NE24 ...... 35 F2 ⊡
  GOS/KPK NE3 .... 56 C1
  MONK NE25 .... 50 B6
  SUNDSW SR3 .... 120 B3
Newlands PI *BLYTH* NE24 ...... 35 F2 ⊡
Newlands Rd *BLYTH* NE24 ...... 35 F2
  DHAM DH1 .... 157 K5
  JES NE2 .... 56 D7
Newlands Rd East
  SEA/MUR SR7 .... 135 H7 ⊡
Newlands Rd West
  SEA/MUR SR7 .... 135 G6
Newlyn Crs *NSHW* NE29 .... 60 C5
Newlyn Dr *CRAM* NE23 .... 33 H7
  JRW NE32 .... 74 B5
Newlyn Rd *GOS/KPK* NE3 ...... 55 J5
Newman Ter *GATE* NE8 .... 11 J7
Newmarch St *JRW* NE32 .... 73 J4
Newmarket St *CON/LDGT* DH8... 123 F4
New Mills *ELS/FEN* NE4 .... 4 E4
Newminster CI *HLS* DH4 .... 131 K5
New Phoenix Yd *MPTH* NE61 ... 20 D5 ⊡
Newport Gv *SUNDSW* SR3 ..... 120 A6 ⊡
New Quay *NSHW* NE29 .... 2 E4 ⊡
Newquay Gdns
  LWF/SPW/WRK NE9 .... 101 F3
New Ridley Rd *PSHWF* NE43.... 79 H6
Newriggs *WASHS* NE38 .... 117 G4
New Rd *BOLCOL* NE35 .... 90 E4
  DUN/TMV NE11 .... 86 B6
  FELL NE10 .... 88 C7
  STLY/ANP DH9 .... 113 K7
  WICK/BNPF NE16 .... 97 J6
Newsham CI
  WD/WHPE/BLK NE5 .... 53 K6 ⊡
Newsham Rd *BLYTH* NE24 ...... 34 E2
Newstead Ct *WASHS* NE38 ..... 116 E1 ⊡
Newstead Rd *CON/LDGT* DH8 ... 122 C2 ⊡
Newstead Rd *HLS* DH4 .... 132 A5
Newsteads CI *MONK* NE25 ...... 50 B4 ⊡
Newsteads Dr *MONK* NE25 ..... 50 A4
Newstead Sq *SUNDSW* SR3 .... 134 A1 ⊡

New Strangford Rd
  SEA/MUR SR7 .... 150 D1
New St *DHAM* DH1 .... 16 B3
  MLFD/PNYW SR4 .... 104 E7 ⊡
  WLSD/HOW NE28 .... 59 H7
Newton CI
  BW/LEM/TK/HW NE15 .... 68 C4
Newton Dr *DHAM* DH1 .... 156 C4
Newton Gv *HAR/WTLS* NE34 .... 74 E6 ⊡
Newton PI *LGB/HTN* NE7 .... 57 G1
Newton St *BDN/LAN/SAC* DH7 .. 155 F1
  DUN/TMV NE11 .... 9 H5
  GATE NE8 .... 10 C7
New York Rd *NSHW* NE29 ...... 59 K1
  SMOOR NE27 .... 49 G7
New York Wy *SMOOR* NE27 ..... 59 J2
Nicholas Av
  CLDN/WHIT/ROK SR6 .... 93 F4
Nicholas St *HLH* DH5 .... 148 A3
Nicholson Ter *LGB/KIL* NE12 ... 58 A1
Nichol St *ELS/FEN* NE4 .... 69 H6
Nickleby Chare *DHAM* DH1 ..... 16 A9
Nidderdale Av *HLH* DH5........ 147 J6
Niddrieside CI *BLYTH* NE24 .... 30 C6
Nidsdale Av *BYK/HTN/WLK* NE6 .. 72 C4
Nightingale CI
  MLFD/PNYW SR4 .... 118 E2
Nightingale PI *STLY/ANP* DH9... 127 F2
Nile CI *BW/LEM/TK/HW* NE15 ... 68 A3
Nile St *CON/LDGT* DH8 .... 123 F5
  NSHW NE29 .... 2 D1
  SSH NE33 .... 2 F9
  SUND SR1 .... 15 G4
Nilverton Av
  ASHBK/HED/RY SR2 .... 120 D3
Nimbus Ct *SUNDSW* SR3 ...... 134 A1 ⊡
Nine Lands *HLS* DH4 .... 132 A7
Ninth Av *BLYTH* NE24 .... 35 F1
  BYK/HTN/WLK NE6 .... 7 G1
  CLSW/PEL DH2 .... 129 H4
  MPTH NE61 .... 21 F6
Ninth St *PLEE/EAS* SR8 .... 175 H3 ⊡
Nissan Wy *WASHN* NE37 .... 103 K6
Nixon St *GATE* NE8 .... 6 C9
Nixon Ter *BLYTH* NE24 .... 35 H1 ⊡
Noble's Bank Rd
  ASHBK/HED/RY SR2 .... 15 J7 ⊡
Noble St *ASHBK/HED/RY* SR2 ... 15 J8 ⊡
  ELS/FEN NE4 .... 9 G1
  FELL NE10 .... 12 D5 ⊡
  PLEE/EAS SR8 .... 162 E4
Noel Av *BLAY* NE21 .... 84 A6
Noel St *STLY/ANP* DH9 .... 112 E7
Noel Ter *BLAY* NE21 .... 84 B5
Noirmont Wy *SUNDSW* SR3 .... 133 J1
Nookside Ct *MLFD/PNYW* SR4 .. 119 G2
The Nook *NSHW* NE29 .... 2 A2
Nora St *HAR/WTLS* NE34 .... 75 G6
  MLFD/PNYW SR4 .... 119 K2
Norburn La *BDN/LAN/SAC* DH7 .. 142 E5
Norburn Pk *BDN/LAN/SAC* DH7 .. 143 F7
Norbury Gv *BYK/HTN/WLK* NE6 .. 7 K7
Nordale Wy *BLYTH* NE24 .... 30 C6
Norfolk Av *CLS/BIR/GTL* DH3 ... 115 J5
  SUNDSW SR3 .... 120 B6
Norfolk CI *ASHGTN* NE63 ...... 23 G1 ⊡
  SEA/MUR SR7 .... 135 G6
Norfolk Dr *WASHN* NE37 .... 103 F3
Norfolk Gdns *WLSD/HOW* NE28 .. 59 G6
Norfolk Rd *CON/LDGT* DH8 ..... 137 G1
  GATE NE8 .... 6 C9
  HAR/WTLS NE34 .... 76 C4
Norfolk St *SUND* SR1 .... 14 F4
  TYNE/NSHE NE30 .... 3 H1
Norfolk Wk *PLEE/EAS* SR8 ..... 174 D2 ⊡
Norfolk Wy
  BW/LEM/TK/HW NE15 .... 68 C5 ⊡
Norham Av *HAR/WTLS* NE34.... 76 A3
Norham Av North
  HAR/WTLS NE34 .... 76 A3
Norham Av South
  HAR/WTLS NE34 .... 76 A3
Norham CI *BLYTH* NE24 .... 30 E7
  DIN/WO NE13 .... 46 A4 ⊡
  MPTH NE61 .... 27 F1 ⊡
Norham Dr *MPTH* NE61 .... 21 F7
  PLEE/EAS SR8 .... 174 D7 ⊡
  WD/WHPE/BLK NE5 .... 54 C7 ⊡
Norham Gdns *STKFD/GP* NE62 .. 23 G4
Norham PI *JES* NE2 .... 70 E2 ⊡
Norham Rd *ASHGTN* NE63 ..... 23 K3
  DHAM DH1 .... 156 D2
  GOS/KPK NE3 .... 56 B4
  MONK NE25 .... 50 D4
  NSHW NE29 .... 60 A5 ⊡
  NSHW NE29 .... 60 A4 ⊡
Norham Rd North *NSHW* NE29 .. 59 K2 ⊡
Norham Ter *JRW* NE32 .... 73 K7
Norhurst *WICK/BNPF* NE16 ..... 84 C7
Norland Rd
  BW/LEM/TK/HW NE15 .... 68 D6
Norley Av *SWCK/CAS* SR5 ..... 106 C3
Norma Crs *WBAY* NE26 .... 51 H5
Norman Av *SUNDSW* SR3 ..... 120 B7
Normanby CI *SEA/MUR* SR7 ... 135 G6
Normandy Crs *HLH* DH5........ 132 C7
Norman Rd *ROWG* NE39 .... 97 G4
Norman Ter *WLSD/HOW* NE28 .. 73 K1
Normanton Ter *ELS/FEN* NE4... 4 D6
Normount Rd *ELS/FEN* NE4 .... 69 J6
Northampton Rd
  PLEE/EAS SR8 .... 174 D2
Northamptonshire Dr
  DHAM DH1 .... 158 A6 ⊡
North Ap *CLSW/PEL* DH2 ...... 129 H3
North Av *GOS/KPK* NE3 .... 56 B6
  HAR/WTLS NE34 .... 75 J5
  LGB/KIL NE12 .... 57 K3
  PLEE/EAS SR8 .... 175 G3 ⊡
  STKFD/GP NE62 .... 22 E6
  WD/WHPE/BLK NE5 .... 68 D1
North Bailey *DHAM* DH1 .... 16 D5
Northbourne Rd *HEBB* NE31 ... 73 J5
Northbourne St *ELS/FEN* NE4 .. 4 A9

GATE NE8 .... 11 H7
North Brancepeth CI
  BDN/LAN/SAC DH7 .... 167 K4 ⊡
North Bridge St
  CLDN/WHIT/ROK SR6 .... 14 E1
  SWCK/CAS SR5 .... 14 E2
North Burns *CLS/BIR/GTL* DH3 ... 129 J3
  HAR/WTLS NE34 .... 75 K5
  RYTON NE40 .... 66 E6
Northcote Av *WICK/BNPF* NE16 .. 84 E7
  WD/WHPE/BLK NE5 .... 68 A2
Northcote St *ELS/FEN* NE4 ..... 4 D6
  SSH NE33 .... 75 H3
North Crs *PLEE/EAS* SR8 ...... 162 D6
  WASHS NE38 .... 116 E5 ⊡
North Cft *LGB/KIL* NE12 .... 58 A3
North Cross St *CON/LDGT* DH8.. 123 J3
  GOS/KPK NE3 .... 56 C5
Northdene *CLS/BIR/GTL* DH3 ... 101 J7
Northdene Av *SEA/MUR* SR7.... 135 K7
North Dr *CLDN/WHIT/ROK* SR6.. 91 J3
  CLS/BIR/GTL DH3 .... 115 K7
  HEBB NE31 .... 72 D6
North Durham St *SUND* SR1 ... 15 H4
Northern Wy *SWCK/CAS* SR5 ... 106 A3
North Farm *BDLGTN* NE22 ..... 28 A5
North Farm Av
  MLFD/PNYW SR4 .... 119 F4
North Farm Rd *HEBB* NE31..... 73 F6
Northfield CI *WICK/BNPF* NE16 .. 84 D7
  MLFD/PNYW SR4 .... 119 F4 ⊡
Northfield Dr *LGB/KIL* NE12 .... 47 H7
Northfield Gdns
  HAR/WTLS NE34 .... 75 K3
Northfield Rd *GOS/KPK* NE3 ... 56 B5
  SSH NE33 .... 75 K2
Northfield Vw
  CON/LDGT DH8 .... 123 G4 ⊡
Northgate *LGB/KIL* NE12 .... 47 K5
North Gra *PONT/DH* NE20 ...... 43 G1
North Gv *CLDN/WHIT/ROK* SR6 .. 106 E2
  RYTON NE40 .... 67 F6
North Guards
  CLDN/WHIT/ROK SR6 .... 92 E4
North Hall Rd *MLFD/PNYW* SR4.. 119 H2
North Hvn *SEA/MUR* SR7 ...... 135 H7
North Hylton Rd
  SWCK/CAS SR5 .... 105 H3
North Jesmond Av *JES* NE2 ... 70 E1 ⊡
North King St *TYNE/NSHE* NE30 .. 61 F4
Northlands *BLAY* NE21 .... 83 K3 ⊡
Northlands Pk *TRIM* TS29 ..... 182 D7 ⊡
Northlands Rd *MPTH* NE61 .... 20 D3
North La *BOL* NE36 .... 91 G5
  HLH DH5 .... 148 C3
Northlea
  BW/LEM/TK/HW NE15 .... 68 C3 ⊡
Northlea Rd *SEA/MUR* SR7 .... 135 G7
North Leech *MPTH* NE61 .... 20 B3
North Magdalene
  CON/LDGT DH8 .... 109 H5
North Mason Ldg *DIN/WO* NE13 .. 44 E7
North Mdw *PRUD* NE42 .... 64 A6
North Milburn St
  MLFD/PNYW SR4 .... 14 A3 ⊡
North Moor Av *TRIM* TS29 ..... 182 E7
North Moor Ct *SUNDSW* SR3.... 119 J5
North Moor La *SUNDSW* SR3 ... 119 J5
Northmoor Rd
  BYK/HTN/WLK NE6 .... 7 M1
North Moor Rd *SUNDSW* SR3 ... 119 J5
Northolt Av *CRAM* NE23 .... 38 C1
North Pde *WBAY* NE26 .... 51 F4
North Railway St
  SEA/MUR SR7 .... 150 E1 ⊡
North Ravensworth St
  MLFD/PNYW SR4 .... 14 A3 ⊡
North Rdg *BDLGTN* NE22 ...... 28 D5
  MONK NE25 .... 50 A4
North Rd *BOL* NE36 .... 91 G5
  BOLCOL NE35 .... 90 C3
  CLS/BIR/GTL DH3 .... 115 J7
  DHAM DH1 .... 16 C3
  HLH DH5 .... 147 H3
  NSHW NE29 .... 60 D2
  PONT/DH NE20 .... 43 G1
  SEA/MUR SR7 .... 135 K6
  STLY/ANP DH9 .... 111 G6
  WLSD/HOW NE28 .... 72 D1
  WNGT TS28 .... 183 J4
North Seaton Rd *ASHGTN* NE63.. 23 K3
  NWBGN NE64 .... 25 F2
Northside PI *MONK* NE25 ...... 40 B6
Northside Rd *CON/LDGT* DH8 .. 122 C2
North Stead Dr *BLAY* NE21 .... 83 J3
North St *BLAY* NE21 .... 83 A3
  CLDN/WHIT/ROK SR6 .... 92 A3
  CNUT NE1 .... 5 K5
  HLH DH5 .... 147 G3
  HLS DH4 .... 132 B3
  JRW NE32 .... 73 K4
  RDHAMSE DH6 .... 178 E5
  SSH NE33 .... 3 G6
  SUNDSW SR3 .... 120 A6
  SWCK/CAS SR5 .... 106 C4 ⊡
North Ter *SEA/MUR* SR7 ...... 135 K7
  SUNDSW SR3 .... 120 A6 ⊡
  WLSD/HOW NE28 .... 73 J1
Northumberland Av
  BDLGTN NE22 .... 28 E5
  GOS/KPK NE3 .... 56 A6
  LGB/KIL NE12 .... 57 K3
  NWBGN NE64 .... 25 G7
Northumberland CI
  ASHGTN NE63 .... 23 G1
Northumberland Dock Rd
  WLSD/HOW NE28.............. 74 A2
Northumberland Gdns
  WD/WHPE/BLK NE5 .... 53 K7
Northumberland PI
  PLEE/EAS SR8 .... 174 C2 ⊡
Northumberland Rd
  BW/LEM/TK/HW NE15 .... 68 A5 ⊡
  CNUT NE1 .... 5 L4

RYTON NE40 .... 66 E5
Northumberland Sq *NSHW* NE29 .. 2 E3
Northumberland St *CNUT* NE1 ... 5 K5
  PLEE/EAS SR8 .... 175 G2
  WLSD/HOW NE28 .... 72 E1
Northumberland Ter
  TYNE/NSHE NE30 .... 61 H3 ⊡
Northumberland Vls
  WLSD/HOW NE28 .... 73 C1
Northumberland Wy
  WASHN NE37 .... 103 F3
  WASHS NE38 .... 117 G3
Northumbrian Rd *CRAM* NE23 .. 33 J7
Northumbrian Wy *LGB/KIL* NE12.. 47 J7
  NSHW NE29 .... 60 C3
Northumbria PI *STLY/ANP* DH9 .. 112 F7
North Vw *BW/LEM/TK/HW* NE6 ... 6 C4
  CLDN/WHIT/ROK SR6 .... 106 D2
  CON/LDGT DH8 .... 122 D3
  JES NE2 .... 45 F2
  HAR/WTLS NE34 .... 75 K3 ⊡
  HLH DH5 .... 148 C7
  JRW NE32 .... 73 J5
  LGB/KIL NE12 .... 57 K2 ⊡
  NWBGN NE64 .... 25 F2
  SWCK/CAS SR5 .... 105 G4
  WBAY NE26 .... 51 G5
  WICK/BNPF NE16 .... 84 E5
  WLSD/HOW NE28 .... 72 E1
North Walbottle Rd
  WD/WHPE/BLK NE5 .... 67 J1
Northway
  BW/LEM/TK/HW NE15 .... 53 F7
  LWF/SPW/WRK NE9 .... 11 J9
  STKFD/GP NE62 .... 23 F6 ⊡
Northwood Ct
  SWCK/CAS SR5 .... 106 C3 ⊡
Northwood Rd *SEA/MUR* SR7 ... 135 H7
Norton Av *RDHAMSE* DH6 ..... 180 A2 ⊡
  SEA/MUR SR7 .... 135 G6
Norton CI *CLSW/PEL* DH2 ...... 129 F6
Norton Rd *SWCK/CAS* SR5 ..... 106 A2
Norton Wy
  BW/LEM/TK/HW NE15 .... 68 C5
Norway Av *MLFD/PNYW* SR4 ... 119 J2
Norwich Av *DIN/WO* NE13 ..... 46 B4 ⊡
Norwich CI *ASHGTN* NE63 ..... 24 C3 ⊡
  CLS/BIR/GTL DH3 .... 145 H1
Norwich Rd *DHAM* DH1 .... 156 E2
Norwood Av *BYK/HTN/WLK* NE6 .. 71 H2
  GOS/KPK NE3 .... 46 C7
Norwood Rd
  BW/LEM/TK/HW NE15 .... 68 B3
  DUN/TMV NE11 .... 9 L9
Nottingham PI *PLEE/EAS* SR8 .. 174 C2
Nottinghamshire Rd
  DHAM DH1 .... 157 K6
Nuneaton Wy
  WD/WHPE/BLK NE5 .... 53 K6
Nunnykirk CI *PRUD* NE42 ...... 64 A7
Nuns La *CNUT* NE1 .... 5 J7
  GATE NE8 .... 11 G2
Nuns Moor Crs *ELS/FEN* NE4 ... 69 J4
Nuns Moor Rd *ELS/FEN* NE4 ... 69 J4
Nuns' Rw *DHAM* DH1 .... 157 G6
Nun St *CNUT* NE1 .... 5 J6
Nunwick Gdns *NSHW* NE29 .... 60 A4 ⊡
Nunwick Wy *LGB/KIL* NE7 ...... 57 K7
Nursery CI *SUNDSW* SR3 ...... 120 A4
Nursery Ct *CHPW* NE17 .... 95 H7
Nursery Gdns *PLEE/EAS* SR8... 162 D6
Nursery La *CLDN/WHIT/ROK* SR6.. 92 A3
Nursery Pk *ASHGTN* NE63 ..... 24 A4
Nursery Rd *SUNDSW* SR3 ..... 120 A4
Nutley PI *BW/LEM/TK/HW* NE15 .. 68 E6
Nye Dene *SWCK/CAS* SR5 ..... 105 F4

O

Oakapple CI *BDLGTN* NE22 ..... 29 F5
Oak Av *DHAM* DH1 .... 17 L4
  DIN/WO NE13 .... 45 G2
  DUN/TMV NE11 .... 9 C9
  HAR/WTLS NE34 .... 76 A6
Oak Crs *CLDN/WHIT/ROK* SR6 .. 93 C3
  CLSW/PEL DH2 .... 144 B5
Oakdale *BDLGTN* NE22 .... 28 B6
Oakdale CI
  BW/LEM/TK/HW NE15 .... 68 B5
Oakdale Rd *CON/LDGT* DH8 .... 123 C4
Oakenshaw
  BW/LEM/TK/HW NE15 .... 68 B5
Oakerside Dr *PLEE/EAS* SR8 ... 174 D6
Oakes PI *ELS/FEN* NE4 .... 4 F6
Oakeys Rd *STLY/ANP* DH9 ..... 112 D5
Oakfield Av *WICK/BNPF* NE16 .. 85 F6
Oakfield CI *SUNDSW* SR3 ...... 133 G1
  WICK/BNPF NE16 .... 85 F6
Oakfield Crs *RDHAMSE* DH6 ... 180 B2
Oakfield Dr *LGB/KIL* NE12 ..... 48 B6
  WICK/BNPF NE16 .... 85 F6 ⊡
Oakfield Gdns
  BW/LEM/TK/HW NE15 .... 69 H6
  WLSD/HOW NE28 .... 58 B7 ⊡
Oakfield Gra *DIN/WO* NE13 .... 45 F2
Oakfield La *CON/LDGT* DH8..... 122 C6
Oakfield North *RYTON* NE40 ... 66 D6 ⊡
Oakfield Rd *DUN/TMV* NE11 .... 86 A6
  GOS/KPK NE3 .... 56 B7
  WICK/BNPF NE16 .... 84 D7
Oakfields *WICK/BNPF* NE16 .... 97 K4
Oakfield Ter *GOS/KPK* NE3 .... 56 B6
  PRUD NE42 .... 80 D2 ⊡
Oakfield Wy *CRAM* NE23 .... 39 G7
Oakgreen Flats
  BDN/LAN/SAC DH7 .... 167 G6
Oak Gv *WLSD/HOW* NE28 ...... 73 F1
Oakham Av *WICK/BNPF* NE16... 84 D6
Oakham Dr *DHAM* DH1 .... 158 A4
Oakhurst Dr *GOS/KPK* NE3 .... 70 A1
Oakhurst Ter *LGB/KIL* NE12 ... 57 K4 ⊡
Oakland Rd *JES* NE2 .... 70 D1 ⊡
  MONK NE25 .... 50 B5
Oaklands *GOS/KPK* NE3 .... 56 C7

PONT/DH NE20 .... 43 F5
  WICK/BNPF NE16 .... 8 A7
Oaklands Ct *PONT/DH* NE20 .... 43 F5
Oaklands Crs *SWCK/CAS* SR5 .. 106 A3
Oaklands Ter
  MLFD/PNYW SR4 .... 120 A1 ⊡
Oakland Ter *MPTH* NE61 .... 18 C2
Oak La *BDN/LAN/SAC* DH7 ..... 143 G7
Oaklea *CLSW/PEL* DH2 .... 129 G3
Oakleigh Gdns
  CLDN/WHIT/ROK SR6 .... 92 A2 ⊡
Oakley CI *CRAM* NE23 .... 47 H1
Oakley Dr *CRAM* NE23 .... 38 D1
Oakmere CI *HLS* DH4 .... 131 K1 ⊡
Oakridge *WICK/BNPF* NE16 .... 84 D6
Oakridge Rd
  BDN/LAN/SAC DH7 .... 155 F7
Oak Rd *NSHW* NE29 .... 59 J3
  PLEE/EAS SR8 .... 162 E6
The Oaks *BDN/LAN/SAC* DH7 ... 155 F7
  RHTLP TS27 .... 184 D6
  RYTON NE40 .... 82 D5 ⊡
Oak St *BDN/LAN/SAC* DH7 ..... 154 B2 ⊡
  CON/LDGT DH8 .... 123 F5
  HLS DH4 .... 131 G6
  JRW NE32 .... 73 J4
  PSHWF NE43 .... 79 J4
  SUND SR1 .... 15 K5
Oak Ter *CLSW/PEL* DH2 .... 114 C7
  SEA/MUR SR7 .... 149 H5
  STLY/ANP DH9 .... 127 F4
Oaktree Av *WLSD/HOW* NE28 .. 72 C2
Oaktree Gdns *MONK* NE25 .... 50 C6
Oakville *ASHGTN* NE63 .... 24 C3
Oakwellgate *GATE* NE8 .... 6 A9
Oakwood *BDN/LAN/SAC* DH7 ... 140 D6
  FELL NE10 .... 88 A7
  HEBB NE31 .... 72 E4
  RDHAMSE DH6 .... 161 G3
Oakwood Av *DIN/WO* NE13 .... 46 C4
  LWF/SPW/WRK NE9 .... 101 G2
  NWBGN NE64 .... 25 F2
Oakwood Gdns *DUN/TMV* NE11 .. 86 B7
Oakwood PI
  WD/WHPE/BLK NE5 .... 69 G2 ⊡
Oakwood St *ASHBK/HED/RY* SR2.. 14 B7
Oatens Bank
  BW/LEM/TK/HW NE15 .... 64 A1
Oates St *MLFD/PNYW* SR4...... 106 A7
Oatfield CI *ASHGTN* NE63 ...... 23 H3 ⊡
Oatlands Rd *MLFD/PNYW* SR4 .. 119 J2
Oatlands Wy *DHAM* DH1 ...... 156 D1
Oban Av *WLSD/HOW* NE28 ..... 59 H6
Oban St *FELL* NE10 .... 12 A6
  JRW NE32 .... 90 C1
Obelisk La *DHAM* DH1 .... 16 A2
Ocean Rd *ASHBK/HED/RY* SR2 .. 121 G4
  SSH NE33 .... 3 H6
Ocean Vw *ASHBK/HED/RY* SR2... 121 F7
  WBAY NE26 .... 51 F4 ⊡
Ochiltree Ct *WBAY* NE26 ...... 41 G2
Octavia CI *BDLGTN* NE22 ...... 28 E4
Octavia CI *WLSD/HOW* NE28 ... 59 G6
Octavian Wy *DUN/TMV* NE11 .. 100 C2
Offerton CI *MLFD/PNYW* SR4 .. 104 D7
Offerton La *MLFD/PNYW* SR4 .. 104 D7
Offerton St *MLFD/PNYW* SR4 .. 106 A7
Office PI *HLH* DH5 .... 147 K5
Office St *PLEE/EAS* SR8 .... 163 G5
Ogden St *MLFD/PNYW* SR4..... 106 A7
Ogle Av *DIN/WO* NE13 .... 46 A5 ⊡
  MPTH NE61 .... 20 C5
Ogle Dr *BLYTH* NE24 .... 34 E1
Ogle Gv *JRW* NE32 .... 89 J1
O'hanlon Crs *WLSD/HOW* NE28 .. 58 C5
Oil Mill Rd *BYK/HTN/WLK* NE6 .. 72 D4
Okehampton Dr *HLS* DH4 ..... 132 K5
Okehampton Sq
  SWCK/CAS SR5 .... 106 A2 ⊡
Old Brewery Sq *PRUD* NE42 ... 63 G7
Old Coronation St *SSH* NE33 .... 3 G5
Old Course Rd
  CLDN/WHIT/ROK SR6 .... 92 A4 ⊡
Old Durham Rd *GATE* NE8 ..... 11 H6
  LWF/SPW/WRK NE9 .... 87 H7
Old Elvet *DHAM* DH1 .... 16 E4
Old Farm Ct *WICK/BNPF* NE16 .. 99 F3 ⊡
Oldfield Rd *BYK/HTN/WLK* NE6 .. 13 H1
Old Fold Rd *FELL* NE10 .... 11 M4
The Old Forge
  BDN/LAN/SAC DH7 .... 176 D2
  PSHWF NE43 .... 62 A6
Old Hall Rd *CON/LDGT* DH8 ... 123 H6
Old Main St *RYTON* NE40 ...... 82 A1
Old Mill La *CLS/BIR/GTL* DH3 .. 145 G2
Old Mill Rd *ASHBK/HED/RY* SR2.. 15 K7
  SWCK/CAS SR5 .... 106 A2
Old Station Ct *PONT/DH* NE20 .. 42 E6
Oldstead Gdns
  MLFD/PNYW SR4 .... 119 J2
Old Well La *BLAY* NE21 .... 83 K3
Oley Mdw *CON/LDGT* DH8 ..... 108 C7
Olive Gdns *LWF/SPW/WRK* NE9 .. 87 G6
Olive PI *ELS/FEN* NE4 .... 69 H4
Oliver Crs *RDHAMSE* DH6 ..... 171 H4
Oliver PI *DHAM* DH1 .... 168 B3
Oliver St *BW/LEM/TK/HW* NE15 .. 69 F6
  SEA/MUR SR7 .... 135 H7
Olive St *STLY/ANP* DH9 .... 126 C3 ⊡
  SSH NE33 .... 75 F5
  SUND SR1 .... 14 D6
Ollerton Dr
  BW/LEM/TK/HW NE15 .... 66 D1
Ollerton Gdns *FELL* NE10 ..... 87 J5
Olney CI *CRAM* NE23 .... 38 E1
Olympia Av *STKFD/GP* NE62 ... 22 E6
Olympia Gdns *MPTH* NE61 .... 20 C5
Olympia HI *MPTH* NE61 .... 20 E4 ⊡
O'neil Dr *PLEE/EAS* SR8 ...... 174 E5
Ongar Wy *LGB/KIL* NE12 ...... 57 K5
Onslow Gdns
  LWF/SPW/WRK NE9 .... 87 F7
Onslow St *MLFD/PNYW* SR4 ... 105 A6 ⊡
Oram CI *MPTH* NE61 .... 21 F5
Orange Gv *CRAM* NE23 .... 38 C7

WICK/BNPF NE16.......... 8 A9
Orb Ct ELS/FEN NE4....... 69 H4
Orchard Av ROWG NE39...... 97 F4
Orchard CI HAR/WTLS NE34... 75 F6
  LGB/KIL NE12.......... 48 B7
  MPTH NE61............ 21 F5
  PRUD NE42............ 80 D2
  ROWG NE39............ 97 F5
  STLY/ANP DH9.......... 128 A1
Orchard Ct RYTON NE40...... 66 E6
  RYTON NE40............ 82 B3
Orchard Dene ROWG NE39.... 97 F4
Orchard Dr DHAM DH1....... 17 G1
Orchard Gdns
  CLDN/WHIT/ROK SR6...... 92 E4
  CLS/BIR/GTL DH3........ 129 J6
  LWF/SPW/WRK NE9....... 101 G1
  WLSD/HOW NE28........ 59 H6
Orchard-leigh
  BW/LEM/TK/HW NE15..... 68 B5
Orchard Pk CLS/BIR/GTL DH3.. 115 J2
Orchard PI JES NE2........ 71 F2
Orchard Priory DHAM DH1.... 16 B5
Orchard Rd ROWG NE39...... 97 F4
  WICK/BNPF NE16........ 8 A9
The Orchards BLYTH NE24.... 30 D6
Orchard St CLS/BIR/GTL DH3.. 115 J2
  CLSW/PEL DH2......... 114 E7
  CNUT NE1............ 5 K8
  MLFD/PNYW SR4........ 105 K6
Orchard Ter CLS/BIR/GTL DH3. 129 K5
The Orchard
  BW/LEM/TK/HW NE15..... 68 B5
  DHAM DH1............ 156 C1
  MPTH NE61............ 27 J1
  WICK/BNPF NE16....... 85 G5
Orchid CI ASHGTN NE63...... 23 J3
Orde Av WLSD/HOW NE28..... 59 G7
Ordley Cl BW/LEM/TK/HW NE15. 68 C5
Ord St ELS/FEN NE4........ 10 A1
Oriel CI CLDN/WHIT/ROK SR6.. 106 D4
Orkney Dr ASHBK/HED/RY SR2. 120 D6
Orlando Rd NSHW NE29...... 60 B4
Ormesby Rd
  CLDN/WHIT/ROK SR6..... 106 D2
Ormiscraig
  BW/LEM/TK/HW NE15..... 68 C5
Ormiston BW/LEM/TK/HW NE15. 68 C5
Ormonde Av
  BW/LEM/TK/HW NE15..... 68 B5
Ormonde St JRW NE32...... 73 K4
  MLFD/PNYW SR4........ 119 K1
Ormskirk CI
  BW/LEM/TK/HW NE15..... 68 B5
Ormskirk Gv CRAM NE23..... 38 D1
Ormston St CRAM NE23...... 33 H4
Orpen Av HAR/WTLS NE34.... 91 G1
Orpine Ct ASHGTN NE63..... 23 J3
Orpington Av BYK/HTN/WLK NE6. 7 L3
Orpington Rd CRAM NE23.... 38 D1
Orr Av SUNDSW SR3........ 134 B1
Orton CI ELS/FEN NE4...... 69 J7
  PLEE/EAS SR8......... 174 C6
Orwell CI HAR/WTLS NE34.... 91 F2
Orwell Gdns STLY/ANP DH9... 126 C3
Osbaldeston Gdns GOS/KPK NE3. 56 D2
Osborne Av JES NE2........ 70 E3
  SSH NE33............ 75 H2
Osborne Gdns NSHW NE29.... 60 E3
  WBAY NE26........... 50 D4
Osborne Rd JES NE2........ 70 E3
  SWCK/CAS SR5......... 104 E6
Osborne St
  CLDN/WHIT/ROK SR6..... 106 D3
  SSH NE33............ 3 L9
Osborne Ter JES NE2....... 5 M2
Osier Ct STKFD/GP NE62.... 23 J6
Oslo CI NSHW NE29........ 59 K6
Osman CI ASHBK/HED/RY SR2. 15 C7
Osprey Cl BDN/LAN/SAC DH7. 165 F2
  NSHW NE29........... 59 J4
Osprey Dr BLYTH NE24...... 35 C3
Osprey Wy HAR/WTLS NE34... 74 E7
Oswald Ct DHAM DH1....... 17 M4
Oswald Ct DHAM DH1....... 16 E6
Oswald Rd HLH DH5........ 147 K3
  MPTH NE61........... 20 E3
Oswald Ter ASHBK/HED/RY SR2. 121 F4
  GATE NE8............ 10 D6
  PLEE/EAS SR8......... 162 E4
Oswald Ter South
  SWCK/CAS SR5......... 105 G4
Oswald Wk GOS/KPK NE3.... 56 E5
Oswestry PI CRAM NE23..... 38 D1
Oswin Cl LGB/KIL NE12..... 58 A2
Oswin Ct LGB/KIL NE12..... 58 A1
Oswin Ter NSHW NE29...... 60 B5
Otley CI CRAM NE23........ 38 E1
Otterburn Av MONK NE25.... 49 K5
Otterburn CI LGB/KIL NE12.. 58 B2
Otterburn Crs HLS DH4..... 132 A6
Otterburn Dr ASHGTN NE63.. 23 H3
Otterburn Gdns
  DUN/TMV NE11......... 86 A5
  HAR/WTLS NE34........ 75 J5
  LWF/SPW/WRK NE9...... 100 E1
  WICK/BNPF NE16....... 85 F5
Otterburn Gv BLYTH NE24... 34 D1
Otterburn Rd NSHW NE29... 60 D3
Otterburn Ter JES NE2..... 70 E2
Otter Burn Wy PRUD NE42... 80 A3
Ottercap CI
  BW/LEM/TK/HW NE15..... 68 B5
Otterington WASHS NE38.... 117 J2
Ottershaw
  BW/LEM/TK/HW NE15..... 68 C5
Otto Ter ASHBK/HED/RY SR2. 14 B7
Ottovale Crs BLAY NE21.... 83 J3
Ottringham CI
  BW/LEM/TK/HW NE15..... 68 B5
Oulton CI CRAM NE23....... 38 E1
Ouseburn CI DIN/WO NE13... 55 H3
Ouseburn CI
  ASHBK/HED/RY SR2..... 121 F6
Ouseburn Rd BYK/HTN/WLK NE6. 6 D2

CNUT NE1............ 6 C5
Ouselaw DUN/TMV NE11.... 100 D7
Ouse St CNUT NE1........ 6 D6
Ouslaw La DUN/TMV NE11... 100 D7
Ousterley Ter STLY/ANP DH9. 127 F5
Ouston CI FELL NE10...... 88 E5
Ouston La CLSW/PEL DH2... 115 F7
Ouston St BW/LEM/TK/HW NE15. 68 D6
Outputs La CON/LDGT DH8.. 137 K4
Outram St HLH DH5........ 132 C6
Oval Park Vw FELL NE10.... 12 D9
  FELL NE10............ 87 K5
The Oval BDLGTN NE22..... 29 J5
  BLYTH NE24.......... 34 D4
  BYK/HTN/WLK NE6...... 7 K9
  CLSW/PEL DH2......... 115 F4
  CLSW/PEL DH2......... 144 C1
  DIN/WO NE13.......... 54 D2
  HLS DH4............. 132 A7
  LGB/KIL NE12......... 57 K4
Overdale Ct STKFD/GP NE62. 22 E7
Overdene
  BW/LEM/TK/HW NE15.... 68 D4
  SEA/MUR SR7......... 150 A3
Overfield Rd GOS/KPK NE3.. 55 K5
Overton CI
  BW/LEM/TK/HW NE15.... 68 B5
Overton Rd NSHW NE29.... 60 C2
Ovingham CI WASHS NE38... 117 H1
Ovingham Gdns
  DIN/WO NE13.......... 46 B3
Ovingham Rd WYLAM NE41.. 65 C5
Ovington Gv
  WD/WHPE/BLK NE5...... 69 G3
Ovington Vw PRUD NE42.... 80 B3
Owen Brannigan Dr
  CRAM NE23........... 47 H1
Owen Dr BOL NE36........ 91 F4
Owengate DHAM DH1...... 16 D4
Owen St HAR/WTLS NE34... 75 F6
Owlet CI BLAY NE21....... 83 J3
Oxbridge St
  ASHBK/HED/RY SR2..... 121 F4
Oxclose Rd WASHS NE38... 117 G2
Oxford Av CRAM NE23..... 38 D1
  SSH NE33............ 75 H3
  WASHN NE37.......... 102 D5
  WLSD/HOW NE28........ 58 C7
Oxford CI SUNDSW SR3.... 119 K6
Oxford Crs HEBB NE31.... 73 H5
Oxford PI CLS/BIR/GTL DH3.. 115 J5
Oxford Rd STKFD/GP NE62.. 23 C6
Oxfordshire Dr DHAM DH1.. 157 K6
Oxford Sq MLFD/PNYW SR4.. 105 J6
Oxford St BLYTH NE24..... 31 H7
  CNUT NE1............ 5 L5
  MLFD/PNYW SR4........ 105 J6
  SEA/MUR SR7......... 150 B1
  SSH NE33............ 75 H3
  TYNE/NSHE NE30....... 61 H3
  WBAY NE26........... 51 F4
Oxley St CON/LDGT DH8.... 122 D3
Oxnam Crs JES NE2....... 4 E2
Oxted CI CRAM NE23...... 38 E1
Oxted PI BYK/HTN/WLK NE6. 12 F1
Oyston St SSH NE33....... 3 G8
Ozanan CI CRAM NE23..... 47 H2

P

Pacific Hall SEA/MUR SR7.... 134 E7
Packham Rd MLFD/PNYW SR4. 119 C1
Paddock CI
  CLDN/WHIT/ROK SR6..... 91 J3
  HLS DH4............. 131 H2
  PRUD NE42........... 80 E2
Paddock HI PONT/DH NE20.. 43 H2
Paddock La SUNDSW SR3... 120 C7
Paddock Ri ASHGTN NE63... 23 H3
The Paddock
  BDN/LAN/SAC DH7...... 140 B5
  BLYTH NE24.......... 30 E7
  BW/LEM/TK/HW NE15.... 67 H2
  CRAM NE23........... 38 E2
  DIN/WO NE13.......... 54 D2
  FELL NE10............ 88 B6
  HLS DH4............. 118 D7
  PSHWF NE43.......... 79 G7
  STLY/ANP DH9......... 112 A6
Paddock Wd PRUD NE42.... 80 E2
Pader CI DIN/WO NE13..... 46 B4
Padgate Rd MLFD/PNYW SR4. 119 G1
Padstow CI
  ASHBK/HED/RY SR2..... 121 F6
Padstow Rd NSHW NE29.... 60 C6
Page Av HAR/WTLS NE34... 75 J4
Page St HEBB NE31....... 73 H4
Paignton Av ELS/FEN NE4.. 69 J6
  MONK NE25........... 50 B7
Paignton Sq SUNDSW SR3.. 119 J4
Painshawfield Rd PSHWF NE43. 79 F7
Paisley Sq SUNDSW SR3... 119 J4
Palace Rd BDLGTN NE22... 29 K4
Palace St ELS/FEN NE4.... 4 F8
Palermo St MLFD/PNYW SR4. 105 K5
Paley St SUND SR1....... 14 C4
Palgrove Rd MLFD/PNYW SR4. 119 G1
Palgrove Sq MLFD/PNYW SR4. 119 G1
Pallinsburn Ct
  WD/WHPE/BLK NE5...... 55 F7
Pallion New Rd
  MLFD/PNYW SR4........ 105 K5
Pallion Pk MLFD/PNYW SR4. 105 K5
Pallion Rd MLFD/PNYW SR4. 105 K7
Pallion Subway
  MLFD/PNYW SR4........ 105 K5
Palm Av ELS/FEN NE4..... 69 H4
  HAR/WTLS NE34........ 76 A6
Palmer Crs HEBB NE31.... 73 H5
Palmer Rd PLEE/EAS SR8... 174 B5
  STLY/ANP DH9......... 111 G5
Palmers Garth DHAM DH1.. 16 E5
Palmers Gn LGB/KIL NE12.. 58 B1
Palmer's Hill Rd
  CLDN/WHIT/ROK SR6..... 14 F2

Palmerston Av
  BYK/HTN/WLK NE6...... 7 M2
Palmerston Rd
  MLFD/PNYW SR4........ 119 F3
Palmer St JRW NE32...... 73 J4
  STLY/ANP DH9......... 126 B2
Palm Lea BDN/LAN/SAC DH7. 167 F6
Palmstead Rd
  MLFD/PNYW SR4........ 119 G1
Palmstead Sq MLFD/PNYW SR4. 119 G1
Palm St BDN/LAN/SAC DH7.. 154 B2
  CON/LDGT DH8......... 123 F4
Palm Ter STLY/ANP DH9.... 127 F4
Pancras Rd SUNDSW SR3... 119 J4
Pandon CNUT NE1........ 5 M7
Pandon Bank CNUT NE1.... 5 M6
Pangbourne CI
  BW/LEM/TK/HW NE15.... 68 A3
Pankhurst Gdns FELL NE10.. 13 K8
Pankhurst PI STLY/ANP DH9. 127 F2
Pann La SUND SR1....... 14 E4
Panns Bank SUND SR1..... 14 F3
The Parade ASHBK/HED/RY SR2. 15 K6
  BYK/HTN/WLK NE6...... 72 C6
  CLSW/PEL DH2......... 128 C1
Paradise Crs PLEE/EAS SR8.. 162 E5
Paradise La PLEE/EAS SR8.. 162 E5
Paradise Rw CRAM NE23... 38 C2
Park Av BDLGTN NE22..... 30 A3
  BLAY NE21........... 84 A2
  CLDN/WHIT/ROK SR6.... 106 E2
  CON/LDGT DH8......... 123 G4
  DUN/TMV NE11......... 8 F9
  GOS/KPK NE3.......... 55 K3
  HAR/WTLS NE34........ 75 K7
  PRUD NE42........... 80 E3
  RDHAMSE DH6......... 180 B4
  SMOOR NE27.......... 49 H6
  SUNDSW SR3.......... 120 B7
  TYNE/NSHE NE30....... 61 G3
  WBAY NE26........... 50 E4
  WICK/BNPF NE16....... 84 C7
Park Chare WASHS NE38... 117 G1
Park CI BDN/LAN/SAC DH7.. 154 C3
  ELS/FEN NE4.......... 4 D8
  STLY/ANP DH9......... 125 J4
Park Crs SMOOR NE27..... 49 H6
  TYNE/NSHE NE30....... 61 G3
Park Crs East TYNE/NSHE NE30. 61 G3
Parkdale Ri WICK/BNPF NE16. 84 D7
Park Dr BDN/LAN/SAC DH7. 154 B3
  BLYTH NE24.......... 34 D3
  GOS/KPK NE3.......... 56 C1
  LGB/KIL NE12......... 58 A2
  MPTH NE61........... 20 E6
  WICK/BNPF NE16....... 8 A9
Parker Av GOS/KPK NE3.... 56 B7
Park Farm Vls BLYTH NE24. 34 C5
Park Fld RYTON NE40..... 66 E6
Park Field Ter WBAY NE26.. 41 F2
Park Gdns WBAY NE26.... 50 E4
Park Ga CLDN/WHIT/ROK SR6. 106 E2
Parkgate La BLAY NE21.... 83 K4
Park Gv SMOOR NE27..... 49 H6
  WASHN NE37.......... 103 F4
Parkham CI CRAM NE23... 33 H6
Parkhead STLY/ANP DH9... 125 C5
Parkhead Gdns BLAY NE21. 83 K4
Park Head Rd GOS/KPK NE3. 71 G1
Parkhouse Av SWCK/CAS SR5. 105 F5
Park House CI
  RDHAMSE DH6......... 158 C7
Park House Rd DHAM DH1.. 168 B3
Parkhurst Rd MLFD/PNYW SR4. 119 F2
Parkland BLAY NE21...... 67 J7
  LGB/KIL NE12......... 57 K4
Parkland Ct SEA/MUR SR7.. 135 H7
Parklands PONT/DH NE20.. 42 D7
  ROWG NE39........... 110 B1
Parklands CI FELL NE10... 88 E3
Parklands Wy FELL NE10... 88 E3
Parkland Ter SEA/MUR SR7. 135 H7
Park La BLAY NE21....... 83 K4
  PLEE/EAS SR8......... 175 H3
  PRUD NE42........... 80 D3
  SEA/MUR SR7......... 149 G5
  SMOOR NE27.......... 49 H6
  SUND SR1............ 14 E6
Park Lea SUNDSW SR3.... 133 F1
Park Lea Rd
  CLDN/WHIT/ROK SR6.... 106 E2
Parkmore Rd
  MLFD/PNYW SR4........ 118 E3
Park Pde CLDN/WHIT/ROK SR6. 106 E3
  WBAY NE26........... 50 E4
Park PI CLS/BIR/GTL DH3... 129 K2
Park Ri BW/LEM/TK/HW NE15. 68 A4
Park Rd ASHBK/HED/RY SR2. 14 E7
  ASHGTN NE63......... 23 H1
  BDLGTN NE22......... 29 G5
  BW/LEM/TK/HW NE15.... 67 H3
  CON/LDGT DH8......... 122 D4
  ELS/FEN NE4.......... 9 K1
  GATE NE8............ 11 K2
  HEBB NE31........... 73 K6
  JRW NE32............ 73 J3
  MONK NE25........... 39 K5
  MPTH NE61........... 18 C2
  PLEE/EAS SR8......... 175 J2
  ROWG NE39........... 97 F3
  SMOOR NE27.......... 49 H6
  STLY/ANP DH9......... 126 B2
  TRIM TS29........... 183 F2
  WBAY NE26........... 50 E4
  WLSD/HOW NE28........ 72 D1
Park Road Central
  CLS/BIR/GTL DH3....... 129 K4
Park Rd North
  CLS/BIR/GTL DH3....... 129 J2
Park Rd South
  CLS/BIR/GTL DH3....... 129 K5
  SWCK/CAS SR5......... 106 A4
Parkshiel HAR/WTLS NE34.. 75 K7

Parkside BDLGTN NE22.... 30 A3
  BDN/LAN/SAC DH7...... 141 H2
  BDN/LAN/SAC DH7...... 143 H5
  BW/LEM/TK/HW NE15.... 67 G2
  DUN/TMV NE11......... 9 H7
  HEBB NE31........... 72 E7
  STLY/ANP DH9......... 112 A5
  TYNE/NSHE NE30....... 61 H1
  WLSD/HOW NE28........ 59 F7
Parkside Av BLAY NE21.... 83 K3
  LGB/HTN NE7......... 57 H5
Parkside Crs SEA/MUR SR7. 150 D3
  TYNE/NSHE NE30....... 61 H2
The Parks CLS/BIR/GTL DH3. 130 A6
Parkstone CI MLFD/PNYW SR4. 118 E4
Park St CON/LDGT DH8.... 122 E3
  SEA/MUR SR7......... 150 E2
Park St South SWCK/CAS SR5. 105 G4
Park Ter BDLGTN NE22.... 29 J5
  DUN/TMV NE11......... 9 G8
  JES NE2............. 5 J2
  PLEE/EAS SR8......... 175 H4
  SWCK/CAS SR5......... 105 K3
  TYNE/NSHE NE30....... 61 G4
  WICK/BNPF NE16....... 84 E3
  WLSD/HOW NE28........ 72 D1
Park Vw ASHGTN NE63..... 23 H1
  BLAY NE21........... 84 A4
  BLYTH NE24.......... 31 H7
  BYK/HTN/WLK NE6...... 72 C6
  CLSW/PEL DH2......... 128 C1
  CON/LDGT DH8......... 123 F4
  HLH DH5............. 147 K5
  JRW NE32............ 73 K7
  LGB/KIL NE12......... 57 K2
  MONK NE25........... 40 A5
  WBAY NE26........... 50 E4
  WLSD/HOW NE28........ 72 D1
Parkway STKFD/GP NE62... 23 F6
  WASHS NE38.......... 116 E1
  WICK/BNPF NE16....... 84 C7
Park Wood Av
  BDN/LAN/SAC DH7...... 155 F6
Parkwood Av PRUD NE42... 81 F1
Parliament St CON/LDGT DH8. 122 E3
Parmeter St STLY/ANP DH9. 126 C3
Parmontley St
  BW/LEM/TK/HW NE15.... 68 D6
Parnaby St CON/LDGT DH8. 122 E5
Parnell St HLS DH4...... 131 K7
Parry Dr CLDN/WHIT/ROK SR6. 92 E3
Parson Rd WYLAM NE41... 65 H5
Parson's Av BYK/HTN/WLK NE6. 72 B6
Parsons Rd PLEE/EAS SR8.. 174 E1
  WASHN NE37.......... 102 D6
Partick Rd MLFD/PNYW SR4. 119 F2
Partick Sq MLFD/PNYW SR4. 119 C2
Partridge CI WASHS NE38.. 116 E3
Partridge Ter WNGT TS28.. 183 J3
Passfield Sq RDHAMSE DH6. 172 B6
Passfield Wy PLEE/EAS SR8. 174 B6
Pasteur Rd RDHAMSE DH6. 160 E2
Paston Rd MONK NE25.... 40 A6
The Pastures BLYTH NE24.. 35 F3
  MPTH NE61........... 20 B6
  PSHWF NE43.......... 79 F4
Pathside MPTH NE61..... 21 J2
Patience Av DIN/WO NE13. 46 C1
Patina CI
  BW/LEM/TK/HW NE15.... 68 A3
Paton Rd SUNDSW SR3.... 119 K4
Paton Sq SUNDSW SR3... 119 K4
Patrick Crs RDHAMSE DH6. 160 D1
Patterdale CI BOL NE36... 91 G5
  DHAM DH1............ 158 B5
Patterdale Gdns LGB/HTN NE7. 57 H7
Patterdale Gv
  SWCK/CAS SR5......... 106 C1
Patterdale Ms
  CON/LDGT DH8......... 123 K3
Patterdale Rd BLYTH NE24. 30 C6
Patterdale St HLH DH5.... 147 K6
Patterson St BLAY NE21... 68 C7
Pattinson Gdns FELL NE10. 12 A4
Pattinson Rd WASHS NE38. 103 K7
Pattison Wk RDHAMSE DH6. 173 F7
Patton Wy MPTH NE61.... 21 J2
Pauline Av
  CLDN/WHIT/ROK SR6.... 106 D2
Pauline Gdns
  BW/LEM/TK/HW NE15.... 68 E4
Pauls Gn HLH DH5....... 147 K2
Paulsway JRW NE32...... 74 C5
Pawston Rd ROWG NE39.. 82 C7
Paxford CI LGB/HTN NE7... 57 F5
Paxton Ter MLFD/PNYW SR4. 106 A6
Pea Flatts La CLS/BIR/GTL DH3. 145 K1
Peareth Gv
  CLDN/WHIT/ROK SR6.... 106 E2
Peareth Hall Rd
  LWF/SPW/WRK NE9...... 102 B4
  WASHN NE37.......... 102 D3
Peareth Rd
  CLDN/WHIT/ROK SR6.... 106 E1
Pear Lea BDN/LAN/SAC DH7. 167 F6
Pearl Rd SUNDSW SR3.... 119 K4
Pearson PI JRW NE32..... 74 A3
  TYNE/NSHE NE30....... 2 F1
Pearson St SSH NE33..... 3 J4
  STLY/ANP DH9......... 112 D6
Peart CI RDHAMSE DH6... 170 D1
Peartree Bungalows
  CHPW NE17........... 95 J7
Peartree Gdns
  BYK/HTN/WLK NE6...... 72 B2
Peary PI WD/WHPE/BLK NE5. 68 D1
Pease Av BW/LEM/TK/HW NE15. 69 G5
Peasemoor Rd
  MLFD/PNYW SR4........ 119 F1
Pease Rd PLEE/EAS SR8... 174 A2
Pecket CI BLYTH NE24.... 34 C2
Peckover St SSH NE33.... 3 J4
Peebles CI NSHW NE29... 59 K2
Peebles Rd SUNDSW SR3.. 119 J4

Peel Av DHAM DH1....... 157 J6
Peel La CNUT NE1........ 5 H8
Peggy's Wicket STLY/ANP DH9. 113 K6
Pegwood Rd
  MLFD/PNYW SR4........ 119 G1
Pelaw Av CLSW/PEL DH2.. 129 H2
  NWBGN NE64.......... 18 E7
  STLY/ANP DH9......... 112 E6
Pelaw Bank CLS/BIR/GTL DH3. 129 J3
Pelaw Crs CLSW/PEL DH2. 129 H2
Pelaw Grange Ct
  CLS/BIR/GTL DH3...... 115 J6
Pelaw Leazes La DHAM DH1. 16 F3
Pelaw PI CLSW/PEL DH2... 129 H2
Pelaw Rd CLSW/PEL DH2.. 129 H2
Pelaw Sq CLSW/PEL DH2.. 129 H2
  MLFD/PNYW SR4........ 105 G6
Pelaw Wy FELL NE10..... 13 K7
Peldon Ct LGB/HTN NE7... 57 J6
Pelham PI GOS/KPK NE3... 55 J5
Peltondale Av BLYTH NE24. 34 C1
Pelton Fell Rd CLSW/PEL DH2. 129 G3
Pelton La CLSW/PEL DH2.. 114 C7
Pelton Ms CLSW/PEL DH2. 128 C1
Pelton Rd MLFD/PNYW SR4. 119 G2
Pemberton Av CON/LDGT DH8. 122 C7
Pemberton Bank HLH DH5. 148 A7
Pemberton CI
  SWCK/CAS SR5......... 106 B4
Pemberton Gdns
  SUNDSW SR3.......... 120 B3
Pemberton Rd CON/LDGT DH8. 122 B5
Pemberton St HLH DH5... 147 K4
Pembroke Av BYK/HTN/WLK NE6. 7 L4
  CLS/BIR/GTL DH3...... 115 K5
Pembroke CI
  SWCK/CAS SR5......... 134 A1
Pembroke Dr PONT/DH NE20. 42 C4
Pembroke Gdns ASHGTN NE63. 24 C4
  WLSD/HOW NE28........ 59 J6
Pembroke Ter SSH NE33.. 75 G4
Pendeford WASHS NE38... 117 J2
Pendle CI WASHS NE38... 116 D3
Pendleton Dr CRAM NE23. 33 G6
Pendower Wy
  BW/LEM/TK/HW NE15.... 69 G5
Penfold CI LGB/HTN NE7... 57 J6
Penhale Dr ASHBK/HED/RY SR2. 121 F7
Penhill CI CLSW/PEL DH2.. 114 E5
Penistone Rd MLFD/PNYW SR4. 118 E2
Penman Sq MLFD/PNYW SR4. 119 F2
Penman St NSHW NE29... 2 C4
Pennant Sq
  MLFD/PNYW SR4........ 105 G7
Pennine Dr ASHGTN NE63. 24 A4
  PLEE/EAS SR8......... 174 C4
Pennine Gdns DUN/TMV NE11. 86 A5
  STLY/ANP DH9......... 126 E2
Pennine Gv BOL NE36.... 91 F5
Pennine Wy LGB/KIL NE12. 57 G4
Penn Sq MLFD/PNYW SR4. 105 G7
Penn St ELS/FEN NE4.... 9 L2
Pennycross Rd
  MLFD/PNYW SR4........ 118 E2
Pennycross Sq
  MLFD/PNYW SR4........ 118 E1
Pennyfine CI NSHW NE29. 60 E2
Pennyfine Rd WICK/BNPF NE16. 99 G2
Pennygate Sq
  MLFD/PNYW SR4........ 118 E1
Pennygreen Sq
  MLFD/PNYW SR4........ 118 E1
Pennymore Sq
  MLFD/PNYW SR4........ 118 E2
Pennywell Rd MLFD/PNYW SR4. 119 G2
Penrith Av TYNE/NSHE NE30. 50 E7
Penrith Gdns
  LWF/SPW/WRK NE9...... 101 H1
Penrith Rd HEBB NE31.... 73 H7
  SWCK/CAS SR5......... 106 C1
Penryn Av SEA/MUR SR7... 149 J3
Penryn Wy BDN/LAN/SAC DH7. 167 H6
Pensford Ct GOS/KPK NE3. 55 G5
Penshaw Cl
  BDN/LAN/SAC DH7...... 154 A3
Penshaw Gn
  WD/WHPE/BLK NE5...... 55 H7
Penshaw La HLS DH4..... 117 K6
Penshaw Vw
  BDN/LAN/SAC DH7...... 143 J6
  FELL NE10............ 88 E4
  HEBB NE31........... 73 K7
  JRW NE32............ 73 K7
Penshaw Wy CLS/BIR/GTL DH3. 116 A2
Pensher St FELL NE10.... 11 M5
  MLFD/PNYW SR4........ 106 A7
Pensher St East FELL NE10. 12 A5
Pentland CI ASHGTN NE63. 24 A4
  CRAM NE23........... 33 H6
  NSHW NE29........... 60 D1
  PLEE/EAS SR8......... 174 B5
  WASHS NE38.......... 116 D3
Pentland Gdns DUN/TMV NE11. 9 J9
Pentland Gv LGB/KIL NE12. 57 H1
Pentlands Ter STLY/ANP DH9. 126 E2
Pentridge CI CRAM NE23.. 38 D1
Penwood Rd MLFD/PNYW SR4. 119 G1
Penyghent Wy WASHN NE37. 102 C7
Penzance Bungs SEA/MUR SR7. 149 J4
Penzance Rd MLFD/PNYW SR4. 119 F2
Percival St MLFD/PNYW SR4. 105 K6
Percy Av WBAY NE26..... 50 D4
Percy Ct NSHW NE29..... 60 B7
Percy Crs NSHW NE29.... 60 B7
Percy Gdns CON/LDGT DH8. 123 H6
  DUN/TMV NE11......... 86 A5
  LGB/KIL NE12......... 57 K7
  MONK NE25........... 50 E5
  STKFD/GP NE62........ 23 C5
  TYNE/NSHE NE30....... 61 J2
Percy La DHAM DH1...... 168 B3
Percy Pk TYNE/NSHE NE30. 61 H2
Percy Park Rd TYNE/NSHE NE30. 61 H2
Percy Rd WBAY NE26.... 51 F4
Percy Scott St HAR/WTLS NE34. 91 G1
Percy Sq DHAM DH1..... 168 B3
Percy St BLYTH NE24.... 31 H6
  BW/LEM/TK/HW NE15.... 68 A5
  CNUT NE1............ 5 J5

CRAM NE23 .... 38 D3
HLH DH5 .... 148 A4
JRW NE32 .... 74 A4
LGB/KIL NE12 .... 58 B1
RDHAMSE DH6 .... 172 C6
RDHAMSE DH6 .... 172 E7
SSH NE33 .... 3 J9
TYNE/NSHE NE30 .... 61 H3
WLSD/HOW NE28 .... 72 E1
Percy St South BLYTH NE24 .... 31 H7
Percy Ter ASHBK/HED/RY SR2 ... 120 E2
DHAM DH1 .... 168 B1
MONK NE25 .... 50 C4
Percy Wy BW/LEM/TK/HW NE15 .. 67 J2
Peregrine Pl LGB/KIL NE12 .... 57 J5
Perivale Rd MLFD/PNYW SR4 ...... 119 F2
Perrycrofts SUNDSW SR3 .... 134 A3
Perry St GATE NE8 .... 11 H8
Perth Av JRW NE32 .... 90 B1
Perth Cl NSHW NE29 .... 60 A2
WLSD/HOW NE28 .... 59 H6
Perth Ct SUNDSW SR3 .... 119 J5
Perth Gdns SUNDSW SR3 .... 119 J5
Perth Rd SUNDSW SR3 .... 119 J5
Perth Sq SUNDSW SR3 .... 119 K4
Pesspool La RDHAMSE DH6 ...... 161 G5
Peterborough Rd DHAM DH1 ..... 157 F3
Peter's Bank STLY/ANP DH9 ...... 111 J7
Petersfield Rd
MLFD/PNYW SR4 .... 119 F2
Petersham Rd
MLFD/PNYW SR4 .... 105 G7
Peth Bank BDN/LAN/SAC DH7 ... 140 C5
Petherton Ct GOS/KPK NE3 .... 55 C4
Peth Gn HLH DH5 .... 148 A7
Peth La BDN/LAN/SAC DH7 .... 141 F4
RYTON NE40 .... 67 F5
Pethside BDN/LAN/SAC DH7 ..... 140 D5
Petrel Cl SSH NE33 .... 3 G6
Petrel Wy BLYTH NE24 .... 35 H3
Petteril WASHS NE38 .... 116 C5
Petterson Dl RDHAMSE DH6 ..... 180 D6
Petwell Crs PLEE/EAS SR8 .... 162 D5
Petwell La PLEE/EAS SR8 .... 162 E4
Petworth Gdns MPTH NE61 .... 21 J2
Pevensey Cl NSHW NE29 .... 60 D1
Pheonix Ct CON/LDGT DH8 .... 122 C4
Philadelphia La HLS DH4 .... 132 K2
Philiphaugh WLSD/HOW NE28 .. 72 D3
Philip Av RDHAMSE DH6 .... 180 A1
Philip Pl ELS/FEN NE4 .... 4 D4
Philipson St BYK/HTN/WLK NE6 .. 72 B5
Philip Sq SUNDSW SR3 .... 119 J4
Philip St ELS/FEN NE4 .... 4 D4
Phillips Av WICK/BNPF NE16 ...... 84 E4
Phoenix Cha NSHW NE29 .... 59 K2
Phoenix Cl BDN/LAN/SAC DH7 .. 153 K3
Phoenix Rd MLFD/PNYW SR4 ..... 105 G7
WASHS NE38 .... 102 A7
Phoenix Wy HLS DH4 .... 147 F1
Piccadilly SUNDSW SR3 .... 119 J5
Pickard Cl PLEE/EAS SR8 .... 175 F3
Pickard St MLFD/PNYW SR4 ...... 106 A6
Pickering Rd MLFD/PNYW SR4 ... 118 E3
Pickering Sq MLFD/PNYW SR4 ... 119 F2
Pickering St WNGT TS28 .... 183 J4
Pickhurst Rd MLFD/PNYW SR4 ... 119 F3
Pickhurst Sq
MLFD/PNYW SR4 .... 119 F3
WASHS NE38 .... 116 A6
Picktree La CLS/BIR/GTL DH3 ..... 129 K3
Picktree Ldg CLS/BIR/GTL DH3 ... 115 K6
Pickwick Cl DHAM DH1 .... 16 A9
Piele Pl CON/LDGT DH8 .... 122 C1
Pier Pde SSH NE33 .... 3 L5
Pier Rd TYNE/NSHE NE30 .... 61 J3
Pier Vw CLDN/WHIT/ROK SR6 .... 107 F3
Pike HI CON/LDGT DH8 .... 108 A7
Pikestone Cl WASHS NE38 .... 116 C3
Pikesyde STLY/ANP DH9 .... 110 D7
Pilgrim St SWCK/CAS SR5 .... 106 C4
Pilgrim St CNUT NE1 .... 5 M8
Pilgrims' Wy DHAM DH1 .... 157 G6
Pilgrimsway JRW NE32 .... 74 C5
LWF/SPW/WRK NE9 .... 11 K9
Pilgrims Wy MPTH NE61 .... 20 B6
Pilton Rd WD/WHPE/BLK NE5 ... 54 D7
Pimlico DHAM DH1 .... 16 C6
Pimlico Rd HLH DH5 .... 148 A7
MLFD/PNYW SR4 .... 119 F2
Pinders Wy RDHAMSE DH6 .... 171 C1
Pine Av DHAM DH1 .... 17 L4
DIN/WO NE13 .... 45 C2
GOS/KPK NE3 .... 55 K3
HAR/WTLS NE34 .... 76 A6
STKFD/GP NE62 .... 22 D6
Pinedale Dr RDHAMSE DH6 ...... 160 E2
Pinegarth PONT/DH NE20 .... 42 E7
Pine Lea BDN/LAN/SAC DH7 ..... 167 F6
Pine Pk BDN/LAN/SAC DH7 ...... 167 G1
Pine Rd BLAY NE21 .... 84 A2
The Pines RYTON NE40 .... 82 D3
Pine St BDN/LAN/SAC DH7 .... 154 B2
CLS/BIR/GTL DH3 .... 115 J1
CLSW/PEL DH2 .... 128 A2
JRW NE32 .... 73 J5
MLFD/PNYW SR4 .... 105 K6
STLY/ANP DH9 .... 126 B3
Pinesway SUNDSW SR3 .... 120 B3
Pinetree BDN/LAN/SAC DH7 ..... 165 G3
Pinetree Gdns MONK NE25 .... 50 C6
Pinetree Wy WICK/BNPF NE16 ... 85 F2
Pine View Vls
BDN/LAN/SAC DH7 .... 165 J2
Pinewood HEBB NE31 .... 72 E4
Pinewood Av CRAM NE23 .... 33 H6
DIN/WO NE13 .... 46 C4
GOS/KPK NE3 .... 46 C4
WASHS NE38 .... 116 E5
Pinewood Cl BYK/HTN/WLK NE6 .. 72 A2
DIN/WO NE13 .... 55 F4
Pinewood Dr MPTH NE61 .... 20 B3
Pinewood Gdns DUN/TMV NE11 .. 86 A7
Pinewood Rd SWCK/CAS SR5 .... 105 K3
Pinewood Sq SWCK/CAS SR5 .... 105 K3
Pinewood Vls HLS DH4 .... 131 G6

Pinewood Vls
HAR/WTLS NE34 .... 76 A5
Pink La CNUT NE1 .... 5 J8
Pinner Pl BYK/HTN/WLK NE6 ..... 7 L8
Pinner Rd MLFD/PNYW SR4 ...... 119 G1
Piper Rd PRUD NE42 .... 64 B6
Pipershaw WASHS NE37 .... 102 B7
Pipe Track La ELS/FEN NE4 .... 69 H7
Pipewellgate GATE NE8 .... 10 D1
Pitcairn Rd MLFD/PNYW SR4 ..... 119 G1
Pithouse La CON/LDGT DH8 ...... 109 H6
HLS DH4 .... 146 B5
Pit La BDN/LAN/SAC DH7 .... 166 C5
DHAM DH1 .... 156 D3
Pittington La DHAM DH1 .... 158 B4
Pittington Rd HLH DH5 .... 158 D1
Pitt St CON/LDGT DH8 .... 123 F5
ELS/FEN NE4 .... 4 F5
Pixley Dell CON/LDGT DH8 .... 138 D1
Plains Rd SUNDSW SR3 .... 119 K4
Plaistow Sq
MLFD/PNYW SR4 .... 105 G7
Plaistow Wy CRAM NE23 .... 33 H6
Plane St CON/LDGT DH8 .... 123 G5
Planesway FELL NE10 .... 88 A7
Planet Pl LGB/KIL NE12 .... 47 J7
Planetree Av ELS/FEN NE4 .... 69 H3
Plane Tree Ct SUNDSW SR3 ...... 133 J1
Plantation Av RDHAMSE DH6 .... 159 G6
WICK/BNPF NE16 .... 84 E4
Plantation Gv FELL NE10 .... 13 M4
Plantation Rd MLFD/PNYW SR4 .. 105 J6
Plantation Sq
MLFD/PNYW SR4 .... 105 J6
Plantation St CON/LDGT DH8 .... 123 K3
WLSD/HOW NE28 .... 72 D3
The Plantation
LWF/SPW/WRK NE9 .... 87 G7
Plantation Vw STLY/ANP DH9 .... 127 K1
Plantation Wk RDHAMSE DH6 ... 160 E2
Plawsworth Gdns
LWF/SPW/WRK NE9 .... 101 J2
Plawsworth Rd
BDN/LAN/SAC DH7 .... 143 H5
Pleasant Vw
BDN/LAN/SAC DH7 .... 141 G4
CON/LDGT DH8 .... 122 B3
Plenmeller Pl WICK/BNPF NE16 .. 98 E2
Plessey Av BLYTH NE24 .... 35 G1
Plessey Crs MONK NE25 .... 51 F5
Plessey Gdns NSHW NE29 .... 60 B5
Plessey Rd BLYTH NE24 .... 31 H6
Plessey Ter LGB/HTN NE7 .... 71 H1
Plough Rd SUNDSW SR3 .... 133 K2
Plover Cl BLYTH NE24 .... 35 G3
Plover Dr WICK/BNPF NE16 ...... 112 A1
Ploverfield Cl ASHGTN NE63 ..... 23 J4
Plunkett Rd STLY/ANP DH9 .... 111 H5
Plunkett Ter CLSW/PEL DH2 ...... 128 D3
Plymouth Cl SEA/MUR SR7 .... 150 A2
Plymouth Sq SUNDSW SR3 .... 119 J4
Point Pleasant Ter
WLSD/HOW NE28 .... 73 G1
Polden Cl PLEE/EAS SR8 .... 174 B5
Polden Crs NSHW NE29 .... 50 C7
Polebrook Rd
MLFD/PNYW SR4 .... 105 C7
Pollard St SSH NE33 .... 3 J6
Polmuir Rd SUNDSW SR3 .... 119 J4
Polmuir Sq SUNDSW SR3 .... 119 J4
Polpero Cl CLS/BIR/GTL DH3 ..... 115 K3
Polperro Cl ASHBK/HED/RY SR2 .. 121 F7
Polwarth Cr GOS/KPK NE3 .... 56 C2
Polwarth Dr GOS/KPK NE3 .... 56 C1
Polwarth Rd GOS/KPK NE3 .... 56 C1
Polwarth Sq SUNDSW SR3 .... 119 K4
Ponds Ct CON/LDGT DH8 .... 122 E5
Pontefract Rd
MLFD/PNYW SR4 .... 119 F3
Ponteland Cl NSHW NE29 .... 60 A3
WASHS NE38 .... 116 B2
Ponteland Rd
BW/LEM/TK/HW NE15 .... 53 F6
DIN/WO NE13 .... 54 E3
ELS/FEN NE4 .... 69 J2
PONT/DH NE20 .... 43 J3
WD/WHPE/BLK NE5 .... 55 F4
Ponthaugh ROWG NE39 .... 97 H2
Pont La CON/LDGT DH8 .... 109 H7
Pontop Pike La STLY/ANP DH9 ... 124 E1
Pontop Sq MLFD/PNYW SR4 ..... 105 C7
Pontop St HLH DH5 .... 147 F4
Pontopsyde STLY/ANP DH9 .... 110 E7
Pontop Vw CON/LDGT DH8 .... 123 H7
ROWG NE39 .... 97 F3
Pont St ASHGTN NE63 .... 23 K2
Pont Vw PONT/DH NE20 .... 43 H2
Poole Cl CRAM NE23 .... 38 D1
Poole Rd MLFD/PNYW SR4 .... 105 C7
Pooley Cl WD/WHPE/BLK NE5 ... 69 F2
Pooley Rd WD/WHPE/BLK NE5 .. 69 F2
Poplar Av BLYTH NE24 .... 31 F5
BYK/HTN/WLK NE6 .... 72 B2
DIN/WO NE13 .... 45 G2
Poplar Crs CLS/BIR/GTL DH3 ..... 115 H1
DUN/TMV NE11 .... 9 G9
GATE NE8 .... 10 E4
Poplar Dr CLDN/WHIT/ROK SR6 .. 93 F3
DHAM DH1 .... 157 H6
Poplar Gv ASHBK/HED/RY SR2 ... 120 E6
BDLGTN NE22 .... 29 H5
HAR/WTLS NE34 .... 75 K6
Poplar Lea BDN/LAN/SAC DH7 .. 167 F6
Poplar Rd BLAY NE21 .... 84 A3
DHAM DH1 .... 158 A5
The Poplars GOS/KPK NE3 .... 56 C7
HLH DH5 .... 148 B2
SWCK/CAS SR5 .... 105 K3
Poplar St CLS/BIR/GTL DH3 .... 129 J4
STLY/ANP DH9 .... 126 B3
Popplewell Gdns
LWF/SPW/WRK NE9 .... 101 G1
Popplewell Ter NSHW NE29 ...... 60 E2
The Populars HLS DH4 .... 117 K6
Porchester Dr CRAM NE23 .... 38 D1
Porlock Ct CRAM NE23 .... 33 G6
Porlock Rd JRW NE32 .... 74 B6

Portadown Rd
MLFD/PNYW SR4 .... 119 F3
Portberry St SSH NE33 .... 75 F2
Portberry Wy SSH NE33 .... 75 F2
Portchester Gv BOLCOL NE35 .... 90 C4
Portchester Rd
MLFD/PNYW SR4 .... 119 G1
Portchester Sq
MLFD/PNYW SR4 .... 119 G1
Porter Ter SEA/MUR SR7 .... 149 H5
Porthcawl Dr MLFD/PNYW SR4 .. 102 C3
Portland Av SEA/MUR SR7 .... 150 B1
Portland Gdns CRAM NE23 .... 38 D1
LWF/SPW/WRK NE9 .... 101 F3
TYNE/NSHE NE30 .... 60 E3
Portland Rd
BW/LEM/TK/HW NE15 .... 67 G1
JES NE2 .... 6 A3
SUNDSW SR3 .... 119 K4
Portland Sq BLYTH NE24 .... 31 F5
ELS/FEN NE4 .... 4 B8
FELL NE10 .... 13 H6
Portland Ter JES NE2 .... 5 M2
Portman Pl BYK/HTN/WLK NE6 .. 12 E1
Portman Sq MLFD/PNYW SR4 ... 119 G1
Portmeads Rd
CLS/BIR/GTL DH3 .... 115 K2
Portobello La
CLDN/WHIT/ROK SR6 .... 106 D4
Portree Sq SUNDSW SR3 .... 119 J5
Portrush Cl WASHN NE37 .... 102 E3
Portrush Rd MLFD/PNYW SR4 ... 105 G7
Portrush Wy LGB/HTN NE7 .... 57 J5
Portslade Rd MLFD/PNYW SR4 .. 119 F2
Portsmouth Rd
MLFD/PNYW SR4 .... 119 F1
NSHW NE29 .... 60 A5
Portsmouth Sq
MLFD/PNYW SR4 .... 119 F2
Portugal Pl
WLSD/HOW NE28 .... 72 D2
Postern Crs MPTH NE61 .... 20 C5
Post Office La NSHW NE29 .... 60 E2
Post Office St BLYTH NE24 .... 31 H6
Potterhouse La DHAM DH1 .... 156 A1
Potter Pl STLY/ANP DH9 .... 127 F2
Potters Bank DHAM DH1 .... 16 A8
Potters Cl DHAM DH1 .... 168 B3
Potter Sq SUNDSW SR3 .... 119 J4
Potter St JRW NE32 .... 73 J4
WLSD/HOW NE28 .... 73 J2
Pottersway LWF/SPW/WRK NE9 .. 87 G6
Pottery Bank
BYK/HTN/WLK NE6 .... 13 H1
MPTH NE61 .... 20 C3
Pottery La CNUT NE1 .... 10 B1
MLFD/PNYW SR4 .... 104 E6
Pottery Rd SWCK/CAS SR5 .... 106 A4
Pottery Yd HLS DH4 .... 132 C7
Potto St RDHAMSE DH6 .... 173 J4
Potts St BYK/HTN/WLK NE6 ...... 7 G4
Powburn Cl PLEE/EAS SR8 .... 129 C6
Powburn Gdns ELS/FEN NE4 ..... 69 J3
Powis Rd SUNDSW SR3 .... 119 K4
Powis Sq SUNDSW SR3 .... 119 K4
Poynings Cl WD/WHPE/BLK NE5 .. 54 D6
Praetorian Dr
WLSD/HOW NE28 .... 72 D3
Prebends Fld DHAM DH1 .... 157 G5
Prefect Pl
LWF/SPW/WRK NE9 .... 87 G5
Premier Rd SUNDSW SR3 .... 119 J4
Prendwick Av HEBB NE31 .... 89 F1
Prendwick Cl CLSW/PEL DH2 .... 129 G7
Prengarth Av
CLDN/WHIT/ROK SR6 .... 106 D2
Prensgarth Wy
HAR/WTLS NE34 .... 90 D1
Prescot Rd MLFD/PNYW SR4 ..... 105 G7
Press La SUND SR1 .... 14 F4
Prestbury Av CRAM NE23 .... 33 G6
Prestbury Rd MLFD/PNYW SR4 .. 118 E2
Prestdale Av BLYTH NE24 .... 30 C7
Presthope Rd MLFD/PNYW SR4 .. 118 E2
Preston Av TYNE/NSHE NE30 .... 60 E3
Preston North Rd NSHW NE29 ... 60 D1
Preston Pk NSHW NE29 .... 60 E3
Preston Rd ASHBK/HED/RY SR2 .. 15 J9
Preston Wd TYNE/NSHE NE30 ... 60 E7
Prestwick FELL NE10 .... 88 A7
Prestwick Av NSHW NE29 .... 60 A3
Prestwick Cl WASHN NE37 .... 102 E3
Prestwick Dr FELL NE10 .... 88 E5
Prestwick Gdns GOS/KPK NE3 ... 55 K6
Prestwick Rd MLFD/PNYW SR4 .. 105 G7
Pretoria Av MPTH NE61 .... 20 D5
Pretoria Sq SUNDSW SR3 .... 119 J4
Pretoria St
BW/LEM/TK/HW NE15 .... 68 E7
Price St HEBB NE31 .... 72 E4
MPTH NE61 .... 20 C4
Priestburn Cl
BDN/LAN/SAC DH7 .... 165 G1
Priestclose Rd PRUD NE42 .... 80 D2
Priestclose Rd SUNDSW SR3 ..... 133 K2
Priestley Ct HAR/WTLS NE34 ..... 90 E1
Priestley Gdns FELL NE10 .... 13 L8
Priestly Crs MLFD/PNYW SR4 .... 14 A2
Priestman Av CON/LDGT DH8 .... 122 C6
Priestman Ct
MLFD/PNYW SR4 .... 105 H7
Primate Rd SUNDSW SR3 .... 119 J4
Primrose Av HAR/WTLS NE34 .... 75 F6
Primrose Cl CRAM NE23 .... 47 G3
Primrose Ct ASHGTN NE63 .... 23 H4
Primrose Crs
CLDN/WHIT/ROK SR6 .... 106 D2
HLS DH4 .... 131 G4
Primrose Gdns
WLSD/HOW NE28 .... 58 C6
Primrose HI
LWF/SPW/WRK NE9 .... 87 G7
Primrose Prec
CLDN/WHIT/ROK SR6 .... 106 D2
Primrose St
MLFD/PNYW SR4 .... 104 E7
Primrose Ter CLS/BIR/GTL DH3 .. 115 K2

JRW NE32 .... 74 A7
Prince Albert Ter JES NE2 .... 6 A5
Prince Charles Av
RDHAMSE DH6 .... 179 K2
Prince Consort La HEBB NE31 .... 73 F5
HEBB NE31 .... 72 E5
JRW NE32 .... 74 A5
Prince Consort Wy NSHW NE29 .. 2 C7
Prince Edward Gv
HAR/WTLS NE34 .... 76 C5
Prince Edward Rd
HAR/WTLS NE34 .... 75 K6
Prince Edward Rd East
HAR/WTLS NE34 .... 76 C5
Prince George Av
CLDN/WHIT/ROK SR6 .... 106 D1
Prince of Wales Cl
HAR/WTLS NE34 .... 75 J6
Prince Philip Cl
BW/LEM/TK/HW NE15 .... 69 C6
Prince Rd WLSD/HOW NE28 ..... 58 D7
Princes Av CLDN/WHIT/ROK SR6 .. 92 E7
GOS/KPK NE3 .... 56 B4
Prince's Gdns SUNDSW SR3 ...... 120 E6
CLDN/WHIT/ROK SR6 .... 92 E7
Prince's Meadow GOS/KPK NE3 .. 56 A5
Princes Pk GOS/KPK NE3 .... 56 B1
Princess Av CON/LDGT DH8 ...... 122 C2
Princess Ct PRUD NE42 .... 64 D7
Princess Dr GATE NE8 .... 9 K6
Princess Louise Rd BLYTH NE24 .. 31 F7
Princess Rd SEA/MUR SR7 .... 150 D1
Princess St ASHBK/HED/RY SR2 .. 14 D7
WICK/BNPF NE16 .... 99 F3
Princess Wy PRUD NE42 .... 80 B1
Prince St SUND SR1 .... 14 E3
Princesway DUN/TMV NE11 ...... 86 C6
Princetown Ter SUNDSW SR3 .... 119 J4
Princeway TYNE/NSHE NE30 ..... 61 H2
Pringle Cl DIN/WO NE13 .... 46 A4
Pringle Gv BDN/LAN/SAC DH7 ... 166 D3
Pringle Pl BDN/LAN/SAC DH7 ... 166 E3
Prinn Pl WICK/BNPF NE16 .... 99 F3
Priors Cl DHAM DH1 .... 156 B7
Priors Gra RDHAMSE DH6 .... 158 E4
Prior's Ter TYNE/NSHE NE30 ..... 61 H3
Priors Wk WLSD/HOW NE28 ..... 73 C1
Priory Av MONK NE25 .... 50 D5
Priory Cl CON/LDGT DH8 .... 122 C2
Priory Ct BDN/LAN/SAC DH7 .... 143 H6
Priory Gra BLYTH NE24 .... 30 E6
Priory Gv MLFD/PNYW SR4 .... 119 K1
Priory Pl DIN/WO NE13 .... 46 A4
STKFD/GP NE62 .... 23 C5
Priory Rd DHAM DH1 .... 156 C4
JRW NE32 .... 74 A6
Priory Wy WD/WHPE/BLK NE5 .. 54 D6
Proctor Sq SUNDSW SR3 .... 119 K4
Proctor St BYK/HTN/WLK NE6 ... 72 C6
Promenade
ASHBK/HED/RY SR2 .... 121 G3
NWBGN NE64 .... 25 C1
SEA/MUR SR7 .... 135 K7
SSH NE33 .... 61 K7
WBAY NE26 .... 50 E3
The Promenade
CON/LDGT DH8 .... 123 F3
Prospect Av MONK NE25 .... 39 K5
WLSD/HOW NE28 .... 58 D7
Prospect Av North
WLSD/HOW NE28 .... 58 D6
Prospect Crs HLH DH5 .... 160 B1
Prospect Gdns BOL NE36 .... 90 E5
Prospect Pl BDN/LAN/SAC DH7 .. 166 D2
CON/LDGT DH8 .... 123 F4
ELS/FEN NE4 .... 4 D6
Prospect Rw SUND SR1 .... 15 J3
Prospect St NWBGN NE64 .... 19 H7
Prospect Ter
BDN/LAN/SAC DH7 .... 166 D2
TYNE/NSHE NE30 .... 61 C4
Prospect Vw HLS DH4 .... 146 C6
Providence Rw DHAM DH1 .... 16 E2
Provident St CLSW/PEL DH2 ...... 128 C1
Provost Gdns ELS/FEN NE4 .... 69 H7
Prudhoe Gv JRW NE32 .... 89 J1
Prudhoe St
MLFD/PNYW SR4 .... 105 H6
NSHW NE29 .... 2 D4
Prudhoe Ter
TYNE/NSHE NE30 .... 61 H2
Pudding Chare CNUT NE1 .... 5 K8
Purbeck Gdns CRAM NE23 .... 38 D1
Purbeck Rd LGB/KIL NE12 .... 57 H4
Purley WASHS NE38 .... 117 J2
Purley Cl WLSD/HOW NE28 ...... 59 H6
Purley Gdns GOS/KPK NE3 .... 55 K6
Purley Rd SUNDSW SR3 .... 119 J4
Purley Sq SUNDSW SR3 .... 119 J4
Putney Sq MLFD/PNYW SR4 ..... 119 F2
Pykerley Rd MONK NE25 .... 50 C4

HAR/WTLS NE34 .... 76 D5
Quarry Rd
BW/LEM/TK/HW NE15 .... 68 A5
HEBB NE31 .... 73 C6
STLY/ANP DH9 .... 112 D7
SUNDSW SR3 .... 120 B7
Quarry Rw FELL NE10 .... 12 C6
Quarry St SUNDSW SR3 .... 120 A7
Quay Rd BLYTH NE24 .... 31 H6
Quayside BLYTH NE24 .... 31 H6
CNUT NE1 .... 5 M8
The Quay HLH DH5 .... 147 K5
Quay Vw WLSD/HOW NE28 ...... 73 H1
Queen Alexandra Rd
ASHBK/HED/RY SR2 .... 60 D3
NSHW NE29 .... 60 D3
SEA/MUR SR7 .... 150 E2
SUNDSW SR3 .... 120 B3
Queen Alexandra Rd West
NSHW NE29 .... 60 C3
Queen Elizabeth Av
LWF/SPW/WRK NE9 .... 87 H7
Queen Elizabeth Dr HLH DH5 .... 160 C1
Queen Elizabeth Ii Br CNUT NE1 .. 10 E1
Queens Av CLDN/WHIT/ROK SR6 .. 92 E7
Queensberry St
MLFD/PNYW SR4 .... 14 B4
Queensbridge LGB/KIL NE12 ..... 57 F3
Queensbury Dr
WD/WHPE/BLK NE5 .... 67 K1
Queensbury Rd SEA/MUR SR7 ... 150 B1
Queen's Ct
BW/LEM/TK/HW NE15 .... 67 J2
GATE NE8 .... 10 A6
GOS/KPK NE3 .... 46 C7
Queen's Crs HEBB NE31 .... 73 F7
HAR/WTLS NE34 .... 120 A1
WLSD/HOW NE28 .... 58 C7
Queen's Dr WBAY NE26 .... 50 E4
WICK/BNPF NE16 .... 85 F7
Queen's Gdns DHAM DH1 .... 168 B3
Queensland Av HAR/WTLS NE34 .. 74 C7
Queens La CNUT NE1 .... 5 K8
Queens Pl NWBGN NE64 .... 19 G7
Queen's Rd BDLGTN NE22 .... 29 K4
BW/LEM/TK/HW NE15 .... 67 J2
CON/LDGT DH8 .... 122 C2
CRAM NE23 .... 38 C7
JES NE2 .... 71 F2
SWCK/CAS SR5 .... 106 B4
WBAY NE26 .... 41 G2
WBAY NE26 .... 50 D3
WD/WHPE/BLK NE5 .... 68 E1
WNGT TS28 .... 183 J3
Queen's Ter JES NE2 .... 71 F2
Queen St ASHBK/HED/RY SR2 ... 121 F6
CLSW/PEL DH2 .... 128 A2
CNUT NE1 .... 5 M8
CON/LDGT DH8 .... 123 F5
GATE NE8 .... 10 A7
HLH DH5 .... 147 K3
NWBGN NE64 .... 19 G7
SEA/MUR SR7 .... 150 D1
SSH NE33 .... 3 G7
SUND SR1 .... 14 D3
TYNE/NSHE NE30 .... 2 F1
Queen St East SUND SR1 .... 15 H4
Queens Wy CON/LDGT DH8 ...... 122 C2
Queensway ELS/FEN NE4 .... 69 H3
GOS/KPK NE3 .... 56 B1
HLH DH5 .... 132 D7
MPTH NE61 .... 20 B6
PONT/DH NE20 .... 43 F7
TYNE/NSHE NE30 .... 61 H2
Queensway North
DUN/TMV NE11 .... 10 A9
Queen Victoria Rd CNUT NE1 .... 5 J4
Queen Victoria St FELL NE10 ..... 13 K6
Quentin Av GOS/KPK NE3 .... 55 H5
Quetlaw Rd RDHAMSE DH6 ...... 182 D1
Quilstyle Rd RDHAMSE DH6 ...... 182 D1
Quin Crs WNGT TS28 .... 183 J3
Quinn Cl PLEE/EAS SR8 .... 174 E5
Quiton Cl WD/WHPE/BLK NE5 .. 55 F6

R

Rabbit Banks Rd GATE NE8 .... 10 D2
Raby Av PLEE/EAS SR8 .... 163 F4
Raby Cl HLS DH4 .... 131 J6
Raby Dr SUNDSW SR3 .... 119 G7
Raby Gdns JRW NE32 .... 73 K7
Raby Rd DHAM DH1 .... 156 D2
WASHS NE38 .... 116 B1
Raby St BYK/HTN/WLK NE6 ...... 7 G5
GATE NE8 .... 11 H7
MLFD/PNYW SR4 .... 14 A6
Raby Wy BYK/HTN/WLK NE6 .... 7 G6
Rachel Cl ASHBK/HED/RY SR2 ... 120 C7
Rackly Wy CLDN/WHIT/ROK SR6 .. 93 F4
Radcliffe Pl
WD/WHPE/BLK NE5 .... 69 H1
Radcliffe Rd SWCK/CAS SR5 ..... 105 J3
Radcliffe St CLS/BIR/GTL DH3 ... 115 J3
Radlett Rd SWCK/CAS SR5 .... 105 H3
Radnor Gdns WLSD/HOW NE28 .. 59 J7
Radnor St CNUT NE1 .... 5 M4
Radstock Pl LGB/KIL NE12 .... 57 J3
Rae Av WLSD/HOW NE28 .... 58 D6
Raeburn Av WASHS NE38 .... 117 G3
Raeburn Gdns
LWF/SPW/WRK NE9 .... 11 M9
Raeburn Rd HAR/WTLS NE34 .... 91 H2
SWCK/CAS SR5 .... 105 J2
Ragian WASHS NE38 .... 116 C1
Raglan Av ASHBK/HED/RY SR2 .. 120 E3
Raglan Pl WICK/BNPF NE16 ...... 97 K7
Raglan St CON/LDGT DH8 .... 123 F5
Railway Pl CON/LDGT DH8 .... 122 E4
Railway Rd DHAM DH1 .... 170 B1
Railway St BDN/LAN/SAC DH7 .. 140 C5
CON/LDGT DH8 .... 123 J3

The Quadrant NSHW NE29 .... 60 C5
SUND SR1 .... 14 D3
Quality Rw BYK/HTN/WLK NE6 ... 6 D6
Quality Row Rd
WICK/BNPF NE16 .... 84 E3
Quantock Cl LGB/KIL NE12 .... 57 G4
Quantock Pl PLEE/EAS SR8 .... 174 B4
Quarry Crs BDN/LAN/SAC DH7 .. 155 F3
Quarryfield Rd GATE NE8 .... 6 B9
Quarryheads La DHAM DH1 ...... 16 B6
Quarry House La DHAM DH1 ..... 168 A1
HLH DH5 .... 147 C4
Quarry La HAR/WTLS NE34 ...... 76 A5

CON/LDGT DH8 .... 123 F5
DUN/TMV NE11 .... 9 G4
ELS/FEN NE4 .... 9 M2
HEBB NE31 .... 73 H4
HLH DH5 .... 147 K4
HLS DH4 .... 132 E5
JRW NE32 .... 73 J4
NSHW NE29 .... 2 D2
STLY/ANP DH9 .... 125 J4
STLY/ANP DH9 .... 127 C5
SUND SR1 .... 15 J5
Railway Ter ELS/FEN NE4 .... 9 L2
NSHW NE29 .... 2 D2
Raine Gv SUND SR1 .... 15 H6
Rainford Av
ASHBK/HED/RY SR2 .... 120 E3
Rainhill Cl WASHN NE37 .... 103 G4
Rainhill Rd WASHN NE37 .... 103 G4
Rainton Cl FELL NE10 .... 88 E6
Rainton Gv HLH DH5 .... 147 H2
Rainton St HLS DH4 .... 117 K6
MLFD/PNYW SR4 .... 106 A7
SEA/MUR SR7 .... 150 E2
Rainton Vw HLS DH4 .... 146 C6
Rake La NSHW NE29 .... 60 A1
Raleigh Cl SSH NE33 .... 75 F3
Raleigh Rd SWCK/CAS SR5 .... 105 H3
Raleigh Sq SWCK/CAS SR5 .... 105 H3
Ralph Av ASHBK/HED/RY SR2 .... 120 E6
Ralph St HEBB NE31 .... 73 H4
Ramilies ASHBK/HED/RY SR2 .... 134 D1
Ramillies Rd SWCK/CAS SR5 .... 105 G2
Ramona Av RDHAMSE DH6 .... 181 F6
The Ramparts
BW/LEM/TK/HW NE17 .... 68 C3
Ramsay Rd CHPW NE17 .... 95 H3
Ramsay St BLAY NE21 .... 83 K3
RDHAMSE DH6 .... 179 K7
Ramsay Ter CON/LDGT DH8 .... 123 H7
PLEE/EAS SR8 .... 174 E2
Ramsey Cl CLS/BIR/GTL DH3 .... 129 J3
Ramsgate Rd SWCK/CAS SR5 .... 105 J2
Ramshaw Cl
BDN/LAN/SAC DH7 .... 153 K3
Ramside Vw DHAM DH1 .... 158 A4
Randolph St JRW NE32 .... 74 A4
Rangoon Rd SWCK/CAS SR5 .... 105 G2
Ranmere Rd
BW/LEM/TK/HW NE15 .... 68 E6
Ranmore Cl CRAM NE23 .... 38 C1
Rannoch Av CLSW/PEL DH2 .... 129 H6
Rannoch Cl FELL NE10 .... 88 E4
Rannoch Rd SWCK/CAS SR5 .... 105 G2
Ranson Crs HAR/WTLS NE34 .... 74 D6
Ranson St MLFD/PNYW SR4 .... 120 A2
Raphael Av HAR/WTLS NE34 .... 91 G1
Rathmore Gdns
TYNE/NSHE NE30 .... 60 E2
Ratho Ct FELL NE10 .... 88 A6
Ravenburn Gdns
BW/LEM/TK/HW NE15 .... 68 D5
Raven Ct BDN/LAN/SAC DH7 .... 165 G2
Ravenna Rd SWCK/CAS SR5 .... 105 F2
Ravensbourne Av BOL NE36 .... 91 H4
Ravenscar Cl
WICK/BNPF NE16 .... 84 C7
Ravenscourt Rd SWCK/CAS SR5 .... 105 G3
Ravensdale Gv BLYTH NE24 .... 30 C7
Ravens Hill Dr ASHGTN NE63 .... 23 G3
Ravenshill Rd
WD/WHPE/BLK NE5 .... 68 B2
Ravenside Rd ELS/FEN NE4 .... 69 J3
Ravenside Ter CON/LDGT DH8 .... 122 D3
Ravenstone WASHN NE37 .... 102 D6
Ravenswood Cl LGB/KIL NE12 .... 58 A2
Ravenswood Gdns
LWF/SPW/WRK NE9 .... 101 F2
Ravenswood Rd
BYK/HTN/WLK NE6 .... 71 J2
SWCK/CAS SR5 .... 105 G2
Ravenswood Sq SWCK/CAS SR5 .... 105 F2
Ravensworh St
MLFD/PNYW SR4 .... 14 A4
Ravensworth
ASHBK/HED/RY SR2 .... 134 D1
Ravensworth Av HLS DH4 .... 131 H6
LWF/SPW/WRK NE9 .... 101 J3
Ravensworth Cl
WLSD/HOW NE28 .... 73 H1
Ravensworth Ct
RDHAMSE DH6 .... 160 E2
Ravensworth Rd
CLS/BIR/GTL DH3 .... 115 H1
DUN/TMV NE11 .... 9 J6
Ravensworth St
WLSD/HOW NE28 .... 73 H1
Ravensworth Ter DHAM DH1 .... 16 F3
DUN/TMV NE11 .... 9 J6
JRW NE32 .... 89 K1
SSH NE33 .... 75 G4
Rawdon Rd SWCK/CAS SR5 .... 105 J2
Rawling Ct GATE NE8 .... 10 C7
Rawlston Wy
WD/WHPE/BLK NE5 .... 55 G7
Rawmarsh Rd
SWCK/CAS SR5 .... 105 G2
Raydale SWCK/CAS SR5 .... 105 J2
Raydale Av WASHN NE37 .... 102 D5
Raylees Gdns DUN/TMV NE11 .... 86 A5
Rayleigh Dr DIN/WO NE13 .... 46 B2
Rayleigh Gv GATE NE8 .... 10 D9
Raynes Cl MPTH NE61 .... 20 B6
Raynham Cl CRAM NE23 .... 38 A5
Rayn Ter RDHAMSE DH6 .... 182 D2
Readhead Av SSH NE33 .... 75 J2
Readhead Dr BYK/HTN/WLK NE6 .... 72 D7
Readhead Rd HAR/WTLS NE34 .... 75 J3
Reading Rd HAR/WTLS NE34 .... 75 H4
SWCK/CAS SR5 .... 105 G2
Reading Sq SWCK/CAS SR5 .... 105 G2
Rea Pl GOS/KPK NE3 .... 56 A5
Reasby Gdns RYTON NE40 .... 66 D6
Reavley Av BDLGTN NE22 .... 30 A3
Reay Crs BOLCOL NE35 .... 91 F4
Reay Gdns WD/WHPE/BLK NE5 .... 68 C1
Reay St FELL NE10 .... 13 L3
Rectory Bank BOL NE36 .... 90 E5

Rectory Ct WICK/BNPF NE16 .... 85 F5
Rectory Dene MPTH NE61 .... 20 D7
Rectory Dr JES NE2 .... 56 E6
Rectory Gn BOL NE36 .... 90 D5
Rectory Gv GOS/KPK NE3 .... 56 D5
Rectory La BLAY NE21 .... 83 K3
WICK/BNPF NE16 .... 85 F6
Rectory Pk MPTH NE61 .... 20 D6
Rectory Pl GATE NE8 .... 10 D5
Rectory Rd FELL NE10 .... 12 B9
GATE NE8 .... 56 D6
GOS/KPK NE3 .... 56 D6
HLH DH5 .... 147 K5
Rectory Rd East FELL NE10 .... 87 K5
Red Admiral Ct
DUN/TMV NE11 .... 86 B5
Red Barnes CNUT NE1 .... 6 B6
Red Berry Wy HAR/WTLS NE34 .... 75 F7
Redburn Cl HLS DH4 .... 132 A7
Redburn Rd WD/WHPE/BLK NE5 .... 56 D5
Redcar Rd BYK/HTN/WLK NE6 .... 71 K2
SWCK/CAS SR5 .... 105 J3
WLSD/HOW NE28 .... 59 J7
Redcar Sq SWCK/CAS SR5 .... 105 J3
Redcliffe Wy
WD/WHPE/BLK NE5 .... 55 F7
Redditch Sq SWCK/CAS SR5 .... 105 H2
Rede Av HEBB NE31 .... 73 G5
Redemarsh FELL NE10 .... 88 C6
Redesdale Av BLAY NE21 .... 83 H4
SWCK/CAS SR5 .... 56 A5
Redesdale Cl LGB/KIL NE12 .... 57 J2
Redesdale Gdns DUN/TMV NE11 .... 9 H9
Redesdale Gv NSHW NE29 .... 60 A4
Redesdale Pl BLYTH NE24 .... 30 D7
Redesdale Rd CLSW/PEL DH2 .... 129 G6
NSHW NE29 .... 60 A4
SWCK/CAS SR5 .... 105 G2
Rede St DUN/TMV NE11 .... 86 C7
JRW NE32 .... 73 J6
Redewater Gdns
WICK/BNPF NE16 .... 84 E6
Redewater Rd ELS/FEN NE4 .... 69 J3
Red Firs BDN/LAN/SAC DH7 .... 167 G6
Redford Pl LGB/KIL NE12 .... 47 J4
Red Hall Dr LGB/HTN NE7 .... 57 K7
Redheugh Bridge Rd
ELS/FEN NE4 .... 10 A1
Redheugh Rd MONK NE25 .... 49 K4
Redhill CLDN/WHIT/ROK SR6 .... 92 E4
Redhill Dr WICK/BNPF NE16 .... 98 C1
Redhill Rd WD/WHPE/BLK NE5 .... 105 H2
Redhills La DHAM DH1 .... 156 B7
Redhills Wy HLH DH5 .... 147 K6
Redhouse Cl
BDN/LAN/SAC DH7 .... 143 J6
Red House Dr MONK NE25 .... 50 A3
Red House Farm BDLGTN NE22 .... 28 C6
Red House Rd HEBB NE31 .... 73 H5
Redland Av GOS/KPK NE3 .... 55 H4
Red Lion La WASHN NE37 .... 102 E3
Redmires Cl CLSW/PEL DH2 .... 114 E5
Redmond Rd SWCK/CAS SR5 .... 105 J2
Redmond Sq SWCK/CAS SR5 .... 105 J2
Rednam Pl WD/WHPE/BLK NE5 .... 69 F1
Redruth Gdns
LWF/SPW/WRK NE9 .... 101 F3
Redruth Sq SWCK/CAS SR5 .... 105 H2
Redshank Cl WASHS NE38 .... 116 B4
Redshank Dr BLYTH NE24 .... 35 G3
Red Wk LGB/HTN NE7 .... 71 G1
Redwell Ct HAR/WTLS NE34 .... 76 C4
PRUD NE42 .... 80 D2
Redwell La HAR/WTLS NE34 .... 76 D4
Redwell Rd PRUD NE42 .... 80 E2
Redwing Cl WASHS NE38 .... 116 B3
Redwood BDN/LAN/SAC DH7 .... 165 G3
BDN/LAN/SAC DH7 .... 167 G6
Redwood Cl HLH DH5 .... 147 J5
LGB/KIL NE12 .... 47 J5
Redwood Ct CON/LDGT DH8 .... 122 E3
Reed Av LGB/KIL NE12 .... 47 J4
Reedham Ct
WD/WHPE/BLK NE5 .... 55 F6
Reedling Ct SWCK/CAS SR5 .... 105 J1
Reedside RYTON NE40 .... 67 F6
Reedsmouth Pl
WD/WHPE/BLK NE5 .... 69 F3
TYNE/NSHE NE30 .... 61 F4
Reedswood Crs CRAM NE23 .... 38 E3
Reestones Pl GOS/KPK NE3 .... 55 H5
Reeth Rd SWCK/CAS SR5 .... 105 H3
Reeth Sq SWCK/CAS SR5 .... 105 H3
Reeth Wy BW/LEM/TK/HW NE15 .... 66 E2
Regal Rd MLFD/PNYW SR4 .... 106 A6
Regency Ct SEA/MUR SR7 .... 150 E1
Regency Dr SUNDSW SR3 .... 120 B6
WICK/BNPF NE16 .... 84 D6
Regency Gdns NSHW NE29 .... 60 C4
Regent Av GOS/KPK NE3 .... 56 B5
Regent Dr WICK/BNPF NE16 .... 98 D1
Regent Farm Rd GOS/KPK NE3 .... 56 A4
Regent Rd ASHBK/HED/RY SR2 .... 135 G2
GOS/KPK NE3 .... 56 C5
JRW NE32 .... 74 A5
WLSD/HOW NE28 .... 58 C7
Regents Ct WLSD/HOW NE28 .... 58 B6
Regents Dr TYNE/NSHE NE30 .... 61 G2
Regents Pk WLSD/HOW NE28 .... 58 A7
Regent St BLYTH NE24 .... 31 G6
HLH DH5 .... 147 K3
Regent Ter ASHBK/HED/RY SR2 .... 121 F4
GATE NE8 .... 10 F5
NSHW NE29 .... 60 C3
Reginald St BOLCOL NE35 .... 90 D4
GATE NE8 .... 11 M6
MLFD/PNYW SR4 .... 105 K7
Regina Sq SWCK/CAS SR5 .... 105 H2
Reid Park Cl JES NE2 .... 71 F1
Reid Park Rd JES NE2 .... 71 F1
Reid's La CRAM NE23 .... 39 F3
Reid St MPTH NE61 .... 20 E5
Reigate Sq SWCK/CAS SR5 .... 105 H2
Rekendyke La SSH NE33 .... 75 F2
Relley Cl BDN/LAN/SAC DH7 .... 167 G1
Relly Pth DHAM DH1 .... 168 B2

Relton Av BYK/HTN/WLK NE6 .... 7 K8
Relton Cl HLS DH4 .... 146 D1
Relton Ter CLS/BIR/GTL DH3 .... 129 J5
MONK NE25 .... 50 C4
Rembrandt Av HAR/WTLS NE34 .... 91 G2
Remscheid Wy ASHGTN NE63 .... 23 J4
Remus Av DIN/WO NE13 .... 46 B4
Rendel St DUN/TMV NE11 .... 9 G5
Rendle Rd BYK/HTN/WLK NE6 .... 72 D7
Renforth St DUN/TMV NE11 .... 9 H7
Renfrew Cl NSHW NE29 .... 60 A2
Renfrew Rd SWCK/CAS SR5 .... 105 H2
Rennie Rd SWCK/CAS SR5 .... 105 H2
Rennie Sq SWCK/CAS SR5 .... 105 F2
Rennington FELL NE10 .... 88 B7
Rennington Av
TYNE/NSHE NE30 .... 61 G1
Rennington Cl MPTH NE61 .... 27 F1
Rennington Pl
WD/WHPE/BLK NE5 .... 69 H2
Renny's La DHAM DH1 .... 17 M2
Renny St DHAM DH1 .... 17 G2
Renoir Gdns HAR/WTLS NE34 .... 91 H2
Renwick Av GOS/KPK NE3 .... 55 J4
Renwick St BYK/HTN/WLK NE6 .... 7 F5
Resida Cl
BW/LEM/TK/HW NE15 .... 68 A3
Retford Rd SWCK/CAS SR5 .... 105 H2
Retford Sq SWCK/CAS SR5 .... 105 H2
The Retreat ASHBK/HED/RY SR2 .... 14 B6
Revell Ter WD/WHPE/BLK NE5 .... 69 J3
Revelstoke Rd SWCK/CAS SR5 .... 105 F2
Revesby St SSH NE33 .... 75 G5
Reynolds Av HAR/WTLS NE34 .... 91 H1
LGB/KIL NE12 .... 47 H7
WASHS NE38 .... 117 G2
Reynolds Ct STLY/ANP DH9 .... 126 C1
Reynolds Ct PLEE/EAS SR8 .... 175 J4
Rheims Ct MLFD/PNYW SR4 .... 105 H6
Rheydt Av WLSD/HOW NE28 .... 72 B1
Rhodesia Rd SWCK/CAS SR5 .... 105 H2
Rhodes St BYK/HTN/WLK NE6 .... 72 C6
Rhondda Rd SWCK/CAS SR5 .... 105 F2
Rhuddlan Ct
WD/WHPE/BLK NE5 .... 55 F6
Rhyl Sq SWCK/CAS SR5 .... 105 J2
Ribbledale Gdns
LGB/HTN NE7 .... 57 H7
Ribble Rd SWCK/CAS SR5 .... 105 G3
Ribblesdale HLS DH4 .... 117 K7
WLSD/HOW NE28 .... 58 B6
Ribblesdale Av BLYTH NE24 .... 30 C6
Richard Av MLFD/PNYW SR4 .... 105 H6
Richard Browell Rd
BW/LEM/TK/HW NE15 .... 67 F2
Richardson Av
HAR/WTLS NE34 .... 74 D7
Richardson Rd JES NE2 .... 4 F2
Richardson St WLSD/HOW NE28 .... 72 E1
Richardson Ter
ASHBK/HED/RY SR2 .... 135 G1
Richard St BLYTH NE24 .... 31 G7
HLH DH5 .... 147 K5
Richmond ASHBK/HED/RY SR2 .... 120 C7
Richmond Av FELL NE10 .... 88 E3
WASHS NE38 .... 103 F7
WICK/BNPF NE16 .... 85 F3
Richmond Cl BDLGTN NE22 .... 28 E4
Richmond Gdns
WLSD/HOW NE28 .... 59 G7
Richmond Gv NSHW NE29 .... 60 C5
Richmond Ms GOS/KPK NE3 .... 56 B7
Richmond Pk
WLSD/HOW NE28 .... 58 B7
Richmond Rd DHAM DH1 .... 156 E2
HAR/WTLS NE34 .... 75 G5
Richmond St SWCK/CAS SR5 .... 14 D2
Richmond Ter RDHAMSE DH6 .... 160 D6
WBAY NE26 .... 9 F5
Richmond Wy CRAM NE23 .... 38 B5
PONT/DH NE20 .... 42 C4
Rickaby St SUND SR1 .... 15 J2
Rickgarth FELL NE10 .... 88 B7
Rickleton Av CLS/BIR/GTL DH3 .... 129 K2
Rickleton Wy WASHS NE38 .... 116 B5
Riddell Av BW/LEM/TK/HW NE15 .... 69 G6
Ridding Ct BDN/LAN/SAC DH7 .... 165 G2
Riddings Rd SWCK/CAS SR5 .... 105 H2
Riddings Sq SWCK/CAS SR5 .... 105 H2
Ridgely Dr PONT/DH NE20 .... 43 J3
Ridge Ter BDLGTN NE22 .... 28 E5
The Ridge RYTON NE40 .... 66 E7
Ridge Wy MONK NE25 .... 40 B7
Ridgeway ASHBK/HED/RY SR2 .... 134 C3
ASHGTN NE63 .... 24 C3
ELS/FEN NE4 .... 69 J3
FELL NE10 .... 13 M9
STKFD/GP NE62 .... 23 G5
Ridgeway Crs SUNDSW SR3 .... 120 B3
The Ridge Wy GOS/KPK NE3 .... 55 K6
The Ridgeway HAR/WTLS NE34 .... 91 K1
Ridgewood Crs GOS/KPK NE3 .... 57 F5
Ridgewood Gdns
GOS/KPK NE3 .... 56 E5
Ridgewood Vls GOS/KPK NE3 .... 56 E5
Riding Cl RYTON NE40 .... 82 A1
Riding Dene PSHWF NE43 .... 79 K3
Riding Hill Rd STLY/ANP DH9 .... 125 H2
Riding La DUN/TMV NE11 .... 114 B2
Riding Lea BLAY NE21 .... 83 J3
The Ridings MONK NE25 .... 50 A3
The Riding GOS/KPK NE3 .... 55 J7
Ridley Av ASHBK/HED/RY SR2 .... 121 F7
BLYTH NE24 .... 31 H7
WLSD/HOW NE28 .... 59 J6
Ridley Cl GOS/KPK NE3 .... 55 K2
MPTH NE61 .... 20 C5
Ridley Gdns WICK/BNPF NE16 .... 84 E3
Ridley Gv HAR/WTLS NE34 .... 76 A4
Ridley Mill Rd PSHWF NE43 .... 79 F7
Ridley Pl CNUT NE1 .... 5 K4
Ridley St BLYTH NE24 .... 31 H6
GATE NE8 .... 10 D7
STLY/ANP DH9 .... 112 D7
SWCK/CAS SR5 .... 106 B3

Ridley Ter ASHBK/HED/RY SR2 .... 15 J8
Ridsdale Av WD/WHPE/BLK NE5 .... 68 B2
Ridsdale Cl MONK NE25 .... 39 K5
WLSD/HOW NE28 .... 58 E6
Rievaulx WASHS NE38 .... 116 E3
Riga Sq SWCK/CAS SR5 .... 105 G2
The Riggs HLH DH5 .... 132 D7
Rignall WASHS NE38 .... 117 J1
Riley St JRW NE32 .... 73 J4
Ringmore Ct
ASHBK/HED/RY SR2 .... 120 C4
Ringway STKFD/GP NE62 .... 23 F5
SWCK/CAS SR5 .... 104 E5
Ringwood Dr CRAM NE23 .... 38 C1
Ringwood Gn LGB/KIL NE12 .... 57 J3
Ringwood Rd SWCK/CAS SR5 .... 105 F2
Ringwood Sq SWCK/CAS SR5 .... 105 F2
Rink St BLYTH NE24 .... 31 H6
Ripley Av NSHW NE29 .... 60 C6
Ripley Cl BDLGTN NE22 .... 28 D4
Ripley Dr CRAM NE23 .... 38 A5
Ripley Ter BYK/HTN/WLK NE6 .... 7 M4
Ripon Cl CRAM NE23 .... 38 A5
Ripon Ct BDN/LAN/SAC DH7 .... 143 G5
Ripon Gdns JES NE2 .... 71 G3
WLSD/HOW NE28 .... 59 G7
Ripon Rd DHAM DH1 .... 156 E1
Ripon St CLDN/WHIT/ROK SR6 .... 106 E4
GATE NE8 .... 10 F6
Ripon Ter SEA/MUR SR7 .... 149 H5
The Rise BLAY NE21 .... 67 J7
CON/LDGT DH8 .... 137 F2
GOS/KPK NE3 .... 55 J6
PONT/DH NE20 .... 42 D7
WBAY NE26 .... 41 G4
Rishton Sq SWCK/CAS SR5 .... 105 G2
Ritson Av BDN/LAN/SAC DH7 .... 155 F6
Ritson Cl NSHW NE29 .... 60 C3
Ritson's Rd CON/LDGT DH8 .... 122 D2
Ritson St CLDN/WHIT/ROK SR6 .... 106 E1
CON/LDGT DH8 .... 122 D3
STLY/ANP DH9 .... 126 C1
River Bank STKFD/GP NE62 .... 23 J5
River Bank East STKFD/GP NE62 .... 23 J6
Riverbank Rd SWCK/CAS SR5 .... 105 H3
Riverdale SWCK/CAS SR5 .... 105 F5
River Dr SSH NE33 .... 3 G5
River La RYTON NE40 .... 66 E7
Rivermead Wy WASHS NE38 .... 117 G5
Riversdale CHPW NE17 .... 95 H7
Riversdale Av STKFD/GP NE62 .... 23 G6
Riversdale Wy
BW/LEM/TK/HW NE15 .... 67 K5
Riverside CON/LDGT DH8 .... 122 C1
PONT/DH NE20 .... 43 G3
Riverside Av STKFD/GP NE62 .... 22 D6
Riverside Ct DUN/TMV NE11 .... 9 J5
Riverside Pk MLFD/PNYW SR4 .... 105 J3
Riverside Rd SWCK/CAS SR5 .... 105 J3
ROWG NE39 .... 97 F5
WICK/BNPF NE16 .... 84 E1
River Vw BLAY NE21 .... 83 K2
CHPW NE17 .... 95 H7
TYNE/NSHE NE30 .... 61 G4
River View Cl BDLGTN NE22 .... 29 K5
Roachburn Rd
WD/WHPE/BLK NE5 .... 68 C1
Robertson Rd SWCK/CAS SR5 .... 105 F2
Robertson Sq SWCK/CAS SR5 .... 105 F3
Robert Sq SEA/MUR SR7 .... 151 F2
Roberts St
BW/LEM/TK/HW NE15 .... 68 E7
Roberts St JRW NE32 .... 73 K6
Robert St MLFD/PNYW SR4 .... 106 A6
SEA/MUR SR7 .... 151 F2
SSH NE33 .... 75 H2
SUNDSW SR3 .... 120 B7
Robert Ter RDHAMSE DH6 .... 180 A1
STLY/ANP DH9 .... 112 D6
Robert Westall Wy NSHW NE29 .... 2 C7
Robin Ct HLH DH5 .... 147 F5
Robin Gv SWCK/CAS SR5 .... 105 G4
Robin La HLH DH5 .... 146 E6
Robinson Gdns
CLDN/WHIT/ROK SR6 .... 93 F3
WLSD/HOW NE28 .... 59 J7
Robinson St SSH NE33 .... 3 J9
SSH NE33 .... 75 H2
Robinson Ter
ASHBK/HED/RY SR2 .... 15 K9
SUNDSW SR3 .... 120 B7
Robsheugh Pl
WD/WHPE/BLK NE5 .... 69 G3
Robson Av PLEE/EAS SR8 .... 174 E3
Robson Crs RDHAMSE DH6 .... 180 A1
Robson Pl ASHBK/HED/RY SR2 .... 135 G1
Robson St BYK/HTN/WLK NE6 .... 6 D4
CON/LDGT DH8 .... 123 G4
LWF/SPW/WRK NE9 .... 87 F7
Rochdale Rd SWCK/CAS SR5 .... 105 H2
Rochdale St HLH DH5 .... 147 K6
WLSD/HOW NE28 .... 72 C2
Rochdale Wy SWCK/CAS SR5 .... 105 H2
Roche Ct WASHS NE38 .... 116 E2
Rochester Cl ASHGTN NE63 .... 24 C3
Rochester Gdns DUN/TMV NE11 .... 9 J8
Rochester Rd DHAM DH1 .... 156 E2
Rochester St BYK/HTN/WLK NE6 .... 72 C6
Rochford Gv CRAM NE23 .... 38 A6
Rochford Rd SWCK/CAS SR5 .... 105 G2
Rockcliffe SSH NE33 .... 75 K2
Rockcliffe Gdns
BW/LEM/TK/HW NE15 .... 68 D4
Rockcliffe St WBAY NE26 .... 51 G4
Rockcliffe Wy
LWF/SPW/WRK NE9 .... 101 J3
Rocket Wy LGB/KIL NE12 .... 58 B2
Rock Gv LWF/SPW/WRK NE9 .... 87 F7
Rockhope WASHS NE38 .... 116 B6
Rockingham Rd SWCK/CAS SR5 .... 105 G2
Rockingham Sq
SWCK/CAS SR5 .... 105 G2
Rock Lodge Rd
CLDN/WHIT/ROK SR6 .... 106 E2
Rockmore Rd BLAY NE21 .... 84 A3
Rock Ter BDN/LAN/SAC DH7 .... 166 E2
JES NE2 .... 6 A4

Rockville
CLDN/WHIT/ROK SR6 .... 106 E1
Rockwood Hill Est RYTON NE40 .... 82 A4
Rockwood Hill Rd RYTON NE40 .... 82 A4
Rodin Av HAR/WTLS NE34 .... 91 H2
Rodney Cl ASHBK/HED/RY SR2 .... 134 C1
TYNE/NSHE NE30 .... 61 H3
Rodney St BYK/HTN/WLK NE6 .... 6 F6
Rodney Wy WBAY NE26 .... 50 B2
Rodridge Pk WNGT TS28 .... 184 A5
Rodsley Av GATE NE8 .... 10 F7
Rodwell St TRIM TS29 .... 182 E6
Roeburn Wy GOS/KPK NE3 .... 55 K7
Roedean Rd SWCK/CAS SR5 .... 105 J2
Roehedge FELL NE10 .... 88 D6
Rogers Cl PLEE/EAS SR8 .... 175 H4
Rogerson Ter
WD/WHPE/BLK NE5 .... 54 C7
Roger St BYK/HTN/WLK NE6 .... 122 E4
Rogues La ROWG NE39 .... 82 B6
Rokeby Av
BW/LEM/TK/HW NE15 .... 68 B5
Rokeby Dr GOS/KPK NE3 .... 55 K6
Rokeby Sq DHAM DH1 .... 168 B3
Rokeby St
BW/LEM/TK/HW NE15 .... 68 B5
MLFD/PNYW SR4 .... 14 A5
Rokeby Ter
BYK/HTN/WLK NE6 .... 71 J2
Rokeby Vw
LWF/SPW/WRK NE9 .... 101 G4
Roker Av CLDN/WHIT/ROK SR6 .... 14 F1
MONK NE25 .... 50 C6
Roker Baths Rd
CLDN/WHIT/ROK SR6 .... 106 E3
Rokerby Av WICK/BNPF NE16 .... 85 G6
Roker Park Rd
CLDN/WHIT/ROK SR6 .... 106 E3
Roker Park Ter
CLDN/WHIT/ROK SR6 .... 107 F3
Roker Ter CLDN/WHIT/ROK SR6 .... 107 F2
Roland Rd WLSD/HOW NE28 .... 73 G1
Rollesby Ct
WD/WHPE/BLK NE5 .... 55 F6
Rolling Mill Rd JRW NE32 .... 73 J3
Romaldskirk Cl
MLFD/PNYW SR4 .... 119 F1
Roman Av BYK/HTN/WLK NE6 .... 7 L3
CLS/BIR/GTL DH3 .... 129 K4
Roman Rd SSH NE33 .... 3 J5
The Roman Wy
WD/WHPE/BLK NE5 .... 68 B2
Romany Dr CON/LDGT DH8 .... 122 E5
Romford Cl CRAM NE23 .... 38 B5
Romford Pl LWF/SPW/WRK NE9 .... 11 K9
Romford St
MLFD/PNYW SR4 .... 105 K7
Romilly St SSH NE33 .... 3 J8
Romley Gv FELL NE10 .... 89 F5
Romney Av
ASHBK/HED/RY SR2 .... 120 E3
HAR/WTLS NE34 .... 91 H1
WASHS NE38 .... 117 G3
Romney Cl HLS DH4 .... 132 A2
Romney Dr DHAM DH1 .... 158 A4
Romney Gdns
LWF/SPW/WRK NE9 .... 11 M9
Romsey Cl CRAM NE23 .... 38 C1
Romsey Dr BOLCOL NE35 .... 90 C3
Romsey Gv
BW/LEM/TK/HW NE15 .... 68 A3
Ronald Dr
BW/LEM/TK/HW NE15 .... 68 E5
Ronald Gdns HEBB NE31 .... 73 F7
Ronaldsay Cl
ASHBK/HED/RY SR2 .... 120 E6
Ronald Sq
CLDN/WHIT/ROK SR6 .... 106 D2
Rookery Cl BLYTH NE24 .... 30 D7
Rookery La WICK/BNPF NE16 .... 98 C1
Rookswood MPTH NE61 .... 20 E7
Rookswood Gdns ROWG NE39 .... 97 G2
Rookwood Dr DIN/WO NE13 .... 46 C1
Rookwood Rd
WD/WHPE/BLK NE5 .... 68 E3
Roosevelt Rd DHAM DH1 .... 17 K1
Ropery La CLS/BIR/GTL DH3 .... 129 K3
CLS/BIR/GTL DH3 .... 130 C5
HEBB NE31 .... 73 F5
WLSD/HOW NE28 .... 73 G1
Ropery Rd GATE NE8 .... 9 L6
MLFD/PNYW SR4 .... 106 A5
The Ropery BYK/HTN/WLK NE6 .... 7 J9
Ropery Wk SEA/MUR SR7 .... 151 F2
Rosalie Ter ASHBK/HED/RY SR2 .... 15 H9
Rosalind Av BDLGTN NE22 .... 29 G6
Rosalind St ASHGTN NE63 .... 23 K1
Rosamond Pl BLYTH NE24 .... 31 H7
Rosa St SSH NE33 .... 3 K9
Rose Av HLS DH4 .... 131 H6
STLY/ANP DH9 .... 126 B2
WICK/BNPF NE16 .... 85 F5
Rosebank Cl
ASHBK/HED/RY SR2 .... 120 E6
Rosebay Rd BDN/LAN/SAC DH7 .... 167 K6
Roseberry Cres RDHAMSE DH6 .... 172 B6
Roseberry Gra LGB/KIL NE12 .... 58 C1
Roseberry St STLY/ANP DH9 .... 113 H7
Roseberry Vls CLSW/PEL DH2 .... 128 C2
Rosebery Av BLYTH NE24 .... 31 J7
GATE NE8 .... 11 J7
NSHW NE29 .... 60 D2
SSH NE33 .... 75 J2
Rosebery Crs JES NE2 .... 6 C1
Rosebery Pl JES NE2 .... 6 C1
Rosebery St SWCK/CAS SR5 .... 106 D4
Rosebery Ter
CON/LDGT DH8 .... 123 F5
Roseby Rd PLEE/EAS SR8 .... 175 G3
Rose Ct BDN/LAN/SAC DH7 .... 153 F7
PLEE/EAS SR8 .... 174 C7
Rose Crs BDN/LAN/SAC DH7 .... 143 J5
CLDN/WHIT/ROK SR6 .... 93 F2
Rosedale BDLGTN NE22 .... 28 E5
WLSD/HOW NE28 .... 58 B6
Rosedale Av
CLDN/WHIT/ROK SR6 .... 92 E6

Ros - Sal 211

CON/LDGT DH8 ... 122 D2
Rosedale Ct WD/WHPE/BLK NE5 .. 68 B2
Rosedale Crs HLS DH4 ... 132 A5 5
Rosedale Rd DHAM DH1 ... 158 A5
RYTON NE40 ... 82 B1
Rosedale St HLH DH5 ... 147 H7
SUND SR1 ... 14 B5
Rosedale Ter
CLDN/WHIT/ROK SR6 ... 106 E1
JES NE2 ... 6 A3
PLEE/EAS SR8 ... 175 C3
TYNE/NSHE NE30 ... 61 F3 2
Roseden Ct LGB/KIL NE12 ... 57 J3 4
Rosedene Vls CRAM NE23 ... 38 E2
Rose Gdns WLSD/HOW NE28 ... 58 D6
Rosegill WASHN NE37 ... 102 D7
Rosehill WLSD/HOW NE28 ... 73 G1
Rosehill Rd WLSD/HOW NE28 ... 73 H1
Rose Hill Wy
WD/WHPE/BLK NE5 ... 69 G2
Rose Lea BDN/LAN/SAC DH7 ... 143 G7
Roselea Av ASHBK/HED/RY SR2 .. 121 F7
Rosemary La PLEE/EAS SR8 ... 162 C5
Rosemary Rd SWCK/CAS SR5 ... 105 H2
Rosemary Ter BLYTH NE24 ... 35 H1
Rosemount DHAM DH1 ... 156 E1
MLFD/PNYW SR4 ... 118 E1
MPTH NE61 ... 20 E6 5
WD/WHPE/BLK NE5 ... 68 D1
Rosemount Cl WASHN NE37 ... 102 E3 5
Rosemount Ct BOL NE36 ... 91 F5 5
Rosemount Wy LGB/HTN NE7 ... 57 J5 5
MONK NE25 ... 50 A4
Roseneath Ct ASHGTN NE63 ... 23 K2
Rose St GATE NE8 ... 10 A4
HEBB NE31 ... 73 F6
MLFD/PNYW SR4 ... 14 B4
TRIM TS29 ... 182 C7
Rose St West HLS DH4 ... 117 K6
Rose Ter WD/WHPE/BLK NE5 ... 69 J2
Roseville St MLFD/PNYW SR4 ... 14 A8
Rosewell Pl WICK/BNPF NE16 ... 98 E1
Rosewood LGB/KIL NE12 ... 48 B6 2
Rosewood Av GOS/KPK NE3 ... 56 D4
Rosewood Crs
BYK/HTN/WLK NE6 ... 72 B2
WBAY NE26 ... 41 G4
Rosewood Gdns GOS/KPK NE3 ... 55 K6
LWF/SPW/WRK NE9 ... 87 H6
Rosewood Sq
MLFD/PNYW SR4 ... 118 E4 1
Rosewood Ter
WLSD/HOW NE28 ... 73 J1 2
Roseworth Av GOS/KPK NE3 ... 56 C6 5
Roseworth Crs GOS/KPK NE3 ... 56 C7
Roslin Pk BDLGTN NE22 ... 29 J5
Roslin Wy CRAM NE23 ... 38 B5 7
Ross CLSW/PEL DH2 ... 115 G4
Ross Av DUN/TMV NE11 ... 9 G6
Rosse Cl WASHN NE37 ... 102 D5
Rossendale Pl LGB/KIL NE12 ... 57 F3 5
Ross Gv CRAM NE23 ... 38 A1
Ross Lea HLS DH4 ... 131 J3
Rosslyn Av ASHBK/HED/RY SR2 .. 121 F7
GOS/KPK NE3 ... 55 J5
Rosslyn St MLFD/PNYW SR4 ... 106 A7
Ross St SWCK/CAS SR5 ... 106 C4 7
Ross Wy GOS/KPK NE3 ... 55 K2
WBAY NE26 ... 50 C2
Rosyth Rd SWCK/CAS SR5 ... 105 J2
Rosyth Sq SWCK/CAS SR5 ... 105 J2
Rotary Pkwy ASHGTN NE63 ... 23 J1
Rotary Wy BLYTH NE24 ... 35 H3
NSHW NE29 ... 60 C7
Rothay Pl WD/WHPE/BLK NE5 .. 69 G1 2
Rothbury ASHBK/HED/RY SR2 ... 134 D1
Rothbury Av BLYTH NE24 ... 34 D1
FELL NE10 ... 13 J5
GOS/KPK NE3 ... 56 B4
JRW NE32 ... 73 H7
PLEE/EAS SR8 ... 175 G2
Rothbury Cl CLSW/PEL DH2 ... 129 G6
LGB/KIL NE12 ... 47 J5 11
TRIM TS29 ... 182 D7
Rothbury Gdns DUN/TMV NE11 ... 86 A7
WLSD/HOW NE28 ... 59 H7
Rothbury Rd DHAM DH1 ... 156 D2
SWCK/CAS SR5 ... 105 H2
Rothbury Ter BYK/HTN/WLK NE6 .. 6 F1
NSHW NE29 ... 60 A6
Rotherfield Cl CRAM NE23 ... 38 C1
Rotherfield Gdns
LWF/SPW/WRK NE9 ... 101 G3 1
Rotherfield Rd SWCK/CAS SR5 ... 105 G2
Rotherfield Sq
SWCK/CAS SR5 ... 105 G2 8
Rotherham Cl HLH DH5 ... 147 G2 2
Rotherham Rd SWCK/CAS SR5 ... 105 G2
Rothlea Gdns STKFD/GP NE62 ... 23 G5
Rothley WASHS NE38 ... 117 H4
Rothley Av ASHGTN NE63 ... 23 K3 2
WD/WHPE/BLK NE5 ... 69 G4
Rothley Cl GOS/KPK NE3 ... 56 D5 5
PONT/DH NE20 ... 43 F2
Rothley Ct SWCK/CAS SR5 ... 105 K1 2
Rothley Gdns TYNE/NSHE NE30 ... 50 E7
Rothley Gv MONK NE25 ... 39 K5 2
Rothley Wy WBAY NE26 ... 50 C2
Rothsay CLSW/PEL DH2 ... 115 F5
Rothwell Rd GOS/KPK NE3 ... 56 C5
SWCK/CAS SR5 ... 105 G2
Roundhill Av
WD/WHPE/BLK NE5 ... 69 G1 5
The Roundway LGB/KIL NE12 ... 57 H3 4
Rowan Av WASHS NE38 ... 116 E5
Rowanberry Rd LGB/KIL NE12 ... 57 H4
Rowan Cl BDLGTN NE22 ... 29 F4
MLFD/PNYW SR4 ... 119 F1
Rowan Ct BDN/LAN/SAC DH7 ... 165 F3
BLYTH NE24 ... 35 F1 5
Rowan Dr DHAM DH1 ... 157 F1
GOS/KPK NE3 ... 55 J4
HLH DH5 ... 147 J4
PONT/DH NE20 ... 43 G2
Rowan Gv PRUD NE42 ... 80 B2
Rowan Lea BDN/LAN/SAC DH7 ... 167 G6
Rowan Tree Av DHAM DH1 ... 157 H5
Rowantree Rd
BYK/HTN/WLK NE6 ... 72 C2
Rowanwood Gdns
DUN/TMV NE11 ... 86 A7
Rowell Cl SUNDSW SR3 ... 134 C1
Rowes Ms BYK/HTN/WLK NE6 ... 7 H9
Rowlandson Crs FELL NE10 ... 12 D8
Rowland Sq SEA/MUR SR7 ... 149 G5
Rowley Bank CON/LDGT DH8 ... 136 E2
Rowley Cl BDN/LAN/SAC DH7 ... 166 D3
Rowley Crs BDN/LAN/SAC DH7 ... 165 G1
Rowley Dr BDN/LAN/SAC DH7 ... 167 G1
Rowley Link
BDN/LAN/SAC DH7 ... 165 G1 5
Rowley St BLYTH NE24 ... 31 G7
Rowntree Wy NSHW NE29 ... 2 C6
Rowsley Rd JRW NE32 ... 74 A6 5
Roxburgh Cl BLAY NE21 ... 83 J4
Roxburgh Pl BYK/HTN/WLK NE6 ... 6 F2
Roxburgh St
CLDN/WHIT/ROK SR6 ... 106 D3
Roxburgh Ter WBAY NE26 ... 50 E4
Roxby Gdns NSHW NE29 ... 60 C5
Roxby Wynd WNGT TS28 ... 183 K2
Royal Crs ELS/FEN NE4 ... 69 J3
Royal Rd STLY/ANP DH9 ... 112 C7
The Royalty ASHBK/HED/RY SR2 .. 14 B6
Roydon Av
ASHBK/HED/RY SR2 ... 120 E3 2
Royle St ASHBK/HED/RY SR2 ... 121 F4
Royston Ter
BYK/HTN/WLK NE6 ... 72 C7 2
Ruabon Cl CRAM NE23 ... 38 B5
Rubens Av HAR/WTLS NE34 ... 91 H1
Ruby St HLS DH4 ... 132 B5
Rudby Cl GOS/KPK NE3 ... 56 D2
Rudchester Pl
WD/WHPE/BLK NE5 ... 69 G3
Rudyard Av
ASHBK/HED/RY SR2 ... 120 E3 5
Rudyerd St NSHW NE29 ... 2 D2
Rugby Gdns
LWF/SPW/WRK NE9 ... 101 K2
Ruislip Pl CRAM NE23 ... 38 A5
Ruislip Rd MLFD/PNYW SR4 ... 118 E1
Runcie Rd RDHAMSE DH6 ... 180 A2 5
Runcorn ASHBK/HED/RY SR2 ... 120 C7
Runcorn Rd SWCK/CAS SR5 ... 105 G2
Runhead Est RYTON NE40 ... 67 F6
Runnymede
ASHBK/HED/RY SR2 ... 120 D7 1
Runnymede Gdns CHPW NE17 ... 95 H6
Runnymede Rd PONT/DH NE20 ... 42 D5
SWCK/CAS SR5 ... 105 H2
WICK/BNPF NE16 ... 84 E6
Runnymede Wy GOS/KPK NE3 .. 55 J6 2
SWCK/CAS SR5 ... 105 H2
Runswick Av LGB/KIL NE12 ... 57 F4
Runswick Cl SUNDSW SR3 ... 120 C7
Rupert Sq SWCK/CAS SR5 ... 105 J2
Rupert St CLDN/WHIT/ROK SR6 ... 93 F3
Rushall Pl LGB/KIL NE12 ... 57 H4
Rushey Gill
BDN/LAN/SAC DH7 ... 167 F6 5
Rushford ASHBK/HED/RY SR2 ... 120 D7
Rushie Av BW/LEM/TK/HW NE15 .. 69 G6
Rushley Crs BLAY NE21 ... 84 A1
Rushsyde Cl WICK/BNPF NE16 ... 84 C7
Rushton Av
ASHBK/HED/RY SR2 ... 120 E3 4
Rushyrig WASHN NE37 ... 102 C7
Ruskin Av ASHGTN NE63 ... 24 B2
CLSW/PEL DH2 ... 128 E4
DUN/TMV NE11 ... 9 H6
HLH DH5 ... 160 B1
LGB/KIL NE12 ... 57 K1 1
Ruskin Cl PRUD NE42 ... 80 B3
STLY/ANP DH9 ... 127 F1
Ruskin Crs HAR/WTLS NE34 ... 91 F1
Ruskin Crs RDHAMSE DH6 ... 172 B6
Ruskin Dr BOLCOL NE35 ... 90 E4
LGB/HTN NE7 ... 72 A1
Ruskin Rd CLS/BIR/GTL DH3 ... 115 J2 1
LWF/SPW/WRK NE9 ... 87 H5
WICK/BNPF NE16 ... 84 E4
Russel Crs TRIM TS29 ... 183 G6
Russell Av HAR/WTLS NE34 ... 76 A5
Russell Cl CON/LDGT DH8 ... 123 G4
Russell Sq DIN/WO NE13 ... 46 C1
Russell St BDN/LAN/SAC DH7 ... 165 F4
JRW NE32 ... 74 A4
NSHW NE29 ... 2 D2
SSH NE33 ... 3 H7
SUND SR1 ... 15 G3
Russell Ter BDLGTN NE22 ... 29 F6
JES NE2 ... 6 A5 1
Ruswarp Dr SUNDSW SR3 ... 134 B1
Rutherford Av SEA/MUR SR7 ... 135 F7
Rutherford Cl STKFD/GP NE62 .. 22 E6 5
Rutherford Pl MPTH NE61 ... 20 C6
Rutherford Rd SWCK/CAS SR5 ... 105 F2
WASHN NE37 ... 103 G4
Rutherford Sq SWCK/CAS SR5 ... 105 F2
Rutherford St BLYTH NE24 ... 35 G1 5
CNUT NE1 ... 5 H7 2
WLSD/HOW NE28 ... 59 K7
Rutherglen Rd SWCK/CAS SR5 ... 105 J2
Rutland Av BYK/HTN/WLK NE6 ... 72 C4
SUNDSW SR3 ... 119 K7
Rutland Pl CON/LDGT DH8 ... 137 G1 1
NSHW NE29 ... 2 A1 1
NSHW NE29 ... 60 C4 1
WASHN NE37 ... 103 F3 2
Rutland Rd CON/LDGT DH8 ... 137 G1
HEBB NE31 ... 89 H1
WLSD/HOW NE28 ... 72 C2
Rutland Sq CLS/BIR/GTL DH3 ... 115 H1
Rutland St HAR/WTLS NE34 ... 75 F5 2
MLFD/PNYW SR4 ... 105 K6
Ryal Cl BLYTH NE24 ... 30 D7
MONK NE25 ... 40 A5
Ryal Ter BYK/HTN/WLK NE6 ... 72 B6
Rydal FELL NE10 ... 13 J7
Rydal Av HLH DH5 ... 160 B1
STLY/ANP DH9 ... 126 B3
TYNE/NSHE NE30 ... 50 E7
Rydal Cl BDN/LAN/SAC DH7 ... 143 G5
BOL NE36 ... 91 G4
LGB/KIL NE12 ... 48 B6
Rydal Crs BLAY NE21 ... 83 K4
PLEE/EAS SR8 ... 175 F4
Rydale Ct TRIM TS29 ... 183 F6
Rydal Gdns HAR/WTLS NE34 ... 75 J5
Rydal Ms CON/LDGT DH8 ... 123 K3
Rydal Mt NWBGN NE64 ... 24 E2
PLEE/EAS SR8 ... 162 E5
SWCK/CAS SR5 ... 104 E5
SWCK/CAS SR5 ... 106 C2
Rydal Rd BW/LEM/TK/HW NE15 .. 68 B3
CLSW/PEL DH2 ... 129 H6
GOS/KPK NE3 ... 56 D5
Rydal St GATE NE8 ... 10 E6
Ryde Pl CRAM NE23 ... 38 C1
Rye Cl BW/LEM/TK/HW NE15 ... 67 G2 5
Ryedale CLDN/WHIT/ROK SR6 ... 93 F5
DHAM DH1 ... 158 A6
WLSD/HOW NE28 ... 58 B5
Ryedale Ct ASHGTN NE63 ... 23 H3
Rye Hl ELS/FEN NE4 ... 4 E8
Ryehill Vw HLH DH5 ... 147 F4
Ryelands Wy DHAM DH1 ... 156 D1
Ryemount Rd
ASHBK/HED/RY SR2 ... 120 D7
Rye View Rd
ASHBK/HED/RY SR2 ... 121 F6
Ryhope Gdns
LWF/SPW/WRK NE9 ... 101 K2
Ryhope Rd ASHBK/HED/RY SR2 ... 14 F9
Ryhope St ASHBK/HED/RY SR2 .. 120 E7
HLH DH5 ... 132 D7
Rymers Cl PLEE/EAS SR8 ... 162 B6
Ryton Ct SSH NE33 ... 75 H2
Ryton Crs SEA/MUR SR7 ... 150 B1
STLY/ANP DH9 ... 112 D6 5
Ryton Hall Dr RYTON NE40 ... 66 E5 5
Ryton Ter BYK/HTN/WLK NE6 ... 72 B7

S

Sackville Rd BYK/HTN/WLK NE6 ... 71 J2
SUNDSW SR3 ... 119 J3
Sacriston Av SUNDSW SR3 ... 119 K3 5
Sacriston La BDN/LAN/SAC DH7 .. 155 F1
Saddleback WASHN NE37 ... 102 D5
Saddler St DHAM DH1 ... 16 D4
Saffron Pl BYK/HTN/WLK NE6 ... 72 C6 5
Sage Cl BW/LEM/TK/HW NE15 .. 68 A3 7
St Agnes' West House
RYTON NE40 ... 66 A7
St Aidan's Av
ASHBK/HED/RY SR2 ... 121 F5
DHAM DH1 ... 156 B4
LGB/KIL NE12 ... 58 E1
St Aidan's Cl NSHW NE29 ... 60 B2 1
St Aidan's Crs DHAM DH1 ... 156 B7
MPTH NE61 ... 20 E7
STLY/ANP DH9 ... 125 H4
St Aidan's Rd SSH NE33 ... 3 J5
WLSD/HOW NE28 ... 72 C2 5
St Aidan's St CON/LDGT DH8 ... 122 E3
GATE NE8 ... 10 D6
St Aidan's Ter HLS DH4 ... 132 C1
St Albans Cl ASHGTN NE63 ... 24 C3
CLS/BIR/GTL DH3 ... 145 J1
St Alban's Crs
BYK/HTN/WLK NE6 ... 71 K1
St Alban's St
ASHBK/HED/RY SR2 ... 120 E3
St Alban's Ter GATE NE8 ... 10 F7
St Albans Vw SMOOR NE27 ... 49 G7
St Aldwyn Rd SEA/MUR SR7 ... 135 H7
St Aloysius Vw HEBB NE31 ... 73 F5
St Andrews HLS DH4 ... 131 K7
St Andrews Av WASHN NE37 ... 102 D5
St Andrew's Cl
CON/LDGT DH8 ... 122 D3 7
St Andrew's Crs CON/LDGT DH8 .. 122 D3
St Andrew's Dr
LWF/SPW/WRK NE9 ... 100 E2
St Andrew's Gdns
CON/LDGT DH8 ... 122 C3
St Andrew's La PRUD NE42 ... 63 H7
St Andrew's Rd CON/LDGT DH8 .. 122 C3
STLY/ANP DH9 ... 112 D5
St Andrew's St CNUT NE1 ... 5 H6
HEBB NE31 ... 72 E4 5
St Andrew's Ter
CLDN/WHIT/ROK SR6 ... 106 E3 5
St Ann's Cl CNUT NE1 ... 6 C6
St Ann's St CNUT NE1 ... 6 B7
St Anselm Crs NSHW NE29 ... 60 A3
St Anselm Rd NSHW NE29 ... 60 A3
St Anthony's Rd
BYK/HTN/WLK NE6 ... 7 M6
St Asaph Cl LGB/HTN NE7 ... 57 K6
St Aubyn's Wy
STLY/ANP DH9 ... 113 F7 1
St Austell Cl
WD/WHPE/BLK NE5 ... 55 G6 1
St Austell Gdns
LWF/SPW/WRK NE9 ... 101 F3
St Barnabas HLS DH4 ... 131 F4
St Barnabas Wy
ASHBK/HED/RY SR2 ... 15 J8
St Bartholomews Cl
ASHGTN NE63 ... 18 B7 1
St Bede Cressent
RDHAMSE DH6 ... 172 B7
St Bede's Cl DHAM DH1 ... 168 B1
St Bede's Ct BDN/LAN/SAC DH7 .. 140 B3
St Bede's Dr GATE NE8 ... 11 H3
St Bedes Pl BLYTH NE24 ... 34 D3
St Bedes Rd BLYTH NE24 ... 34 D3 4
St Bedes Wy
BDN/LAN/SAC DH7 ... 167 K5 1
St Brandon's Gv
BDN/LAN/SAC DH7 ... 167 F6
St Buryan Crs
WD/WHPE/BLK NE5 ... 55 G6
St Catherine's Ct
SWCK/CAS SR5 ... 105 H4
St Chad's Crs SUNDSW SR3 ... 119 F7 1
St Chad Sq RDHAMSE DH6 ... 172 A7
St Chad's Rd SUNDSW SR3 ... 119 F7
St Chad's Vls BOL NE36 ... 91 H5 5
St Christophers Cl
ASHGTN NE63 ... 18 B7 2
St Christopher's Rd
SUNDSW SR3 ... 120 A4
Saint Ct SUNDSW SR3 ... 134 A2
St Cuthbert Av
CLS/BIR/GTL DH3 ... 129 K4
St Cuthbert Rd RDHAMSE DH6 ... 172 B7
St Cuthbert's Av
CON/LDGT DH8 ... 122 C2
DHAM DH1 ... 156 B4
HAR/WTLS NE34 ... 76 A3
St Cuthberts Cl PRUD NE42 ... 80 C2 2
St Cuthberts Ct BLYTH NE24 ... 31 H7 5
St Cuthberts Dr
BDN/LAN/SAC DH7 ... 143 G5
FELL NE10 ... 13 G9
St Cuthberts Pk
WICK/BNPF NE16 ... 98 E5
St Cuthbert's Pl GATE NE8 ... 10 D5 1
St Cuthbert's Rd GATE NE8 ... 10 D4
HLS DH4 ... 132 B4 7
PLEE/EAS SR8 ... 174 E5 1
WD/WHPE/BLK NE5 ... 69 F4
WICK/BNPF NE16 ... 98 E6
WLSD/HOW NE28 ... 59 F7
St Cuthbert's Ter
MLFD/PNYW SR4 ... 14 A3 5
St Cuthberts Wk
BDN/LAN/SAC DH7 ... 167 K5
St Cuthberts Wy BLAY NE21 ... 84 B3
RDHAMSE DH6 ... 170 C1
St Davids Cl ASHGTN NE63 ... 18 B7 5
St David's Wy WBAY NE26 ... 50 D1
St Ebba's Wy CON/LDGT DH8 ... 108 E3
St Edmund's Dr FELL NE10 ... 13 G9
St Edmund's Rd GATE NE8 ... 11 H5
St Gabriel's Av
BYK/HTN/WLK NE6 ... 71 H2
MLFD/PNYW SR4 ... 105 K7
St George's Av SSH NE33 ... 75 J3
St George's Cl JES NE2 ... 70 E1
St Georges Crs MONK NE25 ... 50 D5
NSHW NE29 ... 2 A2
St George's Est WASHS NE38 ... 116 E6 1
St George's Pl
BW/LEM/TK/HW NE15 ... 68 C6 1
CON/LDGT DH8 ... 122 E4
St George's Rd
BW/LEM/TK/HW NE15 ... 68 C6 2
TYNE/NSHE NE30 ... 51 F6
St George's Ter BOL NE36 ... 91 H5
BW/LEM/TK/HW NE15 ... 68 C6 5
CLDN/WHIT/ROK SR6 ... 107 F3
JES NE2 ... 70 E1
St George's Wy
ASHBK/HED/RY SR2 ... 14 E7 1
St Giles Cl DHAM DH1 ... 17 J3
St Godric's Cl DHAM DH1 ... 156 D2
St Godric's Dr HLS DH4 ... 146 D6
St Helen's Crs
LWF/SPW/WRK NE9 ... 86 E7 5
St Heliers Wy STLY/ANP DH9 ... 113 F7
St Hilda's Av
WLSD/HOW NE28 ... 59 G7 2
St Hilda St SSH NE33 ... 3 H8
St Hilds Ct DHAM DH1 ... 17 M2
St Hild's La DHAM DH1 ... 17 G3
St Ignatius Cl
ASHBK/HED/RY SR2 ... 15 H7 5
St Ives' Rd CON/LDGT DH8 ... 123 K3
St Ives Wy WD/WHPE/BLK NE5 ... 55 G6
St James Ct GATE NE8 ... 11 M6
St James' Crs
BW/LEM/TK/HW NE15 ... 69 H7 2
St James' Rd
BW/LEM/TK/HW NE15 ... 69 H6
GATE NE8 ... 11 K4
St James Sq GATE NE8 ... 11 K3
St James' St CNUT NE1 ... 5 H5
GOS/KPK NE3 ... 56 D5
St James' Ter NSHW NE29 ... 60 B7
St Johns SUND SR1 ... 15 J2 1
St John's Av HEBB NE31 ... 73 F6
St John's Cl WBAY NE26 ... 50 D1 5
St John's Crs BDLGTN NE22 ... 29 K3
RDHAMSE DH6 ... 180 A2 4
St John's Gn NSHW NE29 ... 60 B7
St John's Pl BDLGTN NE22 ... 29 K3
CLS/BIR/GTL DH3 ... 115 J2
FELL NE10 ... 12 C7
WBAY NE26 ... 50 D1 4
St John's Rd BDLGTN NE22 ... 29 K4
BDN/LAN/SAC DH7 ... 167 K6
DHAM DH1 ... 168 B1
ELS/FEN NE4 ... 69 J7
St John's St NSHW NE29 ... 60 B7
St John's Ter BOL NE36 ... 91 J5
JRW NE32 ... 73 K4 5
NSHW NE29 ... 60 B7
St John St CNUT NE1 ... 5 J7
St Johns V MLFD/PNYW SR4 ... 118 E2 5
St John's Wk NSHW NE29 ... 60 B7 5
Saint Joseph's Cl DHAM DH1 ... 17 L2
St Joseph's Ct HEBB NE31 ... 89 F1 2
St Joseph's Wy JRW NE32 ... 89 K3
St Jude's Ter SSH NE33 ... 75 G2
St Julien Gdns LGB/HTN NE7 ... 57 K7
WLSD/HOW NE28 ... 59 K7 2
St Lawrence Cl RDHAMSE DH6 ... 159 F4
St Lawrence Rd
BYK/HTN/WLK NE6 ... 6 F7
RDHAMSE DH6 ... 158 E4
St Lawrence Sq
BYK/HTN/WLK NE6 ... 6 E7
St Leonard's Wk MPTH NE61 ... 20 A3
St Lucia Cl
ASHBK/HED/RY SR2 ... 15 G8 2
WBAY NE26 ... 50 C1
St Lukes Cl ASHGTN NE63 ... 18 C7
St Luke's Rd
MLFD/PNYW SR4 ... 105 G6 5
St Luke's St NSHW NE29 ... 60 B7
St Luke's Ter MLFD/PNYW SR4 ... 105 K6
St Margaret's Av
SWCK/CAS SR5 ... 104 E4
St Margaret's Ct DHAM DH1 ... 16 B4 1
St Margaret's Dr STLY/ANP DH9 .. 112 A3
St Margaret's Rd
BW/LEM/TK/HW NE15 ... 69 F7
St Margarets Av
LGB/KIL NE12 ... 57 K4 5
St Mark's Rd MLFD/PNYW SR4 ... 14 A5
St Mark's Rd North
MLFD/PNYW SR4 ... 106 A6
St Mark's St BYK/HTN/WLK NE6 ... 7 G3
MLFD/PNYW SR4 ... 14 A5 2
Saint Mark's St MPTH NE61 ... 20 C4
St Mark's Ter MLFD/PNYW SR4 ... 14 A4
St Mark's Wy SSH NE33 ... 75 G2
St Martin's Cl WBAY NE26 ... 50 C2
St Mary's Av HAR/WTLS NE34 ... 75 K5
WBAY NE26 ... 50 D2
St Marys Cl CLSW/PEL DH2 ... 129 H5
CON/LDGT DH8 ... 122 D3 5
DHAM DH1 ... 169 G4
PLEE/EAS SR8 ... 162 B6 1
St Mary's Crs CON/LDGT DH8 ... 122 C3
St Marys Dr ASHGTN NE63 ... 18 B7
BLYTH NE24 ... 34 D2
HLS DH4 ... 146 D6 2
RDHAMSE DH6 ... 170 C1
St Mary's Pl
BW/LEM/TK/HW NE15 ... 67 G1 5
CNUT NE1 ... 5 K4
St Mary's Rd DHAM DH1 ... 157 K5
St Mary's St CON/LDGT DH8 ... 122 D3
St Mary's Ter BOL NE36 ... 91 H5
St Mary's Wy SUND SR1 ... 14 D4
St Mary's Wynd WBAY NE26 ... 41 H4
St Mathews La PRUD NE42 ... 80 D2 5
St Matthews Vw
SUNDSW SR3 ... 120 A7 4
St Michaels HLS DH4 ... 131 K7
St Michael's Av MONK NE25 ... 40 B2
SSH NE33 ... 75 H2
St Michael's Av North SSH NE33 .. 75 H2
St Michael's Rd
BYK/HTN/WLK NE6 ... 6 E6
St Michaels Wy SUND SR1 ... 14 C4
WICK/BNPF NE16 ... 8 B6
St Monica Gv DHAM DH1 ... 168 B1
St Nicholas Av GOS/KPK NE3 ... 56 C6 4
SUNDSW SR3 ... 120 B3
St Nicholas' Church Yd
CNUT NE1 ... 5 K7 1
St Nicholas Cl ASHGTN NE63 ... 18 B7 7
St Nicholas Dr DHAM DH1 ... 156 A5
St Nicholas Rd BOL NE36 ... 90 E5 5
St Nicholas' St CNUT NE1 ... 5 K7
St Nicholas Ter
PLEE/EAS SR8 ... 162 E5 1
St Omers Rd DUN/TMV NE11 ... 9 G4
St Oswald Av BYK/HTN/WLK NE6 ... 7 L3
St Oswald's Dr DHAM DH1 ... 168 B5
St Oswald's Gn
BYK/HTN/WLK NE6 ... 7 L3
St Oswald's Rd HEBB NE31 ... 73 H4
WLSD/HOW NE28 ... 59 F6
St Oswin's Pl CON/LDGT DH8 .. 122 D3 5
TYNE/NSHE NE30 ... 61 H3
St Oswin's St SSH NE33 ... 75 H4
St Pauls Cl ASHGTN NE63 ... 18 B7
St Pauls Dr HLS DH4 ... 117 G6 2
St Paul's Gdns MONK NE25 ... 50 E5
St Paul's Rd JRW NE32 ... 74 A4
St Peter's Av HAR/WTLS NE34 ... 75 J5
St Peter's Rd BYK/HTN/WLK NE6 ... 7 H8
WLSD/HOW NE28 ... 59 F6
St Peters' Wy
CLDN/WHIT/ROK SR6 ... 15 G2
St Peter's Whf
BYK/HTN/WLK NE6 ... 7 H9
St Philips Cl ELS/FEN NE4 ... 4 E6
St Philips Wy ELS/FEN NE4 ... 4 E6 1
St Ronan's Dr WBAY NE26 ... 40 E1
St Ronan's Rd MONK NE25 ... 50 D5
St Ronans Vw
LWF/SPW/WRK NE9 ... 101 G3
St Simon St HAR/WTLS NE34 ... 74 E7
St Stephen's Cl MONK NE25 ... 39 J5 1
St Stephen's Wy NSHW NE29 ... 74 B1
St Stevens Cl HLS DH4 ... 117 G6 2
St Thomas Cl PLEE/EAS SR8 ... 162 B6 2
St Thomas' Crs CNUT NE1 ... 5 J4
St Thomas Ms PRUD NE42 ... 80 D2
St Thomas' St CNUT NE1 ... 5 J4
LWF/SPW/WRK NE9 ... 87 G7 5
SUND SR1 ... 14 F4
St Vincent Ct GATE NE8 ... 11 K5
St Vincents Cl
BW/LEM/TK/HW NE15 ... 68 C3 5
St Vincent's Pl WBAY NE26 ... 50 D1 5
St Vincent St
ASHBK/HED/RY SR2 ... 15 G7
GATE NE8 ... 11 K5
SSH NE33 ... 75 J2
St Vincent's Wy WBAY NE26 ... 50 D1 5
Salcombe Av JRW NE32 ... 74 B6
Salcombe Cl SEA/MUR SR7 ... 150 B2 5
Salcombe Gdns
LWF/SPW/WRK NE9 ... 101 F3
Salem Av CON/LDGT DH8 ... 123 H7
Salem Hl ASHBK/HED/RY SR2 ... 15 G8
Salem Rd ASHBK/HED/RY SR2 ... 15 G7
Salem St ASHBK/HED/RY SR2 ... 15 G7
JRW NE32 ... 74 A4
SSH NE33 ... 3 G6
Salem St South
ASHBK/HED/RY SR2 ... 15 G8
Salem Ter ASHBK/HED/RY SR2 .. 15 G7 1
Salisbury Av NSHW NE29 ... 60 D3
Salisbury Cl ASHGTN NE63 ... 24 B3
CLS/BIR/GTL DH3 ... 145 H2
CON/LDGT DH8 ... 108 E7 5
CRAM NE23 ... 37 K2
Salisbury Gdns JES NE2 ... 71 G3
Salisbury Pl SSH NE33 ... 3 L7
Salisbury Rd DHAM DH1 ... 157 F2
Salisbury St ASHBK/HED/RY SR2 .. 14 F6
CON/LDGT DH8 ... 123 G4 5
FELL NE10 ... 13 J6
SSH NE33 ... 3 K8
STLY/ANP DH9 ... 126 B2

Salkeld Gdns
LWF/SPW/WRK NE9 .... 11 J8
Salkeld Rd LWF/SPW/WRK NE9 .. 87 C6
Salmon St SSH NE33 .... 3 J5
Saltburn La
WLSD/HOW NE28 .... 59 K7 ☑
Saltburn Rd SUNDSW SR3 .... 119 J3
Saltburn Sq SUNDSW SR3 .... 119 J3
Salterfen La
ASHBK/HED/RY SR2 .... 121 C6
Salterfen Rd
ASHBK/HED/RY SR2 .... 121 C6
Salters Cl GOS/KPK NE3 .... 56 E4
Salter's La HLH DH5 .... 133 J5
HLH DH5 .... 148 D5
LGB/KIL NE12 .... 57 F4
RDHAMSE DH6 .... 160 D3
RDHAMSE DH6 .... 173 H7
SEA/MUR SR7 .... 148 E2
TRIM TS29 .... 182 C5
Salters' Rd GOS/KPK NE3 .... 56 A6
Saltmeadows Rd GATE NE8 .... 6 D9
Saltwell Pl GATE NE8 .... 10 C7
Saltwell Rd GATE NE8 .... 10 C7
Saltwell Rd South
LWF/SPW/WRK NE9 .... 86 E6
Saltwell St GATE NE8 .... 10 D7
Saltwell Vw LWF/SPW/WRK NE9 .. 10 F9
Salvin St RDHAMSE DH6 .... 178 C5
Samson Cl LGB/KIL NE12 .... 47 H7
Sancroft Dr HLH DH5 .... 147 H1
Sandalwood HAR/WTLS NE34 .. 91 H1 ☑
Sandalwood Sq
MLFD/PNYW SR4 .... 118 E4
Sanderling Cl RYTON NE40 .... 67 C7 ☑
Sanderson Rd JES NE2 .... 70 E1 ☑
Sanderson St ELS/FEN NE4 .... 9 I1
Sandfield Rd BDLGTN NE22 .... 30 D2
TYNE/NSHE NE30 .... 51 F6
Sandford Av CRAM NE23 .... 33 H6
Sandford Ms DUN/WO NE11 .... 45 K4
Sandford Rd CON/LDGT DH8 .... 122 B3
Sandgate CNUT NE1 .... 6 A7
STLY/ANP DH9 .... 125 K3
Sandgrove
CLDN/WHIT/ROK SR6 .... 92 A3 ☑
Sandholm Cl
WLSD/HOW NE28 .... 59 H5 ☑
Sandhurst Av TYNE/NSHE NE30 .. 51 F7
Sandmartin Cl ASHGTN NE63 .... 24 A5
Sandmere Pl
BW/LEM/TK/HW NE15 .... 68 E6 ☑
Sandmere Rd
ASHBK/HED/RY SR2 .... 120 E5 ☑
Sandoe Gdns
BW/LEM/TK/HW NE15 .... 69 F6
Sandon Cl SMOOR NE27 .... 48 E4
Sandown MONK NE25 .... 50 A4
Sandown Gdns GATE NE8 .... 10 B8
SUNDSW SR3 .... 119 K6 ☑
WLSD/HOW NE28 .... 59 H6
Sandpiper Cl BLYTH NE24 .... 35 G3
RYTON NE40 .... 67 F7 ☑
Sand Point Rd
CLDN/WHIT/ROK SR6 .... 106 A4
Sandray Cl CLS/BIR/GTL DH3 .. 115 K5
Sandridge NWBGN NE64 .... 19 H7
Sandringham Av LGB/KIL NE12 .. 57 J4
MONK NE25 .... 49 K5
STLY/ANP DH9 .... 125 H2 ☑
WICK/BNPF NE16 .... 84 E5 ☑
Sandringham Gdns NSHW NE29 .. 60 E3
Sandringham Rd
CLDN/WHIT/ROK SR6 .... 106 A3
GOS/KPK NE3 .... 56 E6
WD/WHPE/BLK NE5 .... 68 C3 ☑
Sandringham Ter
CLDN/WHIT/ROK SR6 .... 106 A3
Sandringham Wy
PONT/DH NE20 .... 42 E5
Sandsay Cl ASHBK/HED/RY SR2 .. 120 D6
Sands Rd WICK/BNPF NE16 .... 84 E3
Sandstone HAR/WTLS NE34 .... 90 D1
Sandwell Dr HLS DH4 .... 117 H6
Sandwich Rd NSHW NE29 .... 60 D1
Sandy Chare
CLDN/WHIT/ROK SR6 .... 92 E4
Sandy Crs BYK/HTN/WLK NE6 .. 7 M9
Sandyford Av CLSW/PEL DH2 .. 114 D7
Sandyford Av PRUD NE42 .... 81 F1
Sandyford Rd CNUT NE1 .... 5 L4
JES NE2 .... 5 L3
Sandy La ASHGTN NE63 .... 24 D3
DIN/WO NE13 .... 45 H3
GOS/KPK NE3 .... 46 E5
LWF/SPW/WRK NE9 .... 101 K4
Sandypath La
WICK/BNPF NE42 .... 97 J6 ☑
Sandysykes PRUD NE42 .... 80 B2 ☑
Sans St South SUND SR1 .... 15 G5 ☑
Sarabel Av STKFD/GP NE62 .... 22 E6
Sargent Av HAR/WTLS NE34 .. 91 H2
Satley Gdns SUNDSW SR3 .... 120 B4
Saturn Cl PLEE/EAS SR8 .... 162 D5 ☑
Saturn St SEA/MUR SR7 .... 150 B1
Saunton Ct HLS DH4 .... 132 A4 ☑
Saville St SSH NE33 .... 3 J7
TYNE/NSHE NE30 .... 2 E2
Saville St West NSHW NE29 .... 2 D3
Savory Rd WASHS NE38 .... 59 H7
Sawmill La BDN/LAN/SAC DH7 .. 167 F6
Saxilby Dr GOS/KPK NE3 .... 56 D2
Saxon Cl CLDN/WHIT/ROK SR6 .. 91 J3 ☑
Saxon Crs SUNDSW SR3 .... 119 K3
Saxondale Rd GOS/KPK NE3 .... 55 J5
Saxon Dr TYNE/NSHE NE30 .. 61 G1
Saxon Wy JRW NE32 .... 74 A3
Saxton Gv BYK/HTN/WLK NE6 .. 57 G6
Scafell CLS/BIR/GTL DH3 .. 115 K4
Scafell Ct PLEE/EAS SR8 .... 175 F4
Scafell Dr WD/WHPE/BLK NE5 .. 55 H7
Scafell Gdns DUN/TMV NE11 .. 86 A6
Scalby Cl GOS/KPK NE3 .... 56 D2 ☑
Scales Crs PRUD NE42 .... 81 F2
Scarborough Ct
BYK/HTN/WLK NE6 .... 7 J5 ☑

Scarborough Rd
BYK/HTN/WLK NE6 .... 7 K5
SUNDSW SR3 .... 119 K6
Scardale Wy DHAM DH1 .... 158 B5
Sceptre Pl ELS/FEN NE4 .... 4 C7
Sceptre St ELS/FEN NE4 .... 4 C7
Schalksmuhle Bdg BDLGTN NE22 .. 29 F5
Schimel St SWCK/CAS SR5 .. 106 B3 ☑
School Ap HAR/WTLS NE34 .... 76 A5
School Av DUN/TMV NE11 .... 9 G9
RDHAMSE DH6 .... 181 G5
STKFD/GP NE62 .... 23 F6
School Cl FELL NE10 .... 87 K6
Schoolhouse La
WICK/BNPF NE16 .... 98 C6
School La ROWG NE39 .... 96 C2
STLY/ANP DH9 .... 126 B2 ☑
WICK/BNPF NE16 .... 85 F5
School Loaning
HAR/WTLS NE34 .... 75 F6 ☑
School Rd BDLGTN NE22 .... 29 K3
HLH DH5 .... 147 F4
School St CLS/BIR/GTL DH3 .. 115 J2
HEBB NE31 .... 73 G4
PLEE/EAS SR8 .... 163 F5
RDHAMSE DH6 .... 179 K7
SEA/MUR SR7 .... 150 E3 ☑
WICK/BNPF NE16 .... 84 E5
School Ter STLY/ANP DH9 .... 126 B2
School Vw HLH DH5 .... 160 C1
HLS DH4 .... 146 C7 ☑
Scorer's La CLS/BIR/GTL DH3 .. 130 D7
Scorer St NSHW NE29 .... 2 A2
Scotland Head BLAY NE21 .... 83 J5
Scotland St
ASHBK/HED/RY SR2 .... 135 G1
Scotswood Rd
BW/LEM/TK/HW NE15 .... 68 B6
CNUT NE1 .... 5 G9
ELS/FEN NE4 .... 8 E1
WICK/BNPF NE16 .... 8 A3
Scott Av CRAM NE23 .... 33 F7
Scott Cl CLS/BIR/GTL DH3 .. 145 H1
Scott's Ter HLH DH5 .... 147 K4
Scott St CRAM NE23 .... 33 H4
STLY/ANP DH9 .... 126 C1
Scoular Dr ASHGTN NE63 .... 24 C2
Scripton Gill BDN/LAN/SAC DH7 .. 167 F6
Scripton Gill Rd
BDN/LAN/SAC DH7 .... 166 E7
Scripton La BDN/LAN/SAC DH7 .. 177 F1
Scrogg Rd BYK/HTN/WLK NE6 .. 7 M3
Scruton Av SUNDSW SR3 .... 119 K4
Sea Banks TYNE/NSHE NE30 .. 61 J2
Seaburn Dr HLS DH4 .... 132 A7
Seaburn Gdns
CLDN/WHIT/ROK SR6 .... 106 E1
LWF/SPW/WRK NE9 .... 101 K2
Seaburn Gv WBAY NE26 .... 41 F2
Seaburn Hl
CLDN/WHIT/ROK SR6 .... 106 E1 ☑
Seaburn Ter
CLDN/WHIT/ROK SR6 .... 107 F1 ☑
Seaburn Vw MONK NE25 .... 40 A2
Seacombe Av TYNE/NSHE NE30 .. 51 F6
Seacrest Av TYNE/NSHE NE30 .. 51 F6
Sea Crest Rd NWBGN NE64 .... 19 G6
Seafield Rd BLYTH NE24 .... 35 G7 ☑
Seafields CLDN/WHIT/ROK SR6.. 92 C2
Seafield Ter SSH NE33 .... 3 K6
Seafield Vw TYNE/NSHE NE30 .. 61 H2
Seaforth Rd SUNDSW SR3 .... 120 A3
Seaforth St BLYTH NE24 .... 31 G6 ☑
Seaham CI HAR/WTLS NE34 .. 76 B5
Seaham Gdns
LWF/SPW/WRK NE9 .... 101 J3
Seaham Rd HLH DH5 .... 132 D7
Seaham Gdns SEA/MUR SR7 .. 151 F3 ☑
SUNDSW SR3 .... 120 A7
Sea La CLDN/WHIT/ROK SR6 .. 106 E1
Sea Rd CLDN/WHIT/ROK SR6 .. 106 D1
SSH NE33 .... 3 L5
Seascale Pl LWF/SPW/WRK NE9.. 101 H1
Seaside Ln PLEE/EAS SR8 .... 162 D5
Seaton Av BLYTH NE24 .... 34 E3
HLH DH5 .... 132 E7
NWBGN NE64 .... 25 F1
Seaton Cl FELL NE10 .... 88 D6 ☑
Seaton Crs MONK NE25 .... 40 C6
MONK NE25 .... 50 C4
SEA/MUR SR7 .... 134 E6
Seaton Cft CRAM NE23 .... 47 J1 ☑
Seaton Gv SEA/MUR SR7 .... 134 D7
Seaton La SEA/MUR SR7 .... 134 E6
Seaton Pk SEA/MUR SR7 .... 135 F7
Seaton Pl BYK/HTN/WLK NE6 .. 6 F2
DIN/WO NE13 .... 46 A3
Seaton Rd SMOOR NE27 .... 49 J5
SUNDSW SR3 .... 119 H3
Seatonville Crs MONK NE25 .... 50 C6
Seatonville Rd MONK NE25 .... 50 C6
Sea Vw ASHBK/HED/RY SR2 .. 135 G1
MPTH NE61 .... 18 D2
PLEE/EAS SR8 .... 162 C6
Sea View Gdns
CLDN/WHIT/ROK SR6 .... 106 E2
PLEE/EAS SR8 .... 175 H2
Sea View Pk
CLDN/WHIT/ROK SR6 .... 92 D4
CRAM NE23 .... 38 E2
Sea View Rd
ASHBK/HED/RY SR2 .... 120 A4
Sea View Rd West
ASHBK/HED/RY SR2 .... 120 A4
Sea View St
ASHBK/HED/RY SR2 .... 121 H4
SEA/MUR SR7 .... 149 K4
Sea Wy SSH NE33 .... 3 M7
Second Av ASHGTN NE63 .... 23 K2
BLYTH NE24 .... 35 F1 ☑
BYK/HTN/WLK NE6 .... 7 G1
CLSW/PEL DH2 .... 115 H6
CLSW/PEL DH2 .... 129 H5
DUN/TMV NE11 .... 86 C6
MPTH NE61 .... 21 F6
NSHW NE29 .... 59 K6
Second St GATE NE8 .... 10 C5

Sedgeletch Rd HLS DH4 .... 131 J6
Sedgemoor LGB/KIL NE12 .... 47 K5
Sedgemoor Av
BW/LEM/TK/HW NE15 .... 68 E7
Sedley Rd WLSD/HOW NE28 .. 72 D2
Sedling Rd WASHS NE38 .... 116 D4
Sefton Av BYK/HTN/WLK NE6.. 71 H2
Sefton Ct CRAM NE23 .... 33 K6
Sefton Sq SUNDSW SR3 .... 119 J3
Selborne Gdns CON/LDGT DH8.. 122 D1
JES NE2 .... 71 G3
Selbourne Cl CRAM NE23 .... 37 K2 ☑
Selbourne St SSH NE33 .... 3 K8
Selby Cl CRAM NE23 .... 33 H6
Selby Gdns BYK/HTN/WLK NE6 .. 72 B3
CON/LDGT DH8 .... 122 C6
WLSD/HOW NE28 .... 58 D7
Selby Sq SUNDSW SR3 .... 119 J3
Selkirk Crs CLS/BIR/GTL DH3.. 101 J7
Selkirk Gv CRAM NE23 .... 33 J6
Selkirk Sq SUNDSW SR3 .... 119 H3 ☑
Selkirk St JRW NE32 .... 90 C1
Selkirk Wy NSHW NE29 .... 60 A2
Selsdon Av MLFD/PNYW SR4 .. 118 E4 ☑
Selsey Ct FELL NE10 .... 88 A6
Selwood Ct HAR/WTLS NE34 .. 75 K6 ☑
Selwyn Av MONK NE25 .... 50 B6
Serlby Cl WASHN NE37 .... 102 E4
Seton Av HAR/WTLS NE34 .... 74 D7
Setting Stones WASHS NE38.. 116 C6
Sevenoaks Dr MLFD/PNYW SR4.. 118 E3
Seventh Av ASHGTN NE63 .... 24 A3
BLYTH NE24 .... 35 F1
BYK/HTN/WLK NE6 .... 7 G2
CLSW/PEL DH2 .... 129 H4
MPTH NE61 .... 21 F6 ☑
Seventh St PLEE/EAS SR8 .... 175 H3
Severn Av HEBB NE31 .... 89 C1
Severn Cl PLEE/EAS SR8 .... 174 D6
Severn Dr JRW NE32 .... 90 A2
Severn Gdns GATE NE8 .... 11 L7
Severus Rd ELS/FEN NE4 .... 69 J4
Seymour Cl LWF/SPW/WRK NE9.. 11 M8
Seymour Sq SUNDSW SR3 .... 119 J3 ☑
Seymour St CON/LDGT DH8.. 123 F5 ☑
DUN/TMV NE11 .... 9 J5
NSHW NE29 .... 2 C4
PLEE/EAS SR8 .... 175 J4
Seymour Ter HLH DH5 .... 148 A7
Shadfen Crs MPTH NE61 .... 21 J2
Shadforth Cl PLEE/EAS SR8 .. 174 B6
Shadon Wy CLS/BIR/GTL DH3.. 116 A2
Shaftesbury Av
ASHBK/HED/RY SR2 .... 120 E7
HAR/WTLS NE34 .... 74 C6
JRW NE32 .... 74 B5
WBAY NE26 .... 50 D2
Shaftesbury Crs RHTLP TS27 .. 175 K6 ☑
SUNDSW SR3 .... 119 K3
TYNE/NSHE NE30 .... 50 E6
Shaftesbury Gv
BYK/HTN/WLK NE6 .... 6 E2
Shaftesbury Rd RHTLP TS27 .. 175 K5
Shafto Cl CON/LDGT DH8.. 123 H7
Shaftoe Rd RYTON NE40 .... 82 B1
Shaftoe Rd SUNDSW SR3 .... 119 J4
Shaftoe Sq DIN/WO NE13 .... 44 E2
Shafto St BW/LEM/TK/HW NE15 .. 68 E6
WLSD/HOW NE28 .... 59 G7
Shaftsbury Dr
BDN/LAN/SAC DH7 .... 177 F1
Shakespeare Av HEBB NE31.. 73 G3
Shakespeare St HLH DH5 .... 147 H1
JRW NE32 .... 73 K3 ☑
RDHAMSE DH6 .... 181 G5
SEA/MUR SR7 .... 150 E1 ☑
SSH NE33 .... 75 H2 ☑
SWCK/CAS SR5 .... 106 A2
WLSD/HOW NE28 .... 73 H1
Shakespeare Ter
ASHBK/HED/RY SR2 .... 14 C7
PLEE/EAS SR8 .... 162 D5
Shakespere Ter CLSW/PEL DH2 .. 128 E4
Shalcombe Cl SUNDSW SR3 .. 134 A1
Shallcross ASHBK/HED/RY SR2.. 14 B9
Shallon Ct ASHGTN NE63 .... 23 J5 ☑
Shalstone WASHN NE37 .... 103 H4
Shamrock Cl
BW/LEM/TK/HW NE15 .... 68 A3
Shandon Wy GOS/KPK NE3 .... 55 J5 ☑
Shanklin Pl CRAM NE23 .... 37 K2 ☑
Shannon Ct SWCK/CAS SR5 .. 104 E4 ☑
Shap Cl WASHS NE38 .... 117 F3
Shap La WD/WHPE/BLK NE5.. 68 E2
Shap Rd TYNE/NSHE NE30 .... 50 E7
Sharnford Cl SMOOR NE27 .... 49 F4
Sharon Av RDHAMSE DH6 .... 181 G6
Sharon Cl LGB/KIL NE12 .... 47 H7
Sharp Crs DHAM DH1 .... 17 M1
Sharpendon St HEBB NE31 .. 73 G4 ☑
Sharpley Dr SEA/MUR SR7 .. 134 E7
Shaw Av HAR/WTLS NE34 .... 75 F7
Shawdon Cl
WD/WHPE/BLK NE5 .... 55 F6 ☑
Shaw Gdns FELL NE10 .... 13 L8
Shaw La CON/LDGT DH8 .... 109 F2
Shaw St SEA/MUR SR7 .... 150 E1 ☑
Shaw Wood Cl DHAM DH1 .... 156 B6
Shearlegs Rd GATE NE8 .... 11 K2
Shearwater
CLDN/WHIT/ROK SR6 .... 92 C7 ☑
Shearwater Av LGB/KIL NE12 .. 57 G3
Shearwater Cl
WD/WHPE/BLK NE5 .... 55 F6 ☑
Shearwater Wy BLYTH NE24 .. 35 H3
Sheelin Av CLSW/PEL DH2.. 129 J6
Sheen Cl HLS DH4 .... 146 D6 ☑
Sheen Ct WD/WHPE/BLK NE5 .. 55 F5
Sheepfolds North
SWCK/CAS SR5 .... 14 E2 ☑
Sheepfolds Rd SWCK/CAS SR5 .. 14 E2
Sheepfolds South
SWCK/CAS SR5 .... 14 E2 ☑
Sheep Hl WICK/BNPF NE16 .... 97 K7
Sheepwash Av STKFD/GP NE62.. 22 E6
Sheepwash Bank
STKFD/GP NE62 .... 22 E5 ☑

Sheepwash Rd MPTH NE61 .... 22 E3
Sheldon Gv CRAM NE23 .... 33 H6
GOS/KPK NE3 .... 69 K1
Sheldon Rd HAR/WTLS NE34 .. 75 K2
Sheldon St JRW NE32 .... 73 K4
Shelford Gdns
BW/LEM/TK/HW NE15 .... 68 C4 ☑
Shelley Av BOLCOL NE35 .... 90 E4
HAR/WTLS NE34 .... 76 B6
HLH DH5 .... 160 C1 ☑
LWF/SPW/WRK NE9 .... 102 A4
Shelley Ct CLSW/PEL DH2 .. 128 E4
Shelley Dr GATE NE8 .... 11 J4
Shelley Gdns CLSW/PEL DH2 .. 129 F4
Shelley Rd
BW/LEM/TK/HW NE15 .... 67 H4
WLSD/HOW NE28 .... 58 D7
Shelley St SEA/MUR SR7 .... 150 E1
Shepherd St
MLFD/PNYW SR4 .... 106 A6 ☑
Shepherds Dr BOL NE36 .... 90 E5 ☑
Shepherd Wy WASHS NE38.. 117 G4
Sheppard Ter SWCK/CAS SR5.. 105 F4 ☑
Sheppey Ct SUNDSW SR3 .. 134 A1 ☑
Shepton Cottages
WICK/BNPF NE16 .... 99 G2 ☑
Sheraton FELL NE10 .... 88 C7
Sheraton St JES NE2 .... 4 F1
Sherborne Av NSHW NE29 .... 60 B2 ☑
Sherburn Gra North
JRW NE32 .... 73 J6 ☑
Sherburn Gra South
JRW NE32 .... 73 J7 ☑
Sherburn Gn ROWG NE39 .... 97 G2
Sherburn Gv HLS DH4 .... 132 A6
Sherburn Park Dr ROWG NE39.. 97 G2
Sherburn Rd DHAM DH1 .... 17 M3 ☑
Sherburn Ter CON/LDGT DH8 .. 123 G5
Sherburn Wy FELL NE10 .... 88 D6
Sherfield Dr LGB/HTN NE7 .... 71 K1
Sheridan Gn WASHS NE38.. 116 C5
Sheridan Rd HAR/WTLS NE34 .. 90 E1
Sheridan St MLFD/PNYW SR4.. 105 K6
Sheriffs Cl LWF/SPW/WRK NE9.. 11 M8
Sheriff's Moor Av HLH DH5 .. 160 B1
Sheringham Av NSHW NE29 .... 60 B3
Sheringham Cl SUNDSW SR3 .. 134 A3 ☑
Sheringham Dr CRAM NE23 .... 37 K2
Sheringham Gdns
BW/LEM/TK/HW NE15 .... 66 D1
Sherringham Av NSHW NE29 .. 55 J5
Sherwood Cl CON/LDGT DH8 .. 108 E7
SMOOR NE27 .... 49 K7
WASHS NE38 .... 117 F1
Sherwood Ct SUNDSW SR3 .. 134 A1 ☑
Sherwood Pl GOS/KPK NE3 .... 46 C7
Sherwood Vw WLSD/HOW NE28.. 58 C6
Shetland Ct SUNDSW SR3 .. 134 A1 ☑
Shibdon Bank BLAY NE21 .... 84 B2
Shibdon Crs BLAY NE21 .... 84 B2 ☑
Shibdon Park Vw BLAY NE21 .. 84 B2 ☑
Shibdon Rd BLAY NE21 .... 84 A1
Shibdon Wy BLAY NE21 .... 84 B2 ☑
Shield Av WICK/BNPF NE16 .... 85 F3 ☑
Shieldfield La JES NE2 .... 6 A5
Shield Rd CLDN/WHIT/ROK SR6 .. 92 C7
Shieldrow La STLY/ANP DH9.. 125 J4
Shields Rd BDLGTN NE22 .... 32 B2
BYK/HTN/WLK NE6 .... 7 H3
CLDN/WHIT/ROK SR6 .... 92 B6
CLS/BIR/GTL DH3 .... 129 K2
FELL NE10 .... 13 G7
HAR/WTLS NE34 .... 91 K1
MONK NE25 .... 50 D7
MPTH NE61 .... 20 E6
Shields Rd West
BYK/HTN/WLK NE6 .... 6 D5
Shield St JES NE2 .... 6 A4
Shiel Gdns CRAM NE23 .... 37 J3
Shillaw Pl CRAM NE23 .... 47 H4 ☑
Shilmore Rd GOS/KPK NE3 .... 55 K6
Shilton Cl HAR/WTLS NE34 .... 76 B6 ☑
Shincliffe Av SWCK/CAS SR5 .. 105 G3 ☑
Shincliffe Gdns
LWF/SPW/WRK NE9 .... 101 J2
Shincliffe La DHAM DH1 .... 169 J3
Shinwell Crs RDHAMSE DH6.. 172 B6
Shinwell Ter RDHAMSE DH6.. 182 D1 ☑
SEA/MUR SR7 .... 149 G5
Shipcote La GATE NE8 .... 11 G7
Shipcote Ter GATE NE8 .... 11 H7
Shipley Av ELS/FEN NE4 .... 69 J5
Shipley Rd TYNE/NSHE NE30 .. 61 G3
Shipley St BW/LEM/TK/HW NE15.. 68 E5
Shipton Cl BOLCOL NE35 .... 90 C3
Shire Cha DHAM DH1 .... 156 E1 ☑
Shirley Gdns SUNDSW SR3 .. 120 B3
Shirwood Av WICK/BNPF NE16 .. 84 E7
Shop Spouts BLAY NE21 .... 84 A1 ☑
Shoreham Sq SUNDSW SR3 .. 119 J3 ☑
Shorestone Av TYNE/NSHE NE30.. 51 F6
Shore St
CLDN/WHIT/ROK SR6 .... 106 D4 ☑
Short Gv SEA/MUR SR7 .... 149 F5
Shortridge Ter JES NE2 .... 71 F2
Shot Factory La CNUT NE1 .... 10 B1
Shotley Av SWCK/CAS SR5 .. 106 B2
Shotley Ct ASHGTN NE63 .... 23 H3 ☑
Shotley Gdns
LWF/SPW/WRK NE9 .... 11 J9
Shotley Grove Rd
CON/LDGT DH8 .... 122 B2
Shotton Av BLYTH NE24 .... 35 G1
Shotton Bank PLEE/EAS SR8.. 174 A7
Shotton La CRAM NE23 .... 32 C5
MPTH NE61 .... 32 A7
PLEE/EAS SR8 .... 174 B6
RDHAMSE DH6 .... 173 J4
Shotton Rd PLEE/EAS SR8 .... 173 K3
PLEE/EAS SR8 .... 175 G5
Shotton Wy FELL NE10 .... 89 G6
Shrewsbury Cl LGB/KIL NE12 .. 57 K6
PLEE/EAS SR8 .... 174 C5
Shrewsbury Crs SUNDSW SR3 .. 119 K3
Shrewsbury Dr SMOOR NE27 .. 48 E4
Shrewsbury St DUN/TMV NE11 .. 9 G8
SEA/MUR SR7 .... 150 E3
Shrewsbury Ter SSH NE33 .... 75 G4 ☑

Shrigley Gdns GOS/KPK NE3 .. 55 K5
Shropshire Dr DHAM DH1 .... 157 K7
Shunner Cl WASHN NE37 .... 102 C7
Sibthorpe St NSHW NE29 .... 2 E3
Side Cliff Rd
CLDN/WHIT/ROK SR6 .... 106 D2
Sidegate DHAM DH1 .... 16 C2
Sidlaw Av CLSW/PEL DH2 .. 129 G5
NSHW NE29 .... 60 D1
Sidlaw Ct ASHGTN NE63 .... 24 A4 ☑
Sidmouth Cl HLS DH4 .... 132 A3 ☑
SEA/MUR SR7 .... 150 A2
Sidmouth Rd
LWF/SPW/WRK NE9 .... 101 F2
NSHW NE29 .... 60 A4
Sidney Gv ELS/FEN NE4 .... 4 C5
GATE NE8 .... 10 C6
Sidney St BLYTH NE24 .... 31 F7
BOLCOL NE35 .... 90 D4
NSHW NE29 .... 2 D2
Sidney Ter STLY/ANP DH9 .... 112 B6
Silent Bank RDHAMSE DH6.. 171 H6
Silkey's La NSHW NE29 .... 2 A3
Silksworth Cl SUNDSW SR3 .. 119 K6 ☑
Silksworth Gdns
LWF/SPW/WRK NE9 .... 101 J3
Silksworth Hall Dr
SUNDSW SR3 .... 133 K1
Silksworth La
ASHBK/HED/RY SR2 .... 120 B2 ☑
SUNDSW SR3 .... 119 K6
Silksworth Rw SUND SR1 .... 14 C4 ☑
Silksworth Ter SUNDSW SR3.. 120 A7 ☑
Silksworth Wy SUNDSW SR3 .. 133 H1
Silkwood Cl CRAM NE23 .... 33 H6
Silloth Av WD/WHPE/BLK NE5 .. 68 E3
Silloth Dr WASHN NE37 .... 102 E3
Silloth Pl TYNE/NSHE NE30 .... 51 F7
Silloth Rd SUNDSW SR3 .... 119 H4 ☑
Silver Cts BDN/LAN/SAC DH7 .. 167 G6
Silverdale SUNDSW SR3 .... 134 A3
Silverdale Av FELL NE10 .... 89 F5
Silverdale Dr BLAY NE21 .... 83 H3
Silverdale Rd CRAM NE23 .... 33 H6
Silverdale Ter GATE NE8 .... 11 G8
Silverdale Wy HAR/WTLS NE34.. 90 D1
WICK/BNPF NE16 .... 98 D1
Silver Fox Wy SMOOR NE27 .. 49 K7
Silverhill Dr WD/WHPE/BLK NE5 .. 68 E4
The Silverlink North
SMOOR NE27 .... 59 G1
The Silverlink North SMOOR NE27 .. 59 J3
Silver Lonnen
WD/WHPE/BLK NE5 .... 69 F3
Silvermere Dr RYTON NE40.. 67 F7
Silverstone LGB/KIL NE12 .... 48 A6
Silverstone Rd WASHN NE37 .. 103 G5
Silver St CON/LDGT DH8 .... 122 D3 ☑
DHAM DH1 .... 16 E3 ☑
SUND SR1 .... 15 J2
TYNE/NSHE NE30 .... 61 H3 ☑
Silverwood Gdns
DUN/TMV NE11 .... 86 B7
Simonburn Av ELS/FEN NE4 .... 69 J3
NSHW NE29 .... 60 A4
Simonburn La ASHGTN NE63 .. 24 B3
Simon Pl DIN/WO NE13 .... 46 A4 ☑
Simonside PRUD NE42 .... 80 B3
WBAY NE26 .... 41 G4
Simonside Av STKFD/GP NE62 .. 23 G5
WLSD/HOW NE28 .... 59 H6
Simonside Cl MPTH NE61 .... 20 B6
Simonside Rd BLAY NE21 .... 84 A3 ☑
SUNDSW SR3 .... 119 H3
Simonside Ter
BYK/HTN/WLK NE6 .... 71 H3
NWBGN NE64 .... 19 F7
Simonside Vw JRW NE32 .... 74 A7
PONT/DH NE20 .... 43 F2
Simonside Wy LGB/KIL NE12 .. 48 B5
Simpson Ct ASHGTN NE63 .... 24 C1
Simpson St BLYTH NE24 .... 31 G6 ☑
MLFD/PNYW SR4 .... 14 A2
NSHW NE29 .... 60 C5 ☑
TYNE/NSHE NE30 .... 51 G5 ☑
Simpson Ter JES NE2 .... 6 A5
Sinclair Dr CLS/BIR/GTL DH3.. 115 K6
Sinclair Gdns MONK NE25 .... 40 A5
Sinderby Cl GOS/KPK NE3 .... 56 D2
Six-mile Br DIN/WO NE13 .... 46 C1
Sixth Av ASHGTN NE63 .... 24 A3
BLYTH NE24 .... 35 F1
BYK/HTN/WLK NE6 .... 7 G1
MPTH NE61 .... 21 F6 ☑
Sixth St PLEE/EAS SR8 .... 175 H3
Skaylock Dr WASHS NE38 .. 116 C5
Skelder Av LGB/KIL NE12 .... 57 H4
Skelton Ct GOS/KPK NE3 .... 55 J2
Skerne Cl PLEE/EAS SR8 .... 174 D6
Skerne Gv CON/LDGT DH8.. 123 K2 ☑
Skiddaw Cl PLEE/EAS SR8 .... 175 F4
Skiddaw Dr
CLDN/WHIT/ROK SR6 .... 92 C7 ☑
Skiddaw Pl LWF/SPW/WRK NE9.. 101 H1
Skinnerburn Rd ELS/FEN NE4 .. 10 A2
Skipton Cl BDLGTN NE22 .... 28 D4
CRAM NE23 .... 33 J6 ☑
Skirlaw Cl WASHS NE38 .... 117 F2
Ski Vw SUNDSW SR3 .... 119 K6
Skye Ct SUNDSW SR3 .... 133 K1
Skye Gv JRW NE32 .... 90 C2 ☑
Slaidburn Rd STLY/ANP DH9.. 112 D7 ☑
Slake Rd JRW NE32 .... 74 B3
Slaley WASHS NE38 .... 117 G5
Slaley Cl FELL NE10 .... 88 E5
Slaley Ct BDLGTN NE22 .... 29 G5
SUNDSW SR3 .... 134 A1
Slatyford La WD/WHPE/BLK NE5.. 68 C1
Sled La WYLAM NE41 .... 81 J1
Sledmere Cl PLEE/EAS SR8 .. 174 E2 ☑
Sleekburn Av BDLGTN NE22 .. 29 K3 ☑
Slingley Cl SEA/MUR SR7 .. 134 E7 ☑
Slingsby Gdns LGB/HTN NE7 .. 57 K7
Smailes La ROWG NE39 .... 96 C5 ☑
Smailes St STLY/ANP DH9 .... 126 C2
Smallhope Dr
BDN/LAN/SAC DH7 .... 140 C5
Smeaton St WLSD/HOW NE28.. 73 J2 ☑

Smeaton St *WLSD/HOW* NE28 ... 73 J2 5
Smillie Cl *PLEE/EAS* SR8 ... 174 E3
Smithburn Rd *FELL* NE10 ... 12 E9
Smith Cl *RDHAMSE* DH6 ... 170 B1
Smithfield *DHAM* DH1 ... 156 C1
Smith Gv *ASHBK/HED/RY* SR2 ... 134 E1
Smith St *ASHBK/HED/RY* SR2 ... 135 F1
SSH NE33 ... 75 F3
Smith Ter *GATE* NE8 ... 9 M6
Smithyford
LWF/SPW/WRK NE9 ... 101 G4
Smithy La *DUN/TMV* NE11 ... 100 E4
Smithy St *SSH* NE33 ... 3 H7
Smyrna Pl *SUND* SR1 ... 15 H5
Snaith Ter *WNGT* TS28 ... 183 J3
Snipes Dene *ROWG* NE39 ... 97 G2
Snowdon Gdns
DUN/TMV NE11 ... 86 A6 5
Snowdon Gv *BOL* NE36 ... 91 F5 6
Snow's Green Rd
CON/LDGT DH8 ... 122 C1
Soane Gdns *HAR/WTLS* NE34 ... 91 H1
Softley Pl *BW/LEM/TK/HW* NE15 ... 68 D4
Solingen Est *BLYTH* NE24 ... 35 H2
Solway Av *TYNE/NSHE* NE30 ... 50 E7
Solway Rd *HEBB* NE31 ... 73 G7
Solway Sq *SUNDSW* SR3 ... 119 J3
Somersby Dr *GOS/KPK* NE3 ... 55 J5
Somerset Cl *ASHGTN* NE63 ... 23 G1
Somerset Gdns
WLSD/HOW NE28 ... 58 C7 6
Somerset Gv *NSHW* NE29 ... 60 B2 5
Somerset Pl *ELS/FEN* NE4 ... 4 D7
Somerset Rd *CON/LDGT* DH8 ... 137 F1
HEBB NE31 ... 89 H1 5
SUNDSW SR3 ... 119 H3
Somerset Sq *SUNDSW* SR3 ... 119 H3 2
Somerset St *SUNDSW* SR3 ... 120 A5 1
Somerton Ct *GOS/KPK* NE3 ... 55 G4
Sophia St *SEA/MUR* SR7 ... 150 E1
Sophy St *SWCK/CAS* SR5 ... 106 B3 12
Sorley St *MLFD/PNYW* SR4 ... 106 A7
Sorrel Cl *ASHGTN* NE63 ... 23 J3
Sorrel Gdns *HAR/WTLS* NE34 ... 91 J1
Soulby Ct *DIN/WO* NE13 ... 55 H2
Sourmilk Hill La
LWF/SPW/WRK NE9 ... 87 G6
Souter Rd *GOS/KPK* NE3 ... 56 A5 7
South Ap *CLSW/PEL* DH2 ... 129 J5
South Av *HAR/WTLS* NE34 ... 75 K6
South Bailey *DHAM* DH1 ... 16 D6
South Bend *GOS/KPK* NE3 ... 56 B1
South Bents Av
CLDN/WHIT/ROK SR6 ... 92 E6
South Benwell Rd
BW/LEM/TK/HW NE15 ... 69 G7
Southburn Cl *HLS* DH4 ... 132 A7 2
South Burns *CLS/BIR/GTL* DH3 ... 129 J3
South Cl *HAR/WTLS* NE34 ... 75 K6
HLH DH5 ... 160 C1
RYTON NE40 ... 66 E7
Southcote *WICK/BNPF* NE16 ... 84 E7
South Crs *BOLCOL* NE35 ... 90 D4
SEA/MUR SR7 ... 151 F1
WASHS NE38 ... 116 D6
South Cft *LGB/KIL* NE12 ... 58 A3
Southcroft *WASHS* NE38 ... 117 F5
South Cross St *CON/LDGT* DH8 ... 123 J3
South Dene *HAR/WTLS* NE34 ... 75 F6
South Dr *CLDN/WHIT/ROK* SR6 ... 91 K3 2
DIN/WO NE13 ... 36 D2
DIN/WO NE13 ... 54 D2
HEBB NE31 ... 72 E7
South Eldon St *SSH* NE33 ... 75 F4
Southend Av *BLYTH* NE24 ... 34 E1
Southend Rd
LWF/SPW/WRK NE9 ... 87 H7
SUNDSW SR3 ... 119 J4
Southern Cl *ASHGTN* NE63 ... 24 D2
Southern Rd *BYK/HTN/WLK* NE6 ... 72 B7
Southern Wy *RYTON* NE40 ... 66 E7 1
Southey St *SSH* NE33 ... 75 H3 6
South Farm *BDLGTN* NE22 ... 28 A6
Southfield *CLSW/PEL* DH2 ... 114 E7
Southfield Gdns
WICK/BNPF NE16 ... 85 G5
Southfield La *CHPW* NE17 ... 110 B3
Southfield Rd *HAR/WTLS* NE34 ... 75 K3
LGB/KIL NE12 ... 57 J4
WICK/BNPF NE16 ... 85 G6
Southfields *CRAM* NE23 ... 47 G1 1
Southfield Ter
BYK/HTN/WLK NE6 ... 72 C7 10
Southfield Wy *DHAM* DH1 ... 156 B5
Southfork
BW/LEM/TK/HW NE15 ... 68 A3
South Frederick St *SSH* NE33 ... 75 F4 6
Southgate *LGB/KIL* NE12 ... 47 K7
South Grange Pk *SEA/MUR* SR7 ... 135 F5
South Gv *RYTON* NE40 ... 67 F7
South Hetton Rd *HLH* DH5 ... 160 C1
South Hill Rd *GATE* NE8 ... 10 B6
Southhill Rd *HAR/WTLS* NE34 ... 76 A5
Southlands *JRW* NE32 ... 90 B3
LGB/HTN NE7 ... 71 G1
TYNE/NSHE NE30 ... 61 F2
South La *BOL* NE36 ... 91 G5
South Lea *BDN/LAN/SAC* DH7 ... 155 G1
South Magdalene
CON/LDGT DH8 ... 109 H5
South Market St *HLH* DH5 ... 148 A4
Southmayne Rd
MLFD/PNYW SR4 ... 119 H2 4
Southmead Av
WD/WHPE/BLK NE5 ... 69 F2
South Mdw *STLY/ANP* DH9 ... 111 F6
South Moor Rd *STLY/ANP* DH9 ... 126 C3
South Nelson Rd *CRAM* NE23 ... 32 E7
South Newsham Rd *BLYTH* NE24 ... 34 E4
South Pde *FELL* NE10 ... 13 L4
RDHAMSE DH6 ... 172 C6
WBAY NE26 ... 51 F4
South Preston Gv *NSHW* NE29 ... 2 B2
South Railway St
SEA/MUR SR7 ... 150 E1
South Rdg *ASHGTN* NE63 ... 24 D3
GOS/KPK NE3 ... 56 B2
South Riggs *BDLGTN* NE22 ... 29 F6
South Rd *CHPW* NE17 ... 95 J4
DHAM DH1 ... 168 D4
PRUD NE42 ... 80 D2
South Rw *GATE* NE8 ... 6 D9
South Shore Rd *GATE* NE8 ... 6 B8
South Side *PLEE/EAS* SR8 ... 162 C6
South St *CLSW/PEL* DH2 ... 129 H3
CNUT NE1 ... 5 J9
DHAM DH1 ... 16 C5
GATE NE8 ... 11 H6
GOS/KPK NE3 ... 56 A5 5
HLH DH5 ... 147 F4 2
HLS DH4 ... 132 B4
ROWG NE39 ... 96 B1
SMOOR NE27 ... 49 H5
SUND SR1 ... 14 E4
South Ter *BDN/LAN/SAC* DH7 ... 165 J1
DHAM DH1 ... 156 B4
PLEE/EAS SR8 ... 175 G3
SEA/MUR SR7 ... 151 F1 5
SWCK/CAS SR5 ... 106 B4 7
WLSD/HOW NE28 ... 73 G1
South Vw *ASHGTN* NE63 ... 23 J1 1
BDN/LAN/SAC DH7 ... 167 H7
BLYTH NE24 ... 34 E3
CLDN/WHIT/ROK SR6 ... 106 D2
CLS/BIR/GTL DH3 ... 115 K2
CON/LDGT DH8 ... 122 C3
HLH DH5 ... 160 C2
JRW NE32 ... 73 J5
MPTH NE61 ... 21 J2
RHTLP TS27 ... 184 C2
SEA/MUR SR7 ... 150 A3
STKFD/GP NE62 ... 22 E6 7
STLY/ANP DH9 ... 111 K4
WASHS NE38 ... 117 G5
WD/WHPE/BLK NE5 ... 68 C3
South View Rd
MLFD/PNYW SR4 ... 118 E1
South View Ter *HLS* DH4 ... 131 K7
WICK/BNPF NE16 ... 85 F4
South Vw West
BYK/HTN/WLK NE6 ... 6 D4
Southward *WBAY* NE26 ... 41 G3
Southward Cl *WBAY* NE26 ... 41 G3 3
Southward Wy *MONK* NE25 ... 40 B7
Southway *BDN/LAN/SAC* DH7 ... 140 B4
BW/LEM/TK/HW NE15 ... 68 C4
LWF/SPW/WRK NE9 ... 87 H6
PLEE/EAS SR8 ... 174 D5
Southwick Rd *SWCK/CAS* SR5 ... 14 E1 1
SWCK/CAS SR5 ... 106 D4 5
Southwold Gdns
SUNDSW SR3 ... 119 K6 3
Southwold Pl *CRAM* NE23 ... 37 K2 5
South Woodbine St *SSH* NE33 ... 3 K7
Southwood Gdns *GOS/KPK* NE3 ... 55 K6
Sovereign Pl *ELS/FEN* NE4 ... 4 C8
Spa Dr *CON/LDGT* DH8 ... 108 C7
Spalding Cl *LGB/HTN* NE7 ... 57 J6 7
Sparkwell Cl *HLS* DH4 ... 132 B3 2
Spartylea *WASHS* NE38 ... 117 H5 1
Spa Well Cl *BLAY* NE21 ... 83 K4
Spa Well Dr *SWCK/CAS* SR5 ... 105 G3
Speedwell Ct *ASHGTN* NE63 ... 23 H4
Spelter Works Rd
ASHBK/HED/RY SR2 ... 121 F3
Spelvit La *MPTH* NE61 ... 20 C6
Spen Burn *ROWG* NE39 ... 96 C1
Spencer Cl *STLY/ANP* DH9 ... 127 F1
Spencer Ct *BLYTH* NE24 ... 30 D5
Spencer Dr *MPTH* NE61 ... 21 J2
Spencer Gv *WICK/BNPF* NE16 ... 85 F4 4
Spencer Rd *BLYTH* NE24 ... 30 D5
Spencers Bank
WICK/BNPF NE16 ... 84 E3 5
Spencer St *BYK/HTN/WLK* NE6 ... 7 H1
CON/LDGT DH8 ... 123 F5
NSHW NE29 ... 2 D3 2
Spence Ter *NSHW* NE29 ... 2 B2
Spenfield Rd
WD/WHPE/BLK NE5 ... 55 H7 4
Spen La *ROWG* NE39 ... 96 C2
RYTON NE40 ... 82 B5
Spen Rd *ROWG* NE39 ... 96 B1
Spenser St *JRW* NE32 ... 73 K3 5
Spen St *STLY/ANP* DH9 ... 126 C2
Spetchells *PRUD* NE42 ... 80 D1 4
Spinneyside Gdns
DUN/TMV NE11 ... 85 K5
The Spinney *CRAM* NE23 ... 47 J1
MPTH NE61 ... 20 E7 2
PLEE/EAS SR8 ... 162 B5
WASHS NE38 ... 117 F4
Spire Hollin *PLEE/EAS* SR8 ... 174 D4
Spire Rd *WASHN* NE37 ... 103 H6
Spires La *BYK/HTN/WLK* NE6 ... 7 H5
Spital Crs *NWBGN* NE64 ... 24 E2
Spital Rd *NWBGN* NE64 ... 24 E2
Spital Ter *GOS/KPK* NE3 ... 56 C5
Split Crow Rd *GATE* NE8 ... 11 J7
Spohr Ter *SSH* NE33 ... 75 H2
Spoor St *DUN/TMV* NE11 ... 9 H6
Spout La *WASHN* NE37 ... 103 F6
WASHS NE38 ... 103 F7
Springbank Rd *JES* NE2 ... 6 C2
SUNDSW SR3 ... 119 H3
Springbank Sq *SUNDSW* SR3 ... 119 H3 5
Springdale Av *TRIM* TS29 ... 183 G6 4
Springfield *NSHW* NE29 ... 2 C1 2
PRUD NE42 ... 63 G7
Springfield Av
LWF/SPW/WRK NE9 ... 101 J4
Springfield Cl *PRUD* NE42 ... 63 H7
Springfield Crs *SEA/MUR* SR7 ... 150 D2
Springfield Gdns
CLS/BIR/GTL DH3 ... 129 J2
WLSD/HOW NE28 ... 58 B7
Springfield Gv *MONK* NE25 ... 50 C6
Springfield Pk *DHAM* DH1 ... 156 B6
Springfield Pl
LWF/SPW/WRK NE9 ... 87 G6
Springfield Rd *BLAY* NE21 ... 83 K2
HLS DH4 ... 132 B4 3
WD/WHPE/BLK NE5 ... 69 G2 6
Spring Garden Cl *SUND* SR1 ... 15 H4 3
Springhill Gdns
BW/LEM/TK/HW NE15 ... 69 H5
Springhill Wk *MPTH* NE61 ... 20 C6
Springhouse Cl *CON/LDGT* DH8 ... 108 E4
Springhouse La *CON/LDGT* DH8 ... 108 E5
Spring Pk *BDLGTN* NE22 ... 29 G6
Springside *BDN/LAN/SAC* DH7 ... 143 H5
The Springs *CLS/BIR/GTL* DH3 ... 115 K3
Spring St *ELS/FEN* NE4 ... 4 F5 1
Springsyde Cl
WICK/BNPF NE16 ... 84 C7 4
Spring Ter *NSHW* NE29 ... 2 C1
Springwell Av
BDN/LAN/SAC DH7 ... 154 B3
BYK/HTN/WLK NE6 ... 7 L8
DHAM DH1 ... 156 B6
JRW NE32 ... 74 A5
LWF/SPW/WRK NE9 ... 101 J3 1
Springwell Cl
BDN/LAN/SAC DH7 ... 154 B3 2
Springwell Rd *DHAM* DH1 ... 156 B6
JRW NE32 ... 73 K6
LWF/SPW/WRK NE9 ... 101 K2
MLFD/PNYW SR4 ... 119 H3
Springwood *HEBB* NE31 ... 72 E4
The Square *STKFD/GP* NE62 ... 22 E6 5
Squires Gdns *FELL* NE10 ... 87 K5
Stack Garth *BDN/LAN/SAC* DH7 ... 167 H5
Stadium Wy *SWCK/CAS* SR5 ... 14 D1
Stafford Gv
ASHBK/HED/RY SR2 ... 134 E1 1
SWCK/CAS SR5 ... 106 B3
Stafford Pl *PLEE/EAS* SR8 ... 174 C3
Staffordshire Dr *DHAM* DH1 ... 158 A6
Staffords La
CLDN/WHIT/ROK SR6 ... 93 F4 2
Stafford St *SUND* SR1 ... 15 J2
Stagshaw *LGB/KIL* NE12 ... 47 J4 5
Staindrop *FELL* NE10 ... 88 C7
Staindrop Rd *DHAM* DH1 ... 156 E3
Staines Rd *BYK/HTN/WLK* NE6 ... 7 K8 2
Stainmore Dr *CLS/BIR/GTL* DH3 ... 145 J2
Stainton Dr *FELL* NE10 ... 12 D7
Stainton Gv
CLDN/WHIT/ROK SR6 ... 92 C7
Stainton St East *SSH* NE33 ... 75 H2 11
Stainton Wy *PLEE/EAS* SR8 ... 174 D4
Staithes Av *LGB/KIL* NE12 ... 57 J4
Staithes La *MPTH* NE61 ... 20 E4
Staithes Rd *WASHS* NE38 ... 117 J3
Staithes St *BYK/HTN/WLK* NE6 ... 72 D5
Staith La *BLAY* NE21 ... 67 J7
Staiths Rd *DUN/TMV* NE11 ... 9 J5
Stakeford Crs *STKFD/GP* NE62 ... 23 H6
Stakeford La *STKFD/GP* NE62 ... 23 G6
Stalks Rd *DIN/WO* NE13 ... 46 B3
Stamford Av *MONK* NE25 ... 40 B6
SUNDSW SR3 ... 119 K3
Stamfordham Av *NSHW* NE29 ... 60 B5
Stamfordham Cl
WLSD/HOW NE28 ... 72 C1 3
Stamfordham Ms
WD/WHPE/BLK NE5 ... 69 H2 5
Stamfordham Rd
PONT/DH NE20 ... 52 B2
WD/WHPE/BLK NE5 ... 53 H4
Stampley Cl *BLAY* NE21 ... 83 J4 2
Stamps La *SUND* SR1 ... 15 J3
Stancley Rd *PRUD* NE42 ... 80 E2
Standfield Gdns *FELL* NE10 ... 88 E4 2
Standish St *STLY/ANP* DH9 ... 126 B2
Stanelaw Wy *STLY/ANP* DH9 ... 112 D5
Staneway *FELL* NE10 ... 102 A1
Stanfield Ct *LGB/HTN* NE7 ... 58 A7 4
Stanhope *WASHS* NE38 ... 116 B1
Stanhope Cl
BDN/LAN/SAC DH7 ... 167 H6 5
DHAM DH1 ... 156 E2
HLS DH4 ... 147 G1
Stanhope Pde *SSH* NE33 ... 75 H3 7
Stanhope Rd
CLDN/WHIT/ROK SR6 ... 106 E1
HAR/WTLS NE34 ... 75 F5
JRW NE32 ... 74 B6
SSH NE33 ... 75 H4
Stanhope St *ELS/FEN* NE4 ... 4 D5
SSH NE33 ... 3 H6
Stanley Cl *RDHAMSE* DH6 ... 170 C1
Stanley Crs *PRUD* NE42 ... 80 E1
Stanley Gdns
CON/LDGT DH8 ... 123 F4 13
LWF/SPW/WRK NE9 ... 101 J3
Stanley Gv *BDLGTN* NE22 ... 29 H5
LGB/HTN NE7 ... 57 G7
Stanley St *BLYTH* NE24 ... 31 H6
CON/LDGT DH8 ... 123 F4
ELS/FEN NE4 ... 4 A9 1
HAR/WTLS NE34 ... 75 F6
JRW NE32 ... 74 A4
NSHW NE29 ... 2 D3
SEA/MUR SR7 ... 135 H7
SWCK/CAS SR5 ... 105 F4 5
WLSD/HOW NE28 ... 59 H7
Stanley St West *NSHW* NE29 ... 2 C3
Stanmore Rd
BYK/HTN/WLK NE6 ... 71 J2
Stannerford Rd *RYTON* NE40 ... 66 A6
Stannington Av
BYK/HTN/WLK NE6 ... 6 E2
Stannington Gdns
ASHBK/HED/RY SR2 ... 120 C4 5
Stannington Gv
ASHBK/HED/RY SR2 ... 120 C4
Stannington Pl
BYK/HTN/WLK NE6 ... 6 F2
PONT/DH NE20 ... 43 G1
Stannington Rd *NSHW* NE29 ... 60 A5
Stannington Station Rd
MPTH NE61 ... 27 G7
Stannington St *BLYTH* NE24 ... 31 H7
Stansfield St
CLDN/WHIT/ROK SR6 ... 106 E4
Stanstead Cl *SWCK/CAS* SR5 ... 104 E5 2
Stanton Av *BLYTH* NE24 ... 34 D2
HAR/WTLS NE34 ... 75 J4
Stanton Cl *FELL* NE10 ... 89 F5
Stanton Dr *MPTH* NE61 ... 21 H2
Stanton Rd *SMOOR* NE27 ... 49 G7
TYNE/NSHE NE30 ... 60 D1
Stanton St *ELS/FEN* NE4 ... 4 D5
Stanway Dr *LGB/HTN* NE7 ... 57 G7
Stanwick St *TYNE/NSHE* NE30 ... 61 H2 5
Stapeley Vw *GOS/KPK* NE3 ... 55 H5
Staple Rd *JRW* NE32 ... 73 K3
Stapylton Dr
ASHBK/HED/RY SR2 ... 120 B2
Starbeck Av *JES* NE2 ... 6 A2
Starbeck Ms *JES* NE2 ... 6 A2 1
Stardale Av *BLYTH* NE24 ... 34 C1
Stargate Cl *BDN/LAN/SAC* DH7 ... 153 K3
Stargate La *RYTON* NE40 ... 67 G7
Starlight Crs *MONK* NE25 ... 39 K5 5
Startforth Cl
CLS/BIR/GTL DH3 ... 145 J1 5
Station Ap *BOL* NE36 ... 91 J5
DHAM DH1 ... 16 B3
LGB/KIL NE12 ... 57 K4 5
SSH NE33 ... 3 H6 1
Station Av *BDN/LAN/SAC* DH7 ... 165 H2
BDN/LAN/SAC DH7 ... 167 H6
HLH DH5 ... 147 K5
Station Bank *DHAM* DH1 ... 16 C3 1
PSHWF NE43 ... 79 J2
RYTON NE40 ... 66 E5
Station Crs *SEA/MUR* SR7 ... 135 H7
Station Est East *SEA/MUR* SR7 ... 149 F5
Station Est North
SEA/MUR SR7 ... 149 F5
Station Est South
SEA/MUR SR7 ... 149 F5
Station Field Rd *STLY/ANP* DH9 ... 112 D5
Station La *CLS/BIR/GTL* DH3 ... 115 H2
CLSW/PEL DH2 ... 128 D1
DHAM DH1 ... 17 G2
WNGT TS28 ... 183 K5
Station Rd *ASHBK/HED/RY* SR2 ... 135 G1
ASHGTN NE63 ... 23 J1 2
BDLGTN NE22 ... 29 J4
BDN/LAN/SAC DH7 ... 140 C5
BDN/LAN/SAC DH7 ... 166 E1
BDN/LAN/SAC DH7 ... 167 H6
BOLCOL NE35 ... 90 C2
BW/LEM/TK/HW NE15 ... 66 B1
BW/LEM/TK/HW NE15 ... 67 H4
CLS/BIR/GTL DH3 ... 129 J4
CLSW/PEL DH2 ... 129 J4
CRAM NE23 ... 38 C1 2
CRAM NE23 ... 39 G7
CRAM NE23 ... 47 F1
DIN/WO NE13 ... 55 F4
FELL NE10 ... 13 L3
GOS/KPK NE3 ... 56 E5
HEBB NE31 ... 73 F5
HLH DH5 ... 147 K5
HLS DH4 ... 117 H6
HLS DH4 ... 131 J1 5
HLS DH4 ... 132 B6
HLS DH4 ... 146 C7
LGB/KIL NE12 ... 47 H6
LGB/KIL NE12 ... 57 K4
LWF/SPW/WRK NE9 ... 86 E7
NSHW NE29 ... 60 B6
PLEE/EAS SR8 ... 163 G5
PRUD NE42 ... 80 B1
RDHAMSE DH6 ... 158 D2
RDHAMSE DH6 ... 173 G3
RHTLP TS27 ... 185 H2
ROWG NE39 ... 97 H4
SEA/MUR SR7 ... 135 F7
SEA/MUR SR7 ... 149 F5
SMOOR NE27 ... 49 F6
SSH NE33 ... 3 G8
STLY/ANP DH9 ... 112 D7
STLY/ANP DH9 ... 113 J6
STLY/ANP DH9 ... 126 D3
SWCK/CAS SR5 ... 106 C1
TRIM TS29 ... 182 E5
TYNE/NSHE NE30 ... 51 G6
WASHS NE38 ... 117 G1
WASHS NE38 ... 117 G5
WBAY NE26 ... 51 F5
WLSD/HOW NE28 ... 58 B5
WLSD/HOW NE28 ... 72 C1
WLSD/HOW NE28 ... 72 E2
WLSD/HOW NE28 ... 73 J2
WNGT TS28 ... 183 K5
WYLAM NE41 ... 65 H5
Station Rd North
LGB/KIL NE12 ... 57 K2 5
Station St *BDN/LAN/SAC* DH7 ... 165 F4
BLYTH NE24 ... 31 G6
RDHAMSE DH6 ... 160 E6
SUND SR1 ... 14 E4
Station Ter *TYNE/NSHE* NE30 ... 61 H3
Station Vw *BDN/LAN/SAC* DH7 ... 165 H2
HLH DH5 ... 147 K5
Staveley Rd
CLDN/WHIT/ROK SR6 ... 92 C7
PLEE/EAS SR8 ... 175 F4
Stavordale St *SEA/MUR* SR7 ... 150 E2 5
Stavordale St West
SEA/MUR SR7 ... 150 E3 5
Stavordale Ter
LWF/SPW/WRK NE9 ... 11 K9
Staward Av *MONK* NE25 ... 40 A6
Staward Ter
BYK/HTN/WLK NE6 ... 72 B7 2
Staynebrigg *FELL* NE10 ... 88 C6 5
Stead La *BDLGTN* NE22 ... 29 H5
The Steads *MPTH* NE61 ... 20 E7
Stead St *WLSD/HOW* NE28 ... 59 J7
Steavenson St *RDHAMSE* DH6 ... 180 A3
Stedham Cl *WASHN* NE37 ... 103 G3
Steel St *CON/LDGT* DH8 ... 123 F4
Steep Hl *SUNDSW* SR3 ... 119 F6
Stella Bank *BLAY* NE21 ... 67 H6
Stella Hall *BLAY* NE21 ... 67 J7
Stella La *BLAY* NE21 ... 67 H7
Stella Rd *BLAY* NE21 ... 67 J4
Stephenson Cl *HLH* DH5 ... 148 A4 2
Stephenson Rd
BYK/HTN/WLK NE6 ... 71 H2
PLEE/EAS SR8 ... 174 D1
WASHN NE37 ... 103 G3
Stephenson St *GATE* NE8 ... 10 C8
SEA/MUR SR7 ... 149 H5 5
TYNE/NSHE NE30 ... 2 E1
TYNE/NSHE NE30 ... 61 H3 5
WLSD/HOW NE28 ... 73 K2
Stephenson Ter *FELL* NE10 ... 12 C9
Stephenson Wy *BLAY* NE21 ... 83 K4
STKFD/GP NE62 ... 29 G2
Stephens Rd *SEA/MUR* SR7 ... 149 G5
Stephen St *BLYTH* NE24 ... 31 G6
BYK/HTN/WLK NE6 ... 6 D5
CON/LDGT DH8 ... 123 F4
Stepney Bank *CNUT* NE1 ... 6 C5
Stepney La *CNUT* NE1 ... 6 A6
Stepney Rd *JES* NE2 ... 6 B4
Sterling St *MLFD/PNYW* SR4 ... 106 A7
Steward Crs *HAR/WTLS* NE34 ... 76 B4
Stewart Av *ASHBK/HED/RY* SR2 ... 134 E1
Stewart Dr *BOL* NE36 ... 91 F5 7
WNGT TS28 ... 183 K2
Stewart St *MLFD/PNYW* SR4 ... 106 A7
PLEE/EAS SR8 ... 162 E5
SEA/MUR SR7 ... 151 F2
SUNDSW SR3 ... 120 A7
Stileford *FELL* NE10 ... 13 K9
Stirling Av *JRW* NE32 ... 74 C7
ROWG NE39 ... 97 G4
Stirling Cl *WASHS* NE38 ... 117 H2
Stirling Dr *BDLGTN* NE22 ... 29 J4
NSHW NE29 ... 60 A2
Stirling La *ROWG* NE39 ... 97 G4
Stobart St
BDN/LAN/SAC DH7 ... 143 G1 1
SWCK/CAS SR5 ... 14 D1
Stobhill Vls *MPTH* NE61 ... 20 E6
Stockerley Br *CON/LDGT* DH8 ... 139 G2
Stockerley La
BDN/LAN/SAC DH7 ... 139 G2
Stockerley Rd *CON/LDGT* DH8 ... 123 H6
Stockholm Cl *NSHW* NE29 ... 59 K5
Stockley Av *SWCK/CAS* SR5 ... 105 G3 5
Stockley Ct *BDN/LAN/SAC* DH7 ... 167 H1
Stockley Gv
BDN/LAN/SAC DH7 ... 176 D4 1
Stockley La *BDN/LAN/SAC* DH7 ... 176 C4
Stocksfield Av
WD/WHPE/BLK NE5 ... 69 G4
Stockton Rd
ASHBK/HED/RY SR2 ... 14 D7
ASHBK/HED/RY SR2 ... 135 F2
DHAM DH1 ... 16 E7
NSHW NE29 ... 2 A6
PLEE/EAS SR8 ... 162 B7
SEA/MUR SR7 ... 135 F5
SEA/MUR SR7 ... 162 B1
SUND SR1 ... 14 D6 2
Stockton St *SEA/MUR* SR7 ... 135 H7
Stockwell Gn *BYK/HTN/WLK* NE6 ... 72 B3
Stoddart St *HAR/WTLS* NE34 ... 75 G5 1
JES NE2 ... 6 B4
Stoker Av *HAR/WTLS* NE34 ... 74 D7
Stoker Cressent
RDHAMSE DH6 ... 182 D2 5
Stoker Ter *ROWG* NE39 ... 96 C2 2
Stokesley Gv *LGB/HTN* NE7 ... 57 G7
Stokoe Dr *ASHGTN* NE63 ... 24 C2
Stokoe St *CON/LDGT* DH8 ... 122 E3 2
Stone Cellar Rd *WASHN* NE37 ... 102 D3
Stonechat Pl *LGB/KIL* NE12 ... 57 G3
Stonecroft Gdns *LGB/HTN* NE7 ... 57 K7
Stonecross *ASHGTN* NE63 ... 23 H3
Stonefold Cl
WD/WHPE/BLK NE5 ... 55 F7 5
Stonegate
BW/LEM/TK/HW NE15 ... 64 D2
Stonehaugh Wy *PONT/DH* NE20 ... 42 D7
Stoneleigh *MPTH* NE61 ... 27 J2
Stoneleigh Av *LGB/KIL* NE12 ... 57 G3
Stoneleigh Cl *HLS* DH4 ... 132 A6 1
Stone Rw *CLSW/PEL* DH2 ... 128 A2
Stonesdale *HLS* DH4 ... 117 G6
Stone St *FELL* NE10 ... 87 J6
Stoneygate La *FELL* NE10 ... 12 E6
Stoneyhurst Av
BW/LEM/TK/HW NE15 ... 69 F6 5
Stoneyhurst Rd *GOS/KPK* NE3 ... 56 E6
Stoney La *LWF/SPW/WRK* NE9 ... 102 B4
SWCK/CAS SR5 ... 106 A4 10
Stoneylea Cl *RYTON* NE40 ... 82 A1 5
Stoneylea Rd
WD/WHPE/BLK NE5 ... 68 D3
Stonybank Wy *PSHWF* NE43 ... 79 J4
Stonyflat Bank *PRUD* NE42 ... 80 C2
Stonyheap La *CON/LDGT* DH8 ... 124 D5
Stony La *STLY/ANP* DH9 ... 114 A6
Store Farm Rd *NWBGN* NE64 ... 18 E7
Store St
BW/LEM/TK/HW NE15 ... 68 A5 5
CON/LDGT DH8 ... 123 F4
Storey Crs *NWBGN* NE64 ... 19 F7
Storey La *BLAY* NE21 ... 67 J7 1
Stormont St *NSHW* NE29 ... 2 B3
Stotfold Cl *SEA/MUR* SR7 ... 134 E7
Stothard St *JRW* NE32 ... 74 A4
Stotts Rd *BYK/HTN/WLK* NE6 ... 72 C3
Stowe Gdns *MPTH* NE61 ... 21 J1
Stowell St *CNUT* NE1 ... 5 H7
The Stow *LGB/KIL* NE12 ... 57 G5
Straker St *JRW* NE32 ... 74 B5
Straker Ter *HAR/WTLS* NE34 ... 75 F6
The Strand *SUNDSW* SR3 ... 119 J6 5
Strangford Rd *SEA/MUR* SR7 ... 150 C1
Strangways St *SEA/MUR* SR7 ... 150 E2 7
Stranton Ter
CLDN/WHIT/ROK SR6 ... 106 D3
Stratfield St
MLFD/PNYW SR4 ... 105 J6 5
Stratford Av
ASHBK/HED/RY SR2 ... 120 E3
Stratford Cl *CRAM* NE23 ... 37 K1
LGB/KIL NE12 ... 48 A6
Stratford Gdns
CON/LDGT DH8 ... 123 F3 5
LWF/SPW/WRK NE9 ... 87 F6 5
Stratford Gv West
BYK/HTN/WLK NE6 ... 6 C3
Stratford Rd *BYK/HTN/WLK* NE6 ... 6 D3
Strathearn Wy *GOS/KPK* NE3 ... 55 K3
Strathmore Av *ROWG* NE39 ... 97 G4 1
Strathmore Cl *STLY/ANP* DH9 ... 113 F7
Strathmore Crs *ELS/FEN* NE4 ... 69 J6
Strathmore Rd *GOS/KPK* NE3 ... 56 C3

Strathmore Sq *SUNDSW* SR3 .... 119 J4 🟦
Stratton Cl *ASHBK/HED/RY* SR2 .. 121 G6
Stratus Ct *SUNDSW* SR3................ 134 A1
Strawberry Gdns
   WLSD/HOW NE28 .... 58 C6
Strawberry La *CNUT* NE1 .... 5 H5
   DHAM DH1 .... 169 H6
Strawberry Pl *CNUT* NE1 .... 5 H5
Street Gate Pk *WICK/BNPF* NE16 .. 99 C6
Stretton Cl *HLS* DH4 .... 146 D1 🟦
Stretton Wy *SMOOR* NE27 .... 48 E4
Stridingedge *WASHN* NE37 .... 102 C7
Strothers Rd *ROWG* NE39 .... 82 B7
Stuart Ct *GOS/KPK* NE3 .... 55 F4
Stuart Gdns
   BW/LEM/TK/HW NE15 .... 66 E1
Stubbs Av *WICK/BNPF* NE16 ...... 84 E4 🟦
Studdon Wk *GOS/KPK* NE3 .... 55 H5
Studley Gdns
   LWF/SPW/WRK NE9 .... 87 F7 🟦
   MONK NE25 .... 50 E5
Studley Ter *ELS/FEN* NE4 .... 4 A3
Studley Vls *LGB/KIL* NE12 .... 58 A3 🟦
Sturdee Gdns *JES* NE2 .... 56 E7
Styford Gdns
   BW/LEM/TK/HW NE15 .... 68 C4 🟦
Success Rd *HLS* DH4 .... 131 K2
Sudbury Wy *CRAM* NE23................. 37 K1
Suddick St *SWCK/CAS* SR5 .... 106 B4 🟦
Suez St *TYNE/NSHE* NE30 .... 2 E1
Suffolk Cl *ASHGTN* NE63 .... 23 C1
Suffolk Gdns *HAR/WTLS* NE34 ...... 76 C4
   WLSD/HOW NE28 .... 59 C6
Suffolk Pl *CLS/BIR/GTL* DH3 .... 115 K5
   GATE NE8 .... 6 C9
Suffolk Rd *HEBB* NE31 .... 89 H1
Suffolk St *ASHBK/HED/RY* SR2 ... 15 H8
   JRW NE32 .... 73 K5
Suffolk Wk *PLEE/EAS* SR8 .... 174 D2 🟦
Suffolk Wy *DHAM* DH1 .... 156 E1 🟦
Sugley Dr *BW/LEM/TK/HW* NE15 .. 68 B5
Sugley St *BW/LEM/TK/HW* NE15 .. 68 B5
Sulgrave Rd *WASHN* NE37 .... 103 H4
Sullivan Wk *HEBB* NE31 .... 73 G6
Summerdale *CON/LDGT* DH8 ...... 108 C7
Summerfield *STLY/ANP* DH9 .... 128 A1
Summerfield Rd
   LWF/SPW/WRK NE9 .... 11 H9
   JRW NE32 .... 90 B3
   SUNDSW SR3 .... 119 F7
Summerhill *BLAY* NE21 .... 83 K1
Summerhill Av *GOS/KPK* NE3 .... 56 D1
Summerhill Gv *ELS/FEN* NE4 .... 4 F7
Summerhill Rd *HAR/WTLS* NE34 ... 75 K4
Summerhill St *ELS/FEN* NE4 .... 4 F8
Summerhill Ter *CNUT* NE1 .... 5 G4
Summerhouse Farm
   HLH DH5 .... 147 G3 🟦
Summerhouse La *ASHGTN* NE63 ... 18 D7
Summerson St *HLH* DH5 .... 148 A4
Summerson Wy *BDLGTN* NE22...... 29 K4
Summer St *FELL* NE10 .... 12 C6
Summerville *DHAM* DH1 .... 16 B5
Sunbury Av *JES* NE2 .... 70 E1
Sunderland Av *PLEE/EAS* SR8...... 175 G2
Sunderland Hwy *WASHS* NE38 .... 102 B7
Sunderland Rd *BOL* NE36 .... 91 J5
   CLDN/WHIT/ROK SR6 .... 92 B4
   DHAM DH1 .... 17 K2
   FELL NE10 .... 12 A3
   FELL NE10 .... 89 F4 🟦
   GATE NE8 .... 11 H3
   HAR/WTLS NE34...................... 75 J4
   HLS DH4 .... 132 A6
   PLEE/EAS SR8.......................162 C5
   SEA/MUR SR7....................... 162 C3
   SSH NE33 .... 75 H3
   SWCK/CAS SR5 .... 106 A3
Sunderland St *CNUT* NE1 .... 5 H8
   HLH DH5 .... 132 C6
   HLS DH4 .... 132 C7 🟦
Sundew Rd *LWF/SPW/WRK* NE9 ... 87 J2
Sundridge Dr *FELL* NE10 .... 88 C5
Sunholme Dr *WLSD/HOW* NE28 .... 58 C5
Sunlea Av *TYNE/NSHE* NE30 .... 51 G7
Sunnidale *WICK/BNPF* NE16 .... 84 C7
Sunnilaws *HAR/WTLS* NE34.......... 76 A7
Sunniside Gdns
   BW/LEM/TK/HW NE15 .... 69 F5 🟦
Sunniside La
   CLDN/WHIT/ROK SR6 .... 92 B2
Sunniside Rd *WICK/BNPF* NE16 ... 85 F7 🟦
Sunniside Ter
   CLDN/WHIT/ROK SR6 .... 92 A2
Sunnybank Av
   BW/LEM/TK/HW NE15 .... 69 H6
Sunnybanks *BDN/LAN/SAC* DH7.. 140 B4
Sunny Blunts *PLEE/EAS* SR8.......174 D6
Sunny Brae *RYTON* NE40 .... 82 B4 🟦
Sunnybrow *SUNDSW* SR3 .... 119 K6
Sunnycrest Av
   BYK/HTN/WLK NE6 .... 72 B5
Sunny Ter *STLY/ANP* DH9 .... 112 C7
Sunnyway *WD/WHPE/BLK* NE5 ..... 69 G1
Surrey Av *SUNDSW* SR3 .... 134 A1
Surrey Cl *ASHGTN* NE63 .... 23 C1 🟦
Surrey Crs *CON/LDGT* DH8 .... 137 G3
Surrey Pl *ELS/FEN* NE4 .... 4 D7
Surrey Rd *HEBB* NE31 .... 89 H1
   NSHW NE29 .... 60 B4 🟦
Surrey St *JRW* NE32 .... 73 J5

Surtees Av *RDHAMSE* DH6 .... 180 A2
Surtees Dr *DHAM* DH1 .... 156 B7
Surtees Pl *CON/LDGT* DH8 .... 122 C2
Surtees Rd *PLEE/EAS* SR8 .... 175 F4
Sussex Gdns *WLSD/HOW* NE28.... 59 G7
Sussex Pl *WASHN* NE37 .... 103 C6 🟦
Sussex Rd *SLYTH* NE24 .... 31 H6 🟦
Sutherland Av *ELS/FEN* NE4 .... 69 J4
   NWBGN NE64 .... 25 F1
Sutherland Ct
   HAR/WTLS NE34...................... 91 H2 🟦
Sutherland Gra *HLS* DH4 .... 132 B1 🟦
Sutherland St
   CLDN/WHIT/ROK SR6 .... 106 D3
   SEA/MUR SR7........................ 135 H7
Sutton Cl *HLS* DH4 .... 131 J1
Sutton Ct *WLSD/HOW* NE28 .... 58 B5
Sutton St *BYK/HTN/WLK* NE6 .... 7 M1
   DHAM DH1 .... 16 B3
Sutton Wy *HAR/WTLS* NE34.......... 76 B6
Swainby Cl *GOS/KPK* NE3 .... 56 D2
Swaledale *CLDN/WHIT/ROK* SR6 .. 93 F5 🟦
   WLSD/HOW NE28 .... 58 B5 🟦
Swaledale Av *HLH* DH5 .... 147 H7
Swaledale Cl *HLS* DH4 .... 117 J6
Swaledale Crs *HLS* DH4 .... 117 J6
Swaledale Gdns *LGB/HTN* NE7 .... 57 H7
   MLFD/PNYW SR4 .... 119 K1 🟦
Swallow Cl *ASHGTN* NE63 .... 24 A4
   BDN/LAN/SAC DH7.................165 F1
The Swallows *WLSD/HOW* NE28 .. 59 G3
Swallow Tail Ct
   HAR/WTLS NE34...................... 75 F7 🟦
Swallow Tail Dr *DUN/TMV* NE11 .... 9 M9
Swalwell Bank *WICK/BNPF* NE16.. 84 E3
Swalwell Cl *PRUD* NE42 .... 80 C2
Swan Av *WLSD/HOW* NE28 .... 59 F7 🟦
Swan Dr *GATE* NE8 .... 9 K6
Swan Rd *BYK/HTN/WLK* NE6 .... 72 D7
   PLEE/EAS SR8......................... 174 A5
   WASHS NE38 .... 117 H3
Swansfield *MPTH* NE61 .... 20 C6
Swan St *GATE* NE8 .... 11 G1 🟦
   STLY/ANP DH9 .... 125 G2
   SWCK/CAS SR5 .... 106 C4
Swanton Cl *WD/WHPE/BLK* NE5 ... 55 F6
Swards Rd *FELL* NE10 .... 88 A5
Swarland Av *LGB/HTN* NE7 .... 57 H5
Swarland Gn *MONK* NE25 .... 40 A6
Swarth Cl *WASHN* NE37 .... 102 C7
Sweetbriar Cl *MPTH* NE61 .... 20 B3 🟦
Sweetbriar Wy *BLYTH* NE24 .... 34 E3
Sweethope Av *ASHGTN* NE63 .... 24 A3
   BLYTH NE24 .... 31 F6 🟦
Sweethope Dene *MPTH* NE61 .... 20 E7
Swiftden Dr *MLFD/PNYW* SR4 ... 118 C2
Swinbourne Gdns *WBAY* NE26 ..... 50 D3
Swinbourne Ter *JRW* NE32 .... 89 K1
Swinburne Pl *GATE* NE8 .... 10 F1 🟦
   JRW NE32 .... 74 C5
Swinburne St *GATE* NE8 .... 10 F1
Swinburn Rd *MONK* NE25 .... 40 A6
Swindale Dr *LGB/KIL* NE12 .... 47 J6
Swindon Dr *SUNDSW* SR3 .... 119 H3
Swindon Sq *SUNDSW* SR3 .... 119 J3 🟦
Swindon St *HEBB* NE31 .... 73 F5
Swindon Ter
   BYK/HTN/WLK NE6 .... 71 H2 🟦
Swing Br *CNUT* NE1 .... 5 L8
Swinhoe Gdns *DIN/WO* NE13 .... 46 B2
Swinhope *WASHS* NE38 .... 116 C6
Swinley Gdns
   BW/LEM/TK/HW NE15 .... 68 D5
Swinside Dr *DHAM* DH1 .... 157 K5
Swinton Cl *MPTH* NE61 .... 21 F7 🟦
The Swirle *CNUT* NE1 .... 6 B7 🟦
Sycamore Av *BLYTH* NE24............. 31 F5
   DIN/WO NE13 .... 45 G2
   HAR/WTLS NE34...................... 75 K7
   MONK NE25 .... 50 D5
   PONT/DH NE20 .... 43 F5
   STKFD/GP NE62 .... 22 E6
Sycamore Cl *JES* NE2 .... 71 F1 🟦
Sycamore Dr *SWCK/CAS* SR5 ..... 106 B2
Sycamore Gv *FELL* NE10 .... 12 E8
   LWF/SPW/WRK NE9 .... 102 B4
   PRUD NE42 .... 80 A2
Sycamore Rd *BLAY* NE21 .... 84 A2
   CLDN/WHIT/ROK SR6 .... 93 F3
   CLSW/PEL DH2 .... 144 A5
The Sycamores
   ASHBK/HED/RY SR2 .... 120 E3
   WICK/BNPF NE16 .... 112 A1
Sycamore St
   BW/LEM/TK/HW NE15 .... 53 F7
   WLSD/HOW NE28 .... 72 E2 🟦
Sydenham Ter
   MLFD/PNYW SR4 .... 120 A1
   SSH NE33 .... 3 K7
Sydney Gdns *CON/LDGT* DH8 ...... 123 H7
   HAR/WTLS NE34...................... 90 D1
Sydney Gv *WLSD/HOW* NE28 .... 58 C5
Sydney St *HLS* DH4 .... 131 G5
   STLY/ANP DH9 .... 114 A7
Syke Rd *WICK/BNPF* NE16 .... 97 H7
Sylvan Cl *MPTH* NE61 .... 20 B6
Sylvia Ter *STLY/ANP* DH9 .... 112 D6
Symington Gdns
   SUNDSW SR3 .... 119 K6 🟦
Syon St *TYNE/NSHE* NE30 .... 61 H2
Syron *WICK/BNPF* NE16.................. 84 D6
Syston Cl *HLS* DH4 .... 146 D1

T

Taberna Cl
   BW/LEM/TK/HW NE15 .... 66 A1
Tadcaster Rd *SUNDSW* SR3 .... 119 G5
Tadema Rd *SSH* NE33...................... 75 K1
Tail-upon-end La
   RDHAMSE DH6 .... 180 A1
Talbot Cl *WASHS* NE38 .... 117 F2
Talbot Gn *WD/WHPE/BLK* NE5 ...... 68 D3
Talbot Rd *SEA/MUR* SR7 .... 150 E1

Talbot Rd *CLDN/WHIT/ROK* SR6 .. 106 C2
   HAR/WTLS NE34...................... 75 C5
Talgarth *WASHS* NE38 .... 117 K1
Talisman La *RDHAMSE* DH6 .... 170 C1
Talley Ct *WASHS* NE38 .... 116 E1
Tamar Cl *NSHW* NE29 .... 60 A2
Tamar St *HLH* DH5 .... 160 B1
Tamerton Dr *CLS/BIR/GTL* DH3 ... 115 K4
Tamerton St
   MLFD/PNYW SR4 .... 105 K7 🟦
Tamworth Rd *ELS/FEN* NE4 .... 4 C5
Tamworth Sq *SUNDSW* SR3 .... 119 G5 🟦
Tanfield Gdns *HAR/WTLS* NE34..... 76 B5
Tanfield Pl *LWF/SPW/WRK* NE9 .. 101 J3
Tanfield Rd
   BW/LEM/TK/HW NE15 .... 68 E5
   LWF/SPW/WRK NE9 .... 101 J3
   SUNDSW SR3 .... 119 H5
Tangmere Cl *CRAM* NE23............... 38 D1
Tankerville Pl *JES* NE2 .... 70 E2 🟦
Tankerville Ter *JES* NE2 .... 70 E3
Tanmeads *CLSW/PEL* DH2 .... 144 A4
Tanners' Bank *TYNE/NSHE* NE30 .. 61 G4
Tantobie Rd
   BW/LEM/TK/HW NE15 .... 68 E5
Tarlton Crs *FELL* NE10 .... 12 B8
Tarn Cl *PLEE/EAS* SR8 .... 175 F4 🟦
Tarn Dr *ASHBK/HED/RY* SR2 .... 121 F6
Tarragon Wy *HAR/WTLS* NE34 ...... 91 H1
Tarrington Cl
   WLSD/HOW NE28 .... 59 H5 🟦
Tarset Dr *PRUD* NE42 .... 80 D2
Tarset St *MONK* NE25 .... 49 K4
Tarset St *CNUT* NE1 .... 6 C4
Tasmania Rd *HAR/WTLS* NE34 ...... 90 D1
Tasman Rd *SUNDSW* SR3 .... 119 G6
Tate Av *RDHAMSE* DH6 .... 181 C6
Tate St *BLYTH* NE24 .... 31 H6 🟦
Tatham St *SUND* SR1 .... 15 C5
Tatham Street Back *SUND* SR1 ..... 15 C5
Tattershall *ASHBK/HED/RY* SR2 .. 120 B2
Taunton Av *JRW* NE32 .... 74 C6
   NSHW NE29 .... 60 B2 🟦
Taunton Cl *WLSD/HOW* NE28 .... 59 H5
Taunton Pl *CRAM* NE23................... 33 H7
Taunton Rd *SUNDSW* SR3 .... 119 H5
Tavistock Ct *HLS* DH4 .... 132 A4 🟦
Tavistock Pl *JRW* NE32 .... 74 B6
   SUND SR1 .... 14 F5
Tavistock Sq *SUNDSW* SR3 .... 120 A6
Taylor Av *ASHGTN* NE63 .... 24 D2
   BDN/LAN/SAC DH7.................155 G6
   DIN/WO NE13 .... 46 C3
   ROWG NE39 .... 97 H4
Taylor Gdns *WBAY* NE26 .... 41 G2
Taylor Gv *WNCT* TS28 .... 183 J2
Taylor St *BLYTH* NE24.................... 30 C6
   CON/LDGT DH8........................ 123 F5
   SSH NE33 .... 75 F4
   STLY/ANP DH9 .... 125 G2
Taynton Gv *CRAM* NE23 .... 39 G6 🟦
Tay Rd *SUNDSW* SR3 .... 119 G4
Tay St *CHPW* NE17 .... 95 J4
   HLH DH5 .... 160 B1
Teal Av *BLYTH* NE24....................... 35 H3
Teal Cl *WASHS* NE38 .... 116 B3
Team St *GATE* NE8 .... 9 L5
Teasdale St
   ASHBK/HED/RY SR2 .... 15 J8 🟦
   CON/LDGT DH8...................... 123 G4 🟦
Tebay Dr *WD/WHPE/BLK* NE5 .... 68 B3
Teddington Cl *DIN/WO* NE13 .... 55 F3
Teddington Sq *SUNDSW* SR3 ...... 119 G4 🟦
Tedham Rd
   BW/LEM/TK/HW NE15 .... 68 A4
Tees Cl *PLEE/EAS* SR8 .... 174 D6
Tees Ct *HAR/WTLS* NE34 .... 75 C5
Tees Crs *STLY/ANP* DH9 .... 126 D2
Teesdale Av *HLS* DH4 .... 117 J6
Teesdale Gdns *LGB/HTN* NE7 .... 57 H7
Teesdale Pl *BLYTH* NE24 .... 30 B6
Tees Gv *CON/LDGT* DH8 .... 123 K2
Tees Rd *HEBB* NE31 .... 89 G1
Tees St *HLH* DH5 .... 160 C1 🟦
   PLEE/EAS SR8......................... 175 H3
   SEA/MUR SR7........................ 135 K7
Teign Cl *PLEE/EAS* SR8 .... 174 D5
Teindland Cl *ELS/FEN* NE4............. 69 J7
Tel-el-kebir Rd
   ASHBK/HED/RY SR2 .... 120 E2
Telford Cl *DHAM* DH1 .... 169 J6
   SMOOR NE27 .... 48 E4
Telford Ct *WLSD/HOW* NE28 .... 74 A1
Telford Rd *SUNDSW* SR3 .... 119 H4
Telford St *GATE* NE8 .... 10 D9
   WLSD/HOW NE28 .... 74 A1
Temperance Ter
   BDN/LAN/SAC DH7................. 154 E7
Tempest Rd *SEA/MUR* SR7 .... 150 E1
Tempest St *BLAY* NE21 .... 67 J7 🟦
   SUNDSW SR3 .... 120 A7 🟦
Templar St *CON/LDGT* DH8 .... 122 D3 🟦
Temple Gn *GATE* NE8 .... 10 B7
   HAR/WTLS NE34...................... 75 J6
Temple Park Rd *HAR/WTLS* NE34.. 75 H5
Temple St *CNUT* NE1 .... 5 H8
   FELL NE10 .... 12 D5
   SSH NE33 .... 75 F4
Temple St West *SSH* NE33 .... 75 F3 🟦
Temple Town *SSH* NE33 .... 75 F3
Tenbury Crs *LGB/KIL* NE12 .... 57 J3
   NSHW NE29 .... 60 C5 🟦
Tenby Rd *SUNDSW* SR3 .... 119 G6 🟦
Tenby Sq *CRAM* NE23 .... 33 J7 🟦
Ten Flds *HLH* DH5 .... 147 J5
Tennant St *HAR/WTLS* NE34 .... 74 E7
   HEBB NE31 .... 73 H5 🟦
Tennyson Av *BOLCOL* NE35 .... 91 F4
Tennyson Ct *PRUD* NE42 .... 80 B3
Tennyson Crs
   WICK/BNPF NE16 .... 84 E4 🟦
Tennyson Rd *CLSW/PEL* DH2 ...... 128 E4
   PLEE/EAS SR8......................... 162 E5 🟦
Tennyson St *SWCK/CAS* SR5 ...... 106 A3 🟦

Tennyson Ter *NSHW* NE29 .... 2 E4 🟦
Tenter Ter *DHAM* DH1 .... 16 C3
Tenth Av *BLYTH* NE24 .... 35 F2
   BYK/HTN/WLK NE6 .... 7 G1
   DUN/TMV NE11 .... 100 D3
   MPTH NE61 .... 21 F7
Tenth St *PLEE/EAS* SR8 .... 175 H3
Tern Cl *BLYTH* NE24 .... 35 H3
Terrace Pl *CNUT* NE1 .... 5 H5
The Terrace *CON/LDGT* DH8 .... 122 C1
Terrier Cl *BDLGTN* NE22 .... 29 J5
Tetford Pl *LGB/KIL* NE12 .... 57 J3
Teviot *WASHS* NE38 .... 116 C5
Teviotdale Gdns *LGB/HTN* NE7..... 57 H7
Teviot St *GATE* NE8 .... 11 K7
   HLH DH5 .... 160 B1 🟦
Teviot Wy *JRW* NE32 .... 73 J6 🟦
Tewkesbury *LGB/KIL* NE12 .... 47 K5 🟦
Tewkesbury Rd
   BW/LEM/TK/HW NE15 .... 68 A4
Thackeray Rd *SUNDSW* SR3 .... 119 H4
Thames Av *JRW* NE32 .... 90 A1
Thames Crs *HLS* DH4 .... 131 J7
   STLY/ANP DH9 .... 126 D3
Thames Gdns
   WLSD/HOW NE28 .... 72 D2 🟦
Thames Rd *HEBB* NE31 .... 73 H7
   PLEE/EAS SR8......................... 174 D5
   SUNDSW SR3 .... 119 G6 🟦
Thames St *GATE* NE8 .... 11 K7
   HLH DH5 .... 160 B1
Thanet Rd *SUNDSW* SR3 .... 119 H5
Tharsis Rd *HEBB* NE31 .... 73 F6
Thatcher Cl *WICK/BNPF* NE16....... 84 E7
Thelma St *MLFD/PNYW* SR4 .... 14 A6
Theme Rd *SUNDSW* SR3 .... 119 G6
Theresa St *BLAY* NE21 .... 84 A1
The Sands *DHAM* DH1 .... 16 E1
Thieves Bank *MPTH* NE61 .... 23 F4
Third Av *ASHGTN* NE63 .... 24 A2
   BLYTH NE24 .... 35 F1
   BYK/HTN/WLK NE6 .... 7 G2
   CLSW/PEL DH2 .... 115 H7
   DUN/TMV NE11 .... 86 C7
   MPTH NE61 .... 21 F6
   NSHW NE29 .... 59 K5
Third St *PLEE/EAS* SR8 .... 175 H3
Thirkeld Pl *HLS* DH4 .... 117 K7 🟦
Thirlington Cl
   WD/WHPE/BLK NE5 .... 55 F7
Thirlmere *CLDN/WHIT/ROK* SR6 .. 92 A3
   CLS/BIR/GTL DH3 .... 116 A4
   FELL NE10 .... 13 J7
Thirlmere Av *CLSW/PEL* DH2 ...... 129 H6
   HLH DH5 .... 160 B1
   TYNE/NSHE NE30..................... 50 E7
Thirlmere Cl *LGB/KIL* NE12 .... 48 B6
Thirlmere Ct *HEBB* NE31 .... 73 H7 🟦
Thirlmere Crs *BLAY* NE21 .... 83 K4 🟦
   HLS DH4 .... 131 K1
Thirlmere Rd *PLEE/EAS* SR8 .... 175 F3
Thirlmere Wy *BLYTH* NE24 .... 30 C5
   WD/WHPE/BLK NE5 .... 69 F2
Thirlmoor *WASHN* NE37 .... 102 C7
Thirlmoor Pl *STKFD/GP* NE62 .... 23 G5
Thirlwell Gv *JRW* NE32 .... 89 J1
Thirlwell Rd *GATE* NE8 .... 6 A9
Thirsk Rd *SUNDSW* SR3 .... 119 H4 🟦
Thirston Dr *CRAM* NE23 .... 38 D2
Thirston Pl *NSHW* NE29 .... 60 B3 🟦
Thirston Wy *GOS/KPK* NE3 .... 55 H5 🟦
Thistle Av *RYTON* NE40 .... 66 C7
Thistlecroft *HLH* DH5 .... 147 H1
Thistledon Av *WICK/BNPF* NE16 ... 84 D7
Thistle Rd *BDN/LAN/SAC* DH7 ..... 168 A6
   SUNDSW SR3 .... 119 G6
Thistley Cl *BYK/HTN/WLK* NE6 ..... 72 A3 🟦
Thomas Hawksley Pk
   SUNDSW SR3 .... 120 A3
Thomas St *ASHBK/HED/RY* SR2 .. 135 F1
   CON/LDGT DH8...................... 122 D3
   LWF/SPW/WRK NE9 .... 101 K4
   PLEE/EAS SR8......................... 163 F4
   SSH NE33 .... 3 H7
   STLY/ANP DH9 .... 127 H4
   WICK/BNPF NE16 .... 84 E5 🟦
Thomas St North
   CLDN/WHIT/ROK SR6 .... 14 E1
Thomas St South
   ASHBK/HED/RY SR2 .... 135 F1
   SWCK/CAS SR5 .... 105 F4
Thompson Av *LGB/KIL* NE12 .... 47 J5 🟦
Thompson Crs
   SWCK/CAS SR5 .... 105 F4 🟦
Thompson Gdns
   WLSD/HOW NE28 .... 72 D1 🟦
Thompson Pl *FELL* NE10 .... 12 C7
Thompson St *SWCK/CAS* SR5...... 106 C3
Thompson St *BLYTH* NE24 .... 31 G6 🟦
   BLYTH NE24 .... 31 G5 🟦
   HAR/WTLS NE34...................... 75 F6 🟦
   PLEE/EAS SR8......................... 175 H2
Thorburn St
   CLDN/WHIT/ROK SR6 .... 106 D1 🟦
Thornbank Cl *SUNDSW* SR3 .... 134 A3 🟦
Thornbridge *WASHS* NE38............. 117 J1
Thornbury Av *CRAM* NE23 .... 39 G6
Thornbury Cl *BOLCOL* NE35 .... 90 C3 🟦
   DIN/WO NE13 .... 55 F4
Thornbury Dr *MONK* NE25 .... 50 A3
Thornbury St *MLFD/PNYW* SR4 ... 106 A6
   NSHW NE29 .... 60 C5 🟦
Thorncliffe Pl *NSHW* NE29 .... 2 A2 🟦
Thorn Cl *DIN/WO* NE13 .... 46 A4 🟦
Thorndale Pl *BLYTH* NE24 .... 30 E5 🟦
Thorndale Rd
   BW/LEM/TK/HW NE15 .... 68 D6
   DHAM DH1 .... 158 A6
   SUNDSW SR3 .... 119 G5
Thorne Av *FELL* NE10 .... 13 M8
Thorne Brake *FELL* NE10............... 88 C5 🟦
Thornehill Gdns
   STKFD/GP NE62 .... 23 G5 🟦
Thorne Rd *SUNDSW* SR3 .... 119 G5 🟦
Thornes Rd *PLEE/EAS* SR8 .... 175 G5 🟦

Thorne Sq *SUNDSW* SR3 .... 119 G5
Thorne Ter *BYK/HTN/WLK* NE6...... 7 M3
Thorneyburn Cl *HLS* DH4 .... 132 A5 🟦
Thorneyburn Wy *BLYTH* NE24 ...... 30 E7 🟦
Thorney Close Rd *SUNDSW* SR3 .. 119 H5
Thorneyford Pl
   PONT/DH NE20 .... 43 G2 🟦
Thorneyholme Ter
   STLY/ANP DH9 .... 126 C1
Thornfield Gv
   ASHBK/HED/RY SR2 .... 120 E4 🟦
Thornfield Pl *ROWG* NE39 .... 97 G2 🟦
Thornfield Rd *CON/LDGT* DH8 ..... 122 C6
   GOS/KPK NE3 .... 56 B6 🟦
Thorngill *WASHN* NE37 .... 102 D7
Thornhaugh Av
   WICK/BNPF NE16 .... 84 D6 🟦
Thornhill Cl *MONK* NE25 .... 40 A6
Thornhill Gdns
   ASHBK/HED/RY SR2 .... 14 C9
   PONT/DH NE20 .... 43 G2 🟦
Thornhill Pk *ASHBK/HED/RY* SR2 . 14 C8
   PONT/DH NE20 .... 43 G2
Thornhill Rd *LGB/KIL* NE12 .... 57 K4
   PONT/DH NE20 .... 43 G2
   RDHAMSE DH6 .... 173 H4
Thornhill St *HLS* DH4 .... 132 B7
Thornhill Ter
   ASHBK/HED/RY SR2 .... 14 C7
Thornholme Av *HAR/WTLS* NE34 .. 76 B5
Thornholme Rd
   ASHBK/HED/RY SR2 .... 14 B9
Thornhope Cl *WASHS* NE38 .... 103 H7 🟦
Thornlaw North *RDHAMSE* DH6 ... 172 A6
Thornlea *MPTH* NE61 .... 27 J2
Thornlea Gdns
   LWF/SPW/WRK NE9 .... 87 F6
Thornlea Gv *BDN/LAN/SAC* DH7 .. 140 A4
Thornleigh Gdns
   CLDN/WHIT/ROK SR6 .... 92 A2
Thornleigh Rd *JES* NE2 .... 70 E2 🟦
Thornley Av *CRAM* NE23 .... 38 D2
   FELL NE10 .... 88 D6 🟦
Thornley Cl *BDN/LAN/SAC* DH7 ... 167 G1 🟦
   WICK/BNPF NE16 .... 98 E1
Thornley La *BLAY* NE21 .... 83 J6
   ROWG NE39 .... 97 J1
Thornley Rd *WD/WHPE/BLK* NE5 .. 68 C2
Thornley Vw *ROWG* NE39.............. 97 H3
Thornton Cl *HLS* DH4 .... 117 J7
   MPTH NE61 .... 21 F7 🟦
   RDHAMSE DH6 .... 172 B3
Thornton Ct *WASHS* NE38 .... 116 C1
Thornton Crs *BLAY* NE21 .... 84 A1
Thornton Lea *CLSW/PEL* DH2 ..... 114 D7
Thornton St *CNUT* NE1 .... 5 H8
Thorntree Av *DIN/WO* NE13 .... 37 G7
Thorn Tree Dr *BDLGTN* NE22 .... 29 F4
Thorntree Dr
   BW/LEM/TK/HW NE15 .... 68 E4
   MONK NE25 .... 49 K5
Thorntree Gdns *ASHGTN* NE63 ..... 24 C3
Thorntree Ter *STLY/ANP* DH9 .... 113 F7
Thorntree Wy *BLYTH* NE24 .... 30 B7
Thornwood Gdns
   DUN/TMV NE11 .... 86 B7
Thorp Av *MPTH* NE61...................... 20 E3
Thorp Cl *BLYTH* NE24 .... 34 D2 🟦
Thorpe Cl *ELS/FEN* NE4 .... 4 D5
Thorpe Dr *RYTON* NE40 .... 67 F6
Thorpeness Rd *SUNDSW* SR3 ..... 119 G5 🟦
Thorpe Rd *PLEE/EAS* SR8 .... 162 C6 🟦
Thorpe St *PLEE/EAS* SR8 .... 163 F4 🟦
   PLEE/EAS SR8......................... 175 H3 🟦
Threap Gdns *WLSD/HOW* NE28 .... 59 G6
Three Rivers Ct *BOL* NE36 .... 90 E5 🟦
Threlkeld Gv
   CLDN/WHIT/ROK SR6 .... 92 C7 🟦
Thrift St *NSHW* NE29 .... 2 C4 🟦
Thristley Gdns
   ASHBK/HED/RY SR2 .... 120 C3
Throckley Wy *HAR/WTLS* NE34 ..... 75 F5 🟦
Thropton Av *BLYTH* NE24 .... 34 E2 🟦
   LGB/HTN NE7 .... 57 H5
Thropton Cl *DHAM* DH1 .... 169 J3 🟦
   FELL NE10 .... 88 E5
Thropton Ct *BLYTH* NE24 .... 34 E1 🟦
Thropton Crs *GOS/KPK* NE3 .... 56 B4
Thropton Pl *NSHW* NE29 .... 60 B3
Thropton Ter *LGB/HTN* NE7 .... 71 H1
Thrush Gv *SWCK/CAS* SR5 .... 105 G4 🟦
Thursby Av *TYNE/NSHE* NE30....... 51 F7
Thurso Cl *SUNDSW* SR3 .... 119 F5 🟦
Tiberius Cl *WLSD/HOW* NE28 .... 72 D2 🟦
Tilbeck Sq *SUNDSW* SR3 .... 134 A1 🟦
Tilbury Cl *HLS* DH4 .... 132 A2
Tilbury Gdns *SUNDSW* SR3 .... 119 G6 🟦
Tilbury Gv *MONK* NE25 .... 50 E6
Tilbury Rd *SUNDSW* SR3 .... 119 G6
Tileshed La *BOL* NE36 .... 91 G3
Till Av *BLAY* NE21 .... 83 K2
Tilley Rd *WASHS* NE38 .... 116 B1
Tillmouth Av *MONK* NE25 .... 40 A6
Tillmouth Gdns *ELS/FEN* NE4 .... 69 G5
Tillmouth Park Rd
   BW/LEM/TK/HW NE15 .... 67 F2
Till St *BYK/HTN/WLK* NE6 .... 7 H8 🟦
Tilson Wy *GOS/KPK* NE3 .... 55 K4 🟦
Timber Beach Rd
   SWCK/CAS SR5 .... 105 H4
Timber Rd *PLEE/EAS* SR8 .... 175 H1
Timlin Gdns *WLSD/HOW* NE28 ..... 59 K7
Tindal Cl *ELS/FEN* NE4 .... 4 E6
Tindale Av *CRAM* NE23 .... 38 D2
Tindale Dr *WICK/BNPF* NE16 .... 84 E6
Tindale St *CON/LDGT* DH8 .... 123 J3
Tindal St *ELS/FEN* NE4 .... 4 F7
Tinmill Pl *CON/LDGT* DH8 .... 122 D4
Tintagel Cl *CRAM* NE23 .... 33 H7
   SUNDSW SR3 .... 119 F5 🟦
Tintagel Dr *SEA/MUR* SR7 .... 135 J7
Tintern *WASHS* NE38 .... 116 C3
Tintern Cl *HLS* DH4 .... 132 A5
Tintern Crs *BYK/HTN/WLK* NE6 ...... 6 F2
   NSHW NE29 .... 60 B2
Tintern St *MLFD/PNYW* SR4 .... 14 A5 🟦
Tiree Cl *BDN/LAN/SAC* DH7 .... 167 H5
Tiree Ct *SUNDSW* SR3 .... 134 A1 🟦
Tirril Pl *WD/WHPE/BLK* NE5 .... 68 C2

Titan Rd *BYK/HTN/WLK* NE6 .... 72 C5
Titchfield Rd *WASHS* NE38 .... 116 E2
Titchfield Ter *ASHGTN* NE63 .... 23 K3
Titian Av *HAR/WTLS* NE34 .... 91 G2
Titlington Gv *HEBB* NE31 .... 89 F1
Tiverton Av *ELS/FEN* NE4 .... 69 J6
NSHW NE29 .... 60 A1
Tiverton Cl *WLSD/HOW* NE28 .... 59 H5
Tiverton Gdns
LWF/SPW/WRK NE9 .... 101 F2
Tiverton Pl *CRAM* NE23 .... 33 H7
Tiverton Sq *SUNDSW* SR3 .... 119 G5
Toberty Gdns *FELL* NE10 .... 13 L8
Toft Crs *SEA/MUR* SR7 .... 149 H5
Togstone Pl
WD/WHPE/BLK NE5 .... 69 G2 7
Toll Bar Rd *ASHBK/HED/RY* SR2 .. 120 D5
Toll Bridge Rd *BLAY* NE21 .... 84 D1
Tollerton Dr *SWCK/CAS* SR5 .... 104 D4
Tollgate Flds *HLS* DH4 .... 146 C7 2
Tollgate Rd *ROWG* NE39 .... 110 B1
Toll House Rd *DHAM* DH1 .... 156 A7
Tolls Cl *MONK* NE25 .... 50 A4
Toll Sq *TYNE/NSHE* NE30 .... 3 G1
Tomlea Av *BDLGTN* NE22 .... 29 K5
Tonbridge Av *NSHW* NE29 .... 60 C5
Toner Av *HEBB* NE31 .... 89 F1
Topaz St *SEA/MUR* SR7 .... 150 B1
Topcliff *CLDN/WHIT/ROK* SR6 .... 15 H1
Torcross Wy *CRAM* NE23 .... 33 H7
Toronto Rd *SUNDSW* SR3 .... 119 H4
Toronto Sq *SUNDSW* SR3 .... 119 H4
Torquay Gdns
LWF/SPW/WRK NE9 .... 101 F2
Torquay Rd *SUNDSW* SR3 .... 119 H4
Torrens Rd *SUNDSW* SR3 .... 119 H4
Torrington Cl *HLS* DH4 .... 132 A3 5
Torver Cl *DIN/WO* NE13 .... 46 A4
Torver Crs *CLDN/WHIT/ROK* SR6 .... 92 C7
Torver Pl *LWF/SPW/WRK* NE9 .... 101 H1
Torver Wy *TYNE/NSHE* NE30 .... 50 D7
Tosson Pl *NSHW* NE29 .... 60 B5 4
Tosson Ter *BYK/HTN/WLK* NE6 .. 71 J2 1
Totnes Dr *CRAM* NE23 .... 33 H7
Toward Rd *ASHBK/HED/RY* SR2 .... 15 G9
SUND SR1 .... 14 F5
Toward St *BYK/HTN/WLK* NE6 .... 6 E4 1
Tower Bank *BDN/LAN/SAC* DH7 .. 125 G7
Tower Gdns *RYTON* NE40 .... 66 E6
Tower Pl *ASHBK/HED/RY* SR2 .... 15 H8 5
Tower Rd *BDN/LAN/SAC* DH7 .... 125 J7
STLY/ANP DH9 .... 125 G5
WASHN NE37 .... 103 G6
Towers Av *JES* NE2 .... 56 E7
Towers Cl *BDLGTN* NE22 .... 29 G6
Towers Pl *HAR/WTLS* NE34 .... 74 C6
Tower St *ASHBK/HED/RY* SR2 .... 15 J8
CNUT NE1 .... 5 M7
PLEE/EAS SR8 .... 163 G4
Tower St West
ASHBK/HED/RY SR2 .... 15 H9
The Towne Ga
BW/LEM/TK/HW NE15 .... 66 A1
Townend Ct *HAR/WTLS* NE34 .... 75 G6
Townfield Gdns
BW/LEM/TK/HW NE15 .... 67 H3
Town Hall *MPTH* NE61 .... 20 C4 5
Townley Flds *ROWG* NE39 .... 97 H3
Townley Rd *ROWG* NE39 .... 97 F3 4
Townsend Crs *MPTH* NE61 .... 20 B7
Townsend Rd *SUNDSW* SR3 .... 119 G6
Townsville Av *MONK* NE25 .... 50 B6
Towton *LGB/KIL* NE12 .... 47 K5 11
Toynbee *WASHS* NE38 .... 117 J1
Tracey Av *BOL* NE36 .... 91 F4
Trafalgar Rd *WASHN* NE37 .... 103 H4 2
Trafalgar St *CNUT* NE1 .... 5 M6 1
CON/LDGT DH8 .... 123 F5
Trafford *LWF/SPW/WRK* NE9 .... 101 G3
Trafford Rd *SWCK/CAS* SR5 .... 106 A4
Trafford Wk
WD/WHPE/BLK NE5 .... 54 C7 5
Trajan Av *SSH* NE33 .... 3 J4
Trajan Wk
BW/LEM/TK/HW NE15 .... 65 K1
Tranwell Cl *GOS/KPK* NE3 .... 55 K2 5
MPTH NE61 .... 21 J2
Tranwell Dr *MONK* NE25 .... 40 B6
Treby St *MLFD/PNYW* SR4 .... 106 A6
Tredegar Cl
WD/WHPE/BLK NE5 .... 55 F6 13
Treecone Cl *SUNDSW* SR3 .... 134 A2
Treen Crs *SEA/MUR* SR7 .... 149 J5 1
Trefoil Rd *STLY/ANP* DH9 .... 112 B6
Tregoney Av *SEA/MUR* SR7 .... 149 J5
Treherne Rd *JES* NE2 .... 56 D7 5
Trent Av *HEBB* NE31 .... 89 G1
Trent Dl *CON/LDGT* DH8 .... 123 K2
Trent Dr *JRW* NE32 .... 90 A2
Trent Gdns *GATE* NE8 .... 11 M7
Trentham Av *LGB/HTN* NE7 .... 57 H5
Trentham Gdns *MPTH* NE61 .... 21 J1
Trenton Av *WASHS* NE38 .... 103 F7 1
Trent Rd *SUNDSW* SR3 .... 119 G5
Trent St *HLH* DH5 .... 160 B1
Trevarren Dr
ASHBK/HED/RY SR2 .... 121 F6
Trevelyan Av *BDLGTN* NE22 .... 29 H5
BLYTH NE24 .... 34 E1
Trevelyan Cl *SUNDSW* SR3 .... 119 F5 5
Trevelyan Dr
WD/WHPE/BLK NE5 .... 54 E7
Trevethick St *GATE* NE8 .... 10 C8
Trevone Pl *CRAM* NE23 .... 39 H6
Trevone Sq *SEA/MUR* SR7 .... 149 J5
Trevor Gv *CLDN/WHIT/ROK* SR6 .... 92 A4
Trevor Ter *TYNE/NSHE* NE30 .... 60 E3
Trewhitt Rd
BYK/HTN/WLK NE6 .... 71 J3 5
Tribune Pl *LWF/SPW/WRK* NE9 .... 87 H6
Trident Rd *SUNDSW* SR3 .... 120 A7
Trimdon St *MLFD/PNYW* SR4 .... 14 B3
Trimdon St West
MLFD/PNYW SR4 .... 14 A3
Trinity Ctyd *BYK/HTN/WLK* NE6 .. 7 J9 1
Trinity Gv *CRAM* NE23 .... 39 H6
Trinity Pk *HLS* DH4 .... 131 K2
Trinity Pl *NSHW* NE29 .... 2 D4 1
Trinity St *NSHW* NE29 .... 2 D4
SWCK/CAS SR5 .... 105 K3
Trinity Wk *SSH* NE33 .... 75 F2
Trojan Av *BYK/HTN/WLK* NE6 .... 7 L2
Tromso Cl *NSHW* NE29 .... 59 K5
Trool Ct *SUNDSW* SR3 .... 134 A2
Troon Cl *CON/LDGT* DH8 .... 122 E2
WASHN NE37 .... 102 E3 5
Trotter Gv *BDLGTN* NE22 .... 29 J5 5
Trotter Ter *ASHBK/HED/RY* SR2 .. 135 F1
Troutbeck Av
BYK/HTN/WLK NE6 .... 72 B6 5
Troutbeck Rd
CLDN/WHIT/ROK SR6 .... 92 C7 7
Troutbeck Wy *HAR/WTLS* NE34 .... 90 D1
PLEE/EAS SR8 .... 175 F3 4
Troutdale Pl *LGB/KIL* NE12 .... 57 F4 4
Trout's La *DHAM* DH1 .... 155 J2
Trowbridge Wy *GOS/KPK* NE3 .... 55 K5
Truro Av *SEA/MUR* SR7 .... 149 J4
Truro Gv *NSHW* NE29 .... 60 B2
Truro Rd *SUNDSW* SR3 .... 119 H5 1
Tuart St *CLS/BIR/GTL* DH3 .... 129 J4
Tudor Av *NSHW* NE29 .... 60 C4
Tudor Ct *PONT/DH* NE20 .... 42 E5
RDHAMSE DH6 .... 173 J4
Tudor Dr *STLY/ANP* DH9 .... 112 B3 1
Tudor Gra *PLEE/EAS* SR8 .... 162 B6
Tudor Gv *SUNDSW* SR3 .... 119 K3
Tudor Rd *CLS/BIR/GTL* DH3 .... 129 K2
SSH NE33 .... 2 F9
Tudor Wy *GOS/KPK* NE3 .... 55 G4
WD/WHPE/BLK NE5 .... 55 F5
Tudor Wynd *BYK/HTN/WLK* NE6 .. 71 K2
Tulip St *GATE* NE8 .... 12 A6
Tumulus Av *BYK/HTN/WLK* NE6 .... 72 C3
Tunbridge Rd *SUNDSW* SR3 .... 119 H4
Tundry Wy *BLAY* NE21 .... 68 D7
Tuneside *FELL* NE10 .... 13 L9
Tunis Rd *SUNDSW* SR3 .... 119 J4 5
Tunstall Av *BYK/HTN/WLK* NE6 .... 7 J4
HAR/WTLS NE34 .... 76 B5
RDHAMSE DH6 .... 180 A2
Tunstall Bank *SUNDSW* SR3 .... 120 C7
Tunstall Gv *CON/LDGT* DH8 .... 123 K3 4
Tunstall Hill Cl
ASHBK/HED/RY SR2 .... 120 C4 7
Tunstall Pk *ASHBK/HED/RY* SR2 .. 120 C2
Tunstall Rd *ASHBK/HED/RY* SR2 .... 14 D6
SUNDSW SR3 .... 120 B5
Tunstall Ter *ASHBK/HED/RY* SR2 .. 14 D6
Tunstall Ter West
ASHBK/HED/RY SR2 .... 14 C6
Tunstall V *ASHBK/HED/RY* SR2 .... 14 D9
Tunstall Vw *SUNDSW* SR3 .... 120 B6
Tunstall Village Gn
SUNDSW SR3 .... 120 B7
Tunstall Village Rd
SUNDSW SR3 .... 120 B7
Tunstall Vls *SUNDSW* SR3 .... 120 B7 4
Turbinia Gdns *LGB/HTN* NE7 .... 71 J1
Turnberry *CLSW/PEL* DH2 .... 115 F4
MONK NE25 .... 50 A4
SSH NE33 .... 75 J2 5
Turnberry Cl *CON/LDGT* DH8 .... 122 E1
WASHN NE37 .... 102 E3 5
Turnberry Wy *GOS/KPK* NE3 .... 56 E4 1
Turnbull St *SUND* SR1 .... 15 J2
Turner Av *HAR/WTLS* NE34 .... 91 H1
Turner Cl *RYTON* NE40 .... 67 F7
Turner Crs *GOS/KPK* NE3 .... 56 A5 5
Turner St *CON/LDGT* DH8 .... 122 D4 1
SMOOR NE27 .... 59 G1
Turners Wy *MPTH* NE61 .... 20 B5
Turnham Rd *SUNDSW* SR3 .... 119 G5
Turnstone Dr *WASHS* NE38 .... 116 B3
The Turn *MPTH* NE61 .... 26 D1
Turret Rd *BW/LEM/TK/HW* NE15 .. 68 D4
Tuscan Cl *BDN/LAN/SAC* DH7 .... 166 D3
Tuscan Rd *SUNDSW* SR3 .... 119 G5
Tweddle Ter *RDHAMSE* DH6 .... 179 K2
Tweed Av *CON/LDGT* DH8 .... 123 K2
Tweed Cl *ASHBK/HED/RY* SR2 .... 121 F6
CLSW/PEL DH2 .... 115 F6
PLEE/EAS SR8 .... 174 D5
Tweed Gv *BW/LEM/TK/HW* NE15 .. 68 A4
Tweed St *ELS/FEN* NE4 .... 4 B7
HEBB NE31 .... 73 F5
HLH DH5 .... 160 B1 1
JRW NE32 .... 73 J6
WASHS NE38 .... 117 G2
Tweed Ter *STLY/ANP* DH9 .... 126 D2
Tweedy St *BLYTH* NE24 .... 30 C6 5
Tweedy Ter
BYK/HTN/WLK NE6 .... 72 B6 4
Twelfth Av *BLYTH* NE24 .... 35 F1
CLSW/PEL DH2 .... 129 H3
Twelfth St *PLEE/EAS* SR8 .... 175 G3
Twentieth Av *BLYTH* NE24 .... 35 F2 5
Twentyfifth Av *BLYTH* NE24 .... 35 F2 5
Twentysecond Av
BLYTH NE24 .... 34 E2 6
Twentysixth Av *BLYTH* NE24 .... 34 E2
Twentythird Av *BLYTH* NE24 .... 34 E2
Twickenham Ct *CRAM* NE23 .... 39 G6
Twickenham Rd *SUNDSW* SR3 .... 119 G4
Twizell La *STLY/ANP* DH9 .... 127 J2
Twizell Pl *PONT/DH* NE20 .... 43 G2
Twizell St *BLYTH* NE24 .... 35 H1 5
Twyford Cl *CRAM* NE23 .... 33 H7
Tyldesley Sq *SUNDSW* SR3 .... 119 G5 5
Tyne Ap *JRW* NE32 .... 73 J3
Tyne Av *CON/LDGT* DH8 .... 123 K3
Tynebank *BLAY* NE21 .... 83 K2
Tyne Br *CNUT* NE1 .... 5 M8
Tynedale Av *WBAY* NE26 .... 50 D3
WLSD/HOW NE28 .... 58 D6
Tynedale Cl *WYLAM* NE41 .... 65 H5
Tynedale Crs *HLS* DH4 .... 117 K7
Tynedale Dr *BLYTH* NE24 .... 30 C7
Tynedale Gdns *PSHWF* NE43 .... 79 H6
Tynedale Rd *HAR/WTLS* NE34 .... 75 J3
Tynedale St *HLH* DH5 .... 147 H7
Tynedale Ter *LGB/KIL* NE12 .... 57 K4 7
Tyne Gdns *PRUD* NE42 .... 64 B7
WASHN NE37 .... 103 F4
Tyne Main Rd *FELL* NE10 .... 12 A2
Tynemouth Rd
BYK/HTN/WLK NE6 .... 7 G3
JRW NE32 .... 89 J2
TYNE/NSHE NE30 .... 61 G4
WLSD/HOW NE28 .... 59 K7 4
Tynemouth Sq *SUNDSW* SR3 .... 119 H5 2
Tynemouth Ter
TYNE/NSHE NE30 .... 61 H3 5
Tyne Rd *STLY/ANP* DH9 .... 126 C2
Tyne Rd East *GATE* NE8 .... 10 B3
STLY/ANP DH9 .... 126 C2
Tyneside Rd *ELS/FEN* NE4 .... 9 M1
Tyne St *ASHGTN* NE63 .... 24 A1
BLAY NE21 .... 68 A7
CNUT NE1 .... 6 C7
CON/LDGT DH8 .... 123 G5
FELL NE10 .... 12 F3
HLH DH5 .... 160 B1
JRW NE32 .... 73 K3
SEA/MUR SR7 .... 150 E1 12
TYNE/NSHE NE30 .... 2 F2
Tyne Ter *HAR/WTLS* NE34 .... 75 F6
Tynevale Av *BLAY* NE21 .... 83 K3
Tyne Vw *BW/LEM/TK/HW* NE15 .... 68 A5
HEBB NE31 .... 72 E5
Tyne View Av *WICK/BNPF* NE16 .... 8 A7
Tyne View Pl *GATE* NE8 .... 9 M5
Tyne View Ter *PRUD* NE42 .... 80 D1
WLSD/HOW NE28 .... 73 K2
Tyne-Wear Trail *DUN/TMV* NE11 .... 8 D4
WICK/BNPF NE16 .... 85 H7
Tyzack St *BDN/LAN/SAC* DH7 .... 143 F1

U

Ugly La *CLSW/PEL* DH2 .... 144 A4
Uldale Ct *GOS/KPK* NE3 .... 55 J3 5
Ullerdale Cl *DHAM* DH1 .... 158 B5
Ullswater Av *HLH* DH5 .... 160 B1
JRW NE32 .... 90 B1
Ullswater Cl *BLYTH* NE24 .... 30 A6
Ullswater Crs *BLAY* NE21 .... 83 K4 6
Ullswater Dr *LGB/KIL* NE12 .... 48 B6
Ullswater Gdns *HAR/WTLS* NE34 .. 75 H4
Ullswater Gv *SWCK/CAS* SR5 .... 106 C1 5
Ullswater Rd *CLSW/PEL* DH2 .... 129 H6
NWBGN NE64 .... 24 E2
Ullswater Wy
WD/WHPE/BLK NE5 .... 69 F2
Ulverstone Ter
BYK/HTN/WLK NE6 .... 7 M3
Ulverston Gdns
LWF/SPW/WRK NE9 .... 101 H2
Umfraville Dene *PRUD* NE42 .... 80 D1
Underhill Dr *STKFD/GP* NE62 .... 22 E7
Underhill Rd
CLDN/WHIT/ROK SR6 .... 91 K4
Underwood Gv *CRAM* NE23 .... 33 G6
Union Aly *SSH* NE33 .... 3 G7
Union Hall Rd
BW/LEM/TK/HW NE15 .... 68 A3
Union La *CLSW/PEL* DH2 .... 144 C1
SUND SR1 .... 15 H3 2
Union Quay *TYNE/NSHE* NE30 .... 3 G2
Union Rd *BYK/HTN/WLK* NE6 .... 7 H4
TYNE/NSHE NE30 .... 3 H1
Union St *BLYTH* NE24 .... 31 G6
HLH DH5 .... 147 K4
JES NE2 .... 6 B5
JRW NE32 .... 73 K3
MLFD/PNYW SR4 .... 104 E7 5
NSHW NE29 .... 2 E3
SEA/MUR SR7 .... 150 E2 5
SSH NE33 .... 75 F5 5
SUND SR1 .... 14 E4
WLSD/HOW NE28 .... 72 D3
Unity Ter *STLY/ANP* DH9 .... 111 K4
STLY/ANP DH9 .... 111 G7
Unsworth Gdns *CON/LDGT* DH8 .. 123 F6
Unsworth St *CON/LDGT* DH8 .... 123 F5
Uplands *MONK* NE25 .... 50 B4
The Uplands *CLS/BIR/GTL* DH3 .... 115 K1
GOS/KPK NE3 .... 55 K6
Uplands Wy
LWF/SPW/WRK NE9 .... 102 B4
Upper Camden St
TYNE/NSHE NE30 .... 2 D1
Upper Elsdon St *NSHW* NE29 .... 2 C4 5
Upper Fenwick Gv *MPTH* NE61 .... 20 D3
Upper Norfolk St
TYNE/NSHE NE30 .... 2 E1 2
Upper Pearson St
TYNE/NSHE NE30 .... 2 E1
Upper Queen St
TYNE/NSHE NE30 .... 2 F1 2
Upton St *GATE* NE8 .... 10 A6 1
Urswick Ct *WD/WHPE/BLK* NE5 .... 55 F5
Urwin St *HLH* DH5 .... 148 A5
Ushaw Rd *HEBB* NE31 .... 73 H5
Usher Av *RDHAMSE* DH6 .... 158 C7
Usher St *SWCK/CAS* SR5 .... 106 B4 5
Usk Av *JRW* NE32 .... 90 A1
Usworth Station Rd
WASHN NE37 .... 103 G5 5

V

Valebrooke Av
ASHBK/HED/RY SR2 .... 14 C9
Valebrooke Gdns
ASHBK/HED/RY SR2 .... 14 D8
Valehead *MONK* NE25 .... 50 B4
Valentia Av *BYK/HTN/WLK* NE6 .... 7 L2
Valeria Cl *WLSD/HOW* NE28 .... 59 F4
Valerian Av
BW/LEM/TK/HW NE15 .... 66 B1
Valerian Ct *ASHGTN* NE63 .... 23 H4
Valeside *BW/LEM/TK/HW* NE15 .... 66 E1
Vale St *HLH* DH5 .... 160 A1
MLFD/PNYW SR4 .... 14 A7 5
Vale St East *MLFD/PNYW* SR4 .... 14 A7 5
Vale Vw *BDN/LAN/SAC* DH7 .... 141 H3
Vale Wk *JES* NE2 .... 6 D2
Valley Crs *BLAY* NE21 .... 83 J2
Valley Dene *CHPW* NE17 .... 95 H5
Valley Dr *BDN/LAN/SAC* DH7 .... 165 F1
DUN/TMV NE11 .... 9 G9
LWF/SPW/WRK NE9 .... 11 J9
WICK/BNPF NE16 .... 84 E4
Valley Forge *WASHS* NE38 .... 103 F7
Valley Gdns *CON/LDGT* DH8 .... 122 C3
LWF/SPW/WRK NE9 .... 11 J9
MONK NE25 .... 50 B4
WLSD/HOW NE28 .... 59 F7
Valley Garth *BDN/LAN/SAC* DH7 .. 153 F7
Valley Gv *BDN/LAN/SAC* DH7 .... 140 C5
Valley La *HAR/WTLS* NE34 .... 76 C5
Valley Rd *CLSW/PEL* DH2 .... 128 E3
MONK NE25 .... 40 C6
Valley Vw *BDN/LAN/SAC* DH7 .... 143 G6
BDN/LAN/SAC DH7 .... 167 G1
BW/LEM/TK/HW NE15 .... 68 A4
CLS/BIR/GTL DH3 .... 101 H6
CON/LDGT DH8 .... 122 B2
CON/LDGT DH8 .... 123 J4
JES NE2 .... 71 F2
JRW NE32 .... 73 K7
PRUD NE42 .... 80 E3
ROWG NE39 .... 97 F3
WASHS NE38 .... 117 G5
WICK/BNPF NE16 .... 97 H6
Vallum Rd
BW/LEM/TK/HW NE15 .... 67 G1
BYK/HTN/WLK NE6 .... 7 M4
Vallum Wy *ELS/FEN* NE4 .... 4 E6
Vanborough Ct *MONK* NE25 .... 40 A6 1
Vanburgh Gdns *MPTH* NE61 .... 20 B5
Vancouver Dr *LGB/HTN* NE7 .... 71 K1
Vane St *PLEE/EAS* SR8 .... 163 F5
SUNDSW SR3 .... 120 A7 7
WNGT TS28 .... 184 A6
Vane Ter *ASHBK/HED/RY* SR2 .... 15 K7
SEA/MUR SR7 .... 135 K7 5
Van Mildert Cl *PLEE/EAS* SR8 .. 174 C6 1
Vardy Ter *HLS* DH4 .... 118 C7
Vauxhall Rd *BYK/HTN/WLK* NE6 .... 72 C3
Vedra St *SWCK/CAS* SR5 .... 106 B4 10
Velville Ct *WD/WHPE/BLK* NE5 .... 55 F5 5
Ventnor Av *ELS/FEN* NE4 .... 4 A7
Ventnor Crs *LWF/SPW/WRK* NE9 .. 86 E6
Ventnor Gdns
LWF/SPW/WRK NE9 .... 86 E6
WBAY NE26 .... 50 E3
Vera St *RYTON* NE40 .... 82 B4
Verdun Av *HEBB* NE31 .... 73 G5
Vermont *WASHN* NE37 .... 103 F5
Verne Rd *NSHW* NE29 .... 60 B5
Vernon Cl *SSH* NE33 .... 75 F3
Vernon Dr *MONK* NE25 .... 50 C5
Vernon St *WASHN* NE37 .... 103 F5
Veryan Gdns *SUNDSW* SR3 .... 120 B3
Vespasian Av *SSH* NE33 .... 3 J5
Viador *CLS/BIR/GTL* DH3 .... 129 J3
Viaduct St *WLSD/HOW* NE28 .... 73 G1
Vicarage Cl *CLSW/PEL* DH2 .... 114 E7 1
SUNDSW SR3 .... 119 K7
Vicarage Est *WNGT* TS28 .... 183 K3
Vicarage Flats
BDN/LAN/SAC DH7 .... 167 G6 5
Vicarage La
MLFD/PNYW SR4 .... 104 E7 7
Vicarage Rd *SUNDSW* SR3 .... 120 A7
Vicarage St *NSHW* NE29 .... 2 C3
Vicarsholme Cl *SUNDSW* SR3 .... 133 J2
Vicars' La *LGB/HTN* NE7 .... 57 G5
Vicars Wy *LGB/KIL* NE12 .... 57 F4
Viceroy St *SEA/MUR* SR7 .... 150 E1
Victoria Av *ASHBK/HED/RY* SR2 .. 120 E4
BDN/LAN/SAC DH7 .... 167 H6
FELL NE10 .... 12 A8
LGB/KIL NE12 .... 57 K3
MLFD/PNYW SR4 .... 105 F7
WLSD/HOW NE28 .... 72 D1 5
Victoria Av West
ASHBK/HED/RY SR2 .... 120 E4
Victoria Crs *NSHW* NE29 .... 2 B4
Victoria Ms *BLYTH* NE24 .... 35 F1
Victoria Rd *CON/LDGT* DH8 .... 123 F5 13
GATE NE8 .... 10 A7
SSH NE33 .... 75 G2
WASHN NE37 .... 103 F5
Victoria Rd East *HEBB* NE31 .... 73 H5
Victoria Rd West *FELL* NE10 .... 88 E2
HEBB NE31 .... 88 E2
Victoria Sq *JES* NE2 .... 5 L2
Victoria St
BDN/LAN/SAC DH7 .... 140 B4 2
CON/LDGT DH8 .... 122 E4
DUN/TMV NE11 .... 9 J6
ELS/FEN NE4 .... 4 F8
HLH DH5 .... 147 K4 5
NSHW NE29 .... 2 D5
RDHAMSE DH6 .... 173 J4
RYTON NE40 .... 66 B7 2
SEA/MUR SR7 .... 150 D1
Victoria Ter *JRW* NE32 .... 73 J5
WBAY NE26 .... 51 F4
Victor St *CLS/BIR/GTL* DH3 .... 129 J4
Victory St *MLFD/PNYW* SR4 .... 105 J6
Victory St East *HLH* DH5 .... 148 A4 5
Victory St West *HLH* DH5 .... 148 A4 5
Victory Wy *SUNDSW* SR3 .... 133 G2
Viewforth Dr *SWCK/CAS* SR5 .... 106 C2
Viewforth Rd
ASHBK/HED/RY SR2 .... 135 F2
Viewforth Ter *SWCK/CAS* SR5 .... 106 B2
View La *STLY/ANP* DH9 .... 112 D7
View Pk *MONK* NE25 .... 49 K3
Vigo La *CLS/BIR/GTL* DH3 .... 115 K5
WASHS NE38 .... 116 B6
Village Centre *WASHS* NE38 .... 117 F2 5
Village Ct *WBAY* NE26 .... 50 D4
Village East *RYTON* NE40 .... 66 E5
Village Farm
BW/LEM/TK/HW NE15 .... 67 J2 1
Village La *WASHS* NE38 .... 103 F7
Village Rd *CRAM* NE23 .... 38 D2
The Village *ASHBK/HED/RY* SR2 .. 135 G1
Villa Pl *GATE* NE8 .... 10 E5
Villa Real Rd *CON/LDGT* DH8 .... 123 G3
The Villas *BDN/LAN/SAC* DH7 .... 141 G3
Villa Vw *LWF/SPW/WRK* NE9 .... 87 G6 5
Villette Brook St
ASHBK/HED/RY SR2 .... 15 G9 1
Villette Pth *ASHBK/HED/RY* SR2 .. 15 H9
Villette Rd *ASHBK/HED/RY* SR2 .. 120 E2
Villiers St *SUND* SR1 .... 15 G4
Villiers St South *SUND* SR1 .... 15 G5
Vimy Av *HEBB* NE31 .... 73 G5
Vincent St *PLEE/EAS* SR8 .... 163 F5 1
SEA/MUR SR7 .... 150 E2 5
Vine La *CNUT* NE1 .... 5 K4
Vine Pl *HLS* DH4 .... 132 C7
SUND SR1 .... 14 D6
Vine St *SSH* NE33 .... 75 G5
WLSD/HOW NE28 .... 72 E2
Viola Crs *BDN/LAN/SAC* DH7 .... 143 H6
CLSW/PEL DH2 .... 115 F4
Viola St *WASHN* NE37 .... 103 F5
Violet Cl *ELS/FEN* NE4 .... 69 H7 5
Violet St *HLS* DH4 .... 132 B7
MLFD/PNYW SR4 .... 14 B4
MLFD/PNYW SR4 .... 104 E7
Viscount Rd *SUNDSW* SR3 .... 120 A7 5
Vivian Crs *CLSW/PEL* DH2 .... 129 J5
Vivian Sq
CLDN/WHIT/ROK SR6 .... 106 D2 16
Voltage Ter *HLS* DH4 .... 132 B3 5
Vulcan Pl *BDLGTN* NE22 .... 29 G6

W

Waddington St *DHAM* DH1 .... 16 A3
Wadsley Sq
ASHBK/HED/RY SR2 .... 120 E3
Wagon Wy *WLSD/HOW* NE28 .... 73 F1
Wagonway Rd *HEBB* NE31 .... 73 F4
Wagtail La *STLY/ANP* DH9 .... 126 E6
Wagtail Ter *STLY/ANP* DH9 .... 127 G5
Wakefield Av *HAR/WTLS* NE34 .... 76 B6
Wakenshaw Rd *DHAM* DH1 .... 17 J1
Walbottle Rd
BW/LEM/TK/HW NE15 .... 67 H2
Walden Cl *CLSW/PEL* DH2 .... 114 D5
Waldo St *NSHW* NE29 .... 2 E3
Waldridge La *CLSW/PEL* DH2 .... 129 F5
Waldridge Rd *CLSW/PEL* DH2 .... 129 H5
Waldron Sq
ASHBK/HED/RY SR2 .... 120 E3
Walkerburn *CRAM* NE23 .... 38 C5
Walkergate *DHAM* DH1 .... 16 D3
Walker Pl *TYNE/NSHE* NE30 .... 3 G1 1
Walker Rd *BYK/HTN/WLK* NE6 .... 7 L9
Walker St *RDHAMSE* DH6 .... 180 A3
Wallace Gdns
LWF/SPW/WRK NE9 .... 102 A1
Wallace St *DUN/TMV* NE11 .... 9 J6 1
HLS DH4 .... 132 B7
JES NE2 .... 4 F2
SWCK/CAS SR5 .... 106 C4
Wallingford Av
ASHBK/HED/RY SR2 .... 120 E4
Wallington Av *DIN/WO* NE13 .... 46 A3
TYNE/NSHE NE30 .... 60 E1
Wallington Cl *BDLGTN* NE22 .... 29 J4
Wallington Ct *MONK* NE25 .... 40 A5 5
Wallington Dr
BW/LEM/TK/HW NE15 .... 68 C3
Wallington Rd *ASHGTN* NE63 .... 24 B3
Wallis St *HLS* DH4 .... 117 K6 2
SSH NE33 .... 3 G7 5
Wallnook La *BDN/LAN/SAC* DH7 .. 154 C2
Wallridge Dr *MONK* NE25 .... 40 B7
Wallsend Rd *NSHW* NE29 .... 60 B6
WLSD/HOW NE28 .... 60 A7
Wall St *GOS/KPK* NE3 .... 56 A5
Wall Ter *BYK/HTN/WLK* NE6 .... 7 L3
Walnut Gdns *GATE* NE8 .... 10 A8
Walnut Pl *GOS/KPK* NE3 .... 55 K7
Walpole Cl *SEA/MUR* SR7 .... 150 A2
Walpole Ct *MLFD/PNYW* SR4 .... 105 K7 5
Walpole St *BYK/HTN/WLK* NE6 .... 7 L1
Walsham Cl *BLYTH* NE24 .... 34 D2
Walsh Av *HEBB* NE31 .... 73 G4
Walsingham *WASHS* NE38 .... 116 E3
Walter St *JRW* NE32 .... 73 K3
Walter Ter *ELS/FEN* NE4 .... 4 D3
HLH DH5 .... 148 A7
Walter Thomas St
SWCK/CAS SR5 .... 105 K3 5
Waltham *WASHS* NE38 .... 117 F2
Waltham Cl *WLSD/HOW* NE28 .... 58 B7 4
Waltham Pl
WD/WHPE/BLK NE5 .... 69 F1 5
Walton Av *BLYTH* NE24 .... 30 E6
NSHW NE29 .... 60 D3
SEA/MUR SR7 .... 150 A2
Walton Cl *STLY/ANP* DH9 .... 126 E2
Walton Dr *STKFD/GP* NE62 .... 23 F6
Walton La *SUND* SR1 .... 15 H3
Walton Pk *NSHW* NE29 .... 60 D2
Walton Rd *WASHS* NE38 .... 117 K1
WD/WHPE/BLK NE5 .... 68 E2
Waltons Ter *BDN/LAN/SAC* DH7 .. 166 E2
Walton Ter *WNGT* TS28 .... 183 J2
Walwick Av *NSHW* NE29 .... 60 B4
Walwick Rd *MONK* NE25 .... 49 K4
Walworth Av *HAR/WTLS* NE34 .... 76 C5
Walworth Gv *JRW* NE32 .... 89 K1
Wandsworth Rd
BYK/HTN/WLK NE6 .... 6 E3
Wanebeck *WASHS* NE38 .... 116 C5
Wanlass Ter *DHAM* DH1 .... 16 E2
Wanley St *BLYTH* NE24 .... 31 G6
Wanlock Cl *CRAM* NE23 .... 38 C5
Wanny Rd *BDLGTN* NE22 .... 29 H5 1
Wansbeck Av *BLYTH* NE24 .... 35 G1
STKFD/GP NE62 .... 23 G5
STLY/ANP DH9 .... 126 D2
TYNE/NSHE NE30 .... 51 G6
Wansbeck Cl *CLSW/PEL* DH2 .... 115 F6
WICK/BNPF NE16 .... 98 E2
Wansbeck Crs *MPTH* NE61 .... 21 J2
Wansbeck Gv *CON/LDGT* DH8 .... 123 J2
MONK NE25 .... 40 A2 2
Wansbeck Ms *ASHGTN* NE63 .... 23 H1
Wansbeck Rd *ASHGTN* NE63 .... 23 G3
CRAM NE23 .... 47 F1

JRW NE32 .... 73 J6
Wansbeck Rd North
GOS/KPK NE3 .... 56 A3 🗄
Wansbeck Rd South
GOS/KPK NE3 .... 56 A4
Wansbeck St MPTH NE61 .. 20 E5 🗄
Wansdyke MPTH NE61 ...... 20 B4
Wansfell Av WD/WHPE/BLK NE5 .. 55 H7
Wansford Av
WD/WHPE/BLK NE5 .... 69 F2
Wantage Av NSHW NE29 ...... 60 B6
Wantage Rd DHAM DH1 ...... 158 A4
Wantage St SSH NE33 ...... 75 H4
Wapping St SSH NE33 ...... 3 G4
Warbeck Cl WD/WHPE/BLK NE5 .. 55 F1
Warburton Crs
LWF/SPW/WRK NE9 .... 11 K8
Warcop Ct GOS/KPK NE3 .. 55 J3
Warden Law La SUNDSW SR3.. 133 J1
Wardill Gdns
LWF/SPW/WRK NE9 .... 87 H5
Wardle Av SSH NE33 ...... 75 J2
Wardle Dr CRAM NE23 ...... 47 H1
Wardle Gdns FELL NE10 ...... 12 F9
Wardle St GOS/KPK NE3 .. 56 E5 🗄
STLY/ANP DH9 .... 126 C4
Wardley Ct FELL NE10 ...... 89 F4
Wardley Dr FELL NE10 ...... 89 F4
Wardley La FELL NE10 ...... 88 E3
Warenford Cl CRAM NE23 .. 38 D4 🗄
Warenford Pl
WD/WHPE/BLK NE5 .... 69 G4 🗄
Warenmill Cl
BW/LEM/TK/HW NE15 ...... 67 K4
Warennes St
MLFD/PNYW SR4 .... 105 J6 🗄
Warenton Pl NSHW NE29 .... 59 K1
Waring Av WBAY NE26 ...... 40 E5
Waring Ter SEA/MUR SR7 .. 150 A2
Wark Av NSHW NE29 ...... 60 A4
SMOOR NE27 .... 49 H5
Wark Crs JRW NE32 ...... 89 K2
Warkdale Av BLYTH NE24 .. 34 C1 🗄
Warkworth Av BLYTH NE24 .. 35 C2
HAR/WTLS NE34 .... 76 B4
WLSD/HOW NE28 .... 58 E6
Warkworth Cl WASHS NE38 .. 116 D2
Warkworth Crs ASHGTN NE63 .. 23 J2
GOS/KPK NE3 .... 56 B4
SEA/MUR SR7 .... 149 K1
Warkworth Dr CLSW/PEL DH2 .. 129 G6
DIN/WO NE13 .... 46 C2
MPTH NE61 .... 21 K2
Warkworth Rd DHAM DH1 .. 156 D2
Warkworth St
BW/LEM/TK/HW NE15 ...... 68 A5
Warkworth Ter JRW NE32 .. 89 K1
TYNE/NSHE NE30 .... 61 H2 🗄
Warnham Av
ASHBK/HED/RY SR2 .... 120 E4
Warnhead Rd BDLGTN NE22.. 29 H5
Warren Av BYK/HTN/WLK NE6 .. 72 C3
Warren Cl HLS DH4 .... 132 A3 🗄
Warren Ct ASHGTN NE63 .. 23 J3
Warrenmor FELL NE10 ...... 13 K9
Warren St PLEE/EAS SR8 .. 175 H4
Warrington Rd ELS/FEN NE4 .. 4 D8
GOS/KPK NE3 .... 55 J4
Warton Ter
BYK/HTN/WLK NE6 .... 71 J3 🗄
WICK/BNPF NE16 .... 84 E7
Warwick Av CON/LDGT DH8 .. 137 F1
WICK/BNPF NE16 .... 84 E7
Warwick Cl CRAM NE23 ...... 39 F7 🗄
WICK/BNPF NE16 .... 84 E7 🗄
Warwick Ct DHAM DH1 ...... 168 B3 🗄
GOS/KPK NE3 .... 55 H3
Warwick Dr HLH DH5 ...... 147 H2
SUNDSW SR3 .... 119 G2
WASHN NE37 .... 103 F3
WICK/BNPF NE16 .... 85 F7
Warwick Gv BDLGTN NE22 .. 28 D5
Warwick Hall Wk LGB/HTN NE7 .. 71 K1
Warwick Pl PLEE/EAS SR8 .. 174 C2
Warwick Rd HAR/WTLS NE34 .. 75 H4
HEBB NE31 .... 89 H1 🗄
WD/WHPE/BLK NE5 .... 68 C3 🗄
WLSD/HOW NE28 .... 72 D2
Warwickshire Dr DHAM DH1 .. 158 A7 🗄
Warwick St BLYTH NE24 .. 34 D3
GATE NE8 .... 11 G3
JES NE2 .... 6 B3
SWCK/CAS SR5 .... 106 D4
Warwick Ter SUNDSW SR3 .. 120 A6
Wasdale Cl CRAM NE23 .. 38 C5
PLEE/EAS SR8.................. 175 F4
Wasdale Ct
CLDN/WHIT/ROK SR6 ...... 92 C7 🗄
Wasdale Rd WD/WHPE/BLK NE5 .. 69 F3
Washington Hwy WASHN NE37.. 102 C5
WASHS NE38 .... 116 C4
Washington St SWCK/CAS SR5.. 104 D2
Washington St
MLFD/PNYW SR4 .... 105 K7 🗄
Washingwell La
WICK/BNPF NE16 .... 85 H5
Washingwell Pk
WICK/BNPF NE16 .... 85 G6
Waskdale Crs BLAY NE21 .. 83 K4 🗄
Waskerley Cl WICK/BNPF NE16.. 98 E2
Waskerley Dr RDHAMSE DH6 .. 173 G3
Waskerley Rd WASHS NE38.. 117 H3
Watch House Cl NSHW NE29 .. 2 C7
Watcombe Cl WASHN NE37 .. 103 H3 🗄
Waterbeach Pl
WD/WHPE/BLK NE5 .... 68 C1
Waterbeck Cl CRAM NE23 .. 38 C5
Waterbury Rd GOS/KPK NE3 .. 56 B1
Waterfield Rd BDLGTN NE22 .. 30 D2
Waterford Cl HLH DH5 ...... 147 G4 🗄
WBAY NE26 .... 41 G2 🗄
Waterford Gn ASHGTN NE63.. 23 H5
Waterford Pk DIN/WO NE13 .. 45 K3
Watergate Rd CON/LDGT DH8 .. 136 C2
Waterloo Pl NSHW NE29 .... 60 E4
SUND SR1 .... 14 E5
Waterloo Rd BLYTH NE24 .. 31 G7
MONK NE25 .... 49 J4
WASHN NE37 .... 103 G4

Waterloo Sq SSH NE33 ...... 3 H7 🗄
Waterloo St BLAY NE21 .... 83 J3 🗄
CNUT NE1 .... 5 H8
Waterlow Cl SWCK/CAS SR5 .. 105 K1 🗄
Watermill RYTON NE40 ...... 67 F6
Watermill La FELL NE10 .... 12 E8
Waterside Dr DUN/TMV NE11 .. 8 E4
Waterson Crs
BDN/LAN/SAC DH7 .... 143 G7
Water St BDN/LAN/SAC DH7 .. 143 H5
ELS/FEN NE4 .... 9 L2
Waterville Rd NSHW NE29 .. 60 B6
Waterworks Rd SUND SR1 .. 14 B5
Watford Cl SWCK/CAS SR5 .. 105 K1 🗄
Watkin Crs SEA/MUR SR7 .. 149 H5
Watling Av SEA/MUR SR7 .. 150 A2
Watling Pl
LWF/SPW/WRK NE9 .... 87 H6 🗄
Watling St HAR/WTLS NE34 .. 76 B5
Watling Wy BDN/LAN/SAC DH7 .. 140 B5
Watson Av HAR/WTLS NE34 .. 76 B6
Watson Cl RDHAMSE DH6 .. 173 F7 🗄
Watson Crescent TRIM TS29 .. 183 G6 🗄
Watson Gdns
WLSD/HOW NE28 .... 59 J7 🗄
Watson Pl HAR/WTLS NE34 .. 76 B6 🗄
Watson St CON/LDGT DH8 .. 122 E5 🗄
JRW NE32 .... 74 A3
STLY/ANP DH9 .... 112 D6
WICK/BNPF NE16 .... 97 K7 🗄
Watt's La NWBGN NE64 ...... 19 G7 🗄
Watt's Rd WBAY NE26 ...... 50 E3
Watts St SEA/MUR SR7 ...... 149 H5 🗄
Watt St GATE NE8 .... 10 D9
Wavendon Crs
MLFD/PNYW SR4 .... 119 H2
Waveney Gdns STLY/ANP DH9 .. 126 C1 🗄
Waveney Rd PLEE/EAS SR8 .. 174 C6
Waverdale Av
BYK/HTN/WLK NE6 .... 72 C4
Waverdale Wy SSH NE33 .. 75 F5
Waverley Av BDLGTN NE22 .. 29 J4 🗄
MONK NE25 .... 50 D5
Waverley Cl BLAY NE21 .. 83 H4 🗄
RDHAMSE DH6 .... 173 G3
Waverley Crs
BW/LEM/TK/HW NE15 ...... 68 B4
Waverley Dr BDLGTN NE22 .. 29 J4
Waverley Rd ELS/FEN NE4 .. 4 E9
LWF/SPW/WRK NE9 .... 101 G3
Waverley Ter MLFD/PNYW SR4 .. 105 J6
Waverton Cl CRAM NE23 .. 38 C5
Wawn St SSH NE33 .... 75 H3 🗄
Wayfarer Rd SWCK/CAS SR5 .. 106 A4
Wayland Sq
ASHBK/HED/RY SR2 .... 120 E5
Wayman St SWCK/CAS SR5 .. 106 C4
Wayside ASHBK/HED/RY SR2 .. 14 A9
BW/LEM/TK/HW NE15 ...... 69 F6
RDHAMSE DH6 .... 178 C5
Wealcroft FELL NE10 ...... 88 B7 🗄
Wealleans Cl ASHGTN NE63.. 24 D2
Wear Av CON/LDGT DH8 .. 123 K2
Wear Ct HAR/WTLS NE34 .. 75 G6
Weardale Av BLYTH NE24 .. 30 B6
BYK/HTN/WLK NE6 .... 72 C4
CLDN/WHIT/ROK SR6 ...... 92 E5
LGB/KIL NE12 .... 57 K2
WASHN NE37 .... 102 E5
WLSD/HOW NE28 .... 58 D6 🗄
Weardale Crs HLS DH4 .... 117 K7
Weardale Pk RDHAMSE DH6.. 173 F7
Weardale St HLH DH5 ...... 147 H7
Weardale Wy SPEN DL16 .. 177 G7
Wearfield SWCK/CAS SR5 .. 105 J4
Wear Ldg CLS/BIR/GTL DH3 .. 115 J7
Wearmouth Av
SWCK/CAS SR5 .... 106 D3 🗄
Wearmouth Br SUND SR1 .. 14 E3
Wearmouth Dr SWCK/CAS SR5 .. 106 C3
Wearmouth St
SWCK/CAS SR5 .... 106 A4 🗄🗄
Wear Rd HEBB NE31 ...... 73 G7
STLY/ANP DH9 .... 126 D2
Wearside Dr DHAM DH1 .... 16 E1
Wear St CHPW NE17 ...... 95 J4
CON/LDGT DH8.................. 123 G5
HLH DH5 .... 147 K5
HLS DH4 .... 146 D1
JRW NE32 .... 73 K4 🗄
MLFD/PNYW SR4 .... 104 E6
SEA/MUR SR7 .... 150 E1 🗄🗄
SUND SR1 .... 15 J5
SWCK/CAS SR5 .... 106 A4
Wear Vw DHAM DH1 ...... 16 F2
Weathercock La
LWF/SPW/WRK NE9 .... 87 F7 🗄🗄
Weatherside BLAY NE21 .. 83 K3 🗄
Webb Av SEA/MUR SR7 .... 149 H4
SEA/MUR SR7 .... 149 K1
Webb Gdns FELL NE10 .... 13 K8
Webb Sq PLEE/EAS SR8 .. 175 F1
Wedgewood Cottages
BW/LEM/TK/HW NE15 ...... 68 B5 🗄
Wedgwood Rd SEA/MUR SR7 .. 149 K2
Wedmore Rd
WD/WHPE/BLK NE5 .... 68 B1
Weetman St SSH NE33 ...... 75 F2 🗄
Weetslade Crs CRAM NE23 .. 47 G2
Weetslade Rd CRAM NE23 .. 47 G2
Weetwood Rd CRAM NE23 .. 38 D4 🗄
Weidner Rd
BW/LEM/TK/HW NE15 ...... 69 H6
Welbeck Rd BYK/HTN/WLK NE6 .. 7 H6
STKFD/GP NE62 .... 22 E6 🗄
Welbeck Ter PRUD NE42 .. 64 B6
Weldon Av
ASHBK/HED/RY SR2 .... 120 E4 🗄
Weldon Cl LGB/HTN NE7 .. 71 H1
Weldon Pl NSHW NE29 .... 60 D1
Weldon Rd CRAM NE23 .. 39 F3 🗄
LGB/KIL NE12 .... 57 H4
Weldon Ter CLS/BIR/GTL DH3 .. 129 K5
Weldon Wy GOS/KPK NE3 .. 56 B4
Welfare Rd PLEE/EAS SR8 .. 163 F5

Welfare Crs NWBGN NE64 .. 24 E1
RHTLP TS27 .... 175 K7
Welfare Rd HLH DH5 ...... 147 K4
Welford Av GOS/KPK NE3 .. 56 A5
Welford Rd CON/LDGT DH8.. 122 C7
Welland Cl PLEE/EAS SR8 .. 174 D6
Welland Cl SWCK/CAS SR6 .. 92 E3
Wellands Cl
CLDN/WHIT/ROK SR6 ...... 92 E3
Wellands Ct
CLDN/WHIT/ROK SR6 ...... 92 E3
Well Bank Rd WASHN NE37.. 102 D5
Wellburn Rd WASHN NE37 .. 102 D4
Well Close Wk
WICK/BNPF NE16 .... 84 E6 🗄
Well Dean PRUD NE42 ...... 80 D1
Wellesley St JRW NE32 .... 73 K6
Wellesley Ter ELS/FEN NE4 .. 4 C6
Wellfield Cl
BW/LEM/TK/HW NE15 ...... 66 E2
Wellfield Ct RYTON NE40 .. 82 A2
Wellfield La
WD/WHPE/BLK NE5 .... 69 F1 🗄
Wellfield Rd ELS/FEN NE4 .. 69 H6
ROWG NE39 .... 96 E3
SEA/MUR SR7 .... 149 G5
WNGT TS28 .... 183 K2
Wellhead Dean Rd MPTH NE61 .. 22 E3
Wellhead Ter ASHGTN NE63.. 23 G1
Wellington Av MONK NE25 .. 49 J4 🗄
Wellington Dr SSH NE33 .. 3 G5
Wellington La MLFD/PNYW SR4 .. 14 A2
Wellington Rd DUN/TMV NE11 .. 8 E6
STKFD/GP NE62 .... 23 G6 🗄
Wellington St BLYTH NE24 .. 31 H7 🗄
ELS/FEN NE4 .... 5 C5
FELL NE10 .... 13 B7
HEBB NE31 .... 73 F6
Well La SMOOR NE27 ...... 49 K7
Well Ridge Cl MONK NE25 .. 50 A3
Well Ridge Pk MONK NE25 .. 50 A2
Well Rd PSHWF NE43 ...... 79 F7
Wells Cl LGB/KIL NE12 .... 57 K6 🗄
Wells Crs SEA/MUR SR7 .. 150 A1
Wells Gv LWF/SPW/WRK NE9 .. 101 F3
Well St HAR/WTLS NE34 .... 76 A4
Well St MLFD/PNYW SR4 .. 105 K6
Well Wy MPTH NE61 ...... 20 D4
Wellway Ct MPTH NE61 .. 20 D4
Wellwood Gdns MPTH NE61 .. 20 E4 🗄
Welsh Ter STLY/ANP DH9 .. 125 J4
Welton Cl PSHWF NE43 .... 79 H6
Welwyn Av BDLGTN NE22 .. 29 K2
Welwyn Cl SWCK/CAS SR5 .. 104 E5
WLSD/HOW NE28 .... 58 B6
Wembley Av MONK NE25 .. 50 C2
Wembley Rd SWCK/CAS SR5 .. 105 K2
Wendover Cl SWCK/CAS SR5 .. 105 J1
Wendover Wy SWCK/CAS SR5 .. 105 J1
Wenham Sq
ASHBK/HED/RY SR2 .... 120 B2 🗄
Wenlock WASHS NE38 ...... 116 E2
Wenlock Dr NSHW NE29 .... 60 C2
Wenlock Rd HAR/WTLS NE34 .. 74 E6
Wensley CLSW/PEL DH2 .. 114 C5
Wensleydale
WLSD/HOW NE28 .... 58 B5 🗄
WASHN NE37 .... 102 E5 🗄
Wens Leydale Dr
LGB/KIL NE12 .... 57 K2 🗄
Wensleydale Ter BLYTH NE24 .. 35 H1
Wentworth Cl FELL NE10 .. 87 K5 🗄
Wentworth Ct PONT/DH NE20.. 42 E5
Wentworth Dr WASHN NE37 .. 102 E3
Wentworth Gdns MONK NE25 .. 50 A4
Wentworth Pl ELS/FEN NE4 .. 4 D8
Wentworth Ter
MLFD/PNYW SR4 .... 14 A4
Werdohl Wy CON/LDGT DH8 .. 123 G2
Werhale Gn FELL NE10 .... 13 H9
Wesley Dr LGB/KIL NE12 .. 58 D1
Wesley Gdns CON/LDGT DH8 .. 137 G2
Wesley Gv RYTON NE40 .... 82 A1
Wesley Mt RYTON NE40 .... 82 A1
Wesley St CON/LDGT DH8 .. 122 D3
CON/LDGT DH8.................. 123 F5
LWF/SPW/WRK NE9 .... 87 F7 🗄🗄
PRUD NE42 .... 80 D2
Wesley Wy
BW/LEM/TK/HW NE15 ...... 67 F1
LGB/KIL NE12 .... 58 D1
SEA/MUR SR7 .... 150 A1
Wessex Cl SWCK/CAS SR5 .. 105 K1
Wessington Wy SWCK/CAS SR5 .. 104 D6
SWCK/CAS SR5 .... 106 A4 🗄🗄
West Acre CON/LDGT DH8.. 122 C2
Westacre Gdns
WD/WHPE/BLK NE5 .... 69 G4 🗄
West Acres DIN/WO NE13 .. 45 F1 🗄
Westacres Av WICK/BNPF NE16.. 99 F1
Westacres Crs
BW/LEM/TK/HW NE15 ...... 69 G5 🗄
West Av CLDN/WHIT/ROK SR6 .. 92 E3
GOS/KPK NE3 .... 56 C6
HAR/WTLS NE34................ 75 J5
LGB/KIL NE12 .... 57 K4
NSHW NE29 .... 60 B5
PLEE/EAS SR8.................. 163 F4
ROWG NE39 .... 97 F4 🗄
SEA/MUR SR7 .... 149 H5 🗄
STKFD/GP NE62 .... 22 D6
WASHS NE38 .... 116 D5
West Bailey LGB/KIL NE12 .. 47 K5 🗄🗄
LGB/KIL NE12 .... 47 K6 🗄
Westbourne Av
BYK/HTN/WLK NE6 .... 72 B3
GATE NE8 .... 10 E7
GOS/KPK NE3 .... 56 C3
STKFD/GP NE62 .... 23 G4
Westbourne Dr HLS DH4 .. 131 J1
Westbourne Rd SUND SR1 .. 14 B5
Westburn Gdns
WLSD/HOW NE28 .... 58 B6 🗄
Westburn Ms RYTON NE40 .. 82 A1 🗄

Westburn Ter
CLDN/WHIT/ROK SR6 ...... 106 E3
Westbury Av BYK/HTN/WLK NE6 .. 72 B3
Westbury Rd NSHW NE29 .. 60 D2 🗄
Westcliff Cl PLEE/EAS SR8 .. 162 B6 🗄
Westcliffe Rd
CLDN/WHIT/ROK SR6 ...... 107 F1 🗄
Westcliffe Wy HAR/WTLS NE34 .. 90 D1
West Clifton LGB/KIL NE12 .. 47 J5 🗄🗄
West Copperas
BW/LEM/TK/HW NE15 ...... 68 C4 🗄
Westcott Av SSH NE33 .... 75 J2
Westcott Rd DHAM DH1 .. 156 B4
Westcott Rd HAR/WTLS NE34.. 75 G6
PLEE/EAS SR8.................. 174 E3
West Crs FELL NE10 ...... 88 E4
Westcroft Rd LGB/KIL NE12 .. 58 A2
West Dene Dr TYNE/NSHE NE30 .. 60 E2
West Denton Cl
BW/LEM/TK/HW NE15 ...... 68 B3
West Denton Rd
BW/LEM/TK/HW NE15 ...... 68 B3
West Denton Wy
WD/WHPE/BLK NE5 .... 68 B1
WD/WHPE/BLK NE5 .... 68 B1 🗄
West Dr BDN/LAN/SAC DH7 .. 140 D5
BLYTH NE24 .... 34 E3 🗄
CLDN/WHIT/ROK SR6 ...... 91 J3
CLSW/PEL DH2 .... 129 F5
West End Front St
BDLGTN NE22 .... 29 F6 🗄
Westerdale HLS DH4 ...... 117 G6
WLSD/HOW NE28 .... 58 B6
Westerdale Pl
BYK/HTN/WLK NE6 .... 72 D5
Westerham Cl SWCK/CAS SR5.. 105 K1
Westerhope Gdns
WD/WHPE/BLK NE5 .... 69 H2 🗄🗄
Westerhope Rd WASHS NE38 .. 117 H1
Westerkirk CRAM NE23 .... 38 C4
Western Av SSH NE33 ...... 75 G2
Western Av BDN/LAN/SAC DH7 .. 165 G1
MONK NE25 .... 39 K5
PRUD NE42 .... 80 B2
WD/WHPE/BLK NE5 .... 68 B2
Western Dr ELS/FEN NE4 .. 4 A6 🗄
Western Hwy WASHS NE38.. 116 A6
Western Hl ASHBK/HED/RY SR2 .. 14 A6
CON/LDGT DH8.................. 122 C2
Westernmoor WASHN NE37 .. 102 B7
Western Rd JRW NE32 ...... 73 J4
WLSD/HOW NE28 .... 73 H1
Western Ter BOL NE36 .... 90 E5
CRAM NE23 .... 47 F1
Western Wy BLAY NE21 .. 84 C2
BW/LEM/TK/HW NE15 ...... 52 C2
PONT/DH NE20 .... 42 C5
RYTON NE40 .... 66 E7
WBAY NE26 .... 50 D1
West Farm Av LGB/KIL NE12 .. 57 F4 🗄
West Farm Ct CRAM NE23 .. 38 C1 🗄
West Farm La CON/LDGT DH8.. 109 J4
West Farm Rd BYK/HTN/WLK NE6.. 7 M3
CLDN/WHIT/ROK SR6 ...... 92 A3
WLSD/HOW NE28 .... 59 G7
West Farm Wynd LGB/KIL NE12.. 57 F5
Westfield GOS/KPK NE3 .... 70 B1
MPTH NE61 .... 20 C6
Westfield Av DIN/WO NE13.. 46 A3
GOS/KPK NE3 .... 56 C7
MONK NE25 .... 50 B5
RYTON NE40 .... 82 B1
Westfield Ct
MLFD/PNYW SR4 .... 119 J2 🗄
WLSD/HOW NE28 .... 72 D3
Westfield Crs NWBGN NE64.. 25 F2
RYTON NE40 .... 82 B1
Westfield Dr GOS/KPK NE3 .. 56 B7
Westfield Gv GOS/KPK NE3 .. 56 B7
MLFD/PNYW SR4 .... 119 J2
Westfield La RYTON NE40 .. 66 D5
Westfield Pk WLSD/HOW NE28 .. 72 C1
Westfield Rd
BW/LEM/TK/HW NE15 ...... 69 G6
GATE NE8 .... 10 E7
Westfield Ter GATE NE8 .... 10 F7
West Ford Rd STKFD/GP NE62 .. 23 H4
Westgarth WD/WHPE/BLK NE5 .. 54 C6
Westgarth Gv RDHAMSE DH6.. 173 F6
Westgate MPTH NE61 ...... 20 B6
Westgate Cl MONK NE25 .. 50 A3
Westgate Gv SUNDSW SR3 .. 120 A6
Westgate Hill Ter CNUT NE1.. 5 G7
Westgate Rd CNUT NE1 .... 5 G7
ELS/FEN NE4 .... 69 J5 🗄
West George Potts St
SSH NE33 .... 75 H2 🗄
West Gra SWCK/CAS SR5 .. 106 C2
Westgreen STKFD/GP NE62 .. 28 E3
West Greens MPTH NE61 .. 20 E5 🗄
West Gv MLFD/PNYW SR4 .. 119 F1
Westheath Av
ASHBK/HED/RY SR2 .... 120 E5
West High Horse Cl ROWG NE39.. 97 H1
West Hl MLFD/PNYW SR4 .. 119 J2
MPTH NE61 .... 20 B6
Westhills STLY/ANP DH9 .. 111 J4 🗄
Westhills Cl BDN/LAN/SAC DH7 .. 143 G5
West Holborn SSH NE33 .. 75 F2
Westholme Gdns
BW/LEM/TK/HW NE15 ...... 69 H5
Westhope Cl HAR/WTLS NE34 .. 76 A1
Westhope Rd HAR/WTLS NE34 .. 76 A1
West Jesmond Av JES NE2.. 70 E1 🗄
Westlands
BW/LEM/TK/HW NE15 ...... 68 A2
JRW NE32 .... 90 B3
LGB/HTN NE7 .... 57 G7
TYNE/NSHE NE30 .... 61 F1
WBAY NE26 .... 40 E2
West La BLAY NE21 ...... 83 J4
CHPW NE17 .... 109 H2
CLS/BIR/GTL DH3 .... 129 J5
LGB/KIL NE12 .... 57 K1
RDHAMSE DH6 .... 161 J3
SEA/MUR SR7 .... 162 A2 🗄
WICK/BNPF NE16 .... 98 A4

West Lawn ASHBK/HED/RY SR2 .. 14 D9
West Law Rd CON/LDGT DH8 .. 108 D6
West Lawson St NSHW NE29 .. 2 C5
West Lea BLAY NE21 ...... 84 A3
Westleigh Ct
MLFD/PNYW SR4 .... 105 K7 🗄🗄
Westleigh Rd HLS DH4 .... 132 A3
Westley Av WBAY NE26 .... 41 H7
Westley Cl WBAY NE26 .... 41 H7
Westloch Rd CRAM NE23 .. 38 C5
Westmacott St
BW/LEM/TK/HW NE15 ...... 67 G3 🗄
West Market St MPTH NE61 .. 18 D1 🗄
West Mdw
WD/WHPE/BLK NE5 .... 54 B6 🗄
West Meadows Dr
CLDN/WHIT/ROK SR6 ...... 92 A4
West Meadows Rd
CLDN/WHIT/ROK SR6 ...... 92 A4
Westminster Av NSHW NE29 .. 59 K2
Westminster Crs HEBB NE31 .. 89 C2
Westminster Dr
DUN/TMV NE11 .... 85 K6 🗄
Westminster St GATE NE8 .. 10 E8
Westminster Wy LGB/HTN NE7 .. 57 J6
West Moffett St SSH NE33 .. 75 H2 🗄🗄
West Moor Dr
CLDN/WHIT/ROK SR6 ...... 92 A5
Westmoor Dr LGB/KIL NE12 .. 57 H1
Westmoor Rd MLFD/PNYW SR4.. 105 H6
Westmoreland St
WLSD/HOW NE28................ 72 E1
Westmorland Av BDLGTN NE22.. 28 E5
NWBGN NE64 .... 25 F2
WASHN NE37 .... 103 F3
WLSD/HOW NE28 .... 73 K2 🗄
Westmorland Gdns
LWF/SPW/WRK NE9 .... 87 F7 🗄🗄
Westmorland La CNUT NE1 .. 5 H8
ELS/FEN NE4 .... 4 B9
HAR/WTLS NE34................ 76 C4
NSHW NE29 .... 59 K3
Westmorland Wy CRAM NE23 .. 38 A2
West Mt MLFD/PNYW SR4 .. 119 J1
Westoe Av SSH NE33 ...... 75 J2
Westoe Dr SSH NE33 ...... 75 J2
Westoe Rd SSH NE33 ...... 3 J9
Westoe Village SSH NE33 .. 75 J3
Weston Av WICK/BNPF NE16 .. 84 D7
Weston Vw PLEE/EAS SR8 .. 174 D3
West Ousterley Rd
STLY/ANP DH9 .... 126 E5
Westover Gdns
LWF/SPW/WRK NE9 .... 87 F5
West Pde CON/LDGT DH8 .. 123 F5
ELS/FEN NE4 .... 4 E8
HEBB NE31 .... 73 F7
West Pk MPTH NE61 ...... 20 C6
SUNDSW SR3 .... 133 F1
West Park Gdns BLAY NE21 .. 84 A3
West Park Rd
CLDN/WHIT/ROK SR6 ...... 92 A3
LWF/SPW/WRK NE9 .... 86 E5
SSH NE33 .... 75 G3
West Park Vw CRAM NE23 .. 47 F1
West Pastures ASHGTN NE63.. 23 H3
BOL NE36 .... 90 A7
West Percy Rd NSHW NE29 .. 2 C1
West Percy St NSHW NE29 .. 2 C2
Westport Cl SWCK/CAS SR5 .. 105 K1 🗄
West Quay Rd SWCK/CAS SR5.. 105 K4
West Riggs BDLGTN NE22 .. 29 F6
The West Rig GOS/KPK NE3 .. 55 J6
West Rd BDLGTN NE22 .... 29 K4
CON/LDGT DH8.................. 122 C3
PONT/DH NE20 .... 43 F3
PRUD NE42 .... 80 B2
STLY/ANP DH9 .... 111 J5
STLY/ANP DH9 .... 125 H4
West Salisbury St BLYTH NE24 .. 31 F6
West Stainton St SSH NE33 .. 75 J2 🗄🗄
West Stevenson St
SSH NE33 .... 75 H2 🗄🗄
West Stoneycroft
LGB/KIL NE12 .... 48 A7 🗄
West St CLS/BIR/GTL DH3 .. 115 J2
CLSW/PEL DH2 .... 128 A2
CON/LDGT DH8.................. 123 J3
GATE NE8 .... 10 F1
HEBB NE31 .... 73 G4
RDHAMSE DH6 .... 173 H4
RDHAMSE DH6 .... 179 F6
ROWG NE39 .... 96 B1
SEA/MUR SR7 .... 150 E1
SMOOR NE27 .... 59 F1
STLY/ANP DH9 .... 112 B6
SUND SR1 .... 14 D4
SUNDSW SR3 .... 120 A6 🗄
WICK/BNPF NE16 .... 84 E5
WLSD/HOW NE28 .... 72 C1
West Sunniside SUND SR1 .. 14 F4
Westsyde PONT/DH NE20 .. 42 C6
West Ter DHAM DH1 ...... 16 A2
WBAY NE26 .... 41 G2
West Thorp WD/WHPE/BLK NE5 .. 54 D5
West Vallum
BW/LEM/TK/HW NE15 ...... 68 D4 🗄
West Vw ASHGTN NE63 .... 23 K2 🗄
BDLGTN NE22 .... 29 J3
BDN/LAN/SAC DH7 .... 167 H7
BLAY NE21 .... 84 A1
BW/LEM/TK/HW NE15 ...... 68 A5
CLDN/WHIT/ROK SR6 ...... 106 D2
DHAM DH1 .... 17 H2
DUN/TMV NE11 .... 100 D7
ELS/FEN NE4 .... 4 A9
HLS DH4 .... 131 K3
LGB/KIL NE12 .... 57 K2 🗄🗄
MPTH NE61 .... 21 J2
STKFD/GP NE62 .... 24 C7
SWCK/CAS SR5 .... 105 F4 🗄
West Walls CNUT NE1 ...... 5 H7
West Walpole St SSH NE33 .. 75 F2
Westward Ct
WD/WHPE/BLK NE5 .... 54 C7 🗄
Westward Pl WASHS NE38 .. 116 D5

Westway *BLAY* NE21 ...... 83 K2
  BW/LEM/TK/HW NE15 ...... 53 F7
West Wy *DUN/TMV* NE11 ...... 9 J8
Westway *PLEE/EAS* SR8 ...... 174 D5
West Wy *SSH* NE33 ...... 75 G4
West Wellington St
  NSHW NE29 ...... 2 D2
Westwood Av
  BYK/HTN/WLK NE6 ...... 71 J2
Westwood CI *WICK/BNPF* NE16 ...... 97 K6
Westwood Gdns *GOS/KPK* NE3 ...... 55 J6
  STKFD/GP NE62 ...... 23 F4
Westwood Rd *GOS/KPK* NE3 ...... 56 C1
Westwood St
  MLFD/PNYW SR4 ...... 105 K7
Westwood Vw *RYTON* NE40 ...... 82 A1
West Wylam Dr *PRUD* NE42 ...... 80 E1
West Wynd *LGB/KIL* NE12 ...... 47 K6
Wetheral Gdns
  LWF/SPW/WRK NE9 ...... 101 G2
Wetheral Ter
  BYK/HTN/WLK NE6 ...... 72 B7
Wetherburn Av *SEA/MUR* SR7 ...... 149 C5
Wetherby CI *CON/LDGT* DH8 ...... 108 D7
Wetherby Gv *GATE* NE8 ...... 10 C9
Wetherby Rd
  ASHBK/HED/RY SR2 ...... 121 C5
Wettondale Av *BLYTH* NE24 ...... 30 C7
Weybourne Sq
  ASHBK/HED/RY SR2 ...... 120 E4
Weyhill Av *NSHW* NE29 ...... 60 B6
Weymouth Dr *SEA/MUR* SR7 ...... 150 B2
Weymouth Gdns
  LWF/SPW/WRK NE9 ...... 101 F3
Whaggs La *WICK/BNPF* NE16 ...... 85 F6
Whalebone La *MPTH* NE61 ...... 20 D5
Whalton Av *GOS/KPK* NE3 ...... 56 A4
Whalton CI *FELL* NE10 ...... 88 E5
  RDHAMSE DH6 ...... 170 D1
Whalton St *HAR/WTLS* NE34 ...... 75 J5
Whaper Sq *RDHAMSE* DH6 ...... 182 D2
Wharfdale PI *BYK/HTN/WLK* NE6 ...... 72 B7
Wharfedale *HLS* DH4 ...... 117 J6
  WLSD/HOW NE28 ...... 58 B5
Wharfedale Av *WASHN* NE37 ...... 102 D5
Wharfedale Dr *SSH* NE33 ...... 75 G4
Wharfedale Gdns *BLYTH* NE24 ...... 30 C6
Wharmlands Rd
  BW/LEM/TK/HW NE15 ...... 68 D4
Wharncliffe St *SUND* SR1 ...... 14 B5
Wharnley Wy *CON/LDGT* DH8 ...... 136 E2
Wharrier St *BYK/HTN/WLK* NE6 ...... 72 B7
Wharton St *BLYTH* NE24 ...... 34 D3
  SSH NE33 ...... 3 K9
Wheatall Dr
  CLDN/WHIT/ROK SR6 ...... 93 F2
Wheatfield CI *PRUD* NE42 ...... 64 B6
Wheatfield Gv *LGB/KIL* NE12 ...... 57 H3
Wheatfield Rd
  WD/WHPE/BLK NE5 ...... 54 D7
Wheatley Gdns *BOL* NE36 ...... 90 E5
Wheatley Green La
  BDN/LAN/SAC DH7 ...... 127 H7
Wheatley Ter *RDHAMSE* DH6 ...... 182 D1
Wheatleywell La
  CLS/BIR/GTL DH3 ...... 144 D3
Whernside CI *CRAM* NE23 ...... 38 C5
Whernside Wk *RYTON* NE40 ...... 67 F7
Whickham CI *HLS* DH4 ...... 132 A7
Whickham Hwy *DUN/TMV* NE11 ...... 85 J5
  WICK/BNPF NE16 ...... 8 C9
Whickham Ldg
  WICK/BNPF NE16 ...... 85 G5
Whickham Pk *WICK/BNPF* NE16 ...... 8 A9
Whickham Rd *HEBB* NE31 ...... 73 H6
Whickham St
  CLDN/WHIT/ROK SR6 ...... 15 G1
  PLEE/EAS SR8 ...... 162 E5
Whickham St East
  CLDN/WHIT/ROK SR6 ...... 106 E4
Whickham Vw
  BW/LEM/TK/HW NE15 ...... 68 E5
  LWF/SPW/WRK NE9 ...... 87 G7
Whickhope *WASHS* NE38 ...... 117 G4
Whinbank *PONT/DH* NE20 ...... 43 F7
Whinbrooke *FELL* NE10 ...... 88 C6
Whinbush PI
  BW/LEM/TK/HW NE15 ...... 68 E6
Whinfell CI *CRAM* NE23 ...... 38 D5
Whinfell Rd *PONT/DH* NE20 ...... 43 F6
Whinfield Av *RDHAMSE* DH6 ...... 173 H4
Whinfield Ter *ROWG* NE39 ...... 97 F3
Whinfield Wy *ROWG* NE39 ...... 96 E4
Whinham Wy *MPTH* NE61 ...... 26 E1
Whinlatter Gdns
  LWF/SPW/WRK NE9 ...... 101 G1
Whinmoor PI
  WD/WHPE/BLK NE5 ...... 69 J2
Whinney CI *BLAY* NE21 ...... 83 J4
Whinneyfield Rd
  BYK/HTN/WLK NE6 ...... 72 B4
Whinney HI *DHAM* DH1 ...... 16 F7
Whinny La *CON/LDGT* DH8 ...... 108 E5
Whinny PI *CON/LDGT* DH8 ...... 137 F2
Whinshaw *FELL* NE10 ...... 88 B5
Whistler Gdns *HAR/WTLS* NE34 ...... 91 H1
Whitbay Crs *LGB/KIL* NE12 ...... 57 J4
Whitbeck Rd
  WD/WHPE/BLK NE5 ...... 68 E2
Whitbourne CI *WASHN* NE37 ...... 103 G3
Whitburn Bents Rd
  CLDN/WHIT/ROK SR6 ...... 93 F5
Whitburn CI
  BDN/LAN/SAC DH7 ...... 154 A3
Whitburn Gdns
  LWF/SPW/WRK NE9 ...... 101 K2
Whitburn PI *CRAM* NE23 ...... 38 C5
Whitburn Rd
  CLDN/WHIT/ROK SR6 ...... 91 K4
  CLDN/WHIT/ROK SR6 ...... 107 F1
Whitburn Rd East
  CLDN/WHIT/ROK SR6 ...... 92 B3
Whitburn St
  CLDN/WHIT/ROK SR6 ...... 14 F1
Whitburn Ter *BOL* NE36 ...... 91 H5
  CLDN/WHIT/ROK SR6 ...... 106 D1

Whitby Av *CLDN/WHIT/ROK* SR6 ...... 93 F6
Whitby Dr *WASHS* NE38 ...... 117 F3
Whitby Gdns *WLSD/HOW* NE28 ...... 59 G6
Whitby St *TYNE/NSHE* NE30 ...... 61 F4
Whitchurch CI *BOLCOL* NE35 ...... 90 C3
  SWCK/CAS SR5 ...... 105 K1
Whitchurch Rd *SWCK/CAS* SR5 ...... 105 K1
Whiteacres *MPTH* NE61 ...... 20 E6
Whitebark *SUNDSW* SR3 ...... 133 J5
Whitebridge CI *GOS/KPK* NE3 ...... 56 C2
Whitebridge Ct *GOS/KPK* NE3 ...... 56 C3
Whitebridge Pk *GOS/KPK* NE3 ...... 56 D3
White Cedars
  RDHAMSE DH7 ...... 167 F7
Whitecliff CI *NSHW* NE29 ...... 60 D2
White Crs *RHTLP* TS27 ...... 185 H2
Whitecroft Rd *CRAM* NE23 ...... 47 G7
Whitefield Crs *HLS* DH4 ...... 117 J7
  MPTH NE61 ...... 21 J2
Whitefield Ter
  BYK/HTN/WLK NE6 ...... 71 K2
Whiteford PI *CRAM* NE23 ...... 39 H6
Whitefriars Wy *LGB/KIL* NE12 ...... 57 G5
White Gates Dr *HLH* DH5 ...... 148 A6
Whitegates Rd *RDHAMSE* DH6 ...... 158 C6
Whitehall Rd
  BW/LEM/TK/HW NE15 ...... 67 H1
  GATE NE8 ...... 10 F6
Whitehall St *SSH* NE33 ...... 75 G5
Whitehead St *SSH* NE33 ...... 75 F4
Whitehill *FELL* NE10 ...... 88 B7
Whitehill Crs *CLSW/PEL* DH2 ...... 128 E3
Whitehill Dr *FELL* NE10 ...... 87 K6
Whitehill Hall Gdns
  CLSW/PEL DH2 ...... 129 G3
Whitehill Rd *CRAM* NE23 ...... 33 G6
White Hill Rd *HLH* DH5 ...... 160 B1
Whitehorn Crs
  WD/WHPE/BLK NE5 ...... 69 H1
White Horse Vw
  HAR/WTLS NE34 ...... 76 C5
Whitehouse Av
  BDN/LAN/SAC DH7 ...... 141 G4
Whitehouse Crs
  LWF/SPW/WRK NE9 ...... 102 A1
Whitehouse La
  BDN/LAN/SAC DH7 ...... 154 E7
  NSHW NE29 ...... 60 B2
White House PI
  ASHBK/HED/RY SR2 ...... 15 J6
White House Rd
  ASHBK/HED/RY SR2 ...... 15 H7
Whitehouse Rd
  BW/LEM/TK/HW NE15 ...... 69 F7
Whitehouse Wy *PLEE/EAS* SR8 ...... 174 A4
  RDHAMSE DH6 ...... 174 A6
Whitelaw PI *CRAM* NE23 ...... 38 D4
White Lea CI *PLEE/EAS* SR8 ...... 175 G5
Whiteleas Wy *HAR/WTLS* NE34 ...... 75 G7
White Oaks *GOS/KPK* NE3 ...... 55 J3
White Le Head Gdns
  STLY/ANP DH9 ...... 111 J4
Whiteley CI *RYTON* NE40 ...... 82 C3
Whiteley Rd *BLAY* NE21 ...... 68 C7
Whitemere CI
  ASHBK/HED/RY SR2 ...... 120 E4
White Mere Gdns *FELL* NE10 ...... 88 E4
Whiteoak Av *DHAM* DH1 ...... 157 J6
White Oaks *FELL* NE10 ...... 88 A7
White Rocks Gv
  CLDN/WHIT/ROK SR6 ...... 93 F1
Whites Gdns *HEBB* NE31 ...... 72 E5
Whitesmocks *DHAM* DH1 ...... 156 B5
Whitesmocks Av *DHAM* DH1 ...... 156 A6
White St *BYK/HTN/WLK* NE6 ...... 72 D6
Whitewell La *RYTON* NE40 ...... 66 E6
Whitewell Rd *BLAY* NE21 ...... 84 A2
Whitfield Dr *LGB/KIL* NE12 ...... 57 J4
Whitfield Rd
  BW/LEM/TK/HW NE15 ...... 68 D6
  LGB/KIL NE12 ...... 57 K2
  MONK NE25 ...... 40 A5
Whitfield St *CON/LDGT* DH8 ...... 123 G4
Whitgrave Rd
  WD/WHPE/BLK NE5 ...... 55 H7
Whithorn Ct *BLYTH* NE24 ...... 30 E7
Whitley Rd *LGB/KIL* NE12 ...... 58 A4
  MONK NE25 ...... 49 J4
  WBAY NE26 ...... 51 F5
Whitmore Rd *BLAY* NE21 ...... 84 A1
Whittingham CI *ASHGTN* NE63 ...... 23 C3
Whittingham Rd
  TYNE/NSHE NE30 ...... 51 G7
  WD/WHPE/BLK NE5 ...... 54 D6
Whittington Gv
  WD/WHPE/BLK NE5 ...... 69 G4
Whittleburn *FELL* NE10 ...... 88 B7
Whitton Av *BLYTH* NE24 ...... 34 D2
Whitton Gdns *NSHW* NE29 ...... 60 B3
Whitton PI *LGB/HTN* NE7 ...... 57 G6
  MONK NE25 ...... 40 A5
Whittonstall *WASHS* NE38 ...... 117 H5
Whittonstall Rd *CHPW* NE17 ...... 95 G4
Whitton Wy *GOS/KPK* NE3 ...... 56 B4
Whitwell Acres *DHAM* DH1 ...... 169 J6
Whitworth CI
  BYK/HTN/WLK NE6 ...... 72 C6
  GATE NE8 ...... 86 D1
Whitworth La
  BDN/LAN/SAC DH7 ...... 176 E5
Whitworth Rd *PLEE/EAS* SR8 ...... 174 A4
  WASHN NE37 ...... 102 B6
Whorlton PI
  WD/WHPE/BLK NE5 ...... 54 C7
Whorral Bank *MPTH* NE61 ...... 21 F3
Whygate *FELL* NE10 ...... 88 A7
Whytrigg CI *MONK* NE25 ...... 39 J4
Wicklow Ct *STKFD/GP* NE62 ...... 23 K5
Widderburn Sq *ASHGTN* NE63 ...... 23 J2
Widdrington Gdns
  DIN/WO NE13 ...... 46 C3
Widdrington Rd *BLAY* NE21 ...... 84 A2
Widnes PI *LGB/KIL* NE12 ...... 57 J3

Wigeon CI *WASHS* NE38 ...... 116 B4
Wigmore Av *BYK/HTN/WLK* NE6 ...... 7 L9
Wilber CI *MLFD/PNYW* SR4 ...... 105 K7
Wilberforce St *JRW* NE32 ...... 74 A4
  WLSD/HOW NE28 ...... 72 D3
Wilber St *MLFD/PNYW* SR4 ...... 105 K7
Wilbury PI
  WD/WHPE/BLK NE5 ...... 69 G1
Wilden St *SUNDSW* SR3 ...... 120 B4
Wilden Rd *WASHS* NE38 ...... 117 H3
Wildshaw CI *CRAM* NE23 ...... 38 D5
Wilfred St *BOLCOL* NE35 ...... 90 D5
  BYK/HTN/WLK NE6 ...... 6 D5
  CLS/BIR/GTL DH3 ...... 129 J5
  MLFD/PNYW SR4 ...... 105 J6
Wilfrid St *CLS/BIR/GTL* DH3 ...... 115 J3
Wilkes CI *WD/WHPE/BLK* NE5 ...... 68 D1
Wilkinson Av *HEBB* NE31 ...... 89 F1
Wilkinson St *HAR/WTLS* NE34 ...... 75 G5
Wilkwood CI *CRAM* NE23 ...... 38 D4
Willerby Dr *GOS/KPK* NE3 ...... 56 D2
Willerby Gv *PLEE/EAS* SR8 ...... 174 D3
William Armstrong Dr
  ELS/FEN NE4 ...... 8 F2
William CI *LGB/KIL* NE12 ...... 58 C3
William Morris Av *ROWG* NE39 ...... 96 D3
William PI *DHAM* DH1 ...... 17 J3
Williams CI *STLY/ANP* DH9 ...... 126 E2
Williamson Ter
  CLDN/WHIT/ROK SR6 ...... 14 F1
Williams Rd *SEA/MUR* SR7 ...... 149 H5
William St *BLYTH* NE24 ...... 31 G7
  CHPW NE17 ...... 95 H4
  FELL NE10 ...... 12 D6
  GOS/KPK NE3 ...... 56 E5
  HEBB NE31 ...... 73 F4
  MPTH NE61 ...... 21 K2
  RDHAMSE DH6 ...... 180 A2
  SUND SR1 ...... 14 F3
  WICK/BNPF NE16 ...... 84 E5
William St West *HEBB* NE31 ...... 73 F1
  NSHW NE29 ...... 2 C3
Willington Ter *WLSD/HOW* NE28 ...... 59 G7
Willis St *HLH* DH5 ...... 147 K3
Willmore St *MLFD/PNYW* SR4 ...... 106 A7
Willoughby Dr *WBAY* NE26 ...... 50 C2
Willoughby Rd *NSHW* NE29 ...... 60 B4
Willow Av *BLYTH* NE24 ...... 31 F5
  DUN/TMV NE11 ...... 9 G4
  ELS/FEN NE4 ...... 69 J6
Willowbank Gdns *JES* NE2 ...... 56 E6
Willow Bank Rd
  ASHBK/HED/RY SR2 ...... 120 C3
Willow CI *BDN/LAN/SAC* DH7 ...... 167 F6
  MPTH NE61 ...... 21 F5
Willow Ct *RYTON* NE40 ...... 67 F5
  STKFD/GP NE62 ...... 23 H6
Willow Crs *BLYTH* NE24 ...... 34 E3
  CON/LDGT DH8 ...... 123 K4
  HLH DH5 ...... 148 C7
Willowdene *LGB/KIL* NE12 ...... 58 A1
Willowfield Av *GOS/KPK* NE3 ...... 55 K4
Willow Gdns *LGB/KIL* NE12 ...... 47 J5
Willow Gra *JRW* NE32 ...... 73 J4
Willow Gv *HAR/WTLS* NE34 ...... 75 K6
  PLEE/EAS SR8 ...... 175 J5
  WLSD/HOW NE28 ...... 73 F1
Willow Pk *BDN/LAN/SAC* DH7 ...... 153 K3
Willow PI *PONT/DH* NE20 ...... 43 G5
Willow Rd *BDN/LAN/SAC* DH7 ...... 165 G1
  BLAY NE21 ...... 84 B2
  HLS DH4 ...... 132 A7
Willows CI *DIN/WO* NE13 ...... 46 A4
The Willows
  BW/LEM/TK/HW NE15 ...... 67 F2
  MPTH NE61 ...... 20 E5
  WASHS NE38 ...... 117 H2
Willowtree Av *DHAM* DH1 ...... 157 H5
Willow Tree Av *DHAM* DH1 ...... 169 G4
Willow Wy *PONT/DH* NE20 ...... 43 G7
Wilmington CI
  WD/WHPE/BLK NE5 ...... 55 F4
Wilson Av *BDLGTN* NE22 ...... 30 D2
  CLS/BIR/GTL DH3 ...... 115 J1
Wilson Dr *BOL* NE36 ...... 91 F4
Wilson Gdns *GOS/KPK* NE3 ...... 56 B7
Wilson PI *PLEE/EAS* SR8 ...... 174 E2
Wilson's La *LWF/SPW/WRK* NE9 ...... 87 F7
Wilson St *DUN/TMV* NE11 ...... 9 H8
  MLFD/PNYW SR4 ...... 106 A6
  SSH NE33 ...... 75 G2
  WLSD/HOW NE28 ...... 72 D1
Wilson St North *SWCK/CAS* SR5 ...... 14 D2
Wilson Ter *LGB/KIL* NE12 ...... 57 K2
  SUNDSW SR3 ...... 120 A6
Wilton Gdns North
  BOLCOL NE35 ...... 90 C2
Wilton Gdns South
  BOLCOL NE35 ...... 90 C2
Wiltshire CI *DHAM* DH1 ...... 157 K6
  SWCK/CAS SR5 ...... 105 J1
Wiltshire Dr *WLSD/HOW* NE28 ...... 58 B5
Wiltshire Gdns *WLSD/HOW* NE28 ...... 58 B7
Wiltshire PI *WASHN* NE37 ...... 103 F3
Wiltshire Rd *SWCK/CAS* SR5 ...... 105 K1
Wimbledon CI *SWCK/CAS* SR5 ...... 105 K2
Wimborne CI *BOLCOL* NE35 ...... 90 C4
Wimbourne Av
  MLFD/PNYW SR4 ...... 119 J2
Wimbourne Gn
  WD/WHPE/BLK NE5 ...... 54 D7
Wimpole CI *WASHN* NE37 ...... 103 G3
Wimslow CI *WLSD/HOW* NE28 ...... 58 D7
Winalot Av *ASHBK/HED/RY* SR2 ...... 120 E4
Wincanton PI *CRAM* NE23 ...... 60 C6
Winchcombe PI *LGB/HTN* NE7 ...... 57 G7
Winchester Av *BLYTH* NE24 ...... 31 G7
Winchester CI *ASHGTN* NE63 ...... 24 B3
  CLS/BIR/GTL DH3 ...... 145 H1
Winchester Ct *JRW* NE32 ...... 89 K3
  MLFD/PNYW SR4 ...... 105 K7
Winchester Dr
  BDN/LAN/SAC DH7 ...... 177 F1

  PLEE/EAS SR8 ...... 174 A5
Winchester Rd *DHAM* DH1 ...... 157 F2
Winchester St 3 J7
Winchester Ter *ELS/FEN* NE4 ...... 4 F7
Winchester Wk *DIN/WO* NE13 ...... 46 B4
Wincomblee Rd
  BYK/HTN/WLK NE6 ...... 13 K1
Windburgh Dr *CRAM* NE23 ...... 38 C5
Windermere
  CLDN/WHIT/ROK SR6 ...... 92 A3
Windermere Av *CLSW/PEL* DH2 ...... 129 J6
  FELL NE10 ...... 13 H7
  HLH DH5 ...... 160 B1
Windermere CI *CRAM* NE23 ...... 38 C5
Windermere Crs *BLAY* NE21 ...... 83 K4
  HAR/WTLS NE34 ...... 75 J5
  HEBB NE31 ...... 73 H6
  HLS DH4 ...... 131 K1
  JRW NE32 ...... 90 B1
Windermere Gdns
  WICK/BNPF NE16 ...... 8 B9
Windermere Rd *NWBGN* NE64 ...... 24 E2
  RDHAMSE DH6 ...... 161 G1
  SEA/MUR SR7 ...... 149 K1
  WD/WHPE/BLK NE5 ...... 69 F3
Windermere St
  ASHBK/HED/RY SR2 ...... 121 F4
  GATE NE8 ...... 10 E6
Windermere St West *GATE* NE8 ...... 10 E6
Windermere Ter *NSHW* NE29 ...... 2 B1
Windhill Rd *BYK/HTN/WLK* NE6 ...... 13 H1
The Winding *MONK* NE25 ...... 45 F2
Windlass Ct *HAR/WTLS* NE34 ...... 75 G6
Windlass La *WASHN* NE37 ...... 102 E6
Windmill Ct *JES* NE2 ...... 5 G1
Windmill Gv *BLYTH* NE24 ...... 30 C6
Windmill HI *SSH* NE33 ...... 75 F2
Windmill Sq *SWCK/CAS* SR5 ...... 106 C1
Windmill Wy *HEBB* NE31 ...... 73 G3
  MPTH NE61 ...... 21 F5
Winds La *SEA/MUR* SR7 ...... 149 G6
Winds Lonnen Est
  SEA/MUR SR7 ...... 149 F5
Windsor Av *GATE* NE8 ...... 10 E7
Windsor CI *WICK/BNPF* NE16 ...... 98 D1
Windsor Cottages
  WLSD/HOW NE28 ...... 59 J6
Windsor Ct *BDLGTN* NE22 ...... 29 F6
  CRAM NE23 ...... 33 G6
  GOS/KPK NE3 ...... 55 J3
Windsor Crs *HEBB* NE31 ...... 73 H5
  HLH DH5 ...... 132 D7
  PRUD NE42 ...... 64 B6
  WBAY NE26 ...... 51 G5
  WD/WHPE/BLK NE5 ...... 54 E7
Windsor Dr *CLDN/WHIT/ROK* SR6 ...... 91 J3
  HLH DH5 ...... 147 H2
  RDHAMSE DH6 ...... 160 E1
  STLY/ANP DH9 ...... 125 H2
  SUNDSW SR3 ...... 120 A7
  WLSD/HOW NE28 ...... 59 J7
Windsor Gdns *BDLGTN* NE22 ...... 29 F6
  FELL NE10 ...... 12 A8
  HAR/WTLS NE34 ...... 75 J4
  NSHW NE29 ...... 60 E3
  WLSD/HOW NE28 ...... 59 J6
Windsor Pk *WLSD/HOW* NE28 ...... 58 B7
Windsor PI *PONT/DH* NE20 ...... 42 D5
  RDHAMSE DH6 ...... 173 J3
  SMOOR NE27 ...... 58 E1
Windsor Rd *CLS/BIR/GTL* DH3 ...... 101 H7
  LWF/SPW/WRK NE9 ...... 102 A4
  MONK NE25 ...... 50 C4
  NWBGN NE64 ...... 25 F1
  SEA/MUR SR7 ...... 150 A1
Windsor St *TRIM* TS29 ...... 182 E6
  WLSD/HOW NE28 ...... 72 D1
Windsor Ter *GOS/KPK* NE3 ...... 56 E6
  JES NE2 ...... 5 K2
  PLEE/EAS SR8 ...... 175 J4
  RDHAMSE DH6 ...... 160 D6
  SEA/MUR SR7 ...... 149 J2
  SEA/MUR SR7 ...... 149 K6
  WBAY NE26 ...... 51 G5
Windt St *DIN/WO* NE13 ...... 46 A4
Windy Gyle *ASHGTN* NE63 ...... 24 A1
Windy Nook Rd
  LWF/SPW/WRK NE9 ...... 87 H6
Windy Ridge Vls *FELL* NE10 ...... 87 J5
Wingate CI
  BW/LEM/TK/HW NE15 ...... 68 C5
  HLS DH4 ...... 132 B7
Wingate Gdns
  LWF/SPW/WRK NE9 ...... 101 K1
Wingate La *RDHAMSE* DH6 ...... 182 D2
Wingate Rd *TRIM* TS29 ...... 183 F5
Wingrove *ROWG* NE39 ...... 97 F4
Wingrove Av
  CLDN/WHIT/ROK SR6 ...... 106 E1
  ELS/FEN NE4 ...... 4 A4
Wingrove CI *WNGT* TS28 ...... 183 K2
Wingrove Gdns *ELS/FEN* NE4 ...... 4 A4
Wingrove Rd *ELS/FEN* NE4 ...... 69 J2
Winifred St
  CLDN/WHIT/ROK SR6 ...... 106 E2
Winifred Ter *SUND* SR1 ...... 15 G6
Winshields *CRAM* NE23 ...... 38 D4
Winship CI *HAR/WTLS* NE34 ...... 91 G2
Winship St *BLYTH* NE24 ...... 34 E2
Winskell Rd *HAR/WTLS* NE34 ...... 74 D7
Winslade CI *SUNDSW* SR3 ...... 120 B6
Winslow CI *BOLCOL* NE35 ...... 90 D2
  BYK/HTN/WLK NE6 ...... 72 C5
  SWCK/CAS SR5 ...... 105 K1
Winslow Crs *SEA/MUR* SR7 ...... 150 A1
Winslow Gdns
  LWF/SPW/WRK NE9 ...... 86 E7
Winslow PI *BYK/HTN/WLK* NE6 ...... 72 C5
Winsten *WASHS* NE38 ...... 116 C5
Winston Crs
  MLFD/PNYW SR4 ...... 119 J2
Winston Gn *HLS* DH4 ...... 117 H6
Winton CI *CRAM* NE23 ...... 39 H6
Winton Wy *GOS/KPK* NE3 ...... 55 K5
Wishaw CI *CRAM* NE23 ...... 38 D4

Wishaw Ri
  BW/LEM/TK/HW NE15 ...... 68 C4
Witham Rd *HEBB* NE31 ...... 89 H1
Witherington CI *LGB/HTN* NE7 ...... 58 A7
Withernsea Gv
  ASHBK/HED/RY SR2 ...... 120 D7
Witney CI *SWCK/CAS* SR5 ...... 105 J1
Witney Wy *BOL* NE36 ...... 90 C5
Witton Av *BDN/LAN/SAC* DH7 ...... 143 H5
  HAR/WTLS NE34 ...... 76 A5
Witton Ct *GOS/KPK* NE3 ...... 55 J4
  SUNDSW SR3 ...... 120 B4
Witton Gdns *JRW* NE32 ...... 89 K1
Witton Garth *PLEE/EAS* SR8 ...... 174 D7
Witton Gv *DHAM* DH1 ...... 156 A5
  HLS DH4 ...... 147 F1
Witton Rd *BDN/LAN/SAC* DH7 ...... 143 G6
  HEBB NE31 ...... 73 H3
  SMOOR NE27 ...... 49 H6
Witty Av *HEBB* NE31 ...... 73 H6
Woburn *WASHS* NE38 ...... 117 F2
Woburn CI *CRAM* NE23 ...... 33 G6
  WLSD/HOW NE28 ...... 58 B7
Woburn Dr *BDLGTN* NE22 ...... 29 J4
  SUNDSW SR3 ...... 134 A1
Woburn Wy *WD/WHPE/BLK* NE5 ...... 68 E1
Wolmer Rd *BLYTH* NE24 ...... 35 H2
Wolseley CI *GATE* NE8 ...... 10 A5
  RDHAMSE DH6 ...... 180 A2
Wolseley Gdns *JES* NE2 ...... 6 C1
Wolseley Ter
  MLFD/PNYW SR4 ...... 120 A1
Wolsey Ct *HAR/WTLS* NE34 ...... 75 G5
Wolsey Rd *SEA/MUR* SR7 ...... 149 K2
Wolsingham Ct *CRAM* NE23 ...... 38 E1
Wolsingham Dr *DHAM* DH1 ...... 156 E3
Wolsingham Rd
  BDN/LAN/SAC DH7 ...... 164 E4
  BDN/LAN/SAC DH7 ...... 165 K7
  GOS/KPK NE3 ...... 56 B6
Wolsley Rd *BLYTH* NE24 ...... 31 G6
Wolveleigh Ter *GOS/KPK* NE3 ...... 56 D6
Woodbine Av *WLSD/HOW* NE28 ...... 72 D1
Woodbine CI *ELS/FEN* NE4 ...... 4 A8
Woodbine Rd *DHAM* DH1 ...... 156 B2
  GOS/KPK NE3 ...... 56 C6
Woodbine St *GATE* NE8 ...... 10 E5
  SSH NE33 ...... 3 J5
  SUND SR1 ...... 15 J5
Woodbine Ter *BLYTH* NE24 ...... 35 H1
  FELL NE10 ...... 11 M7
  MLFD/PNYW SR4 ...... 105 K5
Woodbrook Av
  WD/WHPE/BLK NE5 ...... 68 E3
Woodburn *FELL* NE10 ...... 88 A7
  STLY/ANP DH9 ...... 112 A6
Woodburn Av *ELS/FEN* NE4 ...... 69 J2
Woodburn CI *BLAY* NE21 ...... 83 J4
Woodburn Dr *HLS* DH4 ...... 132 A6
  WBAY NE26 ...... 50 C2
Woodburn Gdns *DUN/TMV* NE11 ...... 86 A6
Woodburn Sq *WBAY* NE26 ...... 50 B2
Woodburn St
  BW/LEM/TK/HW NE15 ...... 68 A4
Woodchurch CI *LGB/KIL* NE12 ...... 57 K6
Woodcroft CI *CRAM* NE23 ...... 38 B7
Woodcroft Rd *WYLAM* NE41 ...... 65 G5
Woodend *PONT/DH* NE20 ...... 42 E7
Woodend Wy *GOS/KPK* NE3 ...... 55 G2
Woodfield *PLEE/EAS* SR8 ...... 174 D4
Wood Flds *PONT/DH* NE20 ...... 43 H3
Woodford *LWF/SPW/WRK* NE9 ...... 101 F4
Woodford CI *SWCK/CAS* SR5 ...... 105 K1
Woodgate Gdns *FELL* NE10 ...... 13 M5
Woodgate La *FELL* NE10 ...... 13 M4
Wood Gv *BW/LEM/TK/HW* NE15 ...... 68 D4
Woodhall Spa *HLS* DH4 ...... 131 J3
Woodhead Rd *BYK/HTN/WLK* NE6 ...... 7 M1
  PRUD NE42 ...... 81 F1
Woodhill Dr *MPTH* NE61 ...... 20 C5
Woodhill Rd *CRAM* NE23 ...... 38 D4
Woodhorn Dr *STKFD/GP* NE62 ...... 23 F5
Woodhorn Gdns *DIN/WO* NE13 ...... 46 B3
Woodhorn La *NWBGN* NE64 ...... 19 G7
Woodhorn Rd *ASHGTN* NE63 ...... 24 A1
  NWBGN NE64 ...... 19 F7
Woodhorn Vls *ASHGTN* NE63 ...... 24 B1
Woodhouses La
  WICK/BNPF NE16 ...... 98 C1
Woodhurst Gv
  MLFD/PNYW SR4 ...... 118 E4
Woodland CI
  BDN/LAN/SAC DH7 ...... 155 F6
Woodland Ct *CON/LDGT* DH8 ...... 122 D1
Woodland Crs
  BW/LEM/TK/HW NE15 ...... 69 F7
  RDHAMSE DH6 ...... 181 G6
Woodland Dr *MLFD/PNYW* SR4 ...... 119 J2
Woodland Gra *HLS* DH4 ...... 131 H6
Woodland Ri *SUNDSW* SR3 ...... 133 J1
Woodlands *BDN/LAN/SAC* DH7 ...... 140 C5
  BW/LEM/TK/HW NE15 ...... 66 E1
  GOS/KPK NE3 ...... 56 C7
  NSHW NE29 ...... 60 E2
  PONT/DH NE20 ...... 43 F6
  WASHS NE38 ...... 116 A6
Woodlands Av *RDHAMSE* DH6 ...... 172 E7
Woodlands CI *MONK* NE25 ...... 49 J4
  ROWG NE39 ...... 96 C2
Woodlands Dr
  CLDN/WHIT/ROK SR6 ...... 92 A4
Woodlands Gra *LGB/KIL* NE12 ...... 58 A1
Woodlands Park Dr *BLAY* NE21 ...... 84 B2
Woodlands Rd *ASHGTN* NE63 ...... 24 C3
  BDN/LAN/SAC DH7 ...... 165 G1
  BW/LEM/TK/HW NE15 ...... 68 B4
  CLDN/WHIT/ROK SR6 ...... 91 K4
  CON/LDGT DH8 ...... 122 D1
  ROWG NE39 ...... 97 F3
Woodlands Ter *FELL* NE10 ...... 12 B8
Woodlands Vw
  CLDN/WHIT/ROK SR6 ...... 92 A4
Woodland Veiw *WNGT* TS28 ...... 183 J3
Wood La *MONK* NE22 ...... 29 H5
Woodlea *BDN/LAN/SAC* DH7 ...... 140 B5
Wood Lea *HLH* DH5 ...... 147 K1
Woodlea *LGB/KIL* NE12 ...... 57 K1

Woodlea Cl *HLH* DH5 .... 147 K4
Woodlea Ct *NSHW* NE29 .... 60 C7 ⊡
Woodlea Gdns *GOS/KPK* NE3 .... 56 E3
Woodlea Sq *NSHW* NE29 .... 60 C7
Woodleigh Rd *MONK* NE25 .... 50 C5
Woodleigh Vw
  WD/WHPE/BLK NE5 .... 55 J7 ⊡
Woodman Cl *MPTH* NE61 .... 20 C6
Woodman St *WLSD/HOW* NE28 ..... 56 K7
Woodmans Wy
  WICK/BNPF NE16 .... 98 C1
Woodnansey Cl *PLEE/EAS* SR8..... 174 C3
Woodpack Av *WICK/BNPF* NE6 ...... 84 D6
Woodside *ASHBK/HED/RY* SR2...... 14 D8
  BDLGTN NE22 .... 29 J5
  BLYTH NE24 .... 35 H1 ⊡
  MPTH NE61 .... 20 B5
  PONT/DH NE20 .... 42 E7
  PRUD NE42 .... 80 E2
  RDHAMSE DH6 .... 171 H2
Woodside Av
  BDN/LAN/SAC DH7 .... 155 F6
  BW/LEM/TK/HW NE15 .... 67 G1
  MONK NE25 ....
Woodside Bank *CON/LDGT* DH8.. 124 B7
Woodside Cl *LGB/KIL* NE12 .... 66 D6
Woodside Crs *LGB/KIL* NE12 .... 58 A2
Woodside Dr *CON/LDGT* DH8 ..... 123 H7
Woodside Gdns *DUN/TMV* NE11.. 85 K5
  STLY/ANP DH9 .... 127 F4
Woodside La *HLS* DH4 .... 146 B7
  RYTON NE40 .... 66 D7
Woodside Rd *RYTON* NE40 .... 66 D6
Woodside Ter *SUNDSW* SR3 ...... 133 G1
Woodside Wk *ROWC* NE39 .... 96 E4
Woodside Wy *RYTON* NE40 .... 66 D6 ⊡
  SSH NE33 .... 75 F4
Woods Ter *GATE* NE8 .... 11 H6
  SEA/MUR SR7 .... 149 J5
Woodstock Rd
  BW/LEM/TK/HW NE15 .... 68 E6
  LWF/SPW/WRK NE9 .... 101 G3
Wood St *CLSW/PEL* DH2 .... 114 E7
  CON/LDGT DH8 .... 122 C1 ⊡
  DUN/TMV NE11 ....
  MLFD/PNYW SR4 .... 106 A6 ⊡
Wood Ter *FELL* NE10 .... 13 L4
  JRW NE32 .... 73 J7
  SSH NE33 .... 75 H3
Woodthorne Rd *JES* NE2 .... 56 E7 ⊡
Woodvale *PONT/DH* NE20............. 42 E7

Woodvale Dr *HEBB* NE31 .... 72 E7
Woodvale Gdns
  LWF/SPW/WRK NE9 .... 87 J6 ⊡
  WYLAM NE41 .... 65 G5
Woodvale Rd *BLAY* NE21 .... 84 B3
  LGB/KIL NE12 .... 47 J5
Wood Vw *BDN/LAN/SAC* DH7 .... 154 B2
  TRIM TS29 .... 183 G6
Woodville Ct
  MLFD/PNYW SR4 .... 119 J2 ⊡
Woodville Crs
  MLFD/PNYW SR4 .... 119 J2 ⊡
Woodville Rd
  BW/LEM/TK/HW NE15 .... 68 B3
Wooler Av *NSHW* NE29 .... 60 B6
Wooler Crs *GATE* NE8 .... 9 M7
Wooler Sq *ASHBK/HED/RY* SR2.. 120 E3
  DIN/WO NE13 .... 46 C2 ⊡
Woolerton Dr
  BW/LEM/TK/HW NE15 .... 68 C4
  LWF/SPW/WRK NE9 .... 87 H6 ⊡
Wooler Wk *JRW* NE32 .... 73 J7
Wooley Dr *BDN/LAN/SAC* DH7 ... 167 H1
Wooley St *WLSD/HOW* NE28....... 72 D2
Woolmer Ct *LGB/HTN* NE7 .... 58 A7 ⊡
Woolsington Ct
  MLFD/PNYW SR4 .... 105 K7 ⊡
Woolsington Gdns
  DIN/WO NE13 .... 54 D2
Woolsington Pk South
  DIN/WO NE13 .... 54 D2
Woolsington Rd *NSHW* NE29 .... 60 A3
Woolwich Cl *SWCK/CAS* SR5 ...... 105 K1
Woolwich Rd *SWCK/CAS* SR5 .... 105 K1
Wooperton Gdns
  WD/WHPE/BLK NE5 .... 69 G4
Worcester Cl *CLS/BIR/GTL* DH3 .. 145 H1
Worcester Rd *DHAM* DH1 .... 156 E2
Worcester St
  ASHBK/HED/RY SR2 .... 14 D7 ⊡
Worcester Ter
  ASHBK/HED/RY SR2 .... 14 D7 ⊡
Worcester Wy *DIN/WO* NE13 .... 46 B4
Wordsworth Av *BLYTH* NE24 .... 34 E2
  CLSW/PEL DH2 .... 128 E5
  HEBB NE31 ....
  HLH DH5 .... 160 C1 ⊡
  RDHAMSE DH6 .... 172 E7
  SEA/MUR SR7 .... 149 K1
  WICK/BNPF NE16 .... 85 F4
Wordsworth Rd *PLEE/EAS* SR8 .. 162 D5

Wordsworth St *GATE* NE8 .... 11 J5
Worley Cl *ELS/FEN* NE4 .... 4 D6
Worley St *ELS/FEN* NE4 .... 4 D6
Worm Hill Ter *WASHS* NE38........ 117 G5
Worsdell St *BLYTH* NE24 .... 31 G5 ⊡
Worsley Cl *WLSD/HOW* NE28 .... 58 B7
Worswick St *CNUT* NE1 .... 5 L6
Worthing Cl *WLSD/HOW* NE28 .... 58 B7 ⊡
Worton Cl *RDHAMSE* DH6 .... 173 H5
Wouldhave Ct *SSH* NE33 .... 3 K6
Wraysbury Ct *GOS/KPK* NE3 .... 55 H3 ⊡
Wreigh St *HEBB* NE31 .... 73 F5
Wreken Gdns *FELL* NE10 .... 88 E4
Wrekenton Rw
  LWF/SPW/WRK NE9 .... 101 J3
Wren Cl *WASHS* NE38 .... 116 C3
Wren Gv *SWCK/CAS* SR5 .... 105 C4 ⊡
Wretham Pl *JES* NE2 .... 6 A4
Wright Dr *CRAM* NE23 .... 47 G2
Wrightson St *CRAM* NE23 .... 33 H4
Wright St *BLYTH* NE24 .... 31 F6
Wright Ter *HLS* DH4 .... 131 J2
Wroxham Ct
  ASHBK/HED/RY SR2 .... 120 E4
  WD/WHPE/BLK NE5 .... 55 F6 ⊡
Wroxton *WASHS* NE38 .... 116 E3
Wuppertal Ct *JRW* NE32 .... 73 K5
Wychcroft Wy
  WD/WHPE/BLK NE5 .... 69 G1 ⊡
Wych Elm Crs *LGB/HTN* NE7 .... 57 J7
Wycliffe Av *GOS/KPK* NE3 .... 55 K7
Wycliffe Rd *MLFD/PNYW* SR4.... 119 K2
  SEA/MUR SR7 .... 149 K1
Wye Av *JRW* NE32 .... 90 A1
Wye Rd *HEBB* NE31 .... 89 C1
Wylam Av *MONK* NE25 .... 40 C6
Wylam Cl *HAR/WTLS* NE34 .... 75 J6 ⊡
  WASHN NE37 .... 103 G4 ⊡
Wylam Gdns *WLSD/HOW* NE28.. 59 H6
Wylam Gv *SUND* SR1 .... 15 H6
Wylam Rd *NSHW* NE29 .... 2 A7
  STLY/ANP DH9 .... 112 E7
Wylam St *JRW* NE32 .... 73 K4
  RDHAMSE DH6 .... 180 A3
  STLY/ANP DH9 .... 127 G5
Wylam Ter *STLY/ANP* DH9 .... 112 D6 ⊡
Wylam Vw *BLAY* NE21 .... 83 K2
Wylam Wood Rd *WYLAM* NE41 ... 65 H6
Wynbury Rd
  LWF/SPW/WRK NE9 .... 87 G7 ⊡
Wyncote Ct *LGB/HTN* NE7 .... 71 H1 ⊡

The Wynde *HAR/WTLS* NE34........ 75 C6
  PONT/DH NE20 .... 43 F5
Wyndfall Wy *GOS/KPK* NE3 .... 56 A6
Wyndham Av *GOS/KPK* NE3 .... 55 K7
Wyndham Wy *NSHW* NE29 .... 59 K2
The Wynding *BDLGTN* NE22 .... 28 E4
  CRAM NE23 .... 38 B7
Wyndley Cl *WICK/BNPF* NE16 ...... 84 D7
Wyndley Pl *GOS/KPK* NE3 .... 55 K7
Wyndsail Pl *GOS/KPK* NE3 .... 56 A7 ⊡
The Wynds *BDN/LAN/SAC* DH7 .. 165 G2
The Wynd
  BW/LEM/TK/HW NE15 .... 67 F2 ⊡
  CLSW/PEL DH2 .... 128 E1
  GOS/KPK NE3 .... 56 A6
  TYNE/NSHE NE30 .... 60 E2
Wyndtop Pl *GOS/KPK* NE3 .... 56 A7 ⊡
Wyndways Dr *STLY/ANP* DH9..... 111 G5
Wynn Gdns *FELL* NE10 .... 13 H5
Wynyard *CLSW/PEL* DH2 .... 129 G4
Wynyard Dr *BDLGTN* NE22 .... 29 J3
Wynyard Gdns
  LWF/SPW/WRK NE9 .... 101 J3
Wynyard Sq
  ASHBK/HED/RY SR2 .... 120 E3
Wynyard St *DUN/TMV* NE11........... 9 G8
  HLS DH4 .... 131 J7
  SEA/MUR SR7 .... 150 E3
  SUNDSW SR3 .... 120 A7
Wyvern Sq *ASHBK/HED/RY* SR2 .. 120 E4

Y

Yardley Cl *SUNDSW* SR3............. 134 A2
Yardley Gv *CRAM* NE23 .... 33 G7 ⊡
Yarmouth Cl *SEA/MUR* SR7 .... 150 B2 ⊡
Yarmouth Dr *CRAM* NE23 .... 33 G7
Yatesbury Av
  WD/WHPE/BLK NE5 .... 69 F1
Yeckhouse La
  BDN/LAN/SAC DH7 .... 139 J5
Yelverton Ct *CRAM* NE23 .... 33 G7
Yelverton Crs
  BYK/HTN/WLK NE6 .... 13 G2
Yeoman St *NSHW* NE29 .... 2 E4
Yeovil Cl *CRAM* NE23 .... 33 G7 ⊡
Yetholm Av *CLSW/PEL* DH2........ 129 H5
Yetholm Pl
  WD/WHPE/BLK NE5 .... 54 E6 ⊡

Yetholm Rd *GATE* NE8 .... 9 M5
Yetlington Dr *GOS/KPK* NE3 .... 56 A6
Yewbank Av *DHAM* DH1 .... 157 J6 ⊡
Yewburn Wy *LGB/KIL* NE12........... 57 H4
Yew Ct
  BW/LEM/TK/HW NE15 .... 68 D5
Yewdale Gdns
  LWF/SPW/WRK NE9 .... 101 G1 ⊡
Yewtree Av *SWCK/CAS* SR5 ...... 105 K3
Yew Tree Dr *BDLGTN* NE22 .... 29 F4
Yewtree Gdns
  BYK/HTN/WLK NE6 .... 72 C2
Yewtrees *FELL* NE10 .... 88 A7 ⊡
Yewvale Rd *WD/WHPE/BLK* NE5 .. 69 H2
Yew Wy *WD/WHPE/BLK* NE5 .... 69 H2
Yoden Av *PLEE/EAS* SR8 .... 175 G2
Yoden Crs *PLEE/EAS* SR8 .... 175 G2
Yoden Rd *PLEE/EAS* SR8 .... 174 E3
Yoden Wy *PLEE/EAS* SR8 .... 175 G4
York Av *CON/LDGT* DH8 .... 137 F1
  JRW NE32 .... 89 K1 ⊡
York Cl *CRAM* NE23 .... 33 G7
York Crs *DHAM* DH1 .... 156 E1
  HLH DH5 .... 147 J4
Yorkdale Pl
  BYK/HTN/WLK NE6 .... 72 C5 ⊡
York Dr *WLSD/HOW* NE28 .... 72 C2
York Rd *CLS/BIR/GTL* DH3 .... 115 J5
  CON/LDGT DH8 .... 122 C2
  PLEE/EAS SR8 .... 174 D2
  WBAY NE26 .... 51 F4
Yorkshire Dr *DHAM* DH1 .... 158 A6
York St *ELS/FEN* NE4 .... 4 E7
  FELL NE10 .... 13 J6
  HLH DH5 .... 147 H1
  JRW NE32 .... 73 J5
  SUND SR1 .... 14 E4
York Ter *CLS/BIR/GTL* DH3.......... 129 K5
York Wy *HAR/WTLS* NE34 .... 76 A5
Yorkwood *HEBB* NE31 .... 72 E4
Young Rd *LGB/KIL* NE12 .... 58 B1
Young St *DHAM* DH1 .... 17 K2

Z

Zetland Dr *MONK* NE25 .... 50 D7
Zetland St
  CLDN/WHIT/ROK SR6 .... 106 E4
Zion St *SUND* SR1 .... 15 H4 ⊡
Zion Ter *SWCK/CAS* SR5 .... 106 C2

Index - featured places

Abbeyfields County School
  MPTH NE61 .... 20 C5
Abbey Sports Centre
  DHAM DH1 .... 156 D1
Acre Rigg Junior
  & Infant School
  PLEE/EAS SR8 .... 174 C2
Adamsez West Industrial Estate
  BLAY NE21 .... 68 D7
Adderlane First School
  PRUD NE42 .... 80 E1
Adelaide Row Medical Centre
  SEA/MUR SR7 .... 150 C1
Airport Church
  WD/WHPE/BLK NE5 .... 69 C1
Akhurst Preparatory School
  JES NE2 .... 71 F1
Albert Elliott County
  Junior Mixed School
  HAR/WTLS NE34 .... 91 F1
Albert Road Surgery
  JRW NE32 .... 73 K5
Alexandra Business Park
  MLFD/PNYW SR4 .... 105 J5
Algernon Industrial Estate
  SMOOR NE27 .... 59 H1
All Saints Junior Mixed School
  HAR/WTLS NE34 .... 75 F7
Amberley First School
  LGB/KIL NE12 .... 48 A5
AMF Bowling
  ELS/FEN NE4 .... 4 B6
AMF Bowling
  WASHS NE38 .... 116 E1
Amphitheatre
  SSH NE33 .... 3 M6
Annfield Plain County
  Junior Mixed School
  STLY/ANP DH9 .... 125 J4
Annfield Plain Cricket Club
  STLY/ANP DH9 .... 125 G4
Annfield Plain Infants School
  STLY/ANP DH9 .... 125 H4
Appletree Gardens First School
  MONK NE25 .... 50 C5
Arbeia Roman Fort & Museum
  SSH NE33 .... 3 H4
Archbishop Runcie
  C of E School
  GOS/KPK NE3 .... 56 D4
Archibald First School
  GOS/KPK NE3 .... 56 E5
Arena Business Park
  HLS DH4 .... 147 G2
Argyle House School
  ASHBK/HED/RY SR2 .... 14 C8
The Art Gallery
  SUND SR1 .... 14 E5
Arthurs Hill Clinic
  ELS/FEN NE4 .... 4 F5
Arthur Street Surgery
  BDN/LAN/SAC DH7 .... 154 E7
Ascham House School
  GOS/KPK NE3 .... 56 C6
Ashburne Medical Centre
  ASHBK/HED/RY SR2 .... 15 G9
Ashington Alexandra
  County First School
  ASHGTN NE63 .... 24 B2

Ashington Association
  Football Club
  ASHGTN NE63 .... 23 J1
Ashington Business Centre
  ASHGTN NE63 .... 23 K1
Ashington Coulson Park
  County First School
  ASHGTN NE63 .... 24 B3
Ashington County High School
  ASHGTN NE63 .... 23 J1
Ashington Cricket Club
  ASHGTN NE63 .... 23 J1
Ashington Hirst Park
  County Middle School
  ASHGTN NE63 .... 24 A2
Ashington Hospital
  ASHGTN NE63 .... 23 H1
Ashington Leisure Centre
  ASHGTN NE63 .... 23 H1
Ashington St Aidans RC
  Aided First School
  ASHGTN NE63 .... 24 A4
Ashington Seaton Hirst
  County Middle School
  ASHGTN NE63 .... 24 C3
Ashleigh School
  TYNE/NSHE NE30 .... 2 F1
Ashley Road County JMI School
  HAR/WTLS NE34 .... 75 G5
Astley Community High School
  MONK NE25 .... 39 K5
Atkinson House School
  CRAM NE23 .... 39 G6
Atkinson Road Primary School
  BW/LEM/TK/HW NE15 .... 69 G7
The Avenues Medical Practice
  GOS/KPK NE3 .... 56 C7
Aykley Heads Business Centre
  DHAM DH1 .... 156 C1
Ayton Primary School
  WASHS NE38 .... 116 B3
Backworth County
  First School
  SMOOR NE27 .... 48 E4
Bailey Green First School
  LGB/KIL NE12 .... 47 J5
Balliol Business Park
  LGB/KIL NE12 .... 57 G2
Balliol First School
  LGB/KIL NE12 .... 57 H4
Barley Mow Primary School
  CLS/BIR/GTL DH3 .... 115 K4
Barmston Medical Centre
  WASHS NE38 .... 103 H7
Barmston Village
  Primary School
  WASHS NE38 .... 117 H1
Barnes Junior School
  MLFD/PNYW SR4 .... 119 K2
Barnwell Primary School
  HLS DH4 .... 117 K6
Battle Hill First School
  WLSD/HOW NE28 .... 59 H7
BBC North & Radio Newcastle
  JES NE2 .... 4 D2
Beaconhill County First School
  CRAM NE23 .... 37 K2
Beamish County School
  STLY/ANP DH9 .... 113 H7

Beamish Park Golf Club
  STLY/ANP DH9 .... 113 G4
Beaumont Park Surgery
  MONK NE25 .... 50 B3
Bebside County Middle School
  BLYTH NE24 .... 30 B6
Bebside Social Club House
  BLYTH NE24 .... 29 K7
Bede Infant School
  FELL NE10 .... 11 M4
Bedewell School
  HEBB NE31 .... 73 G7
Bedlington Community
  High School
  BDLGTN NE22 .... 29 K4
Bedlington Station
  County First School
  BDLGTN NE22 .... 29 K3
Bedlington Stead County
  First School
  BDLGTN NE22 .... 29 J5
Belford House Sports Club
  ASHBK/HED/RY SR2 .... 120 D3
Belle Vue Leisure Centre
  CON/LDGT DH8 .... 123 C4
Belle Vue Swimming Centre
  CON/LDGT DH8 .... 123 C4
Bellway Industrial Estate
  LGB/KIL NE12 .... 58 B3
Belmont C of E (Controlled)
  Junior School
  DHAM DH1 .... 157 K6
Belmont Comprehensive
  School
  DHAM DH1 .... 157 K6
Belmont County Infant School
  DHAM DH1 .... 157 K6
Belmont Grange Clinic
  DHAM DH1 .... 157 K5
Belvedere Retail Park
  GOS/KPK NE3 .... 55 G4
Benedict Biscop C of E School
  SUNDSW SR3 .... 133 H2
Benfield Comprehensive
  School
  BYK/HTN/WLK NE6 .... 72 A2
Benfieldside CP School
  CON/LDGT DH8 .... 122 C2
Bensham District Clinic
  GATE NE8 .... 10 D7
Bensham Family Practice
  GATE NE8 .... 10 C6
Bensham Synagogue
  GATE NE8 .... 10 D6
Benton Park Primary School
  LGB/HTN NE7 .... 57 H6
Benwell Hill Cricket Club
  BW/LEM/TK/HW NE15 .... 69 F4
Bernard Gilpin Primary School
  HLS DH4 .... 132 C7
Bessie Surtees House
  CNUT NE1 .... 5 L8
Bewicke Health Centre
  WLSD/HOW NE28 .... 73 J1
Bewick Road Medical Centre
  GATE NE8 .... 11 C5
Bexhill Primary School
  SWCK/CAS SR5 .... 104 D2

Biddick Hall County
  Infant School
  HAR/WTLS NE34 .... 90 E1
Biddick Hall County
  Junior School
  HAR/WTLS NE34 .... 75 F7
Biddick School
  WASHS NE38 .... 117 G3
Bill Quay Cricket Club
  FELL NE10 .... 13 M4
Birtley East Primary School
  CLS/BIR/GTL DH3 .... 101 J4
Birtley Lane Surgery
  CLS/BIR/GTL DH3 .... 115 J2
Birtley Medical Group Practice
  CLS/BIR/GTL DH3 .... 115 J3
Birtley St Josephs RC School
  CLS/BIR/GTL DH3 .... 115 J2
Birtley Swimming Baths
  CLS/BIR/GTL DH3 .... 115 J3
Bishop Ian Ramsey School
  CON/LDGT DH8 .... 109 J4
Blackfell Primary School
  WASHN NE37 .... 102 C7
Blackfriars Craft Centre
  CNUT NE1 .... 5 H6
Blackfyne
  Comprehensive School
  CON/LDGT DH8 .... 123 F3
Black Gate
  CNUT NE1 .... 5 K8
Blackhall Primary School
  RHTLP TS27 .... 175 K7
Blakelaw Health Centre
  WD/WHPE/BLK NE5 .... 69 G1
Blakelaw School
  WD/WHPE/BLK NE5 .... 69 G1
Blaydon Business Centre
  BLAY NE21 .... 84 C1
Blaydon Business Park
  BLAY NE21 .... 68 D7
Blaydon Cricket Club
  BLAY NE21 .... 84 A2
Blaydon Haugh
  Industrial Estate
  BLAY NE21 .... 84 C1
Blaydon Industrial Park
  BLAY NE21 .... 84 B1
Blaydon Rugby Football Club
  WICK/BNPF NE16 .... 84 D3
Blaydon Swimming Pool
  BLAY NE21 .... 84 C2
Blaydon West Primary School
  BLAY NE21 .... 84 A1
Bloemfontein County
  Junior Mixed School
  STLY/ANP DH9 .... 126 E4
Blyth Delaval County
  Middle School
  BLYTH NE24 .... 35 F2
Blyth New Delaval County
  First School
  BLYTH NE24 .... 34 D3
Blyth Newsham County
  First School
  BLYTH NE24 .... 34 E2
Blyth Plessey Road County
  First School
  BLYTH NE24 .... 31 H7

Blyth Spartans AFC
  BLYTH NE24 .... 35 G1
Blyth Sports Centre
  BLYTH NE24 .... 31 F7
Blyth Tynedale County
  High School
  BLYTH NE24 .... 30 C7
Blyth Tynedale County
  Middle School
  BLYTH NE24 .... 30 C7
Blyth Valley Borough Council
  BLYTH NE24 .... 30 D5
Blyth Valley Borough Council
  BLYTH NE24 .... 31 F7
Blyth Valley Borough Council
  MONK NE25 .... 39 K5
Boker Lane Health Centre
  BOLCOL NE35 .... 91 F4
Bolam Business Park
  CRAM NE23 .... 32 D7
Boldon Comprehensive School
  BOLCOL NE35 .... 90 E4
Boldon Lane Health Centre
  HAR/WTLS NE34 .... 75 G7
Bothal County Middle School
  ASHGTN NE63 .... 23 F1
Bowburn County Infant School
  RDHAMSE DH6 .... 180 A3
Bowburn County
  Junior School
  RDHAMSE DH6 .... 180 B2
Bow School
  DHAM DH1 .... 16 D7
Brancepeth Castle
  BDN/LAN/SAC DH7 .... 176 E3
Branch End Surgery
  PSHWF NE43 .... 79 H5
Brandling Primary School
  FELL NE10 .... 12 C6
Brandon & Byshottles
  Parish Council
  BDN/LAN/SAC DH7 .... 167 J5
Brandon Cricket Club
  BDN/LAN/SAC DH7 .... 167 J3
Brandon Modern School
  BDN/LAN/SAC DH7 .... 167 G6
Brandon United Football Club
  BDN/LAN/SAC DH7 .... 167 H5
Brewery
  ELS/FEN NE4 .... 5 G6
Brewery
  SUND SR1 .... 14 D3
Bridges Shopping Centre
  SUND SR1 .... 14 D5
Brighton Avenue
  Primary School
  GATE NE8 .... 10 D6
Brinkburn School
  HAR/WTLS NE34 .... 75 H6
Broadway East First School
  GOS/KPK NE3 .... 56 D3
Broadway Junior School
  MLFD/PNYW SR4 .... 119 H2
Broadwood Junior
  & Infant School
  BW/LEM/TK/HW NE15 .... 68 D4
Brockwell Clinic
  CRAM NE23 .... 33 H7

Brockwell County
Middle School
CRAM NE23 .... 33 H7
Broomley County First School
PSHWF NE43 .... 79 F4
Broomside Lane Surgery
DHAM DH1 .... 157 K5
Brooms RC Primary School
CON/LDGT DH8 .... 123 K3
Browney County
Primary School
BDN/LAN/SAC DH7 .... 167 J7
Browns Gallery
JES NE2 .... 70 E1
Brunswick Beech
Special School
DIN/WO NE13 .... 46 A3
Buddle Industrial Estate
WLSD/HOW NE28 .... 72 D3
Bugatti Industrial Park
NSHW NE29 .... 60 A5
Bullion Lane Primary School
CLSW/PEL DH2 .... 129 H5
Burnhope Primary School
BDN/LAN/SAC DH7 .... 141 G3
Burnmoor Cricket Club
HLS DH4 .... 131 G3
Burnopfield Primary School
WICK/BNPF NE16 .... 97 H7
Burnside County First School
CRAM NE23 .... 33 J6
Burnside High School
WLSD/HOW NE28 .... 73 F1
Burnside JMI School
STLY/ANP DH9 .... 127 F2
Burnside Primary School
HLS DH4 .... 132 B6
Burradon First School
CRAM NE23 .... 47 J4
Byermoor RC Aided
Junior & Infant School
WICK/BNPF NE16 .... 98 B6
Byker Primary School
BYK/HTN/WLK NE6 .... 6 F6
Bywell Estate Office
PSHWF NE43 .... 78 D1
Caedman Primary School
GATE NE8 .... 10 F6
Cambois County First School
BLYTH NE24 .... 30 E2
Camden Square
Secondary School
SEA/MUR SR7 .... 150 D1
Carr Hill Infant & Junior School
LWF/SPW/WRK NE9 .... 11 L9
Cartmel Business Centre
FELL NE10 .... 13 J6
Carville First School
WLSD/HOW NE28 .... 72 D3
Cassop Primary School
RDHAMSE DH6 .... 181 G3
Castle
DHAM DH1 .... 16 D4
Castle Dene Special School
GOS/KPK NE3 .... 57 F6
Castle Keep
CNUT NE1 .... 5 L8
Castle Leazes Halls
JES NE2 .... 4 F3
Castle Morpeth
Borough Council
MPTH NE61 .... 20 D7
Castle Morpeth
Borough Council
MPTH NE61 .... 20 D4
Castleside County Junior
& Infant School
CON/LDGT DH8 .... 136 E2
Castle Surgery
PRUD NE42 .... 80 C1
Castle View School
SWCK/CAS SR5 .... 104 E4
Catchgate Primary School
STLY/ANP DH9 .... 125 G3
Cedars Special School
LWF/SPW/WRK NE9 .... 101 G2
Central County First School
ASHGTN NE63 .... 23 K1
Central First School
WLSD/HOW NE28 .... 73 F1
Central High School
GOS/KPK NE3 .... 56 C6
Central Newcastle High School
JES NE2 .... 5 L1
Central Surgery
SUND SR1 .... 14 F5
Cestria Health Centre
CLSW/PEL DH2 .... 129 F5
Cestria Primary School
CLS/BIR/GTL DH3 .... 129 K4
Chantry Middle School
MPTH NE61 .... 20 C4
Chantry Museum
MPTH NE61 .... 20 E5
Chapel House Middle School
WD/WHPE/BLK NE5 .... 67 K1
Chapel Park Shopping Centre
WD/WHPE/BLK NE5 .... 54 B6
Chase School
WICK/BNPF NE16 .... 85 F5
Chastleton Surgery
DHAM DH1 .... 156 C3
Cherryburn (NT)
PSHWF NE43 .... 79 J3
Chester Le Street
Leisure Centre
CLS/BIR/GTL DH3 .... 129 K4
Chester Le Street C of E
Junior School
CLSW/PEL DH2 .... 129 H3
Chester Le Street Cricket Club
CLS/BIR/GTL DH3 .... 129 K5
Chester Le Street
District Council
CLS/BIR/GTL DH3 .... 129 J3
Chester Le Street
District Council
CLS/BIR/GTL DH3 .... 129 G4
Chester Le Street
Health Centre
CLS/BIR/GTL DH3 .... 129 K3

Chester Road Surgery
MLFD/PNYW SR4 .... 106 A7
Cheveley Park Medical Centre
DHAM DH1 .... 158 A6
Cheveley Park Primary School
DHAM DH1 .... 158 A5
Cheviot County Junior
Mixed School
HAR/WTLS NE34 .... 76 A3
Cheviot First School
WD/WHPE/BLK NE5 .... 54 E6
Chevyside Middle School
WD/WHPE/BLK NE5 .... 54 E6
Childrens Hospital
SUNDSW SR3 .... 120 A2
Chillingham Industrial Estate
BYK/HTN/WLK NE6 .... 7 H2
Chillingham Road
Primary School
BYK/HTN/WLK NE6 .... 7 G1
Choppington County
First School
STKFD/GP NE62 .... 28 E1
Chopwell County
Primary School
CHPW NE17 .... 95 H4
The Chorister School
DHAM DH1 .... 16 C6
Christ Church C of E
Primary School
JES NE2 .... 5 M5
Church of England
Primary School
WLSD/HOW NE28 .... 73 G1
Church View Medical Centre
SUNDSW SR3 .... 120 A7
Cinema
SUND SR1 .... 14 E6
City Council
DHAM DH1 .... 16 F2
City Hall
CNUT NE1 .... 5 L4
City of Sunderland College
ASHBK/HED/RY SR2 .... 120 E4
City of Sunderland College
HLS DH4 .... 131 K2
City of Sunderland College
SUND SR1 .... 14 E4
City of Sunderland College
SWCK/CAS SR5 .... 105 H3
City of Sunderland College
SWCK/CAS SR5 .... 106 C3
City Pool
CNUT NE1 .... 5 K4
Civic Centre
CLS/BIR/GTL DH3 .... 129 K3
Civic Centre
CNUT NE1 .... 5 K4
Civic Centre
GATE NE8 .... 10 F3
Civic Centre
SUND SR1 .... 14 E6
Civic Centre Derwentside DC
CON/LDGT DH8 .... 123 G3
Civic Hall
WLSD/HOW NE28 .... 72 D1
Civil Service Sports Club
LGB/KIL NE12 .... 58 A5
Claremont Footcare Surgery
WBAY NE26 .... 50 C2
Claypath Medical Practice
DHAM DH1 .... 16 F3
Clayton Street Indoor
Mini Market
CNUT NE1 .... 5 J7
Cleadon Village C of E
Infant School
CLDN/WHIT/ROK SR6 ...... 92 B3
Cleadon Village County
JM School
CLDN/WHIT/ROK SR6 ...... 91 K3
Cleasewell Hill School
STKFD/GP NE62 .... 23 F6
Club House
BDN/LAN/SAC DH7 .... 176 E3
Club House
DHAM DH1 .... 168 C4
Club House
HLH DH5 .... 133 F7
C of E Junior Mixed
& Infant School
CON/LDGT DH8 .... 108 E3
Collierley County
Primary School
STLY/ANP DH9 .... 110 E6
Collingwood Primary School
NSHW NE29 .... 60 B5
Collingwood School
MPTH NE61 .... 21 F6
Community College
SEA/MUR SR7 .... 135 J7
Community Health Clinic
RDHAMSE DH6 .... 172 E7
Consett County Court
CON/LDGT DH8 .... 123 F5
Consett County Infant School
CON/LDGT DH8 .... 123 G5
Consett Medical Centre
CON/LDGT DH8 .... 123 G5
Consett RC JMI School
CON/LDGT DH8 .... 123 F4
Coquet Park First School
WBAY NE26 .... 50 E3
Corrymella Scott Gallery
JES NE2 .... 70 D3
Cotsford Junior School
PLEE/EAS SR8 .... 175 J3
County Durham
Health Authority
PLEE/EAS SR8 .... 174 E4
County Hall
MPTH NE61 .... 26 E1
County Hall Durham
County Council
DHAM DH1 .... 156 C5
County Hospital
DHAM DH1 .... 16 B3
County Junior & Infant School
BDN/LAN/SAC DH7 .... 155 D4
County Junior & Infant School
RDHAMSE DH6 .... 160 D6

County Junior Middle
& Infant School
STLY/ANP DH9 .... 127 K1
County Junior Mixed School
RDHAMSE DH6 .... 172 B6
County Junior Mixed School
WNGT TS28 .... 183 K3
Cowgate Leisure Centre
WD/WHPE/BLK NE5 .... 55 H7
Cowgate Primary School
ELS/FEN NE4 .... 69 J2
Coxhoe District Sports Centre
RDHAMSE DH6 .... 180 C7
Coxhoe Medical Practice
RDHAMSE DH6 .... 180 D7
Cragside County First School
CRAM NE23 .... 38 C4
Cragside Primary School
LGB/HTN NE7 .... 57 C7
Craigievar School
CLDN/WHIT/ROK SR6 ...... 106 C2
Cramlington Football Club
CRAM NE23 .... 38 E2
Crawcrook Medical Centre
RYTON NE40 .... 66 B7
Crawcrook RC Junior
& Infant School
RYTON NE40 .... 66 A7
Crook Hall
DHAM DH1 .... 16 D1
Crookhill Junior School
RYTON NE40 .... 67 G6
Crown Court
CNUT NE1 .... 5 L8
Crowtree Leisure Centre
SUND SR1 .... 14 D5
Cruddas Park Health Centre
ELS/FEN NE4 .... 4 D9
Cruddas Park Surgery
ELS/FEN NE4 .... 4 E9
Cullercoats Primary School
TYNE/NSHE NE30 .... 51 G6
Custom House
CNUT NE1 .... 5 M8
Dame Allans Boys School
ELS/FEN NE4 .... 69 J4
Dame Dorothy Street School
CLDN/WHIT/ROK SR6 ...... 15 G1
Davenport Surgery
HLH DH5 .... 147 H2
Deaf Hill Primary School
TRIM TS29 .... 182 E5
Deerness Park Medical Centre
ASHBK/HED/RY SR2 .... 15 H7
Deerness Sports Centre
BDN/LAN/SAC DH7 .... 167 F1
Deerness Valley
Comprehensive School
BDN/LAN/SAC DH7 .... 155 F6
Delaval Primary School
BW/LEM/TK/HW NE15 ...... 69 F6
Denbigh Community
First School
WLSD/HOW NE28 .... 59 J7
Dene House County
Mixed Modern School
PLEE/EAS SR8 .... 175 H4
Deneside Junior
& Infant School
SEA/MUR SR7 .... 150 B2
Deneside Medical Centre
SEA/MUR SR7 .... 150 C1
Denton Park Middle School
WD/WHPE/BLK NE5 .... 68 D1
Denton Road Primary School
BW/LEM/TK/HW NE15 ...... 68 D6
Derwenthaugh Industrial Estate
BLAY NE21 .... 84 D1
Derwent Infant School
GATE NE8 .... 10 A6
Derwentside Business Centre
CON/LDGT DH8 .... 123 H3
Derwentside College
BDN/LAN/SAC DH7 .... 154 A2
Derwentside College
CON/LDGT DH8 .... 123 F5
Derwentside District Council
STLY/ANP DH9 .... 125 J5
Derwentside District Council
STLY/ANP DH9 .... 126 D1
Diamond Hall Junior
& Infant School
MLFD/PNYW SR4 .... 105 K6
Dinnington Village First School
DIN/WO NE13 .... 45 G2
Dipton Surgery
STLY/ANP DH9 .... 110 E6
Dli Museum & Arts Centre
DHAM DH1 .... 156 D6
Donwell Primary School
WASHN NE37 .... 102 E4
Downhill Primary School
SWCK/CAS SR5 .... 105 F1
Dragonville Industrial Park
DHAM DH1 .... 157 J7
Dr Chandys Surgery
PLEE/EAS SR8 .... 175 H3
Dr Dhuny's Surgery
STLY/ANP DH9 .... 127 F4
The Drive Primary School
FELL NE10 .... 12 F7
Dr Krishnans Surgery
GATE NE8 .... 10 C7
Dr Rannus Surgery
DUN/TMV NE11 .... 9 J7
Dr Reg Carrs Surgery
BLYTH NE24 .... 31 H7
Dryburn Hospital
DHAM DH1 .... 156 B5
DSS
SUND SR1 .... 14 C4
Dubmire County Junior
& Infant School
HLS DH4 .... 131 J7
Dudley Surgery
CRAM NE23 .... 47 H1
Dunelm Medical Practice
BDN/LAN/SAC DH7 .... 155 G6
Dunelm Medical Practice
DHAM DH1 .... 17 K2
Dunholme School
DHAM DH1 .... 156 C4

Dunston Federation
Football Club
DUN/TMV NE11 .... 8 F5
Dunston Health Centre
DUN/TMV NE11 .... 8 E8
Dunston Hill Hospital
DUN/TMV NE11 .... 8 F8
Dunston Hill Junior
& Infant School
DUN/TMV NE11 .... 8 F8
Dunston Industrial Estate
DUN/TMV NE11 .... 8 E5
Dunston Riverside
Primary School
DUN/TMV NE11 .... 9 H5
Dunston Swimming Pool
DUN/TMV NE11 .... 8 F9
Durham Baths
DHAM DH1 .... 16 F4
Durham Blue Coat C of E (Aided)
Junior School
DHAM DH1 .... 156 D3
Durham Business Centre
BDN/LAN/SAC DH7 .... 167 K5
Durham Cathedral
DHAM DH1 .... 16 D5
Durham City Amateur
Football Club
DHAM DH1 .... 157 J5
Durham City Cricket Club
DHAM DH1 .... 17 H5
Durham City Rugby Club
DHAM DH1 .... 17 H5
Durham County Constabulary
PLEE/EAS SR8 .... 174 E4
Durham County Council
CLS/BIR/GTL DH3 .... 145 J1
Durham County Council
CON/LDGT DH8 .... 123 F5
Durham County Council
DHAM DH1 .... 156 C4
Durham County Council
DHAM DH1 .... 157 K7
Durham County Council
PLEE/EAS SR8 .... 174 D1
Durham County Council
PLEE/EAS SR8 .... 175 G2
Durham County Council
SEA/MUR SR7 .... 149 H5
Durham County Council
STLY/ANP DH9 .... 126 C1
Durham County Cricket Club
CLS/BIR/GTL DH3 .... 130 A5
Durham County NHS Trust
DHAM DH1 .... 155 K2
Durham Crown Court
DHAM DH1 .... 16 E5
Durham Gilesgate
Comprehensive School
DHAM DH1 .... 157 H6
Durham High School
DHAM DH1 .... 168 C5
Durham Johnston
Comprehensive School
DHAM DH1 .... 17 G6
Durham Johnston
Comprehensive School
DHAM DH1 .... 156 B7
Durham Markets Co
DHAM DH1 .... 16 D3
Durham Newton Hall
County Infant School
DHAM DH1 .... 156 D3
Durham St Hilds C of E (Aided)
Primary School
DHAM DH1 .... 17 M2
Durham School
DHAM DH1 .... 16 B6
Durham Sixth Form Centre
DHAM DH1 .... 16 D2
Earls House Hospital
DHAM DH1 .... 155 K3
Easington C of E School
PLEE/EAS SR8 .... 162 B6
Easington Colliery
Primary School
PLEE/EAS SR8 .... 162 D5
Easington Comprehensive
School
PLEE/EAS SR8 .... 162 B6
Easington District Council
PLEE/EAS SR8 .... 162 C5
Easington District Council
PLEE/EAS SR8 .... 174 A1
Easington District Council
SEA/MUR SR7 .... 149 J5
Easington District Council
SEA/MUR SR7 .... 150 D3
Easington District
Leisure Centre
SEA/MUR SR7 .... 150 C1
Easington Lane
Primary School
HLH DH5 .... 160 C1
East Boldon Junior School
BOL NE36 .... 91 G5
Eastcliffe Grammar School
GOS/KPK NE3 .... 56 D6
East Durham
Community College
PLEE/EAS SR8 .... 174 C4
East Herrington
Primary School
SUNDSW SR3 .... 119 G7
Eastlea First School
CRAM NE23 .... 33 J7
East Rainton JMI School
HLH DH5 .... 147 F4
East Riding Clinic
MPTH NE61 .... 21 F3
Eastwood County
Middle School
PRUD NE42 .... 81 F1
Eden Hall Infant School
PLEE/EAS SR8 .... 175 F3
Edmondsley JMI School
BDN/LAN/SAC DH7 .... 143 G1
Eldon Square Shopping Centre
CNUT NE1 .... 5 K5
Elemore Leisure Centre
HLH DH5 .... 148 B7

Ellison C of E JMI School
JRW NE32 .... 73 K5
Elswick Way Industrial Estate
HAR/WTLS NE34 .... 74 E5
Emmanuel College
DUN/TMV NE11 .... 85 K7
Emmaville Primary School
RYTON NE40 .... 66 B7
Empire Theatre
CON/LDGT DH8 .... 123 F5
Empire Theatre
SUND SR1 .... 14 C4
English Martyrs RC
Primary School
SWCK/CAS SR5 .... 105 J3
Epinay Special School
JRW NE32 .... 74 A5
Eppleton Cricket Club
HLH DH5 .... 147 K2
Esh C of E Aided
Primary School
BDN/LAN/SAC DH7 .... 153 J4
Esh RC Primary School
BDN/LAN/SAC DH7 .... 153 H5
Esh Winning Child
Health Clinic
BDN/LAN/SAC DH7 .... 165 H1
The Evergreen Gallery
CNUT NE1 .... 5 J8
Eye Clinic
CNUT NE1 .... 5 K4
Farne First School
WD/WHPE/BLK NE5 .... 54 E7
Farnham Medical Centre
HAR/WTLS NE34 .... 75 G5
Farringdon School
SUNDSW SR3 .... 119 H7
Farrington Infant School
SUNDSW SR3 .... 119 H6
Farrington Junior School
SUNDSW SR3 .... 119 H6
Fatfield Junior & Infant School
WASHS NE38 .... 117 F4
Felldyke Primary
& Infant School
LWF/SPW/WRK NE9 .... 101 K2
Fellgate JMI School
JRW NE32 .... 89 K3
Felling Business Centre
FELL NE10 .... 12 C3
Fellrose Surgery
CLSW/PEL DH2 .... 128 E3
Fellside County Primary School
WICK/BNPF NE16 .... 84 E6
Fell Tower Medical
Centre Whereis Building
LWF/SPW/WRK NE9 .... 101 F1
Felstead School
MLFD/PNYW SR4 .... 105 H7
Fence Houses Surgery
HLS DH4 .... 131 G5
Finchale County Infant School
DHAM DH1 .... 157 F2
Finchale Priory
DHAM DH1 .... 145 J5
Fire Station
CNUT NE1 .... 5 L6
Fire Station
SUND SR1 .... 14 B5
First School
MONK NE25 .... 39 J4
Fordley Clinic
CRAM NE23 .... 47 G1
Formica Social & Sports Club
NSHW NE29 .... 59 K3
Framwellgate Moor
Comprehensive School
DHAM DH1 .... 156 C3
Framwellgate Moor
Junior & Infant School
DHAM DH1 .... 156 C3
Freeman Hospital
LGB/HTN NE7 .... 57 G6
Front Street Industrial Estate
RDHAMSE DH6 .... 160 E2
Front Street Industrial Estate
RDHAMSE DH6 .... 172 E7
Front Street Junior
& Infant School
WICK/BNPF NE16 .... 84 E5
Front Street Surgery
BLAY NE21 .... 83 K3
Fulling Mill
DHAM DH1 .... 16 C5
Fulwell Grange
Christian School
SWCK/CAS SR5 .... 106 C2
Fulwell Junior School
CLDN/WHIT/ROK SR6 ...... 106 E1
Fulwell Medical Centre
CLDN/WHIT/ROK SR6 ...... 106 D1
Fyndoune Community College
BDN/LAN/SAC DH7 .... 143 H5
The Gables Medical Group
BDLGTN NE22 .... 29 K4
Galactic Zoo
CNUT NE1 .... 5 H8
Gallery of Fine Art
CNUT NE1 .... 5 H4
The Gallery
CLSW/PEL DH2 .... 144 C1
The Gambling Man Gallery
TYNE/NSHE NE30 .... 2 F4
Garden Park Surgery
WLSD/HOW NE28 .... 59 J6
The Garrick Gallery
STLY/ANP DH9 .... 126 C1
Gatehouse Industrial Estate
CON/LDGT DH8 .... 122 E5
Gateshead Area
Health Authority
BLAY NE21 .... 84 D2
Gateshead Area
Health Authority
DUN/TMV NE11 .... 86 A6
Gateshead Area
Health Authority
GATE NE8 .... 10 F4
Gateshead Area
Health Authority
GATE NE8 .... 10 A5

Gateshead Area
Health Authority
LWF/SPW/WRK NE9 ...... 87 H6
Gateshead Area
Health Authority
WICK/BNPF NE16 ...... 85 F5
Gateshead College
LWF/SPW/WRK NE9 ...... 11 G9
Gateshead Complimentary
Health Centre
GATE NE8 ...... 10 E6
Gateshead Fell Cricket Club
LWF/SPW/WRK NE9 ...... 87 G6
Gateshead Health Care
FELL NE10 ...... 88 D6
Gateshead Health NHS Trust
LWF/SPW/WRK NE9 ...... 11 J9
Gateshead Hospitals NHS Trust
GATE NE8 ...... 86 D5
Gateshead
International Stadium
FELL NE10 ...... 12 A2
Gateshead Jewish Boys School
GATE NE8 ...... 10 F5
Gateshead Jewish
Primary School
GATE NE8 ...... 10 F6
Gateshead Leisure Centre
GATE NE8 ...... 11 G7
Gateshead Little Theatre
GATE NE8 ...... 10 F8
Gateshead Magistrates Court
GATE NE8 ...... 11 G4
Gateshead Metropolitan
Borough Council
BLAY NE21 ...... 84 B1
Gateshead Metropolitan
Borough Council
CLS/BIR/GTL DH3 ...... 115 J1
Gateshead Metropolitan
Borough Council
DUN/TMV NE11 ...... 100 D2
Gateshead Metropolitan
Borough Council
FELL NE10 ...... 12 C8
Gateshead Metropolitan
Borough Council
GATE NE8 ...... 10 E4
Gateshead Metropolitan
Borough Council
GATE NE8 ...... 11 L2
Gateshead Metropolitan
Borough Council
LWF/SPW/WRK NE9 ...... 87 F7
Gateshead Metropolitan
Borough Council
LWF/SPW/WRK NE9 ...... 101 G2
Gateshead Metropolitan
Borough Council
ROWG NE39 ...... 96 E3
Gateshead Metropolitan
Borough Council
WICK/BNPF NE16 ...... 85 F5
Gateshead & South Tyneside
Health Authority
SSH NE33 ...... 75 H2
Gateshead Talmudical College
GATE NE8 ...... 10 D6
George Stephenson
High School
LGB/KIL NE12 ...... 47 K7
Gibside School
WICK/BNPF NE16 ...... 84 E7
Gilesgate County
Junior School
DHAM DH1 ...... 17 L1
Glebe School
WBAY NE26 ...... 50 C1
Glebe Village Primary School
WASHS NE38 ...... 117 F1
Glen Dene School
PLEE/EAS SR8 ...... 162 B5
The Globe Gallery
TYNE/NSHE NE30 ...... 2 E2
Glover Industrial Estate
WASHN NE37 ...... 103 H6
Glynwood Primary School
LWF/SPW/WRK NE9 ...... 87 G7
Goathland Primary School
LGB/KIL NE12 ...... 57 J4
Gosforth Central Middle School
GOS/KPK NE3 ...... 56 C4
Gosforth Cricket Club
GOS/KPK NE3 ...... 56 C6
Gosforth High School
GOS/KPK NE3 ...... 56 C4
Gosforth Industrial Estate
GOS/KPK NE3 ...... 56 D4
Gosforth Memorial
Health Centre
GOS/KPK NE3 ...... 56 D5
Gosforth West Middle School
GOS/KPK NE3 ...... 56 B5
Grainger Market
CNUT NE1 ...... 5 J6
Grange First School
GOS/KPK NE3 ...... 56 B4
Grange Park Primary School
SWCK/CAS SR5 ...... 106 C3
Grange Terrace Surgery
ASHBK/HED/RY SR2 ...... 14 D7
Grangetown Family
Dental Health Centre
ASHBK/HED/RY SR2 ...... 120 E4
Grangetown Junior
& Infant School
ASHBK/HED/RY SR2 ...... 121 F3
Grangewood Surgery
HLS DH4 ...... 131 J1
Greencroft
Comprehensive School
STLY/ANP DH9 ...... 125 G3
Greenesfield Business Centre
GATE NE8 ...... 10 E1
Greenfields Special School
HEBB NE31 ...... 73 H4
Greenland County JMI School
STLY/ANP DH9 ...... 126 B3
Greenside Cricket Club
RYTON NE40 ...... 82 C3
Greenside JMI School
RYTON NE40 ...... 82 B3

Grey College
DHAM DH1 ...... 16 D9
Greystoke Surgery
MPTH NE61 ...... 20 D4
Grindon Infants School
MLFD/PNYW SR4 ...... 119 F3
Grove County JMI School
CON/LDGT DH8 ...... 122 F6
Guide Post County
Middle School
STKFD/GP NE62 ...... 23 F6
Guide Post Ringway
County First School
STKFD/GP NE62 ...... 23 F4
Hadrian JMI School
SSH NE33 ...... 3 H4
Hadrian Park First School
WLSD/HOW NE28 ...... 59 G3
Hadrian Park Middle School
WLSD/HOW NE28 ...... 59 G3
Hadrian School
BW/LEM/TK/HW NE15 ...... 69 G5
Halls of Residence
MLFD/PNYW SR4 ...... 14 A6
Hamsteels County Junior
& Infant School
BDN/LAN/SAC DH7 ...... 165 F1
Hancock Museum
JES NE2 ...... 5 K3
Harlow Green Infant School
LWF/SPW/WRK NE9 ...... 101 G3
Harraton Primary School
WASHS NE38 ...... 116 D3
Hartlepool Community
Care NHS Trust
PLEE/EAS SR8 ...... 174 E4
Harton School
HAR/WTLS NE34 ...... 76 A3
Hatfield College
DHAM DH1 ...... 16 D5
Havelock Primary School
MLFD/PNYW SR4 ...... 105 H7
Hawthorn First School
ASHGTN NE63 ...... 23 K4
Hawthorn House
Medical Centre
BYK/HTN/WLK NE6 ...... 7 G4
Hawthorn Primary School
ELS/FEN NE4 ...... 4 D8
Hawthorns Hospital
PLEE/EAS SR8 ...... 175 F5
Hazlewood Community
Primary School
DIN/WO NE13 ...... 46 B4
Headway Theatre
BLYTH NE24 ...... 31 H6
Heaton Manor Lower School
LGB/HTN NE7 ...... 71 G1
Heaton Manor Upper School
LGB/HTN NE7 ...... 57 J6
Hebrew Synagogue
WBAY NE26 ...... 50 E4
Heddon on the Wall C of E
Controlled First School
BW/LEM/TK/HW NE15 ...... 66 A1
Hedworthfield
Comprehensive School
JRW NE32 ...... 89 K3
Heritage Centre
DHAM DH4 ...... 16 E5
Herrington Medical Centre
HLS DH4 ...... 132 A1
Hesleden County Junior
& Infant School
RHTLP TS27 ...... 185 H2
Hetton Health Centre
HLH DH5 ...... 147 K4
Hetton Lyons School
HLH DH5 ...... 147 K6
Hetton Primary School
HLH DH5 ...... 147 J5
Hetton Secondary School
HLH DH5 ...... 147 J5
Hetton UDC Swimming Baths
HLH DH5 ...... 147 J5
Heworth Grange
Comprehensive School
FELL NE10 ...... 13 H8
High Farm Middle School
WLSD/HOW NE28 ...... 58 D5
High Fell Special School
LWF/SPW/WRK NE9 ...... 11 K9
Highfield County Infant School
HAR/WTLS NE34 ...... 76 A2
Highfield County Middle School
PRUD NE42 ...... 80 C3
Highfield Hospital
CLS/BIR/GTL DH3 ...... 129 J2
Highfield Junior
& Infant School
ROWG NE39 ...... 96 B3
High Spen Industrial Estate
ROWG NE39 ...... 82 B7
High Spen Industrial Estate
ROWG NE39 ...... 97 H2
Hillcrest Day Special School
CRAM NE23 ...... 38 C2
Hillsview Surgery
GOS/KPK NE3 ...... 55 J4
Hill Top School
LWF/SPW/WRK NE9 ...... 102 A1
Hillview Clinic
ASHBK/HED/RY SR2 ...... 120 D4
Hill View Infant School
ASHBK/HED/RY SR2 ...... 120 D4
Hill View Junior School
ASHBK/HED/RY SR2 ...... 120 D4
Hilton Primary School
WD/WHPE/BLK NE5 ...... 69 F1
Hindu Temple
ELS/FEN NE4 ...... 69 H5
Hirst High School
ASHGTN NE63 ...... 24 B3
HM Prison
DHAM DH1 ...... 16 F5
HMS Calliope Cadet
Training Centre
GATE NE8 ...... 6 A8
The Hobart Gallery
GOS/KPK NE3 ...... 56 C6
Hollyhurst Medical Centre
BLAY NE21 ...... 83 K3

Holly Park Primary School
WASHS NE38 ...... 116 B3
Holmside & South
Moor Hospital
STLY/ANP DH9 ...... 126 E3
Holy Cross RC Primary School
WLSD/HOW NE28 ...... 59 H6
Holystone First School
SMOOR NE27 ...... 48 E7
Holywell County First School
MONK NE25 ...... 40 C6
Hookergate
Comprehensive School
ROWG NE39 ...... 96 D2
Horden Cotsford
County Infant School
PLEE/EAS SR8 ...... 175 J4
Horden & Easington
RC Primary School
PLEE/EAS SR8 ...... 175 G1
Horton Grange First School
BLYTH NE24 ...... 30 B6
Hotspur Primary School
BYK/HTN/WLK NE6 ...... 6 D4
Houghall College
DHAM DH1 ...... 17 H8
Houghton Colliery
Welfare Cricket Club
HLS DH4 ...... 132 A6
Houghton Health Centre
HLH DH5 ...... 132 C7
Houghton Kepier School
HLS DH4 ...... 132 B7
Howden Green
Industrial Estate
WLSD/HOW NE28 ...... 73 K1
Howletch Lane Junior
& Infant School
PLEE/EAS SR8 ...... 174 C4
Hownsgill Industrial Park
CON/LDGT DH8 ...... 122 E7
Hudson Road Primary School
SUND SR1 ...... 15 G6
Hutton Henry C of E School
WNGT TS28 ...... 184 D6
Hylton Castle
SWCK/CAS SR5 ...... 105 F3
Hylton Castle Health Centre
SWCK/CAS SR5 ...... 105 F3
Hylton Castle Junior School
SWCK/CAS SR5 ...... 104 D3
Imex Business Centre
DHAM DH1 ...... 156 C1
Industrial Estate
BDN/LAN/SAC DH7 ...... 143 H5
Industrial Estate
CON/LDGT DH8 ...... 122 E4
Ivy Road Primary School
LGB/KIL NE12 ...... 58 A2
Jewish Boarding School
GATE NE8 ...... 10 F5
Jewish High School
GATE NE8 ...... 11 G5
Jewish Infant School
GATE NE8 ...... 11 G5
John Spence Community
High School
TYNE/NSHE NE30 ...... 60 E2
Joseph Swan School
LWF/SPW/WRK NE9 ...... 100 E2
Jubilee Infant School
SEA/MUR SR7 ...... 149 J5
Kelloe JMI School
RDHAMSE DH6 ...... 181 H6
Kelvin Grove Primary School
GATE NE8 ...... 10 E8
Kenton Comprehensive School
COS/KPK NE3 ...... 55 H6
Kenton Lodge
Residential School
ELS/FEN NE4 ...... 70 B1
Kepier Clinic
DHAM DH1 ...... 17 L1
Kibblesworth Primary School
DUN/TMV NE11 ...... 100 D7
Killingworth Middle School
LGB/KIL NE12 ...... 47 K7
King Edward Junior
& Infant School
TYNE/NSHE NE30 ...... 61 F3
Kingfisher Industrial Estate
SEA/MUR SR7 ...... 135 G7
King George
Comprehensive School
HAR/WTLS NE34 ...... 91 K1
Kingsmeadow
Comprehensive School
DUN/TMV NE11 ...... 8 E7
Kings School
TYNE/NSHE NE30 ...... 61 H3
Kingston Park Primary School
GOS/KPK NE3 ...... 55 G4
Kingsway First School
BLYTH NE24 ...... 35 C1
Knoplaw First School
WD/WHPE/BLK NE5 ...... 68 C1
Laing Art Gallery
CNUT NE1 ...... 5 L5
Lancaster University
CNUT NE1 ...... 5 K8
Lanchester CP Infant
& Junior School
BDN/LAN/SAC DH7 ...... 140 B4
Lanchester Infant School
BDN/LAN/SAC DH7 ...... 140 B4
Lanchester RC Mixed
& Infant School
BDN/LAN/SAC DH7 ...... 140 B4
Langley Moor Primary School
BDN/LAN/SAC DH7 ...... 167 K4
Langley Park Primary School
BDN/LAN/SAC DH7 ...... 154 B3
Larkspur Primary School
LWF/SPW/WRK NE9 ...... 101 J1
La Sagesse Convent
High School
JES NE2 ...... 56 E7
Laurel Avenue County Junior
& Infant School
DHAM DH1 ...... 17 K4
Law Courts
CNUT NE1 ...... 5 M7

Laygate Lane County
Infant School
SSH NE33 ...... 75 G2
Laygate School
SSH NE33 ...... 75 G2
Leadgate County Junior
Mixed School
CON/LDGT DH8 ...... 123 J4
Leadgate Industrial Estate
CON/LDGT DH8 ...... 124 A5
Leadgate Surgery
CON/LDGT DH8 ...... 123 K3
Leafield House School
CLS/BIR/GTL DH3 ...... 115 K3
Lemington Clinic
BW/LEM/TK/HW NE15 ...... 68 G3
Lemington First School
BW/LEM/TK/HW NE15 ...... 68 G5
Lemington Middle School
BW/LEM/TK/HW NE15 ...... 68 G3
Linden School
LGB/KIL NE12 ...... 57 K2
Lindisfarne County
Primary School
GATE NE8 ...... 11 H3
Lingey House Primary School
FELL NE10 ...... 88 D5
Linhope First School
WD/WHPE/BLK NE5 ...... 68 D1
Little Theatre
CLDN/WHIT/ROK SR6 ...... 92 A3
Live Theatre
CNUT NE1 ...... 5 M8
Lobley Hill Junior
& Infant School
DUN/TMV NE11 ...... 86 A7
Longbenton
Community College
LGB/KIL NE12 ...... 57 J3
Longrigg Medical Centre
FELL NE10 ...... 88 C5
Lord Chancellors Department
CNUT NE1 ...... 5 J8
Lord Lawson of Beamish
Secondary School
CLS/BIR/GTL DH3 ...... 115 K3
Louisa Surgery
STLY/ANP DH9 ...... 126 C1
Low Fell Clinic
LWF/SPW/WRK NE9 ...... 101 G1
Low Fell Junior & Infant School
LWF/SPW/WRK NE9 ...... 87 F7
Ludworth JMI School
RDHAMSE DH6 ...... 172 A3
Lumley County Infant School
CLS/BIR/GTL DH3 ...... 130 C7
Lumley Junior Middle
& Infant School
CLS/BIR/GTL DH3 ...... 145 J1
Lynemouth County First School
MPTH NE61 ...... 18 D1
Lynemouth Surgery
MPTH NE61 ...... 18 C1
Lynnwood Business Centre
ELS/FEN NE4 ...... 4 B7
Maiden Law Hospital
BDN/LAN/SAC DH7 ...... 140 C2
Malvins Close County
First School
BLYTH NE24 ...... 30 E6
Maplewood School
SWCK/CAS SR5 ...... 105 J2
Marden Bridge Middle School
MONK NE25 ...... 50 E5
Marden High School
TYNE/NSHE NE30 ...... 61 F1
Marine Avenue Medical Centre
WBAY NE26 ...... 50 D4
Marine Park JMI School
SSH NE33 ...... 3 K7
Market Place Industrial Estate
HLH DH5 ...... 132 D6
Marlborough Clinic
SEA/MUR SR7 ...... 150 D1
Marley Hill Primary School
WICK/BNPF NE16 ...... 98 E5
Mary Trevelyan
Primary School
ELS/FEN NE4 ...... 9 H1
Masonic Temple
ASHBK/HED/RY SR2 ...... 14 E7
Mayfield Medical Centre
JRW NE32 ...... 73 J5
Mckennas Sports Club
BDN/LAN/SAC DH7 ...... 165 H2
Meadowfield Clinic
BDN/LAN/SAC DH7 ...... 167 J6
Meadowfield Sports Centre
BDN/LAN/SAC DH7 ...... 167 J6
Meadow Well Primary School
NSHW NE29 ...... 60 B6
Megabowl
LGB/KIL NE12 ...... 58 C3
Metrocentre East Business Park
DUN/TMV NE11 ...... 8 D4
Metropolitan Borough
of North Tyneside Council
TYNE/NSHE NE30 ...... 2 E1
Mickley County First School
PSHWF NE43 ...... 79 J3
Millburngate
Shopping Precinct
DHAM DH1 ...... 16 C3
Modern Mixed School
RDHAMSE DH6 ...... 173 H3
Monkhouse Primary School
TYNE/NSHE NE30 ...... 61 F1
Monkseaton Clinic
MONK NE25 ...... 50 C5
Monkseaton High School
MONK NE25 ...... 50 C7
Monkseaton Medical Centre
MONK NE25 ...... 50 B5
Monkseaton Middle School
MONK NE25 ...... 50 C5
Monkton County Infant School
HAR/WTLS NE34 ...... 74 E7
Monkton County Junior
Mixed School
HAR/WTLS NE34 ...... 74 D7
Monkton Hall Hospital
HEBB NE31 ...... 73 H7

Monkwearmouth
Health Centre
SWCK/CAS SR5 ...... 14 E1
Monkwearmouth Hospital
SWCK/CAS SR5 ...... 106 C3
Monkwearmouth Railway
Station Museum
SWCK/CAS SR5 ...... 14 E2
Montagu Junior & Infant School
WD/WHPE/BLK NE5 ...... 55 J7
Moor Edge First School
LGB/KIL NE12 ...... 47 H6
Moorside Community
Primary School
ELS/FEN NE4 ...... 4 D4
Moorside Comprehensive
School
CON/LDGT DH8 ...... 122 B7
Moorside County First School
NWBGN NE64 ...... 19 F7
Moorside County School
CON/LDGT DH8 ...... 137 F1
Morpeth Chantry
Bagpipe Museum
MPTH NE61 ...... 20 E5
Morpeth Cottage Hospital
MPTH NE61 ...... 20 D7
Morpeth County Court
MPTH NE61 ...... 20 D5
Morpeth County First School
MPTH NE61 ...... 20 E5
Morpeth Golf Club
MPTH NE61 ...... 20 D7
Morpeth King Edward
Vi School
MPTH NE61 ...... 20 D3
Morpeth Newminster
County Middle School
MPTH NE61 ...... 20 C4
Morpeth Stobhillgate
County First School
MPTH NE61 ...... 21 F6
Morpeth Town Athletics
Football Club
MPTH NE61 ...... 20 B7
Morpeth Town Council
MPTH NE61 ...... 20 D4
Mortimer
Comprehensive School
HAR/WTLS NE34 ...... 75 H4
Mosque
BYK/HTN/WLK NE6 ...... 71 H3
Mosque
MLFD/PNYW SR4 ...... 14 A6
Mosque
SSH NE33 ...... 75 J2
Mountbatten Medical Centre
HEBB NE31 ...... 73 F6
Mountfield Primary School
GOS/KPK NE3 ...... 55 J5
Mowden Hall (Newton)
School Trust
PSHWF NE43 ...... 62 C4
Murton Primary School
SEA/MUR SR7 ...... 149 J5
Museum & Art Gallery
SSH NE33 ...... 3 H6
Museum of Science
and Industry
ELS/FEN NE4 ...... 4 F8
Music School
DHAM DH1 ...... 16 D5
National Glasscentre
CLDN/WHIT/ROK SR6 ...... 15 H2
The Natural Therapy Clinic
TYNE/NSHE NE30 ...... 60 E4
Nature Reserve
LGB/KIL NE12 ...... 58 E3
Nelson Health Centre
NSHW NE29 ...... 2 C2
Nettlesworth Primary School
CLSW/PEL DH2 ...... 144 A4
Nevilles Cross Primary School
DHAM DH1 ...... 168 A1
Newbiggin by the Sea
County Middle School
NWBGN NE64 ...... 24 E1
Newbottle Primary School
HLS DH4 ...... 132 A4
New Brancepeth
Primary School
BDN/LAN/SAC DH7 ...... 166 E3
Newburn Hall Motor Museum
BW/LEM/TK/HW NE15 ...... 67 H3
Newburn Industrial Estate
BW/LEM/TK/HW NE15 ...... 67 J5
Newburn Leisure Centre
BW/LEM/TK/HW NE15 ...... 67 G3
Newburn Manor First School
BW/LEM/TK/HW NE15 ...... 67 H3
Newcastle Antiques
& Independent Museum
CNUT NE1 ...... 5 J7
Newcastle Area Health
Authority
BW/LEM/TK/HW NE15 ...... 69 F6
Newcastle Area Health
Authority
ELS/FEN NE4 ...... 4 C8
Newcastle Area Health
Authority
JES NE2 ...... 5 H2
Newcastle Arena
ELS/FEN NE4 ...... 10 A1
Newcastle City Council
BW/LEM/TK/HW NE15 ...... 67 F2
Newcastle City Council
BW/LEM/TK/HW NE15 ...... 69 F7
Newcastle City Council
BYK/HTN/WLK NE6 ...... 7 G8
Newcastle City Council
BYK/HTN/WLK NE6 ...... 13 G1
Newcastle City Council
ELS/FEN NE4 ...... 4 B8
Newcastle City Council
ELS/FEN NE4 ...... 69 H6
Newcastle City Council
GOS/KPK NE3 ...... 55 K7
Newcastle City Council
JES NE2 ...... 5 K3
Newcastle City Council
JES NE2 ...... 6 B3

Newcastle City Council
JES NE2 .... 56 E7
Newcastle City Council
WD/WHPE/BLK NE5 .... 54 D7
Newcastle City Council
WD/WHPE/BLK NE5 .... 69 F2
Newcastle City Council
WD/WHPE/BLK NE5 .... 69 H1
Newcastle Clinic
JES NE2 .... 56 E7
Newcastle College
ELS/FEN NE4 .... 4 F9
Newcastle College Concert Hall
ELS/FEN NE4 .... 4 F9
Newcastle Falcons Rugby
Football Club
DIN/WO NE13 .... 55 F3
Newcastle General Hospital
ELS/FEN NE4 .... 4 A6
Newcastle Nuffield Hospital
JES NE2 .... 70 E3
Newcastle Playhouse
& Gulbenkian Studio Theatre
JES NE2 .... 5 J3
Newcastle Preparatory School
JES NE2 .... 5 L1
Newcastle Reform Synagogue
GOS/KPK NE3 .... 56 A6
The New City Medical Centre
SUND SR1 .... 15 C5
New College Durham
DHAM DH1 .... 16 A8
New College Durham
DHAM DH1 .... 156 B4
New College Durham
DHAM DH1 .... 168 B2
Newgate Shopping Mall
CNUT NE1 .... 5 J7
Newker Junior & Infant School
CLSW/PEL DH2 .... 129 H5
New Seaham Primary School
SEA/MUR SR7 .... 135 F6
Newsham Surgery
BLYTH NE24 .... 34 E3
NHS Clinic
SEA/MUR SR7 .... 149 J5
Norfolk Clinic
SUND SR1 .... 14 F4
Norham Community
High School
NSHW NE29 .... 60 B5
North Biddick Club House
WASHS NE38 .... 117 F6
North Blunts Primary School
PLEE/EAS SR8 .... 174 E4
Northburn County First School
CRAM NE23 .... 33 H6
North Durham Community
Healthcare
BDN/LAN/SAC DH7 .... 140 C2
North Durham NHS Trust
CLS/BIR/GTL DH3 .... 129 J5
North East Aircraft Museum
SWCK/CAS SR5 .... 104 B3
Northern Land & Leisure Centre
DHAM DH1 .... 156 C5
Northern Rugby Club
GOS/KPK NE3 .... 56 C2
North Fawdon Primary School
GOS/KPK NE3 .... 55 K3
Northgate District Hospital
MPTH NE61 .... 20 B1
Northgate & Prudhoe NHS Trust
PRUD NE42 .... 80 E4
North Heaton Sports Club
BYK/HTN/WLK NE6 .... 71 J3
North Sands Business Centre
CLDN/WHIT/ROK SR6 ...... 15 H1
North Shields Rugby Club
NSHW NE29 .... 60 D2
North Tyne Industrial Estate
LGB/KIL NE12 .... 58 C2
North Tyneside Area
Health Authority
LGB/KIL NE12 .... 47 K6
North Tyneside Area
Health Authority
NSHW NE29 .... 2 C1
North Tyneside Area
Health Authority
WLSD/HOW NE28 .... 58 E7
North Tyneside Area
Health Authority
WLSD/HOW NE28 .... 59 G3
North Tyneside
Borough Council
NSHW NE29 .... 2 D3
North Tyneside College
WLSD/HOW NE28 .... 59 G5
North Tyneside Council
LGB/KIL NE12 .... 47 H6
North Tyneside Council
LGB/KIL NE12 .... 57 C4
North Tyneside Council
NSHW NE29 .... 2 D2
North Tyneside Council
TYNE/NSHE NE30 .... 2 F1
North Tyneside Council
WLSD/HOW NE28 .... 73 K2
North Tyneside Council
WLSD/HOW NE28 .... 73 F2
North Tyneside Council Offices
WBAY NE26 .... 51 F4
North Tyneside Metropolitan
Borough Council
NSHW NE29 .... 2 A5
Northumberland Area Health
Authority
BLYTH NE24 .... 30 D7
Northumberland Area Health
Authority
PRUD NE42 .... 80 E2
Northumberland
Business Centre
MPTH NE61 .... 26 E1
Northumberland College
of Arts & Technology
ASHGTN NE63 .... 24 A3
Northumberland
Community Health
ASHGTN NE63 .... 23 J1

Northumberland
County Council
ASHGTN NE63 .... 24 C4
Northumberland
County Council
BLYTH NE24 .... 30 B6
Northumberland
County Council
BLYTH NE24 .... 31 H7
Northumberland
County Council
BLYTH NE24 .... 34 E2
Northumberland
County Council
CRAM NE23 .... 37 K1
Northumberland
County Council
CRAM NE23 .... 38 B2
Northumberland
County Council
GOS/KPK NE3 .... 56 D1
Northumberland
County Council
PRUD NE42 .... 80 E2
Northumberland County
Cricket Club
JES NE2 .... 71 F3
Northumberland Mental
Health NHS Trust
CRAM NE23 .... 38 C1
Northumbria Police
STKFD/GP NE62 .... 22 E6
Northumbria Sports Centre
WASHN NE37 .... 103 G2
Novacastrians Rugby
Football Club
LGB/HTN NE7 .... 57 H6
Oakfield College
ELS/FEN NE4 .... 69 H5
Oakfield Junior School
LWF/SPW/WRK NE9 ...... 101 F2
Oaklea School Clinic
WNGT TS28 .... 183 J2
Oakleigh Gardens School
CLDN/WHIT/ROK SR6 ...... 92 B2
Observatory
DHAM DH1 .... 16 B7
The Old Forge Surgery
MLFD/PNYW SR4 .... 105 K6
The Open University
GOS/KPK NE3 .... 56 C4
The Osborne Clinic
JES NE2 .... 71 F2
Our Lady of Peace RC School
HLS DH4 .... 117 J7
Our Lady & St Annes
Primary School
ELS/FEN NE4 .... 4 F8
Ouston County Infant School
CLSW/PEL DH2 .... 115 F5
Ouston Junior School
CLSW/PEL DH2 .... 114 E5
Ovingham C of E First School
PRUD NE42 .... 80 A1
Ovingham Middle School
PRUD NE42 .... 80 A1
Oxclose Community School
WASHS NE38 .... 116 C2
Pallion Health Centre
MLFD/PNYW SR4 .... 105 K7
Pallion Primary School
MLFD/PNYW SR4 .... 105 J5
Palmer Community Hospital
JRW NE32 .... 73 K4
Park House Surgery
BDN/LAN/SAC DH7 .... 140 C5
Parkside Infant School
SEA/MUR SR7 .... 150 C3
Parkside Middle School
CRAM NE23 .... 38 C1
Parkside School
WLSD/HOW NE28 .... 58 C5
The Parks Sports Centre
NSHW NE29 .... 2 B5
Park View Community School
CLS/BIR/GTL DH3 .... 129 K4
Park View
Comprehensive School
CLS/BIR/GTL DH3 .... 115 J7
Parkway Medical Centre
WD/WHPE/BLK NE5 .... 68 A1
Parkway School
WD/WHPE/BLK NE5 .... 68 B1
Pegswood County First School
MPTH NE61 .... 21 K1
Pelaw County Infant School
CLSW/PEL DH2 .... 129 H2
Pelton County Junior
& Infant School
CLSW/PEL DH2 .... 115 F7
Pelton Fell Surgery Building
CLSW/PEL DH2 .... 128 E3
Pelton Health Clinic
CLSW/PEL DH2 .... 115 F7
Pendower Clinic
BW/LEM/TK/HW NE15 ..... 69 F6
Pennywell
Comprehensive School
MLFD/PNYW SR4 .... 119 F1
Percy Main Cricket Club
NSHW NE29 .... 60 B7
Percy Main Primary School
NSHW NE29 .... 74 B1
Percy St Johns Primary School
NSHW NE29 .... 60 C7
Peterlee College
PLEE/EAS SR8 .... 174 D3
Peterlee Leisure Centre
PLEE/EAS SR8 .... 174 E5
Peterlee Town Council
PLEE/EAS SR8 .... 174 C6
Philadelphia Cricket Club
HLS DH4 .... 132 A2
Phoenix Theatre
BLYTH NE24 .... 31 H7
Plawsworth Road
County Infant School
BDN/LAN/SAC DH7 .... 143 H5
Plessey Road County
Junior School
BLYTH NE24 .... 31 H7

Police Headquarters
& Magistrates Court
SUND SR1 .... 14 D4
Ponds Court Business Park
CON/LDGT DH8 .... 122 E5
Ponteland County First School
PONT/DH NE20 .... 43 H2
Ponteland County High School
PONT/DH NE20 .... 43 G4
Ponteland County
Middle School
PONT/DH NE20 .... 43 H4
Ponteland Darras Hall
County First School
PONT/DH NE20 .... 42 E6
Ponteland Health Centre
PONT/DH NE20 .... 43 G2
Ponteland Leisure Centre
PONT/DH NE20 .... 43 H3
Ponteland Parish Council
PONT/DH NE20 .... 43 G3
Portland School
SUNDSW SR3 .... 120 A4
Portobello County Junior
Infant School
CLS/BIR/GTL DH3 .... 115 K4
Primrose Hill Hospital
JRW NE32 .... 74 A1
Princess Louise First School
BLYTH NE24 .... 31 H7
Princess Road Junior School
SEA/MUR SR7 .... 150 D1
Priory Primary School
TYNE/NSHE NE30 .... 61 H2
Priory Theatre
TYNE/NSHE NE30 .... 61 H2
Prospect Business Park
CON/LDGT DH8 .... 123 J4
Prudhoe Castle
PRUD NE42 .... 80 D3
Prudhoe Castle First School
PRUD NE42 .... 80 B2
Prudhoe County High School
PRUD NE42 .... 80 D3
Prudhoe Health Centre
PRUD NE42 .... 80 E1
Prudhoe Town Football Club
PRUD NE42 .... 65 F7
Prudhoe West County
First School
PRUD NE42 .... 80 C2
Queen Elizabeth Hospital
LWF/SPW/WRK NE9 .... 87 H1
Raby Cross Medical Centre
BYK/HTN/WLK NE6 .... 6 F4
Ramside Hall (Hotel)
DHAM DH1 .... 158 B3
Ravenswood Infant
& Primary School
BYK/HTN/WLK NE6 .... 71 J2
Ravensworth Surgery
SSH NE33 .... 75 J2
Ravensworth Terrace
Primary School
CLS/BIR/GTL DH3 .... 115 J2
RC JMI School
BDN/LAN/SAC DH7 .... 143 G5
Recreation Centre
CNUT NE1 .... 5 K6
Redesdale First School
WLSD/HOW NE28 .... 58 B6
Red House Junior
Mixed School
SWCK/CAS SR5 .... 105 H3
Red Rose Primary School
CLS/BIR/GTL DH3 .... 129 K6
Redwell Hills Clinic
CON/LDGT DH8 .... 124 A3
Regent Farm First School
GOS/KPK NE3 .... 56 A4
Regional National Blood
Transfusion Centre
JES NE2 .... 4 E3
Register Office
DHAM DH1 .... 16 F4
Richard Avenue
Primary School
MLFD/PNYW SR4 .... 120 A2
Richard Coates Church
of England Middle School
PONT/DH NE20 .... 43 G2
Richardson Dees First School
WLSD/HOW NE28 .... 73 F1
Rickleton Primary School
WASHS NE38 .... 116 B6
Riversdale Surgery
WYLAM NE41 .... 65 G6
Riverside Leisure Centre
MPTH NE61 .... 20 D5
Riverview House
Business Centre
SUND SR1 .... 14 F3
Roman Road Primary School
FELL NE10 .... 88 C7
Ronald Moore Gallery
TYNE/NSHE NE30 .... 61 F3
Ropery Walk Primary School
SEA/MUR SR7 .... 151 F1
Roseberry Primary School
CLSW/PEL DH2 .... 128 C2
Rowlands Gill Infant School
ROWG NE39 .... 97 H3
Rowlands Gill Junior School
ROWG NE39 .... 97 H2
Rowletch Burn
Industrial Estate
CLS/BIR/GTL DH3 .... 115 H2
Royal College of Nursing
CNUT NE1 .... 5 H5
Royal Grammar School
JES NE2 .... 5 L2
Royalty Theatre
ASHBK/HED/RY SR2 .... 14 B6
Royal Victoria Infirmary
JES NE2 .... 5 H3
Rye Hill Sports Centre
ELS/FEN NE4 .... 4 F8
Ryhope General Hospital
ASHBK/HED/RY SR2 ...... 135 F2
Ryhope Health Centre
ASHBK/HED/RY SR2 ...... 120 E7

Ryhope Junior & Infant School
ASHBK/HED/RY SR2 ...... 120 E7
Ryhope Village C of E
Primary School
ASHBK/HED/RY SR2 ...... 135 F1
Ryton Comprehensive School
RYTON NE40 .... 66 C6
Ryton Industrial Estate
BLAY NE21 .... 67 J6
Ryton Junior & Infant School
RYTON NE40 .... 66 C6
Ryton Rugby Club
RYTON NE40 .... 66 C7
Sacred Heart Primary School
ELS/FEN NE4 .... 69 H4
Sacriston Cricket Club
BDN/LAN/SAC DH7 .... 143 G5
Sacriston Junior School
BDN/LAN/SAC DH7 .... 143 H6
Sacriston Swimming Baths
BDN/LAN/SAC DH7 .... 143 G5
St Aidans College
DHAM DH1 .... 16 B9
St Aidans RC
Comprehensive School
ASHBK/HED/RY SR2 ...... 120 C2
St Albans Medical Group
FELL NE10 .... 12 C8
St Aloysius RC Infants School
HEBB NE31 .... 73 G4
St Aloysius RC Junior School
HEBB NE31 .... 73 G4
St Andrews RC Aided
First School
BLYTH NE24 .... 30 E7
St Annes Mixed High School
SSH NE33 .... 75 J3
St Annes RC Primary School
MLFD/PNYW SR4 .... 119 F1
St Anthonys Health Centre
BYK/HTN/WLK NE6 .... 72 B7
St Anthonys RC School
ASHBK/HED/RY SR2 .... 14 C7
St Augustines RC Infant School
CLDN/WHIT/ROK SR6 ...... 14 F1
St Bede Medical Centre
CLDN/WHIT/ROK SR6 ...... 14 F1
St Bedes First School
BDLGTN NE22 .... 28 E5
St Bedes RC
Comprehensive School
BDN/LAN/SAC DH7 .... 140 B3
St Bedes RC
Comprehensive School
PLEE/EAS SR8 .... 174 D4
St Bedes RC Infants School
JRW NE32 .... 74 A4
St Bedes RC JMI School
JRW NE32 .... 74 A4
St Bedes RC Primary School
BW/LEM/TK/HW NE15 ..... 68 D4
St Bedes RC Primary School
SSH NE33 .... 3 H9
St Bedes RC Primary School
WASHN NE37 .... 103 F4
St Benet Biscops RC
High School
BDLGTN NE22 .... 28 E6
St Benets Primary RC School
CLSW/PEL DH2 .... 115 F5
St Benets RC Primary School
CLDN/WHIT/ROK SR6 ..... 106 D3
St Bernadettes RC First School
WLSD/HOW NE28 .... 58 D5
St Catherines RC
Primary School
JES NE2 .... 6 B1
St Chads College
DHAM DH1 .... 16 D5
St Charles RC Primary School
GOS/KPK NE3 .... 56 B4
St Columbas RC First School
WLSD/HOW NE28 .... 72 C1
St Cuthberts C of E
Junior School
GATE NE8 .... 10 A6
St Cuthberts High School
BW/LEM/TK/HW NE15 ..... 69 F5
St Cuthberts RC Lower School
BW/LEM/TK/HW NE15 ..... 69 F5
St Cuthberts RC Primary School
BW/LEM/TK/HW NE15 ..... 67 H1
St Cuthberts RC Primary School
CLS/BIR/GTL DH3 .... 129 K5
St Cuthberts RC Primary School
GOS/KPK NE3 .... 55 H6
St Cuthberts RC Primary School
NSHW NE29 .... 2 C3
St Cuthberts RC
Comprehensive School
SEA/MUR SR7 .... 134 E7
St Edmunds RC Comprehensive
School
LWF/SPW/WRK NE9 ...... 101 K1
St Georges Hospital
MPTH NE61 .... 20 E3
St Georges RC Primary School
BW/LEM/TK/HW NE15 ..... 68 B6
St Godrics RC Junior
& Infant School
DHAM DH1 .... 156 D3
St Hilda Industrial Estate
SSH NE33 .... 3 G8
St Hildas RC School
SWCK/CAS SR5 .... 106 A3
St Hild & St Bede College
DHAM DH1 .... 17 H3
St James Park
(Newcastle United FC)
CNUT NE1 .... 5 H5
St John Bosco RC
Primary School
SWCK/CAS SR5 .... 104 E1
St John Boste RC
Primary School
WASHS NE38 .... 116 C1
St John Vianney School
WD/WHPE/BLK NE5 .... 68 B2
St Joseph RC Junior
Primary School
BW/LEM/TK/HW NE15 ..... 69 G7
St Josephs Infant School
CLS/BIR/GTL DH3 .... 115 H1

St Josephs RC School
BDN/LAN/SAC DH7 .... 155 F7
St Josephs RC School
DHAM DH1 .... 17 L3
St Josephs RC School
MLFD/PNYW SR4 .... 105 K6
St Josephs RC School
SEA/MUR SR7 .... 149 H6
St Josephs School
NSHW NE29 .... 60 C6
St Josephs School
ROWG NE39 .... 96 D3
St Josephs School
WASHS NE38 .... 103 F7
St Lawrence RC
Primary School
BYK/HTN/WLK NE6 .... 7 H5
St Leonards Junior
& Infants School
SUNDSW SR3 .... 120 B6
St Leonards RC
Comprehensive School
DHAM DH1 .... 16 A1
St Margarets C of E
Infants School
DHAM DH1 .... 168 B2
St Margarets C of E
Primary School
DHAM DH1 .... 16 A5
St Marks RC Primary School
WD/WHPE/BLK NE5 .... 54 D6
St Mary Magdalene RC
Primary School
SEA/MUR SR7 .... 135 J7
St Marys College
ELS/FEN NE4 .... 69 H4
St Marys Hospital
MPTH NE61 .... 26 A7
St Marys Junior
& Infant School
STLY/ANP DH9 .... 126 D3
St Marys Primary School
CON/LDGT DH8 .... 122 C4
St Marys RC
Comprehensive School
LGB/HTN NE7 .... 57 G5
St Marys RC Primary School
ASHBK/HED/RY SR2 ...... 120 B2
St Marys RC Primary School
JRW NE32 .... 90 B1
St Marys RC Primary School
TYNE/NSHE NE30 .... 50 E7
St Marys RC Primary School
WICK/BNPF NE16 .... 8 A9
St Mary's Roman
Catholic Cathedral
CNUT NE1 .... 5 H8
St Matthews RC First School
PRUD NE42 .... 80 C2
St Michaels Industrial Estate
BYK/HTN/WLK NE6 .... 6 E6
St Michaels RC Primary School
ELS/FEN NE4 .... 9 J1
St Michaels RC School
BDN/LAN/SAC DH7 .... 153 J5
St Nicholas Cathedral
CNUT NE1 .... 5 L8
St Oswalds C E Junior Mixed
& Infant School
HEBB NE31 .... 73 H4
St Oswalds Clinic
FELL NE10 .... 12 C8
St Oswalds C of E
Infants School
DHAM DH1 .... 16 D6
St Oswalds RC Infant
& Junior School
LWF/SPW/WRK NE9 ...... 101 J2
St Patricks RC School
ASHBK/HED/RY SR2 ...... 135 F1
St Patricks RC School
BDN/LAN/SAC DH7 .... 167 K5
St Pauls C of E Primary School
ELS/FEN NE4 .... 4 F8
St Pauls RC First School
CRAM NE23 .... 38 C3
St Peter RC Junior
& Infant School
LWF/SPW/WRK NE9 .... 87 G6
St Peters JMI School
JRW NE32 .... 74 A3
St Peters RC Middle School
CRAM NE23 .... 38 C2
St Pius RC School
CON/LDGT DH8 .... 122 C6
St Robert of Newminster RC
Comprehensive School
WASHS NE38 .... 117 F4
St Stephens RC Primary School
LGB/KIL NE12 .... 57 H3
St Teresas RC Primary School
BYK/HTN/WLK NE6 .... 6 E1
St Thomas More RC (Aided)
Comprehensive School
BLAY NE21 .... 83 K1
St Thomas Mores RC School
DHAM DH1 .... 158 A6
St Thomas Street
Business Centre
CNUT NE1 .... 5 J5
St Vincents RC Primary School
BYK/HTN/WLK NE6 .... 7 L9
St Wilfreds RC Junior
& Infant School
FELL NE10 .... 11 M3
St Wilfrids Middle School
BLYTH NE24 .... 31 F7
St Wilfrids RC
Comprehensive School
HAR/WTLS NE34 .... 75 H5
Sam Smiths Sports Ground
BYK/HTN/WLK NE6 .... 72 A2
Sanderson Hospital
GOS/KPK NE3 .... 56 B6
Saville Clinic
CNUT NE1 .... 5 K5
Seaburn Dene Primary School
CLDN/WHIT/ROK SR6 ...... 92 D7
Seaham College
SEA/MUR SR7 .... 150 E1

Seaham
Comprehensive School
SEA/MUR SR7 .... 135 F6

Seaham Town Council
SEA/MUR SR7 .... 150 E1

Seaton Delaval Whytrig
County Middle School
MONK NE25 .... 39 J4

Seaton Sluice Middle School
WBAY NE26 .... 40 E1

Segedunum Business Centre
WLSD/HOW NE28 .... 72 E2

Seghill County First School
CRAM NE23 .... 39 G7

Shanklea First School
CRAM NE23 .... 38 C1

Sherburn Hospital
DHAM DH1 .... 170 A2

Shieldfield Health Centre
JES NE2 .... 6 A4

Shield Row Junior
& Infants School
STLY/ANP DH9 .... 112 E6

Shincliffe C of E Junior
& Infant School
DHAM DH1 .... 169 J5

Shiney Row Primary School
HLS DH4 .... 131 K1

Shipley Art Gallery
GATE NE8 .... 11 J5

Shiremoor First School
SMOOR NE27 .... 49 G6

Shiremoor Middle School
SMOOR NE27 .... 49 H5

Shotley Bridge
General Hospital
CON/LDGT DH8 .... 122 E1

Shotley Bridge Infant School
CON/LDGT DH8 .... 108 D7

Shotley Bridge Junior School
CON/LDGT DH8 .... 108 C7

Shotton Colliery
Primary School
RDHAMSE DH6 .... 173 H3

Shotton Hall
Comprehensive School
PLEE/EAS SR8 .... 174 C6

Shotton Hall Junior School
PLEE/EAS SR8 .... 174 C6

Shotton Parish Council
RDHAMSE DH6 .... 173 J4

Shotton RC JMI School
RDHAMSE DH6 .... 173 G3

The Side Gallery
CNUT NE1 .... 5 L8

Sidegate Gallery
WICK/BNPF NE16 .... 99 F2

Sikh Temple
ELS/FEN NE4 .... 4 C1

Silksworth Health Centre
SUNDSW SR3 .... 120 A7

Silverlink Business Park
WLSD/HOW NE28 .... 59 J4

Simonside First School
WD/WHPE/BLK NE5 .... 54 D5

Simonside Industrial Estate
HAR/WTLS NE34 .... 74 C5

Sir G B Hunter
Memorial Hospital
WLSD/HOW NE28 .... 72 E1

Smiths Surgery
BOLCOL NE35 .... 90 C4

South Benwell Primary School
ELS/FEN NE4 .... 69 J7

Southdene Medical Centre
RDHAMSE DH6 .... 173 J3

South Gosforth First School
JES NE2 .... 56 E6

South Hetton Health Centre
RDHAMSE DH6 .... 160 E2

South Hetton Primary School
RDHAMSE DH6 .... 160 E2

South Hylton Primary School
MLFD/PNYW SR4 .... 104 E7

Southlands Middle School
CRAM NE23 .... 38 C5

Southlands School
TYNE/NSHE NE30 .... 60 E2

Southmoor School
ASHBK/HED/RY SR2 .... 120 E3

Southridge First School
MONK NE25 .... 50 B3

South Shields FC
JRW NE32 .... 74 C5

South Stanley
Comprehensive School
STLY/ANP DH9 .... 126 C2

South Stanley County
Junior Mixed School
STLY/ANP DH9 .... 126 C2

South Street County
Primary School
GATE NE8 .... 11 H6

South Tyneside Area
Health Authority
HAR/WTLS NE34 .... 76 A4

South Tyneside
Borough Council
HEBB NE31 .... 73 F6

South Tyneside College
HEBB NE31 .... 89 F2

South Tyneside College
SSH NE33 .... 75 J3

South Tyneside Health
Care Trust
HAR/WTLS NE34 .... 75 H6

South Tyneside Health
Care Trust
HEBB NE31 .... 73 G6

South Tyneside Health
Care Trust
SSH NE33 .... 3 K6

South Tyneside
Magistrates Court
SSH NE33 .... 3 G9

South Tyneside Metropolitan
Borough Council
HAR/WTLS NE34 .... 76 B4

South Tyneside Metropolitan
Borough Council
SSH NE33 .... 3 J7

South Wellfield First School
MONK NE25 .... 49 K5

Southwick Health Centre
SWCK/CAS SR5 .... 106 A4

Sports Centre
RDHAMSE DH6 .... 170 C1

Springfield Clinic
GATE NE8 .... 11 H8

Springfield
Comprehensive School
JRW NE32 .... 73 K6

Spring Gardens Primary School
NSHW NE29 .... 2 B2

Spring Terrace Health Centre
NSHW NE29 .... 2 C1

Springwell Health Centre
SUNDSW SR3 .... 119 J3

Springwell House Surgery
SUNDSW SR3 .... 119 J1

Springwell Village
Primary School
LWF/SPW/WRK NE9 .... 102 B4

Stanhope County
Infants School
SSH NE33 .... 75 G4

Stanhope County Junior
Mixed School
SSH NE33 .... 75 F5

Stanhope Parade Health Centre
SSH NE33 .... 75 G3

Stanley Health Centre
STLY/ANP DH9 .... 126 C1

Stanley RC Junior Mixed
& Infants School
STLY/ANP DH9 .... 112 C1

Stannington Children's Hospital
MPTH NE61 .... 26 B6

Star Clinic
DHAM DH1 .... 16 D3

Station Industrial Estate
PRUD NE42 .... 80 B1

Stephenson Railway Museum
SMOOR NE27 .... 59 J3

Stephenson Street
TYNE/NSHE NE30 .... 2 E2

Stocksfield Cricket Club
PSHWF NE43 .... 79 G4

Stonelaw County
Middle School
CRAM NE23 .... 38 B4

Studio Gallery
TYNE/NSHE NE30 .... 61 H3

Sunderland AFC Club Shop
SUND SR1 .... 14 E4

Sunderland Area
Health Authority
ASHBK/HED/RY SR2 .... 14 D9

Sunderland Bowling Centre
SWCK/CAS SR5 .... 106 C4

Sunderland City Council
HLS DH4 .... 132 B7

Sunderland City Council
SUND SR1 .... 14 F5

Sunderland
Counselling Services
MLFD/PNYW SR4 .... 119 G1

Sunderland County Court
SUND SR1 .... 14 F5

Sunderland Cricket & Rugby
Football Club House
ASHBK/HED/RY SR2 .... 120 C2

Sunderland District
General Hospital
MLFD/PNYW SR4 .... 105 K7

Sunderland Eye Infirmary
ASHBK/HED/RY SR2 .... 120 D3

Sunderland Football Club
SWCK/CAS SR5 .... 14 D1

Sunderland High School
ASHBK/HED/RY SR2 .... 14 E9

Sunderland Museum
& Art Gallery
SUND SR1 .... 14 F6

Sunderland Retail Park
CLDN/WHIT/ROK SR6 .... 106 D4

Sunderland Royal Hospital
MLFD/PNYW SR4 .... 105 K7

Sunderland Royal Infirmary
ASHBK/HED/RY SR2 .... 14 B7

Sunderland Talmudical College
GATE NE8 .... 11 G7

Sunderland University
SUND SR1 .... 14 F4

Swalwell Cricket Club
WICK/BNPF NE16 .... 84 D3

Talbot House Special School
BW/LEM/TK/HW NE15 .... 67 G1

Tanfield Lea County Junior
Mixed & Infant School
STLY/ANP DH9 .... 112 B6

Tanfield Lea County Junior
Mixed & Infantschool
STLY/ANP DH9 .... 112 A5

Tanfield View Surgery
STLY/ANP DH9 .... 126 C1

Tax Office
SUND SR1 .... 14 D4

Team Valley Business Centre
DUN/TMV NE11 .... 86 D6

Team Valley Trading Estate
Post Office
DUN/TMV NE11 .... 100 E3

Tedco Business Centre
HEBB NE31 .... 73 H3

Tedco Business Park
JRW NE32 .... 73 J3

Theatre Royal
CNUT NE1 .... 5 K6

Thackley First School
BW/LEM/TK/HW NE15 .... 66 E1

Thomas Bewick Birth
Place Museum
PSHWF NE43 .... 79 K2

Thomas Bewick Special School
WD/WHPE/BLK NE5 .... 68 A1

Thomas Hepburn
Community School
FELL NE10 .... 88 A5

Thornhill
Comprehensive School
ASHBK/HED/RY SR2 .... 14 C9

Thornley RC School
RDHAMSE DH6 .... 172 D7

Throckley Industrial Estate
BW/LEM/TK/HW NE15 .... 53 F7

Throckley Middle School
BW/LEM/TK/HW NE15 .... 66 E1

Throckley Surgery
BW/LEM/TK/HW NE15 .... 67 F1

The Toco Gallery
JES NE2 .... 70 E1

Toner Avenue County
Infant School
HEBB NE31 .... 89 F1

Townend Primary School
SWCK/CAS SR5 .... 104 D1

Town Hall & Civic Offices
SSH NE33 .... 3 J8

Trevelyan College
DHAM DH1 .... 16 C9

Trimdon Grange Health Clinic
TRIM TS29 .... 182 D7

Trinity Maritime Museum
CNUT NE1 .... 5 M7

Trinity Medical Centre
SSH NE33 .... 75 G2

Trinity School
BLAY NE21 .... 84 C3

Trouts Lane School
DHAM DH1 .... 155 K2

Tudhoe Colliery
Primary School
SPEN DL16 .... 178 C6

Tynemouth Business Centre
TYNE/NSHE NE30 .... 61 F4

Tynemouth College
NSHW NE29 .... 60 D4

Tynemouth Cricket Club
TYNE/NSHE NE30 .... 61 F2

Tyne Point Industrial Estate
JRW NE32 .... 74 C5

Tyne Tees TV Studios
CNUT NE1 .... 6 B7

Tyne Theatre and Opera House
CNUT NE1 .... 5 G7

Tyneview Primary School
BYK/HTN/WLK NE6 .... 72 C6

Tyne View Primary School
GATE NE8 .... 10 B4

Tyne & Wear County Council
SSH NE33 .... 3 H7

Univeristy Halls of Residence
SUND SR1 .... 15 G3

University College
DHAM DH1 .... 16 C4

University for Industry
SUND SR1 .... 14 E4

University Library
DHAM DH1 .... 16 C4

University of Durham
DHAM DH1 .... 16 C8

University of Durham
DHAM DH1 .... 16 C9

University of Durham
DHAM DH1 .... 16 D5

University of Durham
DHAM DH1 .... 16 E4

University of Durham
DHAM DH1 .... 16 E5

University of Durham
DHAM DH1 .... 16 E9

University of Durham
DHAM DH1 .... 16 F3

University of Durham
DHAM DH1 .... 16 F4

University of Durham
DHAM DH1 .... 16 A9

University of Durham
DHAM DH1 .... 17 G5

University of Durham
DHAM DH1 .... 17 H5

University of Durham
DHAM DH1 .... 17 H8

University of Durham
DHAM DH1 .... 157 J4

University of Durham
DHAM DH1 .... 168 D4

University of Newcastle
Upon Tyne
CNUT NE1 .... 5 J3

University of Newcastle
Upon Tyne
JES NE2 .... 5 G4

University of Newcastle
Upon Tyne
JES NE2 .... 5 L1

University of Newcastle
Upon Tyne
LGB/HTN NE7 .... 57 J7

University of Northumbria
at Newcastle
CNUT NE1 .... 5 L3

University of Northumbria
at Newcastle
LGB/HTN NE7 .... 57 J6

University of Sunderland
ASHBK/HED/RY SR2 .... 14 E7

University of Sunderland
ASHBK/HED/RY SR2 .... 120 D2

University of Sunderland
CLDN/WHIT/ROK SR6 .... 15 G2

University of Sunderland
CLDN/WHIT/ROK SR6 .... 106 E4

University of Sunderland
MLFD/PNYW SR4 .... 105 J7

University of Sunderland
SUND SR1 .... 14 C5

University of Sunderland
SWCK/CAS SR5 .... 105 F5

University of Sunderland
WASHN NE37 .... 102 C6

University of Sunderland
(Library)
SUND SR1 .... 14 C6

University Technology Park
ASHBK/HED/RY SR2 .... 14 C6

Ushaw College
BDN/LAN/SAC DH7 .... 154 C5

Ushaw Moor Cricket Club
BDN/LAN/SAC DH7 .... 166 E1

Ushaw Moor Infant School
BDN/LAN/SAC DH7 .... 154 E7

Ushaw Moor Junior School
BDN/LAN/SAC DH7 .... 155 F7

Usworth Colliery Junior School
WASHN NE37 .... 103 G4

Usworth Grange
Primary School
WASHN NE37 .... 103 H4

Usworth Secondary School
WASHN NE37 .... 103 H3

Valley Road Infant School
ASHBK/HED/RY SR2 .... 15 J9

Valley Road Junior School
ASHBK/HED/RY SR2 .... 15 J9

Valley View County
Infant School
JRW NE32 .... 73 K7

Valley View County
Infant School
JRW NE32 .... 89 K2

Van Mildert College
DHAM DH1 .... 168 C4

Victoria Industrial Estate
FELL NE10 .... 88 C1

Victoria Medical Centre
ASHBK/HED/RY SR2 .... 73 F5

Victoria Road Health Centre
WASHN NE37 .... 103 F5

Viking Gallery
JES NE2 .... 73 K4

Village Gallery
WICK/BNPF NE16 .... 85 F5

Wagonway Industrial Estate
HEBB NE31 .... 73 G3

Walker Comprehensive School
BYK/HTN/WLK NE6 .... 72 B5

Walkerdene Special School
BYK/HTN/WLK NE6 .... 72 B5

Walkergate Hospital
BYK/HTN/WLK NE6 .... 72 A3

Walkergate Infant School
BYK/HTN/WLK NE6 .... 7 M1

Wallsend Business Centre
WLSD/HOW NE28 .... 72 E2

Wallsend Sports Centre
WLSD/HOW NE28 .... 72 B1

Wansbeck Business Centre
ASHGTN NE63 .... 23 H1

Wansbeck Council
NWBGN NE64 .... 25 H1

Wansbeck District Council
BDLGTN NE22 .... 29 F6

Wansbeck District Council
STKFD/GP NE62 .... 23 H6

Wansbeck General Hospital
ASHGTN NE63 .... 24 C1

Wansbeck St Aidan C of E
Aided First School
MPTH NE61 .... 20 B3

Wardley Primary School
FELL NE10 .... 13 L7

War Memorial
SUND SR1 .... 14 F6

Washington Albany
Infants School
WASHN NE37 .... 102 D6

Washington Football Club
WASHN NE37 .... 103 F6

Washington F Pit Museum
WASHN NE37 .... 102 E6

Washington Hospital
WASHS NE38 .... 116 A6

Washington
Secondary School
WASHN NE37 .... 103 F6

Washington Village
Primary School
WASHS NE38 .... 103 G7

Washingwell Primary School
WICK/BNPF NE16 .... 85 G6

Waterhouses JMI School
BDN/LAN/SAC DH7 .... 165 G3

Waterloo Medical Group
BLYTH NE24 .... 31 F6

Waterville Primary School
NSHW NE29 .... 2 B4

Waverley First School
BW/LEM/TK/HW NE15 .... 68 C5

Waygood Gallery & Studios
CNUT NE1 .... 5 K7

Wearside College
SUNDSW SR3 .... 119 K3

Welbeck First School
ASHGTN NE63 .... 24 C2

Welbeck Primary School
BYK/HTN/WLK NE6 .... 7 K6

Wellbank Special School
WASHN NE37 .... 102 D4

Wellfield Comprehensive
School
WNGT TS28 .... 183 K2

West Boldon Junior
Mixed School
BOL NE36 .... 90 E4

Westbourne Surgery
HLS DH4 .... 131 J1

West Denton First School
WD/WHPE/BLK NE5 .... 68 B2

West Denton High School
WD/WHPE/BLK NE5 .... 68 C1

Westerhope Clinic
WD/WHPE/BLK NE5 .... 54 D7

Westerhope First School
WD/WHPE/BLK NE5 .... 54 C7

Westerhope Small
Business Park
WD/WHPE/BLK NE5 .... 54 C6

Western First School
WLSD/HOW NE28 .... 72 C1

Western Infant School
NSHW NE29 .... 2 B4

Western Middle School
WLSD/HOW NE28 .... 72 C2

Westfield School
GOS/KPK NE3 .... 56 B7

West Gate Community College
ELS/FEN NE4 .... 69 H5

Westgate Hill Primary School
ELS/FEN NE4 .... 4 C6

West Jesmond Junior School
JES NE2 .... 70 E2

West Lane Junior
& Infant School
BLAY NE21 .... 83 J4

Westlea Junior School
SEA/MUR SR7 .... 134 E7

West Moor First School
LGB/KIL NE12 .... 57 J1

Westmoor Middle School
LGB/KIL NE12 .... 57 H1

Westmorland Business Centre
ELS/FEN NE4 .... 5 G8

Westoe Gallery
SSH NE33 .... 3 J9

Westovian Theatre Society
SSH NE33 .... 3 L5

West Rainton Primary School
HLS DH4 .... 146 A3

West Sleekburn County
Middle School
STKFD/GP NE62 .... 24 B7

West Walker School
BYK/HTN/WLK NE6 .... 72 C7

Wheatley Hill Primary School
RDHAMSE DH6 .... 182 D1

Whickham
Comprehensive School
WICK/BNPF NE16 .... 84 E6

Whickham Parochial C of E
Junior & Infant School
WICK/BNPF NE16 .... 84 D7

Whinfield Industrial Estate
ROWG NE39 .... 96 E4

Whitburn Comprehensive
School
CLDN/WHIT/ROK SR6 .... 93 G4

Whitburn Cricket Club
CLDN/WHIT/ROK SR6 .... 93 F4

Whitburn Junior Mixed School
CLDN/WHIT/ROK SR6 .... 92 E4

Whitburn Surgery
CLDN/WHIT/ROK SR6 .... 92 E4

Whitehouse Industrial Estate
BW/LEM/TK/HW NE15 .... 69 G7

Whitehouse Primary School
NSHW NE29 .... 60 C2

Whitehouse Primary School
NSHW NE29 .... 60 A3

Whitley Bay Cricket Club
MONK NE25 .... 50 E6

Whitley Bay Football Club
MONK NE25 .... 50 E6

Whitley Bay High School
MONK NE25 .... 50 C3

Whitley Bay Ice Rink
MONK NE25 .... 50 D6

Whitley Bay Rockcliff RFC
MONK NE25 .... 50 E6

Whitley Lodge First School
WBAY NE26 .... 50 C1

Whitley Memorial School
BDLGTN NE22 .... 29 G6

Willington High School
WLSD/HOW NE28 .... 59 H5

Windmill Hills County
Primary School
GATE NE8 .... 10 E4

Windsor County First School
NWBGN NE64 .... 25 F2

Windy Nook Primary School
FELL NE10 .... 87 K6

Wingate RC Junior
& Infant School
WNGT TS28 .... 183 K4

Wingrove Primary School
ELS/FEN NE4 .... 69 J5

Winlaton Park Junior School
BLAY NE21 .... 84 A4

Winlaton Vulcans Rugby Club
BLAY NE21 .... 84 A3

Witherwack School
SWCK/CAS SR5 .... 105 K1

Witton Gilbert County School
BDN/LAN/SAC DH7 .... 155 F1

Woodham Colliery Museum
ASHGTN NE63 .... 18 C7

Woodhorn Church Museum
ASHGTN NE63 .... 18 E6

Woodlands Park Health Centre
DIN/WO NE13 .... 46 B4

Woodlea County
Primary School
HLS DH4 .... 131 G6

Wrekenton Health Centre
LWF/SPW/WRK NE9 .... 101 K2

Wylam County First School
WYLAM NE41 .... 65 H5

Yates Jewish School for Girls
GATE NE8 .... 10 C1

The Yemeni School
SSH NE33 .... 75 F2

Yoden Primary School
PLEE/EAS SR8 .... 175 J4

Page 14

A5
1 Langton Cl
2 St Mark's St
3 Tintern St

Page 47

K5
1 Agincourt
2 Alresford
3 Bannockburn
4 Blenheim
5 Cannock
6 Culloden Wk
7 East Bailey
8 Falkirk
9 Marston
10 Tewkesbury
11 Towton
12 West Bailey

Page 55

F6
1 Brecon Cl
2 Caernarvon Cl
3 Dereham Ct
4 Haggerston Cl
5 Haggerston Ct
6 Hensby Ct
7 Lampeter Cl
8 Reedham Ct
9 Rhuddlan Ct
10 Rollesby Ct
11 Shawdon Cl
12 Shearwater Cl
13 Tredegar Ct
14 Wroxham Ct

C2
1 Hersham Cl

H7
1 Beaufort Cl
2 Bowfell Cl
3 Murrayfield Rd
4 Spenfield Rd

K2
1 Ancroft Wy
2 Boulmer Cl
3 Ingram Av
4 Ridley Cl
5 Tranwell Cl

K3
1 Cornhill Av
2 Ingoe Av
3 Larchwood Av
4 Meldon Av

K4
1 Bellfield Av
2 Bodmin Wy
3 Brandon Rd
4 Brunton Gv
5 Milne Wy
6 Tilson Wy

K5
1 Ambridge Wy
2 Carrfield Rd
3 Colgrove Wy
4 Crantock Rd
5 Hillsview Av
6 Kirkwood Dr
7 Shilmore Rd
8 Winton Wy

K7
1 Aylyth Pl
2 Braebridge Vw
3 Millgrove Vw
4 Montpellier Pl

Page 56

A4
1 Aln Wk
2 Beadnell Wy
3 Embleton Av
4 Falstone Sq
5 Heddon Cl
6 Hepple Wy
7 Matfen Pl
8 Mitford Cl
9 Wansbeck Rd South

A5
1 Agnes Maria St
2 George St
3 Leagreen Ct
4 Mary Agnes St
5 Nelson Av
6 Rea Pl
7 Souter Rd
8 South St
9 Turner Crs

E5
1 Bowes St
2 Bowsden Ct
3 Christon Cl
4 Commercial Rd
5 Donald St
6 Ridgewood Gdns
7 Ridgewood Vls
8 Wardle St

E6
1 Alnmouth Dr
2 Balmoral Av
3 Craghall Dene
4 Craghall Dene Av
5 Hill Crest Gdns
6 Willowbank Av

E7
1 Woodthorne Rd

Page 57

K1
1 Ruskin Av

K2
1 Albany Av
2 Avondale Av
3 Cambridge Av
4 Lynholm Gv
5 North Vw
6 Park Vw
7 Percy Gdns
8 Station Rd North
9 Teasdale Gv
10 Weens Leydale Dr
11 West Vw
12 Whitfield Rd
13 Wilson Ter

K3
1 Hastings Av

K4
1 Belvedere Gdns
2 Eastfield Ter
3 Oakhurst Ter
4 Parkland
5 St Margarets Av
6 Station Ap
7 Tynedale Ter

K6
1 Wells Cl

K7
1 Candelford Cl
2 Halleypike Cl
3 Lark Rise Cl

Page 58

E5
1 Barnwood Cl
2 Basildon Cl
3 Baywood Gv
4 Beamish Cl
5 Beaufort Gdns
6 Beckford Cl
7 Bedale Cl
8 Belford Cl
9 Belper Cl
10 Belsay Cl
11 Berry Cl
12 Briar Cl

Page 59

F5
1 Banbury Gdns
2 Barmouth Cl
3 Barnstaple Cl
4 Barton Cl
5 Bewley Gdns
6 Boreham Cl
7 Bridlington Cl
8 Bromley Gdns
9 Buxton Cl

Page 60

D6
1 Morcott Gdns

D7
1 Hackworth Wy
2 Stockton Rd

E2
1 Argyle Pl
2 Bulman's La
3 Pennyfine Cl
4 Popplewell Ter
5 Post Office La

E3
1 Medway Gdns
2 Osborne Gdns

E4
1 Albion Ter
2 Ashfield Gv
3 Ayre's Ter
4 Church Wy
5 Cleveland Crs
6 Cleveland Ter
7 Frank Pl
8 Lovaine Ter
9 Northumberland Sq
10 Springfield
11 Spring Ter
12 Upper Camden St
13 West Percy Rd

E5
1 Beaumont St
2 Bedford St
3 Brannen St
4 Gardner Pl
5 Lovaine Av
6 Newcastle St
7 Nile St
8 Railway Ter
9 Rudyerd St
10 Saville St West
11 South Preston Gv
12 Spencer St
13 Stanley St
14 West Percy St
15 West Wellington St
16 William St

E6
1 Coronation St
2 Elsdon Pl
3 Elsdon St
4 Hylton St
5 Penman Pl
6 Penman St
7 Thrift St
8 Trinity Pl
9 Upper Elsdon St
10 West Lawson St

E7
1 Atkinson Gdns
2 Hendon Cl
3 Kingdom Pl
4 Watch House Cl

Page 61

H7
1 Brodrick St
2 Catherine St
3 Eastbourne Gv
4 Saville St
5 Shortridge St
6 Sydenham Ter
7 Winchester St
8 Woodbine St

Page 68

A1
1 Ainsdale Gdns
2 Alderney Gdns
3 Anglesey Gdns
4 Arncliffe Gdns
5 Elgar Av
6 Elrick Cl
7 Elston Cl
8 Frenton Cl

A7
1 Cochran St

C2
1 Allerwash
2 Beltingham
3 Burnstones
4 The Garth
5 Harle Cl
6 Highwell La
7 Holborn Pl
8 Knarsdale Pl
9 Linbridge Dr

C3
1 The Close
2 Hedgeley Rd
3 Ilderton Pl
4 Layburn Gdns
5 Northlea
6 St Vincents Cl
7 Sandringham Rd
8 Warwick Rd

D1
1 Barents Cl
2 Bruce Cl
3 Frankham St
4 James St
5 Lordenshaw
6 Nansen Cl
7 Wilkes Cl

D4
1 Castlenook Pl
2 Copperas La
3 Hextol Gdns
4 Legion Gv
5 Legion Rd
6 Overdene
7 Rockcliffe Gdns
8 West Vallum

E3
1 Ashleigh Crs

E5
1 Inglemere Pl
2 Muscott Gdns

E6
1 Sandmere Pl

E7
1 Lightwood Av
2 Pretoria St

Page 69

F1
1 Abercrombie Pl
2 Amersham Pl
3 Blakelaw Rd
4 Bonington Wy
5 Chandra Pl
6 Curzon Pl
7 Lawnhill Wy
8 Waltham Pl
9 Wellfield La

F3
1 Allonby Wy
2 Elrington Gdns
3 Farlam Rd
4 Windermere Rd

G2
1 Blakemoor Pl
2 Deepbrook Rd
3 Hadstone Pl
4 Houndelee Pl
5 Oakwood Pl
6 Springfield Rd
7 Togstone Pl

H1
1 Brieryside
2 Coldingham Gdns
3 Crossbrook Rd
4 Fallodon Gdns
5 Fuchsia Pl
6 Hauxley Gdns
7 Holden Pl
8 Middlegarth
9 Monroe Pl
10 Radcliffe Pl

H3
1 Genister Pl

J7
1 Inchbury Cl
2 Lawson Ter
3 Maryhill Cl
4 Mulben Cl
5 Orton Cl

K4
1 Baldwin Av

K5
1 Agricola Rd
2 Crossley Ter
3 Fenham Rd

K6
1 Eaton Pl
2 Lynnwood Av
3 Mcewan Gdns

K7
1 Ashtree Cl
2 Centenary Ct
3 Chesterfield Rd
4 Croftsway
5 Marie Curie Dr
6 Portland St

G3
1 Granville Gdns
2 Grosvenor Gdns
3 Jesmond Rd
4 Northumberland Gdns
5 Wolseley Gdns

G5
1 Back Stephen St
2 Byker Buildings
3 Claypath St
4 Coquet St
5 Foundry La
6 Hannington St
7 Leighton St
8 Ouseburn Rd
9 Shields Rd West
10 Wilfred St

H5
1 Albion Rw
2 Back Heaton Park Rd
3 Brinkburn St
4 Dalton St
5 Edwin St
6 Flora St
7 Matthew St
8 Molineux St
9 Toward St

H7
1 Crafton St

J4
1 Denmark St
2 Depot Rd
3 Fifth Av
4 Fourth Av

J5
1 Algernon St
2 Denmark St
3 Glendale Ter
4 Headlam St
5 Jane St
6 Michaelgate
7 Robinson St
8 Warkworth St

J6
1 Janet St
2 Mason St
3 Priory Pl

J7
1 Fenning Pl
2 Merchants Whf
3 The Moorings
4 Rowes Ms
5 St Peter's Whf

K1
1 Allerton Gdns
2 Benton Hall Wk
3 Faldonside
4 Kirkleatham Gdns

K2
1 Danby Gdns

K5
1 Blount St
2 Canterbury St
3 Cresswell St
4 Harriet St
5 Scarborough Ct
6 Tunstall Av

K6
1 Bywell St
2 Cresswell St
3 Dunstanburgh Cl

K7
1 Callaly Wy
2 Chatsworth Gdns
3 St Peter's Quayside East
4 Trinity Ctyd

Page 70

B6
1 Buckingham St
2 Colliery La
3 Cookson Cl
4 Cottenham Chare
5 Cottenham St
6 Cross Villa Place No 4
7 Cross Villa Place No 5
8 Douglas Ter
9 Edward Pl
10 Elswick St
11 High Swinburne Pl
12 Lancaster St
13 Mansfield St
14 Quarry Bank
15 Ravensworth Ter
16 St Phillips Cl
17 St Phillips Wy
18 Tindal Cl
19 Tindal St
20 Worley Cl
21 Worley St

B7
1 Belgrave Pde
2 Cambridge St
3 Cross Pde
4 Hawthorn Pl
5 Houston Ct
6 Kirkdale Grn
7 Mather Rd
8 Palace St
9 Victoria St
10 Waverley Rd
11 Wentworth St

C7
1 Back George St
2 Blandford Sq
3 Churchill St
4 Forth Pl
5 Lord St
6 Neville St
7 Peel St
8 Sunderland St
9 Westmorland Rd

D6
1 Mitchell St

E1
1 Alexandra St
2 Croft Av
3 Durham St West
4 Hunters Ct
5 Sunningdale Av

E4
1 Archbold Ter
2 Eglington Rd
3 Gladstone St
4 Gladstone Ter
5 Harrison Pl
6 Osborne Ter
7 Sandyford Rd
8 Windsor Pl

E5
1 Oxford St

E6
1 Broad Chare
2 Carliol Pl
3 Carliol Sq
4 Carliol St
5 Cowgate
6 Croft St
7 Cross Carliol St
8 Manor Chare
9 Melbourne St
10 New Bridge St West
11 Pandon Bank
12 Pilgrim St
13 Trafalgar St

E7
1 Akenside Hl
2 Bridge St
3 Cannon St
4 Castle Garth
5 Dog Bank
6 Hills St
7 King St
8 Lombard St
9 Mirk La
10 Pilgrim St
11 Pipewellgate
12 Quayside
13 Queen St
14 William Iv Yd

Page 71

F4
1 Back Goldspink La
2 Portland Ms
3 Starbeck Av
4 Starbeck Ms

F5
1 Beadnell Pl
2 Bermondsey St
3 Coppice Wy
4 Field Cl
5 Gosforth St
6 Henry Sq
7 Ingham Pl
8 Prince Albert Ter
9 Rock Ter
10 Russell Ter

Page 72

D1
1 Albert Av
2 Clifton Av
3 Diamond St
4 Harle St
5 Harrington St
6 Hopper St
7 Thompson Gdns
8 Victoria Av

D2
1 Atkinson St
2 Benton Wy
3 Border Rd
4 Chadwick St
5 Curzon Rd West
6 Eden St
7 Equitable St
8 Hedley Pl
9 James Ter
10 Portugal Pl
11 Thames Gdns

D5
1 Cartmel Gv
2 Harrison Gdns
3 Wetherby Gv
4 Whitworth Cl

E3
1 Claremont St
2 Ely St
3 Grasmere St
4 Grasmere St West
5 Lincoln St
6 Sedgewick St
7 Villa Pl

E4
1 Westfield Ter

E5
1 Bartram Grn

Page 73

F2
1 Coquet St
2 Ellison St
3 Ropery La

K4
1 Albert Rd
2 Burns St
3 Clayton St
4 Ellison St
5 Hibernian Rd
6 Market Sq
7 Monkton Rd
8 Napier St
9 St John's Ter
10 Wear St

K5
1 Arthur St
2 Bede Burn Rd
3 Humbert St
4 Leopold St

K7
1 Penshaw Vw

Page 75

F3
1 Barnes' Rd
2 Elizabeth Diamond Gdns
3 Temple St West

F6
1 Beattie St
2 Hope St
3 Lucock St
4 Primrose Av
5 School Loaning
6 Thompson St
7 Watling St

G6
1 Afton Ct
2 Awnless Ct
3 Bensham St
4 Browntop Pl
5 Claypool Ct
6 Coxfoot Cl
7 Eavers Ct
8 Eskdale St
9 Hardyards Ct
10 High Moor Pl
11 Loudon St
12 Newland Ct
13 Windlass Ct

H1
1 Beethoven St
2 Berkely St
3 Bolingbroke St
4 Burleigh St
5 Dunelm St
6 Elizabeth St
7 Graham St
8 Handel St
9 Lyndhurst St
10 Percy St
11 Salisbury St
12 Selbourne St

H3
1 Alansway Gdns
2 Albany St East
3 Albany St West
4 Marlborough St
5 Oxford Av
6 Southey St
7 Stanhope Pde
8 Wawn St

J1
1 Aldwych St
2 Fitzpatrick Pl

J2
1 August Pl
2 Catherine Cookson Ct
3 Gleneagles
4 Ingham Gra
5 Sunningdale
6 Turnberry

J3
1 College Dr

J7
1 Armstrong Av
2 Forster Av
3 Hotspur Av

K1
1 Buttermere Gdns
2 Grasmere Gdns
3 Whalton Ct

K2
1 Prince Of Wales Cl
2 Wylam Ct

K3
1 Eastfield Rd
2 North Vw

K4
1 Grinstead Cl

K5
1 Central Gdns
2 Grosvenor Gdns

K6
1 Selwood Ct

K7
1 Myrtle Gv

Page 84

E5
1 Axwell Vw
2 Castle Gn
3 Fellside Ct
4 George St
5 Hawksbury
6 Heathwood Av
7 James St
8 Kestrel Ms
9 Laburnum Gv
10 Sandringham Dr
11 Thomas St
12 William St

Page 86

B1
1 Back Mitford St
2 Blackthorn Pl
3 Charlotte Cl
4 Clasper St
5 Dobson Cl
6 Hornbeam Pl
7 Maiden St
8 Mulberry Pl
9 Tyneside Rd
10 Whitebeam Pl

D4
1 Audouins Rw
2 Chepstow Gdns
3 Goshen St
4 Miller St
5 Newton St
6 Ridley St
7 Stephenson St

E5
1 Alum Well Rd
2 Brackendene Dr
3 St Helen's Crs
4 Winslow Gdns

Page 87

F3
1 Abbey St
2 Camborne Pl
3 Camilla St
4 Cross St
5 Durham St
6 Jedburgh St
7 Marlowe Gdns
8 Milvain Cl
9 Richmond Ct
10 St Alban's Ter
11 St Edmund's Rd
12 Shipley Ct
13 South St
14 Sutherland St
15 Whitby Cl

F7
1 Albert Dr
2 Alum Well Rd
3 Belle Vue Gv
4 Clement St
5 Edmund Cl
6 Elder Gv
7 Lowrey's La
8 Rock Gv
9 Studley Gdns
10 Weathercock La
11 Wesley St
12 Westmorland Rd

G4
1 Chiswick Gdns
2 Conway Sq
3 Grange Ter
4 Highcliffe Gdns
5 Kitchener St
6 Lambeth Pl
7 Lynnholme Gdns
8 Mafeking St
9 Methuen Ter
10 Newman Ter
11 Rosebery Av
12 Teviot St
13 Warburton Crs

H4
1 Bayswater Rd
2 Berkely St
3 Bolingbroke St
4 Burleigh St
5 Landseer Gdns
6 Leyton Pl
7 Trent Gdns

H7
1 Brearley Wy
2 Ellerbeck Cl
3 Flexbury Gdns
4 Millfield Gdns
5 Tarlton Crs
6 Warkworth Gdns
7 Windsor Gdns
8 Woodlands Ter

J5
1 Blackburn La
2 Greenbourne Gdns
3 Heatherwell Cl
4 Windy Ridge Vls

J6
1 Furrowfield
2 Lanercost Gdns
3 Woodvale Gdns

K2
1 Felling House Gdns
2 George Smith Gdns
3 Greenwood Gdns

K3
1 Brandling La
2 Brandling Pl
3 Field St
4 Helmsdale Av
5 Noble St
6 Providence Pl
7 Quarry Rw

K4
1 Croudace Rw
2 Davidson St
3 Elliott Dr
4 Holly Park Vw
5 Park Rw
6 Stainton Dr
7 Thompson Pl
8 Werhale Gn

K5
1 Belgrave Ter
2 Oval Park Vw
3 Picherwell
4 Wentworth Cl

K6
1 College Cl

K7
1 Campion Gdns

Page 88

A5
1 The Cotgarth
2 The Haymyng
3 Highfield Ct
4 Monksfield
5 Parkin Gdns
6 Prestmede
7 Thornygarth

D2
1 Bamburgh Dr
2 Brack Ter
3 Braemar Ct
4 Chreston Wy
5 Elgin Ct
6 Hainingwood Ter
7 Hall Ter
8 Wood Ter

D5
1 Ashridge Ct

D6
1 Alderwyk
2 Beaufront Cl
3 Crophorne
4 Roehedge
5 Seaton Cl
6 Thornley Av

E4
1 Fellgate Gdns
2 Standfield Gdns

E5
1 Berkhamstead Ct
2 Bradbury Ct
3 Meadowbrook Dr

E6
1 Lanchester Cl
2 Rainton Cl

Page 105

F4
1 Alder St
2 Ashwood Gv
3 Elizabeth St
4 The Grove
5 Jennifer Av
6 Joyce Ter
7 Sheppard Ter
8 Stanley St
9 Thompson Crs
10 West Vw

G3
1 Bowburn Av
2 Howley Av
3 Ribble Rd
4 Shincliffe Av
5 Stockley Av

G5
1 Defender Ct

G7
1 Fontburn Ct
2 Rothley Ct
3 Waterlow Ct
4 Watford Ct
5 Westport Cl
6 Whitchurch Ct
7 Wiltshire Ct
8 Woodford Cl

K2
1 Wimbledon Ct

K3
1 Pinewood Sq
2 The Poplars
3 Walter Thomas St

K4
1 Clockwell St

K5
1 Merle Ter
2 Pallion Subway

K6
1 Amethyst Rd
2 Enfield St
3 Garfield St
4 Jacques St
5 Lincoln St
6 Maxwell St
7 Meldon Rd
8 Percival St
9 Pine St
10 Prudhoe St
11 Reginald St

K7
1 Arlington St
2 Bell St
3 Brookland Rd
4 Hazledene Ter
5 Kimberley St
6 Romford St
7 Tamerton St
8 Walpole Ct
9 Washington St
10 Westleigh Cl
11 Westwood St
12 Wilber Cl
13 Wilber St
14 Winchester Ct
15 Woolsington St

Page 106

A3
1 Cato St
2 Churchill Av
3 Clarence St
4 James St
5 Jowett St
6 Julius Caesar St
7 Keats Av
8 Tennyson St

A4
1 Camden St
2 Church Bank
3 Dickens St
4 Kingsley Av
5 Kipling St
6 Lilburn Pl
7 Malaburn Wy
8 Mount Pleasant
9 Park Rw
10 Stoney La
11 Wessington Wy

A6
1 Gilsland St
2 Handel St
3 Oswald St
4 Paxton Ter
5 Pickard St
6 Shepherd St
7 Wood St

B4
1 Attwood Gv
2 Close St
3 Lee St
4 Maypole Cl
5 Pemberton Cl
6 Queen's Rd
7 Suddick St
8 Usher St
9 Vedra St

B6
1 Alliance Pl
2 Alliance St
3 Cirencester St
4 Dryborough St
5 Hyacinth St
6 Hylton Rd
7 Jasmine St
8 Lansdowne St
9 Marguerite Ct
10 Marigold Ct
11 Millburn St
12 North Ravensworth St
13 Queensberry St
14 St Cuthbert's Ter

B7
1 Chepstow St
2 Chester St East
3 Chester St North
4 East Cleft Rd
5 Gilhurst Gra
6 Harlow St
7 Langton Cl
8 The Leazes
9 The Retreat
10 The Royalty
11 St Mark's St
12 St Mark's Ter
13 Tintern St
14 Waterworks Rd
15 Western Hl

C1
1 Cairns Rd
2 Cairns St
3 Patterdale Gv
4 Ullswater Gv
5 Windmill Sq

C6
1 Dun Cow St
2 Dunning St
3 Eden St West
4 Gallery Gill Rd
5 Garden Pl
6 Middle St
7 Paley St
8 Queen St

C7
1 Clanny St
2 Crowtree Rd
3 Crowtree Ter
4 Elwin Ter
5 Green Ter
6 Hope St
7 Mary St
8 St Michaels Wy
9 Silksworth Rw
10 Stockton Rd
11 Tunstall Rd
12 Tunstall Ter West

D2
1 Gildon Av
2 Friarage Rd
3 Hilda St
4 Laburnum Rd
5 Laburnum Rd
6 Marcia Av
7 Marina Ct
8 Marina St
9 Montague St
10 Ormesby Rd
11 Pauline Av
12 Primrose Prec
13 Ronald Sq
14 Vivian Sq

D3
1 Burscough Crs
2 Edgeworth Crs
3 Fairlands East
4 Leeds St
5 Moreland St
6 Wearmouth Av

D4
1 Abbs St
2 Dixon's Sq
3 Fulwell Rd
4 Howard St
5 Monk St
6 Oriel Cl
7 Rosebery St
8 Shore St
9 Southwick Rd
10 Wearmouth St

D5
1 Barclay St
2 Causeway
3 Dundas St
4 George St North
5 Liddell St
6 Lower Dundas St
7 North Bridge St
8 Sheepfolds North
9 Sheepfolds South
10 Southwick Rd
11 Whitburn St
12 Williamson Ter

D6
1 Back Bridge St
2 Bedford St
3 Bridge Crs
4 Bridge St
5 Charman St
6 Fawcett St
7 Frederick St
8 Green St
9 John St
10 Lambton St
11 Pann La
12 Press La
13 Prince St
14 Queen St
15 Sheepfolds South
16 Station St
17 Union St
18 West Sunniside
19 York St

D7
1 Athenaeum St
2 Cowan Ter
3 Fawcett St
4 Frederick St
5 King St
6 Maritime St
7 Park La
8 Tavistock Pl
9 Waterloo Pl

E1
1 Calderbourne Av
2 Cambourne Av
3 Chapman St
4 Cliftonbourne Av
5 Cressbourne Av
6 Rockville
7 Seaburn Hl

E2
1 Claremont Av
2 Lyn-thorpe Gv
3 Merryfield Gdns

E3
1 Association Rd
2 Clockstand Cl
3 St Andrew's Ter

E4
1 Brandling St South
2 Cooper St

E5
1 Huddlestone Ri

E6
1 Cross Pl
2 Donnison Gdns
3 Russell St
4 Spring Garden Cl
5 Zion St

E7
1 Besford Gv
2 Bishop Morton Gv
3 Churchill St
4 Mcmill Pl
5 Winifred Ter

Page 119

H7
1 Galway St
2 Gardiner Sq
3 Geneva Rd
4 Gerrard Rd
5 Glanmore Rd
6 Pickhurst Sq
7 Pontefract Rd
8 Portadown Rd

H7
1 Aldershot Rd
2 Aldershot Sq
3 Aldwych Rd
4 Allendale Rd
5 Anglesey Sq
6 Anthony Rd
7 Appleby Sq
8 Ashford Rd
9 Ashwell Rd
10 Aston Sq
11 Conway Gdns

J2
1 Arncliffe Ct
2 Corry Ct
3 Ingoldsby Ct
4 Maplewood Av
5 Winston Grs
6 Woodville Ct
7 Woodville Crs

J4
1 Grindon La
2 Palgrove Sq
3 Paisley Sq
4 Plymouth Sq
5 Polmuir Sq
6 Pretoria Sq
7 Strathmore Sq
8 Tunis Rd

J6
1 Buckingham
2 Knightsbridge
3 Piccadilly
4 The Strand

K1
1 Dilston Gdns
2 General Graham St
3 Swaledale Gdns

K3
1 Ettrick Gv
2 Portland Rd
3 Sacriston Av

K5
1 Perth Sq
2 Polworth Sq
3 Powis Sq
4 Proctor Sq

K6
1 Sandown Gdns
2 Silksworth Ct
3 Southwold Gdns
4 Symington Gdns

K7
1 Cavalier Wy

Page 120

A3
1 Albyn Gdns
2 Alpine Wy
3 Hanby Gdns
4 Harewood Gdns
5 Haslemere Dr
6 Hatfield Gdns
7 Hathaway Gdns
8 Horsham Gdns
9 Hoseley Gdns
10 Huntingdon Gdns

A7
1 Athol Gv
2 Britannia Rd
3 Comet Sq
4 St Matthews Vw
5 Silksworth Ter
6 Tempest St
7 Vane St
8 Viscount Rd

B2
1 Birchfield Rd
2 Silksworth La
3 Wayside
4 Wenham Sq

B4
1 Brignall Ri
2 Butsfield Gdns
3 Dipton Gdns
4 Frosterley Gdns
5 Mickleton Gdns
6 Wilden St

C5
1 Ashbrooke Cross
2 Ashbrooke Range
3 Fairholme Rd
4 Greystoke Gdns
5 Hillside Gdns
6 Linden Gdns
7 Linden Rd
8 Lulworth Gdns
9 Lynford Gdns
10 Willow Bank Rd

C7
1 Boulby Cl
2 Hawsker Cl
3 Hilltop Gdns
4 Houlskye Cl
5 Levisham Cl

D3
1 The Glen
2 Langport Rd

D4
1 Longridge Sq

D7
1 Runnymede

E1
1 Lindsay Cl
2 Osman Cl
3 St Ignatius Cl

E2
1 Beaumont St
2 Capulet Ter
3 Edith St
4 Villette Brook St

E3
1 Romney Av
2 Roydon Av
3 Rudyard Av
4 Rushton Av

E4
1 Thornfield Gv
2 Weldon Av
3 Weybourne Sq

E5
1 Hardgate Rd
2 Sandmere Rd

E6
1 Ronaldsay Cl
2 Rosebank Cl

E7
1 Murphy Gv

Page 123

B4
1 Barr Hills
2 Barr House Av
3 Clarendon St
4 Collison St
5 Fern St
6 Herbert St
7 Hutchinson Av
8 Jameson St
9 Livingstone St
10 Maple St
11 Palm St
12 Prospect Pl
13 Stanley St

F5
1 Alexandra St
2 Ann St
3 Church St
4 John Street Sq
5 Middle St
6 Nelson St
7 Pitt St
8 Queen St
9 Raglan St
10 Railway St
11 Rosebery Ter
12 Seymour St
13 Wood St

Page 134

A1
1 Arran Ct
2 Delamere Ct
3 Hamsterley Ct
4 Lake Ct
5 Lomond Ct
6 Newstead Sq
7 Nimbus Ct
8 Sheppey Ct
9 Sherwood Ct
10 Shetland Ct
11 Tilbeck Sq
12 Tiree Ct

Page 175

F4
1 Burdon Pl
2 Coniston Cl
3 Duddon Cl
4 Esedale Wk
5 Grisedale Rd
6 Kentmere Pl
7 Langdale Pl
8 Tarn Cl

Notes

Notes